# In the Classroom

## An Introduction to Education

### SECOND EDITION

*A*rthea J. S. Reed, called "Charlie" by her students, family, and friends, lives in Asheville, North Carolina. She has taught at the University of North Carolina at Asheville for sixteen years and is currently professor and chair of the Education Department at the liberal arts, public university. She received her Ph.D. from Florida State University, her M.S. from Southern Connecticut State University, and her B.A. from Bethany College in West Virginia. She has taught in grades two through twelve in the public schools of Connecticut, Ohio, and West Virginia. She is author of *Reaching Adolescents: The Young Adult Book and the School* (Merrill, 1993), *Comics to Classics: A Guide to Books for Teens and Preteens* (Penguin, 1994), and numerous monographs, book chapters, and articles. For six years, she was editor of *The ALAN Review,* a highly-regarded journal in the field of young adult literature. She has been coeditor of the Penguin/Signet Classic teachers guide series since 1988, editing or writing guides to over twenty classic books and most recently coauthoring a teachers' guide to use with a classic book and CD-ROM. She has been the chair of the National Council of Teachers of English Promising Young Writers program since 1990 and was codirector of the Mountain Area Writing Project, a site of the National Writing Project, for eight years. She serves on numerous local, state, and national education committees and in 1985 was named the Ruth and Leon Feldman Professor by the UNCA faculty for her service to education.

*V*erna E. Bergemann is professor emeritus and past chair of the Education Department at the University of North Carolina at Asheville, where she taught for twelve years. She currently lives in Marion, North Carolina. Prior to coming to UNCA, she was a professor of education at the State University of New York at Oswego for thirteen years. She earned her Ed.D. at the University of Maryland, her M.A. at the State University of New York at Buffalo, and her B.A. at the State University of New York at Brockport. She taught elementary school in Niagara Falls, New York, and Los Alamos, New Mexico. She has worked with beginning teachers as a helping teacher, as a cooperating teacher in a university laboratory school, and as a consultant with the North Carolina Department of Public Instruction. She has been a professor of education at three universities and is the author of numerous articles and activity workbooks for teachers. For many years she has worked closely with volunteer organizations that attempt to improve adult literacy. In 1989, she was named Woman of Distinction and Woman of the Year by the city of Asheville for her outstanding contributions to literacy education. In 1992, she chaired a school study committee for private schools in Asheville.

# *In the Classroom*

## An Introduction to Education

### SECOND EDITION

## ARTHEA J. S. REED AND VERNA E. BERGEMANN

*University of North Carolina, Asheville*

The Dushkin Publishing Group, Inc.

*To:*    *Don Reed*

        *Marie Bergemann*

        *Betty McArthur*

        *Elizabeth Hunt*

Printed in the United States of America

Library of Congress Catalog Card Number 94-69040

International Standard Book Number (ISBN) 1-56134-304-8

First Printing

10  9  8  7  6  5  4  3  2  1

This book is printed
on recycled paper

Cover: Pablo Picasso. *Three Musicians.* Fontainebleau, summer 1921.
Oil on canvas, 6′ 7″ × 7′ 3¾″. The Museum of Modern Art, New York.
Mrs. Simon Guggenheim Fund.
Photograph © 1995, The Museum of Modern Art, New York.

Credits continue on pages lviii–lx.

# PREFACE

*L*ike the Clerk in Chaucer's *Canterbury Tales,* we would gladly learn and gladly teach; in fact, we would encourage every student in the foundations course of education or in the introductory course to adopt this motto, too. In writing this book for those courses, we have included a number of features designed to be informative, to provide glimpses of life in the classroom, and to challenge students to analyze points of view that may be different from their own.

This book combines in one volume the features of both a foundations of education text and an introduction to teaching text. The following features of each chapter enhance this dual approach:

**Chapter Objectives** Allow students to understand what information is available in each chapter.

**Opening Anecdotes** Introduce the content of the chapter in story format, an advanced organizer for the material to follow.

**Boldfaced Vocabulary** Introduces students to essential concepts within the context of the chapter; also included in the end-of-book glossary.

**Viewpoints** Range from poetry to excerpts of essays and articles; used to elaborate material in the text, illustrate another point of view, or enhance a concept.

**Taking Sides** Presents two sides of a controversial argument discussed within the chapter; encourages students to question the issues presented and to extend their learning beyond the text.

**Cross-Cultural Perspectives** Broaden the student's perspective through information about education in such cultures as South Africa, France, and Japan.

**In the Classroom** Presents diary entries or stories of real teachers in actual classroom situations, intended to illustrate a specific idea in a chapter.

**Student Atlas of American Education** Sixteen maps in full color that graphically illustrate statistical information about such topics in education as teacher salaries and school populations.

**Points to Remember** Keyed to the chapter objectives; helps students review material during their reading.

**For Thought/Discussion** Questions following each chapter to help students reflect on the content of the chapter.

For Further Reading/Reference  Annotated bibliography at the end of each chapter.

Because students today are expected to spend a fair amount of time observing in classrooms, each copy of our book is accompanied by *A Guide to Participation and Observation In the Classroom,* second edition. This guide is designed to help education students objectively observe teachers, students, and student/teacher interaction, using a variety of field-tested materials. In addition, tools to augment the beginning teacher's technique in tutoring and small group work are included.

We have also written an instructor's resource guide, *Teaching and Testing With In the Classroom,* second edition, to provide a variety of approaches for using the text, including a taking sides approach, an "in the classroom" case-study approach, and a discussions/reflections approach. Course syllabi and teaching ideas and materials are provided for each of the three approaches. We also include summarizing questions for each chapter, classroom activities for small and large group discussion, and individual investigations for independent study. *Teaching and Testing With In the Classroom,* extensively revised for the second edition, contains a test bank of approximately 1,500 items, which are also available on MicroTest III, a powerful but easy-to-use test generating program by Chariot Software Group. MicroTest III is available for DOS, Windows, and Macintosh personal computers.

A set of thirty color transparencies is also available.

## Acknowledgments

Without the help and support of many individuals, a book like this could never be published. First and foremost, each of us thank the other for the contribution she has made. We began the project as friends and colleagues and completed it believing even more strongly in each other. Next, without Marcuss Oslander, the developmental editor of this text, the second edition would be too long and too late. It is hard to explain in a few words all of the encouragement and help she provided us. We will always be grateful! In addition, we cannot help but mention all the terrific people at The Dushkin Publishing Group, Inc. Working with them is what most writers believe publishing a book should be. From our first trip to Connecticut, where we met with Rick Connelly, Irving Rockwood, John Holland, and Marcuss, to the final revisions of the second edition, everyone has been involved in the project. We could not have asked for better support!

We also must thank the staff of UNCA's Ramsey Library. Mel Blowers generously gave us the freedom to use its space, personnel, and resources. Anita White-Carter tirelessly found us books, addresses, phone numbers, government documents, legal case summaries, and more items than we can begin to mention. The rest of the staff cooperated in every way. We feel very privileged to work with such wonderful colleagues.

This book profited greatly from the astute and careful reviews given it by the following professionals in education. We are grateful for their help.

| | |
|---|---|
| Susan L. Adams | King's College |
| Barbara Arnstine | California State University–Sacramento |
| Timothy J. Bergen, Jr. | University of South Carolina |
| Nancy R. Billingsley | Clark College |
| Mosetta S. Cohen | Florida Community College at Jacksonville |
| Lloyd L. Coppedge | Northeastern State University |
| Tom Cuppett | Lake-Sumter Community College |
| Anthony A. DeFalco | Long Island University–C. W. Post Campus |
| Judith A. Green | Kansas State University |
| Douglas Hallatt | University of Wisconsin–Eau Claire |
| J. Merrell Hansen | Brigham Young University |
| William Hedspath | Union University |
| Nancy Kaczmarek | D'Youville College |
| Michael Kamrath | North Dakota State University |
| Joseph T. Kelly | University of Idaho |
| Mike Kelly | Dominican College |
| Catherine Kirby, S.C. | College of Mount St. Joseph |
| Walter H. Klar | Framingham State University |
| Carolyn Lillehaugen | Concordia College–Moorhead |
| Jack Longbotham | Hardin Simmons University |
| Jan McDonald | Phillips University |
| Sharon McNeely | Northeastern Illinois University |
| Linda Metzke | Lyndon State College |
| Barbara A. Peach | Fontbonne College |
| Gene Rhoda | University of North Carolina–Asheville |
| Max L. Ruhl | Northwest Missouri State University |
| David L. Rush | Eastern Kentucky University |
| Carolyn Schoultz | St. Leo College |
| Donald G. Scoles | St. Andrews College |
| Wanda L. Stewart | Juniata College |
| Toni Ungaretti | Johns Hopkins University |

Thanks to the UNCA teacher education students who helped field-test our many observation and participation tools. Special thanks to our colleagues at UNCA, Gene Arnold and Jim McGlinn, who used various drafts of the chapters in their introductory classes and provided us with helpful feedback.

Thanks to Judy Carver who answered numerous telephone calls, and mostly kept the troops at bay while we were writing, and to the students who worked in the Department of Education office.

We could not have written this book without the numerous teachers, administrators, students, and parents, many of whom are mentioned in the text, who provided us with their special insights into teaching, schooling, and learning. We thank each of you. One person at the U.S. Department of Education deserves special mention. W. Vance Grant, statistician specialist, answered our numerous difficult questions and frequently provided us with statistical data long before its publication.

Thanks to the UNCA administrators, particularly Larry Wilson, who gave us the opportunity to complete this work, and to the graphics staff who provided us with many printed materials.

Finally, no author can complete a work of this magnitude without the loving support of friends and family. Particular thanks to Libby and Don who kept up our spirits and read the many drafts of our manuscript.

Arthea J. S. Reed
Verna E. Bergemann

# CONTENTS IN BRIEF

# CONTENTS

## *Chapter 3*

## BECOMING A TEACHER  88

# *Part II*    FOUNDATIONS   130

## *Chapter 4*

## THE HISTORICAL FOUNDATIONS OF U.S. EDUCATION   132

*Chapter 5*

## TWENTIETH-CENTURY U.S. EDUCATION: EQUALIZATION OR EXCELLENCE 170

*Chapter 6*

## THE PHILOSOPHICAL FOUNDATIONS OF EDUCATION  214

*Part III*  SCHOOLS IN A MULTICULTURAL SOCIETY  252

*Chapter 7*

## EFFECTIVE SCHOOLS  254

*Chapter 8*

## THE CURRICULUM IN A MULTICULTURAL SOCIETY 292

*Part IV*

## STUDENTS IN A MULTICULTURAL SOCIETY 340

*Chapter 9*

## STUDENTS IN A MULTICULTURAL SOCIETY 342

## *Chapter 10*

## LEARNING IN A MULTICULTURAL SOCIETY  384

*Part V*    SOCIETY AND SCHOOLS  424

*Chapter 11*

## SOCIETY'S EFFECT ON THE SCHOOLS  426

*Chapter 12*

## SCHOOLS RESPOND TO SOCIAL CHANGE  468

*Part VI* SCHOOLS AND GOVERNANCE 506

*Chapter 13*

### THE POLITICAL INFLUENCES ON EDUCATION 508

## *Chapter 14*

### FUNDING EDUCATION  544

## *Chapter 15*

### LAW AND THE SCHOOLS  586

## Chapter 1

### THE TEACHING PROFESSION

This chapter will explore the teaching profession. We will ask the question: Is teaching an art or a science? We will examine the diversity of students in today's classrooms and discuss such trends in teaching as standards, staff development, and advancement opportunities.

## Chapter 2

### EFFECTIVE TEACHING

Not everyone can teach; not everyone should teach. What is it that makes Mary MacCracken and Jaime Escalante effective teachers? Is it possible to learn how to be an effective teacher? This chapter attempts to answer these questions. As you read it, think about whether you possess the values and can learn the skills that will allow you to become an effective teacher.

## Chapter 3

### BECOMING A TEACHER

This chapter will first examine how contemporary teachers are educated and the importance of fieldwork in the training of teachers. We will then look at alternatives to traditional teacher-training programs. Finally, we will investigate teacher education reform movements of the 1980s and 1990s.

If we accept the status quo and maintain a conservative view toward change, we will not progress. In fact, we'll probably regress. We have an obligation, as educators, to constantly seek better ways of doing things. If that means putting our heads on the chopping block, so be it. Either we stand for something or we stand for nothing. If we stand for something it should be so important that any sacrifice to preserve and further it is worthwhile. And, as educators, we are under a moral and ethical responsibility to stand for something.

Very truly yours,
Jack Crowley

# Part 1

# TEACHERS AND TEACHING

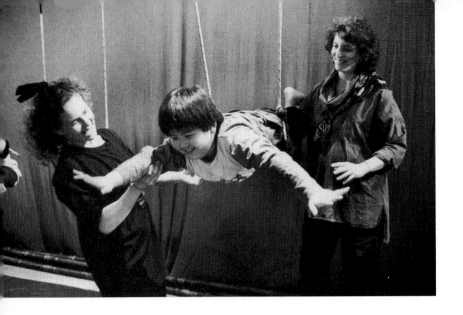

**CHAPTER OBJECTIVES**

After studying this chapter, you should be able to:

- Define teaching from various perspectives.
- Compare teaching as an art and teaching as a science.
- Discuss why teaching requires both art and science.
- Discuss the characteristics of a profession.
- Explain why autonomy and empowerment are important.
- Determine why collegial time is important to teachers.
- Explain the importance of accountability to professionalism.
- Compare and contrast the following incentive pay programs: merit pay, career ladder or differential staffing, and master teacher.
- Trace the changes in teachers' salaries.
- Discuss teaching as a career.
- Describe the diversity of students in today's classrooms.
- Examine why it is important for classroom teachers to know how to teach special needs students.
- Discuss the following trends in teaching: mid-career teaching, staff development, national standards for teaching, and advancement opportunities.

*Chapter 1*

# THE TEACHING PROFESSION

*T*his letter is in response to one written to Margaret T. Metzger by Clare Fox, Metzger's former student, who is interested in pursuing a career in teaching.

Dear Clare,

I look forward to teaching. By mid-August I start planning lessons and dreaming about classrooms. I also wonder whether I'll have the energy to start again with new classes. Yet after September gets under way, I wake up in the morning expecting to have fun at work. I know that teaching well is a worthwhile use of my life. I know that my work is significant.

I am almost 40 years old, and I'm happier in my job than anyone I know. That's saying a lot. My husband, who enjoys his work, has routine days when he comes home and says, "Nothing much happened today—just meetings." I never have routine days. When I am in the classroom, I usually am having a wonderful time.

I also hate this job. In March I want to quit because of the relentless dealing with 100 antsy adolescents day after day. I lose patience with adolescent issues: I think I'll screech if I have to listen to one more adolescent self-obsession. I'm physically exhausted every Friday. The filth in our school is an aesthetic insult. The unending petty politics drain me. Often I feel undermined on small issues by a school system that supports me well on academic freedom. . . .

A curious irony exists. I am never bored at work, yet my days are shockingly routine. I can tell you exactly what I have done every school day for the past 18 years at 10:15 in the morning (homeroom attendance), and I suspect I will do the same for the next 20 years. The structure of the school day has changed little since education moved out of the one-room schoolhouse. All teachers get tired of the monotonous routine of bookkeeping, make-up assignments, 22-minute lunches, and study-hall duties. I identify with J. Alfred Prufrock when

5

he says, "I have measured out my life with coffee spoons." My own life has been measured out in student papers. At a conservative estimate, I've graded over 30,000—a mind-boggling statistic which makes me feel like a very dull person indeed.

The monotony of my schedule is mirrored in the monotony of my paycheck. No matter how well or poorly I teach, I will be paid the same amount. There is absolutely no monetary reward for good job performance, or any recognition of professional growth or acquired expertise. My pay depends on how long I've taught and my level of education. I work in a school district in which I cannot afford to live. I am alternatively sad and angry about my pay. To the outside world it seems that I am doing exactly the same job I did in 1966—same title, same working conditions, same pay scale (except that my buying power is 8 percent less than it was when I earned $5,400 on my first job). To most people, I am "just a teacher."

But this is the outside reality. The interior world of the teacher is quite different. Although you have to come to some terms with the outward flatness of the career, I want to assure you that teachers change and grow. So little research has been done on stage development of teachers that the literature recognizes only three categories—intern, novice, and veteran. This is laughably oversimplified. There is life after student teaching; there is growth after the first year. You will some day solve many of the problems that seem insurmountable during your exhilarating student teaching and your debilitating first year.

Sometimes I am aware of my growth as a teacher, and I realize that finally, after all these years, I am confident in the classroom. On the very, very best days, when classes sing, I am able to operate on many levels during a single class; I integrate logistics, pedagogy, curriculum, group dynamics, individual need, and my own philosophy. I feel generous and good-natured toward my students, and I am challenged by classroom issues. But on bad days, I feel like a total failure. Students attack my most vulnerable points. I feel overwhelmed by paperwork. I ache from exhaustion. I dream about going to Aruba, but I go to the next class. . . .

To me, teaching poses questions worthy of a lifetime of thought. I want to think about what the great writers are saying. I want to think about how people learn. I want to think about the values we are passing on to the next generation. Questions about teaching are like puzzles to me; I can spend hours theorizing and then use my classroom as a laboratory.

I am intellectually challenged by pedagogical problems. I have learned to follow the bizarre questions or "wrong answers." Some questions reveal chasms of ignorance. For example, "Where is Jesus' body?" or "Before movies were in color, wasn't the world dull just being in black and white?"

And then there are all the difficult, "normal" situations: students and parents who are "entitled," hostile, emotionally needy, or indifferent; students who live in chaotic homes, who are academically pressured, who have serious drug and alcohol problems. The list goes on and on. No school of education prepared me for the "Hill Street Blues" intensity and chaos of public schools. I received my combat training from other teachers, from myself and mostly from the students. You will too. . . .

Clare, when you consider a life's work, consider not just what you will take to the task, but what it will give you. Which job will give self-respect and challenge? Which job will give you a world of ideas? Which job will be intellectually challenging? Which job will enlarge you and give you life in abundance? Which job will teach you lessons of the heart?

With deep respect,
Margaret Metzger

POSTSCRIPT: This letter was written to Clare in 1984. In the fall of that year, Clare began her first teaching job at a junior high school in Tucson, Arizona. She left that job at the end of one year, dividing her time between working at a publishing company and teaching in an inner-city high school. In 1986 she wrote to Margaret Metzger explaining why she had left her first teaching job, "I taught at an exceptionally demanding, academically rigorous junior high. By February, I was exhausted, and by June, I had made two friends outside of teaching. Too much of my time outside of school had been spent on papers or in the library."

Margaret was saddened to learn that Clare (now Clare Ringwall) was leaving teaching, but she was not convinced that Clare was abandoning the classroom for good. Margaret was right. Although Clare was enjoying her job in publishing she was beginning to realize that something was missing. In the meantime, Margaret planned to take a two-month parental leave and recommended Clare as a full-time substitute. At first Clare said, "No," but quickly realized she had made the wrong decision. She took the position, but kept her publishing job by working extra hours in the afternoons and on weekends. During the two months of substituting, Clare's attachment to teaching grew stronger. The environment was supportive and stimulating and Clare was encouraged to pursue her love for writing with her students. She was learning to respect her own judgment rather than rely so much on student feedback as she had done in her first year of teaching. At the end of the school year, Clare had to make a difficult choice: teaching or publishing? "Rather than give up on teaching and try to find an alternative career that could give me a fraction of the sense of worth, challenge, and joy that teaching was giving me, I realized that I should stay and figure out how to maintain a satisfying private life." Since that time, Clare has successfully worked as a mentor teacher and has recommended Margaret for a position as an expert teacher.

From: M. T. Metzger and C. Fox, "Two Teachers of Letters" (1986), *Harvard Educational Review* 56 (4), 351–354. M. T. Metzger and C. F. Ringwall, "Friendly Persuasion: How Do You Convince a Doubting Beginner to Remain in the Classroom?" *Teacher Magazine Reader* (1986), 1 (1), 1–5.

---

*T*eacher-training institutions are educating students for a profession in teaching. However, there is much disagreement about what is meant by teaching. Teacher educators argue about whether teaching is an art or a science, and whether a teacher is born with innate skills or can learn to teach. At the same time, not everyone agrees that teaching is a profession because it lacks some qualities generally associated with a profession. In this chapter we will begin by defining teaching from a teacher's perspective, we will explore teaching as an art and a science, review some of the qualities of the teaching profession, and, finally, discuss some developing issues that are certain to have an effect on professionalizing teaching.

## Defining Teaching

Throughout the 1980s, dozens of studies were done, and previous studies were synthesized in an attempt to determine what differentiates effective or good teaching from ineffective or poor teaching and to delineate the characteristics of effective teachers. This body of research has come to be called *effective teaching research.* (The characteristics of effective teachers, as cited in this research, are discussed in chapter 2.) To give you an idea of what teaching is like from teachers' perspectives, the authors of this text asked numerous practicing classroom teachers to write about what teaching means to them. Their definitions include self-examination, guidance, sharing information, as well as drudgery and disappointment.

*Teaching Is Self-Examination*   Scribner Jeliffe, a high school social studies teacher at a midwestern independent school with forty years of teaching experience, says that teachers help students examine themselves, and, therefore, much of what a teacher does cannot be seen or heard.

> At the core of teaching is the sense of bringing to the students what they need to know to advance their self-examination. We must explore the outer reaches of ourselves in order to understand what is within. To that end, a teacher brings written and visual materials together to provide both background content and a central problem for the students and a congregation of interested partners, the class. I have been impressed by how much teaching takes place when the teacher is silent. As a student recently put it, (I have learned that) "I am my own best teacher and my own best student."

*Teaching Is Guiding*   Alida Woods, a fifth-grade teacher with nearly twenty years' teaching experience, says that the teacher is a guide and a partner.

> Teaching is a high calling . . . in education, as the Latin indicates, we "lead out"—(*educare*)—and, in so doing, we guide, facilitate, hold, and light candles as we journey forth, *with* and beside our students.

*Teaching Is Sharing Information*   Mary Futrell, president of the National Education Association from 1979 to 1989 and herself a teacher, believes that the pleasure of sharing knowledge puts teachers in a position to receive the affection and respect of students; teachers become role models. "Having others follow in your example is a heady reward" (Futrell 1989, 26).

Rene Caputo, a first-year elementary school teacher of Spanish, says:

> Teaching is an exciting process of helping students discover new sounds with which they can communicate. It involves creating an environment in which students can safely suspend the absoluteness of their everyday realities to enter a world in which previously learned rules do not apply and everything has a new name.

**Alida Woods is a fifth-grade teacher with nearly twenty years teaching experience. She believes a teacher is a guide and a partner in the process of learning.**

My first year of teaching has been extremely exhausting: teaching between eleven and fourteen classes each day, carrying my materials from room to room, learning the layouts and organizational structures of three schools, and trying to memorize 650 new faces and their accompanying names. There were definite moments when I was ready to give up.

My students kept me coming back. I had never met so many loving, interesting, and inquisitive people before. It was an exhilarating experience to challenge each other in our exploration of another culture and language, to share videos, games and songs, to laugh as we acted out fairy tales together. I learned that a teacher needs to be prepared and flexible, and above all, care deeply about her students and her subject.

***Teaching Is Part Trade, Part Professionalism***   While some teachers feel very positive about what they do and offer inspiring comments about their profession, others feel that teaching has its negative side as well. Heavy workloads, a great deal of paperwork, and low pay have discouraged some who teach. A few of their comments follow.

Educational researcher John Goodlad says, "Teaching functions in a context where the [teacher's] beliefs/expectations are those of a profession but where the realities tend to constrain, likening actual practice more to a trade. . . . By its very nature a profession involves both considerable autonomy in decision making and knowledge and skills developed before entry and then honed in practice" (1984, 194). In Goodlad's three-year "Study of Schooling" in *A Place Called School:*

*Prospects for the Future,* he interviewed 1,350 teachers and found that most went into teaching with professional values but "encountered in schools many realities not conducive to professional growth."

Stephanie Petrovich, a middle school social studies teacher, had similar experiences: "The teaching profession . . . stifles the creative energy of its teachers, often causing immense feelings of despair within the ranks. Teachers are not treated professionally, nor are they allowed to devote their time to the task of teaching. As a result of continued pressure by bureaucrats within the school system, school administrators, and the general public, as well as increasing work loads and low pay, teachers are embittered and apathetic toward their careers."

These personal definitions of teaching corroborate what effective teaching research clearly shows, "teaching is a complex craft, one class never being quite the same as another" (Sizer 1984, 1919). And there is no doubt that David Berliner is correct when he says, "Classrooms are workplaces: complex and dynamic workplaces that require management by an executive of considerable talent" (1989, 105). Inherent in these definitions is also some confusion in the perception of teaching as either art or science.

## Teaching as Art and Science

In a long-standing argument educators still disagree about whether teaching is an art or a science. One's conclusion is particularly important in deciding how teachers are trained and evaluated. One side of the issue asserts, "Teaching is an art, and, therefore, it cannot be taught or evaluated." According to proponents of this point of view, teaching is intuitive; either an individual can do it well or cannot.

The other side of the issue contends that teaching is a science and, therefore, researchers can determine teaching strategies that are successful, which can then be taught and their effectiveness evaluated. As Beverly C. Pestel in the *Journal of Chemical Education* says, "We have an obligation to our students . . . to know what the research [on teaching] says and then apply those principles to our teaching. Our teaching practices require the same attention to the current research as do our laboratory practices, for each is a science in its own right" (June 1990, 490).

### TEACHING AS AN ART

How do teachers who call teaching an art describe it? Perhaps, a visit to the fourth-grade classroom of Jones Ledbetter will help you understand the art of teaching. Everyone agrees that Jones is a master teacher. He has been named teacher of the year. Parents lobby to have their children placed in his class. Carolyn Harris, his principal, appoints him to all the major school committees. However, she must also evaluate his teaching performance. Each time she does so, she agonizes over how to describe what he does.

***The Artist/Teacher Improvises***   Jones seems to break all the traditional rules. He rarely opens his class with an objective or a review, which is required by the evaluation instrument used in his school district. In fact, Carolyn wonders if he ever opens his class at all. When she enters his classroom, all the children are busy. She frequently finds Jones sitting on the floor with four or five children reading an article from the day's newspaper. Sometimes he circulates around the room, stopping to kneel on the floor as he reads a child's classwork. At other times, he works with the children on art projects at the tables in the back of the room. When Carolyn enters, the children rarely notice her; Jones never does. They simply continue their work.

*The Artist/Teacher Focuses on Motivation and Pacing* The children seem happy and rarely misbehave. Jones keeps things continuously moving in the classroom. When a child is off task or appears to be disturbing another, Jones simply looks up at the child and either winks or smiles. Only once has Carolyn observed Jones leave one group of children to deal with a disruptive child, and that time he simply walked over and gently put his hand on the child's arm. The boy looked up at Jones, nodded, walked up to Jones's desk, wrote his name in the notebook there, and returned to his seat.

*The Artist/Teacher Bases Activities on Student Behavior* According to Jones, what works one day may not work the next. He tells Carolyn, "I cannot determine the order of activities. On some days when the children are hyper, quiet time is the most appropriate way to begin the day, whereas on days when they seem down, a physical activity is more appropriate." If he hears an important news report in the morning, this may become the basis of his social studies lesson for the day. When Jones reads a new book to the students, it is frequently one suggested by a child. If the day is sunny and warm, Jones might suggest that it is a perfect day to begin a unit on plant life with a nature walk in the woods. Carolyn has to admit that what he does seems to be effective. Jones's students never visit the office with behavioral problems and attendance in his classroom is the best in the school.

*The Artist/Teacher Is Intuitive and Difficult to Evaluate* What Jones does in his classroom may be difficult to measure. Jones's teaching cannot be evaluated using instruments that examine the content of a lesson. Nor can his teaching be evaluated according to the progress of his students. Jones's students score as well as other students on standardized tests but do not score significantly better.

N. L. Gage, in a lecture given at Teachers College, Columbia University, states that artistry in teaching requires a departure from the rules.

> As a practical art, teaching must be recognized as a process that calls for intuition, creativity, improvisation, and expressiveness—a process that leaves room for departures from what is implied by rules, formulas, and algorithms. In teaching, by whatever method it proceeds—even in the fixed programs of computer-assisted instruction—there is need for artistry: in the choice and use of motivational devices, clarifying definitions and examples, pace, redundancy, and the like.
>
> When teaching goes on in face-to-face interaction with students, the opportunity for artistry expands enormously. No one can ever prescribe successfully all the twists and turns to be taken as the lecturer, the discussion leader, or the classroom teacher uses judgment, sudden insight, sensitivity, and agility to promote learning. (1978, 15)

John Hill, professor of education at the University of Cincinnati, further contends that the artistic teacher is often so "committed in the act of performing that the specific skills have been stylized, personalized, and lost between reflective moments" (1985, 216).

The definition of teaching as art emphasizes the qualities of insight and intuition. These, however, are not the only qualities necessary to successful teaching.

## TEACHING AS A SCIENCE

Proponents of the point of view that teaching is a science contend that most people can learn the skills of teaching, can implement them in the classroom, and can be evaluated based on how well they teach. For example, Margery Montgomery had taught college composition in a small Southern college for three years. Every semester the students read essays and used them as models for their own writing. And every semester Margery graded six compositions written by each student and saw little progress from one to the next. One hot summer she decided to find a remedy.

She reread and analyzed the papers of students from previous semesters, listing common errors and cataloging them into levels of difficulty. While it was easy for students to learn that each paragraph needs a topic sentence, it was difficult for them to understand that the topic sentence need not start the paragraph. The more difficult the writing skill, the more frequently it was incorrect, both in the student's first paper and also the last.

Margery then determined which skills should be taught for the first, second, third, and each subsequent composition. She developed increasingly complex skill checklists, which she gave to the students before they began writing each composition. This not only helped students focus on the skill, but she also used them to grade the papers. Once a skill was taught, the student was expected to have mastered it in each subsequent composition. She also allowed the students to work in pairs and evaluate rough drafts of their compositions using the checklists.

Margery's efforts paid off. When she compared the final compositions of students who had used the new method to final compositions from previous semesters, writing improvement was marked. This, in turn, resulted in an improvement of the students' attitudes and their grades.

Therefore, it could be said that Margery is a scientist/teacher. What she has done in her class is to carefully analyze her students' errors and design an approach to show them how to improve their writing. The technique she employs could be taught to teachers and used by them. In addition her teaching can clearly be evaluated based on the progress of her students, which is exhibited not only in the improved writing in her class, but also on an end-of-the-course writing sample that all students in all composition classes must take at the end of each semester. Jones, on the other hand, is an artist/teacher. It is much more difficult to describe how he teaches, more complicated to teach to other teachers, and very difficult to evaluate.

A visit to another classroom in Carolyn Harris's school may help us better understand the scientist/teacher. Carolyn believes that Mariah Perez is an outstanding teacher. She is like an expert engineer in her first-grade classroom.

*The Scientist/Teacher Organizes Instruction*   In Mariah's classroom it is easy to observe and understand what she is doing. She begins every lesson with a review of the previous lesson and a statement about what is to be learned.

Mariah's class is well organized and orderly. Each day begins the same way: She reads to the children, sometimes a short article from the newspaper, sometimes a poem or a children's book. Then the children take their workbooks from their desks and begin the assignments, which are carefully printed on the chalkboard in the color that represents their learning group.

*The Scientist/Teacher Sets Acceptable Levels of Performance and Behavior* Mariah always begins by working with the red learning group in the small reading circle at the back of the room. She faces the class so that she can observe any rule infractions. Although there rarely are any, Mariah does not hesitate to call a child's name, saying, "Jennifer, you know that it is a rule not to bother another child while he is working. Go write your name on the board." Jennifer understands that if her name is called again, a check will be recorded after it, and she will miss fifteen minutes of recess. This is the **assertive discipline** plan used throughout the county (see chapter 2, p. 83).

When Carolyn asks Mariah why she always begins the day working with the red learning group, Mariah explains that they are nonreaders and cannot follow the instructions on the board, and need her help and encouragement more than the other children. She works with this group for nearly half an hour before moving to the blue learning group, with whom she works for only fifteen minutes. They already know how to read and write.

*The Scientist/Teacher Manages a Classroom*   At the end of the reading period, Mariah and the children review the stories they have read that day, sometimes acting them out. Mariah thinks it is important for each of the small learning groups to talk about what they are learning, but not while they are working on their lessons. Mariah carefully organizes her lesson plans, knows exactly what the students are doing at all times, follows school rules, uses the discipline plan chosen by the county, and carefully monitors and evaluates her students' progress. When Carolyn asks Mariah how she teaches, Mariah replies, "I use the six-point lesson plan. I think it makes sense. It's orderly and young children like routine. It also makes it easy to monitor the students' progress. I think of teaching as a science."

David Berliner, a psychologist, researcher, and writer at Stanford University, agrees with Mariah Perez that the science of teaching must take precedence over the art, since the management of the contemporary classroom is such a difficult task.

> Classrooms are workplaces: complex and dynamic workplaces that require management by an executive of considerable talent. Teachers are not usually thought of as executives. But it's time they became universally recognized as such. . . . Management is "running the place." In the new style of corporate management, less emphasis is on raw materials and manufacturing and more on managing and using the resource of personnel in such a way [as] to create something of value that did not exist before. (Berliner 1989, 105, 106)

## TEACHING IS BOTH AN ART AND A SCIENCE

Is Margaret Metzger, in the opening anecdote, an artistic or a scientific teacher? We do not see her in the classroom, but we read her description of herself as a teacher. It is clear that her rewards come from the artistic aspects of teaching: on the very best days, she reports, her class "sings." She is operating on many levels; she is integrating all aspects of teaching while meeting the needs of her students. At the same time, she is a scientist. She, like Margery, continuously poses questions about teaching and attempts to find answers to pedagogical problems. Linda Darling-Hammond and A. Lin Goodwin, authors and researchers at Columbia University, summarize the two aspects of teaching well. They claim that artistry depends on the marriage of innate talent and a systematic knowledge base or set of delineated skills that are demonstrated through creativity and initiative. According to Darling-Hammond and Goodwin, there is no doubt that much of teaching can be taught and evaluated, but "greatness as a teacher is often characterized by immeasurable qualities that extend beyond content knowledge or specific techniques—intuition, personality or individual dynamism, a sixth sense that 'reads' student needs" (1993, 24). The master teacher must be a scientist of the art of teaching.

The best teachers have clear objectives but improvise tactics for reaching those objectives. They know when it is essential to deal directly with facts and when it is important to enrich lessons to stimulate interest. They design learning activities based on the needs, interests, and abilities of the students. They frequently modify approaches when students appear to be experiencing difficulty. They base the standards they set on the objectives to be reached, but they encourage all students to exceed these objectives. Although substitute teachers and evaluators can follow their lesson plans, when artist/scientist/teachers implement the plans the lessons are varied and subject to change.

## THE ARTIST/SCIENTIST/TEACHER

Landon McMillan is a teacher of ninth-grade social studies who combines the qualities of an artist and a scientist. The ninth-grade curriculum emphasizes U.S. government. Landon believes that the students must be involved in the democratic process if they are to understand how the government works. For the first two weeks of each school year, Landon and his students monitor the local newspapers for an issue of local interest. This fall the students select cutting down of trees for timber in a nearby national forest. For many years the lumber companies have selectively harvested trees and planted new ones to replace them. Recently, however, local environmentalists have expressed concern that the foresting of trees is removing the natural habitats of several endangered species. Landon and his students read as much as they can about this issue and decide to make it the focus of their year's study in government.

### The Artist/Scientist/Teacher Focuses on Objectives but Improvises Tactics
Once the students have selected the topic, Landon gives them a list of objectives for the year that is based on the topic and the state's competency goals for ninth-grade social studies.

Miró, Joan. *Painting.* 1933. Oil on canvas, 68½" x 6'5¼". Collection, The Museum of Modern Art, New York. Loula D. Lasker Bequest (by exchange).

**We can best understand the process of effective teaching as both an artistic and scientific endeavor if we compare it to the process of understanding a painting. In order to appreciate and respond emotionally to this Miró painting, we must first recognize its concepts of color and design.**

1. To understand how the federal government influences environmental issues.
2. To understand how the federal courts affect environmental issues.
3. To understand how the state government influences environmental issues.
4. To understand how the state and local courts affect environmental issues.
5. To understand how local governments influence environmental issues.
6. To understand how interest groups interact with government to affect environmental issues.
7. To understand the role of Joe and Joanne Citizen in environmental issues.
8. To understand the role of the media as the "watchdog" of government.
9. To involve ourselves in government as it relates to this environmental issue.

He tells the students they will learn about how a democratic government works by being actively involved in this social and political issue, but doesn't tell them exactly how to accomplish this goal. Instead, Landon begins the unit by having the students discover what they already know about the issue. Then they make a list of things they need to learn. Landon suggests that they continue reading newspapers and current news magazines. He tells them to search for additional sources as they read. He advises them to write to agencies or individuals mentioned in the articles for more information. He also suggests that they discuss the issue with their families. Later in the unit the students will debate the issue based on their opinions and the new knowledge they have gained. "Ultimately," he tells the students, "the goal of this class is to help you understand the democracy in which you live so that you can take your role as an active citizen of the United States."

*The Artist/Scientist/Teacher Assists Students in Reaching Objectives*    The students are next divided into groups, each with a different aspect of the topic to investigate. One group is to search recent news magazines for related articles from various regions of the country. Another is to develop an annotated bibliography of available resources. A third is to develop a historical timeline of the forestry industry in the United States. Another is to make a list of various business, political, and environmental groups interested in the issue and write to them for information.

*The Artist/Scientist/Teacher Bases Standards on Objectives*    The groups are given nine sheets of paper and told to head each with a different objective. The students will list appropriate information and bibliographic data under each objective. Landon knows that the students are expected to master library research skills in ninth-grade social studies; therefore he incorporates these skills into the unit.

After the students gather information, they post their lists and discuss them with the class, developing a course outline and a bibliography with the help of Landon. As the year progresses Landon will use a variety of evaluation techniques including informal and formal oral presentations, mock court hearings, debates, papers explicating a single point of view, papers explaining several points of view, production of newscasts, interviews with key people, tests, research papers, and a final project requiring each student to take an active role in the issue.

*The Artist/Scientist/Teacher Encourages Students to Exceed Set Standards* Not only will Landon ensure that each of the objectives is met, but also that the students know the terms, concepts, and skills required to do well on statewide tests. They will read and discuss appropriate chapters in the state-adopted text-book, and as they read the chapter on the presidency, for example, they will examine how the president affects environmental policy.

By the end of the year, Landon's students will know the content required in the ninth-grade social studies curriculum based on their own as well as state competency objectives. In addition, they will have become participants in the democratic process.

Landon McMillan, Mariah Perez, and others like them utilize both their artistic and scientific qualities in teaching. They struggle to deal with many different kinds of students who have diverse social and academic needs. They use their knowledge and skills to understand how learning occurs in order to impart information successfully. They see the importance of classroom standards and goals, yet many fail to accomplish them through no fault of their own. Autonomous in their classrooms, they have still to answer to authorities within their own schools, their own cities, states, and even the nation. They hope that

---

**1-1**

**POINTS TO REMEMBER**

- Definitions of teaching include guidance, sharing knowledge, discovery, part trade and part professionalism.
- Artist/teachers are intuitive, improvise tactics, digress from topics, base learning on student behavior, focus on motivation and pacing, and set high standards for self and students.
- Scientist/teachers follow clearly stated objectives, deal directly with objectives and facts, seek order and relationships, guard against wishful thinking, and set expectations for performance based on objectives.
- Teaching as an art is intuitive; teaching as a science is based on developed skills. The training of teachers requires the development of skills; the evaluation of teachers requires the analysis of skills.
- The artist/scientist/teacher helps students understand what their best work can be and teaches them to achieve it by setting attainable goals.

---

ultimately their hard work will result in success, not only for their students, but also for their own professional status, which they expect will rise so that it at least equals that of other professionals.

## Teaching: A Profession

Is teaching a profession? If it is, it should possess the same characteristics of such professions as accounting, medicine, and law. Researchers have identified those characteristics as:

1. *a body of knowledge and the ability to apply that knowledge in the classroom*
   Darling-Hammond and Goodwin 1993; Labaree 1992; Ayers 1990; Feinberg 1990; Darling-Hammond and Berry 1988; Shanker 1987; Stinnett and Huggett 1963; Becker 1962; Bestor 1985
2. *autonomy to make decisions that affect life in the classroom and empowerment to make decisions that affect operation of the school*
   Brandt 1993; Darling-Hammond and Goodwin 1993; Carnegie Foundation 1990; Metropolitan Life Survey 1989; Maeroff 1988; Bennett 1986; Sizer 1984; Becker 1962
3. *a well-established set of collegial and peer relationships*
   Farkas 1993; Darling-Hammond 1992; Carnegie Foundation 1990; Little, 1990; Sockett 1990; Maeroff 1988; Shanker 1987; Bennett 1986
4. *ability to communicate to the public his or her actions, practices, and judgments*
   Labaree 1992; Sockett 1990; Bennett 1986; Sizer 1984
5. *high standards, a code of ethics, and a character and personality that are admired and respected*
   Barringer 1993; Darling-Hammond and Goodwin 1993; Metropolitan Life 1993; National Council of Teachers of Mathematics 1992; Goodlad 1990; Sockett 1990; Shanker 1987; Stinnett and Huggett 1963; Becker 1962; Bestor 1955
6. *commitment to the welfare of students; caring and compassionate relationship with students*

*(continued on p. 20)*

## IS TEACHING A PROFESSION?

### PRO  Jesse F. Haley

It is the purpose of the writer to attempt to show that teaching in both its broad and narrow concepts should be viewed by both educator and layman as a profession. . . . A profession is [according to *Funk and Wagnalls Standard Dictionary*] "an occupation that involves a liberal education, and mental rather than manual labor." To profess means "to announce publicly one's skill in as in art, science, etc.; also to assume the position of teacher or practitioner." We now have, if we accept the above definition, as I believe most educators would, a concise and clear statement of a profession in its general aspect . . .

Some of the outstanding professions are medicine, law, religious calling, dentistry, engineering and teaching. People will certainly admit that the first five are professions.

Teaching, alone, is the one profession mentioned wherein there is sometimes doubt both in the mind of the layman and more so in recent years, in the minds of some teachers. Why is the one profession that makes all the others possible so regarded? Why in the minds of many is the college professor a professional . . . , while the one who teaches the young from kindergarten through secondary school looked upon as belonging to a different group?

Perhaps it may be said because doctors, lawyers and dentists pass uniform standard examinations in the states wherein they practice . . . But college professors certainly do not pass the same examinations, nor do ministers, and yet universally they are regarded as a professional people. Because all teachers in one state do not pass the same examination, although all meet minimum requirements, is not the answer to the question. There must be other causes for this discrimination. . . .

It might be well to state at this point that teaching is really the only profession that for the most part is publicly operated. . . .

What is a teacher? He is more than an instructor. He is one who trains, drills, nurtures, sets an example, informs, indoctrinates, stimulates thought, in short an educator. The process of training for such a profession takes time and necessary experience. The process does not stop when the teacher starts his life work. A real educator is one who expands by means of professional journals, associations, courses, discussions and readings. When we consider how fast many of the educational practices change, because of the varying demands of society, we must realize that a wide awake teacher must be cognizant of these trends at the proper time, not years later. . . . Teaching is a highly skilled profession in that the demands made on it in understanding of the child, the patience and drill required to help this child expand morally, mentally and physically are far greater and more responsible than that of any trade. As a profession it has the right, as any group has, to organize but let it organize as a professional group as other professions have. Let not its organization be one that would take away any of its lofty ambitions and ideals but rather let it help to foster its true professional aims. Let its professional standards and qualifications be raised so that society will give further consideration and respect to it because society knows that it is their children who will benefit.

Excerpt from: J. F. Haley. 1946. "Teaching—A Profession," *The Educational Forum*, 11 (1). Reprinted in 1993. *The Educational Forum*, 57 (Winter), 204–208. Kappa Delta Pi, an International Honor Society in Education.

## POSTSCRIPT

Although these arguments are almost totally parallel, beginning with a disagreement about the meaning of "professional," continuing through the role of teachers as public employees, and finally disagreeing on whether teachers should be grouped with the "elitist" professions of law and medicine, they were written nearly fifty years apart. Their conclusions about whether or not teaching should be considered a profession also differ. Haley con-

# IS TEACHING A PROFESSION?

## CON  Anne Turnbaugh Lockwood

When Kathleen Densmore talks about what it means to be a professional, she begins with a reminder that the word itself needs careful definition. "The word 'professional' has both positive and negative meanings," she explains, "and it's a term that means different things to different people in different ways for different purposes.". . .

"When the word 'professional' is applied to teaching, it suggests an attempt to distinguish teachers from salaried employees."

To Densmore, rather than something positive, this smacks of elitism. "It suggests that some people are more deserving than others, and when it is applied to teachers, I'm concerned that it can suggest that they are set off from public accountability and the people they are supposed to serve." . . .

"Most of the prescriptions for change around professionalism are coming from the top. And most of them contain a meritocracy worldview, that assumes the best teachers will rise to the top. I would like to see more proposals for reform coming from the bottom." . . .

Densmore maintains that the "rhetoric of professionalism" promotes what she calls "the trivialization of teaching."

She explains, "I've seen it recently in the schools in which I work. Teachers have an endless amount of paperwork to manage, and an increasing amount of supervisory duties. The implicit message that often comes from school administrators is that a true professional would perform these tasks uncritically and not question them, and certainly not say they are not part of their job description."

Densmore does not believe that teaching can become a profession in the same sense that law and medicine are professions. "It isn't realistic," she says bluntly. . . .

"The attainment of professionalization would be incompatible with the most important aims of teaching," she says vehemently. "It would create artificial barriers between teachers and low-income parents. Since education is a public enterprise, it should be a participatory and democratic enterprise."

From: A. T. Lockwood. 1992. "Rethinking Professionalization: An Interview with Kathleen Densmore," *Focus in Change*, 9, 12–14.

tends that it is critical that teaching be ranked among the professions if teachers are to be recognized for their skill and contributions. Lockwood, on the other hand, contends that calling teaching a profession smacks of elitism, placing barriers between teachers and low-income parents, and removes from teachers the power they currently possess in their unions and professional organizations. The disagreement about whether teaching is or is not a profession is not new. Nor have the stances changed much in nearly half a century.

Darling-Hammond and Goodwin 1993; Sizer 1992; Ayers 1990; Kohn 1990; Darling-Hammond 1988; Stinnett and Huggett 1963

7. *commitment to a lifetime teaching career*
   Cohen 1991; Freidson 1986; Stinnett and Huggett 1963
8. *accountability for the quality of teaching and the progress of students*
   Darling-Hammond and Goodwin 1993; Nelson and O'Brien 1993; Sockett 1990; Gallup and Elam 1988
9. *membership in professional organizations*
   Murray 1992; Stinnett and Huggett 1963; Becker 1962
10. *opportunity to use his or her own discretion and freedom to teach without direct supervision*
    Cohen 1991; Sockett 1990; Shanker 1987; Bennett 1986

In addition, the field of education, in order to be considered a profession, needs to acquire the following characteristics:

1. *controlled recruitment into the field of teaching and extensive training*
   Zimpher and Ashburn 1992; Feinberg 1990; Goodlad 1990; Freidson 1986; Stinnett and Huggett 1963; Becker 1962
2. *working conditions, salary, benefits, and comparable performance*
   Nelson and O'Brien 1993; Cohen 1991; Sockett 1990; American Federation of Teachers 1989; National Education Association 1989a; Carnegie Forum 1986; Goodlad 1984; Boocock 1980
3. *continuous retraining for intellectual growth and development*
   Darling-Hammond and Goodwin 1993; Espinosa 1992; Sleeter 1992; Stinnett and Huggett 1963
4. *objective evaluation and performance rewards*
   Cornett and Gaines 1993; Wood 1992; Brandt 1990; Southern Regional Education Board 1991; Chance 1986; Rosenholtz 1986; Wise et al. 1984

Perhaps in the 1990s, the best way to look at teaching is as an emerging profession. We can examine the emergence of the teaching profession by analyzing it in relationship to the qualities of a professional, although it is likely that Densmore would argue against this approach. Of the fourteen professional qualities listed above, nine have clearly been attained. However, seven are still being developed. We will examine each of the qualities of the teaching profession that have not been met: autonomy, empowerment, collegial and peer relationships, evaluation and rewards, accountability, sensitivity to student diversity, and standards for the teaching profession.

## TEACHER AUTONOMY

**Autonomy** assumes that teachers have the discretion to make decisions related to the life of the classroom. According to Gary Fenstermacher in *The Moral Dimensions of Teaching* (1990), a teacher must have the autonomy to formulate his or her own plans, act on these plans, assess them, and act again. A teacher who lacks autonomy may be told which books to use, which questions to ask, and which pages in the workbook students are expected to complete, and thus feel in less control than someone with autonomy.

According to Barry Bull in *The Moral Dimensions of Teaching,* teacher autonomy includes both freedom and responsibility: freedom to instruct the young when parents no longer have exclusive rights to do so and responsibility to develop those characteristics, abilities, and understandings expected by the "democratic polity." This responsibility, according to Bull, also requires resisting those policy directives that are not relevant to the purposes of public education. However, he contends that the centralized system of schooling mitigates against directives and regulations of the school board reaching teachers who are seldom aware of all the issues involved in the decisions. If teachers are to be autonomous in their classrooms, there must be decentralization of authority. Bruce Kimball (1988) in his article "The Problem of Teachers' Authority in Light of the Structural Analysis of Professions" agrees. According to Kimball the legal structure of teaching gives the responsibility of decision making to boards of education and the courts uphold their authority. He claims that there is no legal recognition given to teachers' exclusive rights to control education practice. Until this occurs, says Kimball, teaching will not be a profession.

The more autonomy teachers have in making decisions important to their teaching, the more likely they are to have a positive image of their role. The more positive their image of themselves as teachers, the more satisfied and successful they are likely to be. According to David Goslin, teachers in smaller schools usually have a good deal of autonomy in the classroom; however, the larger the school, the less the teacher's autonomy (1965, 29). Sarane Boocock (1980) found that teachers' relatively low status in the school hierarchy (below principals, supervisors, and other administrators) gave them little control over their working conditions, even those in their own class-rooms. C. E. Murray (1992) suggests that because teachers do not have legal authority they need to exert political authority through local teachers' associations in order to gain autonomy. According to Murray, when teachers have autonomy they can exercise personal authority in planning and teaching, which is crucial if students are to learn.

Elementary teachers in a 1986 poll conducted by *Instructor Magazine* suggested that autonomy, along with improved public understanding, respect, and professionalism, were the most important qualities needed in the teach-ing profession. In 1991, 1,007 first-year elementary and secondary teachers in the *Metropolitan Life Survey of the American Teacher* indicated that more opportunities to work with other teachers to enhance their skills, collegial relationships with other teachers, and staff development opportunities are three things that would significantly help their performance (1991, 17). Although elementary teachers found their jobs to be "deeply gratifying" and demanding, some days to the point of exhaustion, they were frustrated by their lack of involvement in decision making. Fewer than 30 percent of those surveyed said they made most of the major decisions about texts and supple-mentary materials. Only 24 percent said they were "meaningfully" involved in the subjects and grades they taught, and only 16 percent said they frequently received useful guidance from the principal on instructional matters (1986, 6). Teachers continue to feel that lack of autonomy, including limited oppor-tunities to make decisions and work with other teachers, is one of the major deficits in teaching.

As professionals, teachers need to possess numerous qualities. Among them are a set of high standards, a personality and character that are admired and respected, and the ability to impart knowledge to a group of diverse students. This teacher leads her first-grade reading group in a lively discussion.

## TEACHER EMPOWERMENT

Gene is a first-year teacher certification student at a large university. However, Gene is not a typical student. He is forty-three years old and has already had a successful career as a banker. On the first day of class, he sits down with Maryjane Montgomery, his adviser, to discuss his decision to make a career change. "Why have you decided to go into teaching?" Maryjane asks.

"I guess I always wanted to teach," replies Gene. "What I liked best about my job at the bank was training and supervising our new employees. A teacher has the power to make a real difference for people. I can't think of a more rewarding profession."

After Gene leaves Maryjane's office, she finds herself wondering if Gene is making the right decision. She respects Gene's decision but is fearful he might be disappointed in teaching. Will he find teaching as rewarding as he hopes? Will he have the "power," as he calls it, to make a real difference? She hopes so; she knows that Gene is the type of person who should be in the classroom.

**Teacher empowerment** is a relatively new phrase that frequently is used as a synonym for professionalism. Empowerment goes a step beyond autonomy. It assumes that teachers are decision makers and that they help make school policy decisions that will influence life in the classroom and the school, including student placement, student evaluation and grading, selection of texts and other materials, attendance procedures, subject matter to be taught, curriculum development, teaching methodology, in-service training, evaluation of peers, and selection of school-based administrators.

According to a survey of 1,850 elementary school teachers in the United States, empowerment will allow them to have some control over their professional destiny (Ashby et al. 1989). However, teachers report that they have a limited role in school decision making. For example, in the *Instructor Magazine* poll, 47 percent said they made none of the decisions regarding their own in-service training; 61 percent had no opportunity to observe their peers teach. Similar results were reported in a 1990 Carnegie Foundation poll of 21,698 public school teachers. Ninety percent of the teachers surveyed indicated that they had no say in issues like teacher evaluation or selection of new teachers and administrators. Just 20 percent felt they had any influence at all in tailoring school budgets (see table 1.1).

A 1990 poll of 21,389 teachers from each of the fifty states and Washington, D.C., conducted by the Carnegie Foundation for the Advancement of Teaching, found "no significant growth in teacher participation [in school decision making], and in some cases . . . a slight decline" (p. 51). When polled, many teachers reported that they were "slightly" or "not at all" involved in setting student promotion and retention policies (71 percent); in setting budgets (8 percent); in the selection of new teachers (90 percent); in the evaluation of teacher performance (92 percent); and in selecting new administrators (93 percent).

## *Viewpoint* Teacher Empowerment

*Peterson and her colleagues are just beginning to experiment with some of the tenets of the school reform movement. She is also experimenting with different instructional strategies in order to engage the attention of every child. "I think we're realizing now that we are going to have to deal with things differently than in the past. At one time I was not receptive to the idea of having different things going on in a classroom. But we must compete against outside forces for a student's attention."*

Let me tell you what a group of teachers is trying to do at Capital Middle School, and you tell me whether or not it's teacher empowerment.

Capital has a high percentage of at-risk students from low socioeconomic situations. The school's success indicators were the lowest of any school in Baton Rouge. When I got here a couple of years ago, morale was very low. A few of us realized that if we were going to do something to boost student morale, the teachers had to boost their own. We had to realize that we were in a position to change a school that everyone did nothing but complain about.

A few of the sixth-grade teachers began to talk about ways to stimulate improvement. At the same time the Southern Regional Council came along with grant money for middle schools with at-risk populations through a local agency called Volunteers in Public Schools (VIPS). We applied for a grant to build achievement, encourage good behavior, and raise academic standards.

While we would have made progress on our own, the grant money was catalytic. It gave us a sense that we could do much more for students than we could have done alone. It also meant that the community and the administration backed us up.

Teachers formed a volunteer steering committee dedicated to changing the school. Some, perhaps, signed up out of curiosity, but many were very determined that we could make a difference.

**TABLE 1-1**

### Secondary School Teachers' Perceptions of Decision Making for Selected School and Classroom Decisions, by Control of School and Type of Community: 1990–91

| | | | Public schools | | | |
|---|---|---|---|---|---|---|
| | | | | Type of community | | |
| Decisions | All schools | Private schools | Total | Rural/small town | Urban fringe/large town | Central city |
| *Percentage of teachers reporting faculty having a great deal of influence over school policies:* | | | | | | |
| Determining discipline policy | 10 | 13 | 9 | 9 | 9 | 11 |
| Determining content of faculty training programs | 12 | 12 | 11 | 10 | 13 | 12 |
| Grouping students by ability | 8 | 14 | 8 | 7 | 7 | 8 |
| Establishing curriculum | 14 | 21 | 13 | 16 | 13 | 11 |
| *Percentage of teachers reporting themselves having complete control over classroom decisions:* | | | | | | |
| Selecting textbooks | 34 | 50 | 33 | 40 | 28 | 25 |
| Selecting course content and topics | 36 | 50 | 35 | 40 | 31 | 30 |
| Selecting teaching techniques | 62 | 76 | 61 | 64 | 59 | 59 |
| Grading students | 62 | 70 | 62 | 63 | 61 | 61 |
| Disciplining students | 35 | 48 | 34 | 34 | 34 | 35 |
| Determining amount of homework | 68 | 74 | 67 | 69 | 66 | 66 |

*From:* National Center for Education Statistics, Schools and Staffing Survey, 1990–91, as reported in *The Condition of Education 1993,* U.S. Department of Education, Office of Educational Research and Improvement (NCES), 93–290, p. 124.

> In 1991, secondary school teachers more often indicated having considerable influence over decisions concerning instruction within their classrooms than over school-level politics regarding student discipline, student tracking, and overall curriculum and staff development. Private school teachers were more likely than public school teachers to perceive themselves having complete control over classroom decisions and a great deal of influence over school policies.

We tackled our problems one by one. For example, kids wouldn't come to class on time so we set up a "tardy room." The idea was this: If kids came to school late, they'd go directly to the tardy room. The teacher on duty would work with the kids in whatever way he or she chose to impress upon them that being on time was important. An important point: Each teacher gives up a prep period to monitor the room.

The tardy room works beautifully. We started out with twenty-five or thirty kids in the room every period. That number was cut at the end of the school year to six. Sometimes this year there aren't any students in the room. We are proud of the success because this is something we made work.

Teacher empowerment is a pretty simple concept: It's active involvement of teachers in the school decision-making process and assuming responsibility for

Teachers who directly participate in the development of school policy, curriculum, and textbook selection have autonomy, a quality necessary for a positive self-image and success in the classroom. These teachers are discussing lesson plans they will use as team teachers.

that involvement. We wanted to cut down on tardiness. We came up with an idea, and we implemented it.

   To make change in a school, there has to be a team approach. You have to find people who are going to work with you. If you take an authoritative attitude, you're going to have the respect that authority commands. But to have authority you have to have credibility. And you have to know how to approach people. If you force your opinion, you're not going to have any success. But if you go into a situation with a genuineness of heart, people will be willing to work with you.

> From: Peterson, 1990. Deborah Peterson began teaching sixteen years ago in Crowley, Louisiana, and returned home to Baton Rouge four years ago to take a job as a sixth-grade teacher at Capital Middle School.

   ***Standardized Approaches Limit Teacher Empowerment***   Teachers in the late 1980s and early 1990s voiced concern that standardized approaches to curriculum development, standardized testing of students, and standardized planning and evaluation of teaching, found in most states, forced them to comply with state and school mandates, thus limiting teacher decision making. According to a mail survey of teachers in all fifty states, teacher morale was low in spite of reforms such as incentive pay plans adopted by many of those states (Carnegie Foundation for the Advancement of Teaching 1988, 11). In fact, careful examination of the survey shows that teacher morale was lowest in states where reforms reflected a top-down administrative structure, which made teachers feel as if they lacked autonomy and had no control over decisions that affected their teaching and evaluation. Linda Darling-Hammond and A. Lin Goodwin suggest that teacher empowerment requires the reshaping of teachers' roles, responsibilities, and teaching conditions and will require the restructuring of schools. Their studies have found that this type of restructuring is beginning to occur. According to Darling-Hammond and Goodwin, "Many school reform efforts have sought to include teachers, along with parents, in school decision making. These include school-based management and shared decision-making initiatives in San Diego, California; Salt Lake City, Utah; Dade County, Florida; Rochester, New York; and New York City, among many others. Other collaborative efforts include the involvement of teachers in developing curriculum and student performance assessments in such states as Vermont and California" (Darling-Hammond and Goodwin 1993, 41).

School membership in Theodore Sizer's Coalition of Essential Schools, as another example, a voluntary consortium of 2 hundred schools in twenty-three states and Canada working together for educational reform, requires for membership that teachers be empowered to jointly develop curriculum, assessments of learning, and plans for professional development. In schools participating in Sizer's coalition, teachers work in teams, integrate subject content in interdisciplinary core courses, and teach fewer students for longer periods of time, thereby getting to know them well.

## COLLEGIAL AND PEER RELATIONSHIPS

Arlene Plevin, a researcher for the National Education Association (NEA), reports that teachers find collegial relationships important to their professional development, particularly at the beginning of each school year, when every member of the educational team essentially starts over again with new students who have diverse personalities and abilities. A 1993 study of four geographically diverse school districts conducted by the Public Agenda Foundation and funded by the Kettering Foundation found that professionals working day-by-day in the schools report that isolation from each other and from the central administration is a major problem in the development of new, different, and exciting lessons. Farkas, the author of the study, reported that "in all four districts teachers seemed to work in a pressure-cooker environment with little time to share resources, information and experience among themselves" (1992, 8).

Plevin (1988) and Little (1990) report that some schools and school districts are attempting to create more opportunities for collegial exchange. Traditional class scheduling and in-service days are being modified to meet this need. In some secondary schools, for example, all teachers in a single subject area have the same planning period so that they can meet together to share ideas and plan the curriculum. Little found that collegiality of teachers resulted in reduced teacher planning time as ideas and materials were pooled in the design of curriculums and tests. The sharing of new practices and ideas inspired more confidence in discussing teaching methods and produced continual self-evaluation. However, Little also cautioned that serious collaboration takes time, training, and patience (1990, 188).

Although it is clear that some schools are working toward developing increased time for collegiality, others are not. For example, the 1989 Metropolitan Life Survey showed that team teaching (two or more professionals teaching a single course together) has increased in 45 percent of the schools and decreased in 25 percent of the schools since 1985. Similarly, 39 percent of the teachers responding to the 1989 survey reported that structured collegial time in their schools had decreased since 1985, whereas 41 percent reported that it had increased.

Another means of providing teachers with more collegial time is planned observation of peers. Thirty-seven percent of those teachers responding to the 1989 Metropolitan Life Survey reported that their school was better in 1989 than in 1986 at having teachers observe one another and provide feedback. However, 33 percent of the teachers said that their school was worse than in 1986.

## INCENTIVE PAY

**Incentive pay** or **performance-based** programs are designed to give teachers increased compensation for success in teaching, for accepting additional responsibilities, and/or for obtaining additional educational degrees. These programs are an outgrowth of the reform reports of the 1980s that suggested that school improvement required better teaching and greater student achievement. Hence, incentive pay programs attempt to link rewards to performance.

In 1990, twenty-five states had increased funding for incentive pay programs that linked financial rewards for teachers and administrators to performance and increased work loads. Ten states had incentive programs that rewarded schools and their staffs for schoolwide innovation or improvement. In 1991, thirty states had increased funding for incentive pay plans and the Southern Regional Education Board reported that most incentive pay programs were focused on increased student achievement and reduced dropout rates. However, by 1992–1993 many states found that their funding reserves were at an all-time low. A large number that had begun incentive pay programs reduced by half their planned monetary growth for elementary and secondary education, including funding of incentive programs. Only six states increased their incentive pay programs while three increased school incentive programs. Two suspended incentive pay entirely and one reduced funding for teacher incentive grants. Two states have not funded their school incentive programs beyond their developmental years in the late 1980s, and two other states reduced their school incentive programs by half.

According to a 1990 study by Richard Brandt and a 1993 study by Cornett and Gaines, the plans have affected teaching in the following ways:

- Teacher evaluation has changed. Because few systematic procedures existed, evaluation schemes were developed not only to help teachers, but to make decisions about performance. . . .
- There are a few instances where incentive pay has been primarily dependent on student achievement—although this is increasing. Most programs continue to move toward incentives for professional development and performing extra work. . . .
- Principals are spending more time in the classroom dealing with instruction; teachers and principals are more involved in joint decision making; some teachers are taking on new roles that expand their responsibility

beyond their own classroom; teachers and principals are planning together when the teachers will be evaluated.
- Programs have caused more differentiation in pay among teachers in a district. Mentor teacher projects are increasingly popular. . . .
- Teacher attitudes have often initially been negative, but have become more positive where programs are seen to have been well implemented.
- Teachers are most hostile to programs that are performance-based and highly selective. . . . (1990, 245–255)

All incentive pay, or performance-based, compensation programs are designed to improve teaching by providing the best teachers with financial incentives.

## TEACHER ACCOUNTABILITY

Teacher evaluation and assessment of student performance are frequently tied to systems of incentive pay. Cornett and Gaines in a 1993 study found that school incentive programs—with rewards for improving student performance—were growing in number. The assumption is that quality teaching leads to greater student achievement and should be rewarded.

**Teacher accountability**, then, means that teachers are responsible for the quality of their instruction and the progress of their students. Usually, teacher performance is measured through classroom-based observation and evaluation by administrators and trained teacher evaluators. Student progress is typically measured by performance on nationally normed standardized tests. In the 1990 Gallup poll of the Public's Attitude Toward the Public Schools, 70 percent of those surveyed favored requiring public schools in their communities to conform to national standards and goals. However, only 36 percent believed national standards and goals could be accomplished by the year 2000. Likewise, in a 1989 survey of two thousand teachers, conducted by the Metropolitan Life Insurance Company, 61 percent of teachers surveyed indicated that they support teacher accountability for the academic success of students (Metropolitan Life Insurance Company 1989, 75).

Despite the support of teacher accountability for student achievement, there is significant disagreement about whether it is possible to evaluate excellence in teaching and whether it is appropriate to assume that teaching excellence necessarily leads to student achievement. For example, assume that Moyra and Roberto teach second grade in the same elementary school. Moyra teaches a class of students who tested above grade level in kindergarten and first grade. Roberto's class tested below grade level. Evaluators believe that both are very good teachers. However, when the standardized tests are administered in the spring, Roberto's students have fallen even further below grade level and Moyra's students have risen further above. Hence, in their incentive pay system, Roberto will receive an average salary increase and Moyra will receive an above average increase. Is this fair? Roberto contends it is not. He says that studies show that children who are below grade level continue to fall further and further behind no matter how good their instruction. He also maintains that his children do not test well because their backgrounds render the tests inappropriate. According to Roberto, the children are unfamiliar with many of the words on the tests because the words are not used in their homes. In addition, Roberto says that he has to work harder than Moyra to be a successful teacher. He also contends that it is not fair to make him accountable when he cannot make decisions about the textbooks and the curriculum he would use. He says that if he could teach these children as he would like to, he would throw away the basal readers, take them on weekly field trips, use written material related to those field trips, introduce them to all kinds of music and visual arts, and read to them at least an hour per day. "Only then," says Roberto, "can I be accountable for the progress of the children."

Linda Darling-Hammond, in a report sponsored by the National Center for Restructuring Education, Schools, and Teaching (NCREST), suggests that neither schools nor teachers can be evaluated purely by student outcomes for these reasons: tests measure the developed abilities and motivations that students bring to school with them; students are influenced by nonschool learning including conditions under which they live; aggregated measures of outcomes such as student achievement and attendance fluctuate with changes in school population and that brings changes in family and community support, school practices and teaching methods change; student performance data is rarely collected or analyzed longitudinally for individual students or groups of students who happen to remain in the same school over a period of time (1992).

## RESULTS OF INCENTIVE PAY PROGRAMS

Historically educators have complained that the only way to advance themselves professionally was to quit teaching and enter administration. One of the goals of incentive pay, or **performance-based**, compensation plans, therefore, is to give teachers increased professional opportunity without requiring them to leave the classroom. For example, in an incentive pay system a teacher's salary is based on seniority and also on educational advancement and teaching excellence. Furthermore, many incentive pay programs offer teachers opportunities to pursue higher education. In some states, school districts provide training for teachers that can lead to merit increases or simply reimburse teachers for educational expenses. Three of the most common incentive pay programs are merit pay, career ladder, and master teacher programs.

*Merit Pay*   One method of financially rewarding teachers for doing their job well is **merit pay**. It does not require a teacher to have increased responsibility or extra assignments. Generally, merit pay is not incorporated into the teacher's base salary but is awarded in the form of an annual bonus. In addition, merit pay programs do not attempt to develop a hierarchy of job classification but simply reward teachers for job-related achievement.

One of the greatest difficulties in a merit pay system has always been in determining the best evaluation system to identify those who deserve a pay increase. Whether conducted by a supervisor, based on student achievement data, or determined by a teacher's portfolio, there is no system that is completely objective. Thus, complaints of favoritism may arise, or worse, moral and ethical complacency may develop in order to appease those in authority who may be scheduled to evaluate a teacher's performance. Furthermore, whatever collegiality exists in a particular school environment may be threatened by the necessity to compete with one's colleagues rather than cooperate with them. As one teacher reported in a study done by Arthur G. Wirth, "In this particular school [merit pay] has destroyed any type of relations. I mean you look at the person next door to you and you say 'I wonder how many points she has.' So instead of encouraging teachers to be more open about what they're doing, there isn't one bit of sharing. When you're in competition with another person for your job, you're pitting one person against another" (1992, 12).

Merit pay is not a new concept. In the early 1920s, 40–50 percent of school districts in the United States had merit pay plans. However, by the 1930s many of these plans had been replaced by more uniform pay scales. Complaints about merit pay systems included questions about the evaluator's judgment and differentials in the salaries of males and females. However, during the school reform movement of the 1950s, merit pay plans, based on teacher performance, were reintroduced. In 1968, 11 percent of all school districts had merit pay programs. By 1976, however, only 4 percent of all schools awarded merit pay. Today, although some merit pay programs exist, most incentive pay programs are not merit or bonus systems but instead base salary differences on measurements of performance, increased responsibilities, and higher levels of education or training. A 1991 survey of teachers and administrators conducted for the Consortium for Policy Research in Education confirmed that incentive pay plans that include job enlargement (extra work such as summer curriculum development and teachers working and planning together) resulted in increased motivation and a broader range of instructional practices and enriching teaching materials, whereas merit pay plans tended to result in standardization of teaching practice (Firestone, 269, 284).

*Career Ladder*   Much more elaborate than merit pay plans are **career ladder** plans that create a new structure for a teaching career, allowing teachers to pass through several stages, each with greater responsibilities and more pay. These plans are also called **differentiated staffing**. Promotion from one level to the next is based on an objective assessment of professional achievements. A hierarchy of job classifications and a differentiated salary schedule result.

For example, as a level-one classroom teacher, or intern, a teacher might be paid at a base of $24,000. Before advancing to level two, the professional level, the teacher would be expected to have successfully completed several years of teaching and to have been evaluated by other teachers and administrators based on a state- or district-designed evaluation instrument. Moreover, he or she would be required to obtain additional education to reach level two. This level also carries increased responsibility, such as curriculum development or teacher mentoring. The base for this level might be $27,000. At level three, the career professional level, the teacher might be required to assume responsibilities as a teacher evaluator or curriculum supervisor. In addition, she or he is likely to be required to obtain a master's degree and additional areas of certification. At this level, the base might be $32,000.

Career ladders are a relatively new concept. (According to Corbett and Gaines, in 1993, six states had fully implemented statewide career ladder plans and one state had a local individual school district initiative career ladder plan.) However, some states have had career ladder programs since the early 1980s. Tennessee's career ladder, instituted statewide in 1983, began as a merit pay program to attract the best candidates and to identify and keep superior teachers.

By 1987, 39 thousand or 84 percent, of Tennessee's teachers had a career ladder certificate, with 62 hundred teachers at the top two levels. Although involvement in Tennessee's career ladder program is no longer mandated by law, the majority of tenured teachers participate and have received training in the evaluation system. Most teachers remain at the lowest level since promotion to the upper levels is done sparingly by outside evaluators. During 1988–1989, only one of five eligible teachers or administrators had achieved levels two or three, and salary supplements ranged from one thousand to 7 thousand dollars for a twelve-month contract. Teachers at levels two and three had additional opportunities for summer employment. But today teachers at all levels have equal opportunities for summer employment, removing one of the incentives for achieving higher levels on the career ladder.

*Master Teacher*    Superior performance can be achieved through **master teacher** plans. According to Corbett and Gaines, in 1993, twenty-one states had master or mentor teacher plans. Although such plans do not establish a graduated career structure, they give one group of teachers increased responsibility for which they are usually provided additional compensation. The programs are also called lead, mentor, or head teacher plans. In California, mentor teachers spend 40 percent of their time working with other teachers on curriculum and instruction and conducting workshops and peer evaluations. Other master teacher plans restructure the teaching pattern of the school. In these plans, the teaching staff might be divided into teams with one master, mentor, head, or lead teacher assuming a leadership function. In other plans, mentor teachers might assume responsibility for the guidance of neophyte teachers in the school. Although these plans are not usually associated with a differentiated staffing pattern, they do highlight differences in teacher performance, responsibility, and salary that run counter to the egalitarian manner in which schools have been traditionally organized.

## OPPOSITION TO INCENTIVE PAY

Although the majority of teachers support some type of teacher accountability for student achievement, a large percentage do not support the current incentive pay plans. In 1989, 48 percent of teachers surveyed by the Metropolitan Life Insurance Company believed that methods used to select teachers for merit pay tended to be unfair and nonobjective. This, however, was down from the 56 percent who found the methods unfair in 1986. Similarly in 1989, 60 percent of teachers surveyed believed that career ladder systems created "artificial and unfortunate distinctions among teachers." This was down from 72 percent in 1986. If so many teachers do not support performance-based compensation plans, can the programs be considered incentives toward improving teaching and keeping the best teachers in the classroom? On the other hand, as these plans are becoming more widely employed, are they more acceptable to the teachers who are participating in them? It will be some time before we know the answers to these questions and the level of success of performance-based compensation plans. Table 1.2 shows the types of incentives favored by teachers.

**TABLE 1-2**

### SASS (Schools and Staffing Survey) Data on Public School Teacher Favorability Rating of Pay Incentives

| Pay incentive program | Statistic[1] | Favorability rating | | | |
| --- | --- | --- | --- | --- | --- |
| | | Strongly favor | Mildly favor | Mildly oppose | Strongly oppose |
| 1. For Added Responsibilities | Percent | 57.8% | 28.7% | 5.7% | 6.9% |
| | Std Error | .33 | .22 | .14 | .16 |
| 2. Teaching in Shortage Field | Percent | 23.7% | 28.6% | 20.6% | 27.0% |
| | Std Error | .20 | .28 | .25 | .26 |
| 3. Teaching in High-Priority Location | Percent | 40.5% | 36.3% | 12.3% | 11.0% |
| | Std Error | .30 | .29 | .18 | .19 |
| 4. Career Ladder Progress | Percent | 39.1% | 30.7% | 12.2% | 18.0% |
| | Std Error | .33 | .27 | .21 | .24 |
| 5. Individual Merit Pay | Percent | 27.0% | 26.2% | 16.5% | 30.4% |
| | Std Error | .31 | .29 | .20 | .28 |
| 6. Group Merit Bonus | Percent | 33.5% | 30.1% | 14.7% | 21.8% |
| | Std Error | .28 | .29 | .18 | .24 |

[1]The unweighted sample sizes on which these data are based are about 40,000 teachers in the public sector and about 6,500 in the private sector. The statistics tabulated pertain to weighted estimates of over 2,200,000 public school teachers and close to 300,000 private school teachers in the United States.

*From:* E. Boe, "Teacher Incentive Research With SASS," paper presented at meeting of the American Education Research Association (April 1990).

**Several programs for determining which teachers should receive pay in addition to their salary have been implemented through the years in various school systems around the country. None have been totally effective or totally acceptable. This table lists the major programs and, by showing the percentage of teachers who approve or disapprove of them, gives a favorability rating for each.**

### SALARIES

Teachers' salaries are increasing both in and out of incentive pay programs. But, are they keeping up with inflation and the salaries of other professionals?

A study of economic principles reveals that an increased demand for teachers and a limited supply, such as we have in the 1990s, should lead to increased salaries. Historically, this has not been the case. In the 1960s, when the demand for teachers exceeded the supply, teaching salaries remained low. Although teaching salaries have risen dramatically in the last several decades, they have not kept pace with those for other professions (see figure 1.1), and have barely kept pace with inflation (see figure 1.2, p. 34).

As early as the mid-1800s, educator and politician Horace Mann recognized the need for improved teacher salaries. Mann claimed that in the 1840s female teachers were paid less than many female laborers in factories. He recognized that the quality of teachers would not improve until salaries improved. If Mann was

**FIGURE 1-1**

## Average Teacher Salary in 1992 Falls Short of Earnings in Other Professions

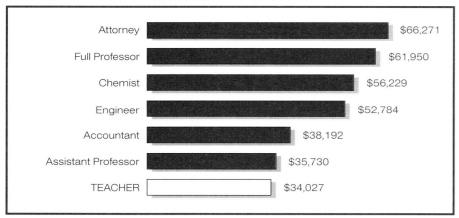

## New Teacher Salaries Lag Behind Beginning Salaries in Other Occupations

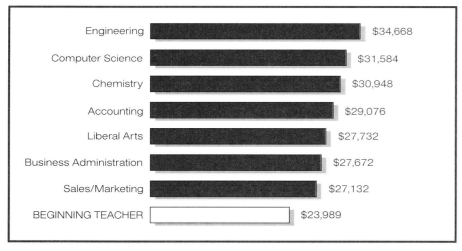

Note: Expected salary of spring graduates. Beginning teacher salary is based on an estimated 3.0 percent increase for the 1993–94 school year.

From: American Federation of Teachers, *Survey and Analysis of Salary Trends* (1993), ix.

**While teachers' salaries have risen considerably in recent years, they remain, for the most part, below the salaries of other professions.**

correct, incentive pay programs will do little to improve the quality of teaching unless overall teaching salaries increase.

Again in the 1980s, as many times before, the call for increased teacher salaries was made by the commissions suggesting reforms in teaching and teacher training. According to a U.S. Department of Education report in 1987, "reports of teacher shortages in selected specialties and the possibility of a general teacher

*(continued on p. 35)*

**FIGURE 1-2**

## Teacher Salaries Keep Even With Inflation

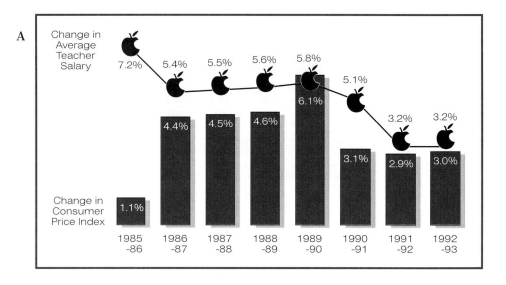

A

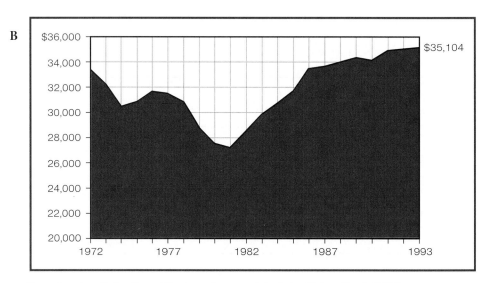

## Average Teacher Salary Exceeds
## 1972 Levels By About $1,700

B

From: American Federation of Teachers, *Survey and Analysis of Salary Trends* (1993).

Teacher salaries have barely kept pace with the cost of inflation as measured by the consumer price index, which shows the percentage of change in cost of goods and services over a given period of time (A). When adjusted for inflation, a teacher's salary in 1992–1993 increased only 19.5 percent from 1979–1980 (B).

shortage in the future have increased the perceived importance of teacher salaries as an incentive in attracting and retaining capable teachers" (p. 50).

In 1992–1993 the highest paid teachers in the United States lived in Connecticut and earned an average of $48,850, while the lowest paid teachers lived in South Dakota and made $24,125. The average teaching salary in 1992–1993 was $35,334, up over 100 percent since 1979–1980 when the average salary was $15,970. However, when adjusted for inflation, the increase over that period was only 19.5 percent, according to the National Education Association. It is also interesting to note that some teachers in some financially troubled school districts have been forced to endure pay cuts. In September 1993, for example, Los Angeles teachers' salaries were cut by 10 percent.

In 1990 when the average base salary was $33,578, male teachers earned an average of $6,000 more than female teachers ($37,895–$31,870). This is partially a result of higher supplemental salaries paid to male teachers: $2,663 for males during the school year, $1,357 to females; $2,328 paid to males during the summer, $1,773 to females. However, male teachers' base salaries were nearly $3,000 higher than female teachers' base salaries (National Center for Educational Statistics 1993a, 82).

Ironically, the inability of teaching salaries to keep ahead of inflation has affected teachers with experience more than it has beginning teachers. In order to attract new teachers to the profession, entry salaries have been kept relatively high when compared to salaries of experienced teachers (see figure 1.3, p. 36). For example, in Connecticut, where teachers have the highest entry salaries, they will reach the top of the pay scale in six or seven years, while in some of the southern states, where entry salaries are relatively low, it may take teachers thirty to fifty years to reach the top, according to the American Federation of Teachers. John Goodlad called the low ratio of teaching salaries after ten years to beginning salaries the "flatness" of the profession. He warned that this trend would ensure that teaching remains a "marginal profession" because the best teachers would leave for better-paying jobs (1984).

In part, as a response to the concern for the flatness of teacher salaries, reform in the allocation of salaries was initiated in many states in the 1980s. This reform, allowing for differentiation in pay based on performance and increased responsibilities, was highly touted by the Reagan and Bush administrations. Reagan's secretary of education, William Bennett, and most of the reform commissions of the 1980s contended that teachers should be paid based on quality of performance rather than seniority. It was hoped that performance-based compensation plans would keep the best teachers in teaching. In 1993, of the one thousand teachers surveyed by the Metropolitan Life Survey 72 percent believed that differential pay should be used to retain teachers who work in urban and isolated rural schools, while 61 percent said differential pay should be available to those who teach science and mathematics. In other words, where a teacher teaches should have more to do with level of pay than how well a teacher teaches.

## Teaching as a Career

When we think in terms of a career, we think in terms of a life's work. According to Alan Eck of the U.S. Bureau of Labor Statistics, the average U.S. adult will change jobs five or six times during his or her working life (telephone conversa-

**FIGURE 1-3**

### The Average Teacher Salary Compared to the Average Experience Level of Teachers

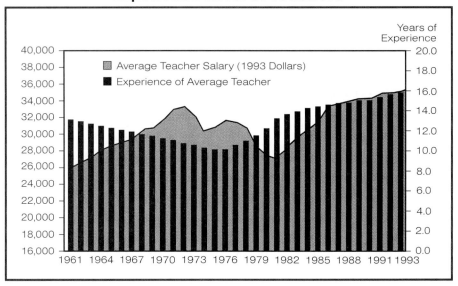

From: American Federation of Teachers, *Survey and Analysis of Salary Trends* (1993).

**In an effort to attract more people to the teaching profession, beginning teachers' salaries have had to keep pace with inflation. The salaries of experienced teachers have not kept pace, however, with the result that many of the best teachers are leaving the profession for higher-paying jobs.**

tion, September 14, 1993). However, it is generally true that the longer the length of training, the longer the individual will remain on the job. Since teaching requires at least four years of academic training and a baccalaureate degree, it is likely that many individuals will remain in classroom teaching or will seek other positions in education. In the 1988 Metropolitan Life Insurance survey of current teachers, 26 percent said they anticipated leaving the profession, but according to Vance Grant of the National Center for Education Statistics, only 5.6 percent of all teachers left teaching in 1988–1989. Of that 5.6 percent, 2.0 percent left the classroom but not education; 0.3 percent left to attend college for further education. This, according to Grant, is up from 4.1 percent in 1987–1988 (telephone conversation, September 15, 1993). In some financially troubled school districts the turnover among teachers is significantly greater. In Los Angeles, for example, so many teachers resigned after the forced pay cut in September 1993 that one thousand non-credentialed teachers filled teacher vacancies at the start of the 1993–1994 school year. Despite this, in *The Metropolitan Life Survey of The American Teacher 1990,* Louis Harris found that most new teachers (90 percent of over one thousand teachers interviewed) view teaching as a long-term career choice, not merely a job.

**1-2**

**POINTS TO REMEMBER**

- The qualities of a profession include a body of knowledge, controlled recruitment, freedom to use one's own discretion, autonomy from direct supervision, empowerment, collegial relations, ability to communicate with the public, high standards and a code of ethics, good working conditions and benefits, commitment to the welfare of students, accountability, continuous retraining, objective evaluation of performance, and membership in professional organizations.

- Teacher autonomy gives teachers the freedom to make decisions related to life in the classroom and to teach without direct supervision.

- Teacher empowerment is the freedom and responsibility for teachers to make decisions regarding the operation of the school that affect life in the classroom.

- Collegial time allows teachers to share ideas with other professionals.

- Incentive pay is awarded for excellent teaching performance, student achievement, and/or increased responsibilities.

- As professionals, teachers are accountable for their own success or failure.

- A merit pay system awards teachers on a scheduled basis for excellence in job performance.

- A career ladder, or differentiated staffing, moves teachers through various professional levels that are related to job performance, increased responsibilities, and additional education.

- Master teacher plans, also called mentor teaching plans, require experienced teachers to work as mentor, lead, or head teachers.

- Incentive pay plans may make the profession competitive but no equitable method of determining who should receive it has been developed.

- Teachers' salaries have been increasing but have not been keeping ahead of inflation.

## WHO ARE TODAY'S TEACHERS?

In 1991 the public schools in the United States had more than 4.5 million employees, 2,431,622 of whom were classroom teachers. While the number of school employees had increased by over .50 million since 1987, the number of teachers had remained relatively constant (National Center for Education Statistics 1993, 163). In 1991, the schools also employed over 200 thousand district and school administrators, nearly 129 thousand administrative support personnel, over 207 thousand school and library support staff, over 410 thousand instructional aides, over 81 thousand guidance counselors, over 49 thousand librarians, and more than one million other support personnel. However, the proportion of teachers to the total public school staff had declined from 65 percent in 1959 to approximately 46 percent in 1991. Of those teachers employed by the public schools in the mid-1980s, 85 percent were white; more than two-thirds were female. Many people believe that teachers' salaries remain lower than those of other professions simply because the majority of teachers are women. The average age of teachers in 1987–1988 was forty years; 32.2 percent were between forty and forty-nine; 18.0 percent were over fifty; only 14.5 percent were under thirty. Of those under thirty, only 8.0 percent were black; while of those over fifty, 22 percent were black. Many between the ages of thirty-six and forty-five had taught for ten to twenty years. The relative maturity of the teaching force means that in the next two decades there will be critical shortages as teachers with twenty or more years of experience begin to retire. Similarly, the decreasing percentage of black teachers means that the teaching force is becoming more white, while the school-age population of people of color is increasing.

According to the Carnegie Foundation for the Advancement of Teaching (1990), the oversupply of teachers experienced in the early 1970s reversed itself by 1982 and the demand will continue to increase relative to the supply

**FIGURE 1-4**

### Elementary and Secondary Classroom Teachers, With Alternative Projections: Fall 1978 to Fall 2003

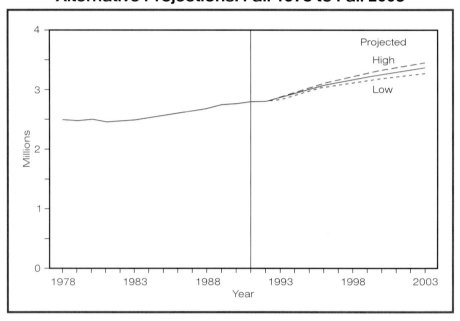

From: National Center for Education Statistics, *Projections of Education Statistics to 2003* (Washington, DC: U.S. Department of Education, 1992), p. 66.

**The number of public school teachers is projected to increase to about 2.93 million by the year 2003, based on the middle, or most likely growth path. The high and low projections are considered reasonable outcomes as well.**

throughout the 1990s (see figure 1.4). By 1994, according to the U.S. Department of Education, the supply peaked with a need for 281 thousand more teachers than there were graduates of teacher-training programs. According to Jewell Gould, director of research for the American Federation of Teachers, 2.5 million teachers will retire from 1994 to the year 2000. Estimates of the retirement rate range from 5 percent to more than 10 percent each year and this is likely to be the largest teacher turnover ever. (Telephone converation with Jewell Gould, June 13, 1994.) According to the National Center for Education Statistics, U.S. Department of Education, the need for public school teachers is projected to increase to 2.93 million by the year 2003, resulting in a 20 percent increase from 1991 (Projections of Education Statistics to 2003, 64).

### TEACHING IN A MULTICULTURAL SOCIETY

One of the challenges career teachers face is the changing school population. While the white population of the United States increased by 6.0 percent in the decade of the 1980s, the black population increased 13.2 percent; the Native American population increased 37.9 percent; the Asian or Pacific Islander population increased by 107.8 percent; and the Hispanic population increased 53

## TABLE 1-3

### Percent Nonwhite Youth* Projections for 2010 for Selected States

| State | Percent nonwhite | State | Percent nonwhite |
|---|---|---|---|
| D.C. | 93.2% | Louisiana | 50.3% |
| Hawaii | 79.5% | Mississippi | 49.9% |
| Texas | 56.9% | New Jersey | 45.7% |
| California | 56.9% | Maryland | 42.7% |
| Florida | 53.4% | Illinois | 41.7% |
| New York | 52.8% | South Carolina | 40.1% |
| U.S. | 38.2% | | |

*Age 0–17 years.

From: H. L. Hodgkinson, *A Demographic Look at Tomorrow* (Washington, DC: Center for Demographic Policy Institute for Educational Leadership, 1992), 2. Based on information in U.S. Census Bureau as cited in *American Demographics,* May 1989.

**The growth in nonwhite school-age population is expected to increase so that by the year 2010 ethnic minorities will constitute 38.2 percent of the entire population. Six states and the District of Columbia will have a nonwhite population of over 50 percent.**

percent (Hodgkinson 1992, 1). While the predicted percentage of U.S. children who will be nonwhite in the year 2010 is 38.2 percent of the entire youth population, six states and the District of Columbia will have a nonwhite youth population of over 50 percent (see table 1.3). Simultaneously, the teaching force has become increasingly white and as teachers who are now over the age of fifty retire, it will be even more white unless new measures for attracting, training, and retaining minority teachers are found.

Although not all states have as large a percentage of nonwhite students as the states listed in table 1.3, Daniel E. Drake (1993), professor of educational administration at Cleveland State University, maintains that all classrooms are becoming more reflective of the diverse U.S. multiracial and multiethnic society. According to James Banks in a lecture at the University of North Carolina at Asheville, students of color constituted the majority in student populations in twenty-five of the fifty largest public school systems in the United States in 1990. By the year 2020, students of color will constitute 46 percent of the nation's public school population (lecture, March 1, 1991). Thus, Drake suggests that if they are to successfully teach in contemporary classrooms, teachers need to:

- be aware of their own personal attitudes toward culturally diverse students
- develop a mind-set that allows them to be accepting of student differences
- solicit the views of students and other advisers who are sensitive to cultural differences

- provide opportunities for critical-thinking and problem-solving activities where no answers are incorrect
- develop a positive relationship between their expectations and students' academic progress
- create the most favorable climate for learning including encouraging positive interpersonal relationships among students, developing positive attitudes of students, and interacting positively with students from other cultures
- select student assessment methods that are appropriate for the diverse student population. (1993, 264–266)

## *Viewpoint* Hidden Minorities

When I was in junior high school, I absolutely loved my history class and I idolized my teacher. That is, until one afternoon.

His lecture that day covered various groups of immigrants that came to America in the early 1900s. He told us that many Greeks arrived during those years. Since their families were so large, there wasn't much time for each individual. Therefore, according to my teacher, the children did not do well in school and many ended up on welfare. The cycle then repeated itself with their children.

As my teacher spoke, I grew numb. I, as well as my brothers and sisters, worked hard to earn As and Bs in all our classes. Our family was not on welfare, and my grandparents were among those Greek arrivals in the early 1900s.

I never did tell that teacher that I was Greek. I did think a little less of him, however, from that point. . . .

Recently, something happened in my own classroom that made me remember those past experiences. My seventh grade speech class was reading poetry aloud. One boy chose Shel Silverstein's *The Gypsies Are Coming*. As he began to read, many students started laughing and staring at Eric in the back of the room. I interrupted and asked for an explanation. After a moment of silence, one of them said, "Eric's a Gypsy" and volunteered negative information about Gypsies.

Eric and I had something in common: we were all members of hidden minorities. Most people are polite (or two-faced) enough to silence their remarks about a racial or ethnic group in the presence of members of that group. We usually know if there is a black person or an Oriental present. But there are many other groups that are not easy to identify. We cannot always tell by a person's name either. Many ethnic surnames were changed to give them a more "American" sound.

I decided to do something about the incident that had happened in my class. That evening I did some research at the library. The next day I gave each of my students an opportunity to talk about his or her heritage. I added my comments on each group and also revealed what I had learned about Gypsies. . . .

Chances are you have hidden minorities in your classroom, too. What can you do to keep these children from being hurt? First of all, let your students know that you expect respect for all ethnic groups. Don't tolerate any ethnic jokes.

Secondly, make stereotypes and prejudice common topics in your classroom. Discuss some common stereotypes. Talk about how ethnic prejudice has led to social injustice, slavery and war throughout history. Devote a bulletin board to a different ethnic group every few weeks. Highlight famous people from the group, facts about the country where the group originated, how they have been treated and special accomplishments.

Finally, schedule an ethnic pride day. Students can bring in flags, clothes, foods, etc., from the countries of their origins. Students who don't know their own ethnic background can choose any interesting group. Some activities may include breaking a piñata, eating Chinese egg rolls, learning to play a Korean game, listening to a student's grandmother speak about early German settlers in your town, and reading Irish folktales. It is amazing what you and your students can learn in one day!

As a teacher, you are in a position to do something about hidden minorities. By taking a little time in the classroom this year, you can help your students develop a lifelong appreciation of our country's rich ethnic heritage.

From: A. Nicholas, 1988. A. Nicholas is a veteran teacher in Cedar Falls, Iowa.

Another challenge for teachers will be dealing with the variety of minority groups attending a single school. According to a 1993 report of the U.S. Bureau of Census, 14 percent of the nation's school children (ages five–seventeen) speak a language other than English (1990). More than half of the nation's non-English speakers are in three states: California, New York, and Florida. However, all regions of the country have some non-English-speaking students, and, although one language may dominate (Spanish being the most prevalent), all states report some percentage of linguistically diverse school children.

*(continued on p. 43)*

**Many American classrooms are becoming ethnically diverse. The teacher must be able to provide opportunities for these students to appreciate their own cultural heritage and at the same time to adjust to their adopted American culture. These fifth graders are performing at a school fair.**

# *Cross-Cultural Perspective*

## Profile: Madeleine Lee

Madeleine Lee's first grade classroom is housed in the older building of Hawthorne Year Round Elementary School in Oakland. The room has high ceilings and a wall of windows which Madeleine likes to keep open so the room doesn't feel stuffy. The room is divided roughly in half. On one side, groups of individual student desks are pulled together to form a table. There are four to five tables depending on the population of this transient neighborhood. The other half of the room has a large area rug and open floor space and then a half table in the farthest end where writing and special projects can be worked on away from the hustle of the class. . . .

Across the full width of the room are strings which look like clothes lines. Art work is hung on those strings. Madeleine explains "Everything that goes up is something the students have contributed. Our work is by themes. We leave the work up and move them around until they are in the far end of the room and are just up for reference to help us remember. We never take it all down. Work stays up and just rotates."

Madeleine explains her evolution as a teacher:

I first started teaching here at Hawthorne Elementary. I had a classroom with a lot of different language children in it. I spoke Spanish from high school, and that was it. So I had to figure out ways to teach the other kids—Vietnamese, Laotian. I just came up with my own style. This year most of them are Cambodian speaking. I have a couple of Tongan speaking children, a Vietnamese girl and a handful of English speaking Black children. It changes all the time; I had more Vietnamese, but they moved. The transiency in Oakland is really high. Kids come and go.

Most of the kids are limited English speaking. You have to do more ESL type things, more visual things, a lot of drawing. You have to start with the basics. If you're talking about something, you have to do the background. I usually teach in the whole language and develop my own curriculum, but I thought I'd give the BASAL reader a try. The story was about the beach. I thought "that's pretty easy because a lot of kids have gone to the beach."

It wasn't as easy as I thought. We had to backtrack and talk about the beach, and about sand, and that the water is very cold, and why you wouldn't want to just go in—the whole thing. Concept development is so important.

In my class I have to do less talking and more showing. I think that's a key thing. If you have pictures, you need to make sure that they understand what that picture is. For example, it's so difficult to explain a rake! In Cambodia I don't think they rake up leaves. What's the difference between a rake and a broom? In a picture, a rake looks like a broom. And what's the difference between a rake, a broom and a mop? So even if you use pictures, sometimes you need to go another step.

I do several things in my class to bridge language and cultural differences. In the morning we have the morning calendar and the weather, and the numbers one to fifteen. We say them in all the different languages of the kids in the class. What's up there (on the wall) is English and Cambodian, because the majority of the kids are Cambodian. But we do it in whatever language there is. Each person gets to be the leader for a day, directing the exercises and taking the lunch count. It's great for building their self-esteem. Whoever the leader is will count from one to fifteen first in English, then in Spanish, or Chinese, or Tongan. That's an awareness thing—that there *are* other languages. When I was little, they used to go "Ching, Chong, Chinaman." That, to them was speaking Chinese. The kids that have gone through my class can at least say the numbers one through fifteen. I think they have an awareness of the different kinds of languages and that they're not just 'bla-bla-bla'. That's good, that they can identify the language and speak a little in it.

From: Olsen and Mullen, 1990. L. Olsen is Immigrant Students Project Director, and N. Mullen is on the staff of California Tomorrow, a nonprofit organization that conducts research and organizes local coalitions to create a fair, working, multiracial, multicultural society.

In 1991–1992, 1,122,903 of the nation's total school population of 42,000,343 were enrolled in bilingual programs. In addition, 1,351,494 students were enrolled in English as a second language (ESL) programs (telephone conversation with Rudolph Munis, specialist bilingual education, U.S. Department of Education, March 25, 1994). In 1988–1989 in Miami, Florida, 166,761 students were registered in bilingual programs and 52,000 in special ethnic heritage programs (National School Boards Association 1990, 24, 39). In Delray Beach, Florida, for example, as many as five different languages may be spoken in one class. The students are the children of migrant workers, illegal aliens, and newly arrived immigrants. In an ESOL (English for Speakers of Other Languages) classroom, the children in Pine Grove Elementary School are given the opportunity to learn English through a computer program called C.A.R.E. (Computer Assisted Reading in English). In California there are 6 million foreign-born residents, one half of whom are recent immigrants, and by the year 2000 one half of the state's school children will be Hispanic or Asian. In the schools, children are encouraged to write about their personal experiences, cultures, and histories in both their native language and in English to help all students learn about backgrounds and cultures that are different from their own. Teachers learn to encourage non-English-speaking or bilingual students to write through an in-service program called the Bay Area Writing Project in which teachers teach teachers about writing and the teaching of writing (Olsen and Mullen 1990) (see chapter 8 for more information on bilingual education).

In Arlington County, Virginia, teacher Teresa Rosegrant had twenty-six students in her 1992 class, among whom fourteen different languages were spoken. Only one of her students was a native English speaker. In Rosegrant's school, thirty-three language groups were represented. She suggests that this presents a challenge to teachers, but also an opportunity to develop a multilingual society (Bredekamp and Rosegrant 1992, 137–138).

As noted above, in California there is no single ethnic minority group that dominates the public schools (Olsen and Mullen 1990). For a report of the "California Immigrant Students Project," thirty-six teachers in multicultural schools were interviewed to determine how they teach across cultural, national, and linguistic diversity. According to the study, teachers report overwhelming challenges but also inspiration from the diversity of California's students. It also found that for every two teachers who retired, seven resigned after one-and-a-half years of teaching or less. The study concludes that teachers must be better trained to deal with the rich diversity of cultures found in the schools.

## TEACHING SPECIAL NEEDS STUDENTS

The diversity of students in today's classrooms requires that teachers learn about their needs and develop teaching methods that will help each individual succeed. Special needs students can be broadly categorized as:

- students with identifiable conditions that interfere with learning and development
- children with developmental delays but with no apparent biological impairments

- students who are at risk for developmental delays or disabilities because of a variety of environmental and/or biological factors. (Wolery, Strain, and Bailey 1992, 94)

The children's problems in any of these categories may be mild, moderate, or severe and may exist in combination with other impairments. Although special needs students share basic needs with all students (physical need for shelter, rest, food, and psychological safety needs), each special student has unique needs, and teachers must be prepared to teach each child as an individual. For instance, developmentally delayed and disabled students need environments that are specially organized and adjusted to minimize the effects of their disabilities and promote learning. Teachers must be helped by parents, professionals in other disciplines, special teachers, and administrators. Therefore, teaching is not a solitary profession. It requires that teachers work with teams of adults to best promote learning for all children.

According to the National Center for Education Statistics (1992), there were 4,641,000 students with special needs (birth to twenty-one years old) being served in the U.S. public schools in 1989–1990. This represented an increase of 949,000 or over 3.0 percent since 1976–1977.

Over 30 percent of all students with special needs are enrolled in regular classrooms. Thirty-eight percent are enrolled in resource rooms with many of these children spending part of the day in the regular classroom. Twenty-four percent are in special classrooms within regular schools; 6 percent are enrolled in separate schools. Regular classrooms are the home base for over 75 percent of speech- and language-impaired children and 19.7 percent of students with specific learning disabilities. Therefore, regular classroom teachers must serve the needs of special students at the same time that they are meeting the needs of regular students (see chapter 9).

Teachers need to be familiar with the laws related to the education of special children. Since services to special children are governed by federal law (P.L. 94–142 and 99–457 are discussed in chapters 9 and 15) rather than locally controlled educational programs, decisions about placement, assessment, and teaching are beyond the control of the classroom teacher. Key provisions include:

- all special needs students are entitled to a free appropriate public education, regardless of severity of disability
- special needs students must be placed in the least restrictive (most normalized) appropriate environment
- to the extent possible, they should be educated with children who do not have special disability needs. (Wolery, Stain, and Bailey 1992, 95)

## Trends in Teaching

Although the ideals of professionalism have yet to be fully implemented in the teaching field, several trends in the 1990s point to an awareness of difficulties and a concerted effort in most parts of the country to improve the conditions under which teachers work. As one indication, an NEA Blue Ribbon Task Force on Educational Excellence established by Mary Futrell, former NEA president, concluded that if teaching is going to be a full-fledged profession, a career in teaching will look like this by the year 2000: (1) teachers will demand more from students and place more responsibility on them; (2) a school's faculty will be deployed in ways that permit individual students to receive help in a timely fashion; (3) the number of students per teacher will be small enough to allow ample time to plan each child's programs; (4) teachers will no longer be isolated from one another; (5) teaching will be an attractive, lifelong profession, and teachers will be professionally compensated; (6) teachers will be encouraged to participate in the development of school policy and programs; (7) there will be no hierarchical staffing systems within the profession, only an exciting mix of equally important roles—such as curriculum development, helping new teachers . . . ; (8) decisions about instruction will be made at the school level, not by bureaucracies in school system central offices and state capitals; and (9) starting salaries will not be less than $24,000 (Futrell 1989, 5–6, 8, 10, 14–15, 25). (In 1992, the average beginning salary was $23,054, up from $19,260 in 1980. U.S. Department of Education National Center for Education Statistics, *The Condition of Education,* 1993, 150).

## MID-CAREER TEACHING

An interesting trend in teaching is the "growing number of professionals . . . turning to teaching in mid-career, taking pay cuts in order to pursue their late-found vocation" (Tifft 1989). This trend can be attributed, in part, to increasing salaries and efforts by many states to speed up the certification process through the development of alternative programs, which frequently count professional experience or expertise toward obtaining teaching credentials. (See chapter 3, pp. 113–114, for a discussion of the controversy surrounding alternative certification routes.)

Although professional rewards, such as salary and autonomy, are important to these career changers, it is clear from the salary cuts they take that these are not the crucial motives. Tom Carlyle, who quit a management job in publishing to teach high school math, says, "Getting these kids through high school is much more satisfying than working behind a desk" (Tifft 1989). A 1993 Metropolitan Life Survey of one thousand teachers found a large majority (75 percent) support this trend of alternative approaches to teacher certification.

## STAFF DEVELOPMENT

After initial certification, all fifty states and the District of Columbia require that teachers meet additional educational requirements at various stages in their teaching careers. In 1991, forty-two states had a second level of teacher certification (required in thirty of the forty-two). Eight states had dropped the requirement since 1987 and four had added it. Requirements for this second level of certification varied among the states and included teaching experience, additional course work, state examinations, and success on assessments of performance. Thirteen states required a master's degree for this second level of certification; four required a fifth year of study; others required from six to thirty semester units of credits. Eight states required an internship for a second stage of certification. Also, in forty-two states a continuing education requirement (education following initial teacher certification) had to be met after the second stage of certification (Mastain 1991). The most common requirement was six semester hours or 120–150 hours of staff development, based on the needs of the individual school district, every five years. Several states, particularly Alaska, California, and the District of Columbia, require that some of the continuing education be in multicultural education. In 1991, 46.7 percent of all teachers had a master's or specialist degree as compared to only 23.1 percent in 1961 (National Center for Education Statistics 1993, 78). The teaching profession has embraced Mortimer Adler's message in *The Paideia Proposal* (1982): "The teacher who has stopped learning is a deadening influence rather than a help to students being initiated into the ways of learning" (p. 59). In-service training programs are specifically designed to improve teaching and management skills. They may be conducted at the school site or in conjunction with a university and involve case studies, films, videos of classroom teachers at work, and role-playing. Recognized authorities in current trends such as student diversity analyze how to deal most effectively with the situations presented.

## NATIONAL STANDARDS FOR TEACHING

In 1987 the Carnegie Forum on Education and the Economy created the National Board for Professional Teaching Standards (NBPTS). Sixty-three representatives from education, industry, and the public were given the task of deciding in five years what excellent teachers should know and be able to do and with developing standards for a system of voluntary, professional assessment and board certification. During the five-year period, the board held state forums on defining standards of professionalism in teaching. They found that teachers defined it in terms of devotion to students and of delivering their best services in the classroom, but that they more often spoke of professionalism in terms of environmental conditions rather than of standards (Barringer 1993, 18).

Since 1987, NBPTS has worked to create policies, processes, and products such as standards and assessment packages to build the professionalism of teachers. In 1992 the National Board issued five core propositions that they claimed are "generic to all excellent teaching" and express "what teachers should know and be able to do."

- Teachers are committed to students and their learning.
- Teachers know their subjects and how to teach them.
- Teachers are responsible for managing and monitoring student life.
- Teachers think systematically about their practice and learn from experience.
- Teachers are members of learning communities. (Barringer 1993, 20)

These propositions will guide the work of the standards committees who, by 1995, will set standards for thirty certification areas of teaching excellence that:

- highlight critical aspects of teaching practice while emphasizing the holistic nature of teaching

- describe how the standard comes to life in different settings
- identify the knowledge, skills, and dispositions that support a teacher's performance on the standard at a high level
- show how a teacher's professional judgment is reflected in observable actions
- reflect the NBPTS policy on "What Teachers Should Know and Be Able to Do." (Barringer 1993, 19)

The work of NBPTS has set in motion a national conversation of teaching standards that goes beyond basic teaching competencies. The discussions have moved out of the committees of the National Board to state Boards of Education, political professional teachers' organizations (examined in chapter 13) such as the American Federation of Teachers (AFT), and professional development organizations such as the National Council of Teachers of Mathematics (NCTM). Many teachers who are members of professional organizations have participated in forums around the country discussing the development of standards. By 1994, standards for each of the curricular areas had been developed (see chapter 8). Exactly how these standards and discussions about them will affect teaching is not yet clear.

The importance of setting educational standards was officially recognized by the U.S. Congress in 1992 when it passed the National Education Standards and Assessment Act (P.L. 102–62). This act grew out of the National Council on Education Standards (NCEST), established by Congress in 1991, and was charged with advising the public about whether national education standards and a system of voluntary national tests or examinations should and can be established. Both questions were answered in the affirmative, and NCEST created the National Education Goals Panel (NEGP).

As with most new trends in public education, the discussion of national standards for teaching and curriculum is not without controversy. Many educators worry that the attention given by the federal government to setting standards will lead to federal control of public education (control of public education will be discussed in chapter 13). Consequently, states and professional organizations are jumping on the standards-setting bandwagon to avoid the noose of federal control.

## ADVANCEMENT OPPORTUNITIES

Of the 5.6 percent of teachers who left the classroom in 1988–1989, 1.5 percent left for an advancement—to become a principal, supervisor, or other type of administrator (Vance Grant, telephone interview, September 15, 1993). Mariah Perez, for example, has been teaching for fifteen years. When she began her career she expected to stay in the classroom no more than five or ten years. But she soon discovered that she was an excellent teacher. After her third year of teaching she began a master's program at a local university. Even after earning her degree she continued to enroll in other educational programs. One summer she went on a tour of the Soviet Union; another summer she was a fellow in a writing project for teachers. All of this made staying in the classroom more and more attractive. And then, her state adopted an incentive pay plan. Within three years her salary jumped nearly 50 percent. During this time she evaluated new teachers as part

---

**1-3**

**POINTS TO REMEMBER**

- The demand for new teachers is likely to exceed the supply throughout the 1990s.
- Today's classrooms are ethnically, racially, and linguistically diverse. Teachers of color and of cultural and linguistic diversity must be recruited and retained in public education. All teachers must receive preservice education and in-service training for working with the diverse student population.
- Special needs children are those with a variety of disabilities and handicaps. Over 30 percent of all special needs children are enrolled in regular classrooms.
- In-service educational expectations vary from state to state. However, all states require that teachers continue their education and training.
- Through incentive pay programs and differentiated staffing, teachers have the potential to advance in status while remaining in the classroom.
- Trends in teaching include mid-career teaching, staff development, national standards for teaching, and advancement opportunities.

---

of her school's mentor teacher program, supervised six preservice teachers from the university, served on the teaching evaluation committee, and worked on the development of a new integrated language arts curriculum. Mariah believes that she is making a real contribution to her profession. And now she has been asked to serve as a teacher evaluator for the district's career ladder program. The pay for this new position is significantly more than for teaching, but it means leaving the classroom. Mariah must make a difficult decision, one facing many excellent teachers who are in a position to advance their careers but at the expense of what they do best—teach.

## For Thought/Discussion

1. Compare and contrast the different definitions of teaching.
2. Discuss why there is a disagreement among educators about whether teaching is an art or a science.
3. How do you feel about making mistakes? How will you react to your students when they make mistakes?
4. Why is it important that your education prepare you to work with ethnically, racially, and linguistically diverse students as well as those with special needs?
5. Do you believe that teacher accountability can be determined by measuring student achievement on a standardized test? Why or why not?
6. What do you think are major considerations for thinking of teaching as a profession?
7. Which, if any, of the incentive pay programs contribute to the professionalization of teaching? How?
8. What are some of the trends in teaching that will contribute to its becoming a full-fledged profession?

For Further Reading/Reference

Brandt, R. M. 1990. *Incentive pay and career ladders for today's teachers: A study of current programs and practices.* Albany: State University of New York. The author presents case studies that discuss implementation of incentive pay programs in various school districts where these programs have been in effect for five or more years.

Cohen, R. M. 1991. *A lifetime of teaching: Portraits of five veteran high school teachers.* New York: Teachers College Press. This work presents case studies of five career public school teachers who have succeeded in remaining enthusiastic about teaching after twenty-five years in the classroom.

Darling-Hammond, L., and Goodwin, A. L. 1993. Progress toward professionalism in teaching. In G. Cawelti (Ed.). *Challenges and achievements of American education: 1993 yearbook of the Association for Supervision and Curriculum Development* (pp. 19–52). Alexandria, VA: ASCD. The authors examine the limitations of teaching as a profession and propose new policies that could contribute to the professionalism of teaching.

Freedman, S. G. 1990. *Small victories: The real world of a teacher, her students, and their high school.* New York: HarperCollins. A true story of a master artist/teacher depicting the joys and frustrations of teaching multicultural and socially deprived students in inner-city Manhattan.

Miller, J. 1991. *Creating spaces and finding voices.* Amherst, NY: SUNY Press. The author presents the journals of five public school teachers who collaborated with a university mentor as part of a teacher empowerment project.

Art Bouthillier in *Phi Delta Kappan.*

*"Lemme guess . . . first day at school with braces, right?"*

## CHAPTER OBJECTIVES

After studying this chapter, you should be able to:

- Identify the characteristics of an effective teacher.
- Discuss how the skills and values of an effective teacher can be developed.
- Explain how effective teaching research contributes to defining teaching skills.
- Discuss how shared identity relates to effective teaching.
- Discuss effective teaching in multicultural classrooms.
- Define teaching style.
- Differentiate teaching style from teaching method and content.

- Identify the characteristics of instructor-centered, content-centered, student-centered, teacher-student-centered, and content-student-centered teaching styles.
- Analyze the potential benefits and dangers of effective teaching research.
- Identify different teachers' job expectations revealed by cultures-of-teaching research.
- Defend teacher diversity.
- Discuss effective discipline procedures and analyze the varied methods of discipline.

# Chapter 2

# EFFECTIVE TEACHING

*Mary MacCracken is a teacher of emotionally disturbed children. She is loving and warm, frequently hugging the children. She wants the children to learn to be independent. She knows they will never achieve great academic success, so she uses her time with them in the classroom to encourage them to be the best they can be. She chronicles one school year in her book* Lovey: A Very Special Child. *The excerpt below tells about the start of the first day in school.*

Brian was the first to arrive. He came so quietly that if I hadn't been watching I wouldn't have known he was there. He came to the hall door and stood just outside it, his hands hidden in his pockets so I couldn't tell whether they were trembling or not. Each year I think I've outgrown the ridiculous soaring excitement I felt the first time I came to the school and saw the children. And then each year I find I'm wrong. The same spin-jolting, rocking delight hits me and spins me around, and I have to be careful not to somersault across the room when the children come.

"Hey, Brian, I'm glad to see you." I walked across the room toward him, waiting for his smile, thin and sweet, to come and warm his pinched little face.

But Brian didn't smile. He didn't even come into the room. "Why are we in here?" he asked. "This isn't our room. This isn't where we were last year."

It's so hard for our children to handle new situations. Their sense of self is so small, their beings so fragile, that if their outer surroundings change, they fear that they themselves will fall apart.

"Listen," I said. "This is the best room we've ever had. Don't spurn luxury. Look, we've got a whole coat closet, instead of just hooks."

Brian took a step or two into the room and peered at the coat closet. "I liked just the hooks," he said.

"And we've got blocks and trucks and a whole toy kitchen—a stove and a sink and tables—and now, look here, our own door. How about that? No more having to go through the office when we want to sneak out before lunch to ride our bikes."

Brian was all the way in the room now. "Do we still have the bikes?"

"Sure. We've even got a couple of new ones." They weren't really new, the church ladies and the Junior Leaguers had donated them, but they were new to us.

Within the next minute Rufus arrived. He looked tan and healthy and had obviously had a good summer.

"Hey, Mary," he announced, "maybe we're going to get a cat. I'm almost not 'lergic any more and my mom says as soon as I'm not 'lergic we can get one." He turned toward Brian. "And I'll bring it in here, Brian, so you can see it."

Rufus walked comfortably around the room, commenting on everything, and I could see Brian loosening up, his fears diminishing. The children did so much for each other without realizing it. Rufus's explorations freed Brian to begin his own, and soon both boys were settled on the floor taking out books and papers and small supplies that I'd put in their individual cubbies.

From: M. MacCracken, 1976, *Lovey: A Very Special Child*, 11–12.

*J*aime Escalante teaches mathematics to Latino students at Garfield High School in Sacramento, California. Many teachers assume these students cannot learn and, therefore, go easy on them. Escalante disagrees, and his results have been well documented in the book Escalante by Jay Mathews and the film Stand and Deliver. These excerpts from the book discuss some initial frustrations Escalante faced in East Los Angeles and later successes.

For his first AP [Advanced Placement] class Escalante collected a few members of the previous year's mathematics analysis course and one or two students who claimed to have taken the prerequisite course at East Los Angeles College. He had fourteen enrolled in the first-period class by the fall of 1978, but many, including Escalante, felt like babes lost in the woods.

Heiland [a student] brought him a copy of an old calculus AP free-response test, the problems requiring written answers that make up the latter half of the three-hour examination. Escalante fingered the green paper gingerly. It had seven questions. He knew this group could not come close to answering any of them. He wondered how far he could take them in just eight months.

He assumed his sharpest look and addressed the class: "You're going to be able to do this class, but you need to brush up your Algebra 2, your math analysis, your trigonometry. You don't know anything in this class. . . .

"First period starts at eight o'clock. We open the doors here at seven. We start at seven-thirty. Then from eight to nine we have regular class. I'd like to change this textbook, but no way. I got to be honest, I don't understand myself this book. So we going to have to give you a lot of handouts and you have to take a lot of notes and keep a folder.

Every morning we have a five-minute quiz. [Now several students began to exchange looks.] And a test on Friday."

He began the routine. To his surprise, in two weeks he was down to seven students.

. . . That day two more boys approached him defiantly. "We gonna drop, Mr. Escalante." They watched closely for his reaction.

"But you gotta *try*," he said.

"Nah," the taller boy said. "I don't want to come at seven o'clock. Why should I?"

. . . Only five students in Escalante's calculus class—three girls and two boys—lasted through the spring. It was a test not only of their patience but of the district's and the principal's. Administrators were not supposed to sanction such tiny classes.

Escalante still insisted the students see him before and after school, but he had to treat them more gently now. He assured them repeatedly they could handle AP questions. He gave them what sample questions he could find from past examinations.

. . . From the beginning Escalante knew he had to soften calculus's granite-hard image. His principal devices were humor, nonchalance, and an appeal to the team spirit. The class motto appeared in a huge poster on his wall: CALCULUS NEED NOT BE MADE EASY; IT IS EASY ALREADY.

In May 1979 all five Escalante students sat down in the English classroom just inside the main door of the school and took the AP calculus examination. One girl, Leticia Arambula, could barely speak. She was mortified. She had panicked and answered only a handful of multiple-choice questions. By the time she opened the free-response booklet, her mind had gone blank.

Escalante knew how quick East LA youths were to wallow in self-doubt. He comforted her. She had not been the best student and was slow in finding her answers to daily quiz questions. But she worked hard and did her homework.

The counseling office called him in July with the results. The Educational Testing Service scored the examination on a five-point scale. A 5 was best, a 1 was worst. A 3 or better meant a student could be said to have passed a college-level calculus course and would receive credit for one at most major universities. In Escalante's class, the grading report said, there were two 4s and two 2s. Leticia Arambula had received a 1.

Escalante resolved to do better. (1988, 100–110, 114–116)

From: J. Mathews, 1988, *Escalante: The Best Teacher in America,* 100–110, 114–116.

---

*E*scalante and his students eventually did do better. In May 1980, all nine of his students who had enrolled in the class took the test in the spring. One student received a 4, five received 3s, and two received 2s. One, who took

Jaime Escalante teaches Latino students high-level mathematics at Garfield High School in Sacramento, California. His persistence and dedication have enabled him to communicate the subject matter to his students effectively and, more importantly, to instill in them a sense of self-confidence that has enabled them to succeed.

the calculus BC exam, reserved only for those with more than a year of preparation, passed with a 3.

In May 1981, fifteen students took the test and the results were: one 5, four 4s, nine 3s, and one 2. By the fall of 1986, there were 151 calculus students in Escalante's school and at least 400 others in the developing process. Escalante, through his persistence and effective teaching, proved that the students of East Los Angeles could learn high-level mathematics. Although Escalante now teaches in a blue-collar neighborhood of Sacramento and is active in television and publishing, he continues to work with teachers and students in East Los Angeles. The students at Garfield still excel on the AP calculus exam. In May 1992, 115 students took the exam, more than at any other school in the L.A. area.

Perhaps you are familiar with the nineteenth-century British playwright and satirist George Bernard Shaw's comment about teachers, "He who can, does. He who cannot, teaches" (1903, 230). This remark makes the assumption that teachers cannot do what they teach. Also inherent in this assumption is that anyone can teach. Shaw was wrong. Teachers like Mary MacCracken and Jaime Escalante prove he was wrong. Although they are entirely different in terms of how they teach, each possesses the attributes and skills of an effective teacher.

Not everyone can teach; not everyone should teach. What is it that makes Mary MacCracken and Jaime Escalante effective teachers? Is it possible to learn how to be an effective teacher? This chapter attempts to answer these questions. As you read it, think about whether you possess the values and can learn the skills that will allow you to become an effective teacher.

# What Is Effective Teaching?

As educational researchers Donald Kauchak and Paul Eggen point out, "Education has always been one of the most rewarding professions—but at the same time, it continues to be one of the most difficult in which to perform well. . . . An effective teacher combines the best of human relations, intuition, sound judgment, knowledge of subject matter, and knowledge of how people learn—all in one simultaneous act" (1989, 3–4). Effective teachers make the very difficult task of teaching appear easy. They are able to teach all kinds of children so effectively that children, in fact, do learn. But although, in theory, effective teaching seems easy to define, its practical aspects are still being researched and analyzed.

## SHARED IDENTITY

According to Philip Jackson in *The Practice of Teaching,* teaching appears simple, except for "the assumption of shared identity." **Shared identity** means that "when teachers are working with students who are very much like themselves,

When teachers do not share an identity with their students, not only do they have to understand the culture and social environment of the children but they also must determine the most effective means of teaching them the material.

there is relatively little to learn about teaching, at least insofar as technique is concerned, that is not supplied either by common sense or by knowledge of the material to be taught. When working with children like themselves, teachers can teach as they were taught, using techniques that worked for them. But when teacher and student are *not* alike in important ways—that is, when the presumption of shared identity is invalid . . . [t]he knowledge called for under those circumstances is genuine knowledge about teaching per se" (1986, 26).

We can see the lack of shared identity between students and teachers in the anecdotes above. Mary MacCracken's students are emotionally and mentally disabled. In order to work with them, she must understand their level of development and select an appropriate means for helping them grow beyond it.

Jaime Escalante's students, in the opening anecdote, are from the East Los Angeles Latino ghetto and, since most of their parents are Mexican immigrants who speak little English, they are the children of two cultures. Escalante says that most of them give up easily in their new environment. However, as a physics teacher in a Catholic high school in Bolivia, he had seen that when students band together to strive for a common goal, they can succeed. Although Escalante's background is very different from those of his students, he has learned about their culture and developed ways to motivate them. Through his hard work, dedication, knowledge of and ability to communicate the subject to his students, he has convinced them that they, too, can succeed.

## EFFECTIVE TEACHING IN A MULTICULTURAL SOCIETY

In today's classrooms most teachers do not share an identity with their students. According to Patricia Larke in a 1992 article in the journal *Equity and Excellence,* one measure of effective teaching is the "ability to work effectively with students of different ethnic backgrounds while integrating the strategies of equity and excellence" (p. 137). James Banks in the book *Multiethnic Education: Theory and Practice* (1994) suggests that these strategies of equity and excellence require that male and female students, exceptional students, and those from diverse cultural, social, racial, and ethnic groups all experience an equal opportunity in school. This means that all students must develop more positive attitudes toward cultural, racial, ethnic, and religious groups (see examples of multicultural and gender-fair curriculums in chapter 8, pp. 319–323).

Effective teachers encourage positive attitudes toward multicultural groups by empowering all students, many who come from "victimized groups" (Banks 1994, 151), teaching them decision-making skills and encouraging cross-cultural learning. Jaime Escalante accomplishes this in the multicultural school in which he now teaches by having students of different cultural and ethnic groups solve mathematical problems together. Gloria Ladson-Billings suggests in a chapter in *Multicultural Education* (Grant 1992) that effective teachers utilize the beliefs and values of the students' cultures rather than the dominant culture as the foundation of teaching; this she calls "culturally relevant teaching." For example, from research involving observation and teachers' journals, Ladson-Billings concludes that African American children are naturally very expressive and verbal and often express themselves in ways that some find out of control, rude, or disrespectful. However, through positive teacher-student communication, teachers begin to understand that the children's verbal expressions are not intentionally rude or disrespectful (p. 113) and can then utilize them to encourage learning.

## *In the Classroom*

Culturally relevant teachers [teachers who teach content and use instruction strategies appropriate to the culture of their students] see teaching as an art as opposed to a science [chapter 1, pp. 10–17] with prescriptive steps and techniques to be learned and demonstrated. Thus, for them, teaching is a creative undertaking:

> . . . I did a lot of substituting of things, too. You know, we didn't have health books so we did health another way . . . There was a period when we didn't have social studies books, soo—well, I never got involved in whether we had the book or not but it was, 'What were some of the skills you need to learn to function in social studies?' . . .

These teachers see themselves as a part of the communities in which they teach and see their role as giving something back to the community. They believe that success is possible for each student and a part of that success is helping students make connections between themselves and their community, national, ethnic and global identities. They believe that black students as a cultural group have special strengths that need to be explored and utilized in the classroom:

> . . . [Black children] have always complemented my classroon because they're willing to express themselves [yet] the way that they express themselves other people think that they're out of control, rude and disrespectful. . . .
>
> Black children bring a sense of cooperation [to the classroom]. They're very willing to help. They're very open-minded. . . . They're very verbal. . . .
>
> . . . they're just full of life . . . enthusiasm. And they're not afraid to show their feelings.
>
> . . . I think that black children are themselves, more than any other type of child. To compare them [with other children], many other children look to see what you want and then they do it, where a black child, at least the ones I've come in contact with, they [sic] look to see what you want and if they agree with it they'll do it but if they don't, they waste no bones in telling you that they don't agree. [Teachers] have to know that. They're [the children] not being rude—that's the way they are.

Culturally relevant teachers understand that the way social interaction takes place in the classroom is important to student success. . . . The pedagogy for producing empowered students must be 'reciprocal interaction-oriented' as opposed to 'transmission-oriented'. Culturally relevant teachers foster classroom social relations that are 'humanely equitable' (Wilson 1972) and extend beyond the classroom. the teacher demonstrates a connectedness with all of the students and encourages each of them to do the same: [In the classroom] there wasn't a lot of competition. Everybody helped everybody to succeed. They were always willing to sit and teach somebody else. . . .

> . . . I start off being a role model. . . . I set the stage, expectations . . . WE collectively, what WE are going to do. . . . WE will.
>      . . . I operate the class on an extended family concept. I try to treat them the way they will be treated at home . . . to love them and discipline them. . . .

Culturally relevant teachers believe that knowledge is continuously re-created, recycled and shared . . . (Torres-Guzman 1989). Through the content, which often is related to students' lives, they help students develop the knowledge base or skills, to build a bridge or scaffolding and often accompany the students across to new and more difficult ideas, concepts and skills (Ladson-Billings 1989a).

> . . . well, I always had the feeling with black children that they were always under . . . we always underestimated what they could do. . . . I found that another avenue for them was sometimes something that didn't necessarily have to do with academics. . . . We always had projects going . . . something that allowed them to have an avenue to be successful. . . . I've never been sold that academics was THE most important thing in the classroom . . . nobody ever measures what the children really are capable of doing.
>      Yesterday, we had a really good lesson on . . . I'm introducing adjectives . . . and I did it with the Halloween words and I put ten words on the board . . . nouns . . . we're getting into nouns and adjectives and for some of them this is so far out of their reach right now but I'm the kind of teacher that I just throw it at you and sooner or later you're going to catch on. And so, they were giving me words like 'bad', 'good' and I said, 'Give me a break! I don't want to hear any more bad witch, good witch, red witch, white witch! Let's think. Let's come on and think!' And it was really interesting how all of a sudden they really got wound up and they really came out with some . . . I mean they started using words like 'gigantic', 'huge', and giving me a compound type adjective like 'green-faced' but see, you gotta press . . . there are some teachers who'll say 'That's good. Red is good for a devil and green is good for a witch'. But that's not what I wanted. I want to keep pushing and pressing because I know they have those kinds of things in them. . . . The lesson went on for a long time. I find that you just can't put minutes on good lessons, you'll never get the best out of your students.

From: Ladson-Billings in Grant, 1992. Ladson-Billings observed in classrooms in California and collected teachers' diaries that include techniques for teaching multicultural children.

Effective teachers in culturally diverse classrooms, according to research reviewed and conducted by Larke, have high expectations for their students. To assist culturally diverse students in reaching these high expectations, these teachers modify their instructional strategies, classroom organization, and whatever else it takes to ensure student success. Likewise, according to Kenneth Zeichner (1993) in a paper funded by the National Center for Research for Teacher Learning, effective teachers of "ethnic- and language-minority" students not only believe that all students can achieve, but make special efforts in communicating this belief to their students. Jaime Escalante helped his East Los Angeles students achieve by convincing them, even when they did not want to believe him, that they not only could learn calculus, but that they could learn it better than other students.

In order to accomplish success with multicultural students, teachers must be sensitive to all the students' needs (Sleeter and Grant 1988; Banks 1989; Larke 1992). Sleeter and Grant in *Making Choices for Multicultural Education* contend that teachers who effectively teach multicultural students do not treat them differently than other students because of race, ethnicity, age, gender, language, or other exceptionality (p. 63). James Banks further suggests that effective teachers treat students equally and provide all students with equal opportunities to learn.

> Adelina Aramburo is a petite woman in her early thirties with long brown hair, sparkling eyes and a playful smile. Adelina teaches at Buena Vista Alternative elementary school, a Spanish Immersion elementary school. The small intimate size of the school and the bright artwork that covers the walls of the sunny halls and rooms, including a masterpiece school quilt hanging in the stairwell, give the sense of a dynamic and creative place to be.

Adelina has traveled far to get to this school. Born in Mexico, Adelina's family immigrated to the San Joaquin Valley [California] where eight-year-old Adelina entered the third grade and after school worked by her parents' side in the fields.

> At that time there was no bilingual education, but I was very lucky in that I had a good teacher who was very sensitive to my situation. She didn't make me feel ashamed to speak Spanish or make me feel stupid. Also, she didn't retain me as teachers did with most immigrant children because she knew I understood the material but I just didn't have all the language yet. By the fourth grade I understood the language but not the nuances. I still didn't know what Thanksgiving was. (Olsen and Mullen 1990)

In addition to a strong academic content, many effective teachers of multicultural students provide them with a basis for exploring and understanding the issues they face: prejudice, oppression, and bigotry (Olsen and Mullen 1990).

> Recognizing our uniqueness, and also our similarities is what connects and binds us. It's central to my teaching—to develop and create an atmosphere of respect where we can share parts of ourselves. Children at this age level (nine and ten) feel a lot of pressure to be the same. They're supposed to wear the same clothes, look the same, listen to the same music. They are terrified to be thought of as different. So I do "Tribes." It helps them recognize who they are as an individual and as part of

a planet full of people. And over time we build a safe, caring environment where they are permanent support groups for each other. It happens by kids beginning to talk in a safe environment, to share what's going on with them, to talk about their feelings and their fears. And once you open things up, once they find they can talk, all kinds of barriers fall aside.
—Roberta Teller, fifth grade, Brookfield Elementary School, Oakland, California. (Olsen and Mullen 1990)

In order for teachers to be effective with students who do not share their identity, it is important to determine the traits and skills of effective teachers. As you read the summary of the research on effective teaching skills, provided in the following pages of this text and in table 2.1 on p. 62, you will see the interrelationship of all these skills with the effective teaching skills required by teachers in multicultural classrooms. Following is an example of an effective teacher: one who can teach *all* students equally well.

I start with them. We talk about it a lot . . . where people are from, who speaks a second language. I work a lot to develop the concepts by using maps and set a context and sense of allowance so that the concepts of different languages and places grow into their own discussions about who they are. . . . they bring in sharing things and talk about where they are made. We have a big globe so you can see the world, and we put dots on all the countries where we find things are made. We start really slow, we start on the world . . . is there more water? more land? we build those concepts first and then the continents and then where we are. We do a lot of oral talk about it before they actually have to come up in front and say "My parents were born in. . . ." That is important, because a lot of times the kids don't have an understanding of what their ethnic title refers to. Even the Indian children did not know the country's name was India. They referred to it as "the old country.". . . So it's a gradual kind of development for them. They can look at the globe and then transfer what they see there.
—Jan Matthews, fourth grade, Meyer Elementary School, San Jose, California. (Olsen and Mullen 1990)

## EFFECTIVE TEACHING RESEARCH

**Effective teaching research** is a relatively new field of study that developed in the early 1980s. Educational researchers are attempting to determine, through extensive observation and interviews of those considered to be effective teachers primarily by their peers and synthesis of research on teaching completed in the 1960s and 1970s, the common characteristics possessed by teachers who are judged to be effective.

Although the term *effective teaching* was coined by researchers in the 1980s, studying what makes teachers successful began in the 1960s. The earlier research focused on the process of teaching by examining a variety of teaching behaviors. For example, from 1959 until 1967, Ned Flanders and his associates focused their research on the effects of teacher indirectness (questioning, praising, and accepting rather than lecturing) on student success. In 1963, Donald Medley and Harold Mitzell's research led to the development of tools for systematically observing and measuring the attributes of teacher behaviors as they relate to changes in student achievement. By 1971, Barak Rosenshine and Norma Furst were actively examining these attributes. This research and other similar studies provided the foundation for the effective teaching research of the 1980s and 1990s, which defined effective teaching as that which leads to student success, usually measured by nationally normed standardized tests. In addition, researchers use evaluation of teachers by administrators and trained teacher observers, teacher-created portfolios, and the opinions of teaching peers, among other means, to determine the common characteristics of successful teachers. In the late 1980s and 1990s research on effective teaching began to focus on multicultural classrooms. The research of Kenneth Zeichner (1993), Patricia Clarke (1992), Laurie Olsen and Nina Mullen (1992), Christine Sleeter and Carl Grant (1988, 1992), and James Banks (1989) defined effective teaching in multicultural classrooms as that which leads to student success as measured by standardized tests, observations, and teachers' journals and diaries. Like most other researchers in the 1980s and 1990s, these also defined effective teaching in multicultural classrooms as related to outcomes.

## EFFECTIVE TEACHING RESEARCH AND TEACHING

Educator Philip Jackson believes that many of the skills and traits identified by researchers in effective teachers can be directly examined, taught, and learned. Many of them relate to the study of pedagogy and the methods of teaching. Because not all studies agree on all the qualities of effective teachers, only those generally acknowledged will be discussed here.

Effective teachers are knowledgeable, have a strong general background, and understand the subject material at a high level. They understand how children and adolescents learn and they know how to encourage learning. Effective teachers have knowledge of ethnic diversity and recognize racism, classism, and sexism and know how to diffuse or deal with them. They have the ability to impart knowledge through appropriate instructional techniques for particular situations. They are flexible in making instructional decisions. They model what is to be learned, set appropriate goal levels for academic achievement, concentrate on a few dominant goals, have a clear instructional focus, offer an overview of each lesson, explain exactly what is expected of students, give time for practice, provide feedback, and allow for review and closure. Effective teachers know how to question, motivate, enrich, and stimulate student learning. They use a limited amount of seat work, teach for mastery, have detailed lesson plans with a variety of activities, and revise and reteach based on student achievement as measured in a variety of ways.

Effective teachers have clear and consistent communication and management skills. They use classroom time effectively and efficiently either on instruction or on student task development. Effective teachers spend limited time in transitions. They are organized, set a brisk instructional pace, monitor student work and progress, are good managers, and help students cope with problems. They are in control of the students and the environment. They use praise more than criticism, are good decision makers, and select and direct activities rather than students.

*(continued on p. 64)*

**TABLE 2-1**

## Effective Teaching Skills

**Measurable**

*has knowledge of subject matter*
Hall 1981; Sizer 1984; Bennett 1986;
Cohen 1991; Labaree 1992;
Darling-Hammond and Goodwin 1993
*has strong general background/*
*understands subject at a high level*
Manatt 1981; Rubin 1985; Bennett
1986; Futrell 1989; Sizer 1992; Brandt
1993
*understands how child/adolescents learn*
Hall 1981; Rubin 1985; Futrell 1989;
Carnegie Council on Adolescent
Development 1989; Olsen and Mullen
1990
*has knowledge of ethnic diversity,*
*recognizes racism, classism, sexism*
Sleeter and Grant 1988; Olsen and
Mullen 1990; Larke 1992; Banks 1993;
Zeichner 1993
*has ability to impart instruction/*
*understands that different approaches are*
*appropriate in different situations*
Walberg et al. 1979; Rubin 1985;
Kauchak and Eggen 1989; Olsen and
Mullen 1990; Larke 1992
*is flexible in instructional decisions*
Flanders 1970; Walberg et al. 1979;
Rubin 1985; Sizer 1992; Swalley 1992
*models what is to be learned*
Manatt 1981; Kauchak and Eggen
1989; Ramsey 1987; Olsen and Mullen
1990
*sets appropriate goal levels of academic*
*achievement*
Brophy and Good 1986; Kauchak and
Eggen 1989; Bredekamp and Rosegrant
1992; Sleeter 1992
*concentrates on a few dominant goals*
Rubin 1985; Sizer 1992
*has clear instructional focus*
Rubin 1985; Kauchak and Eggen 1989;
Cohen 1991
*provides overview of lesson*
Stallings et al. 1972–1978; Brophy and
Evertson 1973; Brophy and Good 1986;
Olsen and Mullen 1990
*explains exactly what is expected*
Bennett 1987; Cohen 1991
*provides for practice*
Hunter 1984; Kauchak and Eggen 1989
*gives feedback*

Stanford Studies, Gage et al.
1960–1982; Good and Grouws 1975;
Stallings et al. 1977, 1978; Kauchak
and Eggen 1989; Larke 1992
*provides for review and closure*
Stallings et al. 1972–1978; Soars and
Soars 1973; Brophy and Evertson 1974;
Kauchak and Eggen 1989
*knows how to question*
Wright and Nuthall 1970; Rosenshine
and Furst 1971; Brophy and Evertson
1973; Soars and Soars 1973; Stallings
1977; Manatt 1981; Kauchak and Eggen
1989; Olsen and Mullen 1990; Sizer
1992; Hammond-Darling and
Goodwin 1993
*motivates students*
Walberg et al. 1979; Rubin 1985;
Cohen 1991; Swalley 1992
*enriches and stimulates student learning*
Rubin 1985; Bredekamp and Rosegrant
1992; Larke 1992; Sleeter 1992
*limits amount of seat work*
Manatt 1981; Olsen and Mullen 1990
*teaches for mastery*
Bloom 1968; Walberg et al. 1979;
Manatt 1981
*gives detailed lesson plans with a variety*
*of activities*
Manatt 1981; Olsen and Mullen 1990;
Larke 1992
*revises/reteaches instruction based on*
*student achievement*
Brophy and Evertson 1974; Good and
Grouws 1975; Walberg et al. 1979;
Cohen 1991
*has clarity of communication*
Wright and Nuthall 1970; Rosenshine
and Furst 1971; Stallings et al.
1972–1978; Soars and Soars 1973; Good
and Grouws 1975; Walberg et al. 1979;
Sizer 1984, 1992; Rubin 1985; Brophy
and Good 1986; Futrell 1989; Kauchak
and Eggen 1989; Swalley 1992
*is consistent in communication*
Kauchak and Eggen 1989;
Ladson-Billings 1992
*has governing powers*
Hall 1981; Darling-Hammond and
Goodwin 1993
*uses time effectively and efficiently; most*
*time spent on instruction and task*
Soars and Soars 1968; Rosenshine and
Furst 1971; Brophy and Evertson 1974,

1979; Denham and Lieberman 1974–1976; Stallings 1974, 1977, 1978; Good and Grouws 1975; Walberg et al. 1979; Manatt 1981; Goodlad 1984; Rubin 1985; Brophy and Good 1986; Bennett 1987b; Kauchak and Eggen 1989

*limits time in transitions*
Brophy and Evertson 1973, 1979; Good and Grouws 1975

*monitors student work and progress*
Brophy and Evertson 1973; Denham and Lieberman 1973–1977; Good and Grouws 1975; Brophy and Good 1986; Olsen and Mullen 1990; Cohen 1991

*is organized*
Denham and Liberman 1973–1977; Kauchak and Eggen 1989; Swalley 1992

*has brisk instructional pace*
Good and Grouws 1975; Evertson et al. 1980; Rubin 1985; Kauchak and Eggen 1989; Dunn and Dunn 1993

*provides good management*
Good and Grouws 1975; Manatt 1981; Rubin 1985; Kauchak and Eggen 1989; Larke 1992; Swick 1992; Ralph 1993

*sets norms of acceptable behavior*
Olsen and Mullen 1990; Larke 1992

*helps students cope with problems*
Rubin 1985; Bennett 1987b; Bredekamp and Rosegrant 1992; Ladson-Billings 1992; Swalley 1992

*is in control and bases control on student behavior*
Flanders 1970; Rubin 1985; Brophy and Good 1986; Cohen 1991; Larke 1992; Dunn and Dunn 1993

*uses praise more than criticism*
Stallings et al. 1972–1978; Rosenshine and Furst 1971; Stallings 1978; Manatt 1981; Olsen and Mullen 1990; Sleeter 1992

*is good decision maker*
Rubin 1985; Kauchak and Eggen 1989; Labaree 1992; Darling-Hammond and Goodwin 1993

*selects and directs activities, not students*
Manatt 1981; Banks 1988; Bennett, C. 1990; Bredekamp and Rosegrant 1992

**Not Measurable**

*has sound moral character*
Hall 1981; Bennett 1986
*likes children and wants to teach them*

Bennett 1986; Olsen and Mullen 1990

*is sensitive*
Banks 1988; Futrell 1989; Olsen and Mullen 1990; Larke 1992; Ladson-Billings 1992; Drake 1993; Zeichner 1993

*has tenacity*
Futrell 1989; Sleeter 1992

*balances the needs of the individual with the needs of the class*
Ramsey 1987; Futrell 1989; Olsen and Mullen 1990; Larke 1992

*has self-confidence*
Sizer 1984; Rubin 1985; Cohen 1991; Dunn and Dunn 1993

*has patience*
Sizer 1984; Olsen and Mullen 1990; Bredekamp and Rosegrant 1992

*has energy*
Sizer 1984, 1992; Cohen 1991; Larke 1992

*is empathic and warm*
Sizer 1984; Kauchak and Eggen 1989; Bennett C. 1990

*has enthusiasm*
Reinhartz and VanCleaf 1986; Mathews 1988; Kauchak and Eggen 1989; Cohen 1991

*sets high goals for themselves and their students*
Rubin 1985; Bennett 1987; Banks 1988; 1990; Larke 1992; Zeichner 1993

*has ability to improvise*
Rubin 1985; Reinhartz and VanCleaf 1986; Olsen and Mullen 1990; Ladson-Billings 1992

*has high expectations and believes all students can succeed*
Olsen and Mullen 1990; Ladson-Billings 1992; Larke 1992; Banks 1993; Zeichner 1993

*is intuitive*
Rubin 1985; Olsen and Mullen 1990; Ladson-Billings 1992; Swalley 1992

*is efficient*
Rubin 1985; Darling-Hammond and Goodwin 1993

*takes pride in what he does*
Rubin 1985; Olsen and Mullen 1990; Cohen 1991

*devotes as much time as possible to what she enjoys about teaching*
Mathews 1988; Rubin 1989; Swalley 1992

---

**Research on effective teaching has discovered many skills that can be measured as well as numerous skills that can't effectively be measured but which, nevertheless, are observed in classrooms where students are learning the material. Both types of skills are listed here with their researchers.**

Although most effective teaching research has emphasized measurable teacher behaviors that produce measurable student learning, much effective teaching research has also identified elements of a teaching personality that cannot be measured. For example, the research has revealed that effective teachers also have sound moral character, like children, want to teach, are sensitive, tenacious, balance the needs of the individual with the needs of the class, are self-confident, patient, energetic, have empathy and warmth, are enthusiastic, set high goals for themselves and their students, improvise, are intuitive, efficient, take pride in what they do, and devote as much time as possible to what they enjoy about teaching. The characteristics of the effective teacher are listed in table 2.1. If you do not already possess them, can you learn them or develop them? In the next section we will discuss how you learn and develop the qualities of effective teaching.

## LEARNING TO BE AN EFFECTIVE TEACHER

Most characteristics of the effective teacher can be taught, learned, and evaluated. For example, there are many ways to ask questions. Far too many teachers simply ask and answer their own questions, or they pose questions that require only factual answers. Students learn little if all questions are answered by the teacher, or if they require only the mere recall of information. (Question: Who was the first president of the United States? Answer: George Washington.) This kind of direct questioning results in low-level cognitive learning. High-level questions, on the other hand, require students to apply their knowledge, analyze, synthesize, and evaluate, and result in higher order thinking skills. (Question: If Thomas Jefferson had been elected the first U.S. president, what differences might we find in our democracy? Answers: As with most high-level questions, there are many possible answers. One might revolve around Jefferson's economic policies, which differed from Washington's. Washington supported Alexander Hamilton's approach of expanding manufacturing in the Northeast, whereas Jefferson supported a westward expansion and an agrarian economy. Another answer might discuss Jefferson's egalitarian view of citizens. It is likely, for example, that Jefferson would have given more power to the states, particularly in education. He would have also encouraged better relations between the president and Congress and opposed a two-term presidency.)

There are some characteristics of effective teachers that are not easy to learn, but because many of them are values they can be developed. In *Taxonomy of Educational Objectives: Affective Domain,* educator David Krathwohl says we develop values by first becoming aware of them. For example, once we recognize that sensitivity toward those of cultures and backgrounds different from our own is an important characteristic of the effective teacher, we can develop it by careful observation and attempted imitation. How does the sensitive teacher respond when children from different backgrounds have difficulty understanding a problem? How does he or she talk to students or react to misbehavior? How does the sensitive teacher incorporate diverse cultural beliefs and values into the classroom?

Finally, according to Krathwohl, we can express the value both orally and in writing.

**Sensitivity is one of the characteristics of the effective teacher that can be developed by observing how sensitive teachers behave in different situations in the classroom. Sensitivity is one way of reaching students who have a tendency to resist learning or who may be intimidated by the learning process, their peers, or their teachers.**

For example, when keeping a log of classroom observations, write about the importance of sensitivity in teaching a diverse population of students and examine how the teacher practices this sensitivity. We can discuss sensitivity in teaching with our instructors and our peers, read about sensitive teachers, like Mary MacCracken and Jaime Escalante, and plan how to be sensitive with our students.

The next stage in developing a value is to organize it within what Krathwohl calls a values complex. In other words, how does one value fit into the hierarchy of values we have already established in our lives? For example, if sensitivity is an important teaching attribute, how is that achieved within a framework of maintaining classroom discipline? How can we sensitively make students aware of the inappropriateness of their behavior? Go back and observe in the classroom of a sensitive teacher. Are the students well-behaved? What does the teacher do to be a sensitive disciplinarian in a classroom with children of different cultures and backgrounds?

It is also helpful to read about teachers who must deal with potential conflicts between two values. Some of the teachers interviewed for the California Tomorrow Immigrant Students Project have developed ways of dealing with conflicting values in the classroom.

> Winnie Porter, a kindergarten teacher [Hawthorne Elementary School] in San Francisco, believes that with young children spending time discussing such incidents [of name calling] are the clearest way to help them understand what prejudice is and how it works.

> Little kids can only learn from things as they happen, when it is concrete and in their experience. Otherwise it's too abstract. so every little incident becomes important as a basis for our learning. I have class meetings *everyday,* whether there has been an overt incident or problem or not. It's important that they know that there is time set aside everyday, regularly, for us to talk about what we are feeling and what has gone on between us as a group of people. That's an essential part of learning in my classroom.

Moyra Contreras, first grade teacher [Melrose Elementary School] in Oakland, responds to each incident and makes it a basis of learning and discussion, though it may not always involve the whole class.

> I always, from day one, make it clear that prejudice and name calling and not playing with kids because of their skin color or language are simply not appropriate ways to behave in school. We have to talk about what is appropriate here. If everybody in the class hears an incident (name calling, etc.) then the discussion includes the whole class, but otherwise I just talk with whoever is involved. I try not to get angry, because it's not the kids' fault. But I *do* try to be clear.

And, indeed, her determination to establish the schoolroom as an alternative environment supportive of diversity is echoed by *all* of the teachers interviewed. Some insist on the importance of teaching children that they are *not* their peers (or sometimes even their families) and that with courage, they can choose behaviors independent and different from those around them. Others choose to clearly and publicly confront intolerance, and indeed let the students sense their outrage and anger at prejudice. Still others may chose a more veiled approach. David Christiano, high school English teacher [Oakland Technical High School] in Oakland, feels it is often a mistake to get confrontational because it's just too charged.

> I speak privately to kids—"what you said may have felt really offensive to these guys . . ." or try to see it from another perspective. One day over the loud speaker a woman was making an announcement, and she was Filipino and had a very heavy accent. It was a strange sound for a lot of the kids. And some of them started to laugh uproariously. I had to stop them. There was a Filipino girl in the class and she was really upset. It really had an impact on her. I talked about the need to be more respectful. She came up later and said she really appreciated that. A lot of that goes on.

Confronting prejudice, responding to incidents of intolerance or name calling, are done in the overall context of human feelings, and respect. Talking about it—and knowing that they will not be attacked while talking about it—is essential (Olsen and Mullen 1990).

According to Krathwohl, the final stage in value development is "characterization by a value complex." This simply means that a value such as sensitivity becomes an integral part of the personality.

This is certainly true of the teachers in the examples above. Sensitivity is so much a part of their personalities that they are able to display it even when they must tell their students that the values they see displayed around them are inappropriate.

**2-1**

**POINTS TO REMEMBER**

- Research shows that effective teachers have sound moral characters, like children, and want to teach them. They are sensitive, tenacious, self-confident, and patient. They possess energy, warmth, and enthusiasm. They work effectively with students from different cultural and ethnic groups and are sensitive to racism and sexism.

- Effective teaching values can be developed by recognizing them, responding to them orally and in writing, observing others who possess the values, and practicing by imitating those who possess them.

- Research identifies effective teachers as knowledgeable, with a strong general background. They are flexible, model what is to be learned, and set appropriate goals. Their lessons have a clear instructional focus. They know how to question and motivate students. They have good communication and management skills.

It is the rare individual who possesses all the attributes of the effective teacher listed in table 2.1, p. 62, but many of them can be developed through teacher-training programs, reflective reading, and careful observation.

## Teaching Style

If we look back to the anecdotes at the beginning of the chapter, we see two effective teachers who approach teaching in very different ways. Both have a similar goal, which is to ensure that their students succeed at the highest possible level. However, each achieves this goal in unique ways based on his or her background, values, knowledge of subject matter and students, understanding of the environment in which he or she teaches, and ability to impart information. Each has developed a personal **teaching style**.

According to Louis Rubin, the author of *Artistry in Teaching,* every teacher has a special way of doing things, a manner or style that makes the teacher what he or she is.

> Style is a composite of the teacher's demeanor and conduct, apparent in the things teachers emphasize, in the procedures they use and in their reactions to opportunity, adversity, failure, success. It is reflected in both good teaching and bad, because each teacher-practitioner goes at his or her work differently. (p. 19)

Rubin further claims that every instructional goal can be accomplished in a variety of ways, depending on one's values, self-image, and conception of teaching role. The teacher's manner or style evolves over a period of time from experience and involves the individual's personality, talent, and ideology. Christine I. Bennett, author of *Comprehensive Multicultural Education: Theory and Practice* (1990), defines style as the "teacher's characteristic approach, whatever the method used" (p. 165). This personal style nourishes the effective teacher. "Great teachers are inspired by the significance they attach to their work and by the pleasure they take in fostering intellectual growth" (p. 20).

*(continued on p. 70)*

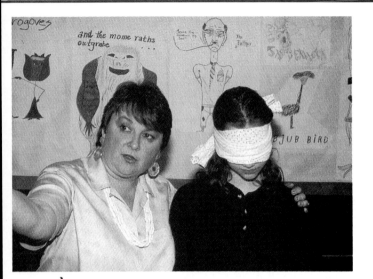

A

B

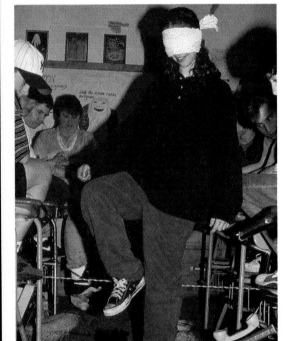

C

An English Teacher at Work

As an English teacher in a Connecticut shoreline high school, Carol Lynn Peterson, a twenty-seven-year veteran in her field with a Master of Arts in English, rarely experiences a peaceful moment once a typical school day gets under way. The following sequence of photographs from the spring of 1994 illustrates the various activities that may involve her and her students both in and out of the classroom:

(A) Freshmen discover that learning can be entertaining as they explore the twelve basic principles of drama in a theatre game called AIRPORT. The teacher first directs a blindfolded student to the game area. (B) Another student communicates directions to the blindfolded student as would an air traffic controller. (C) The blindfolded student tries to avoid obstacles in her path by listening to the directions given by the air traffic controller. (D) Sophomores are called to the podium to give an oral reading of an excerpt from Herman Melville's *Moby Dick.*

D

E

F

(E) Two juniors meet one-on-one with Peterson in the library media center to review their corrected term papers. (F,G) Seniors in an elective entitled "Women in Literature" debate the moral quandary faced by the heroine in *Jane Eyre,* guided by Peterson's questioning techniques. (H) These same students make an afternoon visit to a neighboring town where they are treated to tea and scones in the Front Parlour Tea Room of the British Shoppe in conjunction with their study of the Brontë sisters' lives and writings. (I) Peterson unwinds in her garden while reading from the works of Emily Dickinson and savoring the scent of heliotrope, a perennial flower she grows as a tribute to her favorite American poet.

G

H

I

**METHOD**

Diane Ravitch, a professor at Columbia University and former assistant secretary and counselor to Secretary of Education Lamar Alexander, writes in *The Schools We Deserve*: "Teachers do things in the same way because they all came up through the years of the same type of schooling—they 'model' their own teachers. The pressure in schools is to stay in line with everybody else" (1985, 68–69). John Goodlad's extensive three-year study of 1,350 teachers in thirty-eight very different schools seems to confirm Ravitch's point. His study found that the methods used by all these teachers are more similar than they are different. However, Goodlad's study also concluded that "able teachers, under favorable circumstances, do make an important difference in students' learning, especially in those areas not likely to be attended to in the family" (1984, 167).

Barbara B. Fischer and Louis Fischer, researchers on teaching and learning styles, claim that one of the reasons educators such as Ravitch frequently make the assumption that all teachers are alike is that they tend to think in terms of teaching methods rather than teaching styles. Teaching methods include such techniques as lecturing, asking questions, grouping students, conducting discussions, assigning readings, and giving homework and tests. Most teachers use all these methods at one time or another. A teacher's style is not the specific methods employed but is, instead, the unique way in which the teacher organizes and uses these methods.

For example, two teachers may employ the teaching method of discussion. One teacher acts as the discussion leader, asking directive questions that lead to specific, planned answers. The other allows the students to direct the discussion. This teacher may begin the discussion with an open-ended question and only reenter it to suggest opposing views or alternative solutions or problems. The first teacher expects specific answers from the students; the second wants the students to come up with as many answers as possible. Each teacher's individual teaching style will determine the discussion technique she or he is likely to employ.

**CONTENT**

Teaching style, according to the Fischers, is a "pervasive quality in the behavior of the individual, a quality that persists though the content may change" (p. 245). In other words, two teachers may present the same material but in totally different ways. For example, one may teach the causes of the Civil War by using a simulation in which students play the roles of various social and political groups and attempt to determine the causes of the war based on their interactions. Another may have the students read from a variety of sources to determine the causes of the Civil War. The goals and the content are the same; however, each teacher achieves the goals in a unique way. This constitutes teaching style and is achieved primarily by how content is organized, emphasized, and delivered, based on the teacher's philosophy of learning and teaching.

# Categorizing Teaching Style

In order to understand how individual teachers teach, many educational researchers have attempted to create broad categories under which to group various teaching styles. The five broad categories are instructor centered, content centered, student centered, teacher-student centered, and content-student centered. Within these broad categories, other researchers have described several specific teaching approaches that fall within the major style. See table 2.2 for a delineation of styles and researchers who studied them.

## INSTRUCTOR-CENTERED TEACHING STYLES

**Instructor-centered teaching** and learning implies that the teacher is the model of the way in which a learner should approach a particular field or subject. The teacher is viewed as an ego ideal and a socializing agent. According to Ana Maria Schuhmann (1992) in the article "Learning to Teach Hispanic Students," teachers using instructor-centered styles with multicultural students must communicate clearly when specifying tasks and presenting new information, using outlines, explaining the material, and demonstrating solutions to problems. Further, says Schuhmann, they should monitor student success and provide immediate feedback. Instructor-centered teachers are sometimes dramatic in discussions and lectures with the focus on his or her interpretation of the material. Therefore, evaluation of students is usually more subjective, with both **cognitive** (development of concepts) and **affective** (development of values) orientations to the content and the presentation (Bergquist and Phillips, 18).

According to Fischer and Fischer, the **task-oriented** style assumes that "teachers prescribe the materials to be learned and demand specific performance [related to teacher-determined competencies] on the part of the students." Learning is frequently defined and charted on an individual basis. An explicit system of accounting keeps track of each student's progress (p. 250).

## CONTENT-CENTERED TEACHING STYLES

According to Bergquist and Phillips, **content-centered teaching** and learning implies that the primary task of instruction is to cover the material of the course or subject in a coherent and systematic manner emphasizing student acquisition of the material. The teacher is viewed as an expert or a formal authority; the goals of the course are based on the demands of the material. The teacher's primary methods are lectures and formal discussions. The students' knowledge is usually measured objectively (p. 18).

The **expository style**, according to Blue, involves a variety of lecturing techniques, lecture-recitation being the most prominent. Directive questioning is an important aspect of the expository style as well as is a strong reliance on textbooks and structured assignments. Most of the talk in the classroom is teacher oriented. Teachers impart information, keeping sequence and content under their control. The sequence is determined by the text and subject matter. Teachers are openly didactic, appeal to the learners' rationality, and don't believe that learners

**TABLE 2-2**

## Teaching Styles by Broad Categories

| Instructor-Centered Style | Student-Centered Style |
|---|---|
| *Instructor-Centered*<br>  Bergquist and Phillips 1975<br>*Task-Oriented*<br>  Fischer and Fischer 1979<br>*Emotionally Exciting or Nonemotional*<br>  Fischer and Fischer 1979 | *Student-Centered*<br>  Bergquist and Phillips 1975<br>*Inferential*<br>  Blue 1986<br>*Child-Centered*<br>  Fischer and Fischer 1979 |
| **Content-Centered Style** | **Teacher-Student-Centered Style** |
| *Content-Centered*<br>  Bergquist and Phillips 1975<br>*Expository*<br>  Blue 1986<br>*Subject-Centered*<br>  Fischer and Fischer 1979 | *Cooperative Planning*<br>  Fischer and Fischer 1979<br><br>**Content-Student-Centered Style**<br><br>*Learning-Centered*<br>  Fischer and Fischer 1979 |

**Many educational researchers, listed here, have organized teaching styles first into broad categories, then into various approaches within those categories. Not any one of the teaching styles has proven to be exclusively effective.**

can be left to their own devices. The major goal of expository style teaching is academic achievement related to content taught (pp. 55–56).

The **subject-centered** teacher focuses on the content nearly to the exclusion of the learner. The goal of this type of teaching style is to "cover the subject," even if the student does not learn (Fischer and Fischer, 251). This classification is very similar to Bergquist and Phillips's content-centered teaching style, but there the student's learning is central.

## STUDENT-CENTERED TEACHING STYLES

**Student-centered teaching** and learning, according to Bergquist and Phillips, implies that the teacher is a facilitator and has a person-to-person relationship with each student. This style places a heavy emphasis on learning contracts drawn up between student and teacher that define goals, resources, and means of evaluation. Instruction is tailored to the needs of the student. Student-run group discussions, role playing, simulations, fieldwork, and independent study are key instructional methods. This style emphasizes student-to-student and student-to-teacher interaction. Student experience is an important component. Both cognitive and affective goals are emphasized.

In multicultural classrooms, according to Christine I. Bennett in *Comprehensive Multicultural Education,* teaching style means that teachers provide students with a variety of ways to learn, choosing the one that is most in harmony with their cultural backgrounds. For example, Bennett points out that Native American students often prefer working individually at their desks or in small cooperative groups where the teacher is a facilitator. Thus, small group or individual instruction tends to be far more effective with them than large group instruction.

The **inferential style**, according to Terry Blue, a writer and researcher for the National Education Association, is primarily student centered. The teacher employs inquiry, discovery, discussion, simulations, values clarification, brainstorming, and independent study. The classroom of the inferential-style teacher is characterized by communication in which the teacher (sender) attempts to see the students' (receivers') points of view. The teacher encourages self-directed activities, delegates control to students whenever and wherever possible, attempts to allow for the students' psychological needs, engages the learners' sympathy, resorts to heuristic methods (use of experiment and trial and error), and believes that learners, with guidance, can educate themselves. The goal of this type of instruction is learner independence. In multicultural classrooms in which this style is used effectively, according to Daniel D. Drake in the article "Student Diversity: Implications for Classroom Teachers" (1993), teachers provide opportunities for critical thinking and problem solving, using questioning techniques that personally involve the students and permit them to respond in a way that reflects their cultural diversity.

The **child-centered teaching style**, in its purest form, according to the Fischers, requires the teacher to provide a structure within which children can pursue whatever interests them. Thus, the curriculum emerges from the children's interests. This classification is similar to Bergquist and Phillips's student-centered teaching style, but in that style the curriculum does not emerge from the children; it is planned by the teacher.

For example, in a child-centered classroom in northern Florida Amelia Cano, a third-grade teacher, arranges a walking field trip each Monday morning based on interests expressed by the children. One Monday morning the third-graders, Amelia, the classroom aid, a student teacher from a local university, and several parents walk to a nearby McDonald's. On the way, they discuss how the sidewalks change from cracked ones near the school to smooth ones near the restaurant. The students wonder why, and Amelia asks Tim Lucas, the student teacher, to try to arrange visits to the city offices and, perhaps, a city council meeting. Also on the walk they pass a car dealer. Several of the children comment on the new models in the lot and wonder how much they cost. One little boy says, "I bet that Audi convertible costs at least $1,000." Amelia smiles and responds, "At least!" She mentions to Moyra Christiano, the aid, that they might want to plan a trip to the car dealer on another Monday morning. The children talk to the manager about how the food is prepared, how much is prepared and by whom. A city health inspector arrives at McDonald's, and the assistant manager tells the class how she grades the restaurant. The children talk to her about how to apply for jobs; she shows them a job application and talks about what it takes to become a part of the "McDonald's family." The children ask about Ronald McDonald and other promotional programs, and the assistant manager talks about them. One of the children wants to know more about Ronald McDonald Houses because he knows a child whose family stayed in one when his friend was in the hospital. Amelia jots down a note for future reference. The children leave McDonald's with lots of promotional literature, a nutritional chart, job application forms, coloring books, and a treat for each child. All of this material becomes the focus of this week's lessons. In social studies, the students discuss the city government, including such things as: How are decisions about sidewalk paving made? What do health inspectors do? Why do they do it? What kind of education do you need to become a health inspector? In mathematics, the children compute how many pounds of hamburger meat they need to make enough hamburgers for one day at the local McDonald's. In language arts, they read the comic books and write stories about Ronald McDonald. They also read books about other clowns and watch, discuss, and write about McDonald's television commercials. They search for poems about food and eating, and a group of children create a bulletin board with the poems and their illustrations. In science, the students discuss what kinds of things are important to health in a restaurant. Two of the children call the city health department to invite a health inspector to come and visit the class. Also, in science the students study the nutritional chart and discuss what is needed for good nutrition. They decide it would be fun to keep a log of what they eat for a week and see how nutritious their diets are. One little girl says, "It would really be fun to log the food they serve at breakfast and lunch in the cafeteria." Amelia suggests that a small group work on it. Later in the day, she meets with the group to discuss the best way to accomplish the task. She writes Moyra a note saying that it would be good to use the student logs on food served in the cafeteria as the basis of some lessons on graphing next week and asks her to begin putting together information about graphing.

## TEACHER-STUDENT-CENTERED TEACHING STYLE

In the **teacher-student-centered teaching style** both the teacher and student share equally in the planning of instruction. In this **cooperative planning** teaching style teachers plan "the means and ends of instruction with student cooperation" (Fischer and Fischer, 250). Teachers encourage and support student participation in the learning process, and in guiding students' learning listen to their needs with respect.

Toni Bowman, an elementary school teacher in Davis, California, provides the following example of a student-teacher planned unit that illustrates how students learn to take responsibility for their world at the same time that they learn important mathematical and social skills.

> I want students to feel that working together they can make a difference. This year we worked on a rain forest project for Earth Day. They raised $270 for the rain forest and sent it to the Nature Conservancy to buy acres of the rain forest. My kids were able to purchase 9 acres, which is about the size of our school site. We could go outside and stand and look at the school grounds and say "This is how much rain forest we put into conservation." They raised the money by bringing aluminum cans for recycling; and also by having a toy recycling project where everyone brought toys and we sold them to each other. We were amazed that the quarters and dimes and nickles and pennies really added up to quite a bit of money. I do something every year that focuses on them giving out to the world. It's important. (Olsen and Mullen 1990)

## CONTENT-STUDENT-CENTERED LEARNING STYLE

**Content-student-centered learning styles** balance the objectives of the material to be learned with the needs of the students. The **learning-centered** teacher has equal concern for the students, the curricular objectives, and the material to be learned. These teachers reject the "overemphasis" of the child-centered and subject-centered styles. The goal is to assist students, whatever their abilities, to develop toward curricular goals and autonomy in learning (Fischer and Fischer, 251). According to a study conducted in 1993 by the National Coalition of Advocates for Children, this style is effective in multicultural classrooms because it allows teachers to match the content of the curriculum to the varying rates of student development and to the backgrounds of students, particularly low-income, minority, and limited-English proficient children (p. 110).

Knowing the broad categories of teaching styles allows us to understand how the various approaches facilitate learning. Yet, according to educator Donald C. Orlich, "If there is one truism in teaching, it is there is no *one way* to teach anything or anyone" (1985, 5). In fact, the research indicates that, while there are many characteristics common to effective teachers, there is not yet one definitive style that will work for all teachers, in all situations, all the time.

## INFLUENCE OF EFFECTIVE TEACHING RESEARCH ON TEACHING STYLE

As effective teaching researchers visit classrooms, they attempt to determine whether one style contributes more to effective teaching than another. The results of their studies are, so far, inconclusive.

*Student-Centered Teaching*   The studies of Ned Flanders (1970), Barak Rosenshine and Norma F. Furst (1971), Herbert J. Walberg, Diane Schiller, and Geneva Haertel (1979), and Kenneth Macrorie (1984) found that student-centered teaching styles had a positive impact on student attitudes and achievement. Likewise, the research of Kenneth M. Zeichner (1993), Gloria Ladson-Billings (1993), and Laurie Olsen and Nina Mullen (1990) found that student-centered teaching styles are also effective with students of varied ethnic and racial groups in terms of attitudes, progress, and overall achievement. These students were encouraged to discuss their own cultural backgrounds and experiences as a first step in developing broader concepts. Teachers who allowed students to work on their own and to discover what they were to learn on their own were more effective than teachers who directed student learning. Jere Brophy and Thomas Good (1986) examined and synthesized earlier effective teaching research and reported that one important variable that contributed to student achievement was the involvement of students in organizing and planning their own instruction, an essential component of inferential and student-centered instruction.

*Instructor-Centered Teaching*   Studies conducted by Ana Maria Schuhmann (1992), Robert S. Soars and Ruth M. Soars (1978), Jane Stallings (1974, 1977, 1978), Carolyn Evertson et al. (Junior High Study, 1980), and C. Denham and A. Lieberman (1980), and the Beginning Teacher Evaluation Study conducted between 1973 and 1977, determined that more direct, instructor-centered teaching

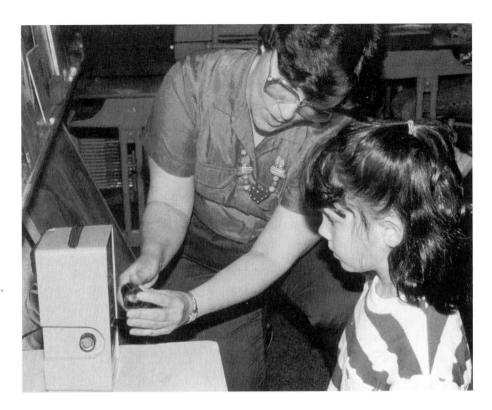

Sally Morrison has been teaching for eighteen years and believes that the best approach is not to utilize one particular teaching style but to be flexible and adapt various styles to the needs of a particular class or to a particular student in a class.

benefits student achievement. In fact, Stallings's research on the teaching of basic skills (reading) in the secondary school study (1978) found a negative correlation between student achievement and choice of activities, one of the most important elements of student-centered instruction. Why do studies on effective teaching disagree on which teaching styles are most likely to promote student achievement?

*Conclusion: Individual Teaching Styles*   These studies of effective teaching seem to prove that, although successful teachers may possess many similar traits and characteristics, they do not necessarily use similar methodologies nor do they have the same combination of styles. In other words, different styles of teaching are appropriate in different settings with different students. According to Ana Marie Schuhmann (1993), "Only recently have demands been made that teachers become more flexible and use a variety of teaching styles in order to respond to the diversity of learning styles among their students" (p. 161).

As Sally Morrison, a second-grade teacher with eighteen years teaching experience, states:

Meeting individual needs should be a full-time job. This includes being aware of individual needs, desires, and problems as well as talents. A teacher asks that the children do work to the best of their abilities, whatever the level, thus accomplishing their full potential. While letting the children be themselves, it is important to bring forth the "best self," bringing out and developing pride, responsibility, self-aware-ness and accomplishment. The teacher expects and gets each child's "best."

It is important for goal setting to be a combined effort of student and teacher. Classes are provided with immediate goals and opportunities to put learning into practice. A teacher should have a sequential and thorough program to provide basic skills with numerous and varied activities which provide zest and flavor to the child's work. This way the child's work is not only *valid* but enjoyable. The teacher uses avenues of approach which appeal most to the child—love and affection, music and rhythm, color and motion, arts and crafts, puppetry, simple humor or whatever the individual best and most effectively responds to.

Morrison acknowledges that effective teachers adjust their teaching styles not only to different groups of students but to individual students within the group. In addition, she notes that there are some elements of instruction that are planned and implemented by the teacher (expository or instructor-centered instruction) and other elements that are jointly planned and implemented by child and teacher (inferential or student-centered instruction). Like all good teachers, Morrison can flexibly adjust pace, methodology, and interactive tech-niques depending on the needs of the individual child.

## Benefits of Effective Teaching Research

Documenting the common, observable attributes of effective teaching is one step toward helping us better understand what it takes to be a good teacher. And for the first time, researchers are using the teacher as the basis for making this determination. In earlier decades, it was not unusual to measure successful teaching by studying what it takes to be successful in business, medicine, or law on the assumption that success in one field automatically extends to success in other fields. For example, in the early 1970s, thousands of educational adminis-trators were trained by the American Management Association for the purpose of adapting the skills used in business management to education. These administra-tors then trained classroom teachers in the use of the management-by-objective concept in their instructional programs and in their classrooms (Chabator and Montgomery 1972).

According to Theodore Sizer, until the qualities that make a teacher good are accessible to everyone, teachers will not be empowered. In other words, teachers must understand from their successful peers what skills and traits are likely to make them successful, and they must be given the opportunity to develop them. Those who are judged to be effective must help other teachers develop essential teaching skills. Until this occurs, Sizer maintains, teaching will fail to be a profession.

***Danger of Conformity in the Implementation of Effective Teaching Research***
Some educators worry that documenting the qualities of effective teachers will lead to a situation where *all* teachers are required to fit into a particular mold. In addition, since most of the researchers select effective teachers based on the achievement of their students, usually measured by standardized tests, they worry

that the immeasurable qualities of teaching, its art, will be left out of the formula for developing effectiveness and rob teachers of their individual spontaneity. If this is the case, critics suggest, teachers will have less control, will be less happy, and the best and brightest of them will leave the profession.

In the 1992 Metropolitan Life Survey of the American Teacher, 19 percent of teachers completing their second year in the classroom reported that they planned to leave teaching within the next five years. The percent of second-year teachers planning to leave teaching was highest at the secondary level, 27 percent; in inner-city or urban schools, 24 percent; in schools with large percentages of minority students, 23 percent; and in schools with large numbers of low-income students, 21 percent. A 1993 survey of American teachers conducted by Louis Harris and Robert F. Wagner, Jr. for the Ford Foundation found that the percentage of all teachers who plan to leave the profession has remained static at 26 percent since 1984. One disturbing aspect of this survey is that the percentage of minority teachers who plan to leave teaching is much higher (29 percent) than the percentage of white teachers who plan to leave the profession (19 percent). Teachers report in these and other surveys that what they find rewarding about teaching is using their own ingenuity, their own unique style, to help students learn. Critics of prescribed teaching content and methodology, including potential misuse of effective teaching research, suggest that this increase in those who want to leave teaching may be a result of less flexibility in making personal teaching decisions. This may be particularly true for minority teachers.

The danger in effective teaching research lies not in the research or in the information gained, but rather in how this research is used by educators. If we attempt to make all teachers clones of a model effective teacher, the danger will be realized. As Richard Turner, professor in the School of Education, University of Colorado, says, "A widespread problem in school districts, in schools of education, and in educational research is the idea that there is a single best style of teaching and that teachers should be highly skilled in that style" (1979, 258). A teacher who served as a subject for Olsen and Mullen's studies of diverse classrooms and reviewed their list of core elements of effective teaching reiterated this concern.

> Looking at any discrete list of what teachers should do worries me. We each have our own styles. That list *does* describe what I do. For example, it's real important to me that my students know me as a human being, and I disclose a lot about my life to my students. But I know another teacher who is very private and doesn't talk about herself with her students. And yet she is very close to them too. I think all of these elements on the list are important. They are critical to my teaching. But teaching isn't really that simple. There are many ways to be a good teacher. (1990, 57)

On the other hand, if the research is considered useful by teachers and prospective teachers in developing their skills, it is likely they will become better at what they do. In fact, the development of one's skills will enhance one's personal teaching style. "Some teachers are superb lecturers, others are excellent discussion leaders, others are at their best in one-to-one tutorial sessions. Some teachers are witty, others impress us with their honesty, others with erudition. Some are firm. Others relaxed and informal. . . . Good teaching is not one way of acting but many ways" (Jackson 1986, 14).

*Effective Research Needs Teachers as Researchers* According to a survey conducted by Gene V. Glass (1993) of over seven hundred distinguished educators and researchers for the Office of Educational Research and Improvement, U.S. Department of Education, effective teaching research should continue. One of the priorities suggested by the researchers was to focus on teachers, "those who labor in the fields, to make them more effective (to do the right things) and more efficient (do things right), that is to improve teaching and learning" (p. 17). According to J. Myron Atkin in the article "Can Educational Research Keep Pace with Education Reform?" (1989), teachers need to become full collaborative partners in effective teaching research if it is going to improve teaching. Teachers surveyed in the Metropolitan Life Surveys of the American Teacher and a 1993 survey of teachers' assumptions about public school reform conducted for the Ford Foundation seem to confirm Atkin's contention. Satisfaction with teaching has risen steadily from 79 percent indicating they were satisfied with teaching in 1984 to 86 percent expressing satisfaction in 1993. Louis Harris and Robert F. Wagner, the researchers who conducted and analyzed these polls, attribute this growth of satisfaction to the school-based decision-making role that has increasingly been given to teachers. In other words, the more opportunity teachers have to be involved, the more satisfied they are with their jobs.

## CULTURES-OF-TEACHING RESEARCH

Another recent trend in research on teaching may mitigate the potential cloning danger of implementing effective teacher research. Sharon Feiman-Nemser and Robert Floden, in reporting on what they call cultures of teaching (how teachers define teaching and describe their own work situations), have found a great deal of variety in how teachers view their work—differences related to age, experience, social and cultural background, gender, marital status, subject matter, and wisdom and ability. However, they are also finding that the extrinsic and intrinsic rewards of teaching are not the same for all teachers (p. 507).

*Extrinsic Rewards* The extrinsic (external) rewards of teaching include relatively high salary, short working hours, elevated status, and significant power. According to cultures-of-teaching studies, "Teachers vary in the importance they attach to both extrinsic and intrinsic rewards. Even the supposedly objective benefits of money and status are not valued equally by all teachers" (Feiman-Nemser and Floden, 510). Frequently these differences stem from the teacher's economic and social status and gender.

The fact that most teachers are women has, according to these studies, negatively affected the status of teaching and the self-image of teachers. Women carry a "double burden in society" by combining career with home and family. "The study of teaching careers using male professionals and businessmen as templates has not done justice to teaching, an occupation dominated by women" (Feiman-Nemser and Floden, 523). Cultures-of-teaching studies have found that the extrinsic rewards that are crucial to those in some professions are not necessarily crucial to all teachers, perhaps because 68 percent are women (83 percent elementary teachers and 49 percent secondary teachers). It is interesting to note that teachers in 1993 were more satisfied with their salaries (66 percent said teaching provided them with the opportunity to earn a "decent living") than

# *Cross-Cultural Perspective*

## Japanese Teachers Do More Than Drill

Many Westerners believe that Japanese educational successes are due to an emphasis on rote learning and memorization, that the classroom is rigidly disciplined. This is far from reality. An American teacher walking into a fourth-grade science class in Japan would be horrified: children all talking at once, leaping and calling for the teacher's attention. The typical American wonders, "Who's in control?"

But if one understands the content of the lively chatter, it is clear that all the noise and movement is focused on the work itself—children are shouting out answers, suggesting other methods, exclaiming in excitement over results, and not gossiping, teasing, or planning games for recess. As long as it is the result of this engagement, the teacher is not concerned over the noise, which may measure a teacher's success. (It has been estimated that American teachers spend about 60 percent of class time on organizing, controlling, and disciplining the class, while Japanese teachers spend only 10 percent.)

A fifth-grade math class I observed reveals some elements of this pedagogy. The day I visited, the class was presented with a general statement about cubing. Before any concrete facts, formulae, or even drawings were displayed, the teacher asked the class to take out their math diaries and spend a few minutes writing down their feelings and anticipations over this new concept. It is hard for me to imagine an American math teacher beginning a lesson with an exhortation to examine one's emotional predispositions about cubing (but that may be only because my own math training was antediluvian).

After that, the teacher asked for conjectures from the children about the surface and volume of a cube and asked for some ideas about formulae for calculation. The teacher asked the class to cluster into its component *han* (working groups) of four or five children each, and gave out materials for measurement and construction. One group left the room with large pieces of cardboard, to construct a model of a cubic meter. The groups worked internally on solutions to problems set by the teacher and competed with each other to finish first. After a while, the cubic meter group returned, groaning under the bulk of its model, and everyone gasped over its size. (There were many comments and guesses as to how many children would fit inside.)

The teacher then set the whole class a very challenging problem, well over their heads, and gave them the rest of the class time to work on it. The class

teachers in 1989 (53 percent) and 1984 (37 percent) (Harris and Wagner, 2–3). Despite this satisfaction, as many teachers plan to leave the profession within five years in 1993 as in 1984. This may be an indication that extrinsic rewards are not what keep teachers in the classroom.

*Intrinsic Rewards* The cultures-of-teaching studies (Lortie 1975; Biklen 1983; Feiman-Nemser and Floden 1986; Cohen 1991) show that the intrinsic (internal) rewards of teaching include knowing that students are learning, having an emotional attachment to them, enjoying interaction with colleagues, deriving satisfaction in performing a valuable service, enjoying teaching activities themselves, and learning from teaching.

Many teachers find that the intrinsic rewards of the classroom outweigh extrinsic rewards. Sari Biklen, professor at Teacher's College, Columbia University, found that women teachers frequently rejected promotions to administrative positions because they were highly committed to teaching and maintained that the quality of their work would suffer. "The point is to offer an array of rewards that will meet many teachers' needs" (Feiman-Nemser and Floden, 523). In a 1991 study of five professional teachers in New York, Rosetta M. Cohen, a professor at

ended without a solution, but the teacher made no particular effort to get or give an answer, although she exhorted them to be energetic. (It was several days before the class got the answer—but the excitement did not flag.)

Several characteristics of this class deserve highlighting. First, there was attention to feelings and predispositions, provision of facts, and opportunities for discovery. The teacher preferred to focus on process, engagement, commitment, and performance rather than on discipline (in our sense) and production.

Second, the *han:* assignments are made to groups, not to individuals (this is also true at the workplace) although individual progress and achievement are closely monitored. Children are supported, praised, and allowed to make mistakes through trial and error within the group. The group is also pitted against other groups, and the group's success is each person's triumph, and vice versa. Groups are made up by the teacher and are designed to include a mixture of skill levels—there is a *hancho* (leader) whose job it is to choreograph the group's work, to encourage the slower members, and to act as a reporter to the class at large.

The regular classroom is a place where the individual does not stick out, but where individual needs are met and goals are set. Children are not held back nor advanced by ability; the cohesion of the age group is said to be more important. Teachers focus

on pulling up the slower learners, rather than tracking the class to suit different abilities.

So where is the competitive selection principle served? In the *juku. Juku* are tough competitive classes, often with up to 500 in one lecture hall. The most prestigious are themselves very selective and there are examinations (and preparation courses for these) to enter the *juku.* Some *juku* specialize in particular universities' entrance exams, and they will boast of their rate of admission into their universities. It is estimated that one-third of all primary school students and one-half of all secondary school students attend *juku.*

The "king of *juku,*" Furukawa Noboru, the creator of a vast chain of such classes, says that *juku* are necessary to bridge the gap of present realities in Japan. He says that public schools do not face the fact of competition, and that ignoring the reality does not help children. While there is considerable grumbling by parents, and while it is clear that the *juku* introduce an inegalitarian element into the process of schooling (since they do cost money), they do, by their separation from the regular school, permit the persistence of more traditional modes of learning, while allowing for a fast track in examinations.

From: White, 1987. M. A. White is a professor at Teacher's College, Columbia University, and an author and researcher on international education.

---

Teacher's College, Columbia University, found that they turned down the opportunity to become department chairs. According to Cohen, "Their first and foremost concern was their effectiveness in the classroom. Job satisfaction, in each case, comes purely from within, from the experience of meeting internal standards of excellence that are infinitely renewing" (p. 100).

## VALUE OF DIVERSITY IN TEACHING

According to Daniel Duke in *Teaching: The Imperiled Profession*, we must begin valuing diversity in teaching instead of acting as if there were one best kind of teacher—there is "no approach to teaching that has been shown to be uniformly effective for all ages of students or all subjects" (p. 138). We must begin thinking of teaching not only as a set of technical skills—such as problem solving, hypothesis testing, decision making, information processing, logical analysis, and resource allocation—but we also must begin thinking of teachers as discipline-based scholars, instructor-teacher-historians, and teacher-child development specialists. Duke suggests that, "Perhaps teachers should be spending more time assessing their different strengths and matching them with the strengths of particular students" (p. 138). He suggests that teachers' schedules could be flexible enough for them to teach late afternoons and evenings. Adult students as well as younger students might be encouraged to attend school at the same time. Duke maintains that at least some teachers should act as coaches so as to learn effective motivating techniques. "Coaches do not rely much on asking questions, yet they often manage to elicit outstanding performances from their players" (p. 140). Duke further suggests that teachers may possess differing skills at age fifty-five than they had at age twenty-two. Therefore, he questions whether it might be possible to give different-age teachers different teaching responsibilities. Perhaps more experienced teachers would assume new teaching roles such as supervisor or adjunct university professor. Duke concludes that his suggestions are only a few of the possible ways in which the teaching profession can begin to value the diversity of its teachers.

## Effective Discipline

Edwin Ralph in an article in the *Middle School Journal* (1993) states that effective teaching and good classroom management are so closely integrated in practice that effective teaching is the basis for effective discipline (see table 2-3). According to Ralph, teachers cannot have effective classroom discipline without first demonstrating a sound grasp of their subject matter. They plan carefully so that material is presented in such a way that it motivates students. When teachers use effective instructional strategies they maximize student attention and participation and this minimizes potential behavioral problems. In their book *Looking in*

**TABLE 2-3**                                    `Research Table`

### Effective Discipline Procedures

*implement effective teaching skills modifying them to meet student needs*
  Ralph 1993; McQueen 1992; Good and Brophy 1991
*develop, explain, enforce, and continually assess classroom rules and procedures*
  Ralph 1993; Mendler 1993; Swick 1992; Brandt 1986
*consistently give positive feedback for merited good conduct and enforce consequences for misbehavior*
  Ralph 1993; Borich 1992; Eby 1992; Hoover 1992; McDaniel 1986

*establish clear norms of acceptable behavior regarding prejudice and respect*
  Larke 1992; Olsen and Mullen 1990
*demonstrate sensitivity to the needs of all students, regardless of gender, race, cultural and ethnic background*
  Zeichner 1993; Ladson-Billings 1992; Larke 1992; Banks 1989
*analyze problems, brainstorm possible solutions and use negotiation skills to set standards of behavior*
  Carlsson-Paige and Levin 1993; Rich 1993; Covaleskie 1992

**Researchers on maintaining discipline in the classroom have determined that the most effective method is to teach students in such a way that they are interested in the material and motivated to learn. Other effective methods are listed in this table.**

*Classrooms* (1991), Thomas Good and Jere Brophy concur, stating that effective teaching requires "proactive problem prevention" (p. 251).

Since schools are microcosms of the greater society, many of society's problems enter the classroom with the students. As the school population has become increasingly diverse and the roles of the home and church in the education of the child have diminished, teachers worry that their roles as models and symbols of authority will be diminished and that student peer groups will control the classroom. The U.S. public considers discipline to be one of three major problems in public education according to the 25th Annual Gallup Poll of the Public's Attitudes toward the Public Schools (1993).

Today, the most accepted definitions of discipline include the words *training* and *self*; **discipline** is the training that leads to the development of self-control, an internal conscience that acknowledges appropriate behavior. However, many of its earlier connotations are still accepted today: submission to authority and a system of rules, and an acceptance of measures intended to correct or punish. Since neither self-discipline nor submission to authority seems to be widely practiced today, discipline in the classroom is a major concern of many teachers.

## METHODS OF DISCIPLINE

Because most educators recognize that a well-managed classroom leads to improved student and teacher performance, more positive relationships with and among students, and less misbehavior, effective methodologies have been developed for managing the classroom that range from those in which the teacher acts as the authority and imposes control from the outside, to those in which the student participates in the development of discipline techniques. The approaches described in the following section reflect a continuum from "external control" to "self-discipline."

*Authoritarian Approaches*   In the **authoritarian**, or teacher-dominant, approach the teacher sets rules and requires the students to submit to his or her authority. The teacher also sets consequences for rule infraction in a fair-minded and consistent manner, fitting the consequences or punishments to the misbehavior. Authoritarian approaches to discipline have had many names; the most popular during the 1980s was the "**Assertive Discipline** Model" (Canter and Canter 1977). This approach assumes that teachers have the right to establish classroom structure and routine, to determine and request appropriate behavior, and to expect and get help from parents and the school administration.

*Analytic Approaches*   The teacher attempts, in the **analytic approach** to discipline, to identify the cause(s) of student misbehavior and then treats the cause(s) rather than the misbehavior. The underlying premise of this form of discipline is that the child's actions frequently do not reveal the underlying problem. For example, the child who is constantly disruptive in class may be insecure, unable to complete the work, may have a psychological need for attention, or a medical problem. In this approach various diagnostic tools are used: test results; social/psychological inventories; attendance records; medical records; cumulative school records; and interviews with student, parents, and previous teachers. Proponents, such as Covaleskie (1992) and Rich (1993), claim

*(continued on p. 86)*

# SHOULD DISCIPLINE PLANS PROMOTE GOOD CLASSROOM BEHAVIOR?

## PRO  Lee Canter

The key to Assertive Discipline is catching students being good: recognizing and supporting them when they behave appropriately and letting them know you like it, day in and day out.

It is vital for classroom teachers to have a systematic discipline plan that explains exactly what will happen when students choose to misbehave. By telling the students at the beginning of the school year what the consequences will be, teachers insure that all students know what to expect in the classroom. Without a plan, teachers must choose an appropriate consequence at the moment when a student misbehaves. . . .

Most important, without a plan teachers tend to be inconsistent. One day they may ignore students who are talking, yelling, or disrupting the class. The next day they may severely discipline students for the same behaviors. In addition, teachers may respond differently to students from different socioeconomic, ethnic, or racial backgrounds.

An effective discipline plan is applied fairly to all students. Every student who willfully disrupts the classroom and stops the teacher from teaching suffers the same consequence. And a written plan can be sent home to parents, who then know beforehand what the teacher's standards are and what will be done when students choose to misbehave. When a teacher calls a parent, there should be no surprises.

I recommend a three-step cycle of behavior management to establish a positive discipline system. First, whenever teachers want students to follow certain directions, they must *teach* the specific behaviors. Teachers too often assume that students know how they are expected to behave. Teachers first need to establish specific directions for each activity during the day—lectures, small-group work, transitions between activities, and so forth. For each situation, teachers must determine the *exact* behaviors they expect from the students. . . .

Second, after teaching the specific directions, teachers—especially at the elementary level—must use *positive repetition* to reinforce the students when they follow the directions. Typically, teachers give directions to the students and then focus attention only on those students who do *not* obey. ("Bobby, you didn't go back to your seat. Teddy, what's wrong with you? Get back to work.") Instead, teachers should focus on those students who do follow the directions, rephrasing the original directions as a positive comment. For example, "Jason went back to his seat and got right to work."

Third, if a student is still misbehaving after a teacher has taught specific directions and has used positive repetition, only then should the teacher use the negative consequences outlined in his or her Assertive Discipline plan. As a general rule, a teacher shouldn't administer a disciplinary consequence to a student until the teacher has reinforced at least two students for the appropriate behavior. Effective teachers are always positive first. Focusing on negative behavior teaches students that negative behavior gets attention, that the teacher is a negative person, and that the classroom is a negative place.

From: L. Canter. "Assertive Discipline—More Than Names on the Board and Marbles in a Jar," *Phi Delta Kappan* (September 1989). Lee Canter has written widely on authoritarian disciplinary approaches and coined the term "assertive discipline."

## POSTSCRIPT

Assertive discipline is probably the most widely used discipline plan in U.S. schools. Teachers claim that they like it because it is easy to use and is usually effective. Critics, such as Covaleskie, contend that its simplicity is one of its biggest problems. Critics suggest that, in the long run, this

# SHOULD DISCIPLINE PLANS PROMOTE GOOD CLASSROOM BEHAVIOR?

## CON John F. Covaleskie

Assertive Discipline has become both the program of choice in many schools and a paradigm of the behavioral approach. Some recent literature reviewing this particular program made clear the extent to which the debate is about means, rather than ends. Rather than endlessly continue the debate about which program best controls student behaviors, we might look at the question from the other end: What is it that we hope to teach children about being good people, and does this mean more than what schools call "discipline"? If we can better define our ends, we might have a better standard by which to evaluate the means to achieve them. . . .

Given the fact that education should have implications for life, the question can be rephrased. It is not, "What is the best way to control student behavior in schools?" but, "What is the best way to prepare our children to live ethical lives?". . .

A program that teaches children that they are simply expected to obey rules . . . fails the children and the larger society, even if it meets the needs of the adults in a school. A discipline program cannot be judged merely by asking whether it does a good job of keeping children out of trouble in school. . . . Children must develop a framework within which they can make good choices about how to act, and we must help them.

It is important in this connection to examine the meaning of two central concepts: "good" and "choices." "Good" is used here in the sense of ethical or moral, not in the sense of practical or advantageous. Children must develop a sense of what it means to be a good person—what it means to choose to do the right thing, especially when circumstances are such that one is faced with the possibility of doing the wrong thing to one's own advantage, and getting away with it. A good choice can, and often will, place the chooser at a disadvantage, and still be a good choice. Further, learning to be a good person is not the same as learning to obey rules; it is more complex than that. . . .

How can we then help children develop this [good] judgment? It is easy to state, but hard to do: we must teach children that the reason they should not do certain things is that those things are wrong; the reason they should prefer to do other things is that those things are right. We must help them see *why* one thing is wrong as against another which is right. *Teaching children that X is wrong because there is a rule against X is not the same as teaching them that there is a rule against X because X is wrong, and helping them understand why this is so.* Children should be taught not to steal because it is wrong. They should not be taught not to steal because there is a rule against stealing. Although they certainly need to know that there is such a rule, the rule is not the reason we teach children not to steal. What they need to understand is that *the rule against stealing exists only because stealing is wrong,* and why this is so. . . .

This voice of conscience. . . is what we must strive to shape in our schools, and this internal voice can best be given shape through external language that models its proper form.

Excerpt from: J. F. Covaleskie. "Discipline and Morality: Beyond Rules and Consequences," *The Educational Forum,* 56 (2), 319 (Winter 1992). Copyright © 1992 by Kappa Delta Pi, an International Honor Society in Education. John Covaleskie writes about the importance of teaching morality in whatever discipline programs schools select.

approach is likely to be counterproductive in that children will not exhibit good behavior unless there is a reward connected to it. They point to grades as an example of this problem. The longer students are in school, these critics suggest, the less willing they are to do work if there is no grade attached. They worry about the kind of life lesson this teaches.

that other forms of discipline do not deal with the causes of the misbehavior and, therefore, provide only temporary solutions; opponents say the approach is too time-consuming and does not deal with immediate problems.

*Behavioristic Approach*    Rooted in the work of psychologist B. F. Skinner, the **behavioristic approach** to classroom management rewards students for good behavior by reinforcing it. In this behavior modification technique, specific misbehavior is identified, performance objectives are identified, and positive behavior is reinforced through rewards appropriate to the child. Negative behavior may be ignored or the student may be removed from the situation that is its cause.

Proponents contend that the approach is successful because it focuses on good behavior and deals with individual children. Opponents say that this approach renders the causes of misbehavior irrelevant and that frequently rewards are inappropriate.

*Teacher-Student Interaction Approach*    A combination of the analytical, the behavioral, and, to some extent, the authoritarian approach is the **teacher-student interaction approach**. In this technique, teacher and student develop a positive relationship that allows them to work together to find the causes of the misbehavior. They engage in structured discussions to help the student build confidence and a strong self-image.

*Student-Centered Approaches*    Students are given maximum freedom within limits in **student-centered approaches**. Teachers observe the students, determine their stages of development, provide work areas and materials appro-

---

**2-2**

**POINTS TO REMEMBER**

- Teaching style is a composite of what the individual teacher believes about teaching and learning and how this philosophy is translated in the classroom.

- Teaching methods are techniques. Teachers can use similar methods and teach identical content even when they have very different teaching styles.

- Teaching styles can be categorized in numerous ways. The most common means is by determining whether the teacher, learner, or content is the central focus of the teaching.

- Some studies of effective teaching claim that teacher-centered teaching is more effective than student-centered teaching; others claim the reverse. Different styles of teaching are effective in different situations with different students.

- Effective teaching research can help teachers develop the traits and skills of effective teachers. On the other hand, if it is assumed that there is one type of effective teacher, the implementation of the research could limit the teacher's ability to develop a personal teaching style.

- Cultures-of-teaching research reveals that some teachers consider job advancement to

- be very important; others are more interested in intrinsic rewards such as interpersonal and professional relationships.

- Teachers develop their own personal teaching styles depending on their strengths and the needs of their students. It is important that there be significant diversity among teachers.

- Methods of discipline can be placed on a continuum from external control to self-discipline. Effective discipline procedures include: implementing effective instructional strategies, setting and enforcing classroom rules, establishing norms of behavior, sensitivity to the needs of all students, and analysis of problems and possible solutions.

priate for the students' stages of emotional and intellectual development, and act as resource persons. Proponents say that this approach allows students to develop naturally and that all students can succeed in this type of classroom, including those with physical or mental handicaps. Opponents contend that many children need limits and that this approach provides none. Legal obligations of teachers and schools related to student discipline will be discussed in chapter 15.

## For Thought/Discussion

1. How can teachers learn to understand their students if they have no shared identity?
2. Must all effective teachers have the same qualities? Why or why not?
3. How can research into teaching styles help teachers improve instruction?

## For Further Reading/Reference

Collins, M., and Tamarkin, C. 1982. *Marva Collins' way.* Los Angeles: J. P. Tarcher. A journalist relates the story of Marva Collins, an inner-city teacher who has successfully taught children and adults whom other educators and schools had given up on.

Conroy, P. 1972. *The water is wide.* Boston: Houghton Mifflin. A moving saga of Pat Conroy's year of teaching the children on isolated Yamacraw Island off the coast of South Carolina. This book was made into the popular motion picture *Conrack.*

Mathews, J. 1988. *Escalante: The best teacher in America.* New York: Henry Holt. This book describes how Escalante, a mathematics teacher in Los Angeles, successfully taught advanced mathematics to Latino students.

McQueen, T. 1992. *Essentials of classroom management and discipline.* New York: HarperCollins. This book clearly describes varied methods of disciplines in varied school settings.

Olsen, L. 1988. *Crossing the schoolhouse border.* San Francisco: California Tomorrow. The author examines how different teachers teach racially and ethnically diverse students.

WRITE THE LARGEST NUMBER YOU CAN:

James Warren in *Phi Delta Kappan.*

**CHAPTER OBJECTIVES**

After studying this chapter, you should be able to:

- Explain what coursework is included in most teacher education programs.
- Explain why fieldwork is important in the training of teachers.
- Define methods of observing teachers.
- Examine some of the technology used in teacher training.
- Describe several means of preparing to teach a diverse student population.
- Identify several different methods of teacher education and training.
- Examine the differences among the teachers' college model, liberal arts model, and competency-based model to teacher training.
- Discuss the variety of five-year programs.
- Examine alternative approaches to teacher training.
- Identify reasons that alternative approaches are controversial.
- Compare and contrast the teacher education reforms suggested by reform commissions of the 1980s and 1990s.
- Discuss outcomes of the reform reports, including changes in coursework required, national certification of teachers, and national accreditation of teacher education programs.

# Chapter 3

# BECOMING A TEACHER

*L*ong before the effective teaching movement of the 1980s, John C. Crowley (1970) wrote this letter to his student teacher. In it Crowley summarizes what it takes to become an effective teacher.

Dear Bill:

Well, your baptism by fire is about over. You have passed through that vague state appropriately mislabelled as "Student Teacher." Soon you will return to the more familiar and secure world of the college campus.

I hope your teaching experience was of some value. Throughout the time we worked together I made repeated plans to sit down with you and have a long talk—a "tell it like it is" type session. Unfortunately, except for between-class chats and noontime gab sessions, our talks never did get down to the nitty-gritty. So, with due apologies for a letter instead of a talk, this will have to do.

If you leave here feeling to some degree satisfied and rewarded, accept these feelings. You have worked diligently and consistently. For your part you have a right to feel rewarded. Teaching offers many intangible bonuses; feeling satisfied when a class goes well is one of them. The day teaching no longer offers to you the feelings of satisfaction and reward is the day you should seriously consider another profession.

Mingled with these feelings is also one of discouragement. Accept this too. Accept it, learn to live with it, and be grateful for it. Of course certain classes flopped; some lesson plans were horror shows; and some kids never seemed to get involved or turned on. This is not a phenomenon experienced only by student teachers. We all encounter this. The good teacher profits from it—he investigates the reasons for failure and seeks to correct himself, his approach, or his students. And in so doing, the good teacher further improves and gets better.

Bad teachers develop mental calluses, blame it on the kids, and sweep the failures under the rug. Always be discouraged and unsatisfied; it's the trademark of a good, professional teacher.

I don't know if you plan to make teaching your career—perhaps, at this point, you don't know yourself—but if you do, I'm sure you will do well; you have the potential. In the event you do elect a teaching career, I would offer these suggestions:

1. Develop a philosophy for yourself and your job. Why do you teach? What do you expect of yourself and your students? Do not chisel this philosophy in stone. Etch it lightly in pencil on your mind, inspect it frequently. Do not be surprised that it changes—that can be a good sign. Be more concerned with the reasons for a change rather than the change itself. Unless you base your teaching on a foundation of goals and ideals, you are wasting time. . . .

2. Do not be just "a teacher," be a professional teacher. Teaching is the most rewarding, demanding, and important job in the world. We deal with the minds of men and the future of the world. It is not a task to be taken lightly. Demand professionalism of yourself and your associates. Do not shut yourself up in a classroom, isolated from and ignorant of the real world. Be prepared to teach at any time, in any place, to anyone. Ferret out ignorance with the zeal of a crusader and the compassion of a saint. Teach as if the fate of mankind rested squarely upon your shoulders and you'll know, in part, what I mean.

3. Always be a learner. Never assume you know all the answers or enough material to teach your class. Read constantly. Do not become an encapsulated specialist. Vary the material. Talk to others. Most of all, learn to listen to your students . . . not to what they say but to what they mean.

A good teacher learns as much from his students as he teaches to them. Do not discourage dialogue. Do not be so dogmatic as to accept only your own views. Do not use the textbook as a mental crutch. . . .

4. Develop the feeling of empathy. Try to feel how the student feels. Do not lapse into the warm complacency of a seating chart, names without faces. Do not accept the cold facts of a rank book, marks without personality. . . .

[See] the boy in the back of the room. Bad teeth, poor complexion, shabby clothes. No known father, a promiscuous mother, and a cold-water flat in a bad part of town. Of course he acts up and appears rebellious; wouldn't you? How have we alleviated his problems by assigning detention time and writing a bad progress report? How does it feel to sit in class day after day hungry, ill, knowing that when the last bell rings it will be back to the sewer?

Is it any wonder that Jacksonian Democracy, the English morality plays, or Boyle's Law leaves these kids cold? But if they are to eventually move into society we must reach them, and the first step comes when we, as teachers, understand them. . . .

5. Finally, alluding to the misadventures of Don Quixote, I would counsel—"Do not be afraid of windmills!" As a conscientious, professional teacher you will find your path constantly bestraddled with windmills of one type or another.

These may come in the form of other teachers, guidance departments, administrators, department heads, school committees, parents, or heaven knows what. They will obstruct, criticize, belittle, and attack you for a variety of reasons and motives. If you think you are right, do not back down! Always be willing to go as far as necessary to defend your convictions and beliefs. Do not avoid experimentation for fear of mistakes or criticism!

If we accept the status quo and maintain a conservative view toward change, we will not progress. In fact, we'll probably regress. We have an obligation, as educators, to constantly seek better ways of doing things. If that means putting our heads on the chopping block, so be it. Either we stand for something or we stand for nothing. If we stand for something it should be so important that any sacrifice to preserve and further it is worthwhile. And, as educators, we are under a moral and ethical responsibility to stand for something.

Well, I hope these words of advice have proved helpful. Repeating an earlier statement, you have great potential and I personally hope you put it to use as a teacher.

I know of no other job that compares with teaching. We need every promising candidate who comes along. It goes without saying of course that should you need a letter of recommendation I will be only too glad to supply it. Having participated in your student teaching experience I also feel morally obliged to assist you should you, at some future date, require and want assistance. It's there for the asking.

Very truly yours,
Jack Crowley

---

*I*n Jack Crowley's letter to Bill the emphasis is on both the skills and attributes of the effective teacher. Crowley would no doubt agree with Robert N. Bush of Stanford University when he asserts, "I am inclined to doubt that genuine artistry in teaching can develop without a thorough underpinning of scholarly, scientific study and training in many of the specific aspects of teaching" (1967, 35). Crowley also tells Bill, "Unless you base your teaching on a foundation of goals and ideals, you are wasting time."

Many critics of teacher education programs believe that teachers are ill-prepared for the challenges of the contemporary classroom. In the 1980s and early 1990s these critics suggested many refroms for teacher training but in the mid-1990s their focus has shifted away from criticizing colleges and universities for lack of teacher preparedness to broadening the mission of teacher-training institutions. They believe we need to train teachers to deal with diverse student populations, to recruit more minority teachers into the profession, and to work collaboratively with public schools and legislators to improve both teacher education and public education simultaneously.

This chapter will first examine how contemporary teachers are educated and discuss the importance of fieldwork in their training. We will specifically examine how today's teacher training programs are preparing teachers to teach in multicultural classrooms. We will then look at alternatives to traditional teacher-training programs, and will investigate the results of teacher education reform movements of the 1980s and 1990s. Finally, this chapter will provide a table illustrating careers in education other than teaching.

# Teacher Education Programs in the 1990s

Most contemporary teachers are educated in colleges and universities. Nearly 1,200, or 70 percent of all four-year colleges and universities in the United States, have state-approved teacher certification programs (Mark Lewis, research assistant, American Association of Colleges for Teacher Education, Nov. 3, 1993, telephone interview). **Certification** is a procedure whereby the state evaluates and reviews a teacher candidate's credentials and provides him or her a license to teach. More than 60 percent of these institutions are private and grant bachelor's degrees only, and 38 percent are public (Lewis, 1993). Although private colleges represent the largest percentage of institutions training teachers, 78 percent of all bachelor-level teachers are trained in public institutions (NCES 1989b, 236). Between the mid-1970s and mid-1980s the number of baccalaureate degrees conferred in education from both private and public colleges and universities declined, while those in computer science, engineering, business, and other technical and professional degrees increased. However, since the mid-1980s, the number of baccalaureate degrees in education has increased while degrees in computer science and engineering have decreased (National Center for Education Statistics 1993).

## COURSEWORK

Teacher education programs generally have three components: general liberal arts, major and minor fields of specialization, and professional studies. In 1993 Cadell Hemphill, specialist at the Council of Chief State School Officers (CSSO), in a telephone conversation confirmed a 1989 American Association of Colleges for Teacher Education (AACTE) report that elementary teacher certification students took, on the average, 40 percent of their coursework in general liberal arts, 32 percent of their coursework in professional studies (methodology, foundations, fieldwork, and psychology), 9 percent in student teaching, and 15 percent in an academic concentration. Secondary teacher certification students took 40 percent of their coursework in general liberal arts, 39 percent in major and minor fields of specialization, and 21 percent in professional studies (AACTE 1989; Hemphill 1993).

There is, however, significant diversity around the country in the number of hours required in academic and professional studies. For example, in 1990, California required eighty-four semester hours in an academic major (general education hours were included in the academic major) and thirty professional education semester hours for elementary certification, while Mississippi required thirty-six academic major semester hours and twenty-seven semester hours in professional education. The highest number of semester hours in professional studies for elementary certification are required by Puerto Rico (ninety), Missouri (sixty), Hawaii (fifty-three), North Dakota, and Pennsylvania (fifty) (CCSO 1990). The highest number of semester hours in general education for elementary certification are required by Iowa (from ninety-five to one hundred), North Dakota (ninety-nine), Maryland (eighty), Indiana and Alabama (sixty) (Hemphill, 1993).

According to the National Association of State Directors of Teacher Education and Certification (NASTEC) (1991), forty-five states and Washington D.C. require general education as one of the broad academic requirements for the initial teaching certificate; in five states general education is a part of an approved program or an individual institution's requirement. All fifty states and the District of Columbia require studies of subject matter and pedagogy; thirty-six require coursework in special education. Sixteen require coursework related to health, drugs, and alcohol abuse; and sixteen require computer education for initial teacher certification (NASTEC 1991, C-1).

In a study of twenty-nine colleges and universities with teacher education programs in eight states, John Goodlad and his associates (1990) found that undergraduate programs leading to teacher certification were usually between 120 and 132 semester hours in length. Of the twenty-nine institutions, which ranged in size from 900 to 35,000 students, twenty-four had four-year undergraduate programs in education. Five required a fifth-year certificate. Most of these programs required two years of general studies, a concentration in an academic discipline for secondary certification students, and some academic coursework for elementary certification students. Goodlad found that the number of methods courses required of teacher certification students had decreased in recent years. His study concluded that fieldwork, however, was increasingly important in the teacher certification programs he reviewed (p. 237).

## FIELDWORK

The dominant approach to teacher training today is based both on **fieldwork**, observing, participating, and teaching in classrooms during a teacher-training program, and the concept that effective teaching requires a combination of teaching skills, knowledge of subject matter, and appropriate personality traits and values. An increase in fieldwork is "one of the most visible changes in teacher education over the past two decades" (AACTE 1990, 12). According to an American Association of Colleges for Teacher Education survey of 713 colleges and universities, candidates in teacher education had an average of four different field experiences for varying purposes and lengths of time. Special education candidates spent an average of one hundred hours in the field; elementary candidates eighty-nine hours; secondary candidates sixty-five hours. According to NASTEC (1991), thirty-seven states require field experiences for initial teacher certification. These requirements vary from a high of three hundred clock hours prior to student teaching in Ohio, to one hundred fifty hours in Kentucky, one hundred in Colorado, Illinois, Nebraska, and Wisconsin and forty-five in Texas, to a low of two required semester hours of field experience in South Carolina.

A survey of former and current teachers, conducted by Louis Harris and Associates for the Metropolitan Life Insurance Company in 1985, found that 50 percent thought it was more important for preservice teachers to spend time on teaching skills than on subject matter; however, 50 percent thought the opposite. A 1991 Metropolitan Life Survey of the American Teacher found that 60 percent of first-year teachers favored more practical training in classrooms as part of their training. The dilemma of how to balance coursework and fieldwork has still not been solved, and the percentage of each varies throughout the country.

According to Louis J. Rubin, author and researcher at the University of Illinois, prospective teachers should observe how mentor teachers exhibit patience, adjust and readjust teaching demeanor to a student's actions, sense how to avoid problems, invent solutions, experiment with numerous instructional and evaluation strategies, and honor individuality (pp. 164–165).

### Educational Research Supports the Importance of Fieldwork

Research supports the belief that classroom-based experiences are important in the training of teachers. A study of forty prestudent teachers (students who observe, participate, tutor in classrooms while taking university coursework before full-time student teaching) found that their observation and participation field experiences positively affected their interpersonal skills as they worked with students, other teachers, and administrators (Austin-Martin, Bull, and Molrine 1981). According to a research study conducted by Marvin Henry, Indiana State University students who participated in a program that required field experiences as teaching aide–observers (twenty–thirty hours), as observers of youth in their cultural setting (ten–twenty hours), as teaching assistants (ten hours minimum), and as reading tutors (ten hours minimum), were better prepared than their peers who had not participated in the field experience. They felt more confident about their ability to assist students with reading problems and perceived themselves as better prepared to teach students with disabilities. In addition, they experienced fewer problems during student teaching (1988).

Preservice elementary education teachers also reported in a research study conducted by Carol Anne Pierson that field experiences were most valuable when there were:

1. clear expectations and objectives (many reported that they missed significant events because they had not been advised what to look for in initial observations)
2. opportunities for feedback and discussion
3. careful correlations with theory and methods taught in the college classroom
4. well-defined procedures for the fieldwork

Martin Haberman and Linda Post, professors and researchers at the University of Wisconsin (1992), confirm in their research that without structure, guidance, and intervention, specific guidelines before fieldwork and follow-up questions, students tend to observe what they expect to see (p. 30). Joan T. Timm, researcher at the University of Wisconsin, and Gregory J. Marchant, professor and researcher at Ball State University (1993), found that when preservice teachers used structured observational instruments designed to provide information about students' behaviors in relation to engagement in learning, they were much more likely to integrate what they were learning in theory with what they had observed in practice. Further, Audrey M. Chasto (1993) found that field experiences in a variety of classrooms are critical if preservice teachers are to see beyond the events or problems of a single lesson or classroom. (See *A Guide to Observation and Participation In the Classroom* for more information on effective fieldwork and forms that provide the student with a means to conduct structured observations in a classroom.)

Although most educators and administrators agree on the importance of classroom-based field experiences for preservice teachers, they frequently disagree on how much is appropriate, when in the student's program it should occur, and what should be accomplished. As John Goodlad's study revealed, the trend in contemporary teacher education programs is toward increasing the number of hours spent in the schools, beginning field experience early in a student's program, and requiring a greater variety of experiences than in the past.

## Observing in Classrooms

One important technique for learning about effective teaching is to observe effective teachers at work in their classrooms. This is a skill, however, that needs to be developed in order to yield the best results. One needs to know what to look for, how to look for it, and how to be objective in one's analysis.

### EFFECTIVE OBSERVATION

Most simply, observation is the act or practice of paying attention to people, events, and/or environment. The difficulty with observation is simply that every individual brings to an event his or her psychological perception of it. Such observations may simply reinforce existing prejudices, thereby "arresting or distorting the growth from further experiences" (Evertson and Green, 95).

However, not all observation is subjective. It also can occur systematically and be conducted fairly objectively. **Systematic observation** is long-term observation involving visiting a classroom many times and observing many different situations. In order to be most effective, it must be planned, objective, and goal or question oriented. The observers identify beforehand what they are looking for and how they will carry it out.

*Objectivity in Observation*   Because teachers and classrooms are so different, observation can be difficult. If the observer tries to do more than record exactly what he or she has seen, the conclusions will be filtered through his or her prejudices and biases.

The criteria for objective observation are (1) observe an entire event or sequence, (2) set goals, limits, and guidelines prior to the observation, (3) record observations completely and carefully, and (4) record objectively without bias or prejudice.

The goal of the systematic observer, then, is to gather as much data as possible over a period of several observations about the classroom, the students, the teacher, and the curriculum. The more data collected, the easier it will be to get a complete picture. The methods of obtaining as objective a point of view as possible involve anecdotal observation, structured observation, and interview. **Anecdotal observations** focus on the situation and specifically on who says or does what rather than on personalities or interpretations of events. **Structured observations** are formal and require that observers look for and record specified

Some of the most accomplished students in Rio Grande City High School in Rio Grande City, Texas, are selected to participate in the B.E.S.T.T. program (Bridging the Education Scene for Teachers of Tomorrow). As part of the program they observe teachers in the classroom and participate in tutoring younger students. Many not only become teachers but also decide to work in Texas.

information that is called for on such things as checklists, sociograms, and profiles. The **interview** is a technique that seeks to find information through direct questioning. This method can be extremely valuable in understanding a procedure one has observed or the rationale behind it. The interview must be planned for and conducted as objectively as possible.

Systematic observation of teachers, students, and classrooms gives preservice teachers the opportunity to learn from effective teachers at work. They can use in their own development what they have learned through their observations.

The specific tools and techniques you need to conduct these observations are available in the observation guide that accompanies this text. Sample forms are filled out by actual students as examples for using the real forms. In addition, two examples of observation logs compiled by university students as they observed teachers at work are also included.

## TECHNOLOGY IN TEACHER-TRAINING PROGRAMS

An increasing number of teacher preparation institutions are utilizing technology in teacher training. Most programs focus on how computer technology can be used to enhance classroom instruction. For example, Austin Peay University in Clarksville, Tennessee, recently opened what it calls a "21st-century classroom." In this classroom there is a computer in, rather than on, every desk. Each desk has a transparent top, allowing students to see the computer monitor situated under them. Keyboards and mice are on rollaway platforms that slide underneath the desktop when not in use. In this classroom, Austin Peay teacher educators are learning not only how to use the computer but how to utilize it in the classroom. Another example is Indiana University's Center for Excellence in Education, which is becoming a national demonstration center for the application of technology to education. For example, it uses videotapes of student teachers to assist them in improving their teaching and to introduce various teaching strategies in methods courses. Also, teleconferencing is allowing university and public school faculties to expand course offerings and consult each other about administrative and instructional issues.

In another example, secondary school student teachers at Elon College in North Carolina were observed by a content specialist while teaching a lesson that was also videotaped. The students utilized the North Carolina Teacher Performance Appraisal Instrument to rate the effectiveness of their teaching. They then compared their self-assessment with the evaluation of the specialist. Results indicated that a combination of the videotape, the self-assessment, and the evaluation of the specialist revealed a more comprehensive and detailed analysis of the effectiveness of the lesson than the evaluation of the specialist alone. Student teachers reported that they were able to solve teaching problems while watching the videotape and also observed student misbehavior they had missed during teaching (Thomson 1992, 20–27).

At the University of North Carolina at Asheville students videotape lessons and later discuss them with peers and faculty advisers. In addition, a microcomputer network allows university students to communicate with students in elementary and middle schools. In one class, for example, university students are assigned the same novel as children in a middle school classroom. In another instance, a university student who is working with two middle school students

These teacher preparation students are utilizing the "21st-century classroom" at Austin Peay University in Clarksville, Tennessee, to become familiar with the computer and how it can be used in the classroom. The computers are placed in, rather than on, every desk, and a transparent top lets students read the screen easily.

in a predominantly black urban school has assigned a novel for them to read. Two other middle school youngsters in a predominantly white rural school have been assigned the same book. The children correspond about the book via the computer network, and the university student monitors their correspondence on a computer at the university, allowing all of them access to ideas and opinions not otherwise easily obtained. In addition, the microcomputer network allows beginning teachers who have completed UNCA's teacher education program to communicate with each other. Each first- and second-year teacher is hooked to the network and communicates with peers and university faculty via electronic mail.

Student teachers at Miami University in Oxford, Ohio, can access a computer network from their student-teaching site that allows them to find curricular information on courses they took in their freshman year. They also have access to videotapes of teachers dealing with classroom management problems that they can use in analyzing their own techniques.

Another use of technology in teacher education is the use of interactive videodiscs. These include software on such topics as management, lesson planning, and learning. The software program appears on the computer screen and students can interact by entering responses verbally or typing them on the keyboard. Interactive videodiscs are being used to enhance focused observation in early field experiences. For example, at Southern Illinois University at Carbondale, unrehearsed classroom sequences are videotaped, edited for significant examples of teaching methodology, and transferred to videodiscs with which students interact. Researchers found that students using these interactive videodiscs were more descriptive in their analysis of all critical classroom events whether on the videodisc or directly observed and were able to support their opinions better than those who simply observed in the classrooms. They were also better able to recall the actions, thoughts, and decisions of both the observed and the videodisc classroom event at a later date in greater detail (McIntyre and Pape 1993).

# Preparation for Diversity

Today's classrooms are increasingly diverse in the cultural, racial, linguistic, and ethnic background of students while the teaching profession remains largely monocultural and monolinguistic. Therefore, researchers agree that teacher educators have two responsibilities: (1) to educate and train preservice and inservice teachers for teaching in multicultural and multilinguistic classrooms and (2) to recruit more ethnically, culturally, racially, and linguistically diverse students into teaching.

### PREPARING TO TEACH IN MULTICULTURAL CLASSROOMS

Antoine M. Garibaldi, a nationally recognized authority on equity in teaching and teacher education, draws on his experience as the Vice President for Academic Affairs at Xavier University in Louisiana and his work revitalizing teacher education programs at historically black colleges when he writes, "Preservice teacher education programs must be reconstructed to accommodate the diverse learning and cultural styles of elementary and secondary students" (1992, 36). They should employ a holistic approach that recognizes the strengths of different cultural orientations and acknowledges that all children, regardless of race or social class, can succeed. Preservice teachers should not take just a single course in multicultural education, but rather should take courses in anthropology, sociology, educational assessment, classroom management and motivational techniques. In addition, they should have field experiences in diverse settings. Jesus Garcia and Sharon L. Pugh of Indiana University concur that preservice teachers need a knowledge base of pluralism, of the nature of different cultures, and of historical and social forces that have affected them. This interdisciplinary knowledge should result in critical thinkers who are multiculturally informed and capable of understanding and meeting the needs of diverse children (1992, 218–219).

James A. Banks suggests that preservice and inservice teachers can be assisted in gaining this pluralistic, holistic knowledge base by:

- clarifying and analyzing their feelings, attitudes and perceptions toward their own and other racial, ethnic and cultural groups
- acquiring knowledge and understanding of the historical experiences and sociological characteristics of ethnic and cultural groups
- increasing instructional skills appropriate in multicultural classrooms
- improving intercultural skills

- developing skills and materials in preparing a culturally and ethnically diverse curriculum

Laurie Olsen and Nina A. Mullen, who observed and interviewed California teachers in multicultural classrooms, were more specific in their recommendations for teacher education. They suggest:

- coursework in second language acquisition
- familiarity with a wide range of materials and literature from different cultures and historical periods
- approaches to creating school and classroom climates that are supportive of diversity
- exposure to the major cultures and background of the target student population (1990, 93)

According to Kenneth M. Zeichner (1993), although "the segregated approach is clearly dominant in U.S. teacher education programs despite a clear preference for an integrated approach" (p. 52), numerous colleges and universities are experimenting with interesting approaches to training monocultural teachers for multicultural classrooms:

- helping preservice teachers understand their own cultural identities by writing autobiographies/life histories (University of Wisconsin-Madison)
- requiring reading of specific books/articles describing successful teaching of students who often do not succeed in school (PROTEACH Program at the University of Florida)
- using case studies to help students examine their attitudes and values toward other groups (University of Washington)
- requiring community field experiences where prospective teachers work in various social service agencies or in economically disadvantaged homes (Knox College, Galesburg, Illinois)
- requiring completion of a minimum number of early field experiences and student teaching in schools serving ethnic and language-minority students
- adding subtopics on multicultural or ethnic studies within education courses

According to NASTEC, in 1991, ten states required that preservice teachers do fieldwork in multicultural settings. Eighty-one percent of preservice teachers who had field experiences in multicultural settings, according to the 1991 Metropolitan Life Survey of the American Teacher, believed that their training had prepared them to teach students from a variety of ethnic backgrounds. However, after one year of teaching experience, only 69 percent agreed that their multicultural field experiences had helped train them to work in multicultural settings.

Patricia J. Larke (1992) reports on an approach to training teachers for multicultural classrooms at Texas A & M University that might prove to be more successful than typical field experiences. Students enroll in a semester-long multicultural seminar to broaden their knowledge base about cultural awareness and sharpen their teaching skills. After the seminar, they are assigned to a

Many teacher preparation institutions are experimenting with programs that require student teachers to do fieldwork in multicultural classrooms as one way of broadening their backgrounds and gaining experience in teaching students of other cultures.

minority student whom they tutor weekly, take to cultural and social events such as concerts and ballgames, take out to dinner or lunch, write letters to and talk to on the telephone. This experience is followed by a second seminar in which the preservice teachers discuss their experience and attempt to solve problems related to it. Larke found in studying the students involved in this program that prior to the seminars and experiences the students' perceptions were largely negative, and that after them, their perceptions had become largely positive (p. 137).

***Recruiting Minorities into Teacher Education***  All the researchers cited previously agree that it is critical that students from a variety of cultures be recruited into teaching. Recruiting New Teachers, Inc., a clearinghouse committed to doing just that, issued a report on state policies that will be needed to improve teacher recruitment based on a working conference co-sponsored by the National Conference of State Legislatures (1993). According to the report, 90 percent of today's teachers are Caucasian and 10 percent are of various minorities. However, 92 percent of current teacher education students are Caucasian and only 8 percent are of minority cultures. The report stated that as long as the racial and ethnic balance of teachers and students is not equal, educational reform will be hindered. Currently, 70 percent of U.S. students are Caucasian and 30 percent are of minority cultures. Three positive initiatives are listed in the report:

- The Southern Regional Task Force on Minority Teacher Recruitment, a project of the Southern Education Foundation, brought five states into a consortium to address minority teacher issues and a recruitment strategy that extends from K–12 through higher education.
- The Consortium for Minorities in Teaching Careers was established in 1989 under the aegis of Jose Mendez, president of the Ana G. Mendez Foundation in Puerto Rico. It consists of two- and four-year colleges, research universities, historically black colleges, and Hispanic-serving institutions in six states and Puerto Rico. The ten-member institutions create local initiatives that draw on each other's resources and experiences.
- A Teacher Cadet Program for High School Students and a ProTeam Program for Middle School Students in South Carolina were started in 1986 by the Center for Teacher Recruitment and now provide nearly one million dollars annually to help recruit minority students into teaching. Two historically black colleges also receive approximately $200,000 in state funding to recruit high school seniors.

A report issued by the Tomas Rivera Center (1993), a national institute for policy studies based in Claremont, California, is more specific in its call for minority teachers. It calls on federal and state governments to develop policies that will encourage Latinos to succeed in school and pursue teaching careers and remove obstacles that keep them from doing so. The report contends that the United States cannot afford to fail its youngest and fastest-growing ethnic group. Further, the report states that Latino teachers are less likely than other teachers to place Latino students in remedial programs and are more likely to identify them as gifted. Therefore, the recruitment of Latino teachers will remove some barriers to success for Latino students.

---

**3-1**

**POINTS TO REMEMBER**

- Most teacher education programs require students to complete a series of courses in general liberal arts, a specialty area or major, coursework in education and psychology, and significant fieldwork.
- Classroom-based fieldwork helps preservice teachers develop their own effective teaching skills and personality traits by allowing them to work with and model mentor teachers.
- Today, more fieldwork is required for prospective teachers. Fieldwork is most effective when there is structure, guidance, well-defined procedures, and correlation with theory.
- Technology in teacher training is used to reinforce fieldwork and to introduce teaching strategies via videotape. In addition, telecommunication networks are employed to allow university faculty, school-based personnel, and teacher education students to confer without leaving their own institutions. Interactive videodiscs using software on topics such as management, lesson planning, and focused observations are also being used.
- Preparing to teach in multicultural settings requires a holistic curriculum in which ethnic topics are woven throughout and varied field experiences are required.

# Approaches to the Training of Teachers

Requirements for state **accreditation** of teacher education programs, a procedure whereby the state evaluates the curriculum and standards of an institution and provides it a professional license to grant degrees (discussed on page 126), have led to a general consistency in requirements for teacher certification. However, within each state there is a great deal of diversity in how these requirements are met by individual institutions. For example, a state may require that all teachers have competency in working with disabled youngsters. Institutions can determine how and when that competency will be met: in a specialized course, during fieldwork, in the education or psychology department, through independent research projects, or other alternative approaches.

The National Council for Accreditation of Teacher Education (NCATE), the national agency that evaluates and accredits teacher education institutions, calls these approaches the "conceptual framework" (NCATE June 16, 1993, 5). It "addresses the philosophy, purposes, coursework, field experiences, student outcomes, student assessment and program evaluation" (5) and assumes that there are many ways to prepare teachers effectively. NCATE's requirement for accreditation is that each institution's "professional education program include the traditional forms of scholarly inquiry and theory development as well as those emerging from the wisdom of practice" (p. 45). It is up to the institution to decide how to interpret these elements. Although all states require a baccalaureate degree from either a nationally or a regionally accredited or state-approved institution for initial certification, fourteen states require that the degree be in professional education, and seven states require that the degree be in another academic area.

Howey and Zimpher (1989) examined a variety of models of teacher education. These are briefly described in the following section.

## TEACHERS' COLLEGE MODEL

The first of these is the **teachers' college model**, which emphasizes a core of professional courses. Historically, they were the largest within the university because the universities themselves were originally normal schools, institutions dedicated to the training of teachers. Contemporary teachers' colleges are usually separate schools or colleges within large universities that have designed model programs for teacher training. One such example is EXEL, Experimental Elementary Education at Ball State University in Muncie, Indiana. This is a cooperative program with the Muncie schools in which students complete a sequence of professional classroom experiences beginning as early as the freshman year. Such early and frequent field experiences are required by most teachers' colleges.

Most students in teachers' colleges major in education, usually in an area of specialty: elementary education, foreign language education, or special education, for example. Frequently, secondary certification students take some or all of the same major courses as others in their discipline. However, most elementary certification students take courses specifically designed to be adapted to the methods employed in the elementary schools.

## LIBERAL ARTS MODEL

The **liberal arts model** features a core liberal arts curriculum in the belief that in order to succeed students must become "capable and cultured human beings" (J. S. Mill). Thus, a large number of courses taken by students in liberal arts programs are interdisciplinary, integrating various arts and sciences disciplines.

All Colorado College teacher education students, for example, major in a discipline within the arts and sciences. At Luther College, elementary certification students complete twenty to twenty-four hours in an area of concentration from anthropology to philosophy. Further, the students' professional studies are heavily based in psychology and include coursework in curriculum, instructional strategies, and foundations of education.

Extensive fieldwork in addition to student teaching is required. For example, at Washington University (St. Louis, Missouri) students are required to do fieldwork in specific courses such as mathematics or anthropology. "Experience in schools is used to illustrate both important ideas in liberal studies and basic educational issues" (Johnston and associates, 128). In Educational Psychology, students observe classroom control for five hours as an example of creating a viable social system. In Sociology of Education, teaching decisions are examined in the context of the school as a political organization, subject to community mores. In this way, the subject matter, the focus of the liberal arts model, can be utilized in developing teaching methods.

According to Joseph S. Johnston Jr. and his associates in a review of liberal arts teacher education programs for the Association of American Colleges, an integrated liberal arts program for arts and sciences majors who are prospective teachers can take many shapes. However, there are several broad characteristics that define the integrated liberal arts teacher education program.

> Each of its principal parts—general education, arts and science major, and professional education—is internally coherent. They also are carefully coordinated and, to an extent, merged with one another. The program emphasizes rigorous and sustained study in the arts and sciences. It also engages undergraduates with this subject matter in ways that specifically support their efforts to prepare themselves as teachers. Study in the liberal arts is improved for all students by a new attention to teaching and learning and to the processes—not merely the products—of disciplinary enquiry. (Johnston and associates 1989, 4)

## COMPETENCY-BASED MODEL

**Competency-based models** center on developing teaching behaviors that are specifically geared to motivate students to learn to the best of their abilities. The goals of the University of Toledo program, for example, were adapted from a statement of quality education from the Pennsylvania State Board of Education. The goals read as follows:

> Each teacher should be prepared to help every child:
>     1. Acquire the greatest possible understanding of himself and an appreciation of his worthiness as a member of society.
>     2. Acquire understanding and appreciation of persons belonging to social, cultural, and ethnic groups different from his own.

3. Acquire to the fullest extent possible for him mastery of the basic skills in the use of words and numbers.

4. Acquire a positive attitude toward school and toward the learning process.

5. Acquire the habits and attitudes associated with responsible citizenship.

6. Acquire good health habits and an understanding of the conditions necessary for the maintenance of physical and emotional well-being.

7. Acquire opportunity and encouragement to be creative in one or more fields of endeavor.

8. Understand the opportunities open to him for preparing himself for a productive life and . . . take advantage of these opportunities.

9. Understand and appreciate as much as he can of human achievement in the natural sciences, the social sciences, the humanities, and the arts.

10. Prepare for a world of rapid change and unforeseeable demands in which continuing education throughout his adult life should be a normal expectation. (Howey and Zimpher 1989, 80–81)

These original goals were later organized into five contexts: organization, education technology, contemporary learning-teaching processes, societal factors, and research. In addition, more than two thousand behavioral objectives related to these broad contexts were generated by the faculty of the University of Toledo College of Education and then specifications were developed to accommodate these objectives.

As in other education programs, students in competency-based programs are required to complete a definite sequence of general education or liberal studies courses that usually includes composition, the humanities, the natural sciences, the social sciences, and mathematics. Moreover, most students must also complete courses in their area of specialization, such as early childhood, language arts, mathematics, science, or social studies. Each course in the competency-based education sequence must bring the preservice teacher closer to reaching the competencies. The University of Toledo accomplishes this by developing a set of educational modules, each designed to help the students reach the specified learning outcome or objective.

An important concept in a competency-based program is the measurement of student success based on behavioral objectives. In the University of Toledo program, for example, students take written tests that are related to the behavioral objectives of each educational module within their education course sequence. The tests may be self-assessments or career explorations. They may also deal with coursework or be based on the student's observation in the schools.

Competency-based teacher education programs, like the one at the University of Toledo, require cooperative relationships between the university and the public schools since a significant portion of the preservice teachers' time must be spent in public school classrooms.

## FIVE-YEAR DEGREE MODELS

In recent years the concept of a **five-year degree** in education, frequently culminating in a master's degree, has gained popularity. However, in 1991 no states required a master's degree for *initial* certification, according to Ted Andrews, president of the National Association of State Directors of Teacher Education. The following eight states required a master's degree for a second stage of certification: Alabama, Colorado, Idaho, Indiana, New York, Nevada, Virginia, and Wyoming. Two states, California and Kentucky, require a fifth year of study for second-stage certification; Montana and Oregon require either a master's degree or a fifth year or thirty semester units. Arizona requires a master's or forty semester units; Maryland and Washington require a master's or thirty semester units.

A 1993 study by Mei Jiun Wong and Russell T. Osguthorpe confirmed that four-year baccalaureate models still dominate teacher training. Ninety percent of the 664 schools, colleges, and departments surveyed offered a baccalaureate degree in elementary education; 89 percent offered it in secondary education, and 67 percent in special education. Only 28 percent offered traditional master's programs leading to certification in elementary education, 31 percent in secondary education, and 39 percent in special education. Less than 16 percent of the institutions offered a five-year baccalaureate degree or a six-year master's program in any of the three areas. Although many institutions had several different degree routes to certification, only half offered training programs at the four-year level. At the end of the traditional master's degree program, usually a fifth-year, the M.Ed. was the most typical degree awarded. The MAT, originally designed for liberal arts baccalaureate graduates wishing to receive certification, has not been widely adopted by institutions.

The master's degree program at the University of New Hampshire provides an interesting model for an integrated undergraduate-graduate five-year program for elementary and secondary teachers. According to University of New Hampshire director of teacher education Michael D. Andrew (March 3, 1994, telephone interview), this five-year, two-degree program begins with the student acting as a teacher assistant during the freshman or sophomore year followed by a required course in the foundations of education. The program concludes with a year-long, twelve-credit teaching internship, at least six credits of electives in education, and a final project or thesis. The baccalaureate degree, with a major in a subject area, not education, is completed in four years. With the exception of the initial teaching assistance experience, the foundations course, a course in human development, and a course titled "Alternative Perspectives on the Nature of Education" (a study of how children and adolescents learn), the rest of the program is completed at the master's level.

A more traditional but not widely employed model for fifth-year programs is the Master of Arts in Teaching (MAT). Students enter the MAT program after completing a bachelor's degree, with or without training in teaching. The basic idea of the Master of Arts in Teaching is that it is primarily a disciplined study of the arts and sciences; at the same time, the student applies this knowledge to theoretical and practical approaches to teaching. The emphasis is on practice teaching as a vehicle for developing methodology. The Association of Master of Arts in Teaching Programs has eight institutional members: Brown University in Rhode Island, the University of Chicago, Claremont Graduate School in California, Colgate University in New York, Duke University in North Carolina, Northwestern University in Illinois, Reed College in Oregon, and Vanderbilt University in Tennessee. Although there are other institutions that offer Masters of Arts in Teaching programs, these eight programs have in common the traditional liberal arts approach to the MAT, a firm commitment to academic excellence in a subject area first, and then its application to teaching/learning methods.

*Cross-Cultural Perspective*

## Teacher Training Around the World

Overall, teachers in the U.S., Canada, Japan, Australia, and the United Kingdom receive similar teacher training as measured by years of training and level of training. Primary and secondary teachers in these nations have about the same number of years of training except in Australia, where most primary teachers have one less year of training than secondary teachers. European nations tend to require higher training standards of their secondary teachers, although training periods for primary teachers have recently been lengthened in some nations such as Finland, France, and Sweden. Many European nations require rigorous national examinations in pedagogy and other subject fields, but due to lack of data, such information is not presented in this section.

Primary teachers in the U.S. need a four-year college degree from a teacher education program, but approximately 45 percent of all U.S. primary teachers earn a master's degree by mid-career.... The four-year training requirement for the U.S. and comparable data from other countries generally include student teaching time. Only Finland (five years) and Germany (four to five years) require more years of teacher training at the primary level. Australia, Austria, Belgium, Ireland, Italy, Norway, Spain and Switzerland require three or fewer years of specialized training after secondary schooling. Many countries still train primary teachers in specialized secondary schools (Italy and some Swiss cantons),

normal schools, or pedagogical institutes. Increasingly, teacher education is being lengthened and upgraded from institute to university status—as in France and Sweden—accompanied by pay increases suitable to the increase in training requirements.

At the lower secondary level, U.S. teachers generally need only a four-year degree, but about 55 percent of lower secondary teachers acquire a master's degree by mid-career. Finland, France, Germany, Ireland, Norway, Sweden, and Switzerland may require more than four years of training and teaching practice *before* becoming a qualified teacher. Only Austria, Belgium, and Spain allow fewer than four years of training.

At the upper secondary level, U.S. teachers almost always major in a subject while simultaneously getting certified through a teacher training program, typically during a single four-year program. About 65 percent of U.S. high school teachers acquire a master's degree by mid-career, but these master's degrees are often attained in the area of educational administration or other non-subject matter areas. No other country requires fewer than four years of postsecondary teacher training. The European standard for upper secondary teacher education is generally around five to six years.

From: Nelson and O'Brien, 1993. Nelson is currently, and O'Brien was, Associate Director of the AFL-CIO.

### ALTERNATIVE APPROACHES

Although the models discussed in the previous section are the most common, there are numerous other approaches to teacher education. Michigan State University, for example, has four alternative approaches to the standard teacher education program. They focus on academic learning, teaching in heterogeneous (mixed group) classrooms, promoting personal and social responsibility, and professional decision making under conditions of multiple and competing demands and expectations. Each of these alternative paths to teacher training requires different coursework designed to lead students toward different teaching situations.

Many of the **alternative approaches** to teacher training have arisen because of shortages of teachers in certain disciplines, such as mathematics and science, and in certain geographic regions of the country. According to a 1992 study, forty states were implementing alternative routes to teacher certification (Feistritzer and Chester). Frequently these programs "strive to reduce or overcome some of the potential barriers to entry into teaching" (Darling-Hammond, Hudson, and Kirby 1989, viii) by taking advantage of revised state certification requirements for entering teaching.

The barriers include coursework in pedagogy, extensive field experiences prior to initial certification, and financial constraints of a career change. The requirements for these alternative routes to certification vary from state to state and program to program. In 1984, New Jersey was the first state to enact legislation for alternative certification. It attempted to bring the best-qualified people into teaching by placing liberal-arts graduates into collaborative school-based/university programs that required them to work with mentor teachers and take university courses. This alternative route to certification has provided the largest number of new minority teachers.

According to Feistritzer and Chester, many of these programs have focused on the retraining of talented professionals in other fields who wish to enter teaching in order to improve the quality of teaching.

## *In the Classroom*

*The following excerpt recounts one incident in Christine Emmel's first year of teaching. Emmel, who had a traditional white, middle-class upbringing, taught five life-science classes to noncollege-bound students in an inner-city Los Angeles high school. She was emergency certified as part of the Los Angeles Unified School District's teacher intern program.*

I prefer to regard myself as a "first-year veteran," having pulled through the horrendous initiation that Maywood [High School] had in store. Gang violence, vandalism, overwhelming rates of teen motherhood, phenomenal records of truancy, student fights, theft, and extreme student hostility in the classroom were just a few of the charms of this particular institution.

I knew I'd be O.K. . . . if I could just turn in my fifth period to the deck and get a new hand. Fifth period was to be my point of surrender—surrender to the frustration of feeling totally powerless over their behavior, surrender to my own feelings of self-doubt and inadequacy.

In the face of my problem with this class, I decided to try "relating" to the students humanistically; this was a suggestion gleaned from several more experienced teachers.

I told the students that I wanted to talk something over with them, meanwhile easing myself into what I hoped was a nonthreatening "I'm your friend" stance. I proceeded to explain, or rather purge, my feelings—how I felt as though they were pitted against me and resistant to what I was trying to teach them, how I felt "real bad" about it and wished we could have a friendlier and more enjoyable class. I finished by "relating" my need for their cooperation, since I wanted to help them, and couldn't under the current terms of our relationship.

What a feeling to finally speak the truth of my feelings—and to them! I looked into their faces, trying to gauge their reaction. Feeling so good about opening up myself, I could only hope for the best. Alas, as usual, reality corrected my forever idealistic expectations, in the form of [her student] Geri's comment: "Well, if you weren't such a bad teacher . . ." This cutting remark, in the face of my vulnerability, plus a few smirks and other unsympathetic comments, were enough to push me past my limit.

And so, I cried in front of fifth period—something I never dreamed I'd do and certainly one of my more horrible imaginings. I'd never let them know I could be pushed that far—and yet, here I was, uncontrollably watering the dirty tile floor! I quickly exited to the hallway, to attempt to regain some equanimity. I hoped no other teachers had decided to keep their doors open that day. After a few moments of agonized "I blew it" thoughts in the empty corridor, I stepped back into my room, heart pounding. In the first second of opening the door, I heard the sound of fake sobs from within. So much for the damned "humanistic" approach! Clearly, neither I nor my students were at a point where this tactic could succeed.

What I learned from this experience is still not altogether clear to me. Once again, however, I was permitted to see that school, just like life, goes on no matter what. I felt I had lost a battle that day and had admitted total defeat in an utterly humiliating way. But a new day of school and fifth period would dawn again . . . and it did. Nothing is irrevocable, and my striving for successful classroom management continued, even though I thought that one day was "The End."

*Patricia Norton, a health teacher for more than twenty-two years and a mentor teacher, reacted this way:*

First of all, I needed to calm down from the outrage I felt upon learning that Christine, with her background and total lack of experience, was sent to such a difficult situation in the first place! I know of no other business where the employers show such a lack of concern about a person's suitability to a particular job. I was beginning to think that the sink-or-swim attitude in education was phasing out with the advent of mentor programs, but I see, as in Christine's dilemma, that the mentality is still alive and well.

Certainly, in a situation like Christine's, a mentor teacher from that school—one who knows the students and the problems—should have spent time with her initially. It was terribly unfortunate that she came to the point of surrender and helplessness.

As to the advice by Christine's colleagues about solving the fifth-period problem by "showing her human side," I think that the interpretation of what that meant needed more defining.

An approach that comes from weakness, as hers was interpreted by the students, never works. She needed to come from whatever strength she had left.

I admire Christine's tenacity to hang in there and learn that experience helps. It sounds as if she really has what it takes to be a teacher. (Shulman and Colbert 1988)

Teachers for Alaska (TFA) at the University of Alaska, Fairbanks, is one interesting alternative approach to teacher certification. It is a fifth-year program designed to train secondary teachers for teaching in small, remote high schools with a myriad of culturally and linguistically varied students as well as in larger high schools serving multicultural populations. The fifteen students who enter TFA each year already have bachelor's degrees in the arts and sciences and are committed to extend their teacher preparation for an additional ten months. TFA is an integrated theory and practice program in which students initially are apprenticed to master teachers in their subject area for two hours per day and take courses designed to help them implement the material in multicultural and minority settings. Students then spend five to ten days in multicultural settings, teach a unit, write case studies of their experience, and return to the university to participate in seminars. The rest of the semester, students continue to work in this manner and become involved in community activities (Noordhoff and Kleinfeld 1993).

TFA emphasizes reflective, inquiring thinking processes, including (1) identification of crucial problems and dilemmas in rural, cross-cultural teaching, (2) developing a wide repertoire of teaching methodologies, (3) using the research base to develop methodologies, (4) tailoring instruction to culturally different students, and (5) reflecting upon and learning from their own practices (Kleinfeld and Noordhoff 1988).

Another alternative teacher-training program that has received a good bit of national publicity is the brainchild of Princeton University liberal arts graduate Wendy Kopp. It is her contention that the best college and university graduates do not go into teaching and that many of them are undecided as to a career. Therefore, with the support of various industries and private foundations, she established Teach for America. The program is designed to train liberal arts graduates to teach in inner-city and rural public schools, where it is difficult to employ quality teachers. Students enrolled in this program possess baccalaureate degrees and take a six-week intensive training course in Los Angeles prior to teaching that includes outcome-based seminars with education specialists from universities and active public school teachers on topics such as classroom management, curriculum development, and parent involvement. Participants do fieldwork in California's year-round public schools. After completing the program, they are qualified to teach in the public schools of twenty states and receive the same salary as other starting teachers. In states in which they are not immediately qualified to teach, they may be required to complete additional coursework prior to teaching or during a probationary period in which they can teach but are not yet certified (Chira 1990). In 1992, the program experienced financial problems, but in 1994 it had promises of $15 million and was able to continue.

Wendy Kopp, the founder of Teach for America, has improved and expanded the training and preparation required of those who participate in her alternative teacher preparation program. Despite its problems, many feel that the program has accomplished its goal of reaching students in areas of the country that desperately need teachers.

*Viewpoint* Alternative Teacher-Education Project Draws Mixed Reviews in First Year of Placing Recent College Graduates in Schools

Soon after Katherine K. Plunkett entered her classroom at Crestworth Elementary School here [Baton Rouge, LA] last fall, she knew she was in trouble. The 1987 graduate of Vassar College couldn't bring her kindergartners under control. Some of the 5-year-olds were running around, several were fighting, and another was climbing a bookshelf.

Ms. Plunkett came here as part of a new program called Teach for America, an alternative teacher-education plan that aims to recruit the brightest graduates from the nation's campuses and send them on two-year teaching stints to some of the nation's toughest schools.

The year was rougher than Ms. Plunkett expected, but it didn't dampen her desire to teach.

"I don't think just because I've had a bad year or a hard month, I'm going to give up," Ms. Plunkett says.

Across town, in an elementary school surrounded by barbed wire, however, Catherine M. Krahnke, a Teach for America recruit from Lehigh University, wants out.

Her year was soured by first graders she couldn't control, and by a few colleagues who resented that she hadn't spent years in college preparing to be a teacher. Teach for America recruits are primarily recent liberal-arts graduates who received just eight weeks of teacher training last summer.

"As hard as I expected it to be, I don't think I was prepared for what it was like," says Ms. Krahnke. One day this spring, she had to break up a fight between two students' mothers. One of the mothers had a gun.

Ms. Krahnke and Ms. Plunkett are among 15 recruits who were sent here last fall by Teach for America. About 500 recent graduates were placed in 25 inner-city and rural school districts throughout the nation that could not find enough certified teachers. The districts accepted and paid the recruits as first-year teachers. In exchange for signing on with Teach for America for two years, the recruits may defer a portion of their student-loan repayments.

The organization says nearly 90 per cent of the new teachers survived their first year in Baton Rouge, New Orleans, Los Angeles, New York City, and several rural towns in North Carolina and Georgia. But the program's first year has drawn mixed reviews. Many of the recruits have been frustrated by their experiences, while others say the program has helped solidify their plans to make teaching a career.

Wendy Kopp, the founder and director of Teach for America, says she realized the first year would uncover lots of difficulties, and says she and her staff are working to improve the program.

"We have learned an incredible amount across the board," says Ms. Kopp. "We're fine-tuning every part of our operation."

Teach for America has drawn tremendous interest across the country, primarily because of its unusual beginnings. Ms. Kopp, a 1989 Princeton University graduate, first proposed the idea in her senior thesis. She was interested in coming up with an innovative way to create a new supply of quality teachers desperately needed by the nation's schools.

Much to the surprise of her professors, and of those who for years have been working to attract people to teaching, Ms. Kopp quickly put the plan into place. She raised more than $1 million by convincing the heads of some of America's largest companies that her idea would work. And she sparked the interest of hundreds more graduates than the program had room for.

Some teacher educators have criticized the plan, saying that underprepared teachers are not what the nation's schools need. They point to the frustrations of some of this year's recruits as evidence of the problems inherent in alternative teacher-education programs.

One of the biggest complaints of the new teachers is that they didn't receive adequate training or have enough time to prepare for their new jobs. Most of those sent here, for example, didn't arrive until a day or two before classes. Some didn't get here until the night before.

On her first day, Lori A. Donoho learned she was the only mathematics teacher at Northdale Magnet Academy. It is an alternative school for students who had trouble in regular classrooms because of learning disabilities or discipline problems. Her students ranged in age from 14 to 21, making Ms. Donoho, a 1990 graduate of Emory University, only two years older than her oldest students. Her challenge didn't end there.

Ms. Donoho was assigned to teach six periods a day, and in three of them she had to divide the class into two subjects. For example, in one period Ms. Donoho had to teach Algebra I to some students and consumer math to others. She ended up writing roughly nine lesson plans each day. She says she had planned and taught no more than 20 lessons in her student-teaching experience at the Teach for America training institute. . . .

Ms. Plunkett says she certainly wasn't ready for what she came up against in her poor school district here. Many of her students were covered with ringworm and lice bites from dirty living conditions. Ms. Plunkett found herself comforting a girl whose abusive mother had burnt her leg with an iron. And the young teacher was frustrated by a youngster who had spent two years in kindergarten but still couldn't write her name. . . .

Many of the new teachers say they also had problems getting guidance from their schools. Some of the districts—because of personnel constraints or budget cutbacks—were unable to follow through on agreements to pair an experienced teacher with each Teach for America recruit. Some recruits grabbed the teacher in the classroom next door for help. But others found they weren't accepted when their colleagues learned how they had been trained. . . .

Officials of the Inglewood Unified School district in California were excited when they first heard of Ms. Kopp's idea, and they signed up for 38 recruits last fall. They say Teach for America offers a new market of highly motivated people with diverse experiences who can bring fresh ideas to the classroom. . . .

Ms. Kopp says expertise will come to those of the recent graduates who stay with teaching. Like all beginning teachers, she says, Teach for America recruits must learn on the job.

"We don't know of a way in this country to prepare people to be expert teachers before they walk into a classroom or to be prepared for what they will see," says Ms. Kopp. "We really believe teachers are made through experience." Ms. Kopp believes some of the recruits will stay long enough to become excellent teachers. A Teach for America survey shows that 23 per cent of the new teachers who survived the first year plan to stay in teaching for at least five years beyond the initial two-year commitment they made to the program.

Teach for America officials say they have made some dramatic improvements as the program enters its second year.

The curriculum for this summer's training institute is being revised to create a better balance between theoretical concepts and classroom management. Experienced teachers from specific regions will travel to the institute to instruct the new recruits on their schools' problems.

Instead of spending all eight weeks at the institute, the recruits will attend a six-week training session in California and will then travel to their schools for a one-to-two-week induction period. Each region also will have a support director—an experienced teacher from the area who will actually observe the new teachers and offer pointers.

The institute projects that 650 to 700 new corps members will be selected from 3,100 applicants this summer. Schools in five new areas—the Rio Grande Valley; Houston; Miami; Oakland, Cal.; and towns in Arkansas—have signed up to accept recruits for the 1991–92 school year.

Teach for America officials say that even the recruits who choose to leave teaching after their two-year commitment can become advocates for education by telling others what they have seen on the front lines of American education.

Says Ms. Kopp: "They are going to take this experience with them and see the world through a whole new lens."

From: Nicklin, 1991

Postscript: Of the 1989 charter group of 342 TFA graduates, 60 percent planned to remain in teaching in 1991: 177 planned to continue in their placement site, 29 planned to teach in other schools, and 11 were pursuing master's degrees (Lawton 1992, 14). As a comparison, of the entire public school teaching force, 5.6 percent left teaching between 1987–88 and 1988–89 (NCES 1991, 5). A report of the Education Commission of the States, authored by Calvin Frazier, concluded that TFA provides candidates with collaborative and evaluative elements appropriate for entry-level teachers, but does not provide for staff development and continuing education nor does it involve the arts and sciences faculties of colleges and universities during the teachers' training at a level necessary for teachers to effectively implement K–12 student performance standards in many states (1993, 6). In other words, the lack of involvement of subject area faculty in the teacher-training process does not give the students the opportunity to integrate subject area knowledge with pedagogy—each are taught in isolation: content area knowledge during the baccalaureate degree program and pedagogy during the TFA training.

*Controversy Surrounding Alternative Teacher-Training Programs*   There is a great deal of controversy surrounding alternative approaches to teacher certification. According to the National Center for Education Statistics (1993), 79 percent of recently hired teachers have a standard baccalaureate degree; 10 percent began traditional teacher training after receiving a baccalaureate degree; 6 percent began their training as undergraduates and completed it in traditional programs after receiving the baccalaureate degree; only 2 percent participated in alternative licensure programs, and 3 percent were certified by other methods such as review of academic/professional background and inservice work to reach specific competencies. Despite the controversy and the small number of teachers trained through alternative approaches, most classroom teachers (73 percent, according to the 1993 Metropolitan Life Survey of the American Teacher) support expanding alternative routes to certification.

One major concern about these nontraditional approaches to teacher training is that the limited pedagogical training they receive may become the norm, and thus, the skills of those entering the profession through college and university programs will be held in lower regard than the nonteaching skills possessed by teachers entering from other professions. The result of this could well be the devaluation of characteristics such as sensitivity and ability to teach for mastery and the loss of empowerment. In addition, many educators resent these programs because the assumption is that the skills learned in professional education programs are unimportant or that they can be learned in a few weeks (AACTE Policy Statement June 1989; Buechler March 1990).

The National Education Association (NEA), the largest professional organization of teachers, endorses what it calls a "*nontraditional route to teacher licensure* while reaffirming its position calling for a fully licensed and qualified teacher in every classroom." The NEA "recognizes that adults will change jobs several times in their lifetimes and that there will be mid-career individuals coming into teaching. . . . [However, NEA's] goal is to avoid substandard licensure programs that will put anyone short of a fully prepared professional at the head of every public-school classroom." To do this, NEA suggests that nontraditional programs be developed that "rigorously prepare an individual to obtain a standard, full teaching license" (NEA July 5, 1990).

Gary Natriello and Karen Zumwalt of Teachers College, Columbia, and Calvin Frazier suggest that if alternative approaches to teacher training are to be successful, the following challenges must be met:

- Maintain and enhance the quality of individuals entering teaching.

- Recruit and retain individuals with an interest in teaching in urban schools.
- Recruit and retain more minorities in teaching.
- Contribute to efforts to make teaching more professional by realizing the need for a specialized knowledge base and controlled entry into the profession.
- Retain alternatively trained teachers who may not have the commitment to teaching because they have not devoted significant time in preparing to teach (Natriello and Zumwalt 1992, 59–60).
- Evaluate alternative programs in terms of what teacher-training programs should be rather than what they are.
- Judge alternative and traditional programs by the same much higher standard of performance than in the past (Frazier 1993, 6).

---

**3-2**

**POINTS TO REMEMBER**

- Requirements for certification of teachers are consistent within individual states. However, institutions are usually allowed to interpret state requirements to meet the needs of their students.
- The foundation of the teachers' college approach is methodology and fieldwork.
- The foundation of the liberal arts approach is the development of critical thinking skills through academic study.
- Competency-based approaches to teacher training contend that there is a series of skills that all successful teachers must be able to meet.
- Fifth-year programs are housed in colleges and universities; some are continuations of bachelor's programs; others are separate master's programs.
- Forty states have implemented alternative routes to teacher education. They are often developed to meet the need for more teachers than traditional programs can supply. Some are within colleges or universities, and students in these programs complete the same basic requirements as traditional students.
- Some educators worry that alternative paths to teacher education will diminish the professionalism of traditionally trained teachers.

---

## Reforms in Contemporary Teacher Training

By most measures, American education is failing to educate its young people. Average SAT scores have fallen fifty-nine points in the last thirty years, and the most recent tests of the National Assessment of Education Progress (NAEP) indicate that serious deficiencies exist in high school seniors' knowledge of English, mathematics, science, history, and geography. Among the many areas of reform suggested to improve American education is that of teacher training.

Despite the commitment of educators to study what it takes to be an effective teacher and to design teacher-training programs that develop a student's knowledge, attributes, and skills, cries for reform came from many educators, politicians, and business leaders during the 1980s and early 1990s. Each of the reports suggested goals of reform such as five-year teacher training programs; an increased number of credits in liberal arts courses; majors or concentrations in arts and sciences disciplines; master's degrees for recertification, professional certification, or permanent certification; and increased length of school-based internships, but how best to train effective teachers remained elusive and much of the content of the reform was controversial. Some of these reports are discussed in the following section.

## HOLMES GROUP

In *Tomorrow's Teachers,* the report of the Holmes Group, a consortium of ninety-six research institutions with deans of education from each state, acknowledged that their suggestions had been made before. In fact, the name of the group honored Henry W. Holmes, dean of Harvard Graduate School, who had suggested many similar reforms in the 1920s. The members of the Holmes Group of 1986 did make many of the same recommendations as Holmes himself in the 1920s and other reform commission reports of the late 1950s and early 1960s. However, they expected different outcomes because the deans of some of the most influential research colleges and universities made up the group. These men and women could influence teacher education reform in their institutions, and, thereby, across the nation.

The Holmes Group identified the following goals for teacher education: to make the education of teachers intellectually more solid; to recognize differences in teachers' knowledge, skills, and commitment, in their education, certification, and work; to create standards of entry to the profession—examinations and educational requirements—that are professionally relevant and intellectually defensible; to connect our own institutions [universities] with the schools; and to make schools better places for teachers to work and to learn (1986, 4).

In order to realize these goals, the Holmes Group proposed a three-tier system of teacher certification. The first tier would include novice instructors who would have a five-year, nonrenewable teaching certificate and would have completed a minimum of a four-year degree in an arts and sciences discipline and several months of intensive pedagogical study (the four-year undergraduate education major would be eliminated). These entry requirements would be flexible to allow professionals from other fields to become teachers. During the first year of teaching, novice instructors would teach under the supervision of a fully certified professional.

Entry to the second tier (professional teacher) would require successful teaching for five years; satisfactory examination scores in general education, professional education, and the individual's arts and sciences discipline; and a master's degree in teaching that would include advanced coursework in the arts and sciences discipline, classroom teaching of children considered to be at-risk in the educational setting, and a full year of supervised teaching. Also, candidates for this level would demonstrate on-the-job performance and would prepare portfolios to document their successful teaching.

To reach the final tier, career professionals, teachers would be able to document extensive and outstanding experience as a professional teacher. Also, they would have completed further specialized study, usually a doctorate, in an arts and sciences discipline or another educational specialty such as supervision or administration. This level of professionalism would require completion of research, oral examinations, and portfolios of practical competence in teaching. Moreover, teachers at this level would act as mentors to novice instructors.

*(continued on p. 118)*

# CAN SCHOOLS OF EDUCATION REFORM THEMSELVES?

## PRO  Donald J. Stedman

Revitalizing the old School will not be enough, simply retooling the old faculty will not be sufficient, rehabilitating the old curriculum is not appropriate. There will be no substitute for a professional School of Education on the campus of the university but its role, function, and organization must be re-invented to undergird the next great leap forward in American education and to sustain new initiatives with a balanced program of effective professional education, research and development, and public service. The question is how?

Some . . . propositions have been put forward, notably John Goodlad's recent work, but none has yet set out the basic reformation that the professional School of Education must undergo. . . . For the university to be a salient part of reform, it must be clear about its role in the effort to strengthen the public schools. . . .

The university, . . . must . . . adopt a clear understanding of its role in strengthening the public schools. It must acknowledge that:

1. The economic, social and cultural development of a state are determined primarily by the quality and effectiveness of its public schools.
2. The principal contribution of higher education toward strengthening the public schools is the preparation of teachers and school leadership. . . .
3. The preparation of teachers and school leadership is a campus-wide responsibility. . . .
4. The preparation and continuing professional development of teachers and school leadership are best carried out through authentic partnerships among colleges, public schools, businesses, and local agencies.
5. The essential ingredients of an effective teacher education program are:

. . . A strong program in the Arts and Sciences.
. . . Effective clinical training. . . .
. . . An intellectually energetic and experienced teacher education faculty to select, prepare, and support prospective teachers and school leadership.

6. Colleges and teacher education programs require strong legislative support and that of the business and corporate community.
7. The improvement of teacher education programs requires long-term support and regular and periodic review and revision by external agencies.
8. The Chief Executive Officers (Presidents or Chancellors), Chief Academic Officers, and Boards of Trustees of colleges or universities preparing teachers must be directly involved in and supportive of school-college partnerships, campus-business relationships, and the operations and accreditation of teacher education programs.
9. There must be broad public support for, and a high value placed on, education for colleges and universities and the public schools to function effectively. . . .

. . . Those [schools of education] that can restructure themselves to a flexible system will not only survive, they will help make a difference.

All of this will require more research and development and a greater federal and state investment in restructuring and strengthening teacher education.

From: Donald J. Stedman. "Re-inventing the Schools of Education: A Marshall Plan for Teacher Education," *Vital Speeches of the Day* (April 15, 1991), 57 (13), 354–358. Donald J. Stedman is a professor of education and Dean of the College of Education at the University of North Carolina at Chapel Hill.

## POSTSCRIPT

Stedman, a dean, suggests that the schools and colleges of education are not to blame for the problems of public education; that they may not be training teachers as well as they could be, but they are doing a good job. Further, he maintains that it is time to let those schools and colleges do what they do best—make their own decisions about how to reform teacher education. Kramer, a researcher and

# CAN SCHOOLS OF EDUCATION REFORM THEMSELVES?

## CON  Rita Kramer

The quest for academic status and acceptance as an equal of the other professional faculties such as law and medicine led to the abandonment on many college and university campuses of the connection with the lowly women who taught children in elementary classrooms. . . . Professors were too busy inventing a discipline of education to concern themselves with the present realities of the public schools. That was left to the less elite—and less selective—institutions. . . .

With a few exceptions, such as Teachers College of Columbia University and the College of Education at Michigan State University, the leading institutions in the field of education largely shy away from identification with the preparation of the elementary school teaching force. . . . The training of primary school teachers thus devolves upon the second-tier institutions, from small private colleges to large state universities, less selective in admissions and less demanding of those they admit. . . .

. . . Almost nowhere did I find teachers of teachers whose emphasis was on the measurable learning of real knowledge. . . .

. . . Among teacher-educators today, the goal of schooling is not considered to be instructional, let alone intellectual, but political. The aim is not to produce individuals capable of effort and mastery, but to make sure everyone gets a passing grade. The school is to be remade into a republic of feelings—as distinct from a republic of learning—where everyone can feel he deserves an *A*.

In order to create a more just society, future teachers are being told, they must focus on the handicapped of all kinds. . . . What matters is not to teach any particular subject or skill, not to preserve past accomplishments or stimulate future achievements, but to give to all that stamp of approval that will make them "feel good about themselves." Self-esteem has replaced understanding as the goal of education.

Thus the education of teachers has not only been politicized; it has been reoriented toward what is euphemistically called "special education.". . . It is no longer acceptable to think in terms of different systems for different kinds of students of differing degrees of ability and motivation, since it is no longer learning that is at the center of the educational enterprise but, increasingly, the promotion of "equity." . . .

Meanwhile, any criticism of this state of affairs is met with the charge of elitism or, worse still, racism. No one in the ed school universe dares publicly to advocate a curriculum that resists the "cooperative learning," the "multicultural" and "global" approach that is often a thinly disguised rejection of individualistic democratic values and institutions and of the very idea that underneath all our variety of backgrounds we Americans have been and should continue to become one nation, one culture. That aim and, in fact, any knowledge or appreciation of that common culture and the institutions from which it derives, I found to be conspicuously absent in the places that prepare men and women to teach in our country's public schools today. . . .

. . . Nowhere in America today is intellectual life deader than in our schools—unless it is in our schools of education.

From: Rita Kramer. *Ed School Follies: The Miseducation of America's Teachers,* Free Press, 1991. Rita Kramer is a researcher who spent several years observing teacher-training institutions. Kramer believes that schools of education have such "politicized" pedagogy that they are not adequately training teachers to teach. Further she implies that teacher-training institutions are neither willing nor able to reform from within.

advocate of reform, claims that the schools and colleges of education have lost their sense of direction and are not educating teachers in how to teach the content, but, instead, are trying to decide what the content of a teacher education curriculum should be. According to Kramer, today's schools and colleges of education are controlled by politics and have lost their ability to make their own decisions about how best to educate teachers.

The second report of the Holmes group, *Work in Progress: The Holmes Group One Year On* (1989), included recommendations on training for student diversity and implementing professional development schools (elementary and secondary schools selected by colleges and universities as sites for teacher training) and teacher education programs in colleges and universities that model effective teaching.

## THE CARNEGIE FORUM ON EDUCATION AND THE ECONOMY TASK FORCE ON TEACHING AS A PROFESSION

The Carnegie Forum on Education and the Economy Task Force on Teaching as a Profession was established in 1985 and consisted of fourteen members from business, education, and politics. Unlike the Holmes Group, only one member of the Carnegie task force represented higher education. In 1986 the task force issued its report, *A Nation Prepared: Teachers for the 21st Century,* which included the following suggested reforms:

1. "Create a National Board for Professional Teacher Standards, organized with a regional and state membership structure made up of a majority of members elected by Board-certified teachers, to establish high standards for what teachers need to know and be able to do, and to certify teachers who meet that standard." The Board would set standards for awarding teacher's certificates attesting to high levels of competence and advanced teacher's certificates for outstanding teaching competence and demonstrated leadership abilities. It would award national certification to teachers that initially would be voluntary.
2. "Restructure the teaching force, and introduce a new category of Lead Teachers with the proven ability to provide active leadership in the redesign of the schools and in helping their colleagues to uphold high standards of learning and teaching.
3. "Require a bachelors degree in the arts and sciences as a prerequisite for the professional study of teaching." States should abolish the undergraduate degree in education and develop Master in Teaching degrees, which should emphasize systematic study of teaching and include extensive school-based experiences.
4. "Develop a new professional curriculum in graduate schools of education leading to a Master in Teaching degree, based on systematic knowledge of teaching and including internships and residencies in the schools." (p. 55)

## NATIONAL COMMISSION FOR EXCELLENCE IN TEACHER EDUCATION

The 1985 report *A Call for Change in Teacher Education* differs from the other reform reports in that it was written by the professional organization of colleges of education, the Association of American Colleges of Teacher Education (AACTE). The seventeen members of the commission included college presidents, chancellors, deans, representatives from the professional organizations of teach-

*(continued on p. 120)*

**TABLE 3-1**                          Research Table

## Recommendations from Major Reports on Teacher Education 1985–1993

1. Advocate consistent standards for strong intellectual, vital programs in professional studies including the study of teaching and schooling as an academic field, knowledge of teaching subject matter, understanding of child adolescent development.
Holmes Group (1986), National Commission for Excellence in Teacher Education (1985), Carnegie Forum on Education and the Economy Task Force on Teaching as a Profession (1986), Southern Regional Education Board (1981, 1983, 1985), Goodlad (1990).

2. Advocate collaboration between colleges of education and K–12 schools, and call for the development of professional schools.
Holmes Group (1986), National Commission of Excellence in Teacher Education (1985), Carnegie Forum on Education and the Economy Task Force on Teaching as a Profession (1986), Southern Regional Education Board (1981, 1983, 1985), Goodlad (1990), Education Commission of the States (1993).

3. Recommend that changes in teacher education involve liberal arts and academic subject area faculties and public school personnel.
Holmes Group (1985), Southern Regional Education Board (1981, 1983, 1985), National Commission for Excellence in Teacher Education (1985).

4. Urge more regulation on selection of teacher education candidates including increasing SAT/ACT or GRE scores, and setting numerical goals for recruitment.
Holmes (1985), Carnegie Forum on Education and the Economy Task Force on Teaching as a Profession (1986), National Commission for Excellence in Teacher Education (1985), Goodlad (1990).

5. Propose a two-tiered system of teacher certification beginning with a provisional entry level (bachelor's degree), followed by professional teacher level that requires successful teaching and a fifth year of study or master's degree.

Southern Regional Education Board (1985), National Commission for Excellence in Teacher Education (1985), Goodlad (1990).

6. Propose a three-tiered system of teacher certification, (1) provisional (bachelor's), (2) professional (master's), and (3) either career professional (doctorate)/or advanced certificate (advanced courses beyond master's).
Holmes (1985), Carnegie Forum on Education and the Economy Task Force on Teaching as a Profession (1986).

7. Recommend diversifying the teaching force by recruiting underrepresented populations into teaching.
Holmes (1989), Goodlad (1990), Education Commission of the States (1993), Recruiting New Teachers, Inc. and the National Conference of State Legislatures (1993).

8. Urge the strengthening and integrating of clinical experiences in teacher preparation, including field experiences before student teaching and internships.
National Commission for Excellence in Teacher Education (1985), Carnegie Forum on Education and the Economy Task Force on Teaching as a Profession (1986), Holmes (1986), Goodlad (1990), Education Commission of the States (1993).

9. Recommend that schools of education model the good teaching they advocate.
Holmes (1989), Goodlad (1990), Education Commission of the States (1993).

10. Recommend research for increased understanding and knowledge of educational processes.
Holmes (1986), Goodlad (1990), Recruiting New Teachers, Inc. (1993).

11. Recommend that the four-year undergraduate education major be abolished.
Holmes (1985), Carnegie Forum on Education Economy Task Force on Teaching as a Profession (1986), Goodlad (1990).

12. Recommend a four-year teacher education program or a liberal arts degree for provisional certification.
Southern Regional Education Board (1985).

13. Recommend a four-year degree program that integrates liberal arts, subject specialization and professional studies.
National Commission for Excellence in Teacher Education (1986).

14. Recommend the creation of a National Board for Professional Teacher Standards.
Carnegie Forum on Education and the Economy Task Force on Teaching as a Profession (1985).

15. Recommend a five-year master's program in teaching be created for initial certification.
Carnegie Forum on Education and the Economy Task Force on Teaching as a Profession (1985).

16. Recommend that alternative certification programs be developed.
Southern Regional Education Board (1985), Education Commission of the States (1993), Recruiting New Teachers, Inc. and the National Conference of State Legislatures (1993).

17. Recommend that teacher education programs work to develop teacher candidates who will have a commitment to the moral, ethical and enculturating responsibilities of teaching.
Goodlad (1990).

18. Urge that the renewal of teacher education be in conjunction with K-12 school reform.
Goodlad (1990), Education Commission of the States (1993), Recruiting New Teachers and the National Conference of State Legislatures (1993).

19. Urge that state initiatives and necessary statutory provisions are needed for the reform reports of 1985–1990 to be further implemented.
Goodlad (1990), Education Commission of the States (1993), Recruiting New Teachers, Inc. and the National Conference of State Legislatures (1993).

20. Urge that state legislatures set standards for skills and knowledge base for candidates receiving state licensure.
Education Commission of the States (1993), Recruiting New Teachers, Inc. and the National Conference of State Legislatures (1993).

21. Advocate that states adopt funding mechanisms for establishing components of a comprehensive teacher education and school renewal program.
Goodlad (1990), Education Commission of the States (1993), Recruiting New Teachers, Inc. and the National Conference of Legislatures (1993).

22. Recommend that states adopt plans for evaluating the effectiveness of the teacher education system that prepare teachers for the schools of the state.
Education Commission of the States (1993).

---

**This table briefly summarizes the reforms that have been proposed for teacher preparation from 1985 to 1993. Following each recommendation is the group or report that supports it.**

ers, state superintendents, a governor, legislators, and a representative from the National School Boards Association.

The report made recommendations related to five themes: supply and demand of teachers, programs for teacher education, accountability for teacher education, resources for teacher education, and conditions necessary to support the highest quality of teaching. Many of the report's recommendations related directly to the training of teachers:

1. "Each teacher education program should be an exacting, intellectually challenging integration of liberal studies, subject specialization from which school curricula are drawn, and content and skills of professional education." The report does not suggest the elimination of the four-year degree in education. Instead, it suggests that education students should have a liberal arts background "equivalent to that of the best-educated members of their community." The report falls short of suggesting the requirement of an undergraduate arts and science major. Instead, it focuses the content of the arts and sciences on practical considerations of teaching and unlike the previous reports discussed, suggests that teachers should gain practical teaching skills during the undergraduate program. (p. 14)
2. "Following their completion of a teacher education program and the awarding of a provisional certificate, new teachers should complete an induction period or internship of at least a year's duration for which compensation is provided." (p. 15)
3. The report suggests that with the help of state funding, colleges and universities should "consider major structural changes, not just course modification; and states should be willing to adjust existing regulations, with appropriate monitoring, to test the new models." (p. 16)
4. Unlike the Carnegie Commission Report, the AACTE report suggests that the states should continue to certify teachers and approve teacher education programs. However, it also contends that voluntary national accreditation of teacher education programs should be strengthened.
5. This report, unlike the others, suggests that funding for research and development in teacher education is essential and must be provided by federal and state governments.

## SOUTHERN REGIONAL EDUCATION BOARD

The Southern Regional Education Board (SREB) produced the report *Improving Teacher Education: An Agenda for Higher Education and the Schools* (1985). The board, made up of representatives from fourteen southeastern states, suggested that:

1. Four-year, undergraduate programs be viewed only as entry to the teaching profession.
2. Four-year, undergraduate programs be revised and higher standards be developed.
3. States, universities, and schools develop collaborative programs to support and monitor teachers in their first years of teaching.
4. Alternative certification programs for liberal arts graduates be developed especially where shortages in the supply of teachers occur.
5. Fifth-year teacher education programs be developed.
6. Establishment of two types of certification, provisional for teachers with three or fewer years of teaching and professional after the completion of a beginning teaching program and advanced coursework.

## TEACHERS FOR OUR NATION'S SCHOOLS

John I. Goodlad authored an important report on teacher education reform. *Teachers for Our Nation's Schools* (1990) was based on a five-year study of twenty-nine representative universities in the United States. Researchers, under Goodlad's direction, observed, interviewed, conducted surveys, and analyzed relevant university and college documents in making the following recommendations for reform:

- Institutions must be committed to teacher education, and it must be shared by the teacher education faculty, the arts and sciences faculty, and the schools.
- A commitment to the moral and ethical responsibilities of teaching is an essential component of teacher education programs.
- The teacher education curriculum must integrate content, teaching knowledge, and understanding of schooling in a democracy.
- Clinical schools should be developed to help train teachers.
- State policies that link teacher education renewal and schooling must be established. (pp. 54–64)

## EDUCATION COMMISSION OF THE STATES

Education Commission of the States (ECS) is a nonprofit, nationwide interstate commission designed to help governors, state legislators, and state education officials develop policies to improve the quality of education at all levels. Forty-nine states, Washington D.C., American Samoa, Puerto Rico, and the Virgin Islands are members. *A Shared Vision: Policy Recommendations Linking Teacher Education to School Reform* (1993) is the reform document of ECS. It results from intensive interviews with teacher educators, school officials, one hundred fifty state legislators, governors, and education agency officials from twenty-five states over a two-year period. The report's recommendations include:

- State leadership is a necessary condition if recommendations from other major reports are to be implemented.
- State legislatures need to adopt statutory provisions for school/university collaboration.
- Legislatures need to designate parties responsible for simultaneous renewal of teacher education and K–12 restructuring.
- States need to set standards for skills, knowledge base, and teaching performance and the funding to do so.
- States need to require recertification programs as needed to accomplish objectives of schools/districts. (pp. 9–27)

## RECRUITING NEW TEACHERS INC. AND THE NATIONAL CONFERENCE OF STATE LEGISLATURES

*State Policies to Improve the Teacher Workforce: Shaping the Profession That Shapes the Future* resulted from discussions with twenty-five legislators and specialists in state policies related to teacher development at a conference co-sponsored by Recruiting New Teachers Inc., a clearinghouse for information about teaching careers, and the National Conference of State Legislatures. Recommendations from this conference include:

- •Continued research on designing and implementing teacher development is needed.
- •America's changing demographics must be considered in the research on teacher development.
- •Governmental responsibility in teacher development must be clarified.
- •Teacher education reform and school reform must be linked and questions of how to fund the reforms must be resolved.

## RESULTS OF THE REFORM REPORTS OF THE MID-1980s AND EARLY 1990s

There is no doubt that the reform reports of the 1980s and 1990s have influenced teacher training, as the Holmes Group had suggested they would. More and more decisions about the training and development of teachers will be collaborative, involving legislatures, state agencies, public schools, business and professional leaders, and colleges and universities. State legislatures will have a much larger role in decision making about teacher education. Few future teachers will have baccalaureate degrees in some form of education but instead will have degrees in arts and sciences disciplines and second majors or minors in education. Some may not begin teaching until they have completed a fifth year of training or a master's degree. Entrance and exit requirements for teaching candidates will be more rigorous. Although professional coursework will decrease, most teacher education students will spend many hours in school field experiences. An increasing number will have paid or unpaid internships after completion of bachelor's degrees but prior to professional licensure (see table 3.2).

*A National Board of Professional Standards*  Other changes in teacher education can be traced to these reform reports. A National Board of Professional Standards, suggested by the Carnegie Forum, was established in 1987. Although the board did not establish a national curriculum for teachers, it developed five core propositions of what teachers need to know and should be able to do (see chapter 1, p. 44). To be board certified, teachers must possess at least a baccalaureate degree at an accredited institution and three or more years of successful teaching experience. The board is developing teaching assessments for various subject areas and age levels. The assessments are based on standards outlined by professional associations (see chapter 1, pp. 44–45), newly developed state standards, and standards set by the National Board. In fall 1993, the National Board field tested assessments for early adolescence/generalist and early adolescence/English-language arts teachers. All subject/age-level field testing was to be completed by 1994 with a final national teaching exam and board certification implemented by 1994-95.

*Levels of Certification*  Another change that can be directly linked to the teacher education reform reports is the creation of a variety of levels of certifica-

*(continued on p. 125)*

**TABLE 3-2**

## Results of Teacher Education Reform 1985–1993

1. Four-year undergraduate programs continue to be the primary initial entry into the profession.

2. More states are reguiring advanced course work or a master's degree and teaching experience for a second stage of teacher certification.

3. More states have at least a two-tiered level of teacher certification.

4. Most states and teacher preparation institutions have made some curricular revisions and entry requirements for initial certification in the past.

5. Most colleges of education have collaborative programs with K-12 schools and increasing numbers of professional development schools have been implemented.

6. At least forty states have implemented some type of alternative certification program, but only nineteen require a bachelor's degree for entry. The rest require analysis of academic and professional backgrounds.

7. More teacher preparation institutions have increased the amount of time for field experiences before student teaching.

8. More states now require a full semester for student teaching. A few more institutions require a full year of internship before initial certification.

9. Relatively little has been done to recruit minorities into teaching.

10. The National Board for Professional Teacher Standards has been established and voluntary national certification is expected in 1994–1995.

11. There continues to be a lack of total campus commitment to undergraduate teacher education in a majority of training institutions, thus causing barriers to needed reform.

12. Many states continue to have regulatory barriers to teacher education renewal rather than a constructive role that defines better methods of accountability, devises new funding mechanisms to encourage campuswide commitment for preparing teachers and supporting policies linking K–12 school reform to teacher education reform.

13. Many states continue to have budgetary shortfalls and school and teacher reform has been slow.

14. The Higher Education Amendments of 1992 (P.L. 102-325) provides funding to states for alternative routes to teacher certification and licensure and for recruitment of minority teachers. In addition it provides funding to the National Board for Profession Standards for research and developmental activities.

SOURCES:

1. National Association of State Directors of Teacher Education and Certification. (1993). *Manual on certification and preparation of educational personnel in the United States.* Dubuque, IA: Kendall-Hunt.

2. Feistritzer, E. & Chester, D. (1992). *Alternative teacher certification: A state by state analysis.* Washington, DC: National Center for Education Information.

3. National Center for Education Statistics, U.S. Department of Education. (1993). *The condition of Education* (NCES 93–290). Washington, DC: US Government Printing Office.

4. Education Commission of the States. (1993). *Improving teacher preparation.* Denver, CO: Author.

5. Education Commission of the States. (1992). *At the crossroads: Linking teacher education to school reform.*

6. Recruiting New Teachers. (1993). *State policies to improve the teacher work force: Shaping the profession that shapes America's future.* (Conference co-sponsored by Recruiting New Teachers and the National Conference of State Legislatures.) Belmont, MA: Author.

7. P. L. 102–325—Higher Education Amendments of 1992.

This table briefly identifies the major educational reforms in teacher training implemented by many institutions of higher learning from 1985 to 1993.

tion, from initial or provisional certification to a permanent or professional one. Each of the reform reports suggested this type of distinction, linking teacher performance and increased responsibility to each subsequent certification level as well as additional training or higher education. Most of the reports suggested that salary increments also be tied to certification levels. According to Ted Andrews, president of the National Association of State Directors of Teacher Education, by 1991 most states had adopted some type of tiered approach to levels of teacher certification (telephone conversation, November 12, 1993).

# Issues of Accreditation of Teacher Education

Because of the diversity of teacher preparation programs around the country, many teacher education reform reports of the 1980s and early 1990s suggested that training programs should be more consistent in their requirements for coursework and field experiences. Thus a move toward national evaluation and accreditation of teacher education programs was suggested.

## NATIONAL ACCREDITATION

The National Council for Accreditation of Teacher Education (NCATE), the major review board for college and university programs in teacher education, in the mid-1980s made its requirements for the accreditation of teacher education programs more rigorous. In 1993 the standards again were revised by NCATE, focusing on improved practice, more attention to individual teaching candidates, increased use of technology in teacher education, and varied opportunities for preservice teachers to work in multicultural classrooms. In addition, the standards encourage "integrative studies" in which teacher education students integrate content and pedagogical knowledge at high levels of competence to create meaningful experiences for all students. The policies also emphasize collaboration with school colleagues, parents, and agencies of the community and encourage professional growth plans for continuous learning (Hall 1993, 1–3). Of the 1,279 state-approved teacher education programs in the country, 521 or 40.7 percent are a part of the NCATE system (Diegmueller 1993, 27).

NCATE requires that each institution receiving accreditation meet nineteen standards under four major headings. These include (1) curriculum of professional education, previously called knowledge base, (design and delivery of the curriculum, professional community of secondary schools and higher education); (2) candidates in professional education (qualifications, monitoring and assessing candidates to ensure competence); (3) professional education faculty (qualifications and composition of faculty, professional assignments and development); (4) the unit (college, school, or department) for professional education (governance and accountability, resources for teaching and scholarship, other resources) (*NCATE* June 16, 1993).

The goal of NCATE's standards for teacher education programs is to ensure that they all meet specific national standards: "(1) to require a level of quality in professional education that fosters competent practice of graduates, and (2) to encourage institutions to meet rigorous academic standards of excellence in

Students who participate in teacher preparation programs may decide to use their skills in areas related to, but not directly involved in teaching. This school librarian files cards in the card catalogue.

professional education." Accreditation by NCATE, however, does not assume that all teacher education programs look alike. NCATE does not require a specific number of hours in liberal arts or in professional courses. Instead, it requires rigorous standards no matter the approach used to the training of teachers. Therefore, even in those institutions accredited by NCATE the debate over the composition of teacher education programs continues.

### STATE ACCREDITATION

NCATE accreditation is voluntary, although an increasing number of states require it. On the other hand, state accreditation of teacher education programs is required, although only two states have formal evaluation processes. Consequently, state education agencies have more control over the content and requirements of teacher education programs than national accreditation agencies. For example, within each state, there are certain requirements that must be met by all teacher-training institutions. In forty-five states and the District of Columbia, assessments of teacher preparation of individual candidates are required prior to initial or provisional certification (NASTEC 1991, 127–C-11). These assessments vary from one test in subject matter to eight different tests in such topics as basic skills, general knowledge, knowledge of teaching, and include an assessment of teaching performance. Seven states use internally developed texts; the others use the National Teachers Examination (NTE). As a result, institutions must prepare students to pass these state-mandated assessments. Therefore, consistency in teacher-training requirements can be seen within the institutions of most states, but not across the nation.

*(continued on p. 128)*

**TABLE 3-3**

## Alternative Careers in Education

| Position | Job Description | Training |
|---|---|---|
| Childcare Specialist | Work with pre-K children in day care centers and pre-schools. | For accredited pre-K day care centers, an associate degree in child study from a community college. |
| Vocational Instructor | Work in high schools and community colleges and state and federal training programs to help students explore the world of work: distributive education, health occupations, technical occupations, automotive repair, computers, robotics, agriculture, etc. | Bachelor's or advanced degrees in specialization; work experience. If position is part-time, degree may not be required. |
| Computer Technologist | Work with students and teachers as specialists in computer education. | Bachelor's degree: work in computers, education, and psychology. |
| Adult Basic Education | Work with adults to meet requirements for high school diploma (GED) and English as a Second Language (ESL), sometimes called English for Speakers of Other Languages (ESOL). | Bachelor's degree from approved teacher-training program. |
| Industry | Develop and run training programs for employees: academic, mental, physical, health, or leisure. | Bachelor's or advanced degrees. |
| Teacher of Special Children | Work with developmentally handicapped, physically, mentally, and emotionally handicapped children in small groups. Work with classroom teachers to plan programs for special children. | Bachelor's and master's degrees in specialty. |
| Bilingual and English as Second Language | Work with students who do not speak English or speak English as a second language. | Bachelor's degree with concentration in variety of languages. |
| Teaching Specialist | Teaching in the arts, foreign languages, reading, mathematics, and writing. | Bachelor's or master's degree in area of specialty. |
| Counselor | Work with faculty to identify student problems, help students make career decisions and give tests. Counsel students in academic and personal concerns. | Advanced degree in guidance/counseling; frequently teaching experience. |
| Educational Social Worker | Liaison between students, families, agencies, and schools to help solve problems and promote learning. | Bachelor's and master's degrees with specialty in sociology and education. |
| Psychometrist and School Psychologist | Administer individual and group tests, develop guidance programs, interpret test results to teachers and administrators, and work with teachers and referred students. | Advanced degree beyond master's in guidance/counseling and psychology. |
| Librarian and Media Specialist | Work in libraries and media centers with teachers and students in the use of books, videos, microfiche, movies, filmstrips, slides, computer, and the library. | Bachelor's degree in library or media education. |
| | Specialists organize and administer the library and media center. | Master's degree in library or media education and professional library experience. |

| Position | Job Description | Training |
|---|---|---|
| School Health Services | Diagnostic work and health care for students: nurses, dental hygienists, speech and hearing specialists, audiologists, and athletic trainers. Also work in preventative health programs. | Bachelor's degree or master's degree in specialty. |
| Dietician | Plan for and provide nutritious meals for students. | Bachelor's degree with specialty in nutrition. |
| School Administrators | Principals have responsibility for daily operation of the school—its finances, discipline, curriculum, and transportation. District-wide administrators are specialists in charge of finance, curriculum, transportation, psychological services, special education, and personnel. Superintendent oversees all aspects of education in school district. | Advanced course work beyond master's degree in curriculum, supervision, and administration. Advanced degree in administration and supervision; usually experience in teaching. |
| Supervisor | Work directly with teachers to improve teaching by helping, counseling, providing inservice workshops on curriculum development, and evaluating teaching. | Advanced degree in supervision; teaching experience. |
| Independent School Personnel | Work in independent/private schools in teaching, admissions, business management, or fund-raising. | Bachelor's or master's degree in specialty. |
| Coach (full- or part-time) | Work with athletic teams | Bachelor's degree. |
| Dean | Provide counseling and discipline. | Bachelor's or advanced degree. |
| Physician | Provide health services. | Medical degree. |
| Attorney | Provide legal services. | Law degree. |
| Director of Student Activities | Direct extracurricular activities. | Bachelor's degree. |

This table lists the numerous career opportunities available in education other than classroom teaching.

---

**3-3**

**POINTS TO REMEMBER**

- The reform reports of the 1980s and early 1990s suggested increased academic training, five-year programs, additional fieldwork, and collaborative training of teachers among schools, colleges, and universities. They stressed commitment to moral and ethical responsibilities, recruiting minorities, and establishing state policies that link teacher education reform and school reform.

- All the reform reports suggest more rigorous entrance and exit requirements for teacher education students, a tiered approach to certification, with a mentoring program in the first years of teaching.

- The Holmes Group and the Carnegie Forum suggest requiring a five-year approach to certification and elimination of the education degree leading to certification.

- The Southern Regional Education Board and the National Commission for Excellence in Teacher Education contend that degrees in education can be maintained with more rigorous standards in all degrees.

- The Goodlad, Education Commission of the States, and Recruiting New Teachers Inc. reports emphasized the need to establish state policies for teacher reform and preparation for diversity.

- National certification of teachers is nearly a reality. No states have adopted the five-year approach to initial teacher certification.

- There are numerous career opportunities available in education other than classroom teaching.

## For Thought/Discussion

1. Which do you believe is more important in the development of teaching skills—fieldwork or coursework? Why?

2. If your teacher preparation program does not include training in teaching students of other cultures, do you feel it is necessary to acquire this knowledge on your own? Why or why not?

3. Do you believe that national standards for teacher preparation would stabilize and upgrade the profession or cause it to stagnate and become predictable? Explain your position.

## For Further Reading/Reference

Good, T. L. 1990. Building the knowledge base of teaching. In *What teachers need to know: The knowledge, skills and values essential to good teaching,* ed. D. Dill and Associates, 17–75. San Francisco: Jossey-Bass. A discussion of how motivation, organization, management, and effective communication are essential for building the knowledge base of teaching.

Goodlad, J. I. 1990. *Teachers for our nation's schools.* San Francisco: Jossey-Bass. A description of teacher education programs in twenty-nine colleges and universities from small, private liberal arts colleges to large research institutions.

Kramer, R. 1992. *Ed School Follies: The Miseducation of American Teachers.* New York: Free Press. The author describes fifteen schools, colleges, and departments of education that she visited across the United States, pointing out deficiencies in the training of teachers.

Natriello, G., and Zumwalt, K. K. 1992. "Challenges to an alternate route for teacher education." In A. Lieberman (Ed.), *The Changing Contexts of Teaching: Ninety-first Yearbook of the National Society for the Study of Education* (pp. 59–78). Chicago: National Society for the Study of Education. This article examines the New Jersey alternative route to teacher certification and presents challenges to alternative certification.

Sirotnik, K. A. 1990. Society, schooling, teaching, and preparing to teach. In *The moral dimensions of teaching,* ed. J. I. Goodlad, R. Soder, and K. A. Sirotnik, 296–326. San Francisco: Jossey-Bass. A discussion of the moral purposes of public schooling and their implications for teacher education.

Art Bouthillier in *Phi Delta Kappan*

*"Think of this as a TV talk show. The band and the audience are off-camera, and you are my guests who'll answer my questions."*

Dear Molly,

Tomorrow the doors of the world begin to open to you. Your father and I have only one request as you begin your college years: Don't close the doors.

You will meet people who are very different from your family and friends. They will look different, have different values, express different ideas, talk differently. . . . Although we do not suggest that you embrace either the person or her ideas, we want you to listen and to think. What does she believe? Where does he come from? How has her life been different from yours? What does he know that you do not know? Listen and learn, Molly.

With love and respect,
Mom

# *Part II*

# FOUNDATIONS

## Chapter 4

### THE HISTORICAL FOUNDATIONS OF U.S. EDUCATION

The past is never totally past. It invariably informs the present. Thus whatever educational problems and issues exist in today's society can be said to be a product of both the recent and distant past. We study the history of education to learn from our past, to learn of our origins. This chapter discusses the historical roots of the American educational system.

## Chapter 5

### TWENTIETH-CENTURY U.S. EDUCATION: EQUALIZATION OR EXCELLENCE

There are no easy solutions to the problems created by the growth of democracy and the concept of equal education for all. As society changes, the system of education must find ways of dealing with a complex and burgeoning student population. This chapter discusses the historical developments of education and the proposals for reform that have been suggested in the twentieth century.

## Chapter 6

### THE PHILOSOPHICAL FOUNDATIONS OF EDUCATION

This chapter focuses on the philosophies that have informed educational thinking and allows teachers to look forward to ways that thinking might be used to creatively restructure what goes on in the classroom and in schools. As Roland Barth says in a recent issue of *Phi Delta Kappan,* "Let go of the trapeze. Think otherwise. Become an independent variable. Lick the envelope. Bell the cat. Fly the cage. Leave your mark" (1991, p. 128).

## CHAPTER OBJECTIVES

After studying this chapter, you should be able to:

- Discuss the importance of studying the history of education.
- Discuss the contributions of the early Greeks and Romans to the history of education.
- Understand how education developed in the medieval period and the Renaissance.
- Explain the influence of Rousseau, Pestalozzi, Herbart, and Froebel.
- Define the terms *popularization, multitudinousness,* and *politicization* as they relate to the history of U.S. education.
- Explain how interpretations of the history of education have changed.
- Explain how the colonial New England schools influenced the popularization of U.S. education.
- Determine how the schools of the Southern colonies influenced the politicization of U.S. education.

- Understand how the schools of the Middle Atlantic colonies developed the concept of multitudinousness.
- Explain the influence of Benjamin Franklin, Thomas Jefferson, and Noah Webster on U.S. education.
- Discuss the impact of Horace Mann and Henry Barnard on the development of U.S. public education.
- Discuss the impact of the common school movement on the popularization of U.S. education.
- Understand how schools in the North during the mid- to late-nineteenth century helped meet the political concerns of the democracy.
- Contrast Northern and Southern schools during the post–Civil War period.
- Discuss the history of education of African Americans, Native Americans, Hispanic Americans, Asian Americans, and women.

# Chapter 4

# THE HISTORICAL FOUNDATIONS
# OF U.S. EDUCATION

*he following letter to Martha Jefferson was written by her father, Thomas Jefferson, in Annapolis on November 28, 1783. In it, he admonishes his daughter to follow a daily plan of study conducted by tutors he provided. Although Jefferson proposed several plans for public education, they ironically did not include girls beyond three years in elementary school.*

Dear Patsy,—After four days' journey, I arrived here without any accident, and in as good health as when I left Philadelphia. The conviction that you would be more improved in the situation I have placed you than if still with me, has solaced me on my parting with you, which my love for you has rendered a difficult thing. The acquirements which I hope you will make under the tutors I have provided for you will render you more worthy of my love; and if they cannot increase it, they will prevent its diminution. Consider the good lady who has taken you under her roof, who has undertaken to see that you perform all your exercises, and to admonish you in all those wanderings from what is right or what is clever, to which your inexperience would expose you: consider her, I say, as your mother, as the only person whom, since the loss with which Heaven has pleased to afflict you, you can now look up; and that her displeasure or disapprobation, on any occasion, will be an immense misfortune, which should you be so unhappy as to incur by any unguarded act, think no concession too much to regain her good-will. With respect to the distribution of your time, the following is what I should approve:

From 8 to 10, practice music.
From 10 to 1, dance one day and draw another.
From 1 to 2, draw on the day you dance, and write a letter next day.
From 3 to 4, read French.
From 4 to 5, exercise yourself in music.
From 5 till bed-time, read English, write, etc.

Thomas Jefferson (1743–1826, member of the Virginia Legislature and the Continental Congress, governor of Virginia, secretary of state, vice president, and president of the United States, believed that the purpose of education was to develop an informed citizenry. Only through education, he believed, would people have the understanding necessary to exercise the rights and responsibilities of a member of a democratic society.

133

Communicate this plan to Mrs. Hopkinson, and if she approves of it, pursue it. As long as Mrs. Trist remains in Philadelphia, cultivate her affection. She has been a valuable friend to you, and her good sense and good heart make her valued by all who know her, and by nobody on earth more than me. I expect you will write me by every post. Inform me what books you read, what tunes you learn, and enclose me your best copy of every lesson in drawing. Write also one letter a week either to your Aunt Eppes, your Aunt Skipwith, your Aunt Carr, or the little lady from whom I now enclose a letter, and always put the letter you so write under cover to me. Take care that you never spell a word wrong. Always before you write a word, consider how it is spelt, and, if you do not remember it, turn to a dictionary. It produces great praise to a lady to spell well. I have placed my happiness on seeing you good and accomplished; and no distress this world can now bring on me would equal that of your disappointing my hopes. If you love me, then strive to be good under every situation and to all living creatures, and to acquire those accomplishments which I have put in your power, and which will go far towards ensuring you the warmest love of your affectionate father.

P.S. Keep my letters and read them at times, that you may always have present in your mind those things which will endear you to me.

From: J. G. DeRoulhac Hamilton (Ed.), *The Best Letters of Thomas Jefferson* (1926).

---

*7*he past is never totally past. It invariably informs the present. Thus whatever educational problems and issues exist in today's society can be said to be a product of both the recent and distant past. We study the history of education to learn from our past, to learn of our origins. Knowing from where we have come enables us to understand who we are and where we are going.

# History of Education

5th Century B.C.

*Greek Roots*

Sophists

According to educational historian Sol Cohen, "We think and behave the way we do because we have traversed this road and not some other" (1978, 1:1). Understanding the history of education helps us think about the course of action we choose and evaluate it in terms of past performance.

## GREEK AND ROMAN ROOTS

An early form of education was provided by the Athenian **Sophists** (490–480 B.C.), who taught grammar, logic, and rhetoric with a view to educating the citizens to become effective legislators. Protagoras used a teaching method by which the students could learn to debate by taking an idea the opponent had conceded and using it as a starting point for argument. Protagoras was probably the first to teach the possibility of arguing for or against any position. Image and impression were important to the Sophists. The Greeks who primarily affected Western thought, however, were Socrates (469–399 B.C., Plato (427–347 B.C.), and Aristotle (384–322 B.C.). Their methods are still part of our teaching vocabulary. The **Socratic method** involves the procedure of systematic doubt and questioning to discover the underlying universal meaning of human life and truth that Socrates believed exists within each individual. It was the job of the teacher to ask the kinds of questions that would lead the students to discover the truth within themselves. Even today, highly regarded scholars and critics of education, like Mortimer Adler in *Paideia Problems and Possibilities* (1983), espouse Socrates's method as the best way to produce an educated society.

Plato continued the pursuit of the ideal, believing it was inherent in the universal concepts of truth, goodness, justice, and beauty, the philosophical basis of idealism. These ideals could not be reached through the imperfect senses but rather had to be attained through the intellect. Because these ideals were universal and permanent, education had to be universal.

In contrast to Socrates, Aristotle believed that reality is physical and exists in objects—the philosophical foundation of realism. Thinking and knowing begin with the sensate perception of objects in the environment, but concepts are formed by the process of deducing pattern and order from specific observation. Teaching and learning are thus based on a body of knowledge and disciplined inquiry into the nature of things. This philosophy was stressed in the eighteenth and nineteenth centuries by such educators as John Locke and Johann Pestalozzi.

An early attempt at formal education occurred when the Roman philosopher and orator Quintilian (A.D. 35–95) trained students to persuade the citizenry to agree with the empirical point of view. In *De Institutione Oratoria* (A.D. 96/1970), which became a manual for teachers, he recognized that education should be based on individual stages of human growth and development. Thus he established four stages of learning: from birth until age seven the child should have as a nurse and pedagogue someone who used correct speech patterns; from seven to fourteen the child formed ideas and learned to read and write; from fourteen to seventeen the student studied the liberal arts such as literature, mythology, music, and grammar; and finally, from seventeen to twenty-one the prospective orator began rhetorical studies such as drama, poetry, history, law, philosophy, and rhetoric. Quintilian's influence extends to the modern teacher's concern for individual differences and the quest to make learning interesting. The Greeks also established the concepts of both the liberal arts and vocational education. They believed that free, aristocratic males should be liberally educated studying disciplines as diverse as drama, philosophy, and rhetoric in order to prepare themselves for the affairs of the state. On the other hand, male slaves or peasants needed to gain skills in a variety of occupations and trades such as shipbuilding which were taught through practical application and physical labor.

The roots of bilingual and private education can be found in Rome. From the second century B.C. to the end of the empire, the Romans had three bilingual levels of schooling. The *ludus* (primary school), the first level, taught young aristocratic boys (and some girls) from ages seven to twelve the alphabet, reading, writing, and counting. Usually housed in a shop in the town forum, the family slave accompanied the boy to the ludus. Should the boy miss a lesson or give a wrong answer he was flogged with the cane of the *ludus magister,* the schoolmas-

Socrates
(469–399 B.C.)

Plato
(427–346 B.C.)

4th Century B.C.

Aristotle
(384–322 B.C.)

1st Century A.D.

*Roman Roots*

Quintilian
(35–95 A.D.)

ter. Because the cost of the ludus was low, its status was also low, and many of the richest Romans had their young sons tutored rather than sending them to the ludus. "This distinction between public and private education—that is, group school versus individual tutorial instruction—remained intact in the United States until the mid-nineteenth century" (Smith and Smith 1994, 37).

The second level, the **grammaticus**, literally meaning grammar teacher, was usually in the home of the teacher. Boys, beginning at age twelve, learned Latin grammar and read the works of Roman poets and dramatists. Boys also learned Greek by studying the Greek classics if they had not already done so in the ludus or with their slaves or tutors. The status of the grammaticus was higher than the status of the ludus because its cost was considerably more and, therefore, fewer students were able to attend. At age sixteen, boys from the most aristocratic families spent a year apprenticeship in what was called **tirocinium fori**. Under the tutelage of a "distinguished man—in some cases their own father—[the boys learned] the duties, manners, and attitudes of senators" (Smith and Smith, 37).

However, by the end of the Roman Empire, formalized instruction had become lifeless. Christians such as Saint Augustine (A.D. 354–430) attempted to revitalize learning by placing greater emphasis on deeds rather than words. Hence, instead of focusing on rules of rhetoric and grammar, Saint Augustine advocated the study of great orations. He claimed that nothing could be learned under compulsion and suggested that students should ask questions to further their own comprehension rather than merely accept the answers provided by scholars. Few followed Saint Augustine's teachings as the Roman Empire declined along with its education, politics, economics, and culture when barbarians invaded from northern Europe. The main thrust of the limited education that existed during the final years of the empire and the early Middle Ages was to preserve the culture. Thus, memorization and imitation were the basic educational methods of this time.

## MEDIEVAL PERIOD

It was not until the end of the Middle Ages and the rise of the medieval university that the systematic development of educational method continued. Pierre Abelard (1079–1142), a monk known as one of the **Schoolmen**, argued with his teachers about interpretations of the Holy Writ. He believed there could be more than one interpretation or argument and that by examining different points of view one could decide which position or interpretation would be more correct. Abelard broke from his contemporaries by suggesting the use of open-ended questions that he published without their proper answers.

Abelard's technique of open questioning influenced Saint Thomas Aquinas (1225–1274), a Christian philosopher and author of the *Summa Theologica,* still the standard work on Catholic theology. In this work, Aquinas discussed **scholasticism**, a method of logical reasoning through the examination of opinions and issues often by raising questions to determine their validity. He is credited with applying Aristotelian logic to Christian theology and justifying both faith and reason, previously considered to be incompatible. Along with Aristotle, Aquinas maintained that that which is incomprehensible to the intellect must be accepted on faith and that knowledge of the world begins with sensation. According to Aquinas, "the finite reason can never comprehend the infinite, but

4th Century A.D.

St. Augustine
(359–430 A.D.)

1100–1400

*Medieval Period*

Pierre Abelard
(1079–1142)

St. Thomas Aquinas
(1225–1274)

it can prove the validity of the preambles of faith and show that faith is not unreasonable" (Smith and Smith, 90). Aquinas rejected the Platonic concept of innate ideas because he believed that they did not exist in actuality but in potentiality. Learning was an actualization of this potential based on the intellect's capacity to form universal concepts from the perception of objects through the senses.

## The Renaissance

By the Renaissance (1330–1500), younger students required teaching methods other than the lecture and disputation approach suggested by early scholars. Dutch philosopher Desiderius Erasmus (1466–1536) was the first of the humanistic scholars, those advocating a return to classical studies of Greece and Rome. He differentiated between innate capacity, those abilities with which we are born, and what learning could be accomplished through instruction. He realized that because no student was endowed with aptitudes in all areas, it was important to develop individual methods of instruction. He realized that students learned in stages and so encouraged teachers to move slowly and not expect students to learn that for which they were not ready.

Historians credit German religious reformer Martin Luther (1483–1546) with the development of a universal educational system for all people without regard to class or "special life work." He believed that schools should be established by the state, not the church as was previously believed, and students should be trained not only in religion but also in science, mathematics, logic, and rhetoric. This change of focus from the church to the individual and secular learning was a major turning point in educational history.

John Calvin (1509–1564), another Protestant reformer, like Luther, affirmed that education was the combined responsibility of the church, the state, and the home. According to Calvin, all three must follow the same strict moral code in teaching, discipline, and training. He placed more emphasis on what we today think of as secondary education (the gymnasium, where older boys were taught Greek, Hebrew, physics, mathematics, oratory, and rhetoric) than on primary education.

John Amos Comenius (1592–1670) of Moravia is frequently called the first modern educator because he devised specific instructional methods whereby the senses could be used to aid the intellect. In *Orbis Pictus* (*The Visible World in Pictures*), he employed the idea of using pictures as a teaching device (1659/1968). Comenius believed that students must learn not merely by seeing and hearing but also by doing. He claimed that schools were for all humanity, not merely for males and the aristocracy. "No reason can be shown why the female sex . . . should be kept from a knowledge of language and wisdom. For they are also human beings, an image of God, as we are . . ." (Comenius 1633/1956, 33).

## EARLY EUROPEAN EDUCATIONAL THEMES

Jean Jacques Rousseau (1712–1778) developed an educational philosophy that has become known as **naturalism**, claiming that environment plays a crucial role in the development of the individual who could be shaped through reason and science. He believed that the aim of education should be to return man to his

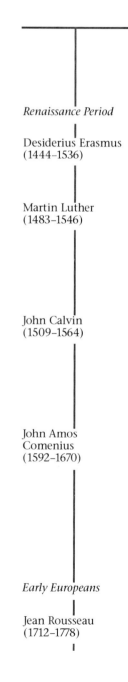

*Renaissance Period*

Desiderius Erasmus
(1444–1536)

Martin Luther
(1483–1546)

John Calvin
(1509–1564)

John Amos
Comenius
(1592–1670)

*Early Europeans*

Jean Rousseau
(1712–1778)

Johann Pestalozzi was a naturalist and a teacher who believed that students learn best when they are emotionally secure, when they use their senses to observe the patterns and laws of their environment, and when they proceed in incremental steps to acquire knowledge. He was particularly sensitive to the poor and disadvantaged; in this engraving, he is teaching orphans.

Johann Pestalozzi
(1746–1827)

"natural state" by developing knowledge based on sensations, natural feelings, and perceptions rather than on books and prescribed curriculums. Rousseau's ideas influenced Pestalozzi.

Although philosophers and scholars had discussed how children should be taught, the first schools devoted exclusively to teacher education were established in early eighteenth-century Prussia during the reign of Frederick the Great by J. Pestalozzi (1740–1786). After the Napoleonic Wars young Prussians traveled to Switzerland to study the work of Johann Pestalozzi (1746–1827) in preparation for establishing seminaries to train teachers in their country.

He was a naturalistic teacher who was influenced by Rousseau and believed that we learn primarily through our senses in observing nature. Thus, he used real, concrete objects to initiate learning before moving to abstract concepts. He urged that the teacher should move from the simple to the complex, the known to the unknown in gradual, cumulative steps respecting the individual differences of the child. He believed that children were born neither good nor evil but were shaped by their environments. Thus, providing children with healthy, supportive environments and a strong family life allowed them to develop their personalities and values to the fullest extent. Pestalozzi put his theory to work in schools based on the concepts of love, understanding, patience for children, a compassion for the poor and disadvantaged, and teaching methods that depended on real objects and an appeal to the senses.

Pestalozzi argued that the schoolmaster was one of the most important people in a community and, as such, must have integrity, understanding, and intelligence. He asserted that the state must assume the responsibility for educating teachers in order to invest the profession with importance.

Johann Friedrich Herbart (1776–1841), who studied under Goethe and Schiller and visited Pestalozzi in Switzerland, believed that education is a process. He asserted that teaching is not an inherent gift but, rather, a science that could be learned.

At Gottingen, Herbart started a pedagogical seminary and demonstration school to experiment with his educational methods, which he called *Vorstellung,* meaning "presentation." According to Herbart, there are five formal steps of teaching: preparation, in which the instructor reminds students of previously learned material; presentation, in which the new material is offered to students; association, in which the new material is systematically related to ideas or information learned previously; generalization, in which specific examples are used to illustrate the concept being taught; and application, in which students are tested to determine if they have understood the material.

Friedrich Wilhelm Froebel (1782–1852) was a philosopher and educator, the founder of the Kindergarten, or child's garden. According to Froebel, childhood was not just a transition toward adulthood, and a child's play was not merely preparation for adult life, but both were something complete and organic. He cultivated self-development, self-activity, and socialization in the child by providing songs, stories, games, "gifts," and "occupations." "Gifts" were objects whose form was fixed, such as balls, cubes, and cylinders, that stimulated the child to make relationships between the object and its concept. "Occupations" consisted of manipulable materials such as clay, paper, or mud. His work led to the establishment of the first German Kindergarten in the United States in 1855 and the first English-speaking kindergarten in 1860.

The work of these philosophers, theologians, and educators influenced early colonial schools and continue to influence U.S. schools today.

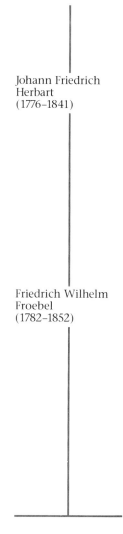

Johann Friedrich Herbart (1776–1841)

Friedrich Wilhelm Froebel (1782–1852)

## Themes of U.S. Education

The study of the history of education in the United States illuminates not only the story of U.S. schools but also that of U.S. society. Lawrence A. Cremin, (1925–1990) whose three historical themes we will use to organize this chapter and the next, was a professor at Teachers College, Columbia, president of Teachers College and of the Spencer Foundation, and the author of nine books (including a three-volume history entitled *American Education* written to celebrate the centennial of the U.S. Office of Education in the mid-1960s) and countless articles and speeches on the history of education. Ellen Condliffe Lagemann, a colleague of Cremin's at Teachers College, and Patricia Albjerg Graham, president of the Spencer Foundation, write in an unpublished manuscript "Lawrence A. Cremin: A Biographical Memoir" that "Cremin's first publications were typical of historical scholarship in education of the late 1940s and 1950s. They focused on the institutional development of the public schools and sought to illuminate how public schools reflected and fit into American society." In 1961, Cremin published *The Transformation of the School.* Lagemann and Graham suggest that "Unlike

Lawrence A. Cremin (1925–1990)

many early works in the history of education, . . . [it] was directed toward, and added to important lines of research in American intellectual, social, and political history," and won the Bancroft Prize in American History in 1962. In a three-volume history, *American Education* (published between 1970 and 1988), the second of which won a Pulitzer Prize, Cremin formulated a broad definition of education: "I have defined education . . . as the deliberate, systematic, and sustained effort to transmit, evoke, or acquire knowledge, values, attitudes, skills, and sensibilities, as well as any learning that results from that effort, direct, or indirect, intended or unintended" (1988, p. x).

In his final book, *Popular Education and Its Discontents* (1990), Cremin develops three themes that he believes are essential in examining the history of U.S. education. The "first, **popularization**, [is] the tendency to make education widely available in forms that are increasingly accessible to diverse peoples; [the] second, **multitudinousness**, [is] the proliferation and multiplication of institutions to provide that wide availability and that increase accessibility; and third, **politicization**, [is] the effort to solve certain social problems indirectly through education instead of directly through politics" (vii–viii). According to Cremin, by themselves none of these themes is uniquely American, but working together in tandem they make the history of U.S. education unique.

Cremin believes that when we examine events chronologically we must reach beyond the events themselves and examine their interaction with the laws, principles, and generalizations that come from outside the discipline of history. Examining history from a thematic approach, for example, allows us to integrate philosophy, politics, psychology, and economics in order to better understand the historical events. Cremin claims that "depending on the particular theory of education that guides and informs the efforts of a particular historian (see the sections, An Idealistic Interpretation of U.S. Education, and A Sociological Interpretation of U.S. Education that follow), one history rather than another will result. But, given a multiplicity of theories and hence a variety of histories, the collective literature that emerges will surely be broader, richer, and in the end more profound than the simplistic accounts of an earlier era" (1977, 163).

To allow you to see the synergy of the history of U.S. education with other disciplines, we will use Lawrence Cremin's three themes as the organizing focus for the remainder of this chapter, which deals primarily with the history of education from the colonial period through the nineteenth century, and for chapter 5, which deals with the twentieth century, a fascinating period of our history when all three themes of education came together in a unique fashion to characterize schools in the United States.

## AN IDEALISTIC INTERPRETATION OF U.S. EDUCATION BEFORE 1960

We can better understand Cremin's point about how examining education from a single point of view leads to different histories of education by briefly discussing the two most prevalent historical perspectives of the twentieth century: idealistic and sociological.

Prior to the 1960s, historical interpretation of U.S. education focused on the perfection of U.S. schools. History was "the story of [the schools'] foreordained, inevitable, and successive triumphs" (Button and Provenzo, xiv). The father of

Popularization

Multitudinousness

Politicization

this historical approach to the study of education was Ellwood P. Cubberley, whose pioneering book, *Public Education in the United States,* was published in 1919. Cubberley and educators influenced by his work viewed the schools as instruments of positive societal change.

Ellwood P. Cubberley (1868–1941)

## A SOCIOLOGICAL INTERPRETATION OF THE HISTORY OF U.S. EDUCATION AFTER 1960

Since the 1960s and the work of historian Bernard Bailyn (*Education in the Forming of American Society,* 1960), the idealistic view has changed. From the 1960s through the 1980s, education was examined more realistically as the "sum of everything intended to enculturate child, youth, and adult—family, church, newspaper, and so on" (Button and Provenzo, xiv). This view, of course, is consistent with that of sociologists, who define education as an enculturation process. Everything the child does under the guidance of an adult including formal schooling is **enculturation**. It occurs when a parent tells a child at the dinner table not to talk with her mouth full, a grocery store clerk gives a child change for a candy bar, or a lifeguard blows a whistle to warn that the water is too deep. Consequently, the sociological approach to a history of education does not look merely at the schools but at the role of society in the education of the young.

Enculturation

Educational historians and sociologists of the 1960s through the 1980s tended to agree that formal education has had its problems. Therefore, many

---

**4-1**

**POINTS TO REMEMBER**

- Studying the history of education helps us understand why schools are as they are today.

- Greek and Roman philosophers provided education with its earliest discourse on teaching. Plato and Socrates developed a method involving systematic doubt and questioning. Aristotle developed the concept of understanding pattern and order through observation of objects in the environment. Quintilian recognized that education should be based on individual patterns of growth.

- In the medieval period, education was the province of the church. Augustine emphasized deeds rather than words. Aqui-

nas believed that students must be considered the primary agents of learning. Luther implemented the first universal educational system in Germany. Calvin claimed that education was the responsibility of the church, the state, and the home. Comenius suggested students must perform a task in order to learn.

- Rousseau was the first to claim that environment plays a crucial role in the development of the individual. Pestalozzi maintained that children learn primarily through their senses. Herbart believed that students must learn to generalize knowledge and apply it to new information. Froebel developed the first Kindergarten and believed in the importance of children's play.

- Interpretations of the history of U.S. education have changed from the pre-1960s' view of the perfectability of U.S. schools to the post-1960s' view of the schools as the reflection of the best and worst in society. Contemporary historians look at the schools and society as influencing each other both positively and negatively.

- Popularization of education is the tendency to make the schools accessible to all. Multitudinousness describes the multiplication of institutions to provide accessibility. Politicization is the effort of schools to solve social problems indirectly. These three characteristics, in tandem, are found only in U.S. schools.

historians have examined education in light of its social, racial, political, and cultural problems, believing that U.S. schools mirror society at the same time that they are subject to societal pressures.

### A SYNERGETIC INTERPRETATION OF U.S. EDUCATION AFTER 1980

In the late 1980s and early 1990s, the approach to the history of U.S. education was again evolving. In the late 1980s historians such as Lawrence A. Cremin began to examine themes that correlated education's history with the history of the United States.

This evolving view of the history of education illustrates how the institutions of education and U.S. society influence each other and work together.

## Roots of Popularization of Education

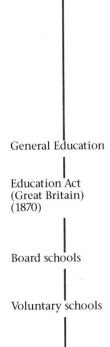

General Education

Education Act
(Great Britain)
(1870)

Board schools

Voluntary schools

Aristotle maintained that the popularization of education was vital for the maintenance of the state. Although we can see the adoption of some of Aristotle's concepts in the general education adhered to by the New England colonists, it did not take root until the common schools movement of the nineteenth century (see p. 153). "And since the whole city has one end, it is manifest that education should be one and the same for all, and that it should be public, and not private . . ." (Aristotle 310 B.C./1984).

### EUROPEAN ROOTS

Prior to the nineteenth century in Europe, the family was central to the education of the young. If the father was a shoemaker, the son usually became a shoemaker. If the family farmed, the children learned to work the farm. Daughters learned to make cloth, sew, cook, and clean. Parents had complete responsibility for the education of their children. Only the wealthy sent their children to private schools or hired someone to educate them in the home.

As industrialization began, however, families no longer were solely responsible for the education of their young. Communities began to train potential employees, passing laws to prevent emigration from one place to another.

By the nineteenth century in much of Europe, **general education** or education for all, which was not necessarily equal in quality, was available to most young people. In Great Britain the Education Act of 1870 provided a state-supported system with two types of schools: "board schools" attended by children of laborers and the lower class, and voluntary schools (precursor of the Latin Grammar School) for middle- and upper-class students. This dual system of education had different curriculums, and only the one for middle- and upper-class students led to higher education. It was the precursor of the dual track educational system of the schools of colonial New England.

## SCHOOLS IN THE COLONIES OF NEW ENGLAND

The educational system developed by the colonists was modeled on the schools of Great Britain. Like the English, the colonists did not believe in total equality of educational opportunity. Children of workers and peasants received minimal training so that they could read the Bible but were not trained in the classics. Boys of the upper and middle classes were expected to attend colleges and universities, often in Europe. The English colonists upheld the tradition of the Old World that the woman's place was in the home, so girls were trained at home rather than at school to be mothers and homemakers. Despite the fact that this system was inherently unequal, it at least planted the seed of general education for all children.

*Religion*   Since the colonists of New England had primarily the same ethnic, linguistic, and religious background, they did not see their approach to education as inequitable. They were intensely religious Puritans who believed that children were savage, primitive beings who had been conceived in sin and born into corruption and that the only way they could be redeemed was through training, discipline, and religious indoctrination. They regarded reading, writing, and mathematics as ways to gain an understanding of religious doctrines and avowed that a general education made all children equal in the eyes of God.

*Higher Education*   Harvard University was founded in Cambridge by a vote of the General Court of the colony of Massachusetts Bay in 1636 to train clergy. The first class entered in 1638. The following year it received its name after John Harvard, a young colonial minister, who willed his 4 hundred-volume library and 780 pounds (half of his fortune) to the new college, becoming the first benefactor of higher education in America. In 1642 the first senior class of nine divinity students graduated, thus establishing the tradition of U.S. higher education in the New England colonies. It also allowed students who could not afford to attend universities in Europe to gain a higher education and, thereby, beginning the popularization of higher education in America.

Harvard University founded, first college in the New World (1636)

*General Education*   By 1642, the Massachusetts General Court enacted the first compulsory education law, which did not establish schools but required parents to be responsible for the education of their children.

First compulsory education law enacted in Massachusetts (1642)

Following the teachings of Calvin and in the tradition of Martin Luther (see pp. 137), in 1647 the Massachusetts General Court passed the Old Deluder Satan Law, by which the state was required to establish schools so that students would learn the teachings and the values of the church and of religion. Hence, they would be protected from their own evil tendencies, thereby defeating that "old deluder, Satan."

Old Deluder Satan Law in Massachusetts (1647)

The law of 1647 not only forced towns to provide schools but established ways to fund them. In addition, it established that elementary schools (for young children in towns of 50 or more families) and grammar or secondary schools (for older children in towns of over 100 families) would be for all students; that the curriculum would require religious and moral training; and that teaching methodology would acknowledge Calvin's belief that children were born in sin.

| | |
|---|---|
| A | In Adam's Fall, We sinned all. |
| B | Heaven to find, The Bible mind. |
| C | Christ crucify'd, For Sinners dy'd. |
| D | The Deluge drown'd The Earth around. |
| E | Elijah hid, By Ravens fed. |
| F | The Judgment made Felix afraid. |

The *New England Primer*, only 2½ by 4½ inches in size, was used extensively in colonial schools until 1800. Based on religious and moral principles, as this page shows, it contained the alphabet, some syllables, and some rhymes.

Hornbook, first elementary textbook

New England Primer (1687)

First Latin Grammar School established in Boston (1634)

Dame schools (1710)

Town schools (1820s–1830s)

*Curriculum*   Colonial schools followed the subject- or instructor-centered approach to curriculum (see chapter 8, pp. 302–304). Children at the elementary level studied the alphabet, the Lord's Prayer, and elements of reading, writing, and counting. By the mid-to-late elementary levels, many boys, especially from less well-to-do families, were apprenticed to someone skilled in the trade of their choice.

Most elementary schools had no textbooks, and the teachers were not trained in methods of teaching. Therefore, the students were taught only what the teacher knew through lecture and recitation. Those with the least formal education tended to teach in elementary schools that received public support and were populated with poor children whereas those who had more formal education taught in elementary schools at which fees were charged or at grammar schools, the secondary schools of the wealthy. There were no formalized requirements for becoming a teacher. Some were unemployed tradesmen, some innkeepers, others members of the clergy. Many teachers in the rigorous secondary schools had achieved high levels of academic distinction. Elijah Corlett, for example, had degrees from the British universities of Oxford and Cambridge.

*Hornbook*   The **hornbook** was the first elementary "notebook" (1630s–1640s). It was not a book, however, but a board and handle covered with transparent paper made by flattening the horns of cattle. On the board appeared the alphabet with vowels listed separately, short meaningless syllables, and the Lord's Prayer, which students were expected to memorize.

The *New England Primer* (1687), the first actual textbook, replaced the hornbook in most New England schools by the late seventeenth century. Its contents were entirely religious with moral verses and poems.

*Types of Schools*   Colonial New England schools developed from places of home-based instruction to larger district-organized institutions.

*Latin Grammar Schools*   In 1635 a **Latin grammar school**, a classical secondary school for young men, was established in Boston. It provided the principal means of college preparation for well-to-do young men. They memorized Latin grammar, a Latin-English phrase book, and Latin vocabulary, and read from Cicero, Virgil, Ovid, and Erasmus. During the last year of study, the boys were required to learn rhetoric and elementary Greek. Saturday afternoons were typically set aside for religious study.

*Dame Schools*   Most of the boys who attended the Latin grammar schools had been educated in their homes, in dame schools, or in town schools. **Dame schools** were private homes in which several children gathered to be taught by the woman of the household. This type of "public" school, however, was soon found to be impractical.

*Town Schools*   Established to provide elementary education to all New England children, most **town schools** received public support, although some charged fees and some received private donations.

*District Schools*   As more and more families moved away from towns and established farms, churches, and villages, they petitioned to become a district

**Dame schools were an extension of the home education that most young people obtained in the early eighteenth century. Those women who became proficient at teaching children in their homes formalized their methods and organized instruction for the children in the community.**

parish or a district with the rights of local government, including the right to control education. As a democratic response to the educational needs of the dispersed population, **district schools** were legalized in Connecticut in 1766 and Massachusetts in 1789. Each district hired its own schoolmaster and set the length of its school term. The teachers rarely had training or educational background and provided only basic instruction in the alphabet, reading and writing, and religion.

District schools (1766)

## Roots of Politicization of Education

The roots of politicization of education can be found in two aspects of the history of education in the colonial South, the education of blacks and of women. While Southern landowners passed laws forbidding the education of slaves in an attempt to keep them subservient, these laws, ironically, acknowledged the potential role of education for social change. Lawrence Cremin, in the essay "Education and Politics" in *Popular Education and Its Discontents,* suggests that "education has always served political functions insofar as it affects, or at least is believed and intended to affect, the future character of the community and the state. He further claims that we can see the synergetic role of politics and education by examining the commentaries of such politicians and educators as Thomas Jefferson, Horace Mann, and John Dewey. "For Jefferson, the goals of education

Role of education in social change

were to diffuse knowledge, inculcate virtue (including patriotism), and cultivate learning . . . to prepare an informed citizenry and a humanely trained leadership" (1990, 85–86). He points to the fact that Jefferson made "no provision for African Americans in his proposals, while Mann stood mute on the matter of racial mixing in the schools, and neither had much to say about the education of women" (p. 86). Mann, according to Cremin, saw the school as an instrument of social reform that prepared young people to make informed, independent judgments and participate actively in the industrial society. Dewey was even more explicit in the relationship of schools and society, seeing the school as "an embryonic community life" (1990, 85).

## SCHOOLS IN THE SOUTHERN COLONIES

Plantation owners

The Southern colonies were sparsely populated. The people of the plantations, who produced rice, tobacco, sugar, indigo, and cotton, were rigidly divided by class and race. Plantation owners, as a class, considered themselves to be descended from Cavaliers, the British landowners who supported the Stuart king in the English Civil War (1642–1649). As such, they reestablished an aristocratic way of life in the New World. They did not see education as a means to a new social order nor did they attempt to provide a general education for all children. Rather they believed that they were responsible for educating their own children, who were often taught by private tutors, or attended denominational schools. As in the New England colonies, the boys were taught subjects to prepare them to attend college later in England, while the girls were taught to manage the household. The Southern plantation owners' greatest need was to maintain the life of the gentleman planter rather than develop education for the masses.

Parsons schools

***Education of Women in the Southern Colonies***   The young women of the Southern colonies fared less well in terms of education than their counterparts in New England. Although a few went to schools outside the home, such as the **parsons schools** (endowed free schools in the parishes or districts) of Virginia, and some were educated by tutors, most women of the Southern colonies were illiterate. One out of every three Southern women in the seventeenth century could sign her name, as compared to three out of five men. After the American Revolution, a few wealthy girls attended private schools but were taught reading, writing, dancing, and arithmetic rather than the Latin, Greek, and philosophy taught to wealthy boys (Spruill 1972). Consequently, college then was not an option for girls.

Plantation slaves

***Training African Slaves***   The plantation economy thrived on cheap labor. By 1619, only twelve years after the settlement of the Jamestown colony, the first slaves were imported from Africa to work the plantations. Because wealthy landowners saw slaves as central to the maintenance of their lifestyle and believed education would make them less subservient and less useful, most were denied an education and never learned to read or write. They were trained to perform the plantation's specific tasks, from fieldwork to household chores. Some received special training or were apprenticed as blacksmiths, wheelwrights, or mill hands. Fearing insurrection, many slave owners forbade blacks from becoming literate.

*Missionary Societies and African Slaves*    In the eighteenth century French and Spanish missionaries organized the first attempt to educate African slaves in colonial America primarily because they considered education a means of increasing the ranks of the Church. The Anglican Missionary Society followed their lead. The Anglican Society for the Propagation of the Gospel in Foreign Parts established charity schools in the 1750s and 1760s that taught Southern slaves to read and write.

But few were educated despite the increasing number of schools where they could develop skills in reading, writing, and religion. By 1770, there were approximately seven hundred thousand African slaves in the colonies. The number increased to over four million by 1860. Although schools such as Samuel Thomas's enrolled sixty students in Goose Creek Parish, South Carolina, in 1705, and the Anglican Society's in New York City enrolled two hundred in 1714, the effort to educate slaves was negligible. Historians estimate that in 1863, at the time of the Emancipation Proclamation, the literacy rate among them was 5 percent (Cohen 1974, 146).

*African Slaves Educated through Informal Channels*    However, some slaves were educated and spread their knowledge to others primarily through informal channels. A common belief at the time, perhaps maintained to justify the denial of education to blacks, was that they were incapable of learning and could not achieve at the level of whites. Still, the education of some slaves, despite incredible odds against them, helped dispel this myth. John Chavis (1763–1838) provides an interesting example. He was sent to Princeton University as part of an experiment to see whether an African slave had the capacity for a college education. Chavis graduated from Princeton, became a preacher who ministered to both blacks and whites, and established a classical school teaching Greek and Latin. Ironically, however, this school trained only the sons of prominent white families for college. Hence, the formal education he received was transmitted only to a limited extent to other blacks.

**Indentured Servants**    White indentured servants in the Southern colonies were only slightly more likely than African slaves to gain an education. It was largely informal and provided by parents who often were illiterate. Hence, the education of poor whites in the South rarely included reading and writing. Poor white boys learned to farm, hunt, and fish from their fathers. Poor white girls learned homemaking from their mothers. The Anglican Missionary Society for the Propagation of the Gospel in Foreign Parts conducted a few schools primarily designed to teach the students to read the Bible. Although most Anglican Missionary Society schools were an early attempt to improve the lot of poor whites and African slaves through education, the majority had no access to schools, so as an initial attempt at politicization, they rarely succeeded.

The Anglican Society for the Propagation of the Gospel in Foreign Parts established charity schools for Southern blacks (1750–1760)

John Chavis (1763–1838)

Indentured servants

## Roots of Multitudinousness of Education

Throughout the history of education in the United States, different themes predominate. During the colonial period we can find the roots of all three themes: popularization in New England, politicization in the South, and multitudinousness in the Middle Atlantic colonies. As with education that became popular in

New England and the political attitude that denied education to some in order to promote particular social goals in the South, the development of a variety of educational institutions stems from the culture, language, and religion of the population of the Middle Atlantic colonies.

## SCHOOLS IN THE MIDDLE ATLANTIC COLONIES

Unlike New England and the Southern colonies, the populations of the Middle Atlantic colonies of New York, New Jersey, Pennsylvania, and Delaware were heterogeneous in terms of ethnicity, language, and religion. The region was colonized by Dutch Calvinists, Anglicans, Lutherans, Quakers, Jews, Presbyterians, and Catholics. They included people of English, Scottish, Dutch, German, Swedish, Danish, and Irish origin. Cultural diversity flourished as these groups attempted to retain their heritage in the New World. These differences made it impossible to establish a single school system, and the density of the population compared to the Southern colonies made home tutoring impractical. Therefore, a multitude of educational options developed.

*Parochial and Private Schools*   In Pennsylvania **parochial schools**, supported by religious organizations, were begun between 1720 and 1740. **Private schools**, supported by individuals rather than by public funds, were begun in Virginia during the same period. In fact, it has been said that if the roots of public education are in New England, then the roots of private education are in the Middle Atlantic region.

The Dutch settlers, mainly members of the Dutch Reformed Church, established **vernacular schools** to teach reading and writing in their native language in New Amsterdam, which later became New York. After taking control of New York in 1664, the English set up Anglican charity schools to teach reading, writing, arithmetic, religion, and catechism to poor children.

*Vocational Education*   By the late seventeenth century the demand for skilled workers such as navigators, surveyors, accountants, and printers was growing in the busy commercial colonies of the Middle Atlantic states. There, lacking a common school system, a number of informal **private venture training schools** were developed by businesses and trades to meet this demand. These private schools met the needs both of those who did not intend to go to college, and of new businesses and industries for a trained workforce. These schools taught such practical courses as writing, arithmetic, geometry, trigonometry, astronomy, and surveying. Frequently, they lasted only as long as the need for workers existed.

*Quaker Schools*   Unlike the Puritans of New England and the Dutch Calvinists of New York, the Quakers rejected corporal punishment as inhuman and cruel; they viewed children as individuals with individual needs and interests.

Quaker elementary schools stressed religion, reading, writing, and arithmetic and were open to all children without restriction. Some African youngsters were housed in Quaker homes while they attended the schools, which were a model of equality for the time. By 1869, there were forty-seven Quaker schools

---

Parochial schools supported by religious organizations (1720–1740)

Private schools supported by individuals (1720–1740)

Vernacular schools founded by Dutch

Private venture training schools developed by businesses for a trained workforce

Quaker school for blacks established in Philadelphia (1700)

throughout the colonies, including one established specifically for blacks in 1700 in Philadelphia.

By 1880, there were twenty-five Quaker secondary schools that were open to all students. Tuition was charged to those who could afford it; the poor attended free. However, despite the equality of the education offered in these schools, they were not funded by public monies and remained private and parochial.

---

**4-2**

**POINTS TO REMEMBER**

- Colonial New Englanders believed in a general education for all white children so that they could learn to read the Bible and develop discipline. Early schools taught reading and basic mathematical skills. Wealthy boys were educated in the classics in Latin grammar schools so that they could attend Harvard or college in Europe. Education in colonial New England thus popularized education in the United States.

- In the South the children of landowners were educated at home. Schools were few and far apart and few children attended them. Blacks and the children of indentured white servants were usually uneducated. However, the seeds of politicization of education were planted by the landowners who passed laws against educating slaves and by the missionary societies that attempted to educate them.

- The Middle Atlantic colonies had a heterogeneous population. Various ethnic groups developed their own parochial and private schools. Industries also developed private venture schools to train students in the trades required in those industries. Consequently, the concept of multitudinousness of education developed in the Middle Atlantic colonies.

---

# Politicization of Education Predominates

As discussed earlier, one of the three historical themes of U.S. education, according to Lawrence Cremin, is politicization, the idea that one of the roles of education is to change society indirectly through the schools rather than directly through politics. This means that rather than making laws or passing bills to alter some aspect of society, we look toward the schools to implement reform through education. Education had been used for political aims in the colonial South, but it was not until the postrevolutionary period that schools were used extensively to educate the young in the skills and knowledge necessary to be active citizens of a common culture.

## EDUCATION OF THE POSTREVOLUTIONARY PERIOD

During the postrevolutionary war period (1776–1830) it became necessary to find a means of developing a single nation from the various backgrounds and beliefs of the colonists. To many early scholars and politicians, the schools were an avenue through which young people could be trained in the rudiments of democracy. Just as the colonists of New England recognized the power of the schools to indoctrinate the young in their religious theory, the thinkers of the new nation recognized the schools' potential in the indoctrination of the young into citizenship in the new republic. Hence the politicization of the schools.

*1776–1830*

*Postrevolutionary War Period*

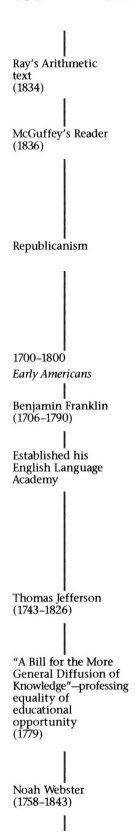

Ray's Arithmetic
text
(1834)

McGuffey's Reader
(1836)

Republicanism

1700–1800
*Early Americans*

Benjamin Franklin
(1706–1790)

Established his
English Language
Academy

Thomas Jefferson
(1743–1826)

"A Bill for the More
General Diffusion of
Knowledge"–professing
equality of
educational
opportunity
(1779)

Noah Webster
(1758–1843)

*Changes in Curriculum*    Although the curriculum changed little in the elementary schools after the Revolution, especially in rural America, new textbooks made the task of teaching reading and arithmetic easier. *Ray's Arithmetic* (1834) and the *McGuffey Reader* (1836) were the common subject-oriented texts used by almost all students through the mid-nineteenth century. Teachers could rely on these texts to set forth the curriculum.

In the secondary curriculum, classical studies were replaced by more practical classes related to everyday life. By the mid-eighteenth century, middle-class settlers, believing that education could effect social change, were advocating a curriculum that would help the country deal with everyday problems.

*Educational Thought of the Postrevolutionary Period*    Various political leaders such as Benjamin Franklin, Thomas Jefferson, and Noah Webster proposed new educational strategies and institutions to educate people in the new republicanism. **Republicanism**, based on the political theories of the Englishman John Locke (1632–1704), was founded on the principle that government arises from the consent of the governed. In this case, the governed needed education to cultivate the skills, knowledge, and values that would be necessary for participating in the new political order, thus giving rise to the concept of education as a means of addressing the country's political needs.

*Benjamin Franklin*    Benjamin Franklin (1706–1790), a highly respected statesman, politician, and philosopher whose own schooling was minimal, developed a prototype for the contemporary secondary school. He considered Latin grammar schools with their focus on Latin and Greek impractical for life in a democracy. His **English language academy**, established in Philadelphia in 1751, included courses in English, oratory, commerce and politics, mathematics as an applied subject, history, and foreign languages as needed for professional training and vocational courses. It introduced into the secondary school curriculum many practical and vocational courses that had previously been part of only private venture schools. Franklin's English language academy served as the precursor to vocational education in contemporary high schools.

*Thomas Jefferson*    Thomas Jefferson (1743–1826) was one of the most influential early American statesmen to profess the importance of equality of educational opportunity. Jefferson, echoing the words of Aristotle, advocated passage of "A Bill for the More General Diffusion of Knowledge" (1779), a law that would provide an education "adapted to years, the capacity, and the condition of everyone, and directed to their freedom and happiness" (Jefferson 1779/1954, 134).

Jefferson advocated three years of free elementary education for all white children in Virginia. For those gifted males who could not afford grammar school (secondary school), a scholarship for an additional three years was provided. Jefferson was the first influential American spokesman for free public education for the masses, at least at the elementary level.

*Noah Webster*    Noah Webster (1758–1843) has been called the "schoolmaster of the Republic." He believed that the development of an American language was essential if a unified national identity were to develop. Toward this end he established a system of phonics to differentiate American from British English and wrote *American Spelling* (1783), later editions of which were to become famous as the *Blue-Backed Speller,* and *American Dictionary of the English Language* (1828). Webster's speller reportedly sold over 24 million copies and, for the most part, replaced the *New England Primer* in the classroom. The popularity and wide use of his speller made his name commonly known in educational circles, and his system of phonics is still an important element in reading instruction today.

*Schooling, the Prerogative of the States*    Schooling was firmly established as the states' prerogative during the postrevolutionary period. In 1787, Congress enacted the *Northwest Ordinance,* by which the lower Great Lakes Region, then known as the Northwest territory, was divided into townships. The newly formed federal government showed its commitment to the principles of education in the Northwest Ordinance, which stated that education is "necessary to good government and happiness of mankind."

The U.S. Constitution, ratified in 1788, failed to mention education. However, under the "reserved powers clause" of the Tenth Amendment to the Constitution, ratified in 1791, educational prerogatives remained with the individual states. Therefore, from the very beginning of the Republic, the legal roles of the states and the federal government in education were firmly established (see also chapter 15).

American Spelling Book, *Blue-Backed Speller* (1783)

Northwest Ordinance—first federal enactment supporting education (1787)

"Reserved powers clause"

# Popularization of Education Predominates

Although many state legislative bodies of the late eighteenth and early nineteenth centuries continued to take a laissez-faire view of education, the American public was beginning to demand that the states take action to ensure wider educational opportunities. Some states moved a few steps toward public education by subsidizing some private and philanthropic schools. In some cases, states allotted revenues from excises, lotteries, and the sale of public lands to the schools. In other cases legislation was passed allowing local agencies to tax themselves for schools.

During this period, then, the concept of the common school was developed in which all children would get an education and more educators began discussing the importance of educating women. Education in the United States was moving irrevocably toward popularization. The road, however, was not always smooth.

## JACKSON'S PRESIDENCY ENHANCES THE STATUS OF THE COMMON MAN

The transition was hastened by a new political, social, and economic spirit in the country. The years between 1812 and 1865 became known as the **age of the common man**, partly due to Andrew Jackson's presidency (1829–1837). Jackson was the first president from a frontier state where vast tracts of land were free and open to all, resulting in equality of economic and political opportunity. Jackson was elected by the common man—farmers, trappers, and laborers.

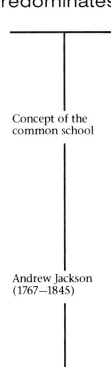

Concept of the common school

Andrew Jackson (1767–1845)

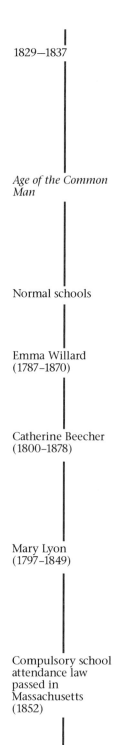

1829—1837

*Age of the Common Man*

Normal schools

Emma Willard
(1787–1870)

Catherine Beecher
(1800–1878)

Mary Lyon
(1797–1849)

Compulsory school
attendance law
passed in
Massachusetts
(1852)

It is no surprise that the rise of the common man, which took place during Jackson's administration, coincided with what has become referred to as the great American revival in education. During this time, state education offices were established, more women entered the schools and the public school system as we know it today was born. It was not long afterward that compulsory attendance laws were passed and high schools were opened. **Normal schools** expressly for the education of teachers were also started during this period.

*Education for Women*   Emma Hart Willard (1787–1870) was a pioneer American educator and author whose work resulted in the foundation of high schools for girls, colleges for women, and coeducational institutions. She was the principal of a girls' academy in Middlebury, Vermont, in 1807. In 1814, she opened a boarding school for girls, and in 1819, she presented the New York state legislature with "A Plan for Improving Female Education." The plan included state aid for opening high schools for girls and suggested that women should have an equal educational opportunity. Although her plan was rejected by the legislature, Governor DeWitt Clinton embraced it, inviting her to move her school to Waterford, New York. In 1821 when the city of Troy, New York, provided a building, Willard moved the school there, calling it the Troy Female Seminary (a school providing a high level of education to females). The seminary became an important center for training teachers prior to the existence of any state-funded normal schools. During the seventeen years in which Willard was principal, more than two hundred teachers graduated from the school. Today it is called the Emma Willard School.

Catherine Esther Beecher (1800–1878) advocated the education of women through her writing and her work. She started a school for girls in Hartford, Connecticut, in 1823, training them in homemaking as well as in academics. In 1830, she began a similar school in Cincinnati, Ohio, and in 1834, she founded the America Women's Educational Association. Also in the 1830s, Beecher trained teachers for one-room rural schools, particularly in the South and West, in what she called the "needy fields" of elementary education and homemaking. She wrote widely on the importance of higher education for women, particularly advocating the establishment of seminaries and normal schools with practice or lab schools in which teachers could train with supervision.

Mary Lyon (1797–1849) began teaching in 1804 at the age of 17 in Shelburne, Massachusetts. She was paid 75 cents a week. In 1821, she taught at Adams Female Academy in Londonderry, New Hampshire. She spent the years between 1830 and 1834 raising money to establish a female higher seminary for poor women. In 1837 she founded Mount Holyoke Seminary. With its ever-rising standards, it became a model for the establishment of similar schools of higher education for women, such as Wellesley and Smith, throughout New England.

*Compulsory Attendance Laws*   Massachusetts enacted the first compulsory attendance statute. Passed in 1852, this law required that all children between eight and fourteen attend school for at least twelve weeks per year, six of which had to be consecutive, and carried penalties for violators.

Throughout the nineteenth and early twentieth centuries, such laws were strengthened by extending age limits, lengthening the school term, and tightening enforcement. However, they did not address equality of educational opportunity and tended to interpret "all children" as meaning all white males of

Prior to the Child Labor Law of 1866, children sometimes worked seventy-two hours a week in factories. This law required that no boys under the age of fourteen could be employed unless they had first attended public or private school for six months.

economic means. Compulsory attendance laws moved the ideal of common education closer to reality.

*The Child Labor Law*    During the age of the common man, a new, unlikely political alliance was formed between the old middle class and those with philanthropic interests who viewed the industrialists as brutalizing their work force, particularly children. Articles about the horrors of child labor began to appear in the press.

As a response to the concerns of a vocal public and press, Massachusetts passed the Child Labor Law in 1866. It required that no child under ten be employed and that no child under fourteen be employed unless he had attended a public or private day school, approved by the school committee, for six months in the year prior to his employment. This law made it possible and, indeed, necessary for boys under the age of fourteen to attend school. Articles in the newspapers, the leadership of the middle class, and the votes of the laborers put pressure on the government to change its laissez-faire approach to education and hastened the movement toward public schools.

Child Labor Law passed in Massachusetts (1866)

## THE COMMON SCHOOL

By the early nineteenth century, as industry became more and more mechanized, it was obvious that workers needed to develop the skills required to operate the increasingly complex machinery. Voluntary philanthropic schools, sponsored by

Establishing the
common school

Rise of district
schools
(1830s–1840s)

Infant schools for
children ages 2–6
emerged
(1800)

Sunday schools
emerged
(1830)

businesses and industries, were inaugurated. Individual workers saw the schools as a way to educate themselves and improve their position in the workplace. The schools, therefore, met the needs of both worker and employer.

Consequently, educators and businessmen began discussing the need for publicly supported education for all children. This ideal was called the **common school**. Of course, to many, the common school was far more than a means of educating the masses for the work force. It was an egalitarian and democratic ideal: a means of preserving and strengthening the culture and conveying and reinforcing American values.

*The District School*    The years immediately after the Revolution until about 1840 have become known as "the period of the district school." Following a New England practice, many states delegated authority over school districts to municipalities. Control of education remained a state function, but much of its power and support derived from local governments and boards such as selectmen (an elected board of officials). In each division of the town the control of the school was delegated to a prudential committeeman, elected by the people of the district. Money needed to support the school was assessed with other taxes and determined by the town.

The early district schools were rather primitive and often overcrowded. Most were heated by fireplaces. Students sat on backless benches placed against the walls. At times as many as one hundred students, between the ages of six and sixteen, attended a school no bigger than thirty feet square taught by one teacher. Supplies were limited. Above the students' benches were a few shelves for books. There were rarely maps or pictures. Blackboards were uncommon until about 1820, and it was not until 1840 that large stoves replaced fireplaces. Children were often required to bring their own firewood to school.

In the earliest district schools, the masters were male. However, after 1820, more young, untrained women teachers who had not attended seminary took over the task. The period of the common man also opened up some jobs to women since it was assumed that any citizen of the community had the qualifications to fill any public office as long as he or she was a loyal American. The employment of women also helped the communities support the district school because women of the nineteenth century earned considerably less than men. The average weekly salary for male teachers in 1841 was $4.15; for women it was $2.51. Therefore, during the period of the district school the tradition of women as teachers was forged, and by the beginning of the U.S. Civil War, the majority of American teachers were women.

*Infant Schools*    In the early 1800s, **infant schools** for children from the ages of two to six whose mothers worked in factories were developed by Welsh educator Robert Owen (1771–1858) in Scotland and later were established in New Harmony, Indiana. These antecedents of modern day care were instituted primarily in the industrial areas of the Northeast to give children, three years and older, moral, intellectual, and physical training.

*Sunday Schools*    Many young children were unable to attend school because they worked at low-paying jobs during the week and on Saturday. Around 1830, the **Sunday school** emerged as a philanthropic endeavor sponsored by the church to help educate these children in the basics of reading, writing, religion,

The public high school began to replace the academies in the 1870s primarily because states were allowed to support their schools by taxes. In addition, the urbanization and industrialization of the United States in the mid-nineteenth century and the specialization of professions required an educated populace. These socioeconomic forces contributed to the growth of the public high school.

and character development. By 1870, Sunday schools were well-established in Protestant churches. However, the focus was moving from teaching basic skills to teaching the Bible.

*Monitorial Schools*   At about the same time that these philanthropic schools were developing, Joseph Lancaster (1778–1838) believed that it was possible to educate large numbers of children effectively, efficiently, and inexpensively. To do so, he developed the concept of **monitorial schools**. In this system, a small number of master teachers trained advanced students to teach beginning students. Lessons were reduced to small elements of basic skills, and each advanced student taught a single phase of each skill. **Ability grouping**, assigning students to groups based on their ability to learn the skill, was established in order to make teaching easier for the advanced students. The first monitorial school in the United States was established in New York City in 1805.

*The High School*   During the nineteenth century statesmen and educators began to question the value of the classical grammar school curriculum for the growing number of children of immigrants. Likewise, they began to look critically at the needs of the burgeoning industrial economy. Clearly, Latin grammar schools met the needs of neither immigrants nor industry.

In the early part of the nineteenth century, the Latin grammar school was replaced by the **academy**. Based on the concept of vernacular (in this case, the

First monitorial school in New York City established (1805)

Academy

English language), education was directed toward the middle class and included young women and men. The academy, following the model provided by Benjamin Franklin, offered a wide range of subjects for college preparatory students as well as those completing their education. Although academies often received some funding from cities and states, most were private. Consequently, they failed to reach the large, growing class of immigrant workers.

By the 1870s, high schools began to replace academies. The development of the high school was aided by a series of court cases such as *Charles E. Stuart et al. v. School District No. 1 of the Village of Kalamazoo* (1874), in which the court ruled that school districts could establish and support public high schools with tax funds. Urbanization and industrialization stimulated the need for training at the same time as specialization in industry increased, so these schools developed quite rapidly. In 1889–1890 there were 2,526 public high schools with a total of 202,063 students.

Ironically, the high school's curriculum remained elite in character. Even though only 5 percent of the students in high school went on to college, the curriculum was primarily for the college-bound. In 1890, for example, the National Education Association (NEA) Committee of Ten recommended that the high school course of study include choices ranging from classical liberal arts to modern languages to science.

## EXPANDING ACCESS FOR FEMALE STUDENTS

In the early years of the twentieth century, an increasing number of female students wanted to attend secondary schools, forcing many educators to debate the value of education for females. Most of the debate, however, focused on practical, economic considerations of female attendance rather than on their potential educational benefits. In 1902, E. E. White, Ohio State commissioner of common schools, sent a report to the United States commissioner of education regarding the need for coeducation in the secondary schools.

> More high schools are needed for both boys and girls; and this immediately presents the question of the uniting or the separating of the sexes in the new high schools. Shall we put up two distinct buildings with two distinct principals and faculties, thus doubling the expense; or shall we erect one building in which the boys and girls shall be educated together, with one principal and faculty for such a school? (Report of United States Commissioner of Education, 1902, cited in Foy 1968, 178–179)

White's 1902 argument for coeducation was won on financial grounds rather than on the basis of equality or educational opportunity. However, when it was decided that girls and boys should be educated in one building, the differentiation of curriculum became an important question. Again, equal opportunity was not the determining factor. In fact, although boys would be allowed to take courses designed primarily for girls, there was no mention of girls being permitted to take courses offered for boys.

Nevertheless, the arguments for coeducation opened the doors of public education to most white females of school age and were another move toward the popularization of U.S. education.

High Schools (1870)

*Kalamazoo* case established support for public high schools (1874)

E. E. White Report on need for coeducation in secondary schools (1902)

## EDUCATIONAL LEADERSHIP AND THE COMMON SCHOOL

Between 1820 and 1850, Horace Mann and Henry Barnard, two influential statesmen, did a great deal through their writings to support the ideal of the publicly supported common school.

*Horace Mann*   Horace Mann (1796–1859), a lawyer and politician, became secretary of the Massachusetts State Board of Education in 1837. During his twelve-year tenure, he produced yearly reports in which he addressed the needs of many different groups and individuals, always emphasizing that common schools met these needs.

Among the many issues he discussed were the development of better school buildings and responsible local boards of education (1837) and the students' need for intellectual development (1838). He advocated the establishment of free circulating libraries in every school district (1839) and argued that the schools should promote a morality that would ensure the protection of the individual's right to property (1841). He discussed the employment of women and the necessity of developing effective teacher-training institutions (1842). Mann asked, "But why should a woman receive less than two-fifths as much as a man, for services which in no respect are of inferior value?" In the tenth (1846) and eleventh (1847) reports he discussed the state's role in education and the power of education to redeem the state. Mann so strongly believed in the common school that he asserted that it "may become the most effective and benignant of all the forces of civilization" (1848).

Mann wrote not only about the popularization but the politicization of education. He was idealistic in his belief in education as a reformer of society, the "great equalizer of the conditions of men." Through education, each individual could become independent and resist the selfishness of others, feelings of social responsibility would expand, and distinction between classes would diminish.

*Henry Barnard*   Henry Barnard (1811–1900) was secretary of the Connecticut Board of Education, commissioner of public schools in Rhode Island, first U.S. commissioner of education, and chancellor of the University of Wisconsin. Whereas Mann's writing was primarily for legislative use, Barnard's was much more accessible to educators and the public through two journals he established: *Connecticut Common School Journal* (1839) and *American Journal of Education* (1848).

Barnard supported Mann's idea that training in civic values and health and diet was as valuable as training in basic skills. He believed that the most important subject to an informed citizenry was the English language. He supported improved teacher education and increased teacher salaries. Barnard's efforts led to the establishment of the first federal office of education in 1867, now called the Department of Education.

Horace Mann
(1796–1859)

Became secretary of
Massachusetts State
Board of Education
(1837)

Henry Barnard
(1811–1900)

Common schools
promoted in Twelve
Annual Reports

Introduced teachers
to views of
European
educational
reformers. First U.S.
Commissioner of
Education
(1867)

## Politicization of Schools Realized: Education of the Post–Civil War Period

In the post–Civil War period, educators in the urban areas of the Northeast and Midwest recognized the economic and social need to educate the large secondary school-aged population, who did not plan to attend college, in vocational subjects and democratic values. In the South it was a time of reconstruction after a war that was disastrous to the region's economy and society. At the same time, popularization of schooling became the rallying cry of the people.

## SCHOOLS TO MEET THE NEEDS OF THE DEMOCRACY

One important example of the politicization of schools to meet society's democratic needs can be seen in the St. Louis public schools of the mid-nineteenth century. Superintendent William Torrey Harris recognized that 46 percent of the students were children of German immigrants. He counted at least ten distinct languages spoken by the expanding European population of the city. His goal was to reduce the differences he observed in manners, customs, and values so that the people of different ethnic backgrounds would "ascend into a new homogeneous nationality . . ." (Harris 1898, 35).

In order to accomplish this, Harris believed that the common national language must be English. However, he realized that a period of transition was necessary when bilingual traditions should be maintained. Gradually students would take all courses in English, although German language courses would remain in the curriculum.

Consequently, children of immigrants enrolled in the schools in large numbers, up from 1,300 in 1860 to more than 20,000 in 1880. Harris believed that in order to assimilate the children of immigrants into U.S. culture, the curriculum must be sequential and structured. For example, students would study U.S. history in German. Moreover, German would be integrated into courses in grammar, literature, art, mathematics, and geography. Harris called these subjects the "six windows of the soul." He believed that their study would allow students to master the mystery and nature of the human mind. At the same time, students would be developing skills in English and learning about the United States. Thereby, the school not only would help students assimilate U.S. culture but also would help them become functioning citizens in the democracy.

## CURRICULUM FOR THE DEMOCRACY

If schools were to educate an increasingly diverse population and help all these students become participating citizens in the democracy, the classical curriculum of the Latin grammar school and teaching by recitation would no longer be appropriate. In an unprecedented manner, educators of the late nineteenth century examined the school curriculum and teaching methodology.

Although the National Education Association (NEA) had clearly asserted in two reports in 1893 and 1895 that the subject-centered approach to curriculum was appropriate in elementary and secondary schools, the educators' commitment to these approaches was diminishing. By 1918, the NEA challenged its earlier convictions by issuing the **Seven Cardinal Principles**. This report recommended a new nonclassical curriculum for the large influx of non-college-bound students. According to this report, all students should be prepared by the schools to be successful in seven endeavors: health, command of fundamental processes, worthy home membership, vocation, civics, worthy use of leisure, and ethical

---

William T. Harris
(1835–1909)

Superintendent of
St. Louis public
schools
(1868–1880)

Immigrants
assimilated into
culture

Seven Cardinal
Principles
(1918)

character. These represented a significant departure from the classical approach of the curriculum of earlier times. The NEA commission that published this report claimed that previous curriculums had served the minority rather than the majority.

The report represented the first attempt to meet the needs of individual students by offering them a variety of different educational options, including several occupational choices in secondary school.

The commission also advocated a significant change in how equality of educational opportunity was viewed. The idea that the same education means equal education was disputed. For example, a boy who was not planning to attend college would now have a curriculum designed specifically for him. However, the report did not address the specific needs of lower-class students, minorities, or women. The beginning of World War I (1914) kept the recommendations from being implemented in the schools.

Despite the limited immediate impact of the Seven Cardinal Principles, curriculum theory and design slowly evolved away from complete subject dominance toward some concern for the needs of the population, including a commitment to different educational options for different students.

## PROGRESSIVISM

Notwithstanding the common school movement of the nineteenth century, the needs of large portions of American society, particularly the poor and immigrant classes, were not being met by the schools. The **progressive movement** was an attempt to improve society by bringing the disenfranchised into the schools. Progressive educators believed that through schooling the poor could rise above their lot and societal problems could be mitigated.

Most contemporary historians see the progressive movement in education as part of the larger reform movement that began in the 1890s. A new, articulated middle class was emerging and began to address the problems of poverty. Jane Addams, who graduated from Rochford College in 1881 and attended Philadelphia Medical School, for example, believed that she could improve the conditions of immigrant slums by developing a sense of community through settlement houses, places of refuge and education for the urban poor. To prove her theory she established Hull House in Chicago in the 1890s where, for example, if the community needed instruction in care of childhood diseases, it was provided. As the educational importance of Hull House grew, a gymnasium, various workshops, a theater, a playground, an art gallery, and a museum were added. In 1894, Hull House was incorporated and supported by endowments and contributions from public-spirited citizens. Through education, the people who operated Hull House attempted nothing less than a renewal of society.

The best-known educator to be associated with the progressive movement was John Dewey (1859–1952), who maintained that the child's course of study should be related to her or his experiences. According to Dewey, schools must reflect society and must actively seek to improve it by allowing students to become effective participants in the democratic process while in school. In 1896, Dewey developed the laboratory school at the University of Chicago beginning the Progressive Education Movement (see also chapter 6, p. 240 and chapter 8, p. 295).

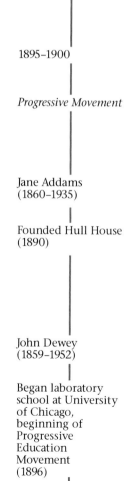

1895–1900

*Progressive Movement*

Jane Addams
(1860–1935)

Founded Hull House
(1890)

John Dewey
(1859–1952)

Began laboratory
school at University
of Chicago,
beginning of
Progressive
Education
Movement
(1896)

*Progressive Education*  Although for some children, Hull House provided an alternative to the public schools, the movement toward politicization of the schools was occurring simultaneously in such places as at John Dewey's University of Chicago Lab School and in the Gary, Indiana, public schools. According to Lawrence Cremin, "To look back to the nineties is to sense an awakening of social conscience, a growing belief that this incredible suffering was neither the fault nor the inevitable lot of the sufferers, that it could certainly be alleviated, and that road to alleviation was neither charity nor revolution, but in the last analysis education" (1957, 59).

The Gary Plan
(1906)

*The Gary Plan*  Although progressive curriculums such as Dewey's, based on the needs of the child and on activity, influenced numerous experimental educational programs, their impact on the public school curriculum was limited, at least initially. Probably the most comprehensive application of Dewey's curriculum can be seen in the Gary Plan. Gary, Indiana, was a new, multicultural city in 1906. The city's populations included immigrants from southern and eastern Europe and African Americans who came from the southern states to work in the steel mills. Under this plan, each school in Gary, Indiana, was organized as an "embryonic community" (Bourne 1916, 144), in some ways similar to Hull House. Each school was a community center designed to serve the educational and social needs of adults and children. Students took vocational and technical courses such as typing, mechanical drawing, drafting, and a series of academic subjects during school hours; adults took similar courses in the evenings or on Saturdays. Work and study were done in a practical, as well as intellectual, setting. Physics laboratories, for example, adjoined machine shops to allow students to apply scientific principles to practical situations. Learning by doing was practically implemented as the children operated the school: The lunchroom was run by students, supplies were ordered and distributed by students, students did accounting for the administration, and younger children became assistants of older children.

School day
organized into a
"platoon system"

To make this program administratively feasible, the school day was departmentalized into what was called the "platoon" system, which allowed for complete use of the facility. While one group of students was studying the basic subjects, another group was studying other disciplines. Ironically, this organizational approach, the one aspect of the plan widely adopted by other public schools, was what defeated it in the end. Departmentalization makes integration between subjects almost impossible (Flexner and Bachman 1918, 77).

## SCHOOLING IN THE SOUTH DURING RECONSTRUCTION

Infrequently in U.S. society, conditions make one section of the country different from another in terms of educational history. The Civil War and the period immediately following it was such a period.

The economic and social climate of the South after the Civil War was very different from that in the North and caused the development of schools in the South to suffer. The plantation economy was in ruins, factories were destroyed, families were separated, banks were insolvent, and civil authority was limited. There was a great deal of poverty, crime, and starvation. Education was of limited concern to Southerners.

The government established in the South by the victorious federal government in Washington, D.C., tended to be corrupt and poorly administered. Over $5 million in federal funds were provided for education from 1865 through 1871. However, because this money was administered by Northerners who did not understand local conditions, most Southerners were indifferent or resisted these attempts to educate their children.

### *Viewpoint* Sadie and Bessie Delany

*At the ages of 101 and 103, Sadie and Bessie Delany told their story to the author Amy Hill Hearth. This excerpt from the book,* Having Our Say: The Delaney Sisters' First One Hundred Years, *illustrates Sadie's account of her first teaching job. Bessie was a dentist.*

The daughters of a man born into slavery and a mother of mixed racial parentage who was born free, the sisters recall what it meant to be "colored" children in the late-nineteenth-century South. They grew up on a college campus, St. Augustine's School in Raleigh, North Carolina, where their father was an Episcopal priest and vice principal. After years of teaching in the rural South to raise money, the Delany sisters managed to put themselves through college and then settled in Harlem, turning down marriage opportunities for careers. . . .

The Delaney sisters tell their story about growing up in the late-nineteenth-century South

**Sadie**

I got my first teaching job in New York in the fall of 1920. I think I was paid fifteen hundred dollars for the year. It was at P.S. 119 in Harlem, which was an elementary school, mostly colored. This was a typical assignment for a colored teacher. They most certainly did not want us in schools where the children were white. The parents would object. One way that the principals kept us out was to say they could not hire anyone with a Southern accent because it would be damaging to the children. Well, most of us colored teachers at the time had Southern accents. So it was just a way of keeping us out.

When my accent was considered a problem, I found a way around that. I signed up with a speech coach, a woman in Manhattan. She was a white woman, a lovely woman. I don't think she had too many colored clients. I remember that when I would go to her apartment for the lessons, the doorman made me take the freight elevator. I didn't make a fuss because I wanted those speech lessons.

You had to decide: Am I going to change the world, or am I going to change me? Or maybe change the world a little bit just by changing me? If I can get ahead, doesn't that help my people? . . .

I had wanted to teach at a high school because it was considered a promotion, and it paid better. But I had to be a little clever to find ways to get around these brick walls they set up for colored folks.

This is what I did when they told me I had to come in for an appointment. I skipped it and sent them a letter, acting like there was a mix-up. Then I just showed up on the first day of classes.

Child, when I showed up that day—at Theodore Roosevelt High School, a white high school—they just about died when they saw me. But my name was on the list to teach there, and it was too late to send me someplace else. So I became the first colored teacher in the New York City system to teach domestic science on the high school level.

The two sisters, Bessie (left) and Sadie Delany, grew up in the late nineteenth century in the South. Strong, independent women, they fought racism and sexism to put themselves through college. Dr. Bessie was a dentist, Sadie a teacher. In 1992, when they were 101 and 103 years old, respectively, they told their story to Amy Hill Hearth.

George Peabody
(1795–1869)

My classes were very demanding because as a colored teacher I always got the meanest kids. Except once. That was the year they had me mixed up with a white woman whose name was also Delany. It was kind of funny. She was just furious because she got all these tough girls, and I got the easy ones—college-bound and motivated. Tell you the truth, I did not mind the tough kids. I loved them all.

From: Delany, and Delany, with Hearth, 1993. Amy Hearth was on assignment for the *New York Times* when she interviewed the Delany sisters.

***George Peabody and Other Philanthropists***   George Peabody (1795–1869), a financier, merchant, and philanthropist, gave $3.5 million for the education of the poor in the South and Southwest. The funds were used to (1) improve state school systems, (2) develop state normal schools, (3) train African American teachers, and (4) strengthen the professional activities of teachers. In 1905 the George Peabody College for Teachers, a model for teacher training in the South, opened in Nashville, Tennessee.

Other philanthropists assisted the cause of education in the South. In 1882 John Slater donated $1 million to provide teacher training and industrial education for African Americans. Anna T. Jeannes created a fund in 1907 to raise their quality of education. In 1917 Julius Rosenwald established a fund to assist all areas of Southern education for 30 years.

In 1901 Southern educational leaders formed the Southern Education Board to guide education in the South. However, by 1918 schools in the South were still far behind the rest of the United States in enrollment, attendance, and funding, especially the high schools. Teachers in the South were poorly trained and paid compared to teachers in other regions of the country.

## Education of Minorities Prior to the Twentieth Century

Following the Civil War it was no longer politically or socially possible to ignore the education of minorities, nor was it possible to leave the education of minorities to a few generous philanthropists or to missionary societies. However, as will be noted in chapter five, although the seeds of public education for all were planted in the late nineteenth century, the issue of how best to meet the needs of the diverse U.S. education are still being argued in the late twentieth century.

### EDUCATION OF SOUTHERN AFRICAN AMERICANS

Freedman's Bureau
(1865)

In 1865 the U.S. Congress established the **Freedmen's Bureau** to work with voluntary organizations to provide basic education to those who had been slaves. Although many did learn to read and write as a result of the Freedmen's Bureau, it did not do much to improve the African's social or economic life, which had been its original goal.

In addition to the philanthropic support of education for African Americans in the Reconstruction South, black educators developed schools and provided inspiration for the education of black children. Booker T. Washington (1856–1915)

Tuskegee Institute was established for the education of black students in Alabama in 1875. Booker T. Washington believed that blacks should be educated in agricultural and occupational skills so as not to compete with and cause conflicts with whites in the professions. While Washington fought for the education and advancement of blacks, he is, nevertheless, sometimes seen as a controversial figure who compromised the position of blacks in society.

established Tuskegee Normal and Industrial Institute in Tuskegee, Alabama, in 1875. It was designed to offer industrial education for African American students and stressed hard work, vocational skills, and economic advancement. Washington contended that it was the kind of education needed for both races, particularly because of the undeveloped material resources of the South. He, however, supported the concept of separate schools for African American students. At the Cotton States Exposition in Atlanta in 1895 he said, "In all things that are purely social we can be as separate as the fingers, yet one as the hand in all things essential to mutual progress" (Harlan 1972).

Frederick Douglass (1817–1895), an orator who spoke for abolitionist groups, supported education for African Americans, especially vocational education, believing, as did Washington, that through vocational education they could most easily advance economically and socially. He contended that the Fourteenth Amendment to the U.S. Constitution, the rights of citizens, and the Fifteenth, the right to vote, were a mockery if they did not ensure equal rights to all citizens.

William E. Burghardt Du Bois (1868–1963), the first African American to receive a Ph.D. degree, attended Fiske University, Harvard University, and the University of Berlin. Du Bois spoke eloquently of the right of black citizens to play an equal role with whites in U.S. society. He argued that they should become prepared for positions of leadership not only in the black community but in society as a whole, and that this required a good education. Du Bois, a sociologist by education, founded the National Association for the Advancement of Colored People (NAACP) to help develop black leadership. His goal was to develop an African American culture that would blend blacks' African backgrounds with American culture.

Booker T. Washington (1856–1915)

Tuskegee Normal and Industrial Institute founded (1875)

Frederick Douglass (1817–1895)

Leader in abolitionist movement and education of blacks

W. E. B. Du Bois (1868–1963)

Promoted education and advancement for blacks

*(continued on p. 166)*

# SHOULD LITERACY BE BASED ON TRADITIONAL CULTURE?

## PRO E. D. Hirsch, Jr.

In recent decades we have assumed that the early curriculum should be "child-centered" and "skill-centered." Yet there is a growing consensus among reading researchers that adequate literacy depends upon the specific information called "cultural literacy," and we should therefore begin to impart traditional literate culture to children at the earliest possible age.

The need to begin such instruction early is based on technical as well as social considerations. From a purely technical standpoint, our children need traditional background information early to make sense of significant reading materials, and thus gain further information that enables them to make further progress in reading and learning. From a social standpoint, the need to start as early as possible is even more urgent. Young children from the middle class sometimes receive necessary literate information outside the school, but disadvantaged children rarely have access to literate background information outside the school. Therefore, to change the cycle of illiteracy that debars disadvantaged children from high literacy, we need to impart enough literate information from preschool through third grade to ensure continued progress in literacy on the part of all our children.

Now that these basic truths are becoming widely known, it is time to question and qualify some educational slogans inconsistent with those truths that have actively hindered the teaching of literate information to young children. . . .

1. *The home is more decisive for literacy than the school.* . . . Parental help is useful not only for motivating students, but also for increasing their time-on-task and attitude to learning. . . . [D]espite the importance of the home, our schools can do a much better job of teaching literacy to all students, even without effective reinforcement from the home. . . .

2. *Schools should stress general skills and broad understanding, not mere facts.* Along with the new child- and skill-centered curriculum went an antipathy to "mere facts." . . .

The negative connotations of terms like "mere facts" and "memorization" arise from the theory that acquiring facts is inferior to "meaningful" learning experiences that cause children to take interest in and understand the significance of what they are being taught. It is assumed that the piling up of information cannot be meaningful, or interesting, or motivational to children. . . .

But expert teaching and well-conceived texts, not modernity of content, are the bridges of relevance that connect reading materials with a child's experience. The life experiences of children who enter American classrooms are much too varied to form a definite content basis for child-centered materials. Moreover, most of the literate culture that children will need for later life consists of traditional, intergenerational materials. Consequently, their literacy is more effectively enhanced when they are successfully taught durable, traditional subjects like Ulysses and the Cyclops than when they are taught ephemera like Dick and Jane at the Supermarket.

From: E. D. Hirsch, Jr., "Restoring Cultural Literacy in the Early Grades," *Educational Leadership,* December 1987/January 1988, 45(4). E.D. Hirsch, Jr., is a well-known critic of public education.

## POSTSCRIPT

From the 1970s through the 1990s educational reformers have argued about the focus of public school curriculum. These two articles reflect the polar ends of that argument: the curriculum should be based on a canon of great works; the curriculum should be inclusive and be transformed to reflect the diversity of U.S. society. In the arguments, we can see three themes or abiding principles of U.S. education suggested by historian Lawrence Cremin. If the schools

# SHOULD LITERACY BE BASED ON TRADITIONAL CULTURE?

## CON  James A. Banks

Most reports urging educational reform in the 1980s paid scant attention to helping citizens develop the knowledge, attitudes, and skills necessary to function effectively in a nation and world increasingly diverse ethnically, racially, and culturally. Two of the most influential works published late in the decade not only failed to describe the need for multicultural literacy and understanding, but also ran counter to the U.S. multicultural movement.

E. D. Hirsch's and Allan Bloom's widely reviewed and discussed books, both published in 1987, were regarded by many as having cogently made the case for emphasizing the traditional western-centric canon dominating school and university curricula, a canon threatened, according to Bloom and other western traditionalists, by movements to incorporate more ethnic and women's content into curricula. . . . Hirsch's formulation of a list of memorizable facts is inconsistent with multicultural teaching, since it ignores the notion of knowledge as a social construction with normative and political assumptions. Regarding knowledge as a social construction and viewing it from diverse cultural perspectives are key components of multicultural literacy.

There is growing recognition among educators and the general public that tomorrow's citizens should acquire the knowledge, skills, and attitudes critical to functioning in a diverse, complex world. Several factors contribute to this growing recognition, including the *demographic imperative,* significant population growth among people of color, and increasing enrollments of students of color in the nation's schools. . . .

Parents and students of color are now pushing for reforms that go beyond separate ethnic studies courses and programs. They are urging public school educators and university faculties to integrate ethnic content into mainstream curricula and to transform the canons and paradigms on which school and university curricula are based. . . .

Feeling that their voices often have been silenced and their experiences minimized, women and people of color are struggling to be recognized in the curriculum and to have their important historical and cultural works canonized. This struggle can best be understood as a battle over who will participate in or control the formulation of the canon or standard used to determine what constitutes a liberal education. The guardians and defenders of the traditional, established canon apparently believe it best serves their interests and, consequently, the interests of society and the nation. . . .

Only a curriculum that reflects the collective experiences and interests of a wide range of groups is truly in the national interest and consistent with the public good. Any other curriculum reflects only special interests and, thus, does not meet the needs of a nation that must survive in a pluralistic, highly interdependent global world. Special interest curricula, such as history and literature emphasizing the primacy of the West and the history of European-American males, are detrimental to the public good, since they do not help students acquire life skills and perspectives essential for surviving in the twenty-first century. . . .

Excerpt from: James A. Banks. "Multicultural Literacy and Curriculum Reform," *Educational Horizons* (Spring 1991), 69 (3), 135–140. James A. Banks is an educator and critic of public education.

Note: References to original article have been omitted.

are popularized, should the curriculum reflect all of the cultures of the students who populate the schools? Should the schools provide opportunities for students to learn about their own culture (multitudinousness); does this include such things as multicultural and bilingual education? Should the function of the schools be to prepare students to participate in the dominant culture of the society; or, should the schools help reform the society so that it reflects a variety of cultures (politicization)?

Mary Bethune
(1875–1955)

Founded Daytona
Normal School
(1904)

Pedro de Gante
founded first
elementary school
on American
continent
(1523)

Indian Civilization
Act
(1819)

Mary McLeod Bethune (1875–1955) was educated at Scotia Seminary in Concord, North Carolina, and Moody Institute in Chicago. In 1904 she founded Daytona Normal School (now Bethune-Cookman College) in Daytona, Florida. The college was developed to provide religious, academic, and vocational programs for African students. Bethune was a strong advocate for the rights of women and of blacks and later became an adviser in the Franklin D. Roosevelt and Harry S. Truman administrations.

## THE EDUCATION OF NATIVE AMERICANS

According to James A. Banks (1991), Native Americans have been on the American continent for at least 16,000 years and perhaps as long as 40,000 years, having migrated across the Bering Strait to what is now Alaska from Siberia. it is estimated that the pre-Columbian North American population was 1,153,000 and that they spoke over 2 thousand different languages. They were diverse in many other ways as well: physical appearance, method of acquiring food (hunting, farming, or fishing), type of housing, and migration patterns. Most, however, held the belief that the universe, which includes all living things, is a harmonious whole because of the Great Spirit. Because of their connection with nature, animals played an important role in their religions.

When Columbus made his fourth voyage to the new world in 1503 he brought with him Spanish friars and priests who settled in Mexico and in the southwestern and western parts of North America. The first elementary school on the American continent was founded in 1523 in Texcoco, now Mexico City, by Pedro de Gante, a Franciscan priest. A similar school was founded in 1525 in what is now San Francisco. The monks and priests learned native languages and taught Native American children reading, writing, arithmetic, singing, and catechism. Later they added agriculture, trades, and crafts. Around the same time, other mission schools were started in Florida and Georgia. These schools were actively maintained by Spanish friars until 1873.

However, by the late nineteenth century, there was little formal education of Native Americans. Most of the tribes not found near Spanish settlements educated their own children at home in such things as survival skills (hunting, gathering, homemaking), linguistic skills, folktales and religious traditions, and the values of cooperation and loyalty to family and tribe. Praise and rewards were given for the children's accomplishments rather than punishment for their wrongdoings. Frequently, these values conflicted with the nineteenth-century European American value of rugged individualism. As European settlers moved west, the U.S. government made treaties with various tribes; included in many of these treaties were provisions for school and health services. In 1819, the Indian Civilization Act appropriated $10,000 to missionary societies to operate Indian schools. Its goal was to christianize and civilize the Native Americans to the same values as European Americans. Contractual agreements with these missionary societies lasted until 1873.

Following the Civil War, the increased westward movement of European Americans forced the federal government to create more and more reservations, land designated for Indian settlements. Often the movement of Native Americans to these reservations was forced and cruel. Some reservation schools were run by missionaries, mainly for sectarian purposes; others were run by the Bureau of Indian Affairs, a federal agency, with white teachers.

Boarding schools, operated by the Bureau of Indian Affairs, existed off the reservations and away from the custom and culture of families and tribes. Native American students were forced to speak English, sometimes under the threat of corporal punishment. They were not permitted to practice their native religions and were often boarded with white families during school holidays. Carlisle Indian School in Pennsylvania was founded by Richard Henry Pratt in 1879. It followed the typical curriculum of reading, writing arithmetic, and religion, but little was done to integrate Native American language or culture into the curriculum. However, by the time the school closed in 1918, more emphasis was being placed on such practical skills as farming and homemaking. According to Smith and Smith, "The history of schooling of Native Americans is a sorry tale. Cultural ignorance and arrogance, political machinations and greed skewed good intentions" (1994, 329).

One bright light in the education of Native Americans in the late nineteenth century was Sarah Winnemucca, a member of the Paiute tribe of Nevada. After working in the home of an army officer, she traveled east in 1875 and met Elizabeth Palmer Peabody, a pioneer in kindergarten education, under whom she studied and worked as a teacher's aide. In 1886, Winnemucca returned to Nevada and founded a school for Paiute children where she taught academics as well as Paiute culture and language. Unfortunately, she could only raise the money to operate the school for two years.

## THE EDUCATION OF HISPANIC AMERICANS

In the early sixteenth century, Spaniards founded colonies in what is now Florida, Louisiana, Texas, New Mexico, Arizona, California, Oklahoma, Nebraska, and Kansas where they also established missionary schools for the Native Americans and their own Spanish-speaking children. The children were taught together in many of the schools where Spanish language, culture, and values were emphasized.

During the common school movement of the 1830s, poorly trained white teachers taught a growing number of Puerto Rican and Mexican immigrant children both in Spanish and English, particularly following the Mexican-American War in the late 1840s. Today, Hispanic Americans make up the fastest growing minority group in the United States. These Spanish-speaking Americans share a past influenced by the Spanish language, Roman Catholicism, and Spanish culture. However, an increasing number of Cuban and Puerto Rican immigrants are black and many Mexican Americans are mestizos with Spanish and Indian blood.

## THE EDUCATION OF ASIAN AMERICANS

Although most Asian Americans came to the United States following World War II, Chinese Americans started immigrating in the mid-nineteenth century. Four hundred and fifty lived in the United States in 1850 according to the census. Most of these young married men settled in California seeking a better life. By 1860, there were 34,933 Chinese immigrants in the United States and by 1880 there were 105,465, according to the census. Most of the Chinese immigrants lived in

Richard Henry Pratt founded Carlisle Indian School (1879)

Sarah Winnemucca founded a school for Paiute children (1875)

Asian immigrants
face limited
educational
opportunities
(1890–1920)

separate cities called Chinatown, but many later moved to other parts of these cities. Their children were educated either in the home or in separate schools. In 1886, Japan legalized emigration, and Japanese immigrants began coming to the United States. In 1890, there were 2,039 Japanese in west coast cities. By 1924, there were over 200,000 Japanese Americans. Like the Chinese, they initially lived in separate settlements where educational opportunities were limited due to racial discrimination, prejudice, and hostility (Banks 1991). It was not until after World War II that Chinese and Japanese American immigrants attended and excelled in U.S. public schools.

By the end of the nineteenth century, the themes of education in the United States were firmly established. Popularization, the concept of schooling for all, was introduced by the New England colonists and developed by those who began the common school movement. The politicization of the schools to solve the problems of society through education rather than through politics was a predominant concern of the mid- to late nineteenth century as the nation attempted to deal with the new industrialization and waves of immigrants. Multitudinousness, the establishment of a variety of educational approaches to meet the needs of a diverse society, was begun in the urban and multiethnic Middle Atlantic colonies and continued as politicians, activists, and educators of the nineteenth century recognized that vast social, economic, and cultural differences required different kinds of schooling if all citizens were to participate in democracy. It was not, however, until the twentieth century that all three themes became integrated in U.S. education. We will examine this unique synergy in chapter 5.

---

**4-3**

**POINTS TO REMEMBER**

• Benjamin Franklin developed the first English language academy for young men in Philadelphia. Thomas Jefferson proposed public education for all males through elementary school and for the ablest students through secondary school. Noah Webster's speller and dictionary were widely circulated, and he developed a system of phonics for American English.

• Horace Mann advocated a system of free education for all students. Henry Barnard edited two journals that further developed the concept of the common school.

• The common school movement provided the framework for publicly supported education for all children.

• After the Civil War schools in the Northeast and Midwest educated children of immigrants in the English language and the manners, customs, and values of the U.S. society. The *Seven Cardinal Principles* broadened the purpose of schooling to include vocational and civic education. The progressive movement encouraged student involvement in their own learning.

• Schools in the northern United States following the Civil War helped integrate immigrants into U.S. society, prepare them for civic duty, and train them for work in industry. The thrust of education during this period was to meet society's democratic needs. African American educators, such as Frederick Douglass and Mary McLeod Bethune, developed schools for blacks in the South.

• During the colonial period, women and blacks were frequently excluded, particularly from secondary schools and universities. The predominant view was that they, and women too, were less able to learn than white males.

• Early nineteenth-century schools for Native Americans forced them to learn the dominant culture rather than their own. In the past few decades schools for Native Americans emphasized both the usual academic subjects as well as native traditions and culture.

• Hispanic Americans were usually taught in separate districts or separate classes. This group is the fastest growing minority group in the United States.

• Most Asian Americans came to the United States following World War II and lived in separate sections of the city, called Chinatown.

## For Thought/Discussion

1. Which aspects of the concept of naturalism are expressed in the educational theory of progressivism?
2. What part did the church play in popularizing education?
3. What role did African slaves play in the politicization of education?
4. How did the report *Seven Cardinal Principles* affect the development of diversity of education?
5. Do you believe that education is primarily a tool for developing a democratic society or a means of accumulating individual knowledge? Explain.

## For Further Reading/Reference

Douglass, F. 1855. *My bondage and my freedom.* New York: Miller, Orton, and Mulligan. Douglass describes the Southern slave community of the mid- to late 1800s with particular attention to slave oppression, his education, and the education of other slaves.

Downs, R. B. 1974. *Horace Mann: Champion of public schools.* New York: Twayne Publishers. This well-documented biography describes Mann's personal life and his mission to establish common schools. The book catalogs his work with legislators and educators in the 1830s and 1840s.

Kaufman, P. W. 1984. *Women teachers on the frontier.* New Haven, CT: Yale University Press. This account describes the work of women teachers in many one-room schools on the western frontier of the late 1800s.

Schlesinger, A. M. 1981. *The birth of a nation: A portrait of the American people on the eve of independence.* Boston, MA: Houghton Mifflin. This work portrays the everyday concerns of Americans during the mid- to late eighteenth century including the role of the family, education of youth, education of girls and blacks, and the social conscience of that period.

Winslow, A. G. 1974. *Diary of Anna Green Winslow: A Boston school girl of 1771,* ed. A. M. Earle. Williamstown, MA: Corner House. This book provides a description of the education and schooling of Anna Green Winslow, who lived in the late eighteenth century.

**William Canty**
*"Don't you recognize us, Bob? We're Dick and Jane!"*

After studying this chapter, you should be able to:

- Define popularization, multitudinous-ness, and politicization of U.S. education in the twentieth century.
- Explain how World War I affected U.S. schools.
- Discuss the impact of the Great Depression on U.S. schools.
- Explain how World War II affected U.S. schools.
- Discuss the impact on U.S. schools of the Soviet Union's launching of Sputnik.
- Explain how the civil rights period affected U.S. schools.
- Discuss the influence of *Brown v. Board of Education of Topeka* on the public schools.

- Define equal educational opportunities after integration.
- Discuss the reasons for the implementation of Head Start.
- Describe the Elementary and Secondary Education Act (1965).
- Discuss changes in schooling for multicultural, bilingual, and female students.
- Discuss changes in schooling for those with disabilities following P.L. 94–142.
- Compare equal educational opportunities in the 1970s, 1980s, and 1990s.
- Contrast the reform movement of the 1980s to the reform movements and legislative acts of the 1990s.

# Chapter 5

# TWENTIETH-CENTURY U.S. EDUCATION: EQUALIZATION OR EXCELLENCE

*The education of women is one of the many changes that occurred during the twentieth century. In the first excerpt, Maryjane Meaker, a well-known author of books for young adults who writes under the pen name M. E. Kerr, tells of her experience at a junior college in the mid-1940s. In the second, Faith O'Brien writes to her daughter, who is about to begin college in 1990.*

Vermont Junior College had decided to take a chance on me. That was the way the dean put it. She was a woman named Ruth Kingsley, whose personality was as far removed from Ape's as Athene's is from Hecate's.

"I know my grades weren't very good," I told Dean Kingsley.

"Your grades were the least of it," she answered. "Listen to this evaluation of you from your boarding school. 'If you tell her to walk, she'll run. If you tell her to run, she'll walk. If you ask her to whistle, she'll sing; to sing, she'll whistle. She delights in stirring up the student body against any/all authority, and at best, her personality might be described as refractory.' " The dean put down my file and said, "You didn't come highly recommended."

"Refractory?" I said.

"Hard to manage," she said.

"How come I got in here?"

"Part of it was my curiosity. Part of it was my interest in psychology. I teach psychology. Some of it was your stated interest in being a writer. I wanted to be a writer once, myself."

"My first choice was the University of Missouri, for journalism," I said.

"You could still make it," she said. "And meanwhile, we're very interested in starting a school newspaper. How would you like to work on the project?"

I knew I was going to like Vermont Junior College. That very first day, down in the basement "smoker," I puffed on cigarettes with my new classmates and heard an old, familiar song:

*We are the girls from V.J.C., you see,*
*There's not a man in this damn nunnery,*
*And every night at eight they lock the door . . .*

I felt like someone who'd been let out of prison. I was finally going to school again with Yankees who talked like me, knew what deep snow was, and owned skis, skates, and toboggans. (Winters you could take skiing for gym, go off on skis before breakfast with the class, and come in to a feast of pancakes with real Vermont maple syrup poured over them.)

From: Kerr, 1983, pp. 147–150, 154–155

**7** *his letter was written to Margaret O'Brien by her mother, Faith, on September 5, 1990, from Asheville, North Carolina. It expresses a parent's hope that education will open new doors and provide intellectual stimulation and growth for her daughter. When compared to Jefferson's letter to his daughter Martha, at the beginning of chapter 4, and with the excerpt above, this letter provides an excellent example of how, through history, people have changed their attitudes toward education for women.*

Dear Molly,

Tomorrow the doors of the world begin to open to you. Your father and I have only one request as you begin your college years: Don't close the doors.

You will meet people who are very different from your family and friends. They will look different, have different values, express different ideas, talk differently. . . . Although we do not suggest that you embrace either the person or her ideas, we want you to listen and to think. What does she believe? Where does he come from? How has her life been different from yours? What does he know that you do not know? Listen and learn, Molly.

It's funny how I can remember things from my first day of college. Sometime during that day President Graham spoke to us and our parents. He said something like, "This great and grand college and her esteemed faculty have one responsibility to you and that is to force you to change your minds; to question your values." At the time I wondered what he meant. But, when he asked us at our senior banquet if they, the faculty and the administration, had forced us to rethink our values and if we had changed our minds, we all agreed that they had and that we had. We were never the same people we had been on that warm September afternoon on the first day of college. We had new knowledge, new ideas, and new skills with which to confront the world.

Your father and I believe we have provided for you a foundation on which to build your own life. We know that the decisions you make will be built on that foundation. We will not always agree with your decisions. But, if each opens a new door, we will support your right to make it.

Molly, you can learn, grow, and change knowing that you have our love and respect. We will always love you. And, more importantly, as you become the person only you can be, you will come to love and respect yourself.

We look forward to watching you open doors, and we pledge to help you in any way we can. We will try to remember to give you the opportunity to ask for our help.

Please allow us our tears as we leave you to your new life, friends, and experiences. We will miss the daily opportunity to share them with you. But, we know you will call and write. We will look forward to discussing with you what you are feeling, experiencing, and learning. We are anxious to get to know you as a friend as well as a daughter.

With love and respect,

Mom

P.S. Sometimes it's better to let a door slam on your toe than to lock it behind you.

Daddy

---

**7**o people of the eighteenth and nineteenth centuries, education was the fire that burned under the melting pot to create a unified democratic nation. It is clear from the opening excerpts that education is still, in the twentieth century, a great force for growth, change, and opportunity.

## The Twentieth Century's Educational Themes

There are no easy solutions to the problems created by the growth of democracy and the concept of equal education for all. As society changes, the system of education must find ways of dealing with a complex and burgeoning student population. How one interprets the historical developments of education, and the suggested proposals for reform, influences what changes will ultimately be implemented. Three such interpretations follow.

### LAWRENCE CREMIN

Lawrence A. Cremin's interpretation of U.S. educational history focuses on the development of democratic trends that combined to make American education unique. He determined that by the twentieth century, popularization, "the tendency to make education widely available in forms that are increasingly accessible to diverse peoples," was close to complete. However, one overriding question was yet to be answered. If the schools or educational programs provided

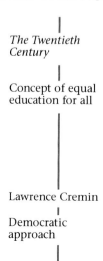

*The Twentieth Century*

Concept of equal education for all

Lawrence Cremin

Democratic approach

to these diverse students are unequal, is quality education accessible to all? The debate over this question continues today.

Attempts to answer this question have also led to concerns about "the proliferation and multiplication of [educational] institutions to provide that wide availability and that increasing accessibility" (1990, vii–viii), what Cremin called multitudinousness. In the twentieth century it became increasingly clear that children's educational needs differ and that not all of them will benefit equally from the same curriculum. Therefore, a growing variety of educational opportunities was offered to the diverse U.S. school population. The schools of today continue this trend but not without inconsistencies and controversies around the country.

Concerns about the equality of educational opportunity and the diversity of opportunity to meet the needs of different populations have increased the politicization of American schools. Cremin defines politicization as "the effort to solve certain social problems indirectly through education instead of directly through politics" (1990, viii). Increasingly, twentieth-century schools were expected to solve many social problems. And, when they were unable to, they were repeatedly criticized. Cremin argued that in order to understand U.S. public education in the twentieth century we must have "a new, more inclusive history [of education, allowing] for cross-fertilization between the history of education and other subfields of American history, for example, the history of science and the history of communication. [The history of U.S. education] should draw from the social sciences for its methods [and] should include comparative studies, contrasting the role of education in the United States with the role of education in other countries, and . . . should allow educational historians to become 'bolder' in their appraisals of the impact on American culture" (Lagemann and Graham, unpublished manuscript, 1994, 8).

## JOEL SPRING–A REVISIONIST VIEW

Of course, there are interpretations of education in the twentieth century other than Cremin's democratic approach. The work of neo-Marxist revisionist historian Joel Spring is most notable. In two important books, *The American School: 1642-1985* (1986) and *Education and the Rise of the Corporate State* (1972), Spring relates the history of nineteenth- and twentieth-century U.S. education to the capitalistic system. According to Spring, schools will not provide equal opportunities to all until the capitalistic system is changed. Spring believes that the purpose of the U.S. school system is what Ivan Illich calls in the foreword to Spring's 1972 book "social control for a corporate state, and for an economy which has as its goal the efficient production and the disciplined consumption of growing amounts of goods and services" (p. x). According to Spring, it was the progressive educators of the early twentieth century (see chapter 4, pp. 159–160) who promoted the rhetoric of schools as a cure for social and economic problems. However, these progressivists, says Spring, were "labor leaders, corporation heads, financiers, politicians, political philosophers, and educators" (1972, xii). They saw the "good society" as "a highly organized and smoothly working corporate structure" (p. xi). This image of society, affirms Spring, shaped and formed the concept of twentieth-century public education.

*Schools expected to solve social problems*

*Joel Spring*

*Neo-Marxist revisionist approach*

*Schools expected to solve economic problems*

## MICHAEL KATZ

Some of Spring's work is based on the revisionist work of historian Michael Katz in *The Irony of Early School Reform* (1968). He claimed that historians had helped to perpetuate a "noble story" of an enlightened working class led by idealistic humanitarian intellectuals "wresting free public education from . . . selfish, wealthy elite and from the bigoted proponents of orthodox religions" (1968, 1), and he asserted that this interpretation was false. Katz arrived at this conclusion by examining the 1860 conflict of Beverly, Massachusetts, voters involving the establishment of a high school. He found that working-class groups voted against it while the well-to-do of the community worked actively for it. He also found that those who lived outside the town opposed a high school serving the entire district. He used his analysis of this 1860 decision to produce a new examination of the common school reforms (see chapter 4) and claimed that the impetus for the common school movement had to do with social and economic conditions of the time: the rise of factories, increase in immigration, and growth of cities. According to Katz, upper-class educational reformers benefited from the development of a common school system that was designed to train workers for factories and inculcate immigrants with the values of the ruling elite. Thus, Katz claimed that schools in the late nineteenth century were factory-like by design.

The interpretations of U.S. educational history by Cremin, Spring, and Katz serve as a background for the numerous studies and proposals for educational reform that have characterized much of the twentieth century. This chapter will examine the major influences on education in the twentieth century and some of the major suggestions for reform.

Michael Katz

Schools trained workers in factory-like conditions

## Politicization of Schools in the Early Twentieth Century

There is no doubt that the schools of the late nineteenth century provided the impetus for social change. During that period educators and politicians believed that education could have a positive impact on society. From this belief came social programs such as Hull House (see chapter 4, p. 159), the progressive education movement (see chapter 4, pp. 159–160), and the NEA's seven cardinal principles (see chapter 4, p. 158).

The belief in the school as a tool for social change continued in the early twentieth century. But the needs of society were changing. Rather than social change, the schools were needed for social recovery both from World War I (1914–1918) and the Great Depression.

Schools as agents for social recovery from World War I and the Great Depression

## CURRICULUM OF THE POST–WORLD WAR I PERIOD

In order to facilitate these social goals, educators made many changes in the high school curriculum early in the twentieth century. In *An Introduction to the Study of Education* (1925), education historian Elwood P. Cubberley points out that it was crowded with new courses designed to prepare students for college and/or for jobs. As an increasingly diverse population attended both elementary and high schools for the first time in the history of U.S. education, the curriculum adapted its aims and purposes to the needs of this population.

Emphasis was placed on the development of citizenship, guidance services, school health services, and vocational education. During this period, nurses and teachers visited the homes of pupils experiencing problems in school. In addition to curricular changes, extracurricular opportunities were developed and parents became more involved in the schools through organizations such as the Parent-Teacher Association.

## Providing Educational Institutions for a Growing Population

**1930–1940**

**Great Depression caused economic cutbacks and increased school enrollments**

The Great Depression of the 1930s was very hard on the public school system. Many schools, particularly in rural areas, were closed. Those that remained open did so with fewer teachers, larger classes, decreased support staff, limited curriculums, and outdated materials. While many young males were forced to leave school and get jobs to help support their families, school enrollment during the Great Depression generally increased as adolescents who could not find jobs entered the schools in greater numbers. (From 1929 to 1934, the number of secondary school students grew from 3,911,000 to 5,669,000. The number of high school graduates per one hundred jumped from 26.2 to 39.2.)

Schools were severely handicapped by economic conditions forcing cutbacks in every area. (During the depression, the gross national product dropped by almost half, from $103.1 billion to $55.6 billion in the three years from 1929 to 1932. Personal income fell from $85.9 billion to $47.0 billion; unemployment increased from 3.2 percent to 24.9 percent. Average teachers' salaries fell from $1,420 to $1,227, a decrease of 13.6 percent.) Because the reform of society was an impossible task for a school system barely able to continue operation itself, progressivism, the concept that schools could reform society through a child-centered, experiential approach that focused on the needs of the individual child and the society, was severely criticized.

**George Counts (1932)**

**Challenged schools to meet societal needs**

George Counts, professor and researcher on educational reform, in *Dare the School Build a New Social Order?* (1932), for example, agreed with progressive educators that the schools should take on the task of social reconstruction. However, he contended that only the liberal-minded, upper middle-class parents sent their children to progressive schools and that if education was to become genuinely progressive, that is, have a commitment to democratic and egalitarian ideals, it had to free itself from this class bias, take on a more realistic view of every social issue, and establish a total relationship with the community. He challenged the schools to put "real content" into such concepts as democracy, citizenship, and ethical character (1932, 3–7, 9–10).

**Robert Hutchins (1936)**

**Education based in the classic disciplines**

On the other hand, Robert Hutchins, president of University of Chicago from 1929 to 1951, in *No Friendly Voice* (1936) and *Higher Learning in America* (1936) criticized the schools for putting too much emphasis on preparation for the future. He proposed general schooling for all based on the classic disciplines of grammar, rhetoric, logic, mathematics, and the great books of the Western world. He took issue with the progressive educator's contention that education must be adapted to the needs of society at a particular time.

## CURRICULUM MOVES TOWARD MULTITUDINOUSNESS

World War I and the Great Depression had convinced the public of the need for more practical courses in the schools to prepare students for jobs. In 1917 the Smith-Hughes Vocational Education Act (P.L. 64–347) provided funding for states to create agricultural and vocational education programs. These courses helped retain many students who would have previously found the college-bound curriculum of the high schools impractical for their career needs.

Ironically, during the Great Depression of the 1930s, more students, particularly young women, remained in school than ever before because jobs were unavailable. However, most of these students needed to obtain jobs upon graduation. Consequently, the secondary curriculum, although still content oriented and primarily designed for college-bound students, shifted its emphasis away from the strictly intellectual to the practical. This was the first actual move of the schools toward multitudinousness, an attempt to develop school programs that were appropriate for various segments of society.

The schools still hadn't established accessibility for all students, however. There was a great deal of difference in the educational opportunities available to poor and rich. High school students of the 1930s had limited diversification of secondary curriculums, which allowed either for occupational training or for college preparation. Lower socioeconomic students spent less time in school, participated in fewer extracurricular activities, and took fewer college preparatory courses. According to a series of studies by sociologists W. Lloyd Warner, Robert J. Havighurst, and Martin B. Loeb, published in *Who Shall Be Educated?* (1944), "The lower class is almost immediately brushed off into a bin labeled 'nonreaders,' 'first grade repeaters,' or 'opportunity class,' where they stay for eight years and then are released through a chute to the outside world to become 'hewers of wood and drawers of water' " (p. 38). The issue of accessibility of education for rich and poor alike continues to be a problem although not in the same way. Today, the problem involves accessibility to educational opportunities. Are all educational opportunities equally available to rich and poor students? Many educators and psychologists say "no." For example, programs for gifted and talented students typically require high IQ test scores for admission. Poor children and minority students are not likely to score well on intelligence tests and, therefore, gifted and talented programs are largely populated with middle- and upper-class white children. Many educators and psychologists, such as Howard Gardner, believe these tests are culturally biased and do not take into account new studies of multiple intelligences that suggest that verbal and analytical intelligence, measured by IQ tests, are only two forms of intelligence; others include spatial intelligence, interpersonal intelligence, and musical intelligence not measured by IQ tests (see chapter 10, pp. 394–395).

***Post–World War I School Populations***    With few exceptions, students who went to high school prior to and immediately following World War I had been carefully selected by their elementary school teachers, who had firm standards of achievement. Admission to U.S. high schools was selective and retention depended on the students' scholastic records.

After World War I this situation began to change. The child labor laws, which removed children from the work force, and compulsory attendance laws, which required them to attend school, were enforced for the first time, increasing

Smith-Hughes Vocational Education Act (1917)

Issue of accessibility of education for both rich and poor

Growth of school populations

Child labor laws of the early twentieth century brought more children into the public schools who previously would have worked in the factories. Not only greater numbers, but greater heterogeneity caused the schools to provide a diverse curriculum.

elementary school enrollment. This new heterogeneous school population forced the schools toward a more diverse curriculum.

## Education of the Post–World War II Period

World War II paved the road to economic recovery after the depression; it instilled a belief in the technological superiority of the United States and it brought newfound economic prosperity to the population as industry retooled after the war.

### NEW SCIENTIFIC IMPETUS

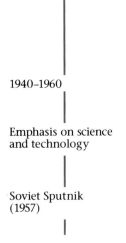

1940–1960

Emphasis on science and technology

Soviet Sputnik (1957)

The needs of a postwar society magnified the necessity for an educational system that equipped students for scientific research. The gigantic leaps made in scientific knowledge, such as the development of the atomic bomb, led to further discoveries in the fields of mathematics and physics and changed the industrial emphasis of the postwar economy. A greater value was placed on scientific research, and more and more industries needed employees trained in the hard sciences and mathematics.

*Soviet Sputnik*   With the launching of the world's first Earth-orbiting satellite, Sputnik, by the Soviet Union in 1957, the feeling of U.S. scientific superiority vanished almost overnight. Criticism of U.S. schools, especially of the progressive philosophy, gained new momentum. It centered on the fact that inadequate numbers of people were being trained to meet the technological needs of an increasingly specialized industrial nation. A direct result of this realization and a fear that the United States would lose its superiority over the Soviet Union in the cold war was the passage of the National Defense Education Act (NDEA), P.L. 85–864, in 1958. It expanded the federal government's role in education by providing categorical aid to improve instruction in science, mathematics, and foreign languages. The federal funds were to be used to develop new curriculums, improve teacher training, purchase equipment for the target subject areas, and supply fellowships and low-interest loans to needy college students. The act was based on the assumption that the defense of the United States depended upon the population's mastery of modern scientific techniques, scientific principles, and new scientific knowledge, and that more adequate educational opportunities must be provided to talented students.

## CRITICAL COMMISSIONS AND REPORTS

Criticisms of the schools were heard in Senate hearings of the late 1950s. Werner von Braun, a German-educated missile expert, testified in 1958 urging the elimination of such courses as "family life" and "human relations," developed during the early years of the twentieth century to meet the needs of students and society, and adoption of the European system of education which, according to von Braun, emphasized technical and scientific subjects and academic excellence. Lee DuBridge, president of California Institute of Technology, testifying before the same Senate committee, recommended that science and mathematics courses be given federal support.

University academicians were the most powerful critics of the curriculum. Arthur Bestor, a University of Illinois historian and author of *The Restoration of Learning* (1956), was particularly critical of a curriculum that attempted to meet the social needs of students. According to Bestor, it was not the job of the school to meet the needs of its students; that was the responsibility of the home.

Columbia University's historian Richard Hofstadter was an even more verbal critic. In *Anti-Intellectualism in American Life* (1963) he decried the availability of public education to all youth, or popularization of education that had

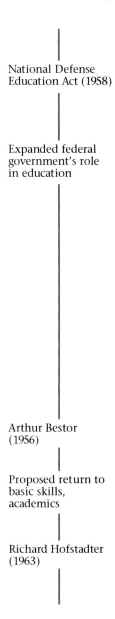

National Defense Education Act (1958)

Expanded federal government's role in education

Arthur Bestor (1956)

Proposed return to basic skills, academics

Richard Hofstadter (1963)

---

**5-1**

**POINTS TO REMEMBER**

- During the twentieth century, U.S. schools were increasingly moving toward popularization. The diverse school population was beginning to require a multitude of offerings. Educators believed that the schools had the ability to affect society through politicization.

- World War I led to a greater need for students to enter the workforce. Thus the curriculum of the high schools became more practical.

- The Great Depression depleted many resources of the public schools. However, since students could not find jobs, the enrollment in schools increased.

- During World War II, industry relied increasingly on science. Consequently, the schools were called upon to improve the teaching of science and mathematics.

- The launching of Sputnik resulted in increased demands on the public schools to train students in mathematics and science.

Development of
the mind should be
the purpose of
secondary education

been the predominant theme throughout most of U.S. education's history. According to Hofstadter, the only aim of secondary education should be development of the mind, not the education of the masses. Hofstadter maintained that intellectuals would be the leaders of the world and that attempting to educate the masses would, of necessity, limit the education of intellectuals.

## Equalizing Educational Opportunity

1950–1970
*Period of Equalizing
Educational
Opportunity*

From the mid-1950s through the early 1970s U.S. public education's major thrust was attempting to equalize educational opportunities for all students no matter gender, race, ethnic group, or disability. The changes in the school population and the developing emphasis in society on equal rights for all citizens led to what Cremin called multitudinousness in the public schools.

### SYNERGY OF EDUCATIONAL THEMES

Although multitudinousness dominates this period of educational history, all the characteristics of education identified by Lawrence Cremin occurred simultaneously for the first time. The schools were increasingly popularized, thereby making education widely available to diverse people. To meet their needs, the schools developed many options, and to bring the disenfranchised minorities into the mainstream of society, they were increasingly politicized, thereby encouraging social change indirectly through education.

### THE CIVIL RIGHTS PERIOD

1955–1968
*Civil Rights Period*

Although the trend toward providing unique opportunities for different students could be seen as early as the NEA's seven cardinal principles of 1918, the beginnings of coeducation in the high schools, and the addition of courses in agriculture and industrial arts following World War I, it was not until the civil rights period, narrowly defined as occurring between 1955 and 1968, that broad-based opportunities for a heterogeneous population became the central theme of public education.

### THE EDUCATION OF MINORITIES: INEQUALITIES

*Plessy v. Ferguson*
(separate but equal
schools)
(1896)

While schools were gradually embracing the democratic ideal of equal education for all citizens, in practice many inequities still existed. In *Plessy v. Ferguson,* 163 U.S. 537 (1896), for example, the Supreme Court ruled in favor of the principle of "separate but equal," implying that students in equal educational facilities were able to attain equal opportunities even if they were separated by race. However, studies of schools from the late nineteenth through the mid-twentieth century show that they were not equal.

In 1945, for example, South Carolina spent three times as much on education for white students as it spent on black students, even though blacks outnumbered whites. Facilities were unequal; educational levels of teachers were unequal; materials were unequal.

The percentage of white students completing four years of high school has always been higher than the percentage of black students, and the difference was particularly great prior to the integration of schools in the 1960s and 1970s. Since the early 1980s the gap has narrowed, but statistics like these make it evident that separate was not equal.

*Funding*   All these inequalities can be attributed, in part, to the amount of money spent educating different groups. In the area of transportation, for example, in 1945 South Carolina spent one-one-hundredth as much to transport blacks as it spent to transport whites, even though the distances from black homes to schools were longer than the distances from white homes to schools. It was not unusual to find that black schools were supplied with discarded textbooks, furniture, and equipment from white schools. If separate meant unequal funding, how could schools be considered equal?

The U.S. Supreme Court recognized inequalities of educational opportunities in the landmark *Brown v. Board of Education of Topeka, Kansas,* 347 U.S. 483 (1954) case, in which it ruled that "separate is not equal." The Court said in its majority opinion: "Separate but equal has no place. . . . Separate educational facilities are inherently unequal and violate the equal protection clause of the Fourteenth Amendment." Perhaps the most vital issue in the decision, according to Chief Justice Earl Warren, was the psychological effect that racial separation had on minority children. It "generates a feeling of inferiority as to their status in the community that may affect their hearts and minds in a way unlikely to be undone." At the time of the *Brown* decision, approximately 40 percent of public school students were enrolled in segregated systems.

*Viewpoint*   Topeka Comes Full Circle

Forty years after the Supreme Court of the United States handed down its landmark ruling on *Brown v. Board of Education,* Topeka Unified School District 501 is finally taking steps to fully integrate the city's elementary schools.

Few people know it, but Topeka didn't feel the effects of the *Brown* ruling with the same immediacy as other school districts around the country. In the fall of 1955 the school district simply started closing its four all-black elementary schools (junior high and high schools were already integrated) and allowed all children to attend neighborhood schools.

Over the next few years, federal urban renewal and low-income-housing dollars flowed into Topeka. City fathers put most of the housing projects on the east side of the city; single-family dwellings grew on the west side. By 1979, east-side schools were serving mostly poor children and had much higher percentages of minority students than those on the west side.

Linda Brown, daughter of Oliver Brown, one of the suit's original plaintiffs, was by that time a mother herself. Claiming that segregation still existed, she was a co-plaintiff in the 1979 resurrected version of the original case. Topeka attorney Richard Jones and ACLU attorney Chris Hansen charged the school district with taking the lazy route to correcting the problem. For its part, the

*Inequitable funding for different groups*

*Brown v. Board of Education of Topeka* (began integration of schools) (1954)

*Brown v. Board of Education of Topeka* (forty years later)

*Cross-Cultural Perspective*

## Apartheid's Legacy to Black Children

[In 1990] few South Africans could have imagined the milestone passed on 17 June 1991. Parliament scrapped the law classifying South Africans by race from birth and thus removed the "final pillar" of statutory apartheid. . . .

Particularly daunting will be school reform. Segregated and unequal education, the main instrument for sorting children into their color-coded niches in society, is deeply embedded in South Africa's social fabric. Indeed, the statutory pillars of apartheid in education remain ironically intact. . . .

One major concern is the character of the curriculum, which is driven by South Africa's system of national exams. To graduate from high school, black students must pass tough, externally administered "matric exams," demonstrating, among other things, that they are bilingual and can answer such questions as the following:

In the last act of the play [Shakespeare's *Antony and Cleopatra*] Cleopatra is determined to die rather than to be carried to Rome as Caesar's captive. Caesar is determined to prevent her suicide and therefore sends Proculeius and Dolabella to her before visiting her himself. Describe the three visits.

Curiously, for all the problems with the exams, black South African children are held to higher graduation standards than are American children in many of our best school systems.

Partly because of test questions like the one above, the curriculum has come under strong attack for being excessively academic and Eurocentric, with too little attention paid to African history or to practical skills that might help youngsters get jobs. . . .

A second problem is that the teachers who were hired to implement the limited goals of Bantu education have only the most meager qualifications. In 1991 about half of the teachers in black primary schools lacked even high school diplomas. . . . While most secondary school teachers are high school graduates, less than 20% have university diplomas. . . .

A third set of problems relates to teaching practice. Many teachers, like many South African families (white and black alike), are highly authoritarian. Teachers are expected to have all the answers, with the students learning by rote the material covered in textbooks and syllabi. . . . There is little experience with group work or with peer teaching. There is no tradition of independent, critical thinking or of asking questions and exploring ideas. Poorly prepared teachers teach as they were taught, and coverage and recall outrank independent thinking. . . .

district claimed that the crux of the original *Brown* case involved Linda Brown's right to attend Sumner Elementary, the neighborhood school four blocks from her home, which was all-white at the time; Topeka's segregated system had forced her to attend all-black Monroe Elementary, more than 20 blocks away. In the second suit the school district further claimed it wasn't responsible for housing patterns that had developed subsequent to the 1954 ruling.

In 1987, U.S. district judge Richard Rogers ruled in favor of the school system, saying "there is no illegal, intentional, systematic or residual separation of races" in Topeka schools. The case then went to the U.S. 10th Circuit Court of Appeals in Denver, which reversed the ruling. In 1990, the school district appealed to the Supreme Court.

It took two years for the Court to respond. During that time, however, it issued two other major desegregation rulings: One supported a move by Oklahoma City to stop busing grade-school children; the other held that De Kalb County, Georgia, wasn't responsible for segregated housing patterns and did not have to implement forced desegregation methods.

One sign of collapse is the total contempt among antigovernment activists for the schools' management structure—a tangled bureaucratic maze that would warm the heart of Rube Goldberg. Depending on who is counting, there are at least 15 major departments of education, each led by its own minister. Eleven control the schooling of blacks: a separate department for each of the 10 homelands (created for the relocation of blacks) and one—the notorious Department of Education and Training (DET)—for blacks in the so-called white areas (i.e., in the 87% of South Africa that lies outside the homelands). In addition, there are separate operating departments for Asian, coloured, and white schooling, as well as a 15th "umbrella" department that coordinates funds and policy. . . .

This centralized structure is racist and unequal by design. . . .

A second sign of collapse is the breakdown of order and authority in the schools, coupled with the politicization of students. Since the Soweto riots of 1976, little sustained schooling has taken place. Black school life has been punctuated by waves of boycotts, school takeovers, and vandalism, as well as by persistent police harassment, detention, and killings. . . .

A third sign of collapse is the breakdown of professional conduct in many black schools. Indeed, in a stinging indictment of teaching in a Soweto high school, Elizabeth de Villiers [in her book, *Walking the Tightrope*] depicts her colleagues—teachers and administrators alike—as self-serving loafers who care little about schooling or children. . . .

De Villiers overlooks systemic reasons for what she encountered and ignores educators who are doing good work. Nonetheless, she describes a lack of professionalism that is widespread. . . .

A final sign of collapse is reflected in black student achievement. Of the 750,000 black students who left formal schooling in 1989, an alarming 26% dropped out of the *first grade,* while only 12% graduated from high school.

What's more, of the small number of blacks who do remain in school through high school—about one in four who started 12 years earlier—only 41% passed the national examinations in 1989, with less than 10% receiving grades high enough to enter the university. . . .

. . . One reason for hope—for both the country and its schooling—is South Africa's economy, which is the wealthiest and most sophisticated in southern Africa. . . .

A second reason for cautious optimism is that there are the signs of real change among the powerful—and still dominant—white minority. At the top, many white government leaders seem determined to share political power with the black majority and to make a new government work. . . .

A third reason for cautious optimism is the remarkable—and unheralded—track record of ordinary black South Africans in bringing apartheid to an end. . . .

From: Murphy, 1992. Jerome T. Murphy is a professor of education and dean of the Graduate School of Education, Harvard University, Cambridge, Massachusetts. He is also a member of the *Kappan* Board of Editorial Consultants.

The Court then kicked the *Brown* ruling back to the 10th Circuit, telling the judges to review their first decision in light of the De Kalb County and Oklahoma City rulings.

It didn't take long for the 10th Circuit to confirm its original finding on the grounds that Topeka, unlike De Kalb County and Oklahoma City, had not implemented a formal desegregation plan. The Topeka school district made one last appeal to the Supreme Court, which in June of last year again refused to review the case.

This meant that Topeka must finally implement some sort of desegregation plan.

Both sides are preparing their proposals for approval by the courts. Two strong options involve the redrawing of school boundaries—a plan that would go into effect this fall—and school consolidation—which would take three to five years. The district could also set up magnet schools, expand its current transfer policy, or start busing, though neither side thinks the latter is likely.

From: Kristen L. Hays, 1994. The author is the education reporter for *The Topeka Capital-Journal.*

*Academic Opportunity*    After the *Brown* decision, the problem became how to enforce integration. On May 31, 1955, the Supreme Court ruled in a second *Brown* decision that the implementation of desegregation of these schools was to be left to local school authorities, subject to the supervision of federal district judges. This ushered in a period of unrest and confusion, with many local authorities and district judges opposed to the rulings of the Court and unwilling to enforce them. Those students who attended the newly integrated schools frequently found that even they did not necessarily ensure equal educational opportunity. Frequently, minority students were placed in tracks with primarily other minority students or were misclassified and placed in vocational tracks rather than in special education or vice versa. **Tracking**, or ability grouping, which separates students by academic ability, often in early elementary school, often limits equal access to knowledge.

James Coleman
(1966)

In 1966 James Coleman conducted a study of schools ordered by the U.S. Congress to determine what recommendations could be made for improving minority education. The study consisted of 645,000 students in grades 1, 3, 6, 9, and 12 in 4,000 schools from five geographic regions. He found that in 1965, 65 percent of all black students in grade 1 attended schools that were 90–100 percent black, and 66 percent in grade 12 attended schools that were 50 percent black. Almost 80 percent of all white students in grades 1–12 attended schools that were 90–100 percent white. He found that blacks in the rural South and whites in the urban Northeast began school much further apart intellectually than blacks and whites in the urban Northeast. Not only did the gap not change during the school years, but in many instances, it widened.

Report on equality
of educational
opportunity

After studying the test results, Coleman concluded that the foremost contributing factor to this eventual gap, and to initial student achievement, was the educational and social background of their families. The second most important factor was the educational and social background of the other children in their school. These two factors were greater contributors to achievement, according to Coleman, than the school, facilities, curriculum, or teachers. He declared that to overcome the disadvantages of a poorer educational and social background, schools must be integrated.

*Hobson v. Hansen*
(found students in
low tracks received
inferior education)
(1967)

*De Facto Segregation*    Many researchers contended that educational opportunities were at least as unequal as they had been before segregation. In its 1967 and 1969 decisions, *Hobson v. Hansen* (269 F. Supp. 401 CDDC, 1967) and *Smuck v. Hobson* (408 F.2d 175 CDC Cir., 1969) and its reconsideration of *Hobson v. Hansen* (327 F. Supp. 844 CDDC, 1971) in 1971, the U.S. Supreme Court found that the Washington, D.C., schools used tracking as a way to ensure **de facto segregation**. This was a subtle though legal means of ensuring that segregation was continued in a school or a district. The Court found, for example, that minority students were usually placed in a low ability track as early as kindergarten, and few moved from that track by high school graduation, if they graduated at all. The judges found that the education offered to students in the low track was inferior to that offered to students in average and upper tracks and it did not push them to higher levels of achievement. As a matter of fact, students in the lower track received little stimulation or curricular enrichment.

*Smuck v. Hansen*
(tracking detri-
mental for those
in low track)
(1969)

## Legislation to Promote Equalization

Despite the failure of the schools to provide a completely equal education for all children, the attitude of Americans toward minorities had begun to change in the late 1950s and early 1960s. It was primarily through a series of legislative acts that some changes were instituted in the educational system.

### ECONOMIC OPPORTUNITY ACT

As part of President Lyndon B. Johnson's War on Poverty, Congress passed the Economic Opportunity Act (EOA) (P.L. 88–452) in 1964. It was designed to help bridge the gap between poverty and prosperity by giving everyone the opportunity for education and training for work, with the chance to live in decency and dignity. This antipoverty bill authorized the creation of the Job Corps, whereby men and women, ages sixteen through twenty-one, could work in conservation camps and training centers. EOA also authorized funding for work-training programs and Volunteers in Service to America (VISTA). Modeled after the Peace Corps, VISTA was designed to provide community service projects for economically poor communities. Also funded under EOA were work-study programs for college students; community action programs to allow state and local governments to develop employment opportunities; adult education grants for those who could not read or write; and loans for low-income families, migrant worker programs, and business incentives to those qualified by age and education to be trained to start their own businesses.

### HEAD START

**Head Start**, which evolved as a result of the Community Action Programs of EOA, was a comprehensive child development program for four- and five-year-olds from low-income homes. It addressed the mental and physical health and intellectual development of children in poverty. Half a million children were initially enrolled in Head Start preschool programs during the summer of 1965, and from 1966 through 1970 an additional 200,000–300,000 were enrolled annually. In 1992, 621,000 children were enrolled in Head Start, which had a total budget of $2.2 billion. The average annual cost per child was $3,415. Congress reauthorized Head Start in 1994, continuing it through 1998 with an annual budget of $3.7 billion (Cohen 1994, 14).

Studies of Head Start children drew conflicting results. A 1968 Westinghouse Learning Corporation and Ohio University study compared differences in intellectual and social-personal development between first, second, and third graders who had and had not participated in Head Start programs. The study concluded that summer-only Head Start programs were ineffective in producing lasting gains in either **affective** (value) or **cognitive** (intellectual) **development** and that year-long programs were ineffective in aiding affective development and only marginally effective in producing cognitive gains. Head Start children were still below national norms on language development tests, but school readiness at grade one did approach the national norms. Another study conducted by Burt

Economic Opportunity Act (1964)

Volunteers in Service to America (VISTA)

Head Start (1965)

*(continued on p. 188)*

# IS HEAD START MAKING A DIFFERENCE IN CHILDREN'S EDUCATION?

## PRO  Children's Defense Fund

With its mounting evidence of solid success, Head Start has earned respect and support from all sectors of American society. . . .

Both the Business Roundtable and the business-led Committee for Economic Development (CED) support Head Start as a program that contributes to the development of a skilled work force that will help American business compete successfully in the global market.

The CED has recommended that the nation expand Head Start until every eligible child has an opportunity to participate. . . .

Today it is clear that Head Start's approach *does* work.

Head Start children start school healthy and ready to learn. Head Start graduates enter kindergarten knowing the basics. They have discovered that learning is fun and have had valuable practice getting along with other children and adults. In addition, they have been immunized against childhood diseases and treated for any medical problems.

The personal stories of Head Start graduates tell of later involvement in school and community activities, high school graduation, college attendance, and successful careers as teachers, physicians, engineers, accountants, and in scores of other jobs important to our country.

Head Start also gives parents opportunities to expand their own horizons, continue their education and training, and become successful breadwinners for their families. Studies show that Head Start parents typically read to their children, take an interest in their children's education, and require their children to help around the house. . . .

Most Head Start programs are excellent, but some programs do need to be strengthened. The research shows that children make great strides in cognitive, social, and emotional development during their time in Head Start. This is because Head Start programs in general provide high quality services.

As might be expected in such an extensive program, however, some local programs need improvement. The weaknesses of some programs can be traced directly to past national policies of increasing the number of children enrolled while ignoring local programs' concerns about quality. President Clinton has proposed to provide the funds and the attention to quality to make sure Head Start offers the best possible programs to all children.

Children receive many long-term benefits from Head Start. These include a sound foundation for good health, reduced risk of being placed in special education classes or being held back during elementary school, and parents who better understand how to help them learn. Moreover, long-term studies of high quality comprehensive early childhood programs like Head Start show that they help children succeed in school and lead productive lives later on. . . .

If our nation expects Head Start to meet the needs of today's families, we have to make sure Head Start has the resources to do it.

Congress must guarantee Head Start enough funding over the next five years to give all eligible children at least two years of Head Start.

From: Children's Defense Fund. *Giving Children a Head Start Now: Leave No Child Behind* (1994) 4, 7, 10 and 14. The Children's Defense Fund, a nonprofit organization, has touted the success of Head Start and supports increased federal funding of the program.

# POSTSCRIPT

The Children's Defense Fund report shows that putting money into early intervention for poor children can save the federal government money that would need to be put into programs to support these children when they become adults and have children of their own. Therefore, Head Start not only makes social sense in terms of helping children and parents, but is also a good investment for federal tax dollars. According to Hood, of the ultra-conser-

# IS HEAD START MAKING A DIFFERENCE IN CHILDREN'S EDUCATION?

## CON  John Hood

Even as public elementary and secondary schools increasingly draw fire from every side, one government-run education program continues to attract substantial political and public support—Head Start. Liberal Democratic and conservative Republican governors tout it. Even disgruntled, frustrated business leaders—willing to back revolutionary change in kindergarten through 12th-grade education—nonetheless sing the praises of Head Start, a Great Society program that spends billions of dollars a year to provide educational, developmental, medical, and nutritional services to poor preschoolers. . . .

However, Head Start's major selling point—early intervention can prevent future dependence and delinquency—rests on several shaky foundations. First, it assumes that policymakers can draw sweeping national conclusions from studies of a few unique and (non-Head Start) preschool programs. Second, it assumes that children's futures are fundamentally malleable and that a brief outside intervention can make an indelible impact on most youngsters' lives despite the continuing influence of both heredity and environment. Third, the Head Start thesis assumes not only that successful early intervention is possible, but that government is an appropriate and effective provider of it.

All three of those propositions are false. Head Start's hucksters, all smiles and promises, have sold the public on a shiny prototype that bears little resemblance to what actually will be provided and, upon closer examination, is an empty shell with nothing under it. Before American policymakers sign anything, they'd better take a good look at what they're getting. . . .

Policymakers should seek a consensus among researchers and academic literature when devising new policies or evaluating old ones. Yet, in the case of Head Start, as in many others, elected officials, bureaucrats, and opinion leaders have mistaken a few special cases for proof of a general thesis that early intervention by the Federal government can keep poor children from growing up into poor adults or criminals. The reason elected officials and others swallow the Head Start hype hook, line, and sinker is that they believe in early intervention as an article of faith, not a proposition to be proven or disproven with facts. . . .

After years of research in developmental psychology, as well as years of experience in running the new social programs of the Great Society, . . . it became apparent that youngsters' minds are so unique, and personal traits so determined by heredity and idiosyncratic relationships between parents and children, that researchers no longer could defend their limitless faith in the efficacy of intervention. . . .

Despite the paucity of evidence that Head Start has a long-term impact on youngsters, there is no doubt that its medical, nutritional, and, to some extent, educational services provide immediate benefits to poor children. It does not follow, however, that a Federal government program is needed to provide those services to preschoolers. A mix of private-sector, nonprofit, church, community group, and extended family providers is a better way to assure such care for children, poor or not.

From: J. Hood. "Caveat Emptor: The Head Start Scam," *USA Today* (May 1993), 76–78. John Hood is the research director of the John Locke Foundation of Raleigh, North Carolina. His article is based on a Cato Institute Policy Analysis.

vative John Locke Foundation, there is no hard data to prove that child care programs improve the later lives of children. Therefore, it cannot be assumed that federal child care programs are good investments. Hood further suggests that the federal government should not be in the business of caring for children. His arguments suggest that the foundation on which Head Start has been built is faulty and that child care, even if there are immediate benefits for poor children, should be a private sector rather than a public sector responsibility.

Conflicting studies on students in Head Start program

S. Barnow for the National Institute of Education of the U.S. Department of Education (1973) revealed different results. This study found that Head Start programs do benefit the cognitive development of minority and white children from mother-headed families.

Studies conducted in the 1970s and 1980s by David Weikart and his colleagues at High/Scope Educational Research Foundation revealed significant results in terms of success of Head Start students in later schooling and ability to obtain and hold employment. However, 1985 and 1990 studies conducted for the U.S. Department of Health and Human Services do not show significant cognitive or socioemotional gains in Head Start children. According to the 1985 study, test scores (cognitive and socioemotional) and health status of those disadvantaged children who attended Head Start did not remain superior to those disadvantaged children who did not attend Head Start. Similarly, a 1990 study concluded that short term gains in intelligence scores and learning skills disappear in Head Start children after two years in school (Hood 1993, 76). In spite of conflicting studies, Head Start continues to gain significant congressional support.

## THE ELEMENTARY AND SECONDARY EDUCATION ACT: 1965

Elementary and Secondary Education Act (ESEA) (1965)

Congress passed the **Elementary and Secondary Education Act (ESEA)** in 1965 (P.L. 89–10). This act and its corollary sections, identified by Titles, may have done more to improve the educational opportunities of all children than any before or since. Long-standing social and economic disadvantages had resulted in great disparities between the educational development of the poor and minorities and those in the middle and upper classes. ESEA helped bring more students into the schools, which in turn created a need for additional facilities to serve the growing student population.

Increased school enrollments

*Title I: Enforcement* Title I of ESEA (1965) mandated a formula by which states and districts, although entitled to a certain amount of money, must make application to receive it. As interpreted by Francis Keppel, then U.S. commissioner of education, it required that schools spend more money for educationally disadvantaged students than for others in order to receive federal funds. Initially, Title I of ESEA received almost 80 percent of the $1.25 billion allocated. Money was provided to local education agencies (school districts) with high concentrations of poverty-level children in the form of basic grants and special incentive grants for programs, projects, equipment, and facilities intended to narrow the intellectual and developmental gap between those who were economically disadvantaged and those who were not. Today, Title I (now Chapter I) is the largest single program of federal aid to education, accounting for approximately 24 percent of the entire Department of Education budget. During 1990–1991, Chapter I provided $5.4 billion to serve approximately 5 million children with special needs. In 1991–1992, there was a 16 percent increase in funding to $6.2 billion (LeTendre 1991, 578), and in 1993–1994, there was an additional 9 percent increase in funding to $6.96 billion (House of Representatives Report 103–275, 1993, 6).

Title I of ESEA (1965)

*Title VII: Race and Ethnic Discrimination* Title VII (1974) of ESEA (P.L. 93–517) gave to the Department of Health, Education, and Welfare (HEW) and to the Office of Civil Rights (OCR) the power to reshape aspects of the educational

Title IX of the Elementary and Second Education Act (ESEA) in 1975 provided athletic opportunities for women equal to those that had been provided for men. Title IX was the first instance of equal opportunity for women being addressed by the federal government. One result is that both boys and girls are given the opportunity to play whatever sport is available at their school.

program such as classification practices, testing procedures, guidance and counseling programs, extracurricular activities, disciplinary procedures, special education, instructional methodology, and the curriculum in general in order to balance the schools racially. The basis for this power was the belief that the federal government has the responsibility to ensure that no student be discriminated against because of race or ethnicity.

*Title IX: Sex Discrimination*   Title IX (1975) of ESEA did for sexual discrimination what Title VII did for racial discrimination. It prohibited schools from discriminating against both women and men in their admission policies and in their classes. Physical education classes had to be integrated by sex but could be segregated for contact sports such as football or wrestling. Schools had to establish women's athletic teams in interscholastic, intercollegiate, or intramural sports, but expenditures for women's and men's sports did not have to be equal. The bill barred discrimination on the basis of sex in all aspects of employment in schools including recruitment; leaves of absence; rates of pay and other compensation; fringe benefits; and tuition, training, and sabbatical assistance. Schools were prohibited from barring pregnant women or placing them in separate classes unless they specifically requested it. Schools were required to treat childbirth, termination of pregnancy, and recovery as any other disability. Pregnant women who left school had to be reinstated to the status they held before they left.

Title VII of ESEA (Racial balance in schools should be maintained) (1974)

Title IX—Women's Education Equity Act (sex discrimination must be eliminated) (1975)

For the first time, federal legislation was directly related to the education of women. Part C of Title IX (P.L. 95–561) is known as the Women's Educational Equity Act, passed in 1978:

> The Congress finds and declares that educational programs in the United States, as presently conducted, are frequently inequitable as such programs relate to women and frequently limit the full participation of all individuals in American society. The Congress finds and declares that excellence in education cannot be achieved without equity for women and girls.

## EDUCATION OF THE DISADVANTAGED

The Civil Rights Act of 1964 was the first federal legislation to extend equal educational opportunity to all Americans. In the early 1970s the definition of disadvantaged was broadened by researchers and bureaucrats to include multicultural, bilingual, and disabled students. This resulted in an increase in the number of students defined as having special needs.

*Funds for Multicultural Students*    The Bilingual Education Act (P.L. 94–247) of 1968 began the trend to expand bilingual programs in schools. This act provided federal funding to those states with large numbers of non-English-speaking students to develop and maintain bilingual programs, provide needed materials and equipment, and develop preservice teacher training. The trend continued in the Supreme Court ruling, *Lau v. Nichols* (483 F.2d, 9th Cir., 1973), which stated that schools must help students who "are certain to find their classroom experiences wholly incomprehensible" because they do not understand English. And in the same year, the Denver school system was required by the court in *Keyes v. School District No. 1, Denver* (414 U.S. 883, 1973) to develop a pilot bilingual-bicultural program.

The capstone to providing equal educational opportunities for bilingual students is Title VI (P.L. 93–380) of the 1974 Civil Rights Act, which called for instruction in two languages for children whose native tongue is not English. School districts that did not meet this provision could not be granted federal aid.

> Where inability to speak and understand the English language excludes national origin minority group children from effective participation in the educational program offered by a school district, [it] must take affirmative steps to rectify the language deficiency to open instructional programs to these students.

Both the Bilingual Acts of 1968 and 1974 caused controversies about the purposes and effects of bilingual education. Should educators help students make transitions to English-speaking classrooms or should they help students develop more fully in their native language and culture? Do bilingual education programs enhance or retard student achievement if and when students enter English-speaking programs?

In spite of these questions, in 1976 California passed legislation requiring all school districts to provide bilingual education for all grades. During the 1970s, congressional appropriations for bilingual education increased from $7.5 million in 1969 to $158 million in 1979. In 1990, federal funding for bilingual education had

---

Civil Rights Act (1964)

Bilingual Education Act (provided funding for bilingual programs) (1968)

*Lau v. Nichols* (ruled that schools should meet needs of non-English-speaking students) (1973)

*Keyes v. School District No. 1 of Denver* (ruled that schools should develop a bilingual-bicultural program) (1973)

Title VI of 1974 Civil Rights Act

increased to over $188 million, and by 1993–1994, funding had increased to $232 million for bilingual and immigrant education (see also chapter 8, pp. 323–328).

*The Handicapped and P.L. 94–142* The cornerstone of federal policies dealing with students who are mentally and physically disabled as well as those who are learning-disabled is the 1975 Education for All Handicapped Children Act (P.L. 94–142) and its 1986 amendments (P.L. 99–457). These acts define disabled students as those who are mentally retarded, hard of hearing or deaf, orthopedically or otherwise health impaired, visually impaired, speech impaired, or emotionally disturbed. P.L. 94–142 mandates that the schools provide free and appropriate education for these children and those with special learning disabilities. The 1986 amendments established services for infants, toddlers, and preschool-aged children (birth to five years) with disabilities.

"Appropriate" programs as defined by P.L. 94–142 required that schools provide specially designed instruction, at no cost to parents or guardians, in the classroom, in the home, or in hospitals and institutions. In addition, schools must offer related services such as transportation, psychological testing, physical and occupational therapy, speech pathology, and medical counseling. An **Individual Education Program (IEP)** is required for each handicapped student (including toddlers to five-year-olds). The program must be written and developed by representatives of the local education agency that supervises the special program, the child's teachers, parents or guardians, and, when appropriate, the child. The 1986 amendments (P.L. 99–457) require states to provide the same, appropriate services to preschool-aged children in appropriate care-giving centers.

As often as possible, schools must allow for the disabled students' participation in the regular educational program. This is called **mainstreaming**. Often it requires the removal of barriers such as stairways and narrow hallways. Furthermore, mainstreaming may stipulate that a special teacher attend the regular classes with the disabled student. For example, a teacher who is trained in sign language may attend the class with a deaf student.

*Changes in Curriculum* To meet the social goal of equal educational opportunity, curricular changes in the 1960s and 1970s moved away from subject orientation toward more emphasis on the needs of the students and society. Many of these changes were affected by federal funding for disenfranchised students, particularly through ESEA and its Titles, P.L. 94–142, and the Civil Rights Act. Some of the curricular revisions that can be indirectly and directly traced to this legislation include:

> (1) adding to existing courses, topics such as environmental protection, drug addiction, black-white inequality, urban problems, aggression and violence, and the meaning of the law; (2) providing educational "alternatives" as a response to the demand for freedom of choice (ranging from the choice of a school with a given curricular focus, to a smorgasbord of electives at the secondary school level, to allowing elementary school pupils to study what interests them); and (3) including out-of-school activities of a social-service nature. (Tanner and Tanner 1975, 365)

These curricular changes occurred at all levels and in all areas of education. One response occurred in the physical environment of many schools, which changed from self-contained classroom space to more open, flexible space with

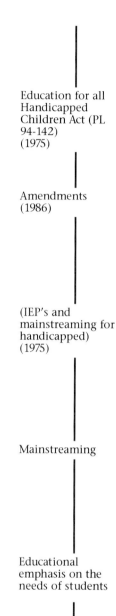

Education for all Handicapped Children Act (PL 94-142) (1975)

Amendments (1986)

(IEP's and mainstreaming for handicapped) (1975)

Mainstreaming

Educational emphasis on the needs of students

room for individual study, as well as small and large group work. Frequently, classrooms, especially in elementary schools, had no walls or movable walls. Schools were more open, not only in terms of physical space and student choice, but also in terms of bringing the community to the school or the student to the community. High school students participated in work-release programs, field trips became increasingly common, and parents and a variety of community resource people were frequently seen in classrooms.

It is important to note that many educators believed that many of these changes were counterproductive. The criticisms can be seen in many of the reform reports of the late 1970s through the early 1990s, which will be discussed later in this chapter.

## Education in the 1970s, 1980s, and 1990s: A Period of Conflicts

**1970–1990**
*A Period of Conflicts*

**Richard M. Nixon** reduced educational funds

**Ronald W. Reagan** shifted educational funds to the states

**Bill Clinton** provided more funding for compensatory public education programs

Education reform in the 1970s through early 1990s was marked by struggle and conflict. On the one hand, there was the attempt to ensure equalization of educational opportunities for all students; on the other, there was decreased federal funding for elementary and secondary schools, making impossible an increase in educational programs for the diverse school population. Richard M. Nixon's election in 1969 followed on the heels of violent protests against the war in Vietnam that spilled over into student protests against all forms of authority. In the resulting social confusion, Nixon's administration questioned whether the War on Poverty's legislation, enacted during the administration of Lyndon B. Johnson (1963–1969), had resulted in improved educational conditions for the poor. Thus, Nixon vetoed three compensatory education and desegregation programs, reducing the total budget for public education reform. President Ronald W. Reagan's (1981–1988) conservative approach to federal spending resulted in a further shift of educational funding from the federal government to the states. Reagan contended that since the schools were controlled by the states, they should be responsible for funding public education. They, however, did not always have the funding necessary to implement the various stipulations of the Elementary and Secondary Education Act and the Civil Rights Act.

In the 1990s, a shift toward more federal funding for compensatory public education programs began during President Bill Clinton's administration. In 1994, Congress approved increases in allocations for Head Start, Bilingual Education, and Chapter I. Ironically, federal funding was also increased for an excellence initiative begun during President George Bush's administration. America 2000, instituted by Bush's Secretary of Education Lamar Alexander, was renamed Goals 2000: Educate America Act by Clinton's secretary of education Richard Riley. Riley's reform proposal had the same goals as American 2000 (see pages 210–212) and carried a price tag of approximately $400 million for fiscal year 1994.

### EQUAL ACCESS

In an attempt to determine if ESEA had made an early impact on equalizing educational opportunities, a study ("A Reassessment of the Effect of Family and Schooling in America") was conducted by Christopher Jencks and seven associates

The right of women to have equal access to education has been challenged at several military institutions in the South including Virginia Military Institute and the Citadel in Charleston, South Carolina. Shannon Faulkner's application for admittance to the Citadel was accepted until it was discovered she was a female. It was then rescinded. She subsequently sued the state-run institution, and a court order declared her eligible to attend. Prior to being admitted to the corps of cadets, Shannon was allowed simply to attend day classes.

from 1968 to 1971. The results compared test scores, educational attainment, occupational status, and income level in different schools. They found that "qualitative differences between schools had relatively little impact on students' test scores, especially at the high school level" (Jencks 1972, 146). Likewise, they found that differences among schools had little to do with a student's eventual educational attainment. Rather, the most important determinants of level of educational attainment were a family's socioeconomic background and cognitive skill, the ability to think, reason, and solve problems.

Their study also found that access to education was far more equal for children between the ages of six and sixteen than for older or younger children. If the results of their study are accurate, they confirm the conclusion of an earlier study by James Coleman (1966) that differences in the school had little impact on student achievement. However, he did find that for average white students, achievement was less influenced by the strengths and weaknesses of the school than for average minority students. Coleman, like Jencks, contended that inequality of educational opportunity was more pronounced before age six, when the child enters school, and after age sixteen, when the child leaves or continues school.

Christopher Jencks
(1971)

A study on reassessment of the effect of family on schooling

John Goodlad, in his 1984 study of thirty-eight elementary, middle, and junior and senior high schools, stated that the central issue of equality of educational opportunity in the 1980s was no longer access to schools but access to knowledge. His studies found, for example, that tracking limits equal access to knowledge. In other words, according to Goodlad, students of the mid-1980s may have had approximately equal opportunity to attend school but not equal access to knowledge in that school.

Partially as a result of studies such as Goodlad's as well as poor academic progress of minority and low socioeconomic students on such national measures as the National Assessment of Educational Progress (NAEP, see chapter 10, pp. 412–421) and high dropout rates of these same students, schools in the late 1980s and early 1990s began to address the issue of tracking. Many elementary and middle schools began using methods such as cooperative learning in which small groups of students of varied ability levels work together and help each other instead of tracking. In addition, Tech Prep programs were begun in many high schools in the 1990s (see chapter 8, pp. 334–337). In these programs, students take a mix of academic, college preparatory courses, and vocational, technological courses, allowing them to pursue various career and college opportunities, rather than limiting them to single job options following graduation. In addition, many of these students participate in paid internship programs.

***Minorities and the Disabled*** The question of equal access to knowledge also involved programs for those with disabilities. Many studies of the 1980s called into question whether P.L. 94–142 was giving equal access to knowledge to all students or was actually limiting it for some disabled students. On the one hand, studies by Mary Moore, L. Walker, and R. Holland (1982) and Margaret Wang, Maynard Reynolds, and Herbert Walberg (1986) concluded that the implementation of P.L. 94–142 had resulted in more equal and appropriate access to education for all disabled students. However, other studies, such as one in 1982 by Kurt Heller, Wayne Holtzman, and Susan Messick, found that there was a disproportionate number of minority and male children in special education programs. This study posed some difficult questions: Are minority males more likely to be emotionally or mentally disabled than any other group of students? Or is placement based on some other factor, such as behavior? Does this placement limit their access to regular academic programs and knowledge?

Several studies indicate that this is so. Since P.L. 94–142, states with greater minority populations have tended to have more students placed in special education programs. In 1990–1991, 11.57 percent of the total public school population was enrolled in special education classes, as compared to 8.33 percent in 1976–1977 (U.S. Department of Education, National Center for Education Statistics 1993, 65). Some say that this rise correlates with the increase in the minority population in the public schools. In Utah, a state with a relatively homogeneous population, for example, there was a 1.5 percent increase in students classified as learning disabled between 1977 and 1981, while in Washington, D.C., a city with a very large minority population, there was a 40 percent increase (Moore, Walker, and Holland 1982). In Washington state there was a 5 percent decrease in students enrolled in emotionally disabled programs from 1977–1978 through 1980–1981, while in Mississippi during the same period, there was a 49 percent increase. If these studies are correct, and if the educators and researchers who claim special education students do not have equal access to

---

John Goodlad study in 1984 determined issue of equal educational opportunity was access to knowledge

Tech Prep programs

Growth in special education programs particularly for minorities

knowledge are also correct, it may be that P.L. 94–142, which was designed to provide equal access to all those with disabilities regardless of severity, may be, in fact, limiting access for some of those who are only mildly disabled.

In addition, Mara Shevin (1989) reported that the proliferation of new categories in special education, such as mildly disabled and mildly retarded, may keep many students out of the regular classroom from which they could profit more. Researchers suggest that the criteria for success in programs for disabled students should be: How many master the competencies of required high school course work? How many leave school as independent, well-educated young adults? How many find jobs to match their talents (Gloeckler and Cianca 1986, 30)?

Barbara K. Keogh (1983) determined that classification of students for special education programs was often influenced by factors other than the children's needs, such as availability of staff; availability of space; and federal, state, and local guidelines and pressures. The issue of the placement of high percentages of minorities and low socioeconomic students in some special education programs has called into question how assignments are being made. According to the research of psychologists Mark Wolery, Philip S. Strain, and Donald Bailey, children have different types of developmental delays related to language and experiential backgrounds. According to a 1993 report from the Office of Special Education Programs, U.S. Department of Education presented to the U.S. Congress, initial formal diagnosis and screening of these children can, therefore, be misleading. This office and these researchers recommend retesting and reclassification of many students utilizing multiple types of diagnostic tests, including: curriculum referenced tests, observation in the home setting, interviews with people who know the child, and teacher informal tests and screening.

*Funding*   Other studies indicated an inequality of resources within and among states (Keppel 1966; Stern 1987; Bastian et al. 1986) and questioned if education can be equal if resources for education are not. In 1963 the average real expenditure per pupil per state was between $317 and $867 a year; in 1969 between $1,402 and $3,715 a year; in 1984 between $2,220 and $7,482 a year; in 1987 between $2,718 and $7,971 a year; and in 1990 between $2,960 and $8,330 a year (National Center for Education Statistics 1993, 163). The more prosperous the state, the more is spent on education.

Francis Keppel in *The Necessary Revolution in American Education* (1966) reported that the way schools are funded has meant that richer school districts get richer, while poorer school districts get poorer. This, according to Keppel, is due to a funding system, called "foundation," in which the states are required to spend a basic minimum amount of money for each student. However, richer communities can easily exceed this basic amount, since local school districts are required to levy property taxes for their share of the foundation amount. Thus, the poorer the district, the poorer the property values, and the lower the revenue produced for schools. The foundation system of funding, although challenged by the courts in several states, remains firmly in place.

There is significant debate about whether dollars spent per pupil have anything to do with educational equality. On the one hand, those who claim that equality can be measured by the attainments of students assert that dollars spent have little effect on it. On the other, those who contend that equality relates to the distribution of democratic opportunity believe that dollars spent do affect it (see also chapter 14).

Proliferation of categories in special education

Francis Keppel Report in 1966 that school funding has resulted in unequal distribution of funds between rich and poor districts

Amy Gutman, a Princeton University researcher, in *Democratic Education* (1987), and Jean Allen, editor of *Business/Education Insider* (1991), exemplify the two sides of the issue. Allen refutes the claim of the Louisiana League of Women Voters in its call for higher spending to improve education in the state, which in 1991 was forty-third in state spending for education with test scores well below national norms: "Studies on school spending conducted within the past two years find no correlation between student achievement and higher spending to reduce class sizes, raise teacher salaries, or construct new buildings" (1991, 2).

Gutman states that the Coleman study, *Report on Equality of Educational Opportunity* (1966), and the Jencks study, *Inequality* (1972)—on which most subsequent studies on financing and school equality have been based—found that differences in spending among schools could not account for differences in average attainment of students. But they failed to look at how these school districts distributed funding among the children. For example, she claimed that the findings "cannot be used to conclude that significant changes in the internal organization of schools—for example, assigning the most experienced and highly paid teachers to the least advantaged children—would make no difference" (1987, 152). Rather, funding makes a great deal of difference to the attainment of equal opportunity. It provides access to the most recent, most up-to-date textbooks, adequate libraries, and the best teachers. Hence, according to this argument, equality should be measured by whether the students' educational opportunities are equal rather than by standardized tests and subsequent income attainment. Interestingly, the Educational Testing Service has examined the relationship between the availability of materials and resources, which can be directly tied to the level of funding, and students' proficiency scores on the National Assessment of Educational Progress (NAEP) grade 8 mathematics tests and have found a direct relationship: the greater the percent of students lacking instructional materials and resources in a given state, the lower the students' proficiency in mathematics as measured by the NAEP (see figure 5.1).

***Americans with Disabilities Act and the Inclusion Argument***   The 1990 Americans with Disabilities Act (P.L. 101–336) prohibits discrimination against any persons with disabilities and encourages the "least restrictive environment possible" for disabled public school students. After the passage of this act, according to Ann Smith, a specialist with the Children's Defense Fund, parents of disabled children, special education teachers, and some educational leaders argued that disabled students, regardless of disability, should have "full inclusion" (permanent placement) in a regular classroom (telephone conversation, December 22, 1993). Mainstreaming allows disabled students to attend some regular classes, whereas full inclusion places disabled students in regular classrooms on a full-time basis. Advocates of full inclusion call it a civil rights issue, while critics say it threatens the education of other children in already overcrowded classrooms and places a big burden on teachers not trained to work with all kinds of disabled students (Henry and Kelly 1993, 1D–2D).

Supporters of inclusion point to schools where it is effective for both disabled and nondisabled students. In some schools in Virginia and California, for example, there are no rigid divisions between regular and special education classrooms. Teachers work together to provide individually suited educational

Amy Gutman Report in 1987 that educational attainment directly tied to funding

Americans with Disabilities Act (1990)

**FIGURE 5-1**

## Relationship Between the Availability of Instructional Materials and Resources and NAEP Mathematics Proficiency, Grade 8, 1990

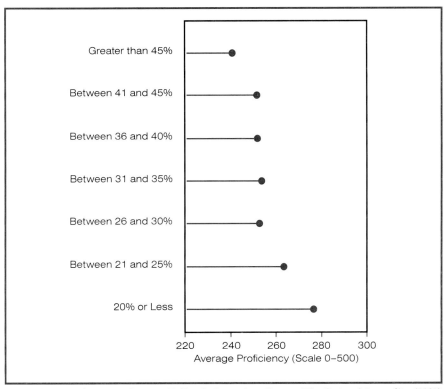

From: Educational Testing Service, Policy Information Center, *The State of Inequality* (1991), Princeton, N.J.

**Students in classrooms lacking instructional materials and resources have lower average mathematics proficiency than those who have adequate materials.**

outcomes for all students. Disabled students may be with their peers in the regular classroom and work with a tutor during the lunch hour, or a speech-impaired student may leave the classroom for specialized work for short periods during the day. Three researchers who examined these schools, which practice cooperative learning and peer tutoring, concluded that "solutions [to the problems of disabled students] are not calculated from label-specific formulas; solutions build on the belief that all students can learn skills that are of value to them, even though these skills will differ from one child to the next. Solutions must include individualized learning goals and the use of teaching strategies devised by teams of regular and special educators looking at individual children and pooling their resources and talents" (Raynes, Snell, and Sailor 1991, 327).

Individualized learning goals best for disabled students

The 1990 Americans with Disabilities Act (P.L. 101–336) provides disabled students with the least restrictive environment. This might mean full inclusion or permanent placement in a regular classroom. Such situations call for teaching strategies that utilize many resources within the institution. In a classroom in Redmond, Washington, Cameron Archibald, left, who suffers from seizures, has become friends with Andy Heilman. They plan to go to summer camp together.

William T. Grant Foundation Commission on Work, Family, and Citizenship (1988)

*Entry into the Workforce*   In 1988 the William T. Grant Foundation Commission on Work, Family, and Citizenship found that public schools were not helping non-college-bound high school students move into the workforce. Therefore, the commission concluded, these students did not receive the same educational opportunity as their college-bound counterparts. It concluded that the schools must do much more to prepare students for work, beginning with preschool education through retraining of already employed adults.

The commission recommended that the federal government invest $5 billion annually for ten years in the following: (1) Head Start, with state and local help, so that the 81 percent of eligible youngsters currently not being served could be included; (2) extension of Chapter I (previously Title I of ESEA) programs into the middle and secondary schools so that earlier educational gains are maintained; (3) expansion of the Job Corps, which was designed to move sixteen-to-eighteen-year-olds into the workforce; (4) redirection of vocational education with hands-on methods to help students acquire basic skills; and (5) provision for monitored work experience such as internships, apprenticeships, reemployment training, and school/industry cooperatives.

## POTENTIAL SOLUTIONS

During the 1970s and 1980s educators tended to agree that not all students had equal educational opportunities despite the increased popularization of the schools for all groups. Frequently, this inequality stemmed not from unequal access but unequal opportunities. Finding solutions to this problem is a complicated and ongoing task.

*Compensatory Education*    One solution to providing equal educational opportunities for all students suggested by Edmund Gordon is for schools to compensate for the unequal learning and experiences that students bring to the classroom. **Compensatory education** needs to be individualized based on the student's unique learning characteristics. In the middle 1970s, when Gordon did his work, there was no evidence that compensatory education was in use or effective.

In *A Place Called School,* a study of thirty-eight elementary, middle, and junior and senior high schools conducted in 1984 by John Goodlad, he concluded that some schools were providing more equal educational opportunities than others and, in some, compensatory education was working. According to Goodlad, earlier studies, such as Gordon's, failed to examine classroom practices within individual schools.

In studying more than one thousand classrooms, Goodlad found similarities in methods, materials, tests, content of curriculum, grouping, modes of learning, and arrangement of classrooms. He found differences, however, in how teachers teach, distribution of resources, how curriculum is designed, and how equality of access to knowledge is regarded by individuals within the schools. Differences in the curricular content for racial and socioeconomic groups included such factors as whether the school emphasized learning facts rather than solving problems, encouraged active rather than passive learning, and working alone rather than in groups. Schools that had more resources, better teachers, and a more flexible curriculum tended to provide more adequate compensatory education than schools that were not adequately funded or flexibly organized.

Title I/Chapter I, for example, was designed to bridge the gap between advantaged and disadvantaged students by supplying the disadvantaged compensatory programs with additional federal and state funds. In a 1986 report, "The Effectiveness of Chapter I Services," Kennedy, Birman, and Demaline reported that the achievement of disadvantaged students relative to the general population had improved since 1965, particularly in reading. The study further concluded that Chapter I had been effective in raising the standardized achievement test scores of the disadvantaged children it served, but had not substantially moved them toward the achievement levels of more advantaged students. It also found that students participating in Chapter I mathematics programs gained more than those in Chapter I reading programs, and that students in early elementary programs gained more than those in later programs. In 1988, Congress mandated, under the Hawkins-Stafford Amendments, a review of Chapter I programs, including a study of their effectiveness. Because, by statute, Chapter I students are to receive more funds and more services than non–Chapter I students, Congress assumed that their performance should improve. By statute, each district receiving Chapter I funds must set realistic goals that can be measured to demonstrate the program's effectiveness. These goals must relate, in part, to student aggregate achievement on nationally normed tests. The federal regulations set minimal standards requiring that Chapter I students should show improvement "beyond what a student of a particular age or grade level . . . would be expected to make during the period being measured if the child had no additional help" (Hawkins and Stafford Elementary and Secondary School Im-

Compensatory
education

John Goodlad

*A Place Called School*
(A study reporting
similarities and
differences among
schools)
(1984)

Hawkins-Stafford
Elementary and
Secondary School
Improvement
Amendments
(1988)

provement Amendment of 1988—P.L. 297–20). Hence, Chapter I programs have tended to set very conservative goals so as not to be found needing improvement. Therefore, Thomas W. Fagan and Camilla A. Heid conclude that if Chapter I students meet all of the program's goals, it is difficult to determine whether it is really helping the students or they are merely meeting low-level goals they could meet without the program's intervention (1991).

In 1990 Congress passed the National Assessment of Chapter I Act (P.L. 101–305), requiring the Secretary of Education to conduct a comprehensive national assessment of programs carried out with assistance under Chapter I of Title I of the Elementary and Secondary Education Act (ESEA) of 1965. According to Marshall S. Smith, undersecretary of education in 1993, after the first year of a longitudinal study, there was some evidence that disadvantaged students gained from being in Chapter I programs, particularly in the primary grades. The study did not show conclusively, however, that students in Chapter I programs, where funding was directed toward working in small remedial groups and one-to-one tutoring, did better academically than students in schoolwide programs in which funding was used to buy materials and limit class size (telephone conversation with Smith, December 28, 1993).

***School-to-Work Opportunities***  Because studies, such as the 1988 William T. Grant Foundation Commission, have found that non-college-bound students did not receive the same educational opportunities as their college-bound counterparts, many states are eliminating the "general track" in the high school curriculum. This track, popular in the 1950s and 1960s, was designed to give students the basic skills they needed to work on assembly-line jobs. As these jobs have been eliminated, new skills are needed by students entering the workforce. Maryland, Oregon, Massachusetts, and Tennessee, for example, have implemented plans requiring all students to prepare for either college or technical school. Other states, including California, Kentucky, Maine, North Carolina, New York, and Washington, are testing similar programs (Marklein 1993, 5D). Tech Prep programs, such as one developed in North Carolina, eliminate the outmoded general, vocational, and college preparatory tracks and replace them with programs in health care, business and management, technology and industry, and college preparation. Each program is designed to prepare students for either technical school, four-year colleges, or the modern workforce. The first three programs include internships in jobs related to the career track.

The School-to-Work Opportunities Act (P.L. 103–239), signed by President Clinton on May 4, 1994, is designed to set up a national system of school-to-work programs in which the 50 percent of students who do not attend college acquire a strong academic preparation for entering a variety of jobs in the workforce, changing jobs several times during their careers, and perhaps, entering college at a later date. It is funded at $300 million.

***Preschool***  In 1988 the Carnegie Foundation for the Advancement of Teaching reported a "disturbing gap between reform rhetoric and results" (p. xi) for black and Hispanic children in urban schools. They recommended that (1) all eligible poverty-level preschoolers be served by Head Start by the year 2000, (2) nutritional programs be increased, (3) poverty parents be given a choice between summer and afternoon programs for their children, and (4) a 5 percent increase be made in Chapter I/Title I to focus on teaching of basic skills. The conclusion of the Carnegie Foundation report was that if the gap between advantaged and disadvantaged children were narrowed before the children entered school, the disadvantaged would have a better chance of success in school. In 1988 Congress allocated $50 million under the Hawkins-Stafford Elementary and Secondary School Improvement Amendments for each fiscal year to the states for a program called Even Start (P.L. 100–297, Title I, Part B). Even Start is for disadvantaged children, including children of migrant workers, and their parents. It is designed to improve child care and education for both children and parents "by integrating early childhood education and adult education for parents into a unified program" (P.L. 100–297, 20 USC 2741). Local education agencies are eligible to apply to the states for grants through this bill. Programs that "assist parents in becoming full partners in the education of their children and assist children in reaching their full potential as learners" (20 USC 2744) include such elements as:

Even Start (Improve adult literacy and early education) (1988)

1. Identification and recruitment of eligible children (those between the ages of one and seven with educationally disadvantaged parents having a basic skills equivalent no higher than fifth grade).
2. Screening and preparation of parents and children (testing and referral for counseling and related services).
3. Programs and support services appropriate to work and other responsibilities (locations that allow joint participation, transportation, and child care).
4. Instructional programs that promote adult literacy, train parents to support the educational growth of their children, and prepare the children for school.
5. Special training for staff.
6. Home-based programs that provide for and monitor integrated instructional services to parents and children.
7. Coordination of Even Start programs with other federally funded programs such as the Adult Education Act, the Education of the Handicapped Act, the Job Training Partnership Act, and Head Start.

There is limited data to establish the level of success of Even Start programs. However, there is anecdotal evidence that seems to indicate that the programs are working. For example, in Asheville, North Carolina, in a five-year period, 50 percent of parents enrolled in the program have earned Graduate Equivalency Degrees (GED). All parents have enrolled in adult literacy programs and all have improved their reading, writing, and spelling skills. It is too early to tell whether the program has long-term positive effects on the children enrolled.

In 1990 Congress passed the Childhood Education and Development Act (P.L. 101–239) authorizing appropriations to expand Head Start programs and programs under ESEA that include child-care services. In 1992, 621,000 children were enrolled in Head Start with a total budget of $2.2 billion and an average cost per child of $3,415 per year. However, it was estimated that only 35 percent of eligible children were being served (Children's Defense Fund 1993, 3). Because of this and the belief of most educators that early education of poverty-level children is critical to their future academic success, the amount of federal dollars allocated for Head Start and other preschool programs is expected to grow. Many long-time supporters of Head Start worry, however, that the growth of Head Start without a system of quality control and emphasis on the management skills and

Childhood Education and Development Act (P.L. 101-239) (1990)

salary of the staff may eventually doom the program to failure (Kantrowitz and Wingert 1993, 57).

*Magnet Schools*    One possible solution to the problem of unequal access to knowledge is the **magnet school**. It allows parents to select among different schools with different educational programs for their children. One magnet school, for example, might stress the theme of multiculturalism; another might be a basic school emphasizing reading, writing, arithmetic, and discipline. Still another might focus on the arts or the sciences and mathematics. In this way, according to proponents, the needs of all children can be met, complete integration can be achieved, and only the best schools will survive since parents will not select inferior schools.

However, reports seem to indicate that new forms of discrimination of poor and minorities are arising as a result of magnet schools. In four urban districts (New York City, Boston, Chicago, and Philadelphia) a 1988 study found that selective admission criteria were employed by many magnet schools, thereby providing opportunities for high achievers but not those who are necessarily disadvantaged. According to the study, these districts had "created a five-tiered school system that offers unequal opportunities to students from different backgrounds." These five tiers were: selective schools based on exams, selective magnet schools, selective vocational schools, nonselective schools drawing students from families with moderate income levels, and nonselective schools drawing students from poor neighborhoods. "Many schools in upper tiers operate as separate, virtually private schools" (Snider 8). The study found that selective schools were given extra resources, had limited enrollments, and sent students who did not do well back to their neighborhood schools (see also chapter 12, pp. 483–486).

Other informal studies are more optimistic about the effects of magnet schools on integration. In 1993 Evans Clinchy, senior associate with the Institute for Responsive Education in Boston, Massachusetts, reported that the federally funded Magnet Schools Assistance program has allowed the applicant local school districts to invent their own voluntary programs to guarantee integration, educational equity, and systemwide improvement for all students. He cites as examples school systems such as New York City's Community School District 4 in East Harlem, and Lowell and Cambridge districts in Massachusetts in which every school, according to Clinchy, is an integrated magnet school of choice and where all students are taught they can succeed (1993, 28).

## A RENEWED SEARCH FOR ACADEMIC EXCELLENCE

The 1980s saw more than a dozen major commission reports focusing on the problem of the U.S. high school, claiming that it was no longer encouraging academic excellence. The second wave of reports focused on elementary and middle school education. The reports seemed to suggest that the schools should change their historical focus.

However, careful reading shows that they are suggesting other means for reaching the goals of U.S. education.

*(continued on p. 205)*

---

Magnet schools allow parents to select among schools with different programs

Magnet Schools Assistance program allows school districts to develop programs to prevent segregation

**TABLE 5-1**

## Summary of Major Reports on Education 1991–1994

| The Report | Source | Recommendations | Implementers |
|---|---|---|---|
| *The State of Inequality (1991)* | Educational Testing Service (ETS) | 1. Provide more equitable funding within and between states and school districts.<br>2. Conduct more research on student learning related to equalization of resources between/among school districts. | 1. Federal government<br>2. State and local officials<br>3. Researchers at federal, state, and local levels |
| *The Good Common School* (1991) | National Coalition for Students (NCAS) | 1. Equal educational opportunity should be supported by provision of greater resources to schools serving students vulnerable to failure.<br>2. Teachers should be fully prepared to meet challenges of diverse classrooms.<br>3. Provide increased support services that address individual needs. | 1. Federal government<br>2. State and local officials<br>3. Colleges and universities |
| *Beyond Rhetoric* (1991) | National Commission on Children | 1. Parents should bear primary responsibilities for meeting their children's physical, emotional and intellectual needs and for providing moral guidance and directions.<br>2. Society should support parents and hold them responsible for the care and support of their children. | 1. Parents<br>2. Local communities<br>3. Social services<br>4. Employers<br>5. Religious organizations<br>6. Charitable and service organizations |
| *Status of School Desegregation: The Next Generation* (1992) | Council of Urban Boards of Education | 1. Federal, state, and local officials should commit to the goal of integrated and equitable schools serving stably integrated communities.<br>2. Government should enact a new federal program to provide financial support for costs of desegregation.<br>3. Develop federal and state policy that offers minority students in highly segregated schools the choice to transfer to integrated schools in neighboring school districts. | 1. Federal, state, and local officials<br>2. Federal government<br>3. Federal and state governments, local school districts, and parents |
| *The State of America's Children* (1992) | Children's Defense Fund | 1. Ensure that all communities have enough doctors, clinics, and basic public health services to provide adequate health care to children and families.<br>2. Ensure that all children reach school ready to learn.<br>3. Ensure that teens have opportunities to develop strong basic skills, a foundation for higher education and have opportunities to acquire work-related skills. | 1. Local communities<br>2. Parents<br>3. Federal, state, and local governments<br>4. Local school districts |
| *The National Education Goals Report: Building a Nation of Learners* (1992) | National Education Goals Panel | 1. Develop standards related to the objectives for each of the six national educational goals.<br>2. Provide federal and state funding to implement the six national education goals. | 1. Professional education organizations<br>2. Federal and state governments<br>3. Local school officials |

| The Report | Source | Recommendations | Implementers |
|---|---|---|---|
| *How Schools Shortchange Girls* (1992) | American Association of University Women Educational Foundation (AAUW) | 1. Require school districts to assess and report on a regular basis to the Office of Civil Rights, U.S. Department of Education on their own Title IX compliance measures.<br>2. Provide funding for Office of Civil Rights that permits reviews and investigations.<br>3. Teachers, administrators, and counselors should be evaluated on the degree to which they promote and encourage gender-equitable and multicultural skills as well as verbal and mathematical skills in both girls and boys. | 1. Local school districts<br>2. Office of Civil Rights, U.S. Department of Education<br>3. Federal government<br>4. Teachers, school administrators, school counselors<br>5. Teacher-training institutions |
| *Horace's School: Redesigning the American High School* (1992) | Theodore Sizer, Brown University | 1. Schools should focus on helping adolescents use their minds well and not attempt to be comprehensive in all aspects of students' life.<br>2. Each student should master a number of essential skills and be competent in certain areas of knowledge.<br>3. School goals apply to all students but means to the goals vary as students vary. | 1. State and local school officials<br>2. Teachers<br>3. Students |
| *Standards of Practice for Learner-Centered Schools* (1992) | National Center for Restructuring Education, Schools, and Teaching (NCREST) | 1. Standards for equitable access should be used to identify key resources that enable students' learning and create incentives for school districts to ensure its availability to all students.<br>2. Standards for accountable school functioning should be used to identify the areas in which schools will create ongoing processes for learning, inquiry, self-evaluation, problem solving, and consultation.<br>3. Standards of practice should be used to identify goals for the organization, management, and teaching practices of schools and to develop approaches for attainment. | 1. State education officials<br>2. Local school officials<br>3. State legislatures<br>4. Federal government<br>5. Teachers and students |
| *Resolving a Crisis in Education: Latino Teachers for Tomorrow's Classrooms* (1993) | The Tomas Rivera Center | 1. Increase greatly the supply of Latino teachers so that representation in the profession may approximate parity with that of Latinos in public school enrollments.<br>2. Improve the preparation of all teachers, especially those who work with poor, culturally diverse students. | 1. Teacher training institutions<br>2. State education officials |
| *National Excellence: A Case for Developing America's Talent* (1993) | Office of Educational Research and Improvement, U.S. Department of Education | 1. Establish challenging curriculum standards for all students including those gifted and talented.<br>2. Establish high-level learning opportunities related to diverse talents and allow students to work in special schools, museums, libraries, and scientific organizations.<br>3. Ensure access to early childhood education, especially minorities and those economically disadvantaged. | 1. State and local officials<br>2. Federal, state, and local governments<br>3. Professional education organizations<br>4. Teachers |
| *A Shared Vision: Policy Recommendations for Linking Teacher Education to School Reform* (1993) | Education Commission of the States | 1. State legislatures should adopt provisions that allow institutions of higher education and public schools to collaborate in the preparation of teachers so that they will be prepared to support and enhance school restructuring. | 1. State legislators<br>2. Teacher training institutions<br>3. Local school districts |

| The Report | Source | Recommendations | Implementers |
|---|---|---|---|
| *Starting Points: Meeting the Needs of Our Youngest Students* (1994) | Carnegie Corporation of New York | 1. Promote responsible parenthood.<br>2. Guarantee quality child-care choices.<br>3. Ensure good health and protection.<br>4. Mobilize communities to support young children and their families. | 1. Schools and parents<br>2. Social services<br>3. Communities<br>4. State and local governments |
| *Changing Systems for Children and Families* (1994) | National Governors' Association | 1. Build accountability structures that target specific child and family outcomes.<br>2. Examine the consequences of failing to offer comprehensive services. | 1. Federal, state, and local governments<br>2. Families and schools |
| *Prisoners of Time* (1994) | National Education Commission on Time and Learning | 1. Recommends a longer school year and school day for academic instruction.<br>2. Give teachers the professional time and opportunities they need to do their jobs.<br>3. Invest in new technologies to enhance student achievement. | 1. State and local education agencies |

**Concern for the quality of education in the United States has risen dramatically in the past few years, resulting in a series of reports suggesting various types of reforms. This table summarizes the recent major reports.**

*Reports Focusing on Secondary Schools*    The titles of the high school reports—*A Nation at Risk* (1983) and *Action for Excellence* (1983)—were indicative of their findings. They emphasized a need to strengthen the curriculum in the core subjects of English, mathematics, science, foreign languages, and social studies. They commonly mentioned a need for courses in the new technologies, such as computers, and they stressed the need for high-level cognitive skills, along with higher standards and more difficult course work.

Several of the reports emphasized that students needed increased homework, more time for learning, more time in school, and more rigorous grading, testing, and discipline. They discussed upgrading teacher education programs by requiring more work in academic disciplines. Although these reports emphasized the secondary school, the commissions believed that their work would spill over into the primary schools, private schools, and colleges. Most of the reports placed the responsibility for implementing these so-called reforms on the states and the local boards of education. Table 5.1 briefly describes the key reports.

*Reports Focusing on Elementary Schools*    The first of the elementary school reports, *First Lesson* (1986), was written by William Bennett, then U.S. secretary of education. Although this report claimed elementary education was in "pretty good shape," it maintained that increased parental involvement was "the single best way" to bring about much-needed improvement.

In addition, the Bennett report suggested that teacher certification "depend on demonstrated knowledge and skills, not on paper credentials," and that the "chronological lockstep" of students through grades be "loosened" to allow for individual progress.

According to Bennett's report, the elementary school curriculum must first teach children to read. The report also said that children should learn that "writing is more than filling in blanks," science should include "hands-on"

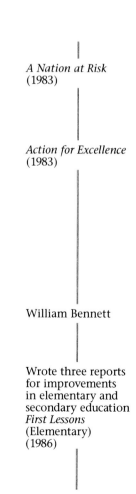

*A Nation at Risk* (1983)

*Action for Excellence* (1983)

William Bennett

Wrote three reports for improvements in elementary and secondary education *First Lessons* (Elementary) (1986)

**FIGURE 5-2**

## The Common Core Curriculum of William Bennett's
*James Madison High School*

THE PROGRAM IN BRIEF: A Four-Year Plan

| Subject | 1st Year | 2nd Year | 3rd Year | 4th Year |
|---|---|---|---|---|
| ENGLISH | Introduction to Literature | American Literature | British Literature | Introduction to World Literature |
| SOCIAL STUDIES | Western Civilization | American History | Principles of American Democracy *(1 sem.)* and American Democracy & the World *(1 sem.)* | |
| MATHE-MATICS | Three Years Required From Among the Following Courses: Algebra I, Plane & Solid Geometry, Algebra II & Trigonometry, Statistics & Probability *(1 sem.)*, Pre-Calculus *(1 sem.)*, and Calculus AB or BC | | | |
| SCIENCE | Three Years Required From Among the Following Courses: Astronomy/Geology, Biology, Chemistry, and Physics or Principles of Technology | | | |
| FOREIGN LAN-GUAGE | Two Years Required in a Single Language From Among Offerings Determined by Local Jurisdictions | | | |
| PHYSICAL EDUCA-TION/ HEALTH | Physical Education/ Health 9 | Physical Education/ Health 10 | | |
| FINE ARTS | Art History *(1 sem.)* Music History *(1 sem.)* | | | |

From: W. J. Bennett, *James Madison High School: A Curriculum for American Students* (Washington, DC: U.S. Department of Education, 1988), 11.

As a response to the reform movement in the 1980s, curriculum became subject centered and less responsive to students' individual needs. In the core curriculum of *James Madison High School,* the emphasis was on basic language and mathematical skills.

experiments, social studies should be broadened to teach the academic disciplines in early grades, mathematics should emphasize problem solving, and instruction in the arts should be an integral part of every elementary school curriculum. Students should gain a grasp of the uses and limitations of computers, health and physical education should be taught, and every school should have a library (p. 2).

In August 1988 Bennett issued a second report on elementary education, *James Madison Elementary School.* Besides referring to the usual elementary school academic subjects, the report suggested a new emphasis on foreign languages, fine arts, physical education, and health. The report also recommended that more emphasis be placed on mathematics and science, beginning in the fourth grade.

*Report Focusing on Middle Schools*　The Carnegie Council on Adolescent Development in the report *Turning Points* (1989) called for a restructuring of middle schools wherein students and teachers would be grouped together as teams with emphasis on intellectual and personal growth. The council suggested a core academic program (integrating English, fine arts, foreign languages, history, literature and grammar, mathematics, science, and social studies); the promotion of cooperative learning (students of varying abilities working together as a team) rather than placement by academic achievement level; staffing middle schools with teachers who are experts at teaching young adolescents; emphasizing the health of the adolescent; and connecting the schools with the community.

*Political Response to the Call for Reforms*　In August 1986 the National Governors' Association conference, chaired by Lamar Alexander, then governor of Tennessee, released a report on education that attempted to deal with some of the demands of the earlier commission studies. *Time for Results: The Governors' 1991 Report on Education* suggested, among other things, that public schools reexamine their organizational structures and provide a choice for parents and students by developing public alternative schools and allowing parents to select the school best suited to their children. According to Richard D. Lamm, then governor of Colorado, author of the "choice" section of the report, "Our task force believes that public education cannot, as presently structured, deal effectively with the nation's diversity and its demand for compulsory education. . . . We propose something in the great American tradition: that you increase excellence by increasing the choices" (*Wall Street Journal* staff 1986, 14). Governor Lamm's task force believed that choice would produce competition, a more responsive system, and a "distinct shared philosophy, mission, and faculty agreement called for in literature on effective schools" (*Time for Results,* 69). The issue of choice continues to be an important method of reform in the 1990s (see also chapter 12, pp. 481–490).

These reforms also addressed issues related to the teaching profession. They set standards for initial certification of teachers, testing requirements for permanent teacher certification, teacher evaluation systems, eligibility requirements for merit pay (salary increments based on evaluation of teaching performance), and requirements for career ladder programs (staffing patterns that award salary levels based on differing responsibilities and levels of success in classroom teaching evaluations).

The goal of these reforms was to improve the quality of schooling. Most of the reformers suggested that this improvement could be measured through student achievement test scores, but the outcome has as yet not been categorically determined. Owing to the cries for reform in the 1980s, the curriculum became increasingly subject centered and less responsive to individual student needs. An example of that curriculum can be seen in William Bennett's *James Madison High School* (see figure 5.2). Changes in the academic programs included more attention to the gaining of basic language and mathematics skills in the elemen-

*James Madison Elementary School* (1988)

Carnegie Council on Adolescent Development (1989)

*Turning Point* (a report for restructuring of middle schools) (1989)

National Governors' Association (1986)

*Time for Results* (established six task forces for improvement of education to be completed by 1991) (1986)

*James Madison High School* (Secondary) (1988)

*(continued on p. 210)*

**TABLE 5-2**

## Federal Legislation in Early 1990s

| Legislation | Year | Provisions |
|---|---|---|
| **Equalizing Educational Opportunities** | | |
| *Individuals with Disabilities Education Act Amendments* (P.L. 102–119) | 1991 | Amends P.L. 94–142 to provide additional programs for infants and toddlers with disabilities. |
| *Rehabilitation Act Amendments* (P.L. 102–52) | 1991 | Reauthorizes funding for vocational rehabilitation services, research and training, supplementary services and facilities. |
| *National Commission on Time and Learning* (P.L. 102–359) | 1992 | Provides appropriations for one year for schoolwide civics education program rather than for just individual educationally disadvantaged children. |
| **Promoting Educational Excellence** | | |
| *The Excellence in Mathematics, Science and Engineering Education Act* (P.L. 101–589) | 1990 | Created a national mathematics and science clearinghouse, established regional mathematics and science consortia, and one new scholarship program for each—mathematics, science, and engineering. |
| *The National Assessment of Chapter I Act* (P.L. 101–305) | 1990 | Required the secretary of education to conduct a comprehensive national assessment of programs carried out under Chapter I and Title I funds from ESEA of 1965. |
| *National Commission on a Longer School Year Act* (P.L. 102–62) | 1991 | Established *The National Education Commission on Time and Learning*; directed the secretary of education to provide grants for research in teaching writing and to educate students about the history and principles of the Constitution; established *The National Council on Education Standards and Testing*. |
| *National Literacy Act* (P.L. 102–73) | 1991 | Established *The National Institute for Literacy, The National Institute Board,* and *The Interagency Task Force on Literacy.* |
| *Ready to Learn Act* (P.L. 102–545) | 1992 | Amended the *General Education Provisions Act* to establish Ready-To-Learn television programs to support educational programming and materials for preschool/elementary school children and their parents, child-care providers, and educators. |
| *Childhood Education and Development Act* (P.L. 101–239) | 1989 | Authorized appropriations to expand Head Start programs carried out under ESEA of 1965 to include child-care services. |
| *Augustus F. Hawkins Human Services Reauthorization Act* (P.L. 101–501) | 1990 | Authorized appropriations for fiscal years 1991–1994 to carry out Head Start programs and others for disadvantaged children and adults. |
| **Preventing School Dropouts and Drug Use** | | |
| *School Dropout Prevention and Basic Skills Improvement Act* (P.L. 101–600) | 1990 | Funding to improve secondary school programs for developing basic skills and preventing dropouts. |

| Legislation | Year | Provisions |
|---|---|---|
| *Anti-Drug Education Act and Drug Abuse Resistance Education* (DARE) (P.L. 101–647) (part of the *Comprehensive Crime Control Act)* | 1990 | Raised funding levels for school personnel training, replication of successful drug education programs, and after-school programs; established a program of grants to HEW for DARE programs to help local education agencies cooperate with law enforcement. |

### Improving Education of Students Entering Workforce

| | | |
|---|---|---|
| *Job Training Reform Amendments Act* (P.L. 102–367) | 1992 | Amended the *Job Training Partnership Act*, the *Carl Perkins Vocational Education Act,* and the *Adult Education Act* |
| *School-to-Work Opportunities Act* (P.L. 103–239) | 1994 | Funded $300 million to set up a national system of school-to-work programs for those students not planning to attend college. |

### Developing Educational Standards by the Year 2000

| | | |
|---|---|---|
| *Goals 2000: Educate America Act* (P.L. 103–227) | 1994 | •All children in America will start school ready to learn.<br>•The high school graduation rate will increase to at least 90 percent.<br>•All students will leave grades 4, 8, and 12 having demonstrated competency over challenging subject matter including English, mathematics, science, foreign languages, civics and government, economics, the arts, history, and geography, and every school in America will ensure that all students learn to use their minds well, so they may be prepared for responsible citizenship, further learning, and productive employment in our nation's modern economy.<br>•U.S. students will be first in the world in mathematics and science achievement.<br>•Every adult American will be literate and will possess the knowledge and skills necessary to compete in a global economy and exercise the rights and responsibilities of citizenship.<br>•Every school in the United States will be free of drugs, violence, and the unauthorized presence of firearms and alcohol and will offer a disciplined environment conducive to learning.<br>•The nation's teaching force will have access to programs for the continued improvement of their professional skills and the opportunity to acquire the knowledge and skills needed to instruct and prepare all American students for the next century.<br>•Every school will promote partnerships that will increase parental involvement and participation in promoting the social, emotional, and academic growth of children. |
| *The Safe Schools Act* (Part of the *Goals 2000: Educate America Act*) | 1994 | Creates a program of federal assistance to local school districts to confront violence and end drug use. |

**Efforts to improve education in the United States in the early 1990s have resulted in federal legislation with applications to specific issues. This table lists the most notable bills and acts in specific categories.**

tary school, increased promotion and graduation standards, development of objectives, measurement of student progress, increased college admission standards, additional academic requirements for high school graduation, and evaluation of teachers based on a set of criteria.

## A RETURN TO CHILD WELFARE AND EQUAL OPPORTUNITIES

Reform reports of the 1990s focused on children

The dozen reports of the early 1990s moved the emphasis of the reforms toward children rather than curriculum and toward equalization of funding rather than academic and professional standards. Perhaps, these later reform reports are a reaction to the reports of the 1980s. They do not suggest that excellence and standards are unimportant; however, they proclaim that excellence cannot be achieved until all children are cared for and all schools are equitably funded.

Teacher reforms focused on teaching diverse populations of students

Curriculum standards proposed

***Reforms Shift toward Equality of Opportunity*** The reform reports of the early 1990s emphasized equal educational opportunity, especially for minorities and women. Reforms in teacher education moved toward preparing teachers to teach a diverse population of students and recruitment of more minority teachers including those of color. Curriculum standards were proposed in the reform reports of the 1990s, as well as improved education of the gifted and talented, and mastery of skills needed for work and higher education for secondary students. However, the reports suggested that the responsibility to educate all children extended beyond the public schools to the parents and to society. Early childhood education was emphasized as were standards to move learning to the higher levels of inquiry, self-evaluation, and problem solving. The reports also suggested that secondary school students can learn by working in challenging internships. The federal government was called upon to provide more funding, particularly in the areas of preschool education, integration of the schools, meeting the goals of America 2000, and developing standards to implement these six educational goals. Likewise, states were called upon to equalize funding formulas and provide choice for minority students attending highly segregated schools.

***Federal Legislation in the Early 1990s*** Federal legislation of the early 1990s (see table 5.2) attempted to equalize educational opportunities, promote excellence through standards and assessment, increase literacy, improve preschool readiness, prevent school dropouts, and improve students' preparation for the world of work. From these legislative acts, it is clear that the themes of popularization, multitudinousness, and politicization were alive and well in U.S. public education in the early 1990s.

## AMERICA 2000

Education Commission of the States (1983)

As a result of the work on the Education Commission of the States, the National Governors' Association outlined six major goals for education in 1990:

- That all children will start school ready to learn
- That 90 percent of all high school students graduate

- That students achieve competence in core subjects in grades 4, 8, and 12
- That American students be "first in the world" in math and science achievement
- That every adult American be literate and have the skills to function as a citizen and a worker
- That all schools will be free of drugs and violence and "offer a disciplined environment conducive to learning"

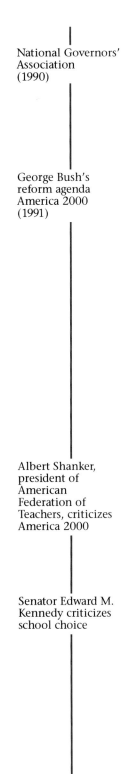

National Governors' Association (1990)

In 1991 President George Bush outlined his agenda for reforming the schools. The plan was designed by Secretary of Education Lamar Alexander, only two months after his appointment to the post, and Assistant Secretary of Education David Kerns, former executive director of the Xerox Corporation. The program, America 2000, utilizing the proposals of the National Governors' Association, called for several reform strategies. They included:

George Bush's reform agenda America 2000 (1991)

- A voluntary national system of examinations in mathematics, science, English, history, and geography
- Incentives to states and communities that develop school choice for parents and teachers
- Differentiated pay for teachers who teach well, teach core subjects, teach in dangerous or challenging settings, and who serve as mentors for new teachers
- Certification of nontraditionally trained teachers and administrators
- Involvement of business and industry in setting job-related skill standards and providing money for new schools

Even before the official announcement of Bush's reform package was made, criticisms were heard. Albert Shanker, president of the American Federation of Teachers, expressed concern about the involvement of business and industry in the plan. According to Shanker, if government officials thought the plan was important, they would pay for it. He expressed concern that the school choice initiative involved private and religious schools as well as public schools. He further suggested that any new plan should involve the continued funding of successful programs such as Head Start and Chapter I rather than developing new, untested initiatives (April 21, 1991, E7).

Albert Shanker, president of American Federation of Teachers, criticizes America 2000

Concerns were also voiced in Congress. Senator Edward M. Kennedy of Massachusetts maintained that school choice involving private schools could become a "death sentence for public schools struggling to serve disadvantaged students" (Chira April 19, 1991, A1). According to Michael Casserly, associate director of the Council of Great City Schools, which represents the nation's largest school districts, Bush's proposed school choice plan, which would allow Chapter I money to follow underprivileged students to private and parochial schools, is probably "unworkable" and "unconstitutional" because poor school districts would be likely to lose Chapter I money. Others objected to the proposal for nationwide tests. Deborah Meier, who runs a school-of-choice that has been cited as a model by Bush, claims that the tests would hamper efforts to create innovative schools and innovative curriculum because they would dictate what must be taught (Chira April 20, 1991, 1). These are serious criticisms of a wide-ranging, complicated proposal to reform the schools. It appears from the legislation passed by the U.S. Congress in the early 1990s that the goals of America

Senator Edward M. Kennedy criticizes school choice

2000 are being taken seriously, while the reform agenda of President George Bush has been ignored.

In September 1991 the National Governors' Association issued its first report card on the progress being made to reach the goals of America 2000. It conceded that little has been achieved in most areas and insisted that more data was necessary in order to make more accurate assessments. However, in spite of these findings, it is possible to see a relationship between the goals of America 2000 and the legislation passed by the U.S. Congress in the early 1990s. Seeing progress toward the goals is another matter. Following the dismal review of the National Governors' Association, President Bush appointed South Carolina Governor Carroll A. Campbell to head a panel to outline objectives for each goal, thereby further defining them. In 1992 the goals panel also issued a report indicating what had been learned about progress toward the goals since 1991 and what still needed to be learned. As in 1991 the goals panel concluded that they still did not have a "direct way to measure the nation's progress" toward the goals (National Education Goals Panel 1992, 19).

Despite criticism of the goals of America 2000 and lack of a means by which to measure progress toward them, in 1993 President Bill Clinton's secretary of education Richard Riley endorsed the goals and added two additional ones. It is now called Goals 2000: Educate America Act (see table 5.2). Tied to the goals, the Clinton administration proposed a $700 million budget for 1994 to implement them and set standards for monitoring progress toward them. It is likely that these eight goals will be the guidepost for federal legislation for many years to come.

---

**5-2**

**POINTS TO REMEMBER**

- As more and more previously disenfranchised students entered the public schools during the civil rights period, the schools offered many educational opportunities to meet their needs.
- The U.S. Supreme Court decision *Brown v. Board of Education of Topeka, Kansas,* which ruled that separate schools were not equal schools, resulted in integration of the public schools.
- After integration many studies revealed that educational opportunities for minorities were still unequal. The students were frequently placed in schools where they were not welcome; funding in poor districts was not equal to funding in prosperous districts; minorities were frequently tracked into lower level classes.
- Head Start, a preschool program, was developed to bridge the educational gap between impoverished and prosperous children. The Elementary and Secondary Education Act of 1965 provided increased opportunities and funding for special programs for minorities, bilingual and multicultural students, and women.
- Public schools were required to educate bilingual and multicultural students in their own language.
- P.L. 94–142 provided funding for public schools to develop equal access and special programs for all those with disabilities.
- Educational opportunities of the 1970s–1990s were increasingly multitudinous but still not equal. Federal funding cuts eliminated many programs for the disenfranchised.
- The reform critics of the 1980s focused on the curriculum, suggesting that schools should do more to ensure excellence. The 1990s reports focused on individual students and stated that school reforms needed the help of communities.
- Federal legislation in the 1990s attempted to equalize educational opportunities, promote educational excellence, and establish goals for developing educational standards by the year 2000.

## For Thought/Discussion

1. Describe the effect on American education of the launching of the Soviet Sputnik in 1957. Do you believe that the scientific achievements of students in the 1990s have kept pace with the achievements of students in the late 1950s? Why or why not?

2. Do you believe that the landmark *Brown v. Board of Education of Topeka, Kansas,* decision has had a net positive or negative effect on equality of American education? Explain.

3. What effects would full inclusion of disabled students have on the regular classroom? Do you support the concept?

4. What connections do you see between the proposals of Goals 2000: Educate America Act and actual changes in the classroom?

5. If you had to choose a school for your child, what specific aspects of the school would influence your decision?

## For Further Reading/Reference

Bell, T. H. 1993. Reflections one decade after *A nation at risk. Phi Delta Kappan 74* (8), 592–597. President Carter's secretary of education looks critically at educational reforms since the publication of *A Nation at Risk,* the report that began the frenzy of reform of the 1980s.

National Commission on Excellence in Education. 1983. *A nation at risk: The imperatives for educational reform.* Washington, DC: U.S. Government Printing Office. An examination of the problems of education in the 1980s and recommendations for attacking the problems in the 1990s.

Ravitch, D. 1983. *The troubled crusade: American education 1945–1980.* New York: Basic Books. A discussion of the concerns and problems of educational opportunity, beginning with progressive education in the 1940s and extending to the growth of the schools in the 1950s and 1960s and finally to the bureaucracy of the schools in the 1980s.

Record, W., and Record, J. S. (Eds.). 1960. *Little Rock, U.S.A.* San Francisco, CA: Chandler Publishing Company. A collection of newspaper accounts, court records, and other documents related to the Little Rock incident of September 1957, when nine black teenagers tried to enroll at an all-white school.

Reisman, F. 1962. *The culturally deprived child.* New York: Harper Brothers. Presents characteristics of the culturally deprived child and explains how the verbally loaded curriculum of the 1950s and 1960s failed to meet the needs of this child.

Tuyack, D., Lowe, R., and Hansot, E. 1984. *Public schools in hard times: The Great Depression and recent years.* Cambridge, MA: Harvard University Press. A discussion of how economic conditions in the 1930s caused cutbacks in education and how these cutbacks led to growing tensions between professional educators and business and industry; also compares education of the 1930s to that of the 1980s.

Martha F. Campbell in *Phi Delta Kappan*

*"When he said* **Klondike,** *I thought he meant bars. When he said* **Quaker,** *I thought he meant oats. When he said* **Philadelphia,** *I thought he meant cheese. I would've done better if the test had been after lunch."*

Drawing by Leo Cullum; © The New Yorker Magazine, Inc.

**CHAPTER OBJECTIVES**

After studying this chapter, you should be able to:

- Define philosophy.
- Discuss metaphysics, epistemology, axiology, and logic.
- Explain why it is important for educators to study philosophy.
- Explain how the categories of philosophy (metaphysics, epistemology, axiology, and logic) relate to the schools of philosophy.
- Discuss the five schools of philosophy: idealism, realism, pragmatism, existentialism, and philosophical analysis.
- Explain how the five schools of philosophy relate to the five theories of education.
- Define the five theories of education: perennialism, essentialism, progressivism, social reconstructionism, and behaviorism.
- Explain how each of the five theories of education relate to educational practice.
- Discuss how philosophy affects education in terms of goal setting, curricular emphasis, and the role of the teacher.

*Chapter 6*

# THE PHILOSOPHICAL FOUNDATIONS OF EDUCATION

**7**his is a classic evaluation of Socrates as a teacher done in a twentieth-century style with twentieth-century attitudes. Intended to be humorous, at the same time it focuses on how philosophies of teaching may change with the times. The ratings go from high to low with 1 being high.

## A. Personal Qualifications
1. Personal appearance
   Rating: 1 2 3 4 ⑤
   Comment: Dresses in an old sheet draped about his body
2. Self-confidence
   Rating: 1 2 3 4 ⑤
   Comment: Not sure of himself—always asking questions . . .
3. Adaptability
   Rating: 1 2 3 4 ⑤
   Comment: Prone to suicide by poison when under duress

## B. Class Management
1. Organization
   Rating: 1 2 3 4 ⑤
   Comment: Does not keep a seating chart
2. Room appearance
   Rating: 1 2 3 ④ 5
   Comment: Does not have eye-catching bulletin boards
3. Utilization of supplies
   Rating: ① 2 3 4 5
   Comment: Does not use supplies

## C. Teacher-Pupil Relations
1. Tact and Consideration
   Rating: 1 2 3 4 ⑤

Socrates (469–399 B.C.), a great teacher, believed in teaching by a method of questioning his students, known as the Socratic Method.

Comment: Places students in embarrassing situations by asking questions

2. Attitude of class

Rating: 1 ② 3 4 5

Comment: Class is friendly

**D. Professional Attitude**

1. Professional ethics

Rating: 1 2 3 4 ⑤

Comment: Does not belong to professional association or PTA

2. In-service training

Rating: 1 2 3 4 ⑤

Comment: Complete failure here—has not even bothered to attend college

3. Parent relationships

Rating: 1 2 3 4 ⑤

Comment: Needs to improve in this area—parents are trying to get rid of him

**Recommendation: DOES NOT HAVE A PLACE IN EDUCATION– SHOULD NOT BE REHIRED.**

From: J. Gauss, "Evaluation of Socrates as a Teacher," *Phi Delta Kappan* (1962).

*I*n the current climate of educational reform, teachers need to look back to the philosophies that have informed their educational thinking and forward to ways that thinking might be used to creatively restructure what goes on in the classroom and in schools. As Roland Barth says in *Phi Delta Kappan,* "Let go of the trapeze. Think otherwise. Become an independent variable. Lick the envelope. Bell the cat. Fly the cage. Leave your mark" (1991, p. 128).

## What Is a Philosophy of Education?

Philosophy and education are closely related fields. Both are vitally concerned with humankind, the nature of humankind, knowledge, relationships, and behavior. But whereas philosophy seeks to understand the fundamental theoretical basis of existence, education seeks to understand the more practical answers. Where philosophy would ask, "Where are we going?" education would ask, "How can we get there?" Where philosophy would ask, "How do we define ourselves as humans?" education would ask, "How do I become self-reliant?" Where philosophy would ask, "Is there life on other planets?" education would ask, "How do we get there?" The various belief systems or schools of philosophy are the foundations on which educational theory is built.

The word *philosophy* comes from the Greek **philos**, which means "love," and **sophos**, which means "wisdom." Hence, philosophy literally means love of wisdom. Philosophy is, therefore, the inquiry into the principles of knowledge, reality, and values that constitute wisdom.

## ORGANIZING KNOWLEDGE

Philosophy seeks to organize and systematize all fields of knowledge as a means of understanding and interpreting the totality of reality. Or put another way, it is a search for truth. Philosophy is composed of the following general categories: metaphysics, epistemology, axiology, and logic. They provide philosophers with questions and specific approaches to examine truth.

*Metaphysics*   The philosopher uses **metaphysics** to speculate on the nature of ultimate reality. Literally, metaphysics means "beyond the physical." Hence it deals with the comparison of "other worldly" to "this worldly" (Brameld 1971, 47), or the relationship of physical substance to its creation. According to William James, "One may say that metaphysics inquires into the cause, the substance, the meaning, and the outcome of all things." He states that the three central metaphysical questions are: "What can I know? What should I do? What may I hope?" (1948, 31). From these stem other metaphysical questions such as: "Is the universe as a whole rationally designed or is it ultimately meaningless? Is what we call mind or spirit nothing more than an illusion bred by the present inadequacy of scientific knowledge, or does it possess a reality of its own? Are all organisms determined [life preordained by the 'other worldly'], or are some, such as man, free?" (Kneller 1964, 5-6).

According to Everett W. Hall, metaphysics affects how humankind acts by shaping people's views of what nature is and how it can and should be controlled. Educational philosopher Theodore Brameld states that metaphysics searches for the principles of human existence, whether physical or spiritual; it does not prejudge what they are.

We can see how metaphysical questions shape action by examining a problem in education. George F. Kneller writes about practical aspects of metaphysics in *Introduction to the Philosophy of Education*.

> Take . . . [a] practical problem in education, which is basically metaphysical. One hears a great deal about teaching the child and not the subject. What does this statement mean to a teacher? Even if the teacher replies, "I prefer just to teach my subject," the question still remains, "Why?" What is the *ultimate* purpose of teaching the subject? (1964, 24)

The answers to these questions are likely to be based on the teacher's metaphysical beliefs. If, for example, the teacher believes that very specific basic knowledge is crucial to the child's intellectual development, it is likely that this teacher will focus on the subject matter. If, on the other hand, the teacher holds that the child is more important than any specific subject matter, it is likely that this teacher will focus on the child and allow the child to provide clues as to how he or she should be instructed. The action that the teacher takes will depend on his or her answer to the metaphysical question, What is the ultimate purpose of teaching the subject?

*Epistemology*    The category of philosophy that inquires into the nature and universality of knowledge is **epistemology**. It attempts to discover what is involved in the cognitive processes of knowing, believing, understanding, supposing, guessing, learning, and forgetting. "It asks such questions as: Is there something common to all the different activities to which we apply the term 'knowing'? Is knowing a special sort of mental act? If so, what is the difference between knowing and believing? Can we know anything beyond the objects with which our senses acquaint us? Does knowing make any difference to the object known?" (Kneller, 8).

The epistemologist neither attempts to gather and classify facts nor attempts to explain how people think scientifically. Rather, the goal of the epistemologist is to understand how we define, and thus acquire, knowledge. Because epistemological questions deal with the essence of knowledge, they are central to education. Teachers must be able to assess "what is knowledge" in order to determine if a particular thing or idea should be included in the curriculum.

Teachers should be able to distinguish this knowledge from opinion and belief. They must determine, for example, if a commonly held belief (**maxim**) is knowledge. Does it meet the standards of reliable knowledge? Is the statement that "all men are created equal" an example of knowledge or a belief? Obviously, this question revolves around the issues of whether all people are created equal in the first place and whether equality in any human endeavor is possible. How one answers the question determines what is included in the curriculum and how one teaches this knowledge.

*Axiology*    The category of philosophy that deals with the nature of values is **axiology**. It is divided into the study of **ethics** (moral values and conduct) and **aesthetics** (values in the realm of beauty and art).

Ethics deals with such questions as: "What is the good life for all men?" and "How ought we to behave?" (Kneller, 15). According to A. R. Lacey in *A Dictionary of Philosophy,* ethical questions generally deal with how people should act and include: What is right? What is wrong? What is my duty? What is desirable? What is good? (1976, 60). An ethical system may be secular, or it may be based on the absolutism of some religions that have fixed rules of conduct that people are expected to obey.

Aesthetics deals with the theory of beauty and art in its broad sense. Aesthetics are concerned with "the creation, value and experience of art and the analysis and solutions of problems related to these" (Lacey, 2). The major questions aesthetics asks are: "What makes something a work of art? Must a work of art exhibit certain formal properties, or express certain emotions and attitudes or do other things?" (Lacey, 2). What are the proper subject matter and scope of art? Should an autumn sunset always be depicted in tones of orange and yellow, or could it be portrayed in black and brown? Is human elimination an appropriate subject for artistic works? Aesthetics, then, determines whether there are principles of art and beauty or if art and beauty are a matter of personal taste.

Both ethics and aesthetics are important issues in education. Should a system of ethics be taught in the public school? If so, should the system be based on religion or should it be totally secular? (Ethics as related to teaching is discussed in chapter 15, pp. 621–625). According to a 1993 Gallup poll, 69 percent of American adults thought it would be possible for their community to agree upon a basic set of values to be taught in public schools. The following were the values these adults thought should be taught: honesty (97 percent), democracy (93 percent), acceptance of people of different races and ethnic backgrounds (93 percent), patriotism and love of country (91 percent), moral courage (91 percent), the golden rule (91 percent), and acceptance of people who hold different religious beliefs (87 percent) (Elam, Rose, Gallup 1994, 143).

One of the most divisive questions of ethics in public education has been the issue of allowing religious practices in the classroom. Should public school children be allowed to participate in exercises during the school day in which the Bible is read and/or a prayer is delivered or recited?

The issue was debated in the Supreme Court case *Abingdon School District v. Schempp* (374 U.S. 203, 1963), in which two Schempp children participated in readings of verses from the Bible and recitation of the Lord's Prayer that were conducted daily over the school intercom. Although participation was voluntary by statute of the Commonwealth of Pennsylvania, the children remained in the classroom during the exercises because their father believed that their relationships with teachers and other students would be adversely affected if they did not. According to the plaintiffs, practicing Unitarians, a literal reading of the Bible was "contrary to the religious beliefs which they held and to their familial teaching."

The Supreme Court ruled in the Schempp case as follows: "Such study of the Bible or of religion, when presented objectively as part of a secular program of education, may not be effected consistently with the First Amendment. But the exercises here do not fall into those categories. They are religious exercises, required by the states in violation of the command of the First Amendment that the government maintain strict neutrality, neither aiding or opposing religion." Thus, the prayers and Bible readings were judged against the law. Others, including a dissenting opinion of the justices of the Supreme Court, disagreed with the ruling, claiming that not permitting prayer and Bible reading in the school impedes the right of free exercise of religion and violates the foundations of the nation. While many of the arguments in favor of prayer and Bible reading are based on questions of ethics rather than law, the Court's decision in this case was based on the Constitution, as it is required to be.

In December 1993, in Jackson, Mississippi, Principal Bishop Knox was fired for allowing a prayer to be read over Wingfield High School's public address system even though 490 of 586 students had voted for it. The prayer, "Almighty God, we ask that you bless our parents, teachers and country throughout the day. In your name we pray. Amen," has caused a furor in Jackson. Jackson school officials stated that allowing the prayer to be read was "an unforgivable trespass by religion into secular territory" (Farley, 41). Knox stated that he believed his action was consistent with a 1992 U.S. Court of Appeals decision in the Fifth Circuit in New Orleans which ruled that prayer was permissible at graduation if it was nonproselytizing, nonsectarian, student initiated, and student led. Mississippi Governor Kirk Fordice expressed support for Knox's decision and school prayer saying, "If we keep on with what started in Jackson, Mississippi, one day, I hope soon, it's not going to be legal to keep prayer out of public schools" (Farley 1993, 41). Mr. Knox, who has been reinstated, is not alone in allowing prayer in his school. In a 1993 survey conducted by Phi Delta Kappa of its 4,231 members who are school superintendents, 1,491 responded to the survey and 71 percent (1,106) reported including prayer in some form at least once during activities associated with high school graduation in 1993; the largest percentage including prayer were in the South (76 percent) and the lowest percentage in the East (34 percent) (Barber 1993, 125).

Aesthetic questions in education involve deciding which works by which artists should be included or not included in the curriculum and what kind of subject matter should be allowed or encouraged in a writing, drawing, or painting class. Are nude figures by Michelangelo more acceptable than those by the photographer Robert Mapplethorpe? [Mapplethorpe is a deceased photographer who had received a National Endowment for the Arts (NEA) grant to support his work, which some people find sacrilegious and offensive. When his work was displayed using NEA funds, it became the focal point of conservative political criticism of use of public funds to support art.] At what age should children be exposed to art that some might consider pornographic? Or does the mere process of selecting pieces of art encourage a liberal or conservative attitude in students? Should teachers compromise their own attitude toward a piece of artwork if it disagrees with that of a parent or a school board? One example occurred recently in a local independent school in North Carolina. An exhibit was displayed in the art gallery, which students also used as classroom space. Because the works dealt with the topic of feminism, several of the pieces used symbols of female genitalia. The artist was asked to remove the exhibit since, according to the headmaster's aesthetic values, it was not appropriate material for the students.

*Logic*   The philosophical category that deals with the nature of reasoning is **logic**. It examines the principles that allow us to move from one argument to the next. There are many types of logic, but the two most commonly used and studied are deductive and inductive. **Deduction** is a type of reasoning that moves from a general statement to a specific instance. For example, the statement "All people are mammals" is a general statement of fact, or a **major premise**. "Jane is a person" is a particular fact, or a **minor premise**, that no one disputes. The conclusion, therefore, is obvious. "Jane is a mammal." Thus the conclusion is logically inferred from the general statements made.

**Induction** is a type of reasoning that moves in the opposite direction, from particular instances to a general conclusion. Certain observations are categorized, and then generalizations are made based on these particulars. One of the dangers of inductive reasoning is jumping to conclusions with too few particular observations. For example, a teacher might reason, "Sammy is having difficulty learning to read. Sammy's mother works. Therefore, Sammy is having difficulty learning to read because his mother works." This generalization is based on the assumption that mothers who work do not devote sufficient time to their children and, therefore, the children are likely to do poorly in school. This reasoning is clearly flawed and dangerous.

Logical reasoning is used all the time in making educational decisions. We use logic when we determine how to order the curriculum. Does it make sense to teach correct spelling before we teach students to compose a story? Does it make more sense to teach history chronologically than thematically? We use logic when we determine how to place students in homogeneous groups. We use logic when we make emergency decisions. Should school be canceled because of the weather? All these are educational questions that use the principles of logic, but it is easy to see how some decisions may be flawed if the basic logical foundation is invalid or flawed.

## THINKING CLEARLY

Philosophy provides us with the tools we need to think clearly. Let's go back to the aesthetic question of the headmaster and the art show to see how philosophy might help us to think clearly about an educational issue.

The headmaster used questions of aesthetics to make his decision to remove the art show. However, if he had asked other philosophical questions earlier, he might have avoided the whole conflict. For example, if he had asked the metaphysical question "What is the purpose of education?" he might have answered, "The purpose of education is to teach students to make ethical and aesthetic decisions for themselves." If he had determined this ahead of time, he would have displayed the show, left it up, and developed curriculums and teaching strategies to help the students make a decision for themselves. On the other hand, he might have answered, "The purpose of education is to teach students what is aesthetically acceptable in polite society." If this had been his answer, it is likely that the show would not have been displayed in the first place.

He also might have asked epistemological questions. For example, going beyond his own subjective judgment, he might ask, "Can we know anything beyond the objects with which our senses acquaint us?" If he had answered affirmatively, he might have decided to exhibit the paintings and then, with his faculty, develop a curriculum that would help the students answer the question.

We've already dealt with this incident in terms of its aesthetic questions, but what of its ethical questions? Suppose the headmaster had asked "How should I behave?" Would he have removed the show after the commitment had been made to the artist? Or would he have allowed it to be displayed prior to carefully reviewing it in terms of other philosophical questions? How would he answer any complaints of parents or school board members?

Finally, he might have dealt with the issue through logic. Deductively he might have concluded, "Painting on canvas is art. This is painting on canvas. Therefore, it is art." It appears that he did deal with the issue inductively, reasoning in this way: "Some of the paintings in this show will be offensive to some people. Therefore, this show is offensive and should be removed." Did he use good logic in his decision-making process? Using the questioning techniques of philosophy, the headmaster would have been helped to arrive at a satisfactory decision.

## Why Study the Philosophy of Education?

Having a philosophy of education is important if educators are going to develop the ability to think clearly about what they do on a day-to-day basis and to see how these things extend beyond the classroom to the whole of humankind and society. Philosophy does not provide us with answers to problems but, instead, gives us a means of inquiry so that we can gain insight into them. People who use the tools of philosophy are more concerned with appropriate questions than with finding the correct answers. William James (1842–1910), a professor of psychology and philosophy at Harvard University from 1872 to 1907, suggests that philosophy provides us with the tools to see beyond ourselves:

*Viewpoint* From: Some Problems of Philosophy

Philosophy, beginning in wonder, as Plato and Aristotle said, is able to fancy everything different from what it is. It sees the familiar as if it were strange, and the strange as if it were familiar. It can take things up and lay them down again. Its mind is full of air that plays around every subject. It rouses us up from our native dogmatic slumber and breaks up our caked prejudices. Historically it has always been a sort of fecundation of four different human interests, science, poetry, religion, and logic, by one another. It has sought by hard reasoning for results emotionally valuable. To have some contact with it, to catch its influence, is thus good for both literary and scientific students. By its poetry it appeals to literary minds; but by its logic stiffens them up and remedies their softness. By its logic it appeals to the scientific; but softens them by its other aspects, and saves them from too dry a technicality. Both types of student ought to get from philosophy a livelier spirit, more air, more mental background . . . A man with no philosophy in him is the most inauspicious and unprofitable of all human mates. (1948, 7-8)

By using the tools of philosophy we can analyze who we are, what we do, and how we do it. Philosophy not only helps us analyze problems, but supplies us with the means for seeking alternative solutions to them. For example, an English teacher is faced with the decision of teaching either the great works of Western literature in the eleventh-grade curriculum or literature that provides a global perspective. He asks many philosophical questions as he ponders his decision: Many of my students come from non-Western cultures. Should they be taught the literature from their cultures or a common core of literature? Is there a common literary terminology that my students can apply to various works of literature? Can we examine both Western and non-Western literature in terms of that terminology? What values should I be teaching my students through literature? Is it more important that they examine the values of different cultures, or of Western culture? Do I intend to encourage the value of reading for pleasure? Or do I hope to help them develop a love of great writing? As the teacher explores many possible answers, he discovers a variety of approaches to the teaching of literature.

Studying the philosophy of education enables you to recognize the philosophical perspectives of educational theory and practice. Education is both changing to adapt to the needs of society and attempting to change it. As you develop your own philosophy of education, you can weigh these changes against your own beliefs and can also determine their likely educational outcomes.

For example, the reform movements of the 1980s suggested a return to a subject-centered curriculum in which students would learn the accumulated knowledge of society. What is the philosophical basis for this reform? What metaphysical questions have been asked and how have they been answered? What is the nature of knowledge according to these reformers? How would these reforms deal with questions of ethics and aesthetics? How do these reforms fit with your own philosophical leaning? How can you justify your opinions based on a philosophical point of view? Knowing how to ask and interpret philosophical questions will not only help you better understand the reforms, but it will help you reevaluate and defend your own philosophical points of view.

## The Schools of Philosophical Thought

The categories of philosophical thought (metaphysics, epistemology, axiology, and logic) yield the questions by which we can derive a system of thought or a school of philosophy. Each of the philosophical schools deals with reality in a different way. The traditional schools of philosophy include idealism, realism, pragmatism, and existentialism. Philosophical analysis is a modern school with a methodological approach. We will discuss how each deals with reality. See table 6.1, page 236, for a comparison of how each school of philosophy deals with the questions of metaphysics, epistemology, axiology, and logic.

### IDEALISM

According to the traditional philosophical school of **idealism**, ultimate reality consists of an idea, a nonphysical essence, that is the foundation of all things. According to the Greek philosopher Plato (427–347 B.C.), the originator of idealism, ideas alone, because they transcend the physical, are genuinely real. The idealist contends, "I think, therefore I am." Plato assumed that the world was made up of "eternal verities," which consisted of the True, the Good, and the Beautiful, and that the universe, which is an expression of will and intelligence, is ordered by this eternal, spiritual reality.

*Viewpoint*  Lesson 1 Plato

This is Plato.
He is trying to separate his mind from his body.
Some trick.
Lots of education will free your reason.
Then you will be a philosopher.
You will uncover the planned order of the world.
You will have knowledge of the pure essences.
Think, think, think.
The material world is imperfect, impermanent and relative.
As a philosopher, you must serve it.
After all that studying.
Too bad.

From: Brandis, B. "A Primer of Educational Philosophy," reprinted in *The Educational Forum,* Winter 1993, 213–214. This cynical poem was written in 1967 when Brandis was a student at Grinnell College in Iowa.

The idealist claims that individuals originated within the mind of a deity, a first cause, or a creator, thus people are finite and limited beings, microcosms of the greater cosmic mind, which is infinite.

According to the idealist, an individual can transcend the physical world and can have knowledge of the spiritual world simply by intuition. The development of the mind and self is primary to the idealist; the development of the physical being is secondary. Since people are the only educable organisms, only humans, along with God, have self-controlled minds.

**Founders and Proponents**   Idealism has numerous proponents. The Greek philosopher Plato (see chapter 4, p. 135) is considered to be the father of idealism.

*René Descartes*   René Descartes (1596–1650), a French Catholic, was influenced by Plato and the works of Saint Augustine (see chapter 4, p. 136). The two main idealistic concepts developed by Descartes are that the self is the most immediate reality in the individual's experience and that the existence of God is proved in that we have an idea of a perfect being.

*Baruch Spinoza*   Baruch Spinoza (1632–1677), a Spanish Jew who lived in Holland, was also an idealist. According to Spinoza, there is an enduring substance that exists now, always has existed, and always will exist. He contended that this substance is correctly called God.

*Immanuel Kant*   The German philosopher Immanuel Kant (1724–1804), in *Metaphysics of Morals* and *Critique of Practical Reason,* spelled out his idealistic philosophy. He believed in freedom, the immortality of the soul, and the existence of God. He believed that there are universal moral laws and man has an obligation to obey them. Kant wrote extensively on human reason. We see the world, the "thing-in-itself," through our senses. Each sensation is an infinitesimal representation of a microscopic part of the physical world. At higher levels of reasoning, the world takes on unity through these sensations. We see objects that are external to us as related to other objects in an orderly way. Reason fits perceived objects into classes according to similarities and differences. Thus, it is through reason that we acquire knowledge of the world.

*Georg Wilhelm Friedrich Hegel*   Georg Wilhelm Friedrich Hegel (1770–1831), another German idealist, enjoyed paradoxes that emerged in his philosophical pattern. Hegel formalized dialectical logic into three stages: thesis, the Idea; antithesis, Nature; and synthesis, Mind or Spirit. The thesis and antithesis, as Hegel sees them, are contradictory. The synthesis unifies the positive aspects of each.

**Idealism and Education**   Although there are few classical idealists (those who believe the ideal rooted in God is central to all things) among contemporary philosophers, idealism has been a major influence in the foundation of Western educational thought. Idealistic educational philosophy centers on epistemology, the theory of knowledge. According to the classical idealist, because the Creator makes Himself evident in the universe, when we understand the nature of knowledge, we will understand the nature of reality and of God.

The classical idealist believes that thinking is an active process of a rational and substantive mind and that values are genuine, absolute, and permanent. The goal of learning is to understand universal ultimate reality.

The educational philosophy of the idealist is ideal—or idea-centered rather than either subject-centered or child-centered—because the ideal, or idea, is the foundation of all things. This knowledge is directed toward "self-hood, self-consciousness, and self-direction" (Bigge 1982, 30) and is centered on the growth of rational mental processes of the individual. One of the major tenets of idealism is that the individual who is created in God's image has free will, thus making learning possible.

The idealist believes that learning comes from within the individual rather than from without. Hence, real mental growth and spiritual growth do not occur until they are self-initiated.

## REALISM

Modern classical realists derive their system of formal reasoning from Aristotle (384–322 B.C.). **Realism** seeks knowledge about the nature of reality and humankind and attempts to interpret people's destiny based on that nature. Aristotle believed that reason was the ability to know the unchanging form of objects through sense experience and then to deduce from these forms the characteristics of the objects themselves.

Realism asserts that we live in a world in which many things, including people and objects, take their form independently of human reason or imagination; they exist in their own right and we experience them through our senses. Our most reliable guide to human behavior is knowledge of the objects, the laws that govern them, and their relationships, since all things behave according to rational, natural laws.

In order to understand an object, we must understand its absolute form, which is unchanging. To the realist, the trees of the forest exist whether or not there is a human mind to perceive them, an example of an independent reality.

Aristotle believed that ideas (or forms), such as the idea of God or the idea of a flower, can exist without matter. However, matter cannot exist without form. Matter has both universal and particular properties. Hence each rose shares universal properties with every other rose and every other flower. However, the particular properties of a rose differentiate it from all other flowers. The same is true of humans, all of whom have properties that distinguish them from other animals but who also have different shapes, heights, and hair colors. Forms (ideas) are nonmaterial representations of universal properties of the material objects that humans define through an examination of material objects that exist apart from themselves.

*Founders and Proponents* Plato first developed the doctrine of ideas, while Aristotle developed the doctrine of forms. According to Plato, ideas are independent of both the mind by which they may be known and the world of particulars in which they may take place. Aristotle, the realist, amended this, claiming that forms have an existence only in things (*in rebus*).

Classical realists maintained that each truth had a First Cause or an Unmoved Mover. The major development of modern realism, which developed

While Plato based his philosophy on the theory that reality exists in ideas, Aristotle based his on the theory that reality exists in forms, an objective world that we can know only through our senses. This is a detail of the fresco *School of Athens* by Raphael that depicts Plato and Aristotle. The fresco is in the Camera della Segnatura, the Vatican, Rome.

*(continued on p. 228)*

## *Cross-Cultural Perspective*

## Shakespeare in the Bush

*Laura Bohannan is an anthropologist who on a trip to West Africa attempted to prove the universality of knowledge by telling the story of* Hamlet *to a group of African tribal leaders. What she found is that truth and wisdom are related to human experience, and the concept of "eternal verities" applies only if individuals exist within the same culture.*

Just before I left Oxford for the Tiv in West Africa, conversation turned to the season at Stratford. "You Americans," said a friend, "often have difficulty with Shakespeare. He was, after all, a very English poet, and one can easily misinterpret the universal by misunderstanding the particular."

I protested that human nature is pretty much the same the whole world over; at least the general plot and motivation of the greater tragedies would always be clear—everywhere—although some details of custom might have to be explained and difficulties of translation might produce other slight changes. To end an argument we could not conclude, my friend gave me a copy of *Hamlet* to study in the African bush: it would, he hoped, lift my mind above its primitive surroundings, and possibly I might, by prolonged meditation, achieve the grace of correct interpretation. . . .

[Bohannan is invited to tell a story of "things a long time ago" to the elders of the tribe.]

Realizing that here was my chance to prove *Hamlet* universally intelligible, I agreed [to tell a story].

The old man handed me some more beer to help me on with my storytelling. Men filled their long wooden pipes and knocked coals from the fire to place in the pipe bowls; then, puffing contentedly, they sat back to listen. I began in the proper style, "Not yesterday, not yesterday, but long ago, a thing occurred. One night three men were keeping watch outside the homestead of the great chief, when suddenly they saw the former chief approach them."

"Why was he no longer their chief?"

"He was dead," I explained. "That is why they were troubled and afraid when they saw him."

"Impossible, began one of the elders, handing his pipe on to his neighbor, who interrupted, "Of course it wasn't the dead chief. It was an omen sent by a witch. Go on."

Slightly shaken, I continued. "One of these three was a man who knew things"—the closest translation for scholar, but unfortunately it also meant witch. The second elder looked triumphantly at the first. "So he spoke to the dead chief saying, 'Tell us what we must do so you may rest in your grave,' but the dead chief did not answer. He vanished, and they could see him no more. Then the man who knew things—his name was Horatio—said this event was the affair of the dead chief's son, Hamlet."

There was a general shaking of heads round the circle. "Had the dead chief no living brothers? Or was this son the chief?"

"No," I replied. "That is, he had one living brother who became the chief when the elder brother died."

The old men muttered: such omens were matters for chiefs and elders, not for youngsters; no good could come of going behind a chief's back; clearly Horatio was not a man who knew things.

"Yes, he was," I insisted, shooing a chicken away from my beer. "In our country the son is next to the father. The dead chief's younger brother had become the great chief. He had also married his elder brother's widow only about a month after the funeral."

"He did well," the old man beamed and announced to the others, "I told you that if we knew more about Europeans, we would find they really were very like us. In our country also," he added to me, "the younger brother marries the elder brother's widow and becomes the father of his children. Now, if your uncle, who married your widowed mother, is your father's full brother, then he will be a real father to you. Did Hamlet's father and uncle have one mother?"

His question barely penetrated my mind; I was too upset and thrown too far off balance by having one of the most important elements of *Hamlet* knocked straight out of the picture. Rather uncertainly I said that I thought they had the same mother, but I wasn't sure—the story didn't say. The old man told me severely that these genealogical details made all the difference and that when I got home I must ask the elders about it. He shouted out the door to one of his younger wives to bring his goatskin bag.

Determined to save what I could of the mother motif, I took a deep breath and began again. "The son Hamlet was very sad because his mother had married again so quickly. There was no need for her to do so, and it is our custom for a widow not to go to her next husband until she has mourned for two years."

"Two years is too long," objected the wife, who had appeared with the old man's battered goatskin bag. "Who will hoe your farms for you while you have no husband?"

"Hamlet," I retorted without thinking, "was old enough to hoe his mother's farms himself. There was no need for her to remarry." No one looked convinced. I gave up. "His mother and the great chief told Hamlet not to be sad, for the great chief himself would be a father to Hamlet. Furthermore, Hamlet would be the next chief: therefore he must stay to learn the things of a chief. Hamlet agreed to remain, and all the rest went off to drink beer."

While I paused, perplexed at how to render Hamlet's disgusted soliloquy to an audience convinced that Claudius and Gertrude had behaved in the best possible manner, one of the younger men asked me who had married the other wives of the dead chief.

"He had no other wives," I told him.

"But a chief must have many wives! How else can he brew beer and prepare food for all his guests?"

I said firmly that in our country even chiefs had only one wife, that they had servants to do their work, and that they paid them from tax money.

It was better, they returned, for a chief to have many wives and sons who would help him hoe his farms and feed his people; then everyone loved the chief who gave much and took nothing—taxes were a bad thing.

I agreed with the last comment, but for the rest fell back on their favorite way of fobbing off my questions: "That is the way it is done, so that is how we do it."

I decided to skip the soliloquy. Even if Claudius was here thought quite right to marry his brother's widow, there remained the poison motif, and I knew they would disapprove of fratricide. More hopefully I resumed, "That night Hamlet kept watch with the three who had seen his dead father. The dead chief again appeared, and although the others were afraid, Hamlet followed his dead father off to one side. When they were alone, Hamlet's dead father spoke."

"Omens can't talk!" The old man was emphatic.

"Hamlet's dead father wasn't an omen. Seeing him might have been an omen, but he was not." My audience looked as confused as I sounded. "It *was* Hamlet's dead father. It was a thing we call a 'ghost.'" I had to use the English word, for unlike many of the neighboring tribes, these people didn't believe in the survival after death of any individuating part of the personality.

"What is a 'ghost?' An omen?"

"No, a 'ghost' is someone who is dead but who walks around and can talk, and people can hear him and see him but not touch him."

They objected. "One can touch zombis."

"No, no! It was not a dead body the witches had animated to sacrifice and eat. No one else made Hamlet's dead father walk. He did it himself."

"Dead men can't walk," protested my audience as one man.

I was quite willing to compromise. "A 'ghost' is the dead man's shadow."

But again they objected. "Dead men cast no shadows."

"They do in my country," I snapped.

The old man quelled the babble of disbelief that arose immediately and told me with that insincere, but courteous, agreement one extends to the fancies of the young, ignorant, and superstitious, "No doubt in your country the dead can also walk without being zombis." From the depths of his bag he produced a withered fragment of kola nut, bit off one end to show it wasn't poisoned, and handed me the rest as a peace offering.

"Anyhow," I resumed, "Hamlet's dead father said that his own brother, the one who became chief, had poisoned him. He wanted Hamlet to avenge him. Hamlet believed this in his heart, for he did not like his father's brother." I took another swallow of beer. "In the country of the great chief, living in the same homestead, for it was a very large one, was an important elder who was often with the chief to advise and help him. His name was Polonius. Hamlet was courting his daughter, but her father and her brother . . . [I cast hastily about for some tribal analogy] warned her not to let Hamlet visit her when she was alone on her farm, for he would be a great chief and so could not marry her."

"Why not?" asked the wife, who had settled down on the edge of the old man's chair. He frowned at her for asking stupid questions and growled, "They lived in the same homestead."

"That was not the reason," I informed them. "Polonius was a stranger who lived in the homestead because he helped the chief, not because he was a relative."

"Then why couldn't Hamlet marry her?"

"He could have," I explained, "but Polonius didn't think he would. After all, Hamlet was a man of great importance who ought to marry a chief's daughter, for in his country a man could have only one wife. Polonius was afraid that if Hamlet made love to his daughter, then no one else would give a high price for her."

"That might be true," remarked one of the shrewder elders, "but a chief's son would give his mistress's father enough presents and patronage to more than make up the difference. Polonius sounds like a fool to me."

"Many people think he was," I agreed. "Meanwhile Polonius sent his son Laertes off to Paris to learn the things of that country, for it was the homestead of a very great chief indeed. Because he was afraid that Laertes might waste a lot of money on beer and women and gambling, or get into trouble by fighting, he sent one of his servants to Paris secretly, to spy out what Laertes was doing. One day Hamlet came upon Polonius's daughter Ophelia. He behaved so oddly he frightened her. Indeed"—I was fumbling for words to express the dubious quality of Hamlet's madness—"the chief and many others had also noticed that when Hamlet talked one could understand the words but not what they meant. Many people thought that he had become mad." My audience suddenly became much more attentive. "The great chief wanted to know what was wrong with Hamlet, so he sent for two of Hamlet's age mates [school friends would have taken long explanation] to talk to Hamlet and find out what troubled his heart. Hamlet, seeing that they had been bribed by the chief to betray him, told them nothing. Polonius, however, insisted that Hamlet was mad because he had been forbidden to see Ophelia, whom he loved."

"Why," inquired a bewildered voice, "should anyone bewitch Hamlet on that account?"

"Bewitch him?"

"Yes, only witchcraft can make anyone mad, unless, of course, one sees the beings that lurk in the forest."

I stopped being a storyteller, took out my notebook and demanded to be told more about these two causes of madness. Even while they spoke and I jotted notes, I tried to calculate the effect of this new factor on the plot. Hamlet had not been exposed to the beings that lurk in the forests. Only his relatives in the male line could bewitch him. Barring relatives not mentioned by Shakespeare, it had to be Claudius who was attempting to harm him. And, of course, it was. . . .

[The story of Hamlet went on at some length with the tribesmen interjecting their own interpretation of the events.]

"Sometime," concluded the old man, gathering his ragged toga about him, "you must tell us some more stories of your country. We, who are elders, will instruct you in their true meaning, so that when you return to your own land your elders will see that you have not been sitting in the bush, but among those who know things and who have taught you wisdom."

From: Bohannan, 1966

---

from classical realism in the sixteenth century, was a method of inductive thinking, which previously had not been adequately addressed.

*Francis Bacon*   Francis Bacon (1561–1626) condemned Aristotelian realism for its theological, nonscientific method of thought, which began with dogma and *à priori* assumptions and then deduced conclusions. Bacon claimed that science must be based on inquiry without preconceived assumptions. We must begin with observable, verifiable instances and then, through reason, arrive at general statements or laws. This approach differed significantly from the theological methods of Thomas Aquinas, in which an axiomatic belief about God's power led to deductions about the use of God's power in the universe and in human affairs.

Bacon pointed to errors caused by this theological approach. A historical example of such an error can be seen in the dispute between Galileo and the Catholic church, in which the church had maintained that the Earth was the center of the universe. The church's position was based on the *à priori* assumption that God created the Earth, and, since God created it, it must be the center of the universe. Galileo, however, argued the position of Nicolaus Copernicus that the sun is the center of the universe, and he employed a telescope to provide empirical proof. Based on this proof, Bacon argued for a new method of inquiry that would not begin with previously assumed knowledge.

*John Locke*   John Locke (1632–1704) supported Bacon's contentions and attempted to explain how we develop knowledge. His major contribution to realism was to dismiss preconceived ideas in human thought. At birth, according to Locke, the mind is a *tabula rasa,* a blank slate, upon which ideas are imprinted. Hence, all knowledge is acquired from sources independent of the individual's mind and from experience by way of sensation and reflection. Locke claimed that some primary qualities of objects were objective or directly connected with the object whereas others were subjective or dependent upon an individual's experiencing them. Many scholars believe that the work of Francis Bacon and John Locke opened the door for the scientific revolution.

*Alfred North Whitehead*   Alfred North Whitehead (1861–1947) attempted to reconcile some aspects of idealism and realism. As a mathematician, he is typically thought of as a realist. He was the coauthor of *Principia Mathematica* (1903) with another realist, Bertrand Russell (1872–1970). Process is the central aspect of Whitehead's concept of realism. Unlike Locke, he did not see objective reality and subjective mind as separate; he saw them as an organic unity that operates by its own principles in process.

*Bertrand Russell*   Russell agreed with Whitehead that the universe was characterized by patterns, but he believed that these patterns could be verified and analyzed through mathematics. Russell contended that philosophy is both analytical, based in science because science has the only genuine claim to knowledge, and synthetic, because it must provide hypotheses that science has not yet determined. Russell did not necessarily accept the results of science, but he did accept its methods.

Realism differs from idealism in that the idealist believes that the only genuine reality comes from the nature of the mind, whereas the realist contends that physical entities exist in their own right.

***Realism and Education***   According to the classical realist, the ultimate goal of education is advancing human rationality. Aristotle held that the goal of education is to aid human beings in attaining happiness through the cultivation of their potential for excellence. Schools, according to contemporary realists, can do this by requiring students to study organized bodies of knowledge, by using teaching methods that help students arrive at this knowledge, and by assisting students to reason critically through observation and experimentation.

According to the realist, the objects that comprise reality can be classified into categories based on their structure or form. Consequently, contemporary advocates of classical realism contend that the logical ordering of the curriculum is by disciplines or subjects, which, according to Gerald L. Gutek, "consist of clusters of related concepts and of generalizations that interpret and explain interactions between the objects which these concepts represent" (p. 47).

Teachers, therefore, must have specific knowledge about a subject so that they can order it in such a way as to teach it rationally and must also have a broad liberal arts background in order to show clearly and logically the correlations that exist in all fields of knowledge. Therefore, teachers must know and use a variety of methods to communicate the subject to the student. Students, according to the realist, are expected to be ready and willing to learn what is being taught.

## PRAGMATISM

Coming from the Greek word *pragma,* meaning "work," **pragmatism** encourages processes that allow individuals to do those things that lead to desired ends. It is primarily a twentieth-century American philosophy that examines traditional ways of thinking and doing and reconstructs them to fit modern life.

Pragmatists agree with realists that a physical world exists in its own right, not as merely a projection of the mind. However, unlike the realist, they neither believe that this world is permanent nor that it exists independent of humans. Instead, the pragmatist contends that humans and their environment interact and that both are equally responsible for that which is real. If humans cannot experience something, according to the pragmatist, it can't have reality for humankind. Thus, the mind is active and exploratory rather than passive and receptive; humans do not simply receive knowledge, they make it.

Problem solving is the primary methodology of the pragmatist. Human intelligence proposes hypotheses in order to explain or solve problems, then collects data to support each hypothesis. The hypothesis that solves the problem most successfully is regarded as true. However, the resolution to problems may change as new methods emerge and data are collected. Hence, truth is relative and subject to change.

***Founders and Proponents*** The pre–twentieth-century European background of pragmatism can be found in the work of Francis Bacon, John Locke, Jean-Jacques Rousseau, and Charles Darwin. Bacon's influence on pragmatism is primarily his method of induction, which serves as the basis of the scientific method. The pragmatists extended Bacon's scientific approach beyond solving simple material problems to include those in economics, politics, psychology, education, and ethics. Locke influenced pragmatism through his concept of experience as the source of knowledge. He emphasized the idea of placing children in the most desirable environment for their education. Further, he described the ideal education as being exposed to many experiences. However, his concept of the *tabula rasa* was rejected by the pragmatists because it implied that the mind is passive.

*Jean-Jacques Rousseau* Rousseau's major contribution to pragmatism was a belief that knowledge was based on the sense experience of the natural world. He thought of individuals as basically good but corrupted by civilization, which included art and science. He argued not that humans should give up technology but that its corrupting influences should be controlled. Daniel Defoe's Robinson Crusoe was his model for the "noble savage" Emile, in a novel of the same name. Crusoe returned to his shipwrecked vessel many times to remove only what he needed for survival in his natural life. Rousseau did not see children as miniature adults but as humans passing through various stages of development. His work led to questions about what was natural for children and opened the door for modern psychological studies of childhood and contemporary child-centered education.

*Charles Darwin*   Charles Darwin (1809–1882) had the greatest scientific impact on pragmatism. Reasoning from scientific evidence, Darwin argued that species evolve naturally through a universal struggle for existence. Through the interaction of organism and environment based on available food supply, absence of predators, and geographic conditions, the strongest of the species survives. Favorable characteristics of the species are maintained and unfavorable characteristics are eliminated. Darwin's view helped foster the concept that humans are in the process of developing and becoming, as is the universe. This led to the pragmatists' belief that reality is an open-ended process.

*Charles S. Peirce*   The work of these individuals set the stage for the development of pragmatism, which was formalized in the United States in the early part of the twentieth century. Charles S. Peirce (1839–1914), although little known in his day, influenced other pragmatists such as William James and John Dewey. Peirce accepted Aristotle's idea that the mind is different from material reality. However, he also declared that what we know about objective reality resides in the ideas we give objects and that true knowledge depends upon verification of ideas in experience. Therefore, it is essential that our ideas be as clear as possible.

*William James*   Peirce's friend and contemporary William James (1842–1910) had a much greater impact on pragmatism. James used Peirce's concept of reality as a consequence of ideas to form his theory of truth, which he saw in terms of its "workability." He did not view truth as an absolute but rather as a variable based on real-life events. Truth lies in individual experiences and cannot be verified objectively by someone else.

*John Dewey*   John Dewey (1859–1952) was the most notable pragmatist in education because he applied his theory in the schools. Because Dewey considered nature and human affairs changeable, he viewed education as a constant "reorganizing and reconstruction of experience" (1928, 89). Dewey agreed with Rousseau that nature in education is essential, but he differed from Rousseau in that he believed that the child should not be removed from the social environment in order to be educated. Dewey maintained that nature includes not only physical objects but also social relationships.

**Pragmatism and Education**   At Dewey's Laboratory School at the University of Chicago, he put his theory into practice by organizing three levels of learning based on his philosophy: development of the senses and physical coordination; use of materials and tools found in the environment; and use of intelligence to discover, examine, and use ideas. In this way students observed, planned, and prepared for the consequences of their actions. He abandoned the idea of a fixed subject matter outside the children's experience. Rather, he believed that the curriculum should be continuously restructured so that it moved from the child's experience into what he called "the organized bodies of truth" (1902, 11).

Since pragmatists believe that change is the essence of reality, the curriculum must be flexible. Likewise, since reality is defined as the interaction of humans with their environment, the curriculum must assist students in learning how the world affects humankind and how people affect one another. Because the mind is actively engaged with experience, the curriculum and teaching methodologies should encourage activity, exploration, and problem solving.

The school, as a social institution, should not be viewed as separate from life itself. According to the pragmatist, education is part of life, not a preparation for it. Schools should use real situations, not just formal academic subjects, to help students learn how to interact with their biological and social environments.

## EXISTENTIALISM

Those who believe in **existentialism** believe that reality is lived existence, and final reality resides within the individual. Reality begins with being aware of one's own existence; it is, therefore, human-made. It is not a state of being, but a process of becoming.

The existentialist believes that people live on earth for a short time, are born by chance in a chance place, and are affected by situations beyond their control. According to existentialist philosopher Jean-Paul Sartre (1905–1980), "Existence precedes essence." He means by this that things exist before we may give any definition to them. Thus, knowledge, like all things, exists only in light of human consciousness.

Similarly, the universe is without meaning or purpose. Humans are not part of a great cosmic "design," because design is merely a concept of the mind. The purposes humans think they detect in the universe are merely projections of humans' desire for order. We are placed in an alien universe in which we will sooner or later die. The existentialist talks about *angst*, the German word for dread, which comes from people's awareness of the absurdity of the human condition—we are free and yet finite; we are in the world and yet apart from it; we are condemned to death. According to the existentialists, humans transcend the world through their freedom and submit to it through their death.

They also believe that humans, having free choice, can either conform and accept society's norms or revolt against and reject them. As individuals make various choices, they engage in defining who they are, their reality. A person is what a person does. According to Van Cleve Morris in *Existentialism in Education: What It Means* (1966), the existentialist says:

1. I am a *choosing* agent, unable to avoid choosing my way through life.
2. I am a *free* agent, absolutely free to set the goals of my own life.
3. I am a *responsible* agent, personally accountable for my free choices as they are revealed in how I live my life. (p. 135)

***Founders and Proponents*** Existentialists claim ancient roots extending back to some Greek philosophers of the fifth and fourth centuries B.C. However, existentialism is basically a philosophy of nineteenth-century thought that allowed humans the freedom to define their own essence based on their existence in a moment in time. It was explored in the philosophical writings of such men as Søren Kierkegaard (1813–1855) and Jean-Paul Sartre and the literature of such writers as Albert Camus (1913–1960).

*Søren Kierkegaard*　Kierkegaard, a Danish theologian, examined the life of the lonely individual against the objective, scientific world. He criticized science, contending that its objectivity was an attempt to drive society away from the Christian faith. He described three stages of life: the aesthetic stage, in which humans live in sensuous enjoyment and emotions dominate; the ethical stage, in which humans achieve understanding of their place and function in life; and the religious stage, for Kierkegaard the highest, in which humans stand alone before God. It is only through faith that humans can bridge the gap between man and God. He believed that individuals must come to understand their souls, their destinies, and the reality of God through education. Kierkegaard also maintained that individuals must accept responsibility for their choices, which they alone can make.

*John-Paul Sartre*　Sartre published *L'Etre et le Nèant* (*Being and Nothingness*) in 1943 in France. In it he spelled out his existentialist philosophy, which differed significantly from Kierkegaard's because it was basically secular rather than religious. Sartre believed that objects exist prior to any essence or definition humans may give them. The world exists, is concrete and particular, and any interpretation humans give to it is less real than the data from which the interpretation is abstracted. By itself the universe is meaningless; human interpretation of meaning is nothing more than a desire for order.

Sartre affirmed that man possesses absolute freedom. Since man is free, he "makes himself." Freedom is merely potential until man acts; man is "nothing" until he acts. In Sartre's words, "If man, as the existentialist sees him, is indefinable, it is because at first he is nothing. Only afterwards will he be something and he himself will have made what he will be" (1957, 18). Because man is free, he is always potentially in conflict with others. This is because humans must either dominate or be dominated by the other. In the first case, he treats the other as an object by denying the other's freedom. In the second, he denies his own freedom, thereby "objectifying" himself.

*Existentialism and Education*　Existentialism in education is an outgrowth of twentieth-century existential thought and psychological counseling. According to philosopher Paul Tillich, twentieth-century existentialists had many different and even contradictory philosophical thoughts; however, they were unified in that they opposed the life and thought developed by Western industrial society. They believed that "the implications of this system had become increasingly clear: a logical or naturalistic mechanism which seemed to destroy individual freedom, personal decision, and organic community: an analytical rationalism which saps the vital forces of life and transforms everything, including man himself, into an object of calculation and control" (Kurtz 1966, 516). The school, according to many modern existentialists, is a part of this Western industrial society and has become a mechanism for promoting this life and thought.

Existentialism has been translated into educational thought by the humanistic psychologists Carl Rogers (see chapter 8, p. 317) and Abraham Maslow (see chapter 9, p. 369). Rogers believed that teachers should seek the potentiality and wisdom of their students by helping them work for self-directed change. The teacher must trust the learner and serve as a facilitator for learning.

*Abraham Maslow*    Maslow contended that individuals have a hierarchy of needs beginning with basic needs and culminating in what he called "metaneeds." Basic survival needs include such things as food, health, shelter, and protection. Metaneeds are the individual's strivings to transcend basic needs. They include such things as acceptance, understanding, and aesthetics. According to Maslow, meeting these needs is essential if an individual is to become self-actualized and reach his or her full potential. The work of these psychologists has been implemented in the schools through counseling and instructional methodologies that strive to help students reach their full potential.

The existentialist believes that most schools, like other larger corporate symbols, deemphasize the individual and the relationship between the teacher and the student. As educators attempt to predict the behavior of students, they turn individuals into objects to be measured quantitatively. They feel that grouping, measurement, standardization, and scheduling all work against creating opportunities for self-direction and personal choice.

Since the final goal of existentialism is the development of a completely autonomous self-actualized person, the existentialist suggests education without coercion or prescription. Students should be active and encouraged to make their own educational choices. According to Morris L. Bigge, "There is no existential learning *system*. Instead, existentialists have an ever-shifting vision of what transpires in conscious minds; human mentalities are always in process. As long as one lives, one's unfinished experience is always shifting and changing" (1982, 140).

The existentialist educator rejects the philosophical schools of idealism, realism, and pragmatism. The existentialist approach, never widely accepted in its more extreme forms, has lost favor in contemporary schools. However, its several legacies include the practice of basing instruction on an assessment of student interests, abilities, and needs; counseling with students about academic and/or discipline problems; allowing students to make choices about books to read or exercises to complete; developing a variety of learning centers from which students can select activities; and contract grading.

## PHILOSOPHICAL ANALYSIS

**Philosophical analysis** classifies and verifies phenomena in order to define reality. Unlike existentialists, philosophical analysts attempt to remove the personal and the subjective from the search for truth and therefore base their information on whatever can be confirmed through the senses; knowledge gained in this way takes the form of empirically verified propositions, grounded in experiment and observation. Truths about the universe, reality, and humankind are thus empirical, not philosophical matters. The branch of philosophical analysis based on experiment and observation is known as **logical empiricism**.

Knowledge founded on empirical evidence satisfies the **theory of verification**, which states that empirical propositions may be verified either directly or indirectly. Direct verification is tested through sense perception. "I feel the rain." But logical empiricists rely most often on indirect verification. This is the scientific method in which tests can be developed to determine whether some-thing is true. George F. Kneller provides this description of indirect verification.

> Proposition P1: This book is made of paper. Such a proposition is not *directly* verifiable, but we may set up the following premises in order to test it:
>     P2: "If fire is placed under paper, it burns." This is a physical law, already directly verified.
>     P3: "This flame is fire." This proposition is also directly verified; that is, we can see flame or feel it.
>     P4: "The fire is placed under the book." This proposition is *now* directly verified by observation.
>     We may now deduce the conclusion from our premises:
>     P5: The book will now burn. (1964, 74)

According to Kneller, the final proposition is a hypothesis that may be tested by observation. If observation and further tests support the hypothesis, we can be more certain that the book is made of paper. But we can never be absolutely certain. According to the empiricist, statements about the material world can carry only a "very high degree of probability" (p. 75). For example, the book also will burn if it's made of plastic or cloth.

Unlike the major schools of philosophy, analytical philosophers attempt to clarify language and thought rather than develop new theories or, in other words, to verify that which is already believed to be true. The analysts' tools are language, particularly grammar and structural linguistics, and logic. This branch of philo-sophical analysis is known as **linguistic analysis.**

*Founders and Proponents*    The historical roots of philosophical analysis can be traced to ancient Greek philosophers Anaximander and Anaximines and the ancient atomists, who believed the universe was made of tiny, simple particles that could not be destroyed or divided. In the eighteenth century Auguste Comte was one of the first to assert that philosophy could be used to clarify the concepts of science, which are both testable and universal. However, modern analytical philosophy was developed in the early and mid-twentieth century. The propo-nents of this philosophy included George Edward Moore, the architect of linguis-tic analysis, and Bertrand Russell, a proponent of the use of mathematical logic for scientific analysis and meaning.

*George Edward Moore*    George Edward Moore (1873–1958) in "The Defence of Common Sense" in *Main Problems of Philosophy* (1953) focused on common speech as the most logical extension of common sense. Moore claimed that in both philosophy and ordinary language there are things that cannot be proved or disproved; therefore, it made sense to analyze commonly used terminology to assess what is meant by words such as *good, know,* and *real.* Moore believed that knowing the concept of the word and analyzing the meaning of the word are two different things. Analysis would help the user determine what Moore called the "goodness of fit" of the word.

*Bertrand Russell*    Bertrand Russell (1872–1970) developed a logical system of philosophical analysis incorporating a precise vocabulary. In *Principia Mathe-matica* mathematics was reduced to a logical language. Russell's logic dealt with

*(continued on p. 237)*

**TABLE 6-1**

## Schools of Philosophical Thought

|  | Idealism | Realism | Pragmatism | Existentialism | Philosophical analysis |
|---|---|---|---|---|---|
| Metaphysics (Reality) | Reality consists of ideas, thoughts, minds, and selves. It is essentially spiritual. | Reality is the absolute form or idea of physical objects, experienced through our senses. It is permanent, unchanging. | Reality is the total of the individual's experience; the interaction with his/her surroundings; it is forever changing. | Reality is a process of becoming; an awareness from within one's self; from his/her own existence. | Reality is common sense; it is classifying and verifying much as in a scientific analysis. |
| Epistemology (Knowledge) | Knowledge is an active process of a rational and substantive mind. | Knowledge is direct contact with objects and the laws that govern them; their relationships. | Knowledge comes from actively exploring, solving problems, and from interaction with others. | Knowledge results from free choices made in the process of becoming, and from accountability for choices made. | Knowledge results from observations, experiments, and analysis. |
| Axiology (Values) | Values are genuine, absolute, rooted in deity, and permanent. | Values are permanent, objective. | Values change as situations change; they are relative. | Values are individual decisions; selective. | Values are based on reasoning. |
| Logic | People come from an existing infinite God, having a mind and soul: i.e., people grow in the image of God. | People are biological existing organisms in a real world: i.e., all people have power to acquire and use knowledge. | People are biological and social beings, interacting with their environment: i.e., people continually discover knowledge. | People are born by chance in a chance place; they have free choice to accept or reject: i.e., people gain knowledge of self. | Analysis involves classifying and verifying: i.e., people can reason, solve problems, and think empirically. |
| Educational Implications | Education is idea centered. Learning leads to self-initiated mental and spiritual growth. Based on intuition and recall. | Education's goal is to develop potential for excellence through organized sequencing of subjects/disciplines. Teachers must know both subject and student. Students must be receptive to learning/achievement. | Education involves real-life problem-solving activities. Teachers should be knowledgeable in child/adolescent development and in the group process. Students must interact, solve problems, creating knowledge. | Education should emphasize development of selfhood—of an autonomous person. Students should have an environment where they are free to make choices and to be active. | Education should emphasize the scientific method and analysis of language. Students should be taught to observe, experiment, think critically, and observe rules of formal logic. |

Philosophical theories derive their concepts of reality from basic approaches to philosophical inquiry. These approaches are listed in the left-hand column along with their educational implications. Listed horizontally are the philosophical interpretations of each of these approaches and their practical application to education.

the relationship of propositions to each other. For example, "If the temperature is below freezing, the water on the road will freeze." This statement consists of two propositions, each with a relationship to the other. According to Russell, language has a basic logical structure similar to mathematics, which can be used to clarify the meaning of language.

*Philosophical Analysis and Education*   Philosophical analysis teaches students two different sets of skills to verify propositions. The first is the scientific method of logical empiricism and the second is the critical examination of language, or linguistic analysis.

The goal of education is to teach students to think empirically by seeking evidence to confirm propositions. The logical empiricist directs students to find true knowledge by observing and doing. According to analytical philosopher Gilbert Ryle (1900–1976), educators often confuse "knowing that" and "knowing how to." "Knowing that" may simply mean filling the student's head with information. This, according to Ryle, is not "knowing." "Knowing" requires "knowing how to," or being able to perform tasks using available data. An individual may know, for example, that driving a car requires turning the key in the ignition, shifting gears, putting the foot on the accelerator, and steering. However, this individual does not know how to drive a car until he or she has had the experience of driving. This is the basis for liberal arts education, in which students are taught not only specific facts but also how to think and question within disciplines.

Linguistic analysts encourage the critical examination of language. Students are taught to establish meaning in language and clarify assumptions of different points of view. They attempt to defuse propaganda and examine the substance of slogans to clarify ambiguous terms and phrases.

Analysts try to develop a scientific language that orders and evaluates propositions. To this end, they study language games, symbolic language, metaphorical language, and other forms of expression in order to establish veracity based on a common understanding of terminology. For example, middle school students might examine television advertisements to find overstatements such as "an extra large quart size"; "lite dinners are lower in calories" (what the ad doesn't tell us is they are also smaller in size); and "the best steak dinner east of the Mississippi."

---

**6-1**

**POINTS TO REMEMBER**

- Philosophy is the love of wisdom. It is an inquiry into the principles of knowledge.
- Metaphysical questions deal with the nature of reality, epistemological with the nature and source of knowledge, axiological with the nature of values and aesthetics. Logic deals with the nature of reasoning.

- It is important for educators to study philosophy because it helps us think clearly about educational issues and gives educators a theory with which to back up practice.
- The categories of philosophy (metaphysics, epistemology, axiology, and logic) provide philosophers with questions to ask about reality, knowledge, values, aesthetics, and reasoning.

- Idealists contend that reality consists of ideas, thoughts, minds, and selves. Realists believe that many things, including people, exist without benefit of human knowledge; pragmatists say that reality is constantly changing. Existentialists believe that reality is defined by lived existence, and final reality exists within the self. Philosophical analysts hold that things are not real unless they can be classified and verified.

## Philosophical Theories of Education

Theories of education are based on the schools of philosophy: idealism, realism, pragmatism, existentialism, and philosophical analysis. The anecdote at the beginning of this chapter represents a satirical glimpse at the difference between a school of philosophy and a theory of education. The young teacher Socrates is not rehired. Of course, John Gauss, the author of this anecdote, was poking fun at systems of evaluation that would keep a teacher like Socrates from being hired by the schools. However, the anecdote can be used to illustrate another point: schools of philosophy are NOT theories of education but are instead the foundations for theories of education. Philosophers ask questions about knowledge, truth, and education, whereas educators develop the ideas of philosophers into specific theories of teaching and learning.

The theories of education based on the schools of philosophy include perennialism, essentialism, progressivism, social reconstructionism, and behaviorism. See table 6.2 (p. 246) for a comparative illustration of how each theory of education deals with curricular focus, methodology, and the role of the teacher.

### PERENNIALISM

**Perennialism** is based on the philosophical schools of classical idealism and realism. Perennialists stress the permanence of time-honored ideas, the great works of the intellectual past, and the human ability to reason. They attempt to develop both the intellectual and spiritual in students through study of the traditional disciplines of history, language, mathematics, logic, and literature, which survive from one generation to the next and provide insights into the true, the good, and the beautiful and develop the intellect.

Perennialism, according to George F. Kneller, has six basic principles: (1) Human nature is constant; therefore the nature of education is constant. (2) Humans' distinguishing characteristic is reason; therefore education should help students develop rationality. (3) Education should lead students to the truth, which is eternal, rather than to an understanding of the contemporary world, which is temporal. (4) Education is a preparation for life rather than an imitation of life. (5) Students should be taught basic subjects that will lead them to an understanding of the world's permanence. (6) Students should be introduced to the universal concerns of humankind through the study of great works of literature, philosophy, history, and science.

Perennialists most often cite the classical realist philosophies of Aristotle and Saint Thomas Aquinas. More recent educational proponents include Robert Maynard Hutchins, former president of the University of Chicago who wrote scathing attacks on progressive education, and Mortimer J. Adler, who developed his own perennial philosophy and teaching methodologies based on great books and questioning techniques. Adler's best-known educational work is *The Paideia Proposal: An Educational Manifesto* (1982), in which he asserts that all students should be taught to deal with great literary works through well-developed questioning techniques.

Perennialists expect teachers to use Socratic methods of questioning and well-organized lectures. Students are coached to recite information correctly.

Therefore, teachers are the most essential element in perennialism. According to Hutchins in *The Higher Learning In America* (1936), "Education implies teaching. Teaching implies knowledge. Knowledge is truth. The truth is everywhere the same. Hence education is everywhere the same" (p. 66).

## ESSENTIALISM

The educational theory of **essentialism** is, like perennialism, based in the philosophical schools of idealism and realism. Unlike perennialism, however, essentialism began as an educational rather than a philosophical movement. The essentialist believes that there are certain basic facts having permanent value, that all students must know, and that the school's role is the transmission of these essential facts and, thus, of a common culture. The primary function of the school is academic in providing broad general knowledge. This core knowledge, according to Theodore Brameld in *Patterns of Educational Philosophy: Divergence and Convergence in Culturological Perspective,* gives students the fundamental information they need to help them to live a better life.

There are four basic principles of the essentialist: (1) Learning, by its very nature, requires hard work and often unwilling application. (2) The initiative toward education lies with the teacher, not with the student. (3) The student's absorption of the prescribed subject matter is the heart of the educational process. (4) The school should employ traditional methods of mental discipline. There- fore, the teacher must be the central classroom authority in terms of discipline, motivation, and curriculum. She or he must know what is to be learned and must administer discipline to ensure that it is.

Like perennialism, the philosophical foundation of essentialism lies in the classical philosophies of idealism and realism. The principles are those of Plato and Aristotle, and the teaching methodologies are consistent with those of Socrates. The best-known contemporary proponent is E. D. Hirsch, Jr., William R. Kenan professor of English, University of Virginia, who spelled out his essentialist theory in *Cultural Literacy: What Every American Needs to Know* (1987). According to Hirsch in the preface to the 1988 edition of the book: "This book focuses on the background knowledge necessary for functional literacy and effective national communication. . . . American literacy has been declining at a time when our changed economy requires that our literacy should rise" (xi). In part, Hirsch maintains that in order to have effective communication, we must have a national language and a national culture. He states that since our culture changes slowly, students should learn the works on which it is based. His alphabetical list of authors who must be taught includes Aristophanes, Aristotle, Bacon, Cicero, Dryden, Homer, Locke, Milton, Pope, Rousseau, Shakespeare, and Virgil.

Hirsch's work is one example of the neoessentialist or essentialist revival movement of the 1980s. In addition to Hirsch's book, this movement included many of the reform reports of the decade, including *A Nation at Risk* (National Commission on Excellence in Education 1983) and *Action for Excellence* (Task Force on Education for Economic Growth 1983). (See chapter 5 for a discussion of these and other neoessentialist reports and books.)

A contemporary interpretation of the theory of essentialism can be seen in the development of The Coalition of Essential Schools in 1984 by Theodore Sizer

and his associates at Brown University. This group of schools from across the United States espouses a philosophical theory, based on five years of research conducted by Sizer and associates, that there is a set of ideas "that . . . should inform all good schools" (Sizer 1991, 207). These principles, set forth in *Horace's School: Redesigning the American High School* (Sizer 1992), include:

- helping adolescents use their minds well
- teaching for the mastery of essential skills and competence in certain areas of knowledge
- recognizing the student as worker rather than the teacher as deliverer
- provoking students to learn how to learn
- reflecting values of trust, decency, tolerance, and generosity in the tone of the school
- expecting much from the students without threatening them

Each of the schools in the coalition uses these ideas and principles as they best relate to their community and the strengths of the school's faculty—no essential school is exactly like any other essential school. Likewise, although there is a common traditional core of knowledge and skills to be mastered, each school's program is shaped by the intellectual powers and competencies the students need (Sizer 1992, 207–208).

Progressivists believe that education is a part of life itself, not a preparation for life. Thus, children learn more quickly if the classroom is structured in such a way as to resemble the real world. These students are learning math and reading by pretending they are in a grocery store.

## PROGRESSIVISM

**Progressivism**, rooted in the philosophical school of pragmatism, is the counterpoint to both essentialism and perennialism. According to the progressive educator, the child should be the focal point of the school, and therefore the curriculum and teaching methodology should relate to the students' interests and needs. Moreover, progressivism contends that children want to learn and have many questions if they are not frustrated by adults; therefore, teachers should act merely as guides to student learning and, in order to respond to different requests for knowledge, must possess significant knowledge and experience. Progressivists believe that children learn how to think by solving problems and experimenting. Therefore, they espouse the scientific method of learning rather than the more directed teaching for mastery of essential knowledge and skills of the essentialists.

The school, according to the progressive movement, is a microcosm of society, and learning experiences should occur in the school as they do in society; they should not be artificially divided into time, space, and content. English and social studies, for example, should be integrated and focus on problem solving rather than simple memorization of content. According to the progressivist, education is part of life itself, not a preparation for life; this is the exact opposite of the perennialist's point of view. Thus, learning should be cooperative as it is in a democratic environment. Teachers and students should be involved in the operation of the school. Teachers should participate in such things as curriculum planning and assignment of students to groups.

According to George F. Kneller, the basic principles of progressivism include the following: (1) Learning should be active and related to the interests of the child. (2) Individuals handle the complexity of life more effectively if they break experiences down into specific problems. Therefore, learning should involve the solving of problems rather than memorization of subject matter. (3) Since education is a reconstruction of experience, education is synonymous with living. So education should be like life itself rather than a preparation for life. (4) Because interests of the child are central to what is taught, the teacher should act as a guide rather than a figure of authority. (5) Individuals achieve more when they work with others than when they compete. Therefore, the schools should encourage cooperative learning practices. (6) In order to grow, individuals need the interplay of ideas and personalities. Since this is best achieved in a democratic system, the school must operate within the principles of a democracy.

Progressivism was an attempt to reform the essentialist and perennialist views of schooling in the late nineteenth and early twentieth centuries. In the 1870s educator Colonel Francis W. Parker was one of the first to argue that schools were too authoritarian, relied too heavily on textbooks and passive learning, and isolated learning from social reality. In *Schools of Tomorrow* (1915) John Dewey spelled out his pragmatic philosophy by explaining how progressive methodology functioned in the classroom. In 1919 the Progressive Education Association was founded. But its rise corresponded with World War I and, as a result, its influence on the schools was not as great as it might have been. However, its influence has been far-reaching, particularly in elementary education. Some of the legacies passed down to contemporary schools from progressive education include manipulatives in science and mathematics, field trips, projects related to study of community issues, and classroom stores and kitchens.

During the years of the Great Depression and those immediately following it, progressivists moved away from emphasis on the individual child toward emphasis on education for the good of society. They advocated that schools be heavily immersed in solving society's problems and issues. Progressivists take the pragmatic view that change is the essence of reality, and therefore, education is always in the process of changing; it is a positive, continual reconstruction of experience. The more radical wing of the progressive movement became known as reconstructionists.

## SOCIAL RECONSTRUCTIONISM

Those who follow the ideas of **reconstructionism** believe that the purpose of education is to reconstruct society. As such, it is built upon the foundation of progressivism and, like progressivism, derives from the philosophical school of pragmatism. Reconstructionists view the educational theories of perennialism and essentialism as mere reflections of societal patterns and values and urge educators to originate policies and programs to reform society.

George S. Counts is considered to be the first and foremost proponent of reconstructionism. Counts, a professor at Columbia University, stated, in *Dare the School Build a New Social Order?* (1932), that the great crises of the twentieth century (World War I and the Great Depression) were a result of profound transition and rapid change. According to Counts, it is not change itself but, rather, the inability of humans to deal with change that promotes crisis. Hence, Counts believed, the educational system must prepare students to deal cognitively and attitudinally with change that occurs multilaterally (changes in one arena of society affect changes in other arenas).

*(continued on p. 244)*

## SHOULD EDUCATION PREPARE STUDENTS FOR THE WORKFORCE?

### PRO  Tracie M. Rider and Annette Craig

"Put away your literature books, class. Today we need some novices," stated Mrs. Mary McAlister, English teacher at Westside High School. . . .

Ryobi Motor Products, Westside's business partner, is continually searching for new ways to improve the products they manufacture for Sears. "An important part of a product," says Tom Magruder, manager of human resources, "is the instruction manual. Ryobi produces several Craftsman tools for Sears. One of the most popular of these is the Craftsman electric drill." After reviewing the instruction manual . . .

Ryobi approached Westside for assistance. When Mrs. McAlister learned of Ryobi's request to have students review the manual, she was delighted her students would participate in a real life exercise. "It wasn't designed by a teacher. It was a way our students could provide a valuable service to the business world," said Mrs. McAlister. . . .

Problems associated with the manual ranged from small print to an unclear explanation of how to hold the drill. Students also reported that there was a lack of consistency in the terminology and there were several words that needed to be defined. . . .

We, in education, need to take a closer look at what we are teaching our students. We need to ask ourselves some important questions:

**Exactly what are the skills needed for future success? What are employers looking for in a future employee? Are we teaching our students these skills?**

If we take a closer look, the answer to the last question is "NO!"

We are teaching the same skills that we learned and our parents learned years ago. The educational system has not kept up with our changing society. . . . —we are not teaching our students what they need to be competitive in a global economy. . . .

We [in Pickens County, South Carolina] started by looking at classified advertisements. I suggest you do this, too. Do you know what a sleep technician does; a histology technologist; a wafer fabrication process technician? More importantly, if one of your students wants to become one, can you tell him [her] what courses s/he needs to take? . . .

When you consider that approximately 25 percent of students enroll in a college prep curriculum, approximately 25 percent in occupational training, and the remaining 50 percent in general education courses, the question of what we are training our students for takes on a new perspective. There are no "general" jobs, but we are allowing our students to take general courses. . . .

Courses of a general nature are being phased out and we are offering courses that are workplace-oriented—that give students hands-on examples and hands-on, "real-world" experiences. Our students select one of two curriculum options—College Prep or Tech Prep. These options are unique in that students are not locked into one curriculum; they can move between the curricula without being penalized.

From: T. M. Rider. "Students Help Business Partner Grade Instruction Manual," *Tech Prep News* (Fall 1993), VI (1), and A. Craig. "Tech Prep and Youth Apprenticeship: Opening New Doors to Success," *Palmetto Administrator* (Winter 1993), 31 & 33. Tracie Rider is a student at Westside High School in Pickens County, South Carolina, and Annette Craig is the director of the B. J. Skelton Career Center in the Pickens County School District.

## POSTSCRIPT

Tracie Rider and Annette Craig contend that a high school education should not only prepare students for entering the workforce, but should help them identify the skills they need for specific jobs. The South Carolina program they describe can be said to be based on the philosophical schools of pragmatism and philosophical analysis and the progressive and behaviorist theories of education.

# SHOULD EDUCATION PREPARE STUDENTS FOR THE WORKFORCE?

## CON Patricia Kean

During the past year I've listened quietly as education professors ballyhooed school reforms with a familiar Sixties ring—everything from cooperative group learning to student-centered, hands-on curricula. . . . Buzzwords like "critical thinking," "problem-solving," "benchmarks," and "competencies" have become the mantras of education professionals, shiny, high-tech wrappers dressing up the pedagogical theories of the tie-dyed era. . . .

As barriers between vocational and academic education fall, a curious hybrid called "applied learning" is emerging, stressing real-world pertinence for all subjects. But while applied learning seems likely to enhance math and science instruction, it strikes this English teacher as having a chilling effect on what's left of the liberal arts. And as schools reinvent themselves, change will inevitably work its way up the academic ladder. . . .

The demand for work-related learning arises from undeniably ugly realities. Standardized test scores are plummeting; urban schools have become battle zones; and desperate educators are latching on to applied education as a way to increase motivation and stem skyrocketing dropout rates, particularly for students from low-income families who sometimes see little connection between their schools and their futures.

Business leaders have complained for years that public school graduates can neither read, write, add simple sums, nor manage to show up on time. Corporate benefactors, no longer satisfied to donate computers or participate in the "adopt-a-school" programs that proliferated during the Eighties, now demand that schools turn out a "product" that can meet the needs of industry. . . .

And who's going to complain? Liberals are happy, and conservatives who gleefully skewer the PC movement are unlikely to take on the workplace correct. Cardinal Newman's truly radical notion that "knowledge is its own end" lacks a natural constituency, especially against the backdrop of economic emergency. After all, no one is suggesting that the liberal arts be dropped, merely that they be twisted into useful shapes. And the only elements lost in a hands-on, applied education are the very things that already tend to slip right through a student's fingers—beauty, pleasure, surprise, personal enlightenment and enrichment—the abstractions at the heart of the classic liberal-arts ideal.

From: P. Kean. "Building a Better Beowulf: The New Assault on the Liberal Arts," *Lingua Franca*, (May/June 1993), 22–25. Patricia Kean has written for *The New York Times, New York Newsday,* and *The Washington Monthly.*

Patricia Kean, on the other hand, suggests that knowledge for its own sake is the most important goal of public education. She claims that an "applied" approach to teaching and learning, such as that described by Rider and Craig, is narrow and pigeon-holes students into training for specific jobs. Her defense of the liberal arts is based in the philosophical schools of idealism and realism and the perennialist and essentialist theories of education.

Social reconstructionists believe that a society's culture does not keep pace with its dynamic technology. Students should be taught, therefore, to reconstruct and reform society so that, for example, it can efficiently use the products of technology without endangering the environment.

According to Gerald L. Gutek, social reconstructionism is founded on the following principles: (1) All philosophies, ideologies, and theories are culturally based. Each culture is influenced by the living conditions of a specific time and place. (2) Culture is dynamic, continually changing and growing. (3) Humans can change the culture so that it reflects their growth and development. Therefore, educational theories, according to reconstructionists, are a product of the particular historic period and culture at the time in which they existed.

Social reconstructionists believe that society itself must be reformed since it is in severe crisis caused by the unwillingness of humans to reconstruct institutions and values to meet the changing needs and demands of contemporary life. Modern technological society still clings to the values of an agrarian, preindustrial society, leading not only to problems in adapting to change but also to what the reconstructionist calls **social disintegration**. Consequently, humans need to reexamine their institutions and values in order to adapt them to the new society.

Thus, the task of education is twofold. First, educators must reconstruct the theoretical base of the United States' cultural heritage. Second, they must develop school programs with a clearly thought-out curriculum of social reform to deal with extreme cultural crisis and social disintegration. The new social order of the school must be democratic yet the teacher must persuade students of the importance of the reconstructionist point of view. Theodore Brameld, in *Patterns of Educational Philosophy: Divergence and Convergence in Culturological Perspective* (1971), says, "The teacher of reconstructionist inclination, being an important member of cooperative learning, is subject to the same guiding principles of practice as is any other group member. His [or her] classroom (whether enclosed by walls or embraced by a community) affords continuous opportunity for unrestricted, impartial study just because he [or she] and [the] students cannot otherwise reach effective agreements that are themselves partial" (p. 474).

## BEHAVIORISM

Although **behaviorism** is a psychological and educational theory of the twentieth century, it is rooted in the philosophical schools of realism and philosophical analysis. Early behaviorists, psychologists in the mid-twentieth century, based their theories on the philosophies of Locke and Bacon who professed a belief in the scientific method of observable behavior rather than in assumptions about behavior. Behaviorists believed in the scientific method, objectivity, immediate results, efficiency and economy, and positiveness. John B. Watson was the first to elaborate on behaviorism. Its major contemporary proponent, until his death in 1990, was B. F. Skinner.

Skinner maintained that applying science to human nature should lead to advances equivalent to those in other scientific fields. He believed that scientific knowledge could lead to teaching improvements as educators and psychologists developed what he called a "technology of teaching." Skinner based much of his work on the assumption of Locke that the newborn's mind is a blank slate and that all that is learned is acquired through experience. Therefore, he concluded that those who arrange experiences control behavior and shape personality, primarily by means of reinforcement. In a series of laboratory experiments with animals, he showed how repeated rewards affected the animal's behavior. He applied the results of these experiments to children, saying that the child's tendency to repeat certain acts is a function of which acts have been rewarded. Skinner wrote in *The Technology of Teaching* (1968):

> Some promising advances have recently been made in the field of learning. Special techniques have been designed to arrange what are called contingencies of reinforcement—the relations which prevail between behavior on the one hand and the consequences of the behavior on the other—with the result that a much more effective control of behavior has been achieved. It has long been argued that an organism learns mainly by producing changes in its environment, but it is only recently that these changes have been carefully manipulated. (p. 9)

Humans need to learn the laws of behavior, to be taught to act in specific ways through either reward or punishment. In simple terms, those behaviors that are rewarded are increased, those that receive no rewards diminish, and those that are punished are more rapidly lessened. The task of education is to develop learning environments that lead to desired behaviors in students for which they are rewarded so that they are motivated to continue to learn.

*(continued on p. 247)*

**TABLE 6-2**

## Theories of Education

| | Perennialism | Essentialism | Progressivism | Social reconstructionism | Behaviorism |
|---|---|---|---|---|---|
| Origins | Idealism | Idealism/Realism | Pragmatism/Science | Pragmatism/Events of History/The Great Depression | Realism/Philosophical Analysis/Science |
| Goals | Development of intellectual and spiritual potential. | Preserve and transmit the basic elements of human culture. | Reconstruct experiences related to needs and interests of students and society. | Reconstruction of existing society. | Provide experiences that develop intellectual and moral dispositions in the form of desired behavioral patterns. |
| Curriculum | A curriculum based on great works of literature, history, science, philosophy. Basic skills that are constant and a preparation for life. | Subject-centered curriculum. Basic skills of literacy and math (elementary), content of history, English, math, science, literature, foreign language (secondary). | Child-centered curriculum, emphasizing problem solving, activities, projects related to child's interests, integration of subject areas, and social issues. | A curriculum based on social reform. Emphasis on social sciences and process. | A curriculum based on problem areas in life situations rather than on subjects. Most conventional courses taught but through the problems to be solved. (Communication, city planning) |
| Methods and Teachers | Didactic methods developing rationality. Teacher is knowledgeable and asks probing questions and has directed discussions. | Directed teaching for mastery of essential skills. Teacher must be competent in subject matter and method. | Problem solving, active group-learning activities. Teachers should be stimulators, consultants to students, and active in the curriculum planning and operation of the school. | Democratic cooperative learning. Teachers should identify major social problems and direct students to study them impartially. | Use behavioral objectives to direct teaching and learning programmed materials. Teachers encourage objectivity, inquiry, and stimulate each student's participation for desired behavioral outcomes. |

**Goals, curriculums, and methods of instruction are based on a specific theory of education that is, in turn, derived from a philosophical school of thought. This table compares the approaches of the major theories of education.**

Behaviorists believe that the school environment must be highly organized and the curriculum based on behavioral objectives. They strongly contend that empirical evidence is essential if students are to learn and that the scientific method must be employed to arrive at knowledge. Student progress must be observed so that it can be verified.

Behaviorists have these eight educational goals:

1. To develop a world view devoid of all dualisms that separate humankind from nature, spirit from flesh, purpose from mechanism, and morals from the conditions of living.

2. To promote the integration of the development of human values and intelligence through furthering a rich appreciation of the forms and qualities of things in their connection with one another as a positive resource for the development of intellectual powers.

3. To promote the primary mode of experiencing, which involves feeling, doing, and undergoing; and learning from that which is done, suffered, and enjoyed.

4. To emphasize dealing with both things and words. An educational program that emphasizes things and not words is as defective as one that emphasizes words and not things.

5. To give students a balance of primary experience and learning through the use of literary materials.

6. To develop in students the ability to preserve a characteristic pattern of activity through a process of continuous adjustment with surroundings.

7. To help biological organisms become selves, which are inherently social in nature, through their participation in the ways of life and thought of a community that include language, history, knowledge, and practical and fine arts.

8. To develop the kinds of persons who will be responsible citizens in a democratic society, not obedient, submissive subjects of an autocratic leadership who carry out the functions that are imposed upon them. (Bigge, 158)

In order to fulfill these goals, behaviorists contend that the classrooms should represent the world of problems, and teachers should serve as directors of the students' social and intellectual learning. The behaviorists agree with the progressivists that education is life itself rather than a preparation for life. Instead of teaching formal subjects, the curriculum should revolve around problem areas such as the environment or housing. Students and teachers should analyze and evaluate how communities evolve and change. Thereby, education takes an active role in social change, and students learn the "intrinsic connection between freedom of thought and inquiry and the maintenance of a society that is cooperatively controlled in the interest of the good life of all its members" (Bigge, 159).

## How Does Philosophy Affect Education?

As we discussed earlier, philosophy cannot be directly translated into teaching. Philosophy is the love of wisdom seeking answers about knowledge and reality, humankind's relationship to nature and the deity, and morals and beauty.

Philosophy does, however, provide the basis for theories of learning that address such issues as how best to teach a subject area, problem solving, and values. Unlike theories of learning that are based on psychology, those based on philosophy do not attempt to explain systematically how students learn but, instead, direct educators toward goals and methodologies that explore the nature of knowing.

## GOAL SETTING

According to George R. Knight in *Issues and Alternatives in Educational Philosophy* (1982), how individuals view reality, knowledge, and values will determine the educational goals they set for their students. The goals in turn will determine the curricular emphasis.

For example, if an individual believes that the universe exists independently of humankind and humans have limited control over it (realism), then it is likely that the educational goals will emphasize teaching the students about the existing universe. On the other hand, if an individual believes that reality is continuously changing and that humans can affect how it changes (pragmatism), then it is likely that these goals will involve teaching the students to deal with the changing universe and assisting them in becoming agents of change. See figure 6.1 for a graphic representation of how philosophy affects education.

Knight points out that in addition to philosophy, politics, economic conditions, and social factors influence education. He suggests that differing philosophical beliefs do not always lead to different goals and hence different educational practices. Some people arrive at the same destination from different starting points. In other words, in spite of differing educational philosophies, two teachers might employ the same teaching methodology. Conversely, people with similar philosophical orientations will not always have the same goals or teach in the same way.

## CURRICULUM

Based on a teacher's philosophical beliefs, he or she establishes educational goals and designs the curriculum. For example, if a teacher believes that it is essential for the students to learn universal and unchanging truths (idealism) that must be communicated to them through the study of the great works of humankind (perennialism), she or he may adopt the curricular focus of Mortimer Adler's *Paideia Proposal*.

*Paideia* is the Greek term for the "upbringing of children." Adler's proposal states that all humans should have a similar general educational background. According to Adler, schooling has three major goals: "(1) it should provide the means by which people can grow and develop mentally, morally, and spiritually; (2) it should cultivate the civic knowledge and virtues needed for responsible and participatory citizenship; (3) it should provide the basic skills that are common to and which are needed for work rather than a particular job training that limits a person to a single occupation" (Adler 1982, 10–12). The *paideia* proposal attempts to accomplish this through a common

**FIGURE 6-1**

## The Relationship of Philosophy to Educational Practice

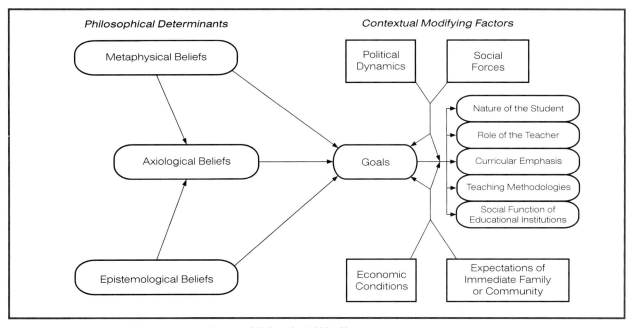

From: G. Knight, *Issues and Alternatives in educational Philosophy* (1982), 33.

**A teacher's view of reality (metaphysics), knowledge (axiology), and values (epistemology) leads to the setting of educational goals, which in turn leads to a curricular emphasis. This curriculum, however, is also influenced by outside forces such as political dynamics and expectations of families and communities.**

curriculum of twelve years of basic schooling. In this curriculum students acquire knowledge, develop learning and intellectual skills, and enlarge their understanding of ideas and values.

## PHILOSOPHY AFFECTS THE ROLE OF THE TEACHER

Just as individuals' philosophical beliefs affect their goals and curricular emphases, they also influence how these individuals view themselves as teachers. Those who believe in the classical philosophies of realism and idealism are likely to view themselves as authoritarian figures giving the students the skills and the information they need to succeed. The educational theories of essentialism and perennialism, based on these philosophies, see teachers as central to the educational process, which cannot proceed without their knowledge, instruction, and modeling.

On the other hand, teachers who believe in the philosophies of pragmatism, existentialism, and philosophical analysis contend that students should work together, have the ability to direct change, and must observe and experiment in order to determine what is real. These teachers believe that it is their responsibility to guide rather than to direct the students' learning. They therefore lean toward

---

**6-2**

**POINTS TO REMEMBER**

- The theories of education discussed in this chapter are based on the schools of philosophy. They attempt to describe educational practice, whereas the schools of philosophy attempt to categorize and systematize reality, knowledge, values, aesthetics, and reasoning by asking metaphysical, epistemological, axiological, and logical questions.

- The five theories of education are perennialism, which emphasizes great works; essentialism, which emphasizes bodies of knowledge; progressivism, which emphasizes the changing nature of knowledge and the child as the curricular focal point; social reconstructionism, which emphasizes the need to help children become social change agents; and behaviorism, which emphasizes the importance of the scientific method, objectivity, immediate results, efficiency and economy, and positiveness.

- Each theory relates to educational practice. Perennialism and essentialism focus on an unchanging curriculum based on great books and content determined by scholars. Teaching methodology is instructor centered. Progressivists and social reconstructionists contend that the curriculum must change continually to meet the needs of the child. Teaching methodology focuses on the needs and interests of the students and society. Behaviorists believe that students must be actively involved in their own learning through observation and experimentation and must be rewarded for appropriate behavior. Teaching methodology focuses on the students, with the teacher setting behavioral objectives.

- Personal educational philosophies are essential to effective teaching. They affect the teacher's goals, curricular focus, and perceived role.

---

the educational theories of progressivism, social reconstructionism, and behaviorism. They tend to believe that much of learning comes from student interaction, discovery, and experimentation. Education in this scenario can, in part, proceed without a teacher's direct intervention. In fact, educators who profess these beliefs frequently describe their role as a facilitator who designs an environment in which students can learn. Their most important role is observation of student progress.

## For Thought/Discussion

1. How did existentialism affect modern educational methods?

2. Is it possible to teach without a philosophy of education? Why or why not?

3. The high school you attended had an educational philosophy even if you weren't aware of it. Can you determine now, what it was? Do you think it was effective? Why or why not?

4. Which educational theory do you think will have the most influence on education in the future?

## For Further Reading/Reference

Counts, G. S. 1932. *Dare the school build a new social order?* New York: John Day. A description of the transition from a rural, agrarian society to an industrialized, technological society and a call for schools to prepare students to resolve the social crisis by reconstructing ideas and beliefs in light of changing conditions; an example of social reconstruction educational theory.

Dewey, J. 1900. *The school and society.* Chicago: University of Chicago Press. A description of the author's earliest revolutionary emphasis on education as a child-centered process; an example of the educational theory of progressivism.

Hirsch, E. D. 1987. *Cultural literacy: What every American needs to know.* Boston: Houghton Mifflin. A treatise that suggests that in order for America to produce a literate, skilled population, schools must emphasize teaching of basic skills and classical content; an example of the essentialist theory of education.

Hutchins, R. M. 1968. *The learning society.* New York: Praeger. A treatise that suggests that liberal education will prepare students for manhood rather than manpower. According to the author, the aims of education should be the development of a capacity to think; an example of a perennialist theory of education.

Rogers, C. 1983. *Freedom to learn for the 80s.* Columbus, OH: Charles E. Merrill. A presentation of several case studies of the relationships between teachers and students, which the author defines as the facilitation of learning based on the philosophy of existentialism.

Sizer, T. 1992. *Horace's school: Redesigning the American high school.* Boston: Houghton Mifflin. A fictional account, based on five years of research, of how high school instructors can teach students to use their minds by mastering a common core of essential information and skills. The book is based on the essentialist philosophy.

© 1990 Malcolm Hancock ("Mal")

For moments then, the room was still. From the bilingual class next door to the south came the baritone of the teacher Victor Guevara, singing to his students in Spanish. Through the small casement windows behind Chris came the sounds of the city—Holyoke, Massachusetts—trailer truck brakes releasing giant sighs now and then, occasional screeches of freight trains, and, always in the background, the mechanical hum of ventilators from the school and from Dinn Bros. Trophies and Autron, from Leduc Corp. Metal Fabricators and Laminated Papers. It was so quiet inside the room during those moments that little sounds were loud: the rustle of a book's pages being turned and the tiny clanks of metal-legged chairs being shifted slightly. Bending over forms and the children's records, Chris watched the class from the corner of her eye.

From: Kidder 1989, pp. 6–7, 12–13.

# Part III

# SCHOOLS IN A MULTICULTURAL SOCIETY

## Chapter 7

### EFFECTIVE SCHOOLS

Since the school is the institution in which most people are educated and which has a profound influence on the individual and ultimately on society, it is important to define a school in which the vast majority of students succeed. Researchers have begun to identify the attributes of effective schools by observation, testing, and comments of students. In this chapter we will examine the results of the research—part science, part art—and identify what makes some schools more effective than others.

## Chapter 8

### THE CURRICULUM IN A MULTICULTURAL SOCIETY

In this chapter we will define curriculum from a variety of points of view. We will attempt to illustrate how the individual's definition of curriculum helps determine its organization. We also will examine the philosophical basis of a curriculum and discuss its major organizational structures. Finally, we will examine the social and economic forces that have affected how curriculum is defined, developed, and implemented.

**CHAPTER OBJECTIVES**

After studying this chapter, you should be able to:

- Define effective schools research.
- Describe what is meant by the social organization of the school.
- Explain what is meant by a school's positive ethos.
- Identify those things that make a classroom climate conducive to learning.
- Define the role of the leader in a good school.
- Discuss student involvement in a good school.
- List those elements that make schools ineffective.
- Discuss how students' definitions of school relate to their experiences in school.
- Explain how classroom organization is affected by the teacher's definition of school.
- Explain why most adults define school in terms of students and learning.
- Discuss how examining another culture's definition of school helps us better understand U.S. schools.

# Chapter 7

# EFFECTIVE SCHOOLS

*F*ifth-grade teacher Chris Zajac prepares for the opening of school long before the students arrive and begins the year with a new group of students and a student teacher. Here's how Tracy Kidder describes the scene.

When Chris had first walked into her room—Room 205—back in late August, it felt like an attic. The chalkboards and bulletin boards were covered up with newspaper, and the bright colors of the plastic chairs seemed calculated to force cheerfulness upon her. On the side of one of the empty children's desks there was a faded sticker that read, OFFICIAL PACE CAR. A child from some other year must have put it there; he'd moved on, but she'd come back to the same place. There was always something a little mournful about coming back to an empty classroom at the end of summer, a childhood feeling, like being put to bed when it is light outside. . . .

Chris looked around her empty classroom. It was fairly small as classrooms go, about twenty-five by thirty-six feet. The room repossessed her. She said to herself, "I can't believe the summer's over. I feel like I never left this place." And then she got to work.

She put up her bulletin board displays, scouted up pencils and many kinds of paper—crayons hadn't yet arrived; she'd borrow some of her son's—made a red paper apple for her door, and moved the desks around into the layout she had settled on in her first years of teaching. She didn't use the truly ancient arrangement, with the teacher's desk up front and the children's in even rows before it. Her desk was already where she wanted it, in a corner by the window. She had to be on her feet and moving in order to teach. Over there in the corner, her desk wouldn't get in her way. And she could retire to it in between lessons, at a little distance from the children, and still see down the hallway between her door and the boys' room—a strategic piece of real estate—and also keep an eye on all the children at their desks. She pushed most of the children's small, beige-topped desks side by side, in a continuous perimeter describing three-quarters of a square, open at the front. She put four desks in the middle of the square, so that each of those four had space between it and any other desk. These were Chris's "middle-person desks," where it was especially hard to hide, although even the back row of the perimeter was more exposed than back rows usually are.

When the room was arranged to her liking, she went home to the last days of summer. . . .

There was a lot of prettiness in the room, and all the children looked cute to Chris.

So did the student teacher, Miss Hunt, a very young woman in a dress with a bow at the throat who sat at a table in the back of the room. Miss Hunt had a sweet smile, which she turned on the children, hunching her shoulders when they looked at her. At times the first days, while watching Chris in action, Miss Hunt seemed to gulp. Sometimes she looked as frightened as the children. For Chris, looking at Miss Hunt was like looking at herself fourteen years ago.

The smell of construction paper, slightly sweet and forest-like, mingled with the fading, acrid smell of roach and rodent spray. The squawk box on the wall above the closets, beside the clock with its jerky minute hand, erupted almost constantly, adult voices paging adults by their surnames and reminding staff of deadlines for the census forms, attendance calendars, and United Way contributions. Other teachers poked their heads inside the door to say hello to Chris or to ask advice about how to fill out forms or to confer with her on schedules for math and reading. In between interruptions, amid the usual commotion of the first day, Chris taught a short lesson, assigned the children seat work, and attended to paperwork at her large gray metal desk over by the window.

For moments then, the room was still. From the bilingual class next door to the south came the baritone of the teacher Victor Guevara, singing to his students in Spanish. Through the small casement windows behind Chris came the sounds of the city—Holyoke, Massachusetts—trailer truck brakes releasing giant sighs now and then, occasional screeches of freight trains, and, always in the background, the mechanical hum of ventilators from the school and from Dinn Bros. Trophies and Autron, from Leduc Corp. Metal Fabricators and Laminated Papers. It was so quiet inside the room during those moments that little sounds were loud: the rustle of a book's pages being turned and the tiny clanks of metal-legged chairs being shifted slightly. Bending over forms and the children's records, Chris watched the class from the corner of her eye.

From: Kidder 1989, pp. 6–7, 12–13.

*S*ince the school is the institution in which most people are educated and which has a profound influence on the individual and ultimately on society, it is important to define a school in which the vast majority of students succeed. Researchers have identified the characteristics or correlates of effective schools by observation, testing, and comments of students. In this chapter we will examine the results of the research—part science, part art—and identify what makes some schools more effective than others.

# What Is a Good School?

In 1936 scientist Albert Einstein defined the school by focusing on its most important goals in an address given in Albany, New York.

> Sometimes one sees in the school simply the instrument for transferring a certain maximum quantity of knowledge to the growing generation. But that is not right. Knowledge is dead; the school, however, serves the living. It should develop in the young individuals those qualities and capabilities which are of value for the welfare of the commonwealth. But that does not mean that individuality should be destroyed and the individual become a mere tool of the community, like a bee or an ant. For a community of standardized individuals without personal originality and personal aims would be a poor community without possibilities for development. On the contrary, the aim must be the training of independently acting and thinking individuals, who, however, see in the service of the community their highest life problem. (Einstein 1954, 60)

Therefore, according to Einstein, the good school serves two essential and interrelated functions. First, the development of an acting and thinking individual. And, second, service to the community by these individuals. Einstein, like most people who attempted to define a good school prior to the 1980s, defined it based on what the school should do. Also, like most writers, Einstein had difficulty determining how the school should accomplish its lofty goals.

We can develop a good school by implementing what makes the school good. But what is it that makes a school good? Einstein goes on to say that it is "actual performance" based on personal motivation to succeed rather than on "fear and compulsion." He claims that the good school cannot work with "methods of fear, force, and artificial authority" (p. 61).

Einstein spends a great deal of time explaining what he means by a personal motivation to succeed. In the end he has brought his definition of school back full circle to the individual. He concludes that "the most important motive for work in the school and in life is the pleasure of work, pleasure in its result, and the knowledge of the value of the result to the community" (p. 62). He never makes it clear how the good school develops motivation based on pleasure in its students. After reading Einstein's definition, one might conclude that a good school is simply one that is populated with good students who are motivated to do good work.

## EFFECTIVE SCHOOLS RESEARCH

Most attempts to define a good school prior to the 1980s resulted in descriptions like the one above. And, like Einstein's definition, they tended to be what Einstein warned against, "moralizing . . . lip service to an ideal." However, in the 1980s

*(continued on p. 260)*

**TABLE 7-1**

## Summary of Effective Schools Research and Opinions, 1979–1994

| Findings | Practice |
|---|---|
| *Effective schools have:* | |
| 1. *A positive ethos*<br>Edmonds (1979), Goodlad (1984), Brown (1984), Grant (1985), Stedman (1988), Feinberg (1990), Lockwood (1990), Hill, Foster, and Gendler (1990), Sizer (1992), Banks (1994) | Students and teachers are expected to achieve and are told they can<br>Standards for achievement are related to individual differences<br>Lines of communication among administrators, teachers, students, parents, and community are kept open<br>Students from varied backgrounds and cultures study and socialize together<br>Required subjects, varied curriculum, and choices are available<br>Teachers and administrators are role models for developing honesty and respect<br>Literature is used to nurture qualities of good character |
| 2. *A classroom climate conducive to learning*<br>Brown (1984), Goodlad (1984), Ravitch (1984), Bennett (1987), Fiske (1991), Goeller (1992), Cartwright and D'Orso (1993), National Coalition of Advocates for Students (1993) | Teachers are involved in decision making<br>Students are more interested in learning than in sports and socializing<br>Teachers spend more time on instruction than on controlling behavior<br>Parents volunteer or keep in close contact with teachers<br>Attendance is high<br>Classrooms have few interruptions<br>A caring, humanistic approach to furthering student development fostered |
| 3. *Clearly understood goals*<br>Wynne (1981), Persell and Cookson (1982), Goodlad (1984), Carnegie Foundation for the Advancement of Teaching (1988), Levine and Lezotte (1990), Sizer (1992), Swan and Nixon (1992), Horenstein (1993) | Students, teachers, parents, and administrators agree on goals for academic achievement and broad goals for the school<br>Administrators and teachers monitor progress toward goals<br>Students and teachers can verbalize the goals of the school |
| 4. *Effective teachers*<br>Wynne (1981), Ravitch (1984), Bennett (1987), National Governors' Association (1990), Shanker (1990), Banks (1991), Ladson-Billings (1992), Martin (1992), National Coalition of Advocates for Students (1993), Zeichner (1993) | Schools recruit and keep knowledgeable and talented teachers<br>Schools recruit and keep talented minority teachers<br>Teachers use time wisely<br>Teachers set objectives and learning strategies related to student needs<br>Teachers use materials in addition to textbooks<br>Teachers are firm but friendly<br>Teachers are culturally sensitive |
| 5. *Clear and effective leadership*<br>Edmonds (1979), Wynne (1981), Brown (1984), Ravitch (1984), Carnegie Foundation for the Advancement of Teaching (1988), Conrath (1992), Easterbrook (1992), Findley and Findley (1992), Lezotte (1992) | Goals are established, agreed upon, and followed through on<br>Policies and procedures are initiated and carried out<br>A climate of high expectations for students and teachers is developed<br>The staff members work hard and cooperate with one another<br>Academic achievement is monitored<br>Leader and staff committed to learning for all |

| Findings | Practice |
|---|---|
| 6. *Good communication*<br>Wynne (1981), Brown (1984), Stedman (1988), National Governors' Association (1990), Hill, Foster, and Gendler (1990), Carnes (1992), Little (1992), Cartwright and D'Orso (1992) | Principals visit classrooms<br>Teachers have time during school day to communicate with one another<br>Parents are informed of student life and growth in school<br>Teachers respond to students' personal problems<br>Principal and teachers communicate with varied types of family units |
| 7. *Active student involvement*<br>Wynne (1981), Goodlad (1984), Findley and Findley (1992), Horenstein (1993), National Coalition of Advocates for Students (1993) | Students participate in special interest clubs, sports, honor societies, student government, and the performing arts<br>Students tutor one another<br>Students are assistants to teachers and administrators |
| 8. *Positive incentives and awards*<br>Brookover et al. (1977), Bennett (1987), National Governors' Association (1990), Shanker (1990), Levine and Lezotte (1990), Sizer (1992), Swan and Nixon (1992) | Students receive honor awards and badges for academic achievement and other accomplishments<br>Teachers of the year are recognized<br>Students are given remedial attention if needed<br>Parents recognize all teachers during Education Week<br>Professional development days are provided for teachers<br>Schools have flexible semesters that provide academic incentives |
| 9. *Order and discipline*<br>Edmonds (1979), Wynne (1981), Brown (1984), Bennett (1987), National Governors' Association (1990), Levine and Lezotte (1990), Fiske (1991), Horenstein (1993), U.S. Congress (1994) | Rules that are a happy medium between strong discipline and the growing student are established<br>Rules are clearly stated to students and parents so that standards, rewards, and punishments are clearly understood<br>There is follow-through on agreed-upon rules<br>There are goals and programs to remove drugs and violence from the school<br>A safe and orderly environment is established<br>A mental health team of internal and external personnel work with students |
| 10. *Focus on instruction and curriculum*<br>Edmonds (1979), Brown (1984), Ravitch (1984), Bennett (1987), Carnegie Foundation for the Advancement of Teaching (1988), National Governors' Association (1990), Hill, Foster, and Gendler (1990), Levine and Lezotte (1990), Banks (1991), Committee for Economic Development (1991), National Education Goals Panel (1992), Sizer (1992), Horenstein (1993) | Schools have large media centers that students use<br>More time is spent on instruction than on keeping an orderly classroom<br>There is an emphasis on basic skills and academic subjects<br>Technological innovations are implemented, particularly for the disadvantaged<br>There is a multicultural emphasis to the curriculum<br>Standards on what students should know and be able to do are established<br>Higher level thinking skills are emphasized |

In an effort to define an effective school, many studies have been conducted on those schools that have already proven to be effective in one area or another. Rather than arrive at one specific definition of an effective school, research has instead identified qualities that cumulatively result in an effective school.

educators developed a body of research that began to describe the specific correlates of effective schools. The first phase of this research was carried out through careful observation of schools and classrooms judged to be effective. Two former directors of the National Center for Effective Schools Research, Daniel U. Levine and Lawrence W. Lezotte, call this first phase of effective schools research *identification.*

A variety of measures was used to determine effectiveness during the identification phase: test scores, other measures of student achievement, perceptions of students and parents, and panels of experts. Of course, the means used to select the effective schools often dictated the results of the study. For example, if researchers used test scores as a measure of the schools' effectiveness, the schools found to be effective exhibited high test scores, high academic achievement of students, a curriculum emphasizing skills required on the tests, and, many educators argued, a population that tended to be successful taking standardized tests, largely white and middle or upper class.

From this body of research, no specific definition of a good school was developed; however, educators and researchers identified many characteristics of an effective school. Levine and Lezotte refer to this second phase of effective schools research as *description.*

The third phase of effective schools research, according to Levine and Lezotte, "crossed the bridge" from describing characteristics of effective schools to developing guidelines and approaches for improving school effectiveness. In the 1990s, effective schools research entered its current phase of *addressing issues of organization context,* which includes such things as examining school districts and coordinating efforts with state education agencies, state government, federal government, and other agencies external to the single school (1990, 71). See table 7.1 for a summary of effective schools research. A description of each finding follows in the text.

## SOCIAL ORGANIZATION OF A GOOD SCHOOL

Most studies of effective schools found that there is little difference in instructional patterns between schools that are considered good and those that are not. Instead, the difference seems to come from things such as goals, high expectations, climate and atmosphere, and leadership. Levine and Lezotte, authors of *Unusually Effective Schools,* reviewed seven characteristics or correlates that were identified by earlier researchers:

- safe and orderly environment
- clear school mission
- instructional leadership
- high expectations
- opportunity to learn and student time on task
- frequent monitoring of student progress
- positive home-school relationships (1990, 2)

***A Positive Ethos***   Gerald Grant, a professor of sociology and education at Syracuse University, defined quality in terms of a school's positive ethos: the school teaches both intellectual and moral development (1985). Academic achievement as evidenced by high test scores is only one of the aims of "schools that make an imprint." Also needed is the development of character, or ethos, evident in the high expectations teachers have for students and reflected as much in what people *do* as in what they say.

The school's ethos, to be adequately developed, must be shared by the community, a situation more commonly found in private schools in which, in this largely homogeneous population, parents share intellectual and moral values with the faculty and staff. In public schools a shared ethos is more difficult to achieve because teachers and students are, by definition, diverse and possess different values. However, according to Grant, these differences can be overcome through the common core of a democratic society's beliefs. He observed that a positive ethos does not necessarily require a particular moral content. He cited examples of the common positive ethos in the United States: "Decency, fairness, the minimal order required for dialogue, the willingness to listen to others, the rejection of racism, honesty, respect for truth, recognition of merit and excellence . . . a sense of altruism and service to others and respect for personal effort and hard work" (1985, 143). James A. Banks, professor at the University of Washington and researcher in multicultural education, suggests that students learn compassion and democratic ideals from influential teachers. According to Banks, "The classroom should be a forum of open inquiry, where diverse points of view and perspectives are shared and analyzed reflectively. In democratic classrooms both students and teachers should have the freedom to express their values and beliefs but should be required to defend them and to point out ways in which their moral choices are related to overarching democratic ideals, such as human dignity, justice and equality" (1994, 189).

William J. Bennett, former U.S. secretary of education and author of *The Book of Virtues* (1993), suggests in *What Works: Research About Teaching and Learning* (1987) that high expectations for both students and teachers are required if schools are to develop a positive ethos. Arthur W. Steller in *Effective Schools Research: Practice and Promise* (1988) agrees with Bennett's contention that teachers' expectations for good or poor student performances are self-fulfilling prophecies. Steller quotes George Bernard Shaw's *Pygmalion:* "The difference between a lady and a flower girl is not how she behaves but how she's treated." He cites Robert Rosenthal and Lenore Jacobson in *Pygmalion in the Classroom* (1968), saying that teachers' expectations of achievement influence students' levels of achievement. Anne Turnbaugh Lockwood, an assistant director of the National Center for Effective Schools, suggests that "children can succeed, but they need love and understanding . . . not only academics" (1990, 6). According to Bruce R. Joyce, Richard H. Hersh, and Michael McKibbin in *The Structure of School Improvement* (1983), "High expectations carry several messages. First, they symbolize the demand for excellence and tell the student, 'I think you ought to and can achieve.' . . . Second, they communicate to the student that the teacher *cares* by saying, in effect, 'The reason I have high expectations for you is that I believe in you.' Third, high expectations serve as the adult world's professional judgment which is translated to the student as, 'I am really more capable than even I at times think I am' " (p. 26). According to Grant, schools that achieve these positive goals provide quality education for their students. Theodore Sizer, chairperson of the Coalition of Essential Schools and a strong advocate for effective schools implementation, sums up all of the above when he writes, "The tone of the school should explicitly and self-consciously stress the values of unanxious expectation ('I won't threaten you, but I expect much of you'), of trust (unless it is abused), and of decency (the values of fairness, generosity, and tolerance)" (1992, 208).

## *Viewpoint* Billy Paris

Mel Glenn teaches high school English in Brooklyn, New York. He writes poems about his students who he says are often misunderstood. This poem is about Billy Paris. The Spanish classroom of which Glenn writes is one that displays a positive ethos.

This term I don't have a lunch period.
Too many subjects to make up.
So while I learn new nouns in Mr. Brewer's Spanish class,
I munch on some potato chips.
Two days ago he laid down the law:
"No snacking while speaking Spanish."
Yesterday I got even.
I pulled out from my bag
A checkered tablecloth,
Two candlesticks,
One bowl,
One spoon,
And a thermos full of soup.
I slowly set the table,
Said a blessing (in Spanish) over the food,
And named every object with perfect accent.
Mr. Brewer stood there, dumbstruck.
Then he began to laugh.
The class joined in.
You know, school doesn't have to be so grim.

From: Glenn, 1982

*A Classroom Climate Conducive to Learning*   John Goodlad (1984) in his observation of over one thousand classrooms found that differences in the quality of schools have little to do with teaching practices. Differences come instead from what he called classroom climate. The most satisfying schools are ones with favorable conditions for learning; parent interest in, and knowledge of, the schools; and positive relationships between principals and teachers, and teachers and students. According to Karen A. Goeller, in doctoral research conducted at Indiana State University, a school climate refers to "shared perceptions of the school" (1992, 153).

In a National Institute of Education publication, *Reaching for Excellence: An Effective Schools Sourcebook* (1985), Steven Bossert claimed that 1,750 school districts identified as promoting effective practices at the building and district levels had in common "a school climate conducive to learning—one free from disciplinary problems and vandalism; the expectation among teachers that all students can achieve; an emphasis on basic skills instruction and high levels of student **time-on-task**; a system of clear instructional objectives for monitoring and assessing students' performance" (p. 7). In "A Good School" (1984), Diane Ravitch further defines positive school climate as "relaxed and tension-free. Teachers and students alike know that they are in a good school, and this sense of being special contributes to high morale" (p. 493). Goeller took the study of climate a step further into the community by completing what she called a "climate audit" of a high school in Terre Haute, Indiana, in which she examined students' and parents' perceptions of the school. She determined that if their perceptions of the school matched what the school believes about itself, reflected in its mission statement, then the school climate is shared, and is more likely to be conducive to student learning.

Shared perception is also important among school staff. Edward Fiske, visiting scholar, School of Education, Stanford University, in his book *Smart Schools, Smart Kids* (1992), determined that teachers must share not only in the mission of the school, but in decision making about the school if there is to be a climate conducive to student learning. In his study of Drew Elementary School in Dade County, Florida, he found that teachers and parents there, those who were historically at the bottom of the school hierarchy, had a sense of school ownership because of their shared decision making. He calls the process the "democratization" of the school. According to Fiske, when this occurs, as it has at Drew Elementary School, there is a sense of enthusiasm, that "there is nothing we can't do" (1991, 49). In another example, at Blaine Elementary School in North Philadelphia, the positive results of this democratization process can be seen. Prior to Madeline Cartwright's principalship, the school was troubled and run-down. Today, largely as a result of shared decision making, and complete cleaning and painting of the entire building, test scores have increased, daily attendance has grown to 92 percent, teachers feel an ownership of the school, and students express a sense of belonging (Cartwright and D'Orso, *For the Children: Lessons from a Visionary Principal,* 1993).

In addition to a shared climate and democratization, researchers from the National Coalition of Advocates for Students conducted comprehensive national studies to determine characteristics of schools that support the success of young immigrants. According to their studies, schools that successfully encourage learning and social development in young immigrants have a "culturally supportive school climate" and a staff that makes it clear through their words and actions that racist behavior will not be tolerated. These successful schools provide "a harmonious environment in which respect for the diverse makeup of the school community is promoted" (1993, 34).

***Clearly Understood Goals***   Edward Wynne, professor of education, University of Chicago, in a survey of schools considered "good," found that their principals, teachers, and parents had developed, knew, and could articulate the school's academic and social behavior goals. Likewise, he found that "the staff—especially the teachers/administrators and even the students and parents evolved a clear idea of what constitutes good performance" and knew what was expected of them. He also found that good schools are generally small and have highly visible staffs (1981, 377). John Goodlad further stated in *A Place Called School* (1984) that when parents and teachers reported congruence between their preferred goals for the school and its actual goals, they were largely satisfied with the school's program. In order to have congruence in goal perception, researchers have found that the most effective goals are sharply focused and targeted, concentrating on one or two measurable outcomes per year, and developed through a democratic process (Levine and Lezotte 1990; Sizer 1992; Swan and Nixon 1992; Horenstein 1993).

*Effective Teachers* According to Joyce, Hersh, and McKibbin, effective schools have a strong sense of teacher efficacy, which arises from the conviction that " 'I *know* I can teach any and all of these kids.' Efficacy is a sense of potency, and it is what provides a teacher with the psychic energy to maintain a high task orientation by the students" (1983, 26).

Wynne's study also determined that teachers who are rated as good care about teaching and their students in observable ways. They have regular and timely attendance, well-organized lesson plans, reasonably orderly classes, routinely assigned and appropriately graded homework, friendly but authoritative relations with students, purposeful use of class time, and supportive relations with colleagues (p. 378). According to Wynne, good teachers are more frequently found in schools in which they are required to set performance goals for their students and translate these goals into objectives. He found that the principals in these schools also set goals. According to William Bennett, good teachers are enthusiastic and confident, have high standards, demand mastery of materials from all students, have instructional management skills that give students maximum time for instructional tasks (time-on-task), and enforce discipline consistently and fairly.

The National Coalition of Advocates for Students determined that effective schools have a plan to hire minority teachers. According to their studies, "A multicultural school staff presents students with positive adult role models from their own cultural background and displays the schools' commitment to serve all students" (1993, 37). Further, researchers Kenneth M. Zeichner (1993) and Gloria Ladson-Billings (1992) found that effective teachers in effective schools are knowledgeable about ethnic diversity and sensitive to cultural differences. Teacher effectiveness is discussed in depth in chapter 2.

*Clear and Effective Leadership* Wynne's study also found that, in good schools, staffing roles are clear; staff members and volunteers, including parents, know their jobs and work hard at them. He found that administrators are able to conceptualize goals; are tactful, tough, and ambitious; believe in education; and are determined to get things under control.

Bennett's study found that successful schools have "successful principals [who] establish policies that create an orderly environment and support effective instruction" (1987, 64). Good administrators keep teachers' instructional time from being interrupted, supply necessary materials, create opportunities for faculty/staff development, encourage new ideas, involve teachers in formulation of school policies and selection of materials, and provide aides or volunteers for routine work.

In addition, Robert Estabrook, professor and researcher from Indiana University, found that leaders of effective schools have a "multiple vision coupled with a targeted response" for their schools. They utilize the varying degrees of skill and motivation within the staff for realizing this vision, and implement a plan of action following careful analysis. The effective school leader, according to Estabrook, helps staff members to mature and is flexible in responding to the environment of the school (1992, 91–92). Further, Lezotte, who has researched

Effective schools have principals who provide clear direction to their staff, involve them in decision making where appropriate, and encourage creativity.

effective schools for over 25 years, suggests effective schools are led by those with "the vision that learning in a democracy must be inclusive—learning for all" (1992, 12). This vision must be communicated to and shared by the school staff.

Jerry Conrath, who has taught and studied disadvantaged students in effective schools, concurs with Lezotte, stating that an effective school is a place where all children enter believing that they are expected to learn and therefore, will. He suggests that the vision of the effective leader and the staff of the effective school understands that "equity means different treatment for different kids with different needs" (1992, 140). This vision, according to researchers Beverly Findley and Dale Findley, keeps leaders of effective schools "focused on activities which pave the way for high student achievement, both academically and personally" (1992, 102). This focus is communicated to faculty, school district personnel, the school board, and the community.

Ron Edmonds found in a 1979 study, "Effective Schools for the Urban Poor," that even in schools populated by economically disadvantaged youngsters, students can achieve at levels equal to middle-class students if there is "strong leadership and a climate of expectation that students will learn" (p. 15). According to Edmonds, "There has never been a time in the life of the American public school when we have not known all we needed to in order to teach all those whom we chose to teach" (p. 16). Edmonds asserts that leaders of ineffective urban schools often chose not to teach poor students. Edmonds cites a 1974 State of New York Office of Education Performance Review study of the academic performance of students in two inner-city schools, both with a predominantly poor pupil population, but one with high-achieving students and the other with low-achieving students. Edmonds found that student performance in these two schools could be "attributed to factors under the schools' control," which included administrative behavior, policies, and practices. In the school where students had achieved at high levels, the administrative team "provided a good balance between both management and instructional skills; developed a plan for dealing with the reading problem and had implemented the plan throughout the school"; and created an environment in which the students were expected to succeed (pp. 16–17).

*Good Communication*    Wynne's study further showed that in schools rated as good there is a constant information flow among principals, teachers, students, and parents. Principals frequently visit classrooms, usually unannounced, and monitor teacher performance in other areas such as hall duty, attendance records, report cards, lesson plans, records, and test scores. Principals communicate the results of their evaluations to the teachers and allow teachers to respond. In effective schools the line of communication not only extends from the principal's office to the classroom but also from one classroom to another, according to researcher and University of California at Berkeley professor Judith W. Little. Teachers in effective schools give up their individualistic view of teaching and become more collaborative. They see the need, and have been given time, to communicate with their colleagues on a daily basis. They "embrace a common set of priorities and . . . organize a collective response to the complexities of teaching" (1992, 158).

According to researchers Paul T. Hill, Gail E. Foster, and Tamar Gendler, all of the connections between staff and students within the school can be characterized as a "social contract" that communicates the reciprocal responsibilities of the administration, teachers, and students. Likewise, the contracts "establish the benefits that each derives from fufilling the contract faithfully" (1990, vii).

According to B. Frank Brown in *Crisis in Secondary Education: Rebuilding America's High Schools* (1984), communication between parents and schools is needed today more than ever before. Wynne, in his studies, also confirms the importance of the active role of parents in effective schools. As one way to accomplish this, Brown claims that schools must recognize that American families are in transition and that the two-parent family no longer represents the norm. Effective schools "must revise their calendars to make certain that working single parents have regular access to school personnel and activities after working hours" (p. 140). The National Governors' Association in its report, *Educating America: State Strategies for Achieving the National Education Goals* (1990), agrees. Parents must become equal partners in their children's learning and schooling if schools are to be effective, beginning during early childhood with programs such as Head Start and continuing as children progress through the public schools (see also chapters 11 and 12). According to William J. Carnes, superintendent of Oak Hill Unit School Corporation in Converse, Indiana, this means that leaders and teachers in effective schools not only talk to parents but listen to them. His research showed that when school personnel actively listened to parents, they became more involved in the educational process and there was a general overall improvement in student test scores and schoolwide morale (1992, 129).

   *Active Student Involvement*   In good secondary schools, Wynne's study found that students are actively involved in the school's governance. Findley and Findley (1992) found that in effective schools students are encouraged to initiate ideas through an established mechanism. Mary Ann Horenstein featured twelve of the 1991 Blue Ribbon High Schools selected in an annual competition by the U.S. Department of Education in the book *Twelve Schools that Succeed* (1993). She found that these schools not only prize classroom learning, but also place a high value on the arts, athletics, and a variety of student clubs and other activities that allow students to function in leadership capacities. According to Horenstein, these effective schools had bands, orchestras, theater programs, choruses, dance classes, and instrumental ensembles. Says Horenstein, "Scholarly learning is seen as only one kind of growth" (p. 3). However, many activities in effective schools focus on the achievements of students in award assemblies, pep rallies, and science fairs.

   According to a 1993 study reported by the Office of Educational Research and Improvement, U.S. Department of Education, successful schools have students who participate in extracurricular activities such as athletics, cheerleading, music, academic, and vocational clubs. In 1990, the study found, 30 percent of high school sophomores participated in academic clubs, 52 percent in athletic clubs, and 22 percent in musical activities (p. 88).

   The National Coalition of Advocates for Students found that effective schools also have buddy systems, peer discussion groups, and peer tutoring programs that often pair students from different cultures. Benjamin Banneker High School, one of the twelve Blue Ribbon Schools, has a mentor program in which new freshman are paired with upperclassmen.

*In the Classroom*

---

### Benjamin Banneker High School

Imagine walking into a school and finding students' books and other possessions sitting in the halls in front of lockers because the students did not have time to open their lockers and put their belongings away between classes. Then take into consideration the school's location in a rough neighborhood in Washington, D.C. Will those possessions be intact three hours later?

   They will if the school is Benjamin Banneker High School. Thievery and vandalism are virtually unknown in the school. The students are urged to take their books out of the hall over the weekend so the floors can be cleaned.

   When I asked students what they liked best about Banneker, the first thing they were likely to say was, "It's safe here." And, of course, the school is much more than safe. Banneker is truly a family for students, teachers, administrators, secretaries, and custodians. People trust each other, and visitors can sense it the moment they enter the building. . . .

The population of the District of Columbia is predominantly African American, a fact that is echoed in the student body, which is 97 percent African American. A handful of Hispanic and Asian American students also attend Banneker. The year I visited, there was one white student. During her application interview with Principal Linette Adams, she asked, "Will I be all right here?"

"If you're expecting to be discriminated against, you'll be disappointed," was Mrs. Adams' reply. "Everyone at Banneker is special one way or another; your difference just stands out more."

Being part of the Banneker family means that new students get support from older students and staff even before they arrive on the first day of ninth grade. Each incoming student is assigned an older student as a mentor. The mentor calls and sometimes visits the new student during the summer. Then, on the day before school opens in September, the senior class sponsors a reception for new students; part of the day is devoted to informal gatherings of mentors with their students. After that, the relationship is maintained informally to meet the younger students' needs.

Another way that new students are eased into the school is through Banneker's Summer Institute, established in 1990. For five weeks, at a time when other schools offer remedial instruction, Banneker offers a series of non-credit, enrichment courses ranging from language arts and foreign language to math and science, including field trips. About 75 percent of the participants are ninth-graders. Since they come from a variety of sending schools, the institute gives them a chance to get to know each other and Banneker. . . .

A less formal support system is the Advisory Group, held for one hour on two afternoons a week, in which each faculty member meets with a group of students. This system replaces the typical homeroom. But the Advisory Group, with its extended time, can do much more. The students study, play games, and discuss academic and personal problems with their advisors.

The teachers also have a support system. All new teachers are assigned a mentor, a master teacher with whom they meet at least once a week and who helps them solve the myriad problems that face every new professional.

Teachers receive support from the administration as well: in dealing with students, starting new courses, and becoming part of the school's decision-making process. Administrative support also extends to secretaries and maintenance people. "I'm treated with dignity and am part of the decision-making process," the school's head custodian told me. "It's like I've died and gone to heaven."

Another ingredient in the Banneker success story is visibly supportive parents. They value their children's unique educational opportunities at Banneker and are willing to give their own time in order to maintain the high standards. Parents volunteer as attendance aides, assist in classes, help raise money and, in short, sell the Banneker idea. . . .

The Banneker family and support system does not stop at the walls of the school; a number of outside organizations and individuals also are involved. Banneker was established, for good reason, a half-block from Howard University, one of the nation's largest and most prestigious African American institutions of higher learning. The two institutions have had a partnership since Banneker's founding. Banneker students have regular access to the university library, and many of them take courses at Howard. They use the pool and the gym and hold their annual commencement exercises at the university.

Another important partnership for Banneker is with the National Science Foundation. Members of the NSF frequently visit the school to speak to classes, provide materials, discuss career opportunities, and serve as role models for the teenagers. Students sometimes have opportunities to visit NSF-funded facilities, such as Woods Hole. One student went to Hawaii with the NSF to visit an active volcano and see the engineering feat of creating a new observatory. . . .

Banneker develops links to the larger community in a number of ways. For example, the school library is electronically linked with the computerized card catalog of the Martin Luther King Library in downtown Washington, which enables students to access needed research materials. Students often are assigned to do research at the many museums in Washington. A required course in global perspectives for sophomores provides an overview of modern world history from 1500 to the present. . . .

Banneker students also interact with the community in other ways. They have a long history of community service. All students are required to complete 270 hours of community service in order to graduate. Every other Wednesday, school closes early to permit them to leave for various community sites. . . .

Banneker is a curious mixture of the new and the traditional. It is on the cutting edge of educational thinking by requiring community service. There are no bells to disrupt classes; teachers just end their classes at the same time. At the end of lunch, someone simply walks through the cafeteria announcing, "Time to go." But the curriculum is a conservative one. Every student must study Latin to help with SAT preparation and with their understanding of English. Requirements are so stringent that there is room for neither substitutions nor failure in the curriculum. There are no study halls. A few students who want an extra class come to school early for an extra period.

But the teaching is anything but traditional. Teachers incorporate an abundance of discussion and small-group work where students report to each other. And the students have lots of homework. They average more than three hours of homework each night. If students are late to school, someone calls their parents; it usually does not happen twice. I found that most students feel that the extra work pays off. All Banneker graduates are accepted in four-year colleges each year. (Horenstein 1993, 53–58)

---

*Positive Incentives and Awards*   In effective schools incentives and rewards are given to students and staff in the form of honor societies, honor rolls, mentioning accomplishments in daily announcements and school newspapers, displaying photographs of successful students, and awarding them pins, badges, and ribbons in special assemblies. Good schools retain rather than automatically promote students with learning problems, preferring to work with them to achieve promotion. Theodore Sizer, chairperson of the Coalition for Essential

When students feel they have an important voice in the government of the school, they are likely to view their school experience as positive. This attitude contributes to high morale, positive school spirit, order, and discipline.

Schools, found that effective schools also provide intensive remedial work for students who have not met appropriate levels of competence for a particular grade or subject (1992).

Staff incentives include, according to the National Governors' Association, increased involvement for teachers in school governance, which allows them to participate in school decision making. According to Levine and Lezotte's summary of 25 years of effective schools research, these schools provide substantial staff development time, stipends for inservice training, early dismissal days so staff members can work together on planning, and teams of experienced substitute teachers to allow regular classroom teachers to attend staff development sessions during school time. Other staff incentives that have been investigated in studies of effective schools include incentive pay and differentiated staffing and pay for differing responsibilities (see chapter 1, pp. 27–31).

*Order and Discipline*    According to Wynne's study, good schools develop discipline by "maintaining effective physical boundaries [creating a sense of safe haven], especially in disorderly urban areas" (p. 381). Students remain in the buildings and recognize their rights and obligations. Symbolic boundaries such as uniforms are also found in many good schools. According to Wynne's study, good schools have well-enforced dress codes and use mottoes, school songs, colors, ceremonies, parades, assemblies, athletic events, faculty and student social events, and dances to develop this safe haven for students.

According to Brown (1984) and Fiske (1991), the measures of a well-disciplined school include good student behavior, high attendance rates, fewer suspensions, minimal delinquency, and achievement as confirmed by examination. In addition, Fiske found that in effective schools parents were actively involved as student advocates with teams of teachers, counselors, psychologists, social workers, special teachers, and administrators. Good discipline and safe schools, according to Steward C. Purkey and Marshall S. Smith in *Review of Effective Schools* (1983), comes from effective school governance. The Carnegie Foundation for the Advancement of Teaching report *An Imperiled Generation: Saving Urban Schools* (1988) agrees, and further states that effective governance of urban schools requires that principals not be "crippled by mindless regulations" (p. xv). Schools must be decentralized in terms of decision making and they must be accountable for the decisions they make. In addition, the National Governors' Association task force report asserts that schools must make a commitment to eliminate drugs and violence. This may require significant school reorganization, including establishing a curriculum to motivate students to learn and calendar revisions to help keep students in school throughout the year. Many students, particularly those who are not college bound, are shortchanged by the schools, according to the report, and many quit school in order to work. If schools are to become safe havens of academic achievement, they must recognize the needs of all students, not just those who are college bound (pp. 15–16). Horenstein found in her study that effective schools empower teachers to help decide issues related to at-risk students and encourage students to bring their problems to strong student councils for deliberation. Levine and Lezotte summarized effective schools research saying that the orderly environment of schools is enhanced when discipline derives from the students' sense of "belonging and participating" rather than from simply the imposition of "rules and external controls" (1990, 9). (See chapter 2, pp. 82–86 for more information about discipline.)

The federal government is increasingly becoming involved in promoting safe schools. Money was targeted at the problems of violence and drugs in the schools through the Safe School Act of 1993. Other federal funds, through the School-to-Work Opportunities Act (1993), provide youth apprenticeships for students who do not plan to attend college.

## INSTRUCTION AND CURRICULUM IN GOOD SCHOOLS

Although most of the studies that identified common characteristics of effective schools focused on the social organization of the schools, some attempted to examine common features of instruction and curriculum. Frank Brown in *Crisis in Secondary Education* found that highly effective schools differ from less effective schools in several ways: they have a balanced blend of classroom instruction, discipline, and sound administration; they have better teacher salaries, smaller class size, and larger libraries with greater student use; they effectively manage time spent on instruction, determine who makes decisions about learning, and have positive relationships with the school district authorities. According to Levine and Lezotte, effective schools give explicit curricular attention to issues involving multicultural sensitivity. James Banks in his studies of effective schools confirms this and adds that the curriculum in effective schools includes the experiences of different ethnic groups and presents them from

*(continued on p. 274)*

# CAN RESEARCH IDENTIFY QUALITIES OF EFFECTIVE SCHOOLS?

## PRO B. R. Joyce, R. H. Hersh, and M. McKibbin

For the past two years we have been reviewing research to determine what, if anything, makes some schools and teachers more effective than others. Happily, there emerges from such research a variety of clues, which when put together into a coherent whole, make a great deal of intuitive sense. What is particularly pleasing is that different researchers in a variety of studies are reaching similar conclusions about teachers and administrators who bring to research programs the critical eyes of experience. Be-cause of the conjunction of researchers' knowledge and professional educators' wisdom we optimistically believe that we can improve education in America both on its current terms and by using technology and fresh curriculum alternatives more extensively. . . .

What is important is that [beliefs about effective schools] are shared by educators who otherwise espouse and have developed very different approaches to the creation of an effective education.

From: Joyce, Hersh, and McKibbin. *The Structure of School Improvement* (1983).

## Postscript

Joyce, Hersh, and McKibbin believe that the cumulative and interactive effects of research and practice confirm the importance of effective schools research. They point to a parallel from the 1960s, when federal educational programs for economically poor children were developed based on specific beliefs about early childhood education such as "education should begin where children are ready to learn. . . . Instruction should be individualized to a large extent. . . . Goals should be clear to all. . . . All children need to learn how to learn. . . . Emotional development must be enhanced" (p. 31). When this cumulative and interactive effect of research and practice occurs, they contend, we should use the research as the basis for the improvement of education.

# CAN RESEARCH IDENTIFY QUALITIES OF EFFECTIVE SCHOOLS?

## CON  T. L. Good and J. E. Brophy

School effects data are limited in several respects. First, most effective schools research has been conducted in urban schools, so its application to suburban schools is unknown. Second, the description of effective schools is based largely on their effectiveness in obtaining high student performance on standardized achievement tests. This is a narrow definition of school effectiveness. Although there is some evidence that schools can simultaneously achieve several goals (e.g., high attendance rates, high student engagement rates, high achievement), for the most part the question of school success on cognitive criteria other than standardized achievement (e.g., decision-making skills) has been ignored. There is no evidence that schools that teach the basic skills relatively well can also teach computer skills, science, and writing relatively well. Furthermore, process measures usually have been limited to a few global dimensions of schooling, and these examine *form* more than *quality.* Often, data are collected on only a few teachers per school, and the information about what even these teachers do is sketchy. . . .

Another major constraint on effective schools research is that existing evidence is largely correlational. Whether active leadership precedes or follows the development of high expectations or whether student achievement precedes or follows high expectations for performance is uncertain. . . .

Although certain aspects of the school effects literature may help practitioners to identify their problems and alternatives and thus allow them to think more systematically about their instructional programs, this research does not yet yield answers. . . . The research completed to date shows that individual school variance is an important dimension that can be influenced by selected actions and resources. Despite this progress, the next step does not involve application. Rather, it requires further extending the basic knowledge in this field by completing new studies that help us to understand more the fully qualitative aspects of schooling.

From: Good and Brophy. "School Effects," in *Handbook of Research on Teaching,* 3rd. ed. (1986).

On the other hand, Good and Brophy suggest caution in implementing effective schools research before researchers have had time to examine it. Should we proceed with the information we have, despite the fact that it might not be complete? Or should we seek additional information to further confirm what we have found?

We agree with Joyce, Hersh, and McKibbin that the research is broad based enough and has such potential for improving education that it should be implemented. On the other hand, we also agree with Good and Brophy that many important aspects of what makes a school effective have yet to be examined. Therefore, we suggest the middle road. Use what you know about effective schools to examine the schools in which you observe, to develop your own definition of the word *school,* and to think about how your classroom will be organized.

diverse perspectives and points of view (1994, 184). Hill, Foster and Gendler in their study of thirteen urban high schools in New York City and Washington, D.C., suggest that effective schools have what they call a *centripetal curriculum,* which draws all students toward a common core of skills and perspectives (1990, viii). Likewise, Sizer found that curricular decisions in effective schools are related to the students' attainment of mastery of essential skills and that the design of the curriculum is shaped by "intellectual and imaginative powers and competencies the students need" (1992, 207). Levine and Lezotte's studies confirm that the emphasis in effective schools is on high level comprehension skills such as analysis and synthesis, and problem solving. Frequently, according to Horenstein's studies, the curriculum in these schools focuses on interdisciplinary studies such as team-taught history and English, and physics and industrial technology. Characteristics of curriculum and instruction in schools found to be effective will be more specifically examined in chapter 8.

## SOME REASONS WHY SOME SCHOOLS ARE NOT EFFECTIVE

Because determining what makes schools good is so difficult and subjective, many educators have reverted to examining why schools are not as effective as they could be. We will look at the results of some of these studies below.

*Lack of Innovation*   John Goodlad (1983) contends that most people teach as they were taught, modeling their practices on what they observed for sixteen or more years. Teacher training, he says, is of short duration and students discuss innovations but rarely get to observe them. Once on the job, teachers conform to social pressures that support inadequate teaching. The cards are stacked against innovation, he says, because the pressures teachers face to maintain control over a large group in a small room pushes them into methods that seemed to work for their teachers. According to Goodlad, teachers are torn between professional beliefs and on-the-job realities; they need more incentives and support to be innovative. Levine and Lezotte (1990) confirm Goodlad's conclusion saying that it takes considerable time and practice to try out innovative and improved practices at the classroom level. Schools that are less effective do not provide the needed staff development and coaching for the faculty and other school staff. Something other than standardized tests, which only measure lower level comprehension skills, must be found or teachers, who must teach to the test, will have no incentive to be innovative. David A. Gilman, editor of *Contemporary Education,* in his comparison of effective and ineffective schools, agrees, but also found that when incentives such as new equipment, released time, reduced schedules, extra materials, and other advantages were granted only to a select group of teachers, the motivation of the others was upset and their morale was diminished. This, in turn, also led to lack of willingness to innovate (1992, 89).

*Inadequate Funding*   The Carnegie Foundation also pointed to another roadblock in making all schools effective: inadequate funding. "We strongly urge that states fulfill their legal and moral obligations by achieving equity in the financing of urban schools. Once a standard of expenditures for effective schools is determined, the goal should be at least to meet the standard for all schools. Unless big city schools are given more support, much of what we propose will remain a hollow promise" (1988, 51). For the first time in the twenty-five-year history of the Phi Delta Kappa/Gallup poll on problems in public education, the number one educational problem perceived by the public in 1993 was lack of proper financial support. A report by the Educational Testing Service (ETS) suggests another financial impediment to effective schools: funding inequalities between and within states across the nation that affect the adequacy of instructional materials and other resources needed to teach classes. ETS found that lack of funding was especially glaring in disadvantaged urban and rural districts. Quoting from the NAEP study that focused on educational materials and mathematics, ETS stated that students in schools that lacked instructional materials had lower average mathematics proficiency in eighth grade than those with adequate resources (1991, 14). (See chapter 14 for an in-depth discussion of funding.)

*Mindless Regulations*    John Goodlad also found that states set broad educational goals for schools but do not articulate them to the schools or to the public vigorously or clearly. Similarly, the Carnegie Foundation found that urban school principals were crippled by mindless regulations; schools were viewed as one more administrative unit to be controlled rather than inspired. According to the Carnegie Foundation report, here is how one New York City principal described her situation:

> As I stare at the piles of memos and forms that confront me as a school principal, the job appears somewhere between a joke and an impossibility. The staff and I are directed instantly to implement new programs to resolve current crises, to use the latest research on teaching, to tighten supervision, increase consultation, and to report back in detail on all the above. There are pages of new rules and regulations to study: It would take a few months to make sense of the Regents plan alone. Responding to it would take a lifetime. Meanwhile, finding the funds to buy paper, repair our single rented typewriter, fix a computer, or tune the piano requires most of my time and imagination. (p. 6)

The foundation learned that purchasing, from pencils to textbooks, was centralized in district offices, giving individual schools little discretion in how to spend tax dollars to best meet the needs of their students. Levine and Lezotte

---

**7-1**

**POINTS TO REMEMBER**

- Effective schools research involves the observation of schools using a variety of measures such as standardized tests and public opinion to establish what makes a school effective.
- The social organization of the school includes such things as goals, levels of expectations, reward systems, and leadership.
- A positive ethos in a school requires the teaching of both intellectual and moral development.
- A classroom climate that is conducive to learning is fostered by a family's interest in the school and positive relationships among teachers, administrators, parents, and students.
- Good school leaders develop clear roles for all school employees. They establish an orderly environment and communicate effectively with teachers and students.
- Students in a good school are actively involved in its governance and in school activities.
- Staff development, practice, and time are needed components of effective schools.
- Schools are ineffective when teachers are not innovative, funding is inadequate, and regulations get in the way of administration.

further noted that ineffective schools rely on "bureaucratic processes that stress forms and checklists" in response to state mandates rather than a "collaborative collegial process designed specifically to empower and change the process" (1990, 71).

## Schools from Different Perspectives

Notwithstanding the research on effective schools, educators frequently do not agree on what schools should do to be more effective. These differences can be seen in various definitions of school. "Schools should be a place where children learn what they most want to know, instead of what we think they ought to know" (Holt 1964, 175). Martin Carnoy and Henry M. Levin express a different point of view in *Schooling and Work in the Democratic State* (1985). "The school . . . contributes to the making of competent adults. . . . Schools are . . . functional institutions that satisfy the needs of adult society" (pp. 19, 20).

What skills must the schools teach so that their students can become competent adults? On this, too, educators disagree. Arthur G. Wirth, author of several books on education, suggests that symbolic analysis skills are needed by adults in order to function within an electronic global economy (1992, 200–201). Howard Gardner, professor of education at Harvard Graduate School of Education, on the other hand, claims that schools must go far beyond "the mastery of written or numerical literacy. They have become the logical site for the transmission of rapidly accumulating wisdom as well as the inculcation of skills that will permit further discoveries to be made and deeper understandings to emerge" (1991, 130). William A. Donahue, author of *The New Freedom,* adds another role for the school in developing adult competence: the development of character. "A good school can be defined . . . as a place where the values of self-discipline and hard work are consistently nurtured by both teachers and administrators" (1990, 167).

Holt, and Carnoy and Levin each define school in terms of its function. However, Holt emphasizes that school is "a place where children learn," whereas Carnoy and Levin believe that schools *make* competent adults. In other words, Holt defines school as a place for students and learning, and Carnoy and Levin define school as a place of instruction and subject matter. The distinction between school as a locus for learning and school as a locus of instruction is a critical one in terms of how schools are defined and organized. Holt's school, for example, would be organized with the student as its focus, what researcher Linda Darling-Hammond calls "learner-centered schools" (1992); Carnoy and Levin's school would be organized with instruction and content as its focus.

Further, although both Wirth and Gardner agree that schools must develop competent adults, their definitions of competence differ as would the curriculum and teaching methods in a school wholly embracing each definition of adult competence. Schools embracing Wirth's definition will be filled with advanced technological equipment and have a curriculum in which mathematics and sciences predominate with instructional strategies in which students solve analytical problems. (Some good contemporary examples of schools based on Wirth's definition are the tech-prep programs discussed in chapter 8, pp. 334–337.) A school based on Gardner's definition of adult competence will certainly teach the sciences and mathematics, but its curricular offerings are likely to be broader and include many more offerings in the humanities and the arts. This school will expect students to learn the accumulated wisdom of humankind through classical books and other time-tested resources, at the same time it will require students to be active participants in all aspects of their learning—practicing artists as well as scientific researchers. Donahue suggests another way in which the schools must develop adult competence, character building. A school adopting this definition is likely to have a curriculum emphasizing how values are developed. For example, students may read books and discuss the values expressed in the books or they may be required to participate in school activities designed to accomplish such objectives as improved leadership skills or active volunteerism. Although a list of courses may look very similar to those in a school based on Gardner's definition, it is likely that the approach to teaching them will differ. In practice, however, most schools focus on both the student and on instruction. Similarly, most schools incorporate many goals toward development of adult competence, and Wirth's, Gardner's, and Donahue's goals, as well as many others, could be incorporated into a single curriculum.

While experts in the field disagree on the definition of a school, we wondered what the people directly involved in the school believed. So we interviewed students, educators, and adults from a variety of walks of life, from various geographic regions of the United States, in a range of communities from urban to rural to obtain definitions of a school. We also examined various studies of schools to try to achieve a balance to these definitions. We selected the following as a representative group.

## THE CONTEMPORARY STUDENT'S PERSPECTIVE

The students' perspective on school depends largely on their experiences there. Ryan Eller, age seven, from a suburban southern community, says that "school is a place where you learn things, like how to read." His eight-year-old brother, Justin, says, "In a way, school is fun. It's a place where you learn science, math, English and geography." Ten-year-old Justin Vieira from Hilo, Hawaii, makes the same point metaphorically, "School to me is where I play with my friends and where my brain is a junior vacuum sucking up information." Ryan's definition is of the place, as are both Justins', but Justin and Justin add that school is fun, "in a way" and a place to learn. Both Justins are commenting on the social, as well as the instructional, organization of the school.

Nine-year-old Sharon Elliman from a small New England community thinks of school as "a place where you learn about science, social studies, geography, and much more. In school they also teach you math, spelling, and how to read. I like school a lot." Her best friend, nine-year-old Christina Marie Caviello, says, "I think school is great. Because the teachers make the work fun. . . . At the end of the year I feel sad because I had so much fun during the year." Chace Noguchi, a fourth grader from Hawaii, agrees, "To me school is about learning and knowing new things and meeting new friends to play with up field. I have learned new things in school. I am learning a lot. I am having fun in school and I like it. School is important to me and so is play time!!! I like small classrooms and a place to have different people in class." Her classmate Elizabeth Cross says, "I really like school because summer is usually boring, but school is always fun!" Sharon and Christina think about the curriculum when they think

A student's perception of school may range from sheer joy to sheer disaster, depending on her or his experiences there, both in the classroom and out of it. These students enjoy reading their group-composed essay to the class, making learning meaningful and happy.

about school, while Chace and Elizabeth think in terms of what they are learning and how much fun both the work and the play are. To all these elementary school students, school is working and learning and having fun. Being with their peers is yet to become a primary purpose of going to school.

Eight-year-old Ellen Stanley, who attends school in a small rural community, says of school, "It's where there's kids and teachers and you learn stuff." Alicia Hall, age seven, who lives in a small southern town, also recognizes that school is more than a place; it is a place with people. "It's a building where we work and people go there to play with things and go on field trips." Her thirteen-year-old brother, Eric, has a slightly more sophisticated view of school based on his experiences. "It's a place to learn from books and about basketball, and there are lots of friends there, but you don't get to see them often." To Eric, as to most thirteen-year-olds, learning is important only if it relates to current interests, and school is a place where you meet your friends.

In recent years, the school may have assumed a new role, particularly for students in urban centers. Ryan Newth, a middle school student in Charlotte, North Carolina, calls it "a safe haven. It is a place where children can socialize and learn under the safety of a watchful eye." Jim Martin, a schoolmate of Ryan's, also thinks of school as a safe place where you "feel comfortable and are accepted." Rett Matthews, another student from the same school calls it "a second home where students look forward to going." Polly Cline, a junior at New Trier Township High School in Winnetka, Illinois, makes the same point eloquently.

Some will say to you that a school is a sifter, merely separating those people who will succeed from those who will fail. And some will say a school is a beehive often overcrowded with uncaring, unaffected students. And still others will contend that a school is an echo, mindlessly repeating pointless lessons. But I, I don't think like other people. In my eyes, a school is a blanket which protects me from the real traumas of the outside world.

Some young students already look at school in terms of their futures. Lori Hirayama, a ten-year-old from Hawaii, writes, "School to me is a place to learn as much as you can, so when you grow UP you will have a great job." However, looking at school in terms of the future is more typical of older students. Jason Whitaker, a sixteen-year-old high school sophomore in a consolidated rural high school, describes school as "a place where you and your friends go to learn what you will use later on." Sixteen-year-old sophomore Mary Russell, also a student in a rural high school, says, "School is a place where you work, get an education, have friends. It's like a family to me, where there are teachers, and you have fun, but sometimes it's boring." To these high school students, learning, in terms of future directions, begins to take on importance, but peers and social interaction remain an essential part of the school experience.

Not all students find school a positive experience, however. In fact, in New York City, at a high school geared to prepare students for college, one student reported to the Carnegie Foundation for the Advancement of Teaching in *An Imperiled Generation: Saving Urban Schools*, "I made guest appearances when I was enrolled." Another student said, "The environment there was not one in which the kids wanted to learn. They just wanted to hang out on the streets." The Carnegie Foundation refers to this as the school's "culture of cutting" (p. xiii).

Other students depict the school experience as mixed. Caroline Owens, a twelve-year-old seventh grader in an urban middle school, said, "Some of the students have bad attitudes—like wanting to fight. They are school bullies. It's just the way they learned. They can't help it." However, Caroline says that for her, the "classes are great . . . I like the teachers because they are understanding, funny, and treat you like a person." David Smith, another twelve-year-old urban middle schooler, confirms Caroline's concern about the students. "Lots of kids pick on other kids—put them down. They're mean; they don't want to be social." He also finds school less satisfying than Caroline. "I like the social part of school, like the thirty minute breaks so we can visit. . . . The health classes are good, but you need teachers you can talk to and ask questions—teachers have to be open so you can ask questions about sex and drugs and alcohol—not just read it in the books." Ten-year-old Todd Saxon from Hawaii may suggest one of the reasons many students either do not like or have mixed feelings about school. "School is a place to learn more about science and get better at other subjects. School is fun when you do good." And, by suggestion, not fun when you don't.

The Carnegie Foundation for the Advancement of Teaching found that a student's experience in school depended, at least in part, on the curriculum. According to the commission, the school's curriculum tends to put students in boxes: academic, vocational, and general. The North Carolina Task Force on Excellence in Secondary Education reported in an unpublished series of research reports that students in general tracks are caught in an educational wasteland; they are less likely to succeed than their peers in more goal-oriented academic and vocational tracks. The Carnegie Foundation for the Advancement of Teaching says in the prologue to its report that "a reform movement launched to upgrade the education of *all* students is irrelevant to many children—largely black and Hispanic—in our urban schools" (p. xi).

Fifteen-year-old Aisha Washburn, a student in an urban high school, confirms their view. "I don't see much point in going to school. The teachers don't care whether I'm there or not. It's a waste of time; I learn more watching TV. What good is reading Shakespeare gonna' do me? I gotta' kid to take care of. As soon as I'm sixteen, I'm gonna quit."

By the time most students are ready to graduate from high school, they define school primarily in terms of preparation for college or life. Peers, of course, do not diminish in importance. According to Marc Bart, an eighteen-year-old senior in a city high school, who was taking a Scholastic Aptitude Test (SAT) preparation course when he wrote this definition, "School is a place that either prepares you for life directly outside of high school or prepares you for further education, and it also gives you the basic skills to get along in the world."

However, those students who do not see school as leading them toward their future careers or education tend to define and describe school as a waste of time. The Carnegie Foundation for the Advancement of Teaching concludes in its 1988 report that although most "Americans talk of providing a quality education for all children, we found that many people, both in and out of schools, simply do not believe this objective can be reached" (p. xv). Rather, many believe that urban students from underprivileged economic and social backgrounds cannot succeed. Hence, the report begins with the following declaration: "An urban school will be successful only as teachers, administrators, and community leaders have confidence that all students can succeed" (p. 1).

As students develop, their definitions of school evolve. Younger students think in terms of the activities of the classroom. Their friends are important, but they rarely define school in terms of relationships.

Older students, particularly in middle school and early high school, tend to define school in terms of both relationships and school activities. However, relationships take on primary importance, and activities are described in terms of what the student did or how the learning relates to the student's current interests.

As students mature, the importance of school to their future jobs or education takes precedence, but peer interactions remain a central focus of how they view schools. By the time students are completing their secondary education, their educational focus moves from peer interaction to preparation for jobs or college—life beyond school.

Note that all the students view school from the perspective of the learner. None of them talks about school as a place of instruction but rather as a place where learning happens.

## THE EDUCATOR'S PERSPECTIVE

Although teachers and administrators spend much of their lives inside school buildings, they are rarely asked to define school. What they believe about schooling, their philosophy of education, is the basis for the organizational structure of their schools and classrooms.

Alice Evans, a retired early childhood teacher from Los Alamos, New Mexico, answers her own question.

> What is a school? A school is the raveling and unraveling of life. It is not confined to four walls. It is ever present from the day we are born to the day we die.
>
> What is a school? A school is a place where students and teachers meet to interact, to learn and grow together, to experience the excitement of curiosity and knowledge.

It is likely none of us were in Ms. Evans's classroom. However, we can imagine what it was like. Ms. Evans claims that school is a place that is "not confined to four walls," and the interactions between students and teachers take precedence over the specifics of the content. Ms. Evans's classroom had walls, but the walls didn't keep the outside out or the inside in. The classroom was filled with critters in boxes and cages; in one corner was a microenvironment of a stream. Every spring the ant colony revisited the room. The children observed the activities of the animals and kept a class journal. They wrote books for the classroom library about their animal friends and life along the stream. The children freely wandered out the classroom door to gather samples of grass or dirt. On fine days they frequently sat in circles on the lawn and wrote poems about the sounds of spring or the tastes of winter. Parents and other adults often visited the classroom. A trip to the local fire station, accompanied by the station dalmatian, was the highlight of one walking field trip; another was to a corner grocery store, to reinforce addition and subtraction skills.

Lee Fowler has taught high school social studies and Latin for twenty-four years in Du Page County, Illinois. She says of school:

> A school is a place to instill WONDER—about the student's own life, the community, and the whole world. If the school sees itself *only* as a training place so that the students can make a living, the children are diminished.
>
> A child starts out life with such a tremendous amount of curiosity, and school should take that motivation to develop an awareness of self-importance as well as the individual's relationship to others and the world—both the physical world and the world of ideas and feelings.
>
> I've seen children begin school with such anticipation and eagerness. Why do those two marvelous traits seem to so often get killed off?

Ms. Fowler's definition tells us a great deal about the structure of her classroom. As a social studies teacher, she believes that individuals grow in self-importance through their interaction with one another. Her classroom is an active place. Groups of students work on projects. The group project is planned by Ms. Fowler, but the students' interaction is frequently unplanned. Ms. Fowler has an objective in mind for the group work; however, she is never sure of the exact direction the students will take. Will their study of "The Aging of America" lead a group of students to conduct interviews with residents of a local retirement home? Will their study of the Civil War lead to a reenactment of the Battle of Gettysburg? You never know where students will go when you give them a direction and send them on their way.

Cleveland Smith, a high school science teacher in Asheville, North Carolina, believes that "a school is a place where students learn academically, as well as through extracurricular activities and socially, a place where learning is nurtured in many different ways." Mr. Smith places a high value on both the knowledge

However they define school, most teachers are positive about their interactions with students and encourage them to develop their talents in many different ways. While their problems may be different, teachers in both urban and suburban schools believe that they must try to meet the needs of the individual student.

his students gain in his science classroom and the time he spends working with them outside class. His choice of the word *nurture* shows how he views the role of the teacher—he or she is one who works closely with the students, continuously encouraging them, helping them feel good about themselves.

Ron Eller is an associate professor of history at the University of Kentucky in Lexington. According to Mr. Eller, "School is a place where the values of the community are passed on to the next generation." Mr. Eller is a scholar who researches the past and examines the values that have created communities. His classes reflect his beliefs. He encourages his students to become scholars of their cultures, to investigate their communities, to learn about their past, and thereby understand their present and future.

Earlier in this chapter you read an "In the Classroom" about an effective school, Banneker High School in urban Washington, D.C. Listen to what Banneker teachers say about their school. We believe you will not be surprised by their definitions.

> School is the crucible in which strong minds are forged by interaction with other minds. At the school where I teach, I watch as lives change, and disciplined characters emerge from the careful, dedicated pressure of the crucible. Mind and character are considered equally here, and the "product" is a highly individualized personality. (Eileen Davis, English)
>
> School is a nurturing environment which takes a child at whatever level he/she may be and nurtures and encourages him to develop to the pinnacle of his ability. In order to do this, the school must relate whatever is done to the real world in which the child lives and to which he is obligated to contribute for the rest of his life. (Barbara Bennett, Spanish)
>
> School is the first and last place one encounters in life that apportions opportunity equally. (Dennis Brent, English)
>
> School is a supportive environment which fosters the mental, emotional, and physical growth of children. (Jodi Improta, speech and drama)
>
> School is a refuge from ignorance and want. (Edward H. Smilde, English and European history)

Moyra Contreras, a teacher at Melrose Elementary School in Oakland, California, talks of another aspect of the school that she has embodied in her own work as a mentor teacher to other teachers and a consultant to the Bay Area Writing Project, an in-service staff development project in which teachers work together to improve their own writing and their teaching of writing. According to Ms. Contreras, "School is the opportunity for all of us, students, teachers, parents and other members of the school community, to teach each other what we know and support each other in our quest to discover what we need to learn."

The teachers quoted above have largely positive definitions of school. Some, however, are negative in their descriptions. In the Carnegie Foundation for the Advancement of Teaching report on urban schools, the task force members discovered that many educators described school in terms of "failures." They talked about students who were merely "marking time" in school. "A social studies teacher in a Los Angeles high school confided somewhat sheepishly that her students were using a book written on a third-grade level because it was 'all they could handle.' 'It's a game we play,' said a teacher in Houston. 'If we held them all back, the system would get clogged up. So we water down the curriculum and move them along' " (1988, 1).

Teachers in urban schools further reported to the Carnegie Commission task force that school is "paper work." As one urban teacher said to the task force:

> Paper work is one of the things that competes for my time. You have to check roll in homeroom and then you have to see if anyone is tardy. In second period, you have to fill out an attendance report that is audited for average daily attendance. You have to keep those records in your grade book. Then, if a student is absent three times you have to list him on a special form that goes to the principal with your lesson plans. And you have to call the student. On the fourth day, you have to send a letter to the student's parents, and send another form into the office when the student is absent the sixth time. I think that is a lot of time that surely could come from some other source, like from the attendance office. It is an every period activity. (1988, 6–7)

Another problem urban teachers related to the task force was lack of materials and supplies. Here is how one urban teacher described the problem:

> I sometimes wonder how we're able to teach at all. A lot of times there aren't enough textbooks to go around; the library here is totally inadequate; and the science teachers complain that the labs aren't equipped and are out-of-date. We're always running short on supplies. Last year we were out of mimeograph paper for a month, and once we even ran out of chalk.
>
> After a while you learn to be resourceful. But it's still frustrating to try to teach under these conditions. I mean, talk about teaching the basics! We don't even have the basics to teach with. (1988, 7)

It is not only in urban schools in which teachers define schooling negatively. Paul Houts, director of the Carnegie Foundation's Study of the American High School, summarized the study's findings in a conference in Racine, Wisconsin, in 1982.

> They [high school teachers] have little time to prepare for what they do each day, no authority to make decisions, frequent interruptions by disruptive students and by principals with nearly incessant public address announcements, and pay so low that moonlighting on second jobs is often necessary. In many places, teachers also lack the support and respect of the community in which they work. And after the school year ends, many must take jobs as clerks, waitresses, house painters, or other non-professional work in order to make ends meet. There is considerable demoralization out there.

Similar conclusions were reached in a 1994 report of the National Education Commission on Time and Testing, chaired by Murfreesboro, Tennessee, City School Superintendent John Hodge Jones. After a two-year study of and interviews with one hundred fifty teachers in nineteen geographically distributed schools, the commission concluded, "educators do not have the time they need to do their job properly" (p. 13). They do not have time to read, plan, practice what they will teach, and collaborate with other teachers. For some reason, professional development is viewed as a "waste of time," concluded the 1994 study titled *Prisoners of Time* (p. 17).

Recently we asked students who had just finished their student teaching at an urban high school to define school. One of them summarized his impressions.

> It is like there are two (or maybe more) schools. There is a school for the good students. These kids are largely economically advantaged and white. They get a good

education in my school. They take advanced classes; some of them take Advanced Placement courses [classes that provide college credit depending on the results of a national test]. These kids could compete anywhere. Then, there is the other school, the school of the disenfranchised kids. These kids are largely economically disadvantaged and nonwhite. They get a poor education in my school. They take low-level classes. They study a curriculum which helps prove to them that there are no people of color who do work that is worth studying. Do you know, that in spite of the fact that my school is over forty percent black, the English curriculum has no black writers—even in the classes which are largely black? In history, the students do not study great African or native Americans. Many of these kids drop out, and those that don't are prepared for little when they graduate. There are at least two schools in my school, one very good and one very poor.

A report funded by the William T. Grant Foundation Commission on Work, Family and Citizenship, *The Forgotten Half: Pathways to Success for America's Youth and Young Families* (1988), states, "Educators have become so preoccupied with those who go on to college that they have lost sight of those who do not. And more and more of the non-college-bound now fall between the cracks when they are in school, drop out, or graduate inadequately prepared for the requirements of the society and the workplace" (p. 3). Hence, the report tends to confirm the student teacher's impression: school must be defined from the perspective of the background of the students.

## THE ADMINISTRATOR'S PERSPECTIVE

As the leader of the school, the principal affects the school's organization by his or her definition of school. This can be seen clearly in Linette M. Adams's definition of school. She is the principal of Benjamin Banneker High School in Washington, D.C. "This school provides a safe and nurturing environment where children must come first and sensitive committed adults provide opportunities for students to learn to their fullest potential in preparation for world citizenship." Larry Liggett has been a principal of a small-city high school for nearly twenty years. According to Mr. Liggett, "A school is a family of people, gathered together to learn." Mr. Liggett's high school is large, but students and teachers are encouraged to think of themselves as part of a family.

The superintendent's definition of school affects not only a single school but potentially the entire school district. According to Culver R. Dale, retired superintendent of a small-town school district, "A school is an institution of formal instruction where a person learns in order to grow into a happy, productive, self-supporting, reliable, contributing individual. A school enables a person to develop to the fullest extent whatever talents and abilities he or she possesses. Thus, leaves this world a better place than he or she found it."

Sam Haywood, area superintendent in the Charlotte/Mecklenburg, North Carolina, schools, defines schools in a way that reflects the altruistic goals of the schools and the realistic problems of the schools.

Schools are places where knowledgeable and committed administrators and teachers help great kids learn how to think about important and even less important issues and problems. Schools are places where students learn basic skills.

Schools are places where students from many different economic and ethnic backgrounds come together. The school is a melting pot of the world and students are exposed to many things their parents had not taught them—like inappropriate sexual behavior, profanity, fighting, drugs, and using guns. The parents try to help, but sometimes it's too late.

Schools are places where kids have fun playing in sports, participating in band and chorus, experimenting in labs and just plain socializing together.

All these educators have different definitions of school; however, all of them agree that it is a place in which students learn. How that learning is to be carried out, the activities of the classroom, vary according to their personal definition.

## THE CONTEMPORARY ADULT'S PERSPECTIVE

None of the people whose interviews follow is an educator. The one thing they have in common is that they all attended school. Some of them are parents of children currently in school; some of them have children who have completed school; some work inside the home; others pursue careers outside the home. Their definitions of school reflect their own experiences and those of their children. In addition, their definitions express their adult concerns about what schools should do.

Anne Coviello is a mother and homemaker from a small town in Massachusetts. She says of school:

A school is one of the greatest influences in an individual's life. For those who are receptive, school acts as a foundation for the many paths we choose to follow as adults.

In talking with many friends, we all agree that "school" is the main thing that we wish we could "do again" and, somehow, "make right."

We, the homemakers and mothers, who for the most part work a minimal amount of time outside of the home, have a real thirst for knowledge at this stage of our lives. School takes on a new and much more valuable meaning for us now, perhaps because we're so caught up in the education of our children. The same "school" that we, as children, trudged through (all too often reluctantly and with little appreciation) has become a primary focus in our lives in terms of wanting the best in education for our children. We would love to be in the position to "learn it all," again. Consequently, we become frustrated when our children don't approach the learning process with the same enthusiasm that we would now were we given the opportunity.

Ms. Coviello, like most parents, wants more from school for her children than she got from it. In fact, she longs for the opportunity to go to school again, and, this time around, take all that it has to offer. She worries that her children are not eager to learn, perhaps no more eager than she was as a young student. Ms. Coviello places the greatest importance on what the students learn in school, calling that learning the "foundation" for life's choices. She does not say what should be included in that foundation, but she believes that it involves the gaining of knowledge. To Ms. Coviello, the instructional organization of the school takes precedence over the social. However, it is likely if we had asked her what she remembers most from her own schooling, she would recall those aspects that involve interaction with her peers.

Foster Evans, a theoretical physicist from New Mexico, says school is "a place where a person may go to learn. A successful school is one that provides an environment conducive to learning. [A school is a group of teachers that provides such an environment.]" Mr. Evans recognizes that a school is a place where a person "may" go to learn. He makes it clear, through the use of the word *may,* that learning is not the only reason why people go to school, and that not all people who go to school will learn. In addition, Mr. Evans acknowledges that a school is successful only if the environment is conducive to learning.

Doris Phillips Loomis, an attorney and mother from North Carolina, says that "a school is an arena is which the inquisitive can thrive and the complacent can absorb. It sets those two groups apart. In order for this definition to be accurate, however, a school must be construed to be not only an educational institution but also the world in general." Ms. Loomis's definition looks at school as more than a place with four walls. She refers to school as an "arena" and acknowledges that if school is to allow the "inquisitive to thrive" it must be viewed as more than an institution; it must be viewed as the "world in general." In Ms. Loomis's ideal school, the world will be brought into the classroom, and the students will be taken into the world.

Although all these adults, who at one time were students, have different definitions of a school, all of them recognize the centrality of the learner to the learning process. None of them places instruction at the forefront but each recognizes that some interaction between student and teacher must occur. All these adults speak from their own experiences, the experiences of their children, and what their lives have taught them school should be. For all of them, schools in the United States are far more than "buildings where instruction takes place."

## SCHOOLS FROM A CROSS-CULTURAL PERSPECTIVE

To help us better understand the contemporary view of schools in the United States, we asked Japanese, Argentinean, and Chinese high school exchange or immigrant students to discuss the schools in their home countries and compare them to the American public schools they were attending. We also examined quotes of immigrant students from *Achieving the Dream: How Communities and Schools Can Improve Education for Immigrant Students* (NCAS 1993) and an editorial written by a Nigerian immigrant. Through these cross-cultural comparisons we can see how *all* the definitions above differ from those of these students.

Ayumi Moro, a nineteen-year-old high school graduate visiting an American high school, says of schools in Japan:

> School [one term] begins in April. There are three terms. Most of the Japanese students wear school uniforms. They go to school by train, bus, or bicycle. Some walk. There is no school bus. People under eighteen years of age cannot drive cars. In addition, they cannot go by car to school.
>
> School usually begins at eight thirty and finishes at three o'clock. There is a ten minute break between classes for the teacher to change rooms. The students don't

change rooms, but they have different schedules every day. They have five big exams a year. This decides the grades on the report card.

Summer vacation lasts about forty days. School [another term] begins in September. In autumn, there are many school events—a culture festival, an athletic meet, and a school excursion for seniors only. This is a very big event.

The winter vacation starts at Christmas and lasts about two weeks. In March seniors graduate from school.

According to Chikako Yokogawa, an eighteen-year-old senior visiting an American high school as an exchange student:

I go to a public school in Japan. After students finish compulsory education through junior high school, most go on to complete high school so that they can get a good job. This is because the Japanese society puts so much emphasis on one's educational background, and most Japanese companies demand people to have a high educational background. To attend a high school, each student must pass an entrance examination; however, the number of applicants for admission is far greater than the number actually accepted. This makes it very difficult.

The students must study very hard, since the school has major exams often. Over half the students go to a private tutoring school in the afternoons after regular school. This is especially true for seniors, as they have to study even harder than anyone else to get into a university. It is referred to as "Examination Hell."

Kyoko Shogetsu frankly says of her experience as a Japanese public school student, "I like school, but there are so many programs, I have to study very hard. Japanese schools are boring. I come here to an American high school so I won't be so bored in school. I have many friends in school [in America], then it's not so boring."

Claudio Bottero, a seventeen-year-old exchange student from Argentina, compares schools in Argentina to the one he is visiting in the United States.

School is a place to learn many things. There are more possibilities to learn in America—like many science labs and electronic labs. There is a lot of opportunity to practice. Practice is better here. In Argentina, I had to study very hard, like five hours to study for a calculus test. Here I study about thirty minutes and can get B's and A's. Theory is much harder there.

Students here waste a lot of time. Many don't do their homework. They like to have parties and drink to get drunk. In Argentina, we like to drink because we enjoy it, but not to get drunk. Every day when I go into the bathrooms [in the school] I can smell the pot, but I don't see any of that in classrooms or the halls.

Quingfei Zhang is an eighteen-year-old high school senior who came to the United States two years ago with his parents. He compares U.S. schools to those in mainland China.

Schools in America have lots of free choices of subjects to take. In China, in my first two years of high school, I had to take just those classes that I need to have to get into an engineering college. Here I can take those classes but other ones too, like swimming and advanced English. There is more leisure time here—lots of activities

## *Cross-Cultural Perspective*

## The Secret of Japanese Education

It is scarcely necessary to provide references to document the wonderful impression that Japanese education has made on the American press. Article after article extols the efficiency and effectiveness of Japanese public schools. The only sour note ever sounded has to do with the pressures students suffer in preparing for entrance examinations. However, after 15 years of teaching in the schools of Japan (public and private), I can say that a great many things Americans think they know about Japanese schooling turn out to be myths.

The problem, as Merry White [professor of education] points out, is that the observers are usually Americans, and their observations are colored by their familiarity with the American model of education and the almost irresistible tendency to compare.[1] For example, an observer visits a math class in a Japanese high school. Walking around the room, the observer notices that textbooks are open to a page of calculus. The observer then erroneously concludes that the students are learning calculus and writes a report about how advanced Japanese students are when compared to American students.[2]

What observers don't seem to know is that Japanese textbooks target high-achievers, not average students; that upwards of 95% of the students do not understand what the teacher is talking about; that a passing score in the prerequisites is 35%; and that most students are studying calculus without having passed the prerequisites.

The same situation can be found in English class, another popular class for observers to visit. Third-year students are studying third-year English because they are third-year students, not because they have passed second-year or even first-year English.[3]

Americans think they know that a Japanese student must pass an entrance exam to attend high school. What most Americans don't know is that the test is a test of elimination. If there are 300 freshman slots available and 304 students apply, the test is given to eliminate four students. "Passing" scores can be as low as 5%, which means that the student correctly responded to only 5% of the questions. Failing a high school entrance exam is truly a catastrophe for Japanese students.

On the other hand, the competition for admission to universities and even to some prestigious high schools is truly fierce, because there are so few slots and so many applicants for each one. Students preparing for a university entrance exam study not only academic material, but also statistics on the minimum passing score for each major in each college of interest to them—in order to determine where their best chances lie.

Many "facts" long accepted by the Western press are misleading. For example, students may spend more time in school, but they don't necessarily spend that time studying. The three hours of classes students have on Saturday morning make up for the three nonacademic hours during the week that are spent on homeroom activities, teachers' meetings,

and clubs. The clubs are good if you do something, but some students join clubs that meet during the school day to get out of going to class, and in the clubs they sit there and just talk. I guess that's o.k. It depends on what your career aspirations are. I want to be an engineer, so I don't want to waste my time that way.

Jide Nzelibe, now a graduate student at Princeton University, remembers his high school experience in Hyattsville, Maryland, after having emigrated from Nigeria in 1988.

I looked on with bemusement as an attractive female passed a note to a young man in the first row. Some trite vulgarities were exchanged, my more restive classmates started singing, and the teacher was all but completely ignored.

club activities, and so on. In a typical school year some 65 to 70 days' worth of afternoons are either free time or given over to nonacademic activities. Students are also required to attend school in uniform for one day in the middle of summer vacation so that teachers can take the roll and send them home. Three or four school days per year are devoted to cleaning the school.

Although Japanese high schools are mostly untracked,[4] the comprehensive high school as Americans understand the term is virtually unknown. Junior high schoolers are guided by their teachers into applying for the type of high school that the teachers feel will reflect best on the junior high school. Statistics on the success rate of students taking the high school entrance exams determine the status of the junior high school. Teachers do not want students applying for schools where there is a good possibility of failure, not because of a concern for students' self-esteem, but because it would hurt the statistics. . . .

There are basically three kinds of high schools in Japan: academic high schools, vocational high schools, and commercial high schools. These institutions are wholly independent of one another and do not even share the same grounds. The mission of the academic high schools is to prepare students for college entrance examinations. When Americans read about Japanese high schools, they are usually reading about academic high schools.

Students at the vocational high schools are mostly male, and the academic program is much less rigorous. The students expect to graduate and to go on to work as skilled or semiskilled apprentices. . . .

Students at the commercial high schools are for the most part female. These students expect to graduate, to work for a few years in an office, and then to marry (and leave the work force permanently). They learn such useful skills as the ins and outs of serving tea and bowing to customers, as well as the operation of business machines and a little bookkeeping. Overall, their education is not academically rigorous.

Japanese students *are* tracked, not into different programs within one school, but into entirely different schools. Moreover, this tracking rigidly determines a student's future career possibilities.

The fact is that Japanese public schools are doing a pathetic job of educating the people. Virtually 100% of public school graduates would fail college entrance exams if they depended on the public schools alone to prepare them.[5] A high school diploma represents nothing more than a certificate of attendance. The poor quality of public schools in Japan motivated Prime Minister Nakasone to form the ad hoc Commission on Educational Reform while he was in office.

1. Merry I. White, review of James J. Shields, Jr., ed., *Japanese Schooling: Patterns of Socialization, Equality, and Political Control,* in *Teachers College Record,* Winter 1990, pp. 312–14.

2. D. B. Willis, "Japan's Success: Some Lessons for Educators," *Japan Times,* 21 April 1983, p. 11.

3. Peggy Lukens, "Probing the 'Myths' About Japanese Education," *Education Digest,* vol. 54, May 1989, pp. 13–16.

4. E. O. Reischauer, *The Japanese* (Tokyo: Tuttle, 1977).

5. Susan C. Lucas, "Measures of Learning: Japan and America," unpublished manuscript, University of Maryland, College Park.

From: Goya, 1993, 126–129. Ms. Goya taught for fifteen years in the schools of Japan.

Welcome to the civics course at Northwestern High School.

. . . Though the above scene is commonplace to American students, as a recent immigrant raised in a poor but industrious village in Nigeria, I was more than a little shocked.

My initial impressions . . . were a jumble of mixed messages: mini-billboards and placards constantly advertised the dangers of unsafe sex and drug abuse. The school's public-address system constantly eulogized students who made it through a month or week without any absences, or those who were only marginally competent in their studies.

By contrast, Nigeria's public school system—which I attended through grammar school and most of high school—closely mirrors its parent British system in its emphasis on merit-based results and rigid codes of conduct. . . .

At Northwestern High School, most of the teachers appeared eager to help with my homework and career plans, the library in the school was well stocked and accessible, and there were plenty of sporting facilities. What I found lacking was an atmosphere among students—reinforced by family—that was congenial to academic excellence and social growth. (1994, 9A)

Many immigrant students have not found U.S. schools particularly welcoming. A Filipino student in Jersey City, New Jersey, said, "I can't speak English very well. I have difficulty understanding if they talk fast. On the first day I felt so left out that I went home and cried in the bathroom." A Haitian student in Queens, New York, claimed, "Teachers put me down by giving me lower grades and discouraging me from taking courses because they doubt my ability" (NCAS 1993, 33).

It is interesting to compare the exchange and immigrant students' descriptions of school with the American secondary school students' definitions. School, to the foreign students, is an academic endeavor filled with studying, tutoring, long hours of work, and tests, "Examination Hell," as one student calls it. None of these students mentions what he or she learns in school but rather what is required. The distinction is important. In every definition provided by U.S. students, educators, and noneducator adults, what the student learns is the most important element. However, in the exchange and immigrant students' descriptions of schools in their home countries, what the student learns is not mentioned. Instead, whether or not the student meets the demands of the educational system and/or business appears to be the central element of schooling.

It can be said, then, that one's experience in school can influence not only one's definition of school but also one's perception of the school's effectiveness. As the student teacher in this chapter said, a school may be very good for some students and not good for others. Is it possible for a school to be effective for *all* students? Scholars and educators who have examined schools judged to be effective say that it is.

---

**7-2**

**POINTS TO REMEMBER**

- Students' definitions of school relate to their experiences there. Elementary school students tend to define school in terms of what they are learning to do. By late elementary school, students define school in terms of peer relationships, by late high school, in terms of

their future goals for employment or higher education.

- Teachers' definitions of school are reflected in the organization of their classrooms. If they think of school as a community in which students work together to learn, their classroom organizations will encourage student interaction and participation in learning.

- Most adults define school from their own personal experien-

ces. Because they remember from the perspective of a learner, they define school in these terms.

- Examining how individuals in other cultures define schools helps us see how they relate to experience and school organization and helps us better understand U.S. schools by knowing how they differ from schools in other cultures.

## For Thought/Discussion

1. Do you think most U.S. schools teach a common positive ethos? If yes, what effect is it having on today's students? If no, why isn't it being implemented in all schools?

2. From your knowledge about schools and from information in this chapter, describe some elements that make schools ineffective.

3. What is your definition of a school from the perspective of a student and from the perspective of a teacher? How will this definition affect your classroom organization?

## For Further Reading/Reference

Brandt, R. S. (Ed.). 1989. *Readings from educational leadership: Effective schools and school improvement.* Alexandria, VA: Association for Supervision and Curriculum Development. A collection of articles about effective schools that first appeared in *Educational Leadership,* the journal of ASCD. Articles by R. Edmonds and R. S. Brandt are particularly noteworthy.

Fiske, B. 1991. *Smart schools, smart kids: Why do some schools work?* New York: Simon and Schuster. A description of on-site visits to public school classrooms that have made recent innovative structural changes. The author suggests that smart schools blend elements of change that fit the school's particular circumstances.

Horenstein, M. A. 1993. *Twelve schools that succeed.* Bloomington, IN: Phi Delta Kappa Educational Foundation. A discussion of why these twelve schools, each a Blue Ribbon School identified by the U.S. Department of Education, are effective.

Levine, D. U., and L. W. Lezotte. 1990. *Unusually effective schools: A review and analysis of research and practice.* Madison, WI: National Center for Effective School Research and Development. A summary of twenty-five years of research on effective schools. In addition, it describes how to develop effective schools and compares and contrasts numerous effective schools.

"Our teacher told us about sex today. As I understand it, we were bees before we were born."

Fred Thomas in *Phi Delta Kappan*

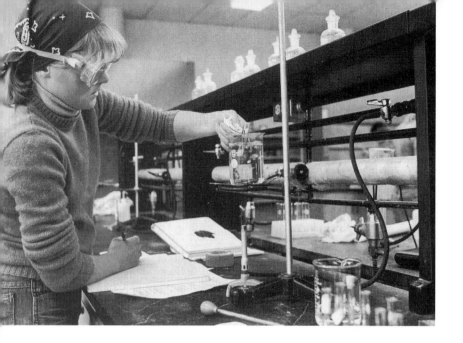

## CHAPTER OBJECTIVES

After studying this chapter, you should be able to:

- Define curriculum from the point of view of the essentialist.
- Define curriculum from the point of view of the progressivist.
- Describe how curriculum of the twentieth century has evolved.
- Discuss the hidden curriculum.
- Explain how psychologists have influenced curriculum.
- Compare how the schools of philosophy and the theories of education relate to curricular organization.
- Describe the subject-centered curriculum.

- Explain the similarities and differences between competency-based and outcome-based curriculum.
- Define mastery learning.
- Describe the broad fields curriculum.
- Define core curriculum.
- Describe the child-centered or activity curriculum.
- Discuss the humanistic curriculum.
- Explain how society's economic needs affect the curriculum.
- Discuss how women and minorities affect the curriculum.

*Chapter 8*

# THE CURRICULUM IN A MULTICULTURAL SOCIETY

*H*enry has been teaching high school English for almost thirty years. A friend asked him to appear on a panel at a professional meeting to discuss how teaching English has changed during that period. In reflecting upon his topic, Henry realized that there had been many changes in the students, the way the school is administered, how teachers are treated, and requirements for certification. But, most of all, Henry thought, the curriculum pendulum continues to swing. That's what Henry decided to talk about.

When I began teaching in the mid-1960s, I was assigned to three sections of average eleventh-graders, one section of remedial students, and one section of advanced students. By the late 1960s I had been "promoted" to three sections of advanced and two sections of average. The better I became as a teacher, the better the students I was given to teach.

I taught all three levels the same eleventh-grade material, using the same textbooks, the same Shakespearean plays. The differences were in how quickly we got through the material, how frequently I lectured, and how many essays I asked each group to write. The better the students, the more we read, the more difficult the questions I asked, the more in-depth their answers, and the longer their writing assignments and tests.

By the late 1960s the students began protesting. Was this material relevant? How did Shakespeare relate to the real world of Vietnam, segregation, and street riots? So, I tried to make the literature more relevant. In some of my classes we turned Hamlet into modern street dialect. That was fun; but was it more relevant? The teachers began to talk about the students' concerns. Thus, we read more contemporary books like *Black Like Me* and *Catcher in the Rye*. Soon, the teachers decided to reorganize the curriculum into minicourses primarily in areas of personal interest with titles such as "Myth and Legend" and "Who 'Dun' It?" The students and teachers as well selected courses they were interested in. At first, nearly everyone was happy. I particularly enjoyed the humanities courses I was team teaching with the history, music, and art teachers. I think the best humanities course we taught was based on the theme of "War and Peace."

However, before a generation of high school students had passed through the minicourses, concerns were voiced: Were the students selecting courses that would teach them to write? Were the students selecting only "gut" courses? How was reading adolescent literature going to help them understand great literature? Were advanced students penalized by having remedial students in the same class? What about spelling and grammar; where did they fit in?

The teachers began to make changes again. All students were required to take one quarter of composition and grammar each year. Advanced students were required to take one quarter of "the classics" each year. Within a few years, minicourse electives had become no more than required quarter courses. Allowing students to select among the required courses was an administrative headache. We decided then to go back to full-year courses. At first, they were similar to the minicourses. Most teachers organized the year into units based on themes or types of literature; most still taught one quarter of grammar and composition.

But, then, along came competency tests and concern that advanced students were not doing well on college entrance exams. So, we added more grammar, composition, and vocabulary to each class. National studies in the 1980s seemed to indicate that all students needed to be aware of a common "classical" body of literature. Consequently, the curriculum in my classes in the 1980s looked remarkably like the curriculum I taught in the mid-1960s. The only difference was in the state-provided course of study that included thirty or forty pages of competencies that the students must meet.

And, now, in the mid-1990s, the curriculum pendulum seems to be swinging again primarily because the students I am teaching today are not the same kind of students I taught in the 1960s. Then my classes were made up of mostly white students, more like I was at their age. Today, my classes are very different. I have many students of diverse cultures primarily of Asian and African American heritage. I enjoy the mix and the variety of perspectives in my classes, but I find teaching primarily western literature to these students difficult at best and unjust at worst. So, I've decided it's time to help my dendrites grow and enroll in some college courses that were not offered when I was an undergraduate. This summer I am taking two: African American Literature and Adolescent Literature. In the fall, I plan to take a course in Asian Literature. I am looking forward to the intellectual challenge and to changing my classes so they can be relevant to my students.

*H*enry wonders. "What is curriculum, anyway?" Is it simply a set of courses to be taught? Is it a response to social demands? Is it in any way related to the students' needs? Who defines students' needs? In this chapter we will define curriculum from a variety of points of view. We will attempt to illustrate how the individual's definition of curriculum helps determine its organization. We also will examine the philosophical basis of a curriculum and discuss its major organizational structures. Finally, we will examine the social and economic forces that have affected how curriculum is defined, developed, and implemented.

# What Is a Curriculum?

According to William Schubert, professor and college administrator at the University of Illinois in Chicago, "curriculum is shrouded in definitional controversy" (1993, 80). Literally, by dictionary definition, curriculum is what is taught in an educational institution, usually a series of courses. However, since learning is the presumed product of teaching, curriculum is also used to describe what is learned. Therefore, Schubert suggests that curriculum can be most simply defined as "whatever is advocated for teaching and learning" (p. 81). Herein lies the difficulty in defining curriculum. It is easy to describe what is planned to be taught. It is far more difficult to determine what is actually taught, and even more difficult to assess what has been learned. In fact, many schools do not have a formal curriculum. Instead, the curriculum consists of the textbooks taught, the tests given, and the instructional decisions made by individual teachers behind classroom doors.

## AN ESSENTIALIST DEFINITION

The word *curriculum* is derived from the Latin word *currere* meaning "the course to be run." Its derivation implies that curriculum is like a track with a beginning, a series of steps, and an end. The school sets the order of these steps, the essential building blocks of learning, making them increasingly difficult to achieve. Students must successfully complete each stage before being allowed to tackle the next. This definition is based on the essentialist theory of learning, which focuses on the basic, or essential, courses such as reading, writing, and arithmetic at the elementary level, and subject-matter disciplines such as mathematics and language at the secondary level.

## A PROGRESSIVE DEFINITION

However, the essentialist definition limits curriculum to what is taught and/or what is planned to be taught. Learners, and even teachers, are left out of this interpretation of curriculum. John Dewey in *Democracy and Education* (1928) criticizes the essentialist definition of curriculum.

The notion that the "essentials" of elementary education are the three R's mechanically treated, is based upon ignorance of the essentials needed for realization of democratic ideals. Unconsciously it assumes that these ideals are unrealizable; it assumes that in the future, as in the past, getting a livelihood, "making a living," must signify for most men and women doing things which are not significant, freely chosen, and ennobling to those who do them; doing things which serve ends unrecognized by those engaged in them, carried on under the direction of others for the sake of pecuniary reward. (p. 226)

Many educators believe that curriculum is far more than the development of a course to be run. Instead, curriculum includes, according to Elliot W. Eisner, "all the experiences the child has under the aegis of the school" (1985, 40).

This definition became popular during the progressive education movement of the 1920s. (For a discussion of progressivism, see chapter 6, pp. 240–241.) According to progressive educators, the "real" curriculum includes not only what goes on in the classroom within the planned lesson but also what goes on in the hallways and on the playground. Dewey and other progressive educators define curriculum as "continuous reconstruction of experience, an idea which is marked off from education as preparation for a remote future, as unfolding, as external formation, and as recapitulation of the past" (Dewey 1928, 93). The progressive definition of curriculum assumes that every student has his or her own curriculum because every student has different experiences.

## THE "HIDDEN CURRICULUM"

The "hidden curriculum" is that which occurs in the school but is not a part of the formal curriculum or course of study. John D. McNeil defines the hidden curriculum as including the "unofficial instructional influences [of schooling], which may either support or weaken the attainment of manifest goals" (1977, 209). Observers who gathered data in 129 elementary, 362 junior high, and 525 senior high classes for John I. Goodlad's study *A Place Called School: Prospects for the Future* defined the hidden curriculum as the many informal aspects of life in the school environment such as student-to-student interaction, student-to-teacher interaction, the lunchroom environment, the aesthetics of the school building, the use of technological equipment, students' involvement in decision making about their own learning, percentage of class time in which students talk and teachers talk, the use of small groups in the classroom, use of praise and laughter, and hands-on activity and physical movements (pp. 226–230).

John P. Portelli, a professor at Mount Saint Vincent University in Nova Scotia, further explains that the hidden curriculum consists of unpublished, unofficial expectations of students and teachers, unintended learning outcomes or messages, implicit messages arising from the structure of schooling, and the curriculum that is created by the students (1993, 345). According to Jackson, these factors give rise to norms and values that "collectively form a hidden curriculum which each student and teacher must master if he is to make his way satisfactorily through school" (p. 34). Often, says Jackson, when students do not do well academically, their failure can actually be attributed to a failure to successfully manage the hidden curriculum.

Apple and King, in "What Do Schools Teach?" (1977), believe the hidden curriculum is the tacit teaching of social and economic norms and expectations. They claim that it is not as hidden or "mindless" as many educators believe since much of what the school does is to "certify adult competence" for involvement in an advanced industrial society.

Therefore, educational knowledge dispensed by the schools must be considered in light of the larger distribution of goods and services in society. Neo-Marxists such as Michael F. D. Young state there is not only an unequal distribution of economic capital in society but also an unequal distribution of cultural capital. The school plays a critical role in dispensing this capital because school personnel make decisions about what is to be included in the curriculum and which students are to study which topics. "Principles of selection, organization, and evaluation of this knowledge are valuative selections from a much larger universe of possible knowledge and collection principles" (Young 1971, 31). Therefore, deciding that college-bound students will study Shakespeare, physics, foreign language, and world civilization and non-college-bound students will not, is part of the hidden curriculum in that these decisions determine to whom specific cultural capital will be given.

Neo-Marxists also discuss "access to power" as part of the hidden curriculum. There are numerous ways that this access to power can be seen in the school curriculum: Who develops the curriculum? Who has access to aspects of the curriculum that encourage development of power? Which students can make curricular choices? Do students work in small groups in some classes while being lectured to in other classes? Which students have access to positions of power in the school? Which students participate in important extracurricular activities such as interscholastic sports?

Philip W. Jackson in *Life in Classrooms* (1968) says that we can examine the hidden curriculum in terms of the amount of time students spend in school, the settings in which they perform, and the fact that they are in school whether they want to be or not. He maintains that in most classrooms "the social composition is not only stable, it is also physically arranged with considerable regularity" (1968, 7). Students typically have assigned seats and usually can be found in them. He further claims that despite diversity of subject matter content, "the identifiable activities are not great in number. The labels: 'seat work,' 'group discussion,' 'teacher demonstration,' and 'question-and-answer-period' (which would include work 'at the board'), are sufficient to categorize most of the things that happen when class is in session" (p. 8).

What then is the hidden curriculum if schools are so similar? Jackson's definition includes such things as how time is spent by the student in the classroom, how the environment of the classroom affects the students' roles, and how the instructional techniques employed by the teacher involve the students. Whereas the neo-Marxist definition examines curricular decisions that affect groups of students differently based on social and economic norms.

***Multicultural Curriculum*** James Banks, a professor at the University of Washington, writes of the need for a "transformative curriculum." This means students need to develop critical thinking skills so they can discover how knowledge is constructed and then construct knowledge itself. Banks contends that it is not enough to add content to the current curriculum, setting aside a month as black history or women's history month, for example. Instead, the

The hidden curriculum influences a student's education almost as much as does the obvious selection and organization of subject matter. Such things as time spent in class, the physical structure of the school building, student-to-teacher interaction, and implicit messages in the particular activity can all be considered a part of the hidden curriculum. These students are visiting the New York State assembly as part of a classroom project.

entire curriculum must be transformed in order to empower students, especially those from victimized and marginalized groups. (See table 8.2, pp. 324–325.)

A multicultural curriculum must help students develop the knowledge and skills needed to critically examine the current political and economic structure and the myths and ideologies used to justify it. Such a curriculum must also teach students critical thinking skills, so they can understand the basic assumptions and values that undergird knowledge systems and thus learn how to construct knowledge themselves (1994, 151).

## INFLUENCE OF U.S. PSYCHOLOGISTS

The curriculum in U.S. schools has been influenced by several psychologists. In this section of the chapter, we will examine some of their theories.

***G. Stanley Hall***   G. Stanley Hall (1846–1924), considered by many to be the father of educational psychology, developed a field that has come to be called **child-centered psychology.** Significantly influenced by the work of biologist Charles Darwin, the premise of his theory, which he called **paidocentric** (from Greek **pais, paidas** meaning "the upbringing of the child"), was that various stages in the history of organic evolution are repeated in the gestatory period of the human embryo. He expanded this theory further to the social stages in history, claiming that each stage of man's progress from savagery to civilization is mirrored in the child's development.

Although the research he conducted is considered today to be handicapped by serious inaccuracies, his work forced educators to examine the stages of children's physical, intellectual, and behavioral development. In addition, Hall was the first to describe the characteristics of adolescence with any scientific accuracy. He noted the rapid physiological and psychological growth during this period, especially sexual differentiation and maturation. Hall's research led to examination of how children develop and eventually to curriculum and teaching strategies designed for the developmental stages of the child. Hall's major contribution to modern curriculum development can be seen in the child-centered or activity curriculum (see pp. 287–289).

***William James***   William James (1842–1910), a pragmatist from the United States, was also influenced by the theories of Charles Darwin, particularly the theory of evolution. James believed that the human mind was a latecomer in the evolutionary stages of development. He contended that the mind biologically adjusts to the environment; the learner is not a passive receptacle but rather one who reacts to what is received in an instinctive order, the first based on repetitive physical movements. The student is then ready to acquire the ability for rationally conceptualizing material. James's major contribution to curriculum is the idea that teaching requires a specific sequence of skills. Consequently, the teacher must know the student well enough to be aware of his or her previously learned skills. His major contribution to teaching can be seen in the child-centered or activity curriculum.

***Edward L. Thorndike***   Edward Lee Thorndike (1874–1949), through studies of animals, theorized that learning is connecting the correct stimulus to the correct response, and that the correct response is to a large degree accidental, a matter of trial and error. His theory has come to be known as *stimulus-response (S-R)* and *conditioning*. Another contribution of Thorndike was in the area of measurement. Because progress in learning is a series of decreases in errors and increases in successes, Thorndike was able to plot, mathematically, a *learning curve*. At the turn of the century, he offered the first university course in the application of statistics to education. For the first time educators examined how teaching and learning could be measured through the use of concepts such as averages, means, probable errors, and correlations. Thorndike's major contribution to modern curriculum development can be seen in the competency-based curriculum (see pp. 305–307).

*William H. Kilpatrick*    William H. Kilpatrick (1871–1965) believed that education required a social emphasis that included all the formative influences and agencies that help induct the person into the life and culture of the group. Instructing students to work with groups "becomes even the more necessary because for some two decades now the dominant stress in study and research has been laid upon the scientific and impersonal aspects of education, with a resulting accumulation of techniques and procedures that largely ignore any social outlook and bearing" (Kilpatrick 1933, 257). Kilpatrick's major contribution to modern curriculum development can be seen in the project method. This curriculum included such things as the development of school newspapers, student gardens, and student construction of buildings.

*Howard Gardner*    Although there have been numerous twentieth century psychologists who have contributed to the curriculum (most notably Benjamin Bloom who developed the concept of the cognitive domain), the recent work of Howard Gardner on learning has the potential to revolutionize the curriculum. (For more detail on Howard Gardner's theory, see chapter 10, pp. 394–395.) In his 1991 book *The Unschooled Mind: How Children Think & How Schools Should Teach*, Gardner, a professor at Harvard Graduate School of Education, discusses the concept of multiple intelligences (MI), the many combinations of unique and individual intelligences that humans have. He suggests that they include: interpersonal (ability to interact with others), introspective (ability to analyze oneself), spacial (ability to understand relationships of objects and space), bodily (ability to control the body in multiple ways), musical (ability to hear and create sound), verbal (ability to understand and communicate orally and through writing), and mathematical or analytical (ability to solve complex problems). The potential impact of his studies on the curriculum go beyond questioning the appropriateness of standardized tests of intelligence and even concepts such as IQ (intelligence quotient) to developing curriculum and teaching methodologies that encourage students to use and develop multiple intelligences.

## TWENTIETH-CENTURY U.S. DEFINITION

During the twentieth century the curriculum pendulum has swung between the polar definitions of essentialism and progressivism, as illustrated by Henry in the opening chapter anecdote. Many educators contend that today's definition of curriculum is again moving from the essentialist view expressed in

David Gardner's reform reports, *The Nation At Risk* (1983) and Secretary of Education William Bennett's *American Education: Making It Work* (1988a), to a more progressive view of an inclusive curriculum that meets the needs of the diverse student population.

The *competency-based education* (CBE) movement, popular in the late 1970s and early 1980s, and the outcome-based education movement of the 1990s also illustrate the essentialist approach to curricular organization (for more information on essentialism see chapter 6). CBE, for example, assumes that there is a series of increasingly complex skills or competencies that students must meet as they progress through each discipline. Curriculum developers decide on these competencies. Although CBE and OBE are based on the learning theory of behaviorism (see chapter 6, pp. 245–247), many educators argue that CBE emphasizes only what is to be learned, ignoring the needs of the students and the skills of teachers in the process. It approaches the essentialist view of curriculum and the "course to be run" definition.

On the other hand, many educators contend that *open education,* an approach to curricular organization made popular by Carl Rogers and others during the 1960s and early 1970s, pushed the definition of curriculum beyond progressivism. Rogers, who changed the term *teacher* to *facilitator,* believed students should be asked, What do you want to learn? not told what they should learn (1983, 35). Hence, the term *curriculum* became obsolete because, as many critics of open education maintain, Rogers's approach removed not only the content but the professional from the teaching and learning process.

A broader, more inclusive definition of curriculum can be seen in the 1990s in the work of scholars such as Theodore Sizer of the Essential Schools Coalition (see chapters 2 and 7). Sizer's curricular definition focuses on what is essential in U.S. secondary schools, but not on particular subjects and works as stated in the 1980s reform reports.

1. The schools should focus on helping adolescents learn to use their minds well. Schools should not attempt to be "comprehensive" if such a claim is made at the expense of the school's central intellectual purpose.
2. The school's goal should be simple: each student should master a number of essential skills and be competent in certain areas of knowledge. Although these skills and areas will to varying degrees reflect the traditional academic disciplines, the program's design should be shaped by the intellectual and imaginative powers and competencies that students need, rather than by conventional "subjects." The aphorism "less is more" should dominate: curricular decisions are to be directed toward the students' attempt to gain mastery rather than by the teachers' effort to cover content.
3. The school's goals should apply to all students, but the means to these goals will vary as these students themselves vary. School practice should be tailor-made to meet the needs of every group of adolescents. (1992, 207–208)

It could be said that definitions of curriculum appearing in the 1990s combine the educational theories of essentialism and progressivism, and even have some elements of social reconstructionism and behaviorism.

## *Viewpoint*  Substance and Standards

"What's the curriculum to be?" asked the young English teacher. Horace feared that his neophyte colleague was groping for the List of Things to Cover, that beginning teacher's salvation. Mercifully, Green rode in on her hobbyhorse: "We've agreed to plan backward. Tell me what the student should be able to Exhibit, and I'll give you your curriculum."

Others broke in: "How can there be only one curriculum? We've spent hours agreeing that kids differ. If they do, then what we give them should also differ.". . .

"How you teach is itself a form of curriculum. It's not just the stuff I put forward; it's how I put it forward . . . how the kids receive it." The remark was flipped mischievously in Horace's direction.

Patches: "There's too much in the curriculum now, too many courses, too many promises, too much stuff. We know that most of it is covered superficially, and we know how confused the kids are—those kids who bother to think about what we teach them." Patches was referring to what the committee members had learned from "shadowing" individual students over the course of a day, an experience that had radicalized more than a few of them. At the end of trekking behind a student for seven periods, their behinds were sore, they had been bored by being talked at so much, they had witnessed the cumulative intellectual chaos of a typical sequence of courses, French to physics to English to phys ed to mathematics, none planned with any reference to any of the others, and all before lunch. There was, most of them had agreed, no coherent sum to be totted up from these disparate parts.

"So what's the solution?" a parent member asked. "A core curriculum [specific required subjects]?"

"Back to basics?" The second student snorted at that. "Give us a break." This assertion was expressed not as a plea but as an attack.

Patches: "What's wrong with a core curriculum?"

The student: "We deserve some choice. We don't want to learn just what you want us to learn."

Patches, scornfully: "How do you know what you want to learn when you don't know anything to begin with?" The student flushed but held his tongue. The teachers stiffened.

The mathematics teacher: "Franklin is trying to do too much. We have no priorities. The curriculum is there because it's always been there. It's completely divided up by departments, and tested accordingly. Somehow we've got to break all that."

"You can talk that way because you know that math will always be there, and you'll have a job. Art is just as important as math, but when people get into core curriculum and the basics and all that stuff, art gets cut out. Goodbye to my job." Others nodded, all teachers of "elective" subjects—art, foreign language, the vocational courses.

The first student, quietly: "The curriculum that *we* have to take really reflects *your* jobs, and whether or not you'll keep them. Nobody asks what *we* like and need. That's not fair." Her remark slapped across faculty faces. . . .

"Where are we going?" Frustration.

"It's a mess, I agree," Horace admitted. "Getting hold all at once of the various pieces—the courses and their syllabi, the Exhibitions and the ways we teach—is very tough. But let's not be too hard on ourselves: we've never really tried before. Planning backward is new and hard."

Excerpt from: Sizer, 1992.

## The Organization of Curriculum

Since philosophy organizes and systematizes all fields of knowledge as a means of interpreting this knowledge, curricular organization itself is a philosophical process. Throughout this chapter we will identify a variety of different curricular organizations and show how they are based on a particular school of philosophy, which was discussed in chapter 6 (see table 8.1).

### SUBJECT-CENTERED CURRICULUM ORGANIZATION

The type of curricular organization of which Henry, in the opening anecdote, was a part in the 1960s and again in the 1980s is the *separate subject,* or *subject-centered,* curriculum. This organizational approach has its roots in the philosophical schools of idealism and realism and the educational theories of perennialism and essentialism.

Separate subject, or subject-centered, is the most widely used form of curricular organization. Its roots are in ancient Greece and Rome, where learning was divided into the seven liberal arts: the *trivium* (grammar, rhetoric, and logic) and the *quadrivium* (arithmetic, geometry, astronomy, and music). Although the subjects have changed somewhat, the concept of separation of the subjects has remained. In colonial America the typical division of subjects was reading, writing, religion, and arithmetic at the primary level; classics, language, trigo- nometry, geometry, and botany at the secondary level. In the subject-centered form of curricular organization, the material is compartmentalized into bodies of knowledge taught in isolation from other material based on the belief that each subject has a separate series of essential skills and concepts that must be learned.

The curriculum within each subject is sequentially organized from the simple to the complex and based on previous learning. Typically, this curricular organization divides subjects into two groups: required courses and electives. The assumption is that certain subjects are so important that all students must study them to acquire a common body of knowledge and a common set of skills, hence

**TABLE 8-1**

### Curricular Organizations Influenced by Schools of Philosophy and Theories of Education

| Curricular organization | School of philosophy | Theory of education |
|---|---|---|
| Subject Centered/Separate Subjects | Idealism/Realism | Perennialism/Essentialism |
| Competency Based | Realism/Analysis | Essentialism/Behaviorism |
| Mastery Learning | Realism/Analysis | Essentialism/Behaviorism |
| Broad Fields | Pragmatism | Progressivism/Reconstructionism |
| Core | Pragmatism | Progressivism/Reconstructionism |
| Activity/Child-Centered | Pragmatism | Progressivism |
| Humanistic | Existentialism | Progressivism |

The organization of curriculum is influenced both by a school of philosophy and a theory of education. The educational theory and the philosophy from which it is derived are discussed in chapter 6.

the terms *essential* and *perennial,* which are the foundation of the essentialist and perennialist theories of learning.

Typically, core or required courses include reading, language, composition, literature, arithmetic or mathematics, computer science (beginning in the 1980s), science (at the secondary level divided into separate sciences), social studies (usually divided into separate disciplines such as history, economics, civics or government, geography, and less frequently sociology and psychology), foreign language (historically in the secondary school but during the late 1950s, early 1960s, and late 1980s in the elementary school as well), and health and physical education.

Other subjects are less important. Therefore, they can be elected by students who are interested in them. Electives include the arts (divided into separate disciplines), home economics, and industrial arts and other vocational courses at the secondary level.

***Attributes of the Subject-Centered Curriculum***   Subject-centered organization has many attributes. It is a logical, effective way to organize new knowledge and allows logical progression from one level of education to the next. With this rather simplified organization of material, all students should meet basic, minimal levels of achievement and possess a common knowledge. With this type of organization, teachers can be trained in various subject areas.

***Problems of the Subject-Centered Curriculum***   Of course, many questions arise when educators attempt to determine which are the core courses and what is essential within these courses. New knowledge has increased the problem of what to include within the core.

*Viewpoint* The Poor Scholar's Soliloquy

No I'm not very good in school. This is my second year in the seventh grade and I'm bigger and taller than the other kids. They like me all right, though, even if I don't say much in the schoolroom, because outside I can tell them how to do a lot of things. They tag me around and that sort of makes up for what goes on in school. . . .

I guess I can't remember names in history. Anyway, this year I've been trying to learn about trucks because my uncle owns three and he says I can drive one when I'm sixteen. I already know the horsepower and number of forward and backwards speeds of twenty-six American trucks, some of them Diesels, and I can spot each make a long way off. It's funny how that Diesel works. I started to tell my teacher about it last Wednesday in science class when the pump we were using to make a vacuum in a bell jar got hot, but she said she didn't see what a Diesel engine had to do with our experiment on air pressure so I just kept still. The kids seemed interested though. I took four of them around to my uncle's garage after school and we saw the mechanic, Gus, tearing a big Diesel down. Boy, does he know his stuff!

I'm not very good in geography either. They call it economic geography this year. We've been studying the imports and exports of Chile all week but I couldn't tell you what they are. Maybe the reason is I had to miss school yesterday because my uncle took me and his big trailer down state about two hundred miles and we brought almost ten tons of stock to the Chicago market.

He had told me where we were going and I had to figure out the highways to take and also the mileage. He didn't do anything but drive and turn where I told him to. Was that fun! I sat with a map in my lap and told him to turn south or southeast or some other direction. We made seven stops and drove over five hundred miles round trip. I'm figuring now what his oil cost and also the wear and tear on the truck—he calls it depreciation—so we'll know how much we made.

I even write out all the bills and send letters to farmers about what their pigs and beef cattle brought at the stockyards. I only made three mistakes in 17 letters last time, my aunt said—all commas. She's been through high school and reads them over. I wish I could write school themes that way. The last one I had to write was on "What a Daffodil Thinks of Spring," and I just couldn't get going.

I don't do very well in school in arithmetic either. Seems I just can't keep my mind on the problems. We had one the other day like this:

*If a 57 foot telephone pole falls across a cement highway so that 17 $\frac{3}{6}$ feet extend from one side and 14 $\frac{9}{17}$ feet from the other, how wide is the highway?*

That seemed to me like an awfully silly way to get the width of a highway. I didn't even try to answer it because it didn't say whether the pole had fallen straight across or not. . . .

Even in shop I don't get very good grades. All of us kids made a broom holder and a bookend this term and mine were sloppy. I just couldn't get interested. Mom doesn't use a broom anymore with her new vacuum cleaner and all our books are in a bookcase with glass doors in the parlor. Anyway, I wanted to make an end gate for my uncle's trailer but the shop teacher said that meant using metal and wood both and I'd have to learn how to work with wood first. I didn't see why but I kept still and made a tie rack at school and the tail gate after school at my uncle's garage. He said I saved him $10. . . .

Dad says I can quit school when I'm fifteen and I'm sort of anxious to because there are a lot of things I want to learn how to do and, as my uncle says, I'm not getting any younger.

From: Corey, 1944

## COMPETENCY-BASED AND OUTCOME-BASED EDUCATION

Competency-based education (CBE) is a fairly recent curricular pattern, common during the 1970s and 1980s. In the 1990s, a new term for competency-based curriculum, "outcome-based education" (OBE), was coined by William Spady, a sociologist and director of the High Success Network on Outcome-Based Education in Eagle, Colorado. Its philosophical foundations are in the schools of realism and philosophical analysis and the educational theories of essentialism and behaviorism. CBE differs from subject-centered curriculum in that its approach is to help students develop competencies, bits of knowledge related to a particular subject. OBE is similar to CBE in structure and approach; however, all of the outcomes that students must successfully perform are related to skills and concepts they need to function as effective adults in the real world rather than as students studying traditional school subjects such as history and literature. In both OBE and CBE subjects tend to be isolated from one another, as in subject-centered curriculums; however, in CBE and OBE students move from the simple to the complex within the material. The underlying assumption of CBE and OBE is that there are certain identifiable, measurable skills and concepts within the subjects or set of adult performances that students must learn in order to master them.

Development of a CBE or OBE curriculum begins with the identification of **competencies** or outcomes, usually by professional educators. In the OBE curriculum this is known as a design down process—moving from exit outcomes, or what students must know at the end of a course of study, to lesson outcomes. Once competencies or outcomes have been identified, teaching methodologies are devised to help students achieve them. Finally, students are tested using *criterion-referenced tests* to determine if the competencies or outcomes have been reached. Tests typically are given several times during elementary and junior high school and at the end of high school.

Outcome-based education adds a mastery approach (see p. 307) to competency-based education by expanding the number of ways and times students get to learn, and to demonstrate at a very high level whatever they are expected to learn (Brandt 1992–1993, 68). In addition, as in mastery learning, a term coined by psychologist Benjamin Bloom, outcome-based education eliminates the bell-curve approach in which students are evaluated by comparing their results to other students in the same class or school. Outcome-based education assumes that all students can reach the desired outcomes if given enough time and enough ways to express their learning.

Competency-based education has as its foundation the behavioral philosophy of B. F. Skinner, which assumes that competencies can be expressed in terms of student behavior and, thereby, can be observed and measured. Using this form of curricular organization, schools and teachers, as well as students themselves, can be held accountable for the students' reaching predetermined levels of competence. Herein lies the major difference in the CBE and OBE approaches and the subject-centered approach. CBE and OBE emphasize student outcomes, whereas the subject-centered approach emphasizes teacher input.

### Attributes of the Competency-Based and Outcome-Based Curriculums
Hildreth H. McAshan in *Competency-based Education and Behavioral Objectives* (1979) has outlined some of the attributes of competency-based curriculum.

CBE, in its purest form, has been designed to overcome perennial problems that have plagued experience-based programs prior to the behavioral objective era. [A *behavioral objective* is a goal that can be measured by behavioral change in the students.] These problems were based upon the following needs:

1. To avoid duplication of content within a program
2. To establish and maintain consistency of competencies taught with courses, regardless of the instructor teaching the course
3. To revise and implement appropriate systems of evaluation and reporting of student achievement
4. To better communicate to the students the learning tasks that they are expected to achieve and how their success will be determined
5. To better provide students with ongoing information regarding their personal progress
6. To be better accountable to the general public for the educational program standards accepted by educational institutions
7. To better determine student achievement through more systematic procedures of evaluation. (pp. 31–35)

Proponents of CBE contend that it is a real-life orientation to curriculum development as expressed in life roles (Parnell 1978). Frequently, students are asked to read newspapers, balance checkbooks, make out budgets, design menus, and seek employment as a way to perform identified competencies. By breaking down the curriculum into small instructional modules, according to proponents of CBE, educators and students can address skills and concepts with increasing complexity. Albert Shanker, president of the American Federation of Teachers, examines the attributes of OBE saying that the traditional way of looking at inputs, how many courses a student has taken and how many years she or he has spent in school, does not tell us how much the student has learned. Says Shanker, "Set time is no gauge of educational attainment" (1993, E7). He agrees that measuring outcomes rather than inputs is a sound practice.

***Problems of Competency-Based and Outcome-Based Curriculums***    Critics of CBE contend that it is not possible to break all disciplines into small instructional modules; students can miss seeing the forest if all they are required to do is look at the trees. According to critics of CBE, many things, such as appreciation of art or creativity in writing, cannot be measured or stated in a behavioral manner. Frequently, only easy-to-teach, easy-to-test bits of knowledge are tested, and a student's understanding of a larger whole is ignored. For example, a standardized test can measure if a student has memorized the presidents of the United States, but it can't determine if the student understands the democratic process.

Albert Shanker also sees some of the same problems in outcome-based curricular reforms. According to Shanker, OBE standards are vague, and they can be satisfied at any level of achievement, from top-notch to minimal. For example, he cites a Pennsylvania writing outcome that calls for "all students to write for a variety of purposes, including to narrate, inform, and persuade in all subjects." According to Shanker, in an excellent school this could mean thousand word essays, in a poor school it could mean three short paragraphs loaded with misspellings (1993, E7). Ironically, critics from the radical right make the same contention. Spokesperson Phyllis Schlafly is concerned that parents will have no input. She writes, "Parents who are trying to rear their children with strong religious values are concerned that willingness to go along with the crowd is taught by OBE as a positive rather than a negative attitude" (1993, 2).

Likewise, critics maintain that making schools and teachers accountable for student learning is a dangerous practice. They point to the differences among students from class to class and district to district. They contend that basic competencies are not the same for all children. That, for example, in an urban district an important competency may be street sense; whereas in a rural district a basic competency might be water conservation. These critics also worry about the tendency to teach for the test so that students score well and so that, thereby, teachers and schools appear to be doing their jobs successfully. And, finally, critics of CBE and OBE ask such questions as, What is a minimum competency or an appropriate outcome, anyway, and, how can we avoid making the minimums become maximums if the tests test minimums?

## MASTERY LEARNING

An outgrowth of CBE is *mastery learning.* Like CBE, it is based on the philosophical schools of realism and philosophical analysis and the educational theories of essentialism and behaviorism. Its major proponent is Benjamin Bloom. Many mastery learning approaches can also be seen in OBE (see above).

Like CBE and OBE, the mastery approach to curriculum development is based on the belief that objectives can be predetermined. However, it contends that each student will move toward mastery of specific skills and concepts in different ways and according to different timetables.

Mastery learning differs from CBE and OBE in that it places more emphasis on instruction than on objectives and assessment. In fact, it assumes that what is an objective for one student may not be an objective for other students. Consequently, mastery learning requires that students be treated individually and that teachers avoid preoccupation with the group. Like CBE and subject-centered curriculums, mastery learning groups skills and concepts by subject. However, it also assumes that the vast majority of students "can learn selected subjects up to as high a level as the most able students in the group" (Bloom 1976, 223).

***Attributes of Mastery Learning***    The most important attribute of mastery learning is the belief that the vast majority of students can succeed on any given task if given enough time and appropriate instruction. Benjamin Bloom believes it is essential that schools in the United States require mastery learning.

John Miller in *The Educational Spectrum* (1983) delineates the major characteristics of mastery learning.

1. Mastery of any subject is defined in terms of sets of major objectives which represent the purposes of the course or unit.
2. The substance of the subject matter is then divided into a larger set of relatively small learning units, each one accompanied by its own objectives, which are part of the larger ones or thought essential to their mastery.

Mastery learning is a concept that assumes all students can learn any subject matter or any skill if given enough time and individual instruction. One way of implementing mastery learning successfully is to provide one-on-one instruction in the form of tutors or teacher aides where appropriate or necessary.

3. Learning materials are then identified and the instructional strategy selected.
4. Each unit is accompanied by brief diagnostic tests to measure the student's developing progress (the formative evaluation) and identify the particular problems each student is having.
5. The data obtained from administering the tests are used to provide supplementary instruction to the student to help him overcome his problem. (p. 26)

According to studies conducted by Bloom, more than 90 percent of all students could learn a skill or concept if given instruction that takes into account individual differences and gives the student enough time to learn. Bloom claimed that the common use of the bell curve to illustrate the distribution of student performance assumed that only a small percentage could master a skill or concept at a high level, and that this was erroneous. The **bell curve** is a bell-shaped symmetrical distribution in which most scores or human attributes (for example, height and weight) fall near the mean (arithmetic average), with only a small percentage of scores or attributes extending well above or below the mean. A bell-curve distribution does not account for individual differences in learning style and time needed to master a skill or concept. Mastery learning individualizes large group instruction so that appropriate instructional methods are selected for

**FIGURE 8-1**

## Achievement Distribution for Students Under Conventional, Mastery Learning, and Tutorial Instruction

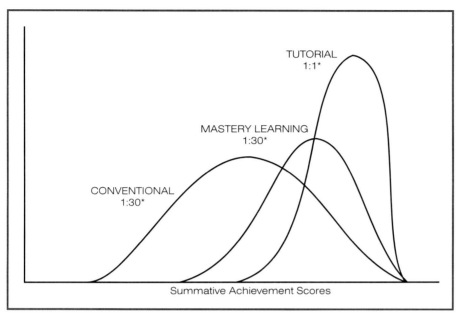

*Teacher:Student Ratio
From: B. Bloom, "The Search for Methods of Group Instruction as Effective as One-to-One Tutoring," *Educational Leadership* (May 1984), 5.

**Bloom's research indicates that a large percentage of students can reach mastery of a skill and concept when appropriate instructional methods are employed and can achieve at even higher levels when the ratio of student to teacher is one-to-one, as it would be in a tutorial situation.**

individuals or small groups of students. See figure 8.1 for achievement distribution of students under conventional (bell-curve), mastery learning, and tutorial (one-on-one) instruction. Bloom and his associates have spent nearly three decades studying teaching methodologies that are most likely to produce mastery. As late as the early 1990s, the results of Bloom's research have had little impact on the schools. Although some elementary schools have utilized limited aspects of the mastery learning approach, most still use large group conventional instruction as the primary mode and assume that student performance will distribute along a normal bell curve.

*Problems of Mastery Learning* Critics of the mastery approach maintain that although its goals are laudable and that probably every child can achieve mastery in a given subject, its procedures are cumbersome and likely to be inconsistent. For example, how is it possible to give students unlimited time to master a skill when there is not unlimited time in the school day or school year? They also express concern about the articulation among classes, levels, and schools. For example, a typical student may change schools a minimum of three

*(continued on p. 312)*

# IS OUTCOME-BASED EDUCATION A GOOD WAY TO REFORM THE SCHOOLS?

## PRO William G. Spady

Outcome-Based Education (OBE) means organizing for results: basing what we do instructionally on the outcomes we want to achieve, whether in specific parts of the curriculum or in the schooling process as a whole. Outcome-based practitioners start by determining the knowledge, competencies, and qualities they want students to be able to demonstrate when they finish school and face the challenges and opportunities of the adult world. Then, with these "exit outcomes" clearly in mind, they deliberately design curriculums and instructional systems with the intent that *all* students will ultimately be able to demonstrate them successfully. OBE, therefore, is not a "program" but a way of designing, developing, delivering, and documenting instruction in terms of its intended goals and outcomes. . . .

In Outcome-Based Education, exit outcomes are a critical factor in designing the curriculum: you develop the curriculum *from* the outcomes you want students to demonstrate, rather than writing objectives *for* the curriculum you already have. I encourage districts to develop exit outcomes that go far beyond the narrow subject-matter emphasis that characterizes most state testing and reform efforts. Districts such as Sunnyside Unified in Tucson, Arizona, and Township High School District 214 in Mt. Prospect, Illinois, have defined exit outcomes that reflect our emphasis on the broad opportunities and challenges students will face when they leave school and assume adult responsibilities. We want students to be equipped to lead enriched and successful lives—not just to meet conventional curriculum demands or college admission requirements.

This broad perspective provides a rich range of possibilities for the development of high-level, cross-disciplinary, experiential curriculum, teaching, and learning. By defining competencies of all kinds in both functional and higher-order terms, . . . districts know that their outcome goals and indicators need not be limited to basic skills, low-level cognition, and narrow objectives. For example, District 214 has identified 10 "General Learner Outcomes" as the keys to its instructional design and delivery processes. Among the things this district expects all graduates to demonstrate are (1) skills in problem solving and decision making; (2) skills in expressing themselves creatively and responding to the creative works of others; (3) concern, tolerance, and respect for others; (4) skills in adapting to and creating personal and social change; (5) capacity for enhancing and sustaining self-esteem through emotional, intellectual, and physical well-being; and (6) skills necessary to be self-directed learners.

The design and development strategies of OBE flow from an equally straightforward principle: that all other levels of outcomes in an instructional system—program outcomes, course outcomes, unit outcomes, and, ultimately, lesson outcomes—should be derived directly from, and align with, these visionary exit outcomes. In other words, we design *down* from broadly defined exit outcomes to define coherent, thematic programs that directly support them, then determine what the appropriate segments of the program should be (what educators almost always call a course or grade level), and then determine the appropriate units to facilitate those course outcomes. . . .

From: W. G. Spady. "Organizing for Results: The Basis of Authentic Restructuring and Reform," *Educational Leadership* (October 1988) *46* (2), 4–8. William G. Spady is the founder of the outcome-based education reform movement and is currently the director of the High Success Network on Outcome-Based Education in Eagle, Colorado.

## Postscript

William Spady argues that OBE will result in student achievement because educators select outcomes students need to reach and instructional approaches that will lead to achieving these outcomes. The curriculum is designed by educators from the outcomes backwards and is based on the theories of progressivism and behaviorism.

# IS OUTCOME-BASED EDUCATION A GOOD WAY TO REFORM THE SCHOOLS?

## CON  Janet Parshall

Carbon monoxide gas: you cannot smell it, see it, or taste it; nonetheless, it can kill. In much the same way, a new teaching concept is seeping into America's public classrooms, and while on the surface it may look and sound innocent, it will prove toxic to the children who are exposed to it.

Outcomes Based Education (OBE), as it is widely known, is a lethal shift in educational philosophy *away* from the old notion that Johnny should learn his math facts and spelling words to the radical new notion that Johnny should not compete with other students, but rather learn in his own way and at his own pace. Sound good? Perhaps too good to be true.

All across the country we are seeing the traditional educational curriculum concepts systematically replaced with "learning outcomes" like attitudes and values. By replacing fact-based skills with a focus on feelings and emotions, schools are opening the door to classroom chaos. There is an objective, academic standard of measurement for math, spelling, and history, but how does a teacher measure a child's attitude about citizenship in a global society?

Pam Shellenberger, Area Representative for CWA of Pennsylvania, warns about the intrusion of OBE in her state. "The [education] goals [proposed] have nothing to do with testing based on self-worth, information and thinking skills, learning independently and collaboratively, adaptability to change and ethical judgment. I'm not quite sure how this program could improve our academic excellence." . . .

Lest you think Outcomes Based Education has not yet arrived at your neighborhood school, think again! This chameleon curriculum goes by many names: mastery learning, critical thinking, and exit behaviors, just to name a few. And in the state of Kansas, this poisonous program is called Quality Performance Accreditation (QPA). . . .

OBE brings with it a very hefty price tag with no proven track record. Mastery Learning (another OBE program) blew into the windy city of Chicago a long time ago costing the city several million dollars. After five years of watching educational confusion, the Board of Education decided to abandon the program. After this failed experiment, it was former U.S. Secretary of Education William Bennett who called the Chicago OBE model the "worst" in the nation. . . .

Perhaps the most repugnant aspect of OBE is the overriding philosophy that children "belong" to the state. More and more schools have tried to assume the role of co-parent with all the vestiges of that high calling. The movement toward collaboration of all social service agencies through the public school can be readily fostered through anti-parent and subjective programs like OBE. . . .

Solid education is comprised of concrete learning—reading, writing, and arithmetic. Toxic education, like that undetected gas, can choke and kill the value system we, as parents, instill daily in our children.

From: J. Parshall. "Outcomes Based Education: Toxic Teaching," *Family Voice, Concerned Women for America* (April 1993), *15* (4), 15. Janet Parshall is a writer for *Family Voice, Concerned Women for America,* a journal whose mission is to "preserve, project, and promote traditional and Judeo-Christian values through education, legal defense, legislative programs, humanitarian aid, and related activities."

Janet Parshall, writing for a conservative political journal, expresses the concern that "learning outcomes," like attitudes and values, focus on students' feelings and emotions. She worries that curriculums like OBE are replacing agreed-upon skills with outcomes selected by educators. She suggests that OBE is another example of the state attempting to wrest control of children from parents.

times during his or her educational career. How is the middle school to know what has been mastered by each child at each level? If individual teachers are setting the goals, won't goals change with each teacher? Isn't this likely to produce confusion? What about record keeping; how is it possible to communicate each student's progress to another school or another teacher?

Robert E. Slavin, in *Mastery Learning Reconsidered* (1987), found no evidence to support the claim that mastery learning improved student performance. Students did not achieve at higher levels on standardized tests after participating in group-based mastery learning programs, and improvement on experimenter-made tests was moderate and not maintained over a long period of time. Slavin pointed to the problem of allowing students to take as much time as needed to master an objective. "If some students take much longer than others to learn a particular objective, then one of two things must happen. Either corrective instruction must be given outside of regular class time, or students who achieve mastery early on will have to waste considerable amounts of time waiting for their classmates to catch up" (p. 6). In addition, spending significant time mastering an objective means that students must select content mastery over content coverage. Slavin also found that the amount of time spent on remediation was not sufficient for students needing it. These conditions, Slavin suggested, might negatively influence scores on standardized tests.

## BROAD FIELDS CURRICULUM

The *broad fields* approach to curricular organization combines several related subjects into larger fields of study. It is based on the philosophical school of pragmatism and employs the educational theories of progressivism and social reconstructionism. For example, language arts might include reading, literature, composition, grammar, spelling, penmanship, vocabulary, speaking, and listening. Similarly, geography, history, civics, economics, sociology, and psychology are taught within the general subject matter of social studies. At times the number of disciplines included within a broad field can be even greater. Broad field curriculum is multidisciplinary (many) rather than interdisciplinary (interrelated and integrated).

In this approach, which is used more frequently in elementary and middle schools than in high schools, students may spend two hours per day dealing with the language arts. During that time they may read or have read to them a story. Then they might write about it or produce an informal skit related to it. During their study of the story they might examine vocabulary words, develop spelling lists, and participate in other activities related to the story.

***Attributes of Broad Fields Curriculum*** Proponents of the broad fields approach claim that it is more natural than separating the various components of the discipline. They claim, for example, that writers do not simply write a book. They research the material, talk to others about what they plan to write, write letters to publishers, check words in dictionaries, and participate in numerous other activities that eventually, through a long process, may result in a book. Therefore, the natural approach of the writer and most other professionals is dealing with broad fields of learning rather than single subjects in isolation.

*Problems of Broad Fields Curriculum* Opponents of the broad fields approach contend that it can be chaotic. Students do not know what they are supposed to learn from the activities. Frequently the products of their efforts lose significance. Students do not know whether a paper or an art project is well done or poorly done. For example, in the writing process approach mentioned in the paragraph above, students may spend so much time researching, talking to others, developing topics, and illustrating their writing that they might lose sight of the importance of a grammatically correct final paper.

Critics also claim that the approach is too general. There is not a careful study of any aspect of the discipline and, consequently, the student's learning is hit or miss. Depending on the teacher, students may or may not be taught specific skills and concepts. Those using this approach do not believe that there are some things so important that everyone must learn them.

## CORE CURRICULUM

An even broader approach to curriculum than the broad fields is the *core curriculum*. A core or **integrated** approach, unifies a number of subjects or fields of study into one topic. In the 1970s, for example, Henry, of the opening anecdote, participated in a curricular organizational pattern known as the core curriculum. Henry's program taught minicourses in English and the humanities related to specific themes.

Core, as it relates to curriculum, is used in two ways. It can be used to describe a required set of subjects, or core courses, to be taken in common by all students. This approach is single subject centered, not integrated. When core is used in this way it is based on the philosophical school of realism and the educational theory of essentialism. However, this is not how the term *core* is being employed here.

The core curriculum, as it is used here, is the integration of a variety of disciplines around a single core, often a theme or a problem. The core curriculum is based on the philosophical school of pragmatism and the educational theories of progressivism or social reconstructionism. This approach to curriculum is student centered because it focuses on a topic of interest to the learner. For example, if the topic being studied is pollution, the students might study ecology, biology, statistics, mathematics, political science, history, psychology, reading, writing, and literature. In other words, all subjects are studied simultaneously to better understand the theme or solve the problem. The possibilities are limited only by the imagination of the teacher or teachers involved in the planning process. Cores usually involve broad, preplanned problem areas. However, it is also possible to develop a core curriculum around a theme, such as "People Against People," wherein students might read fiction (perhaps a work such as John Hersey's *The Wall*) and nonfiction (perhaps a work such as Milton Meltzer's *Never to Forget: The Jews of the Holocaust*); they might pursue research projects on various aspects of the theme; they might study the history of political movements that pitted people against each other; they might examine the psychology that allowed a Hitler to gain power. The key to the success of the core curriculum, say its proponents, is that it must relate to the interests of the students and be planned collaboratively by faculty and students.

The core curriculum organizes a number of subjects into an integrated study of a theme or problem. These students in a sixth grade science class are using skills learned in botany, biology, and mathematics to conduct a plant distribution survey.

*Attributes of the Core Curriculum*   Although the core approach to curricular organization has many influential proponents, it has not been widely employed by the schools. In a study done in 1984 of 38 schools, 1,000 classrooms, and 1,350 teachers, John Goodlad concluded that the "major shortcomings of the schools' subject offerings is the common failure of the learning activities to connect the student with the 'structure and ways of thinking'" (1984, 291). According to Goodlad, in many schools, topics such as magnets and batteries are unrelated to the concept of energy. He suggests that all students study a common set of concepts, principles, skills, and ways of knowing, rather than a common group of subjects (1984, 284). These can be taught within cores, such as the preplanned problem areas mentioned on page 313.

Integrative, core curricular approaches can also be seen in the multicultural curriculums of the 1990s. James Banks, who proposes a transformative curriculum (see p. 323), suggests the use of thematic units that allow students to "struggle for voice" and discover "different voices" (quoting Starrs 1988). The units might be on such topics as "Christopher Columbus and the Arawak Indians" (Banks with Sebesta 1982) or " 'Nii-maa-moo-chi-ge-min': A Coming Together," a multisensory unit on the Ojibwe culture taught in Deer River, Minnesota (National Foundation for the Improvement of Education 1992, 11).

James A. Beane, a professor at National-Louis University in Madison, Wisconsin, points out that in the late 1980s and early 1990s there was an increased use of the core curriculum. He cites the 1992 National Council of Teachers of Mathematics (NCTM) call for teaching mathematics in the context of communication, integration, exploration, and problem solving as an example. In addition he suggests that the 1992 National Council of Teachers of English (NCTE) call for a wholistic language arts curriculum is likely to lead to more core approaches to curriculum development.

The attributes of a core curriculum are many:

- Skills and concepts are no longer isolated within disciplines but are taught in a more natural way across disciplines.
- Problem solving can be emphasized within a variety of preplanned problem area units.
- Integration of content across disciplines allows for the development of multicultural approaches to teaching.
- Teaching methodology can be multisensory.
- Students and teachers are excited about learning and motivated to learn.
- Skills and concepts that did not fit neatly into subject division can be taught in the core curriculum.
- Content of the core curriculum can relate to the "real world" in ways that are frequently not possible in other curriculum organizations.

***Problems of the Core Curriculum***    The core approach has many critics. Many find the integrated core approach too broad and not likely to produce specific knowledge, or to provide a systematic approach to gaining knowledge—complaints similar to those raised against the broad fields or multidisciplinary approach. Critics are concerned that students will know "how to," but they will not know "what," that the outcomes of such an approach cannot be measured, and that it requires teachers who are specifically trained in integrating subjects.

In addition, as an incident at Furnace Woods Elementary School in Peekskill, New York, points out, parents frequently do not understand how their children will learn important skills within a core curriculum and resist moving the curriculum away from the separate-subject approach with which they are familiar.

> [Principal Joanne Falinski's] troubles can be traced back several years to her efforts to base the Furnace Woods curriculum on whole language principles. . . . Under the whole language curriculum, children began to write and read more, to generate spelling lists from their own work, and to correct each other's work. Rather than report cards, teachers sent letters home to parents that detailed their children's activities and accomplishments and emphasized those areas in which the children needed more attention. . . .
>
>     As outlined in a letter to . . . Superintendent James Frenck, . . . disgruntled parents believed that what was going on at Furnace Woods was that "fundamental skills of mathematics, spelling, sentence structure, handwriting, and reading comprehension are severely lacking in our children's education."
>
>     "They wanted a lot of 'drill and practice,' " Falinski said. "They equate that kind of activity and learning. They didn't understand how those skills were embedded in the more holistic activities in which the children were engaged." (Flanagan 1994)

Not only do critics of the core curriculum point out potential problems, so do its advocates. James Beane, for example, suggests that it is difficult for teachers to develop a curriculum based on thematic content since it is difficult to be sure what knowledge and skills fit into each theme. In addition, he found that teachers have loyalties to particular subject areas and their content that ultimately inhibits the use of integrative approaches. Beane claims that this a part of the hidden curriculum of the colleges in which these teachers were educated.

According to opponents of multidisciplinary approaches (broad fields) and integrated approaches (core curriculum), they fail to delineate what is essential material for all students. These critics advocate subject-centered curricular organizations in the belief that they ensure that all students have a common base of knowledge.

## CHILD-CENTERED OR ACTIVITY CURRICULUM

The *activity,* or *child-centered,* curriculum is rooted in the philosophical school of pragmatism. Progressivism, the theory of education rooted in pragmatism, was based on the work of John Dewey. The child-centered or activity curriculum differs from the broad fields and core curriculums in that the experience of the student is central to its development. As proponent Hilda Taba states, "People learn only what they experience" (1962, 401).

By the early twentieth century Dewey was working to counteract what he saw as passivity in the subject-centered curriculum. The approach he developed at the University of Chicago Laboratory School saw children as active problem solvers, envisioned the interrelationship of subjects, believed that children gained skills as they needed them, and contended that they learn best what they experience.

Dewey pointed out that because the child is a beginner, he or she is not able to approach learning with the completed experiences of adulthood. Thus, the teacher must organize the curriculum to capitalize on the child's experiences.

It is essential that teachers assess what the needs and interests of the students are rather than trying to determine what they should be. This requires that the teacher have a thorough knowledge of the theories of childhood and adolescent growth and development. The curriculum should not be preplanned by the teacher, but rather cooperatively planned by both students and teacher. Since problem solving is its central focus, subjects are viewed as resources instead of as bodies of knowledge that are ends in themselves. Thus, the structure of the child-centered or activity curriculum is determined by the needs and interests of the students.

*Attributes of the Child-Centered or Activity Curriculum* Attributes of the child-centered or activity curriculum are many.

- The content of the curriculum and the skills taught relate to the needs, interests, and abilities of the particular students.
- The curriculum is designed by the professionals who know the students best rather than by far-removed authors and publishers.
- The curriculum utilizes all the senses and multiple intelligences (see chapter 10, pp. 394–395).
- Students are active participants in their own learning.
- Students are engaged in solving problems that relate to real-life situations and adult living.
- Children are motivated to learn more because they are actively involved in learning.

- All children can succeed no matter what their experience or knowledge base.
- Students can work together in teams or as individuals.
- Technology is employed in all subject areas to enhance student learning.

Activity or child-centered curriculum has been reinstated in many forms since Dewey's earliest writings. The impact of his work, particularly on the elementary curriculum, cannot be overemphasized. His influence changed the direction of elementary education, which even today, through several generations of subject-centered reform, remains largely child centered; elementary teachers usually base instructional strategies on the developmental stage of the students (see chapter 6, pp. 230–232).

*Problems of the Child-Centered or Activity Curriculum*    According to many opponents of the child-centered or activity curriculum, the complexity of Dewey's theories makes them impractical in most school settings. The teacher must be an expert not in a single subject but in all subjects and able to subdivide them into their component parts. She or he must be able to deal with all subjects or themes in a problem-solving approach. In addition, the teacher must be thoroughly grounded in developmental psychology, knowing what children can and should be able to do at any given time, and he or she must know the interests, needs, and abilities of each student. Finally, the teacher must continually restructure the curriculum based on the changing child. Consequently, most programs that have emulated Dewey's curricular approach have either turned his definition of experience into overt activity and focused on physical contact with objects (Taba 1962, 404), reverted to the logical organization of the subject-matter curriculum (Brubacher 1966, 293), or romanticized Dewey's philosophy as a "sentimental regard for the child's interests and needs" (Brubacher, 294).

## HUMANISTIC CURRICULUM

The *humanistic curriculum* is based on the philosophical school of existentialism and the educational theory of progressivism. Like the activity curriculum, the humanistic curriculum is student centered. The teacher's primary task is to permit students to learn how to learn. Teachers in the humanistic curriculum are what psychologist Carl Rogers calls "facilitators." Although the general material of the course and some requirements may be defined by the facilitator, most of the curriculum emerges through interaction among the students, teacher, and content in a climate of trust "in which curiosity and the natural desire to learn can be nourished and enhanced" (Rogers 1983, 31, 33).

The humanistic curriculum is based on Gestalt psychology and therapy, whose principles are openness, uniqueness, awareness, and personal responsibility. Hence, curriculums that are consistent with this theory of psychology deemphasize competition and emphasize personal responsibility. In the humanistic curriculum there are no right or wrong answers; its goal is personal development and change. Because Gestalt psychology contends that discrete elements are meaningful only in relationship to the whole, humanistic curriculums attempt to integrate the student's behavior with course content.

Implementation of the curriculum requires an emotional relationship between the students and their teachers who must be warm and nurturing to facilitate learning. They do not require students to do anything they do not want to do; they simply provide materials and opportunities for learning.

*Attributes of the Humanistic Curriculum*  The humanistic curriculum, according to its advocates, helps all children succeed in school by not setting objectively defined criteria for achievement. Because the humanistic curriculum is interested in personal growth no matter how it is measured or defined, all children are considered successful. Evaluation of the activities in which students are engaged, process, is at least as important as evaluation of the student's achievement, product. Teachers examine activities in terms of whether they lead to student openness and independence. Success of the curriculum is based on subjective assessments by both teachers and students.

*Problems of the Humanistic Curriculum*  By the beginning of the 1980s few proponents of the humanistic curriculum remained, primarily because its implementation was impractical and disorganized. How could teachers develop a curriculum based on the needs of all the children in the classroom? How could teachers ensure that students learned what they needed to, if the students themselves determined the curriculum? Would students know what was best for them?

---

**8-2**

**POINTS TO REMEMBER**

- The separate subject, or subject-centered, curriculum contends that each subject should be taught separately and its components organized sequentially.

- In competency-based curriculum each subject can be divided into essential elements of knowledge and students can be evaluated on what they learned. In outcome-based curriculum students develop discrete knowledge and skills required for a successful adult life.

- Mastery learning assumes that all students can master concepts if provided with appropriate instruction and an adequate amount of time.

- The broad fields, or multidisciplinary, curriculum combines several related subjects into larger fields of study such as language arts (reading, literature, writing, speaking, and listening).

- The core curriculum, or integrated approach, arranges various subjects or fields into a related, unifying topic.

- The activity, or child-centered, curriculum contends that children learn best through experience.

- The humanistic curriculum believes that the role of the teacher is to permit students to satisfy their own curiosity.

---

## Social Forces That Influence Curriculum

Numerous social forces influence the development of curriculum in the schools. Among these are the economic and business needs of society, disenfranchised groups such as women and people of other cultures, textbooks and tests, and technological developments. This section of the chapter will deal with these curricular influences.

## ROLE OF ECONOMY

Perhaps the primary influence on the curriculum of schools in the United States is the economy. During the colonial period, when the needs of society were agrarian, the schools prepared students for a life on the land and in the home. As industry grew in the mid-nineteenth and early twentieth centuries, the schools prepared students to work on the assembly lines.

By the middle of the twentieth century the U.S. workforce was again changing. More workers were needed at middle levels of management. In addition, an increasing number of skilled laborers were required as assembly lines became computerized, using fewer and fewer unskilled workers. The schools again responded to this change, adding more courses in science, mathematics, and technology. More and more students attended institutions of higher education as the needs of the workplace could no longer be met in four years of high school.

Many argue that in this final decade of the twentieth century the needs of business and industry are again changing. As traditional businesses employing large numbers of unskilled laborers are downsizing, others are changing the way labor works by requiring that all workers know all jobs and be able to effectively utilize sophisticated technology and work together to solve complex problems. In addition, more and more workers are in white collar positions in which they solve sophisticated problems often requiring high level mathematics, computer, and communication skills. They must be able to work cooperatively with others in order to make decisions and solve problems, many of which are increasingly technical in nature. How the curriculum will meet the demands of the contemporary workplace is not completely clear, but the ubiquitous computer in the schools is one way.

Schools respond not only to business and economic needs of the U.S. society but also to other social changes and demands such as the changing role of women and the influence of people of other cultures.

## ROLE OF GENDER

During World War II as U.S. men went off to war, women replaced them on the assembly lines and at the cash registers. As men returned from the war, they took their original places in the workforce and women returned to maintaining home and family (Sleeter and Grant 1988, 153). In fact, as recently as the 1950s most middle-class men considered themselves failures if their wives worked. However, many sociologists believe that although women were replaced in the workplace by returning soldiers, they never totally moved back into the home.

The women's movement of the late 1960s and 1970s is a result, at least in part, of women discovering their potential as workers. Women also found new rewards, including increased family income and autonomy, through the roles they played in business and industry. In 1992, 63 percent (53 million) of all U.S. women worked full-time outside the home (The U.S. Department of Commerce, Bureau of Census, *Statistical Abstract of the United States,* 1990). Likewise, a majority of African American women are employed outside the home; however, Hispanic and Native American women are less likely to be in the workforce, and working-age women are less likely to be employed than men and more than twice as likely as men to be out of the labor force (Population Reference Bureau, Inc. 1993). Also, mothers with children under age eighteen are increasingly likely to be working. In 1990, for the first time, the majority of women with young children were in the workforce. In every state, except West Virginia, a majority of mothers of preschoolers were in the labor force; in seven states two-thirds of these mothers were in the workforce (Population Reference Bureau, Inc. 1993, 10–11).

Likewise, although women's salaries have increased, they have not equaled those of their male counterparts. A large proportion of women managers, for example, are in professions that have been traditionally low paying, such as education and nursing, rather than in business, industry, and medicine, where the pay is generally higher. This seems to be confirmed by statistics. Of all registered nurses, 94.3 percent are women, whereas of all physicians, only 20.4 percent are women. In teaching, excluding the college and university level, 74.8 percent are women who are paid significantly less than men (Bureau of Census 1993). According to the 1993 Digest of Educational Statistics, female elementary and secondary teachers were paid an average of $31,870, whereas male teachers were paid an average of $37,874 (1993, 82). The American Association of School Administrators reported in *Women and Racial Minority Representation in School Administration* (1993) that only slightly more than 35 percent (up from 30 percent in 1990) of all school administrative positions, only 4.8 percent of superintendencies, and only 27.7 percent of principalships were occupied by women. Likewise, in 1991, only nine of fifty chief state school officers were women (American Association of University Women Educational Foundation 1992, 7). The percentage of women in high-level positions in education is increasing, however. In 1993, 7.1 percent of super-intendents and 34.2 percent of principals were women. According to the U.S. Department of Education, in 1990–1991, the average female principal was paid $52,099, whereas the average male principal was paid $52,990 (1993). It is possible, though, that this difference is probably related more to seniority on the job than the gender bias.

The schools have only partially responded to the needs of women workers. Today, more female students take academic courses to prepare them for college; fewer take courses such as home economics. However, high school secretarial courses are still primarily populated by women students. This, too, is supported by statistics. The National Center for Education Statistics, *Digest of Education Statistics,* 1993, reported that female high school graduates completed slightly fewer Carnegie Units in 1990 than their male counterparts. In 1987 female high school graduates completed slightly more units in vocational education (3.67) than their male counterparts (3.64). (Carnegie Units represent the amount of course time spent in each subject; credit for high school graduation, in some school districts, is based on Carnegie Units.) However, in 1990, most of the units earned in vocational education by female students were in traditionally female-dominated programs such as business or secretarial studies (0.83 Carnegie Units for females as compared to 0.32 for males) and occupational home economics (0.14 Carnegie Units for females as compared to 0.04 for males).

*Gender and the Curriculum* Changes in attitudes about the role of women in society have not always been directly reflected in the number of women in leadership positions or in their salary; however, changes in attitudes can be seen in textbooks. In the nearly twenty years since the funding of the Women's Educational Equity Program (Title IX, P.L. 95–561; see chapter 5, pp. 189–190), textbooks have almost completely eliminated the use of sexist language, such as the male pronoun "he" referring to people in occupations such as physician or lawyer and the female pronoun "she" referring to people in occupations such as teacher and nurse. Likewise, few textbooks in the late 1990s stereotype men and women into particular societal roles.

However, since the 1980s little has been done to develop gender-fair curriculums. For example, a 1991 study of high school social studies textbooks conducted by Gretchen Wilbur, then a Commission of Education researcher for the Wellesley College Center for Research on Women, concluded that while more women are included in textbooks than in the past, they tend to be famous women such as Betsy Ross or Marie Curie or those who participated in protest movements. Rarely is there a balanced treatment of men and women. For example: What role did women play during the Revolution and the Civil War? What was the role of Native American women in their culture during the eighteenth and nineteenth centuries? Typically, according to Wilbur's study, gender-fair courses fall into the following categories: pull-out curriculums, targeting a problem group such as pregnant teenagers, or fragmented curriculums, adding units on women's issues to the already existing curriculum. She confirms James Banks's view of the same situation in multicultural curriculums (see p. 322), stating that these approaches fall short of genuine gender-fair integration into central course content (1992, 63–66).

However, around the nation there are numerous pilot projects attempting to implement gender-fair curriculums. One such project is Seeking Educational Equity and Diversity (SEED), a national project headed by Peggy McIntosh, associate director of the Wellesley College Center for Research on Women, and Emily Style, an English teacher and diversity coordinator in Madison, New Jersey. This project provides K–12 teachers with the opportunity to consider gender issues that relate to curriculum and teaching. "The project seeks to engage teachers in curricular change by bringing issues of race, gender, class, and ethnicity into their classrooms" (Nelson 1991, 66).

*Attributes of a Gender-Fair Curriculum*   According to Wilbur, a genuine gender-fair curriculum has six benefits.

- It acknowledges and affirms *variation,* i.e., similarities and differences among and within groups of people.
- It is *inclusive,* allowing both females and males to find and identify positively with messages about themselves.
- It is *accurate,* presenting information that is data-based, verifiable, and able to withstand critical analysis.
- It is *affirmative,* acknowledging and valuing the worth of individuals and groups.
- It is *representative,* balancing multiple perspectives.
- It is *integrated,* weaving together the experiences, needs, and interests of both males and females. (Wilbur 1992, 64)

## ROLE OF MULTICULTURAL SOCIETY

There have been only minimal changes in the schools to meet the needs of minorities. Although the schools of the 1980s were more culturally heterogeneous than ever before, the curriculum only minimally reflected these changes. Some schools added bilingual studies and some offered courses in black history; however, the role of minorities in U.S. society was scarcely included in existing courses such as history, science, and English. In addition, the curriculum of such subjects as English required an increased number of prescribed classic works, which tended to limit the number of works by minorities and women that were included.

Although more minority students attended college in the 1990s than in the middle years of the twentieth century, they still did not attend at the rate of their white counterparts. In 1992, 63.4 percent of college-age whites enrolled in college, whereas only 47.9 percent of blacks and 54.8 percent of Hispanics did. From 1982 to 1992, enrollments of blacks had increased 7.7 percent, Hispanics 5.5 percent, and whites 9.5 percent (U.S. Department of Education, *The Condition of Education*, 1993, 24). Despite increases in enrollment, black and other minority students did not achieve at the level of their white counterparts. In 1992, for example, only 11.9 (down from 16.4 in 1988) percent of blacks over the age of twenty-five had completed four or more years of college, whereas 22.1 (up from 20.9 in 1988) percent of whites had. Many educators contend that the poor records of many minority students indicate that public education has not changed sufficiently to meet their needs.

James Banks, in *Teaching Strategies for Ethnic Studies* (1991), states that while the United States has always "held tightly to the idea that ethnic cultures would melt or vanish" (p. 3), this has not been the case. "Discrimination prevents many individuals and groups with particular ethnic, racial, and or cultural characteristics from attaining full structural inclusion into U.S. society" (pp. 3–4). Banks claims that the schools have attempted to *Americanize* or *Anglicize* the curriculum. He suggests that until the schools recognize the important accomplishments of individuals from various racial, cultural, and ethnic groups and incorporate these into the curriculum, minority students will not achieve at levels equal to white students. He suggests that simply adding a lesson about minorities here and there in the curriculum will not help. Instead, of "merely adding low-level facts about ethnic content to a curriculum already bulging with discrete and isolated facts about mainstream history [resulting] in overkill, [schools must] integrate content about ethnic groups meaningfully into the total curriculum [and] must undertake more substantial and innovative curriculum reform" (1994, 210).

The increasing cultural diversity of the school population has caused problems of its own for students unfamiliar with both American customs and language. This has led to the call for multicultural education, which James A. Banks believes, is "an idea, an educational reform movement, and a process whose major goal is to change the structure of educational institutions so that male and female students, exceptional students, and students who are members of diverse racial, ethnic, and cultural groups will have an equal chance in school" (1993, 1).

*The Multicultural Curriculum*   In the 1970s the dominant approach to multicultural education was a "culturally disadvantaged model," which was predicated on the concept that "different is disadvantaged" (Puglisi and Hoffman 1978, 495). The authors (just cited) suggest that what is needed is a "culturally different model," based on "cultural variations [that] enrich a person's academic, intellectual and social experiences and contribute to the social and political qualities of a society" (p. 497).

James Banks suggests that the following curricular approaches can be used to develop a culturally different curriculum: contributions, additions, transformations, and decision making and social action (see table 8.2). Banks believes these approaches form a hierarchy for integration of multiculturalism in the curriculum, the "contributions" approach being the least inclusive. It is often a first step in developing a multicultural curriculum by simply mentioning the contributions of specific ethnic people in a field. The "additive" approach, the second level in the hierarchy, simply adds ethnic content to the already existing curriculum without changing the curriculum's basic structure. For example, students might study *The Color Purple* by Alice Walker in an American literature class. Or, in an elementary school, children might read literature that deals with various cultures, such as Isaac B. Singer's *The Power of Light: Eight Stories for Hannukah, Indian Tales and Legends* retold by J. E. B. Gray, *The Secret of Gumbo Grove* by Eleanora Tate, or *Three Stalks of Corn* by Leo Politi.

The "transformation" approach changes the structure of the curriculum by allowing students to view ideas from several ethnic perspectives. One example might be that rather than studying merely "standard English," students would study the regional, cultural, and ethnic influences on language.

The "social action" approach incorporates transformation with student action and decision making related to concepts, issues, or problems of ethnicity. For example, students might explore topics such as how to reduce prejudice in the school, how to ensure that women can participate equally in sports, or whether African American students should sponsor their own prom. Students would then not only suggest a plan of action but actually implement it.

## THE ROLE OF BILINGUALISM

According to the 1990 U.S. Census, one in seven U.S. residents (31.8 million speakers over five years of age) speaks a language other than English at home. This number is up from 21.8 million in 1980. Spanish is spoken by 17.3 million Americans, more than any other language except English. Yet the fastest growing language spoken in the United States from 1980 to 1990 was Mon-Khmer, spoken by Cambodians. The second fastest growing language spoken was French Creole.

The number of limited-English-proficient (LEP) students in U.S. schools has increased significantly since 1980. In 1991, there were 2.3 million students actually enrolled in LEP classes in grades K–12, an increase of 25 percent since 1980 when there were 1.84 million students enrolled in LEP classes (phone conversation with Rudy Coreaga, specialist at the National Clearing House for Bilingual Education, June 3, 1994). Approximately 64 hundred of the nation's 15 thousand school districts enrolled LEP students in 1991 with Los Angeles Unified School District having the largest number, 242,000 (telephone interview with Rudolph Munis, specialist, Bilingual Education and Minority Affairs, U.S.

*(continued on p. 326)*

TABLE 8-2

## Approaches for the Integration of Multicultural Content

| Approach | Description | Examples | Strengths | Problems |
|---|---|---|---|---|
| Contributions | Heroes, cultural components, holidays, and other discrete elements related to ethnic groups are added to the curriculum on special days, occasions, and celebrations. | Famous Mexican Americans are studied only during the week of Cinco de Mayo (May 5). African Americans are studied during African American History Month in February but rarely during the rest of the year.    Ethnic foods are studied in the first grade with little attention devoted to the cultures in which the foods are embedded. | Provides a quick and relatively easy way to put ethnic content into the curriculum.    Gives ethnic heroes visibility in the curriculum alongside mainstream heroes.    Is a popular approach among teachers and educators. | Results in a superficial understanding of ethnic cultures.    Focuses on the lifestyles and artifacts of ethnic groups and reinforces stereotypes and misconceptions.    Mainstream criteria are used to select heroes and cultural elements for inclusion in the curriculum. |
| Additive | This approach consists of the addition of content, concepts, themes, and perspectives to the curriculum without changing its structure. | Adding the book *The Color Purple* to a literature unit without reconceptualizing the unit or giving the students the background knowledge to understand the book.    Adding a unit on the Japanese American internment to a U.S. history course without treating the Japanese in any other unit.    Leaving the core curriculum intact but adding an ethnic studies course, as an elective, that focuses on a specific ethnic group. | Makes it possible to add ethnic content to the curriculum without changing its structure, which requires substantial curriculum changes and staff development.    Can be implemented within the existing curriculum structure. | Reinforces the idea that ethnic history and culture are not integral parts of U.S. mainstream culture.    Students view ethnic groups from Anglocentric and Eurocentric perspectives.    Fails to help students understand how the dominant culture and ethnic cultures are interconnected and interrelated. |

| Approach | Description | Examples | Strengths | Problems |
|---|---|---|---|---|
| Transformation | The basic goals, structure, and nature of the curriculum are changed to enable students to view concepts, events, issues, problems, and themes from the perspectives of diverse cultural, ethnic, and racial groups. | A unit on the American Revolution describes the meaning of the revolution to Anglo revolutionaries, Anglo loyalists, African Americans, Indians, and the British.<br><br>A unit on twentieth-century U.S. literature includes works by William Faulkner, Joyce Carol Oates, Langston Hughes, N. Scott Momoday, Saul Bellow, Maxine Hong Kingston, Rudolfo A. Anaya, and Piri Thomas. | Enables students to understand the complex ways in which diverse racial and cultural groups participated in the formation of U.S. society and culture.<br><br>Helps reduce racial and ethnic encapsulation.<br><br>Enables diverse ethnic, racial, and religious groups to see their cultures, ethos, and perspectives in the school curriculum.<br><br>Gives students a balanced view of the nature and development of U.S. culture and society.<br><br>Helps to empower victimized racial, ethnic, and cultural groups. | The implementation of this approach requires substantial curriculum revision, inservice training, and the identification and development of materials written from the perspectives of various racial and cultural groups.<br><br>Staff development for the institutionalization of this approach must be continual and ongoing. |
| Social Action | In this approach, students identify important social problems and issues, gather pertinent data, clarify their values on the issues, make decisions, and take reflective actions to help resolve the issue or problem. | A class studies prejudice and discrimination in their school and decides to take actions to improve race relations in the school.<br><br>A class studies the treatment of ethnic groups in a local newspaper and writes a letter to the newspaper publisher suggesting ways that the treatment of ethnic groups in the newspapers should be improved. | Enables students to improve their thinking, value analysis, decision making, and social-action skills.<br><br>Enables students to improve their data-gathering skills.<br><br>Helps students develop a sense of political efficacy.<br><br>Helps students improve their skills to work in groups. | Requires a considerable amount of curriculum planning and materials identification.<br><br>May be longer in duration than more traditional teaching units.<br><br>May focus on problems and issues considered controversial by some members of the school staff and citizens of the community.<br><br>Students may be able to take few meaningful actions that contribute to the resolution of the social issue or problem. |

From: J. A. Banks, "Approaches to Multicultural Curriculum Reform." In J. Banks and C. A. M. Banks (Eds.), *Multicultural Education: Issues and Perspectives* (2nd ed.) (1993), 208–209.

**This table describes the various approaches that might be employed to integrate multicultural material in the classroom.**

Department of Education, March 11, 1994). In Alaska, 65.1 percent of students are enrolled in bilingual education programs and 68.3 percent in English as a second language programs. In California, the numbers are 60.1 percent and 84.2 percent respectively. By contrast, in Kentucky, only 2.7 percent are enrolled in bilingual programs and 14 percent in English as a second language (U.S. Department of Education, Center for Education Statistics, *The Condition of Education 1993*, 373).

*Bilingual Education Programs*    Bilingual education is one form of multicultural education that is based on a paradigm that values diversity, "challenging melting pot assimilationist notions" (Garcia 1978). The 1968 Bilingual Education Act, the U.S. Supreme Court decision *Lau v. Nichols* (1973), and the 1978 amendments to the Bilingual Education Act, which provide a legal basis for equitable treatment of limited-English-proficient (LEP) students in the United States, set the stage for bilingual education. In 1994 Congress reauthorized the 1968 Bilingual Education Act. Federal funding for bilingual education continues to increase, but not at the rate of need. According to the National Coalition of Advocates for Students, of the estimated 3.5 million to 5.5 million LEP students in the public schools only one-third are receiving language assistance needed to succeed in school (1991, 113).

Carlos J. Ovando in "Language Diversity in Education" states that "about 206 Native American languages have survived the overwhelming powers of the English language" (1989, 211). These, along with non-native languages, make the United States what he calls a truly remarkable "language laboratory." Ovando points out that both Spanish and French are the "communicative and cultural instruments in various regions of the country" (p. 212). The range of languages still spoken in the United States today extends from Navajo to Hmong, the latter spoken by people from Laos and Cambodia. These do not include the numerous indigenous language varieties known as Creole, pidgin, and dialect. According to Ovando, pidgin was the means of communication among slaves who came to the plantation speaking a variety of languages. When these slaves became free, pidgin was the only language they shared, and, consequently, it became the first language of the community. Creole is the adoption of pidgin as an accepted language of a community. He cites three examples of creole varieties: Gullah, an English- and West African-based Creole spoken on the barrier islands from South Carolina to northern Florida; Louisiana French Creole, spoken in Louisiana and coexisting with two local variations of French and another variation of English; and Hawaiian Creole, which was influenced by the many languages of the islands (p. 212). Dialect is a variation of the English language. Black English is one example.

LEP students come from a wide range of backgrounds. Foreign-born students may enter U.S. schools speaking only their native languages; other students may have been born in the United States but do not speak English or speak some English and a native language. In 1987 it was estimated that in the Los Angeles schools, for example, there were seventy-nine different languages spoken and in the Anchorage, Alaska, schools, over one hundred.

*The Bilingual Curriculum*    Because of the wide variety of different languages spoken, even in a single school district, some believe there must be an equally wide variety of bilingual programs to meet the needs of LEP students and English-speaking students. Ricardo Garcia in *The Multiethnic Dimension of Bilin-*

*gual-Bicultural Education* states that the purpose of bilingual education is to create an educational environment that is compatible with the student's home environment (1978, 492). He and many other proponents of bilingual education claim that placing Spanish-speaking children, for example, in an Anglo curriculum dominated by the English language creates an impossible stumbling block for the students.

Rudolph C. Troike in *Improving Conditions for Success in Bilingual Education Programs* suggests certain elements essential in a bilingual curriculum, including:

- development of native language skills, including reading; the overall amount of English used should not exceed 50 percent
- teachers trained in the language of the students
- a program extending over at least five grades
- support from the community and parents
- high standards for student achievement

Instruction for LEP students, often called English as a Second Language (ESL), includes remedial instruction in either the native language or in English; linguistic enrichment by teaching in more than one language; teaching in both the native language and in English; and immersion, speaking the native (or target) language entirely.

## THE BILINGUAL CONTROVERSY

The road of bilingual education has not been smooth. It has been surrounded by controversy ever since the Supreme Court's 1974 *Lau* decision, which ruled that a young San Francisco boy, Kinney Lau, who spoke only Chinese, had to receive special language attention. During the 1970s, proponents contended that bilingual education for Hispanics, for example, would improve their educational performance. However, the dropout rates for Hispanics changed little from the mid-1970s to the late 1980s. Therefore, many questioned whether bilingual education worked. In a 1993 Phi Delta Kappa/Gallup poll of the American public, 46 percent said that students should be required to learn English in the public schools before they receive instruction in any other subject. Only 27 percent believed that students should be taught in their native language, and 25 percent believed that special English instruction should be provided at the parents' expense (Elam, Rose, Gallup 1993, 146). Public school teachers also expressed reservations in a 1993 Metropolitan Life Survey. Sixty-four percent of the one thousand teachers surveyed felt that substantive subjects such as mathematics, science, social studies, and language arts should be taught in English to students whose native language is not English, and only 34 percent felt that the schools should provide bilingual instruction in these subjects.

Others wonder how it is possible to provide adequate instruction in all the languages that are spoken by U.S. children. Cynthia Gorney, an editor at the *Washington Post National Weekly,* asks, "Where do you find a teacher who speaks Hmong?" And, if you find a teacher, how can the schools afford to pay for someone who may teach only one or two students? Opponents of bilingual education often cite its high cost as one of its problems.

Another concern is expressed by some English-speaking white parents who worry that their children are being shortchanged because the time spent learning Spanish or any other language will take away from time spent learning English, and conversely, many non-English-speaking students are less likely to learn English if they do not have to. Others are concerned that American patriotic values will be lost if schools emphasize the values of other cultures. Thus, in Fillmore, California, the city council adopted an English as the Official Language Resolution.

# Role of Materials and Technology

In 1990 Arthur Woodward and David L. Elliott in the *Yearbook of the National Society for the Study of Education* reported that commercially produced instructional materials were the basis for 67 percent of classroom instruction; 22 percent of classroom instruction was based on nonprint materials (p. 179). Thus, 89 percent of instructional time was structured around commercially produced materials, primarily textbooks. According to Woodward and Elliott, 98 percent of first-grade teachers and 92–94 percent of second-grade and third-grade teachers structured their reading curriculums around basal readers (elementary reading textbooks).

## TEXTBOOKS

Textbooks are the single most important instructional tool in the classroom. Educator Allan C. Ornstein claims that "the textbook has had the longest and most obvious influence on curriculum, to the extent of, in effect, standardizing teaching and instructional practices" (1992, 167). Many teachers refer to the textbook, the teacher's guide, workbooks, and other instructional materials as a "curriculum package," acknowledging its impact. Elliott and Woodward suggest that multigrade textbook programs constitute a virtually national curriculum in the basic subjects in elementary and junior high school (1990, 222).

In addition, as educator Michael W. Apple points out in "Making Knowledge Legitimate: Power, Profit, and the Textbook," the textbook also influences the social climate of the classroom. According to Apple, "The impact of textbooks on the social relations of the classroom is also immense." It is estimated, for example, that 75 percent of classroom time and 90 percent of homework time are spent with text materials (1985, 75). Hence, Apple concludes that social interaction between students and students, and teachers and students is limited.

*Benefits of Textbooks*   While some may decry the text as the basis of the curriculum, many educators point to its benefits. These include organized and sequential instruction of the material, articulation between grade levels and schools about the curriculum, benefits of the latest knowledge and research, assistance provided to teachers who cannot know everything about a subject, and teachers working together to utilize the material in curriculum packages. In addition, according to Ornstein, textbooks provide a common resource for all students. They include pictures, graphs, maps, and other illustrations that facili-

In many schools, teachers select the curriculum package that best meets the needs of their students and most nearly matches their own teaching approach and focus. In some schools, a committee of teachers may make a selection of texts for an entire department or grade level.

tate learning. The reading level and knowledge base of most textbooks match the developmental level of the students (1992, 168).

*Problems of Textbooks*   On the other hand, critics of statewide textbook adoption systems claim that the quality of the books is not as good as it could or should be. Benjamin Bloom claims that his examination of textbooks revealed that many of them were as alike as "peas in a pod" (1981, 144). Many educators suggest that this lack of diversity in textbooks is a result of marketplace demands: schools will purchase books that are more alike than they are different. Likewise, Ornstein points out, textbooks summarize large quantities of information and often make it too general and superficial, thus discouraging conceptual thinking, critical analysis, and evelution. To add to this problem, Woodward and Elliott suggest that textbooks avoid controversial topics and found that up to 30 percent of the content pages of textbooks are photographs and illustrations, which often do not serve instructional purposes (1990, 183).

Critics of the curriculum's reliance on textbooks cite the role of special interest groups in textbook adoption as problematic. For example, in several court cases in the 1980s, Christian fundamentalist groups attacked books for including the theory of evolution and humanistic literature for not including information about Christianity. According to Anita Manning in an article in *USA Today,* special interest groups, such as the Texas Council for Family Values, succeeded in deleting nearly 300 items from proposed health texts in Texas in 1994. The deleted items included issues such as population control, safe or safer sex, and homosexuality (p. A1). Other groups condemned texts for being too simplistic and not scientific enough in their approach.

John Goodlad, in his study of effective schools *A Place Called School: Prospects for the Future* (1984), evaluated texts and found that many emphasized the rudiments of reading and computation at the expense of skills such as comprehension, analysis, problem solving, and drawing conclusions (pp. 205–209). According to Goodlad, some leave out enrichment activities in the arts and humanities; many simply repeat and extend material rather than teaching new material (1984, 206). Other researchers found that texts presented only shallow knowledge in order to appeal to a wider audience (Newman in Rothman 1988a, 1). Many of these researchers condemned texts for prejudice and misinformation, especially when reporting on other cultures, and others claimed that texts were written at very low reading levels in order to appeal to the widest range of students.

***What Can be Done to Improve Textbooks?***   David Gardner in *A Nation at Risk* says that texts should be (1) upgraded and updated to assure more "rigorous content," (2) available in "thin markets" for groups such as disadvantaged and gifted, (3) based on results of field trials and creditable evaluation, (4) reflective of the most current application, the best scholarship, the best teaching and learning in each discipline, and (5) evaluated by state and school districts on the above criteria (1983, 25–26). Woodward and Elliott claim that textbooks can be improved if they have less emphasis on lower-level memorizing of facts and more emphasis on problem solving and higher-order cognitive processes. Likewise, according to Woodward and Elliott, textbooks need broader coverage of topics to promote deeper understanding of knowledge fields, particularly in history and science (1990, 223).

Whatever is included in the textbooks has an undeniable impact on the public school curriculum. How to balance the criticism of groups who want less scientific inquiry in texts and groups who demand more is a difficult problem, but one that textbook publishers will continue to attempt to solve.

## TESTS

Tests also have a huge impact on the public school curriculum, and, like textbooks, their production is a very profitable business. According to Elliot Eisner in *The Education Imagination: On the Design and Evaluation of School Programs* (1985), since the late 1970s, testing has become the most powerful control on educational practice in U.S. public schools. According to a 1994 report from the Educational Testing Service (ETS), there has been an explosion of testing in the United States in the last twenty years, and in some circles, according to ETS, educational reform has come to mean more testing (1994, 2). The Scholastic Aptitude Test (SAT), is one example. In recent years the SAT has become the benchmark for how the secondary schools are performing. If scores fall, it is assumed the schools are doing poorly. Consequently, most schools, school districts, and states take seriously the performance of their students as compared to those in other schools, districts, and states.

*Attributes of Tests*   Standardized tests designed to examine levels of knowledge in specific content areas also have an impact on curriculum. The largest of these testing programs, designed more as an evaluation of groups of students and the nation as a whole than of individual students, is the National Assessment of Educational Progress (NAEP). It is a program in which third-, seventh-, and eleventh-grade students have been tested every two years since 1969 in reading, writing, mathematics, science, and other subjects given on a rotating basis.

The NAEP, administered by the National Assessment Governing Board, which was established by Congress in 1988, is the only regular national assessment of what U.S. students know in various subject areas. The results of these tests are used to examine areas of student weakness and recommend curricular change (see chapter 10).

In 1986, NAEP tests showed that "relatively few students were knowledgeable about computer programming" (Rothman 1988b, 1), a finding that seemed to contradict earlier industry studies. Also, the 1986 test seemed to indicate that students knew little about American history. As a result, many states adopted new requirements in computer education at all levels and emphasized history content beginning in the early grades, a direct shift from the previous sociological approach of studying the individual, the family unit, and the community before dealing with specific historical content. As a result of increased emphasis on higher standards in all curricular areas, the NAEP in 1992 made significant changes in both the content of the tests and assessment questions. For example, on the reading test, students are required to read long and difficult passages for three different purposes: inferring, making connections, and understanding point of view (U.S. Department of Education, National Center for Education Statistics 1993, 1–2). Therefore, if NAEP test results continue to be used to suggest curriculum reform, it is likely that the curriculum will emphasize more high level thinking skills than rudimentary skills and knowledge. Similar changes in state testing programs (forty-five states have tests in language/reading, thirty-five in writing, thirty-four in science, twenty-nine in social studies) are moving standardized tests away from the traditional multiple choice items to short-answer, open-ended items and items that require explanations for selection of multiple-choice responses (ETS 1994).

In addition, most educators realize that when test scores are appropriately used they allow teachers to make sound decisions about students and the curriculum. For example, careful analysis of answers permits reading teachers to determine if a student's reading problem is in word recognition or comprehension. Similarly, if a teacher compares the results of a standardized reading test to the results of an oral IQ test and discovers that a student has a very high IQ and a low reading test score, this may influence the type of reading material the teacher assigns. It may also lead the teacher to ask important questions: Are the results of the tests accurate? Should the student be retested? Does the student have a physical problem that is affecting his or her test score? Is a learning disability negatively affecting test results? When did the student's scores begin to decline? Is the student experiencing social or emotional stress that might be affecting achievement? The importance of tests to assist teachers in asking and answering these questions cannot be overemphasized.

Many educators also believe that tests such as the NAEP are leading the United States closer to a national test of achievement and, hence, a national curriculum. In April 1991, President George Bush and Secretary of Education

Lamar Alexander proposed a national system of achievement testing. In 1994 Congress passed the Goals 2000: Educate America Act (proposed by President Bill Clinton and Secretary of Education Richard Riley) delineating what U.S. students should know and on what they should be tested. States were encouraged to adopt content standards in numerous subject areas and develop tests based on these standards.

*Problems of Tests*   Opponents of the 1980s educational reformers' call for national achievement tests suggest that nationwide testing would lead to centralized control over what children learn, and they fear that all children, no matter what their ethnic or racial background, will be required to learn the same content so that they can successfully pass the tests.

Critics, such as Elliot Eisner, maintain that the emphasis on testing removed from the curriculum that which could not be measured: appreciation, self-worth, motivation, commitment, problem solving, and creativity, for example. Many educators, including Philip Jackson, Michael Apple, and Vincent Rogers, voiced concern that the teaching, testing, teaching process was a meaningless series of steps in which only easy-to-teach and easy-to-test material was included in the curriculum, and that frequently teachers taught to the test rather than to the student's development.

Educator Theodore Sizer suggested that using tests to achieve accountability and thus high standards is a dangerous practice. According to Sizer, "[This practice] clouds our thinking about those high standards themselves. To assume that national examinations provide the only way to improve the system is both arrogantly to overrate our ability to create decent mass tests and—when we make international comparisons—to engage in a tricky non sequitur, to argue that because those nations we think produce better school graduates have national examinations, it is therefore the central presence of those examinations which primarily creates the quality we admire" (1992, 112–113).

Many educators wondered if standardized tests were statistically valid and reliable. A widely publicized 1988 study by the psychologist John Jacob Cannell reported that most students performed above the norm on many standardized tests, a statistically impossible occurrence (Watters 1988). Cannell's survey, in *How Public Educators Cheat on Standardized Achievement Tests: The "Lake Wobegon" Report* (1989), reported that the standards used by many test companies to establish "averages" were outdated and misleading. Critics of many standardized tests maintained that since the test results were so important to the schools' reputation and standing in the community, administrators would not buy a test on which they could be reasonably sure that their students would not perform well. Therefore, as in Garrison Keillor's comedy routines about Lake Wobegon, all the children would be above average. Many claimed that this apparent misrepresentation of results allowed the public and schools to believe that the current competency-based approach was working, when, in fact, it was not.

Further criticism came from a three-year (1987–1990) study on the testing practices in schools and workplaces funded by the Ford Foundation and chaired by George F. Madaus, director of testing and evaluation at Boston College. The study charged that in terms of minorities and women, the U.S. testing system had become a "hostile gatekeeper," that is, yet another method of keeping them out of opportunities for advancement, and called for a new system that would "open the gates of opportunity for America's diverse population" (Rothman

*(continued on p. 334)*

# *Cross-Cultural Perspective*

## Mexicans Look Askance at Textbooks' New Slant

For 20 years, Mexican fourth graders have been taught that Porfirio Díaz, the turn-of-the-century dictator, "was very bad for the life of Mexico, because the people were not given the chance to elect their leaders."

This month they began to learn that, despotism aside, Díaz achieved stability and peace, tolerated the Roman Catholic Church, built railroads, fostered industrial growth and attracted foreign investment.

Among historians, such revisionism is standard fare. Since it hit the fourth grade, however, it has detonated a political scandal in which educators, intellectuals and opposition legislators have all accused the Government of President Carlos Salinas de Gortari of rewriting the country's history to suit its political needs.

The charges range from rehabilitating Díaz, a man who the critics say was like Mr. Salinas in putting economic reform first, democracy second, to painting warts on the once-heroic peasant revolutionary Emiliano Zapata, a patron saint of those who oppose the President's agricultural changes. . . .

In the new texts for fourth, fifth and sixth graders—as in Mexican society—"what is in dispute is the very essence of the nation," exclaimed Luís Javier Garrido, a lawyer and political analyst.

Education officials say that as part of their long-overdue modernization of the country's public education system, they simply tried to update and improve the texts that are distributed to all private and public schools. If the new books have included a revisionist view or two, they add, it is only because those interpretations have gained currency since the last ones were written in 1972. . . .

The previous Government texts, issued under Mr. Echeverría in 1972, set off conservatives with laudatory accounts of Fidel Castro's Cuba, Salvador Allende's Chile, and other causes of the third world. But they included virtually nothing of the revisionist currents that were then gaining strength among students of Mexican history.

By emphasizing the country's economic modernization under Díaz, critics say, the new histories show a subtle bias toward Mr. Salinas's own priorities. By citing the shortcomings of revolutionary heroes like Zapata, they contend, the books support the Government's recent changes in the land-tenure system that

These sixth graders in Colonia Ramos Millán in Mexico City are reviewing a lesson from a new Mexican history textbook. The text caused great controversy in the schools since its revisionist attitude now portrays Porfirio Díaz's dictatorship in a positive light.

had long been celebrated as a revolutionary achievement.

The debate has taken little account of the treatment the new books give the Spanish conquest. The earlier social science texts described it as violent and seemingly unjust, but also in some ways positive for the indigenous peoples. The new sixth-grade history book describes the years following the conquest as "terrible," and recounts that for three centuries Indian peoples "resisted" efforts to wipe away their cultural traditions.

The sharpest critics of the books have focused on their depiction of more recent events. Although the texts offer the first mention of the 1968 army massacre of scores of students in Mexico City, for example, the critics note that they avoid mentioning that the Government ordered soldiers to confront the protesters and skirt the still-contentious issue of how many died.

From: Golden, 1992

1990, 1). Researcher and educator James A. Banks (1994, 12) reconfirmed this effect of standardized tests for racial minorities as did Herbert and Suzanne Grossman (1994, 29) for female students. One article reporting on the study claimed that schools and businesses increasingly rely on standardized, multiple-choice tests to make judgments about individuals and institutions, and that these tests tend to be biased in terms of race and gender.

The study claimed that each year elementary and secondary school students take 127 million separate tests as mandated by states and school districts. This testing costs over $1 billion annually. "The opportunity costs of missed instructional time used to drill students in the narrow skills measured by standardized tests are even greater than financial costs. Such time could be better used to develop students' higher order skills" (Rothman, 12). Lorrie A. Shepard, who has done extensive research on standardized testing, claims that if national tests are developed in advance of curriculum change, without teacher training, and are externally imposed, it is likely that we will continue to have: inflation of scores, high stake tests that narrow the curriculum to teach the content of the tests, and more hard-to-reach students rejected by the system (1991, 233–234, 238).

The Association for Childhood Education International (ACEI) published an international position paper on standardized tests in the spring of 1991. It stressed the inappropriateness of standardized tests to make any judgment about a child. It set forth unequivocally the belief that all testing of young children in preschool and grades K–2 and the practice of testing every child in elementary school should cease. According to ACEI, standardized testing:

- Results in increased pressure on children.
- Leads to harmful tracking and labeling of children.
- Compels teachers to spend time preparing children to take the tests, rather than providing developmental programs related to interests and needs. (Perrone 1991, 141)

## TECHNOLOGY

It is impossible to overemphasize the impact of technology on the curriculum. Ask someone who has been teaching for more than a decade how the use of technology in the classroom has changed, and you might hear something like the following:

> When I began teaching in the late 1960s the extent of the technology we used was motion pictures and filmstrips. Within a decade we had moved to videotapes and sound-slide shows. Today, almost every classroom in my school has a computer, and a computer lab is usually available to students most periods of the school day. I use the computer to keep track of student assignments, to average grades, to keep attendance records, and to do all of my lesson planning. All of my handouts are typed and duplicated on the computer. This year, with the help of a college class, I developed a system for having my students write essays on the computer and use it to check for spelling and grammatical errors. This allows me to read the essays for content only. Recently, my students read Arthur Miller's play "The Crucible." Using a CD-ROM disc, I made overheads of maps of Salem, Massachusetts, and we watched film clips of Arthur Miller appearing before the House Un-American Activities Committee. We were also able to watch parts of the play itself. Individual

students use the CD-ROM program for reinforcement and individual research. I can't begin to tell you how much technology has changed my teaching.

Of course, this scenario does not exist in all schools, but the computer is playing an important role in more and more of today's classrooms. According to a 1992 study by Ron Anderson of the University of Minnesota, over 90 percent of elementary and secondary schools in the United States have installed computers and over 85 percent of students use them during the school year. In 1992 many schools had multimedia peripherals such as CD-ROMs, videodiscs, and computer networks. Likewise, U.S. schools had one computer for every thirteen students (U.S. Census Bureau). According to Anderson, about one-half of school computer time is spent learning to use the computer, the other half is spent using the computer to enhance learning in other subjects.

*Benefits of Technology*   The benefits of technology are obvious in the teacher's statement above. In addition, Henry Jay Becker, in "The Computer in the Elementary School," states that the microcomputer in the classroom has had more effect on the social organization of the classroom than on learning. In a 1983 survey of 2,209 elementary and secondary schools, teachers reported that microcomputers led to increased student enthusiasm toward school, improved academic learning for above-average students, and more students working independently, helping others with questions, and working at their own ability levels. In 1991 a *U.S. News & World Report* article examined the use of new compact videodisc and CD-ROM technology in the classroom stating that the technology is bringing classrooms to life and turning students into enthusiastic learners by allowing them to use computers to do such things as "paint" in art class and conduct sophisticated science experiments in chemistry and physics (Toch 1991, 176–179). Teachers also report that they are able to give struggling students more attention by using the computer to help students master basic skills (Toch 1991, 178). In addition, computer technology may help equalize student learning. In grades eight and eleven, boys and girls performed equally well on computer skills, and ethnic minorities scored only slightly lower than whites on computer knowledge.

*Problems of Technology*   There are, however, numerous potential problems with technology in the schools. One of the most difficult is how best to use technology in the curriculum. Should there be separate courses for students in how to use computers? Should programming languages be taught in high schools? When in the curriculum should these things be added? Who should have access to computers? Should calculators be used in mathematics classrooms? If they are used, how and when should they be used?

Studies show that the students with high academic achievement have greater access to computers in their homes than poorer achieving students (Becker 1985, 32–33). Given the cost of computer technology, students who live in districts with a lower funding base may also be shortchanged in school. If schools were to purchase all of their own computers, it would cost $4 billion annually to have one computer for every three students (Toch, 78). Does this further separate opportunities for able and less able students? Moreover, how should computers and other technologies be purchased for the schools?

Anderson's study concludes that schools have taken a "hit or miss" approach to teaching students how to use computers. He states that it is the school's responsibility to rethink and reinvent ways to address forthcoming waves of computer-based technology (1993, xxvii–xx).

*Technology and Curriculum*    There is no doubt that technology directly and indirectly affects curriculum in many ways. In the early 1990s a new curricular approach was developed in which technology was the central focus. Tech-Prep is a result of the National Governors' Association's (NGA) concern about student progress as exhibited on such tests as the NAEP and one of the six national goals set by NGA in 1989 and adopted by Congress in 1992 (see section on "Role of Standards," p. 337). According to this goal, "all workers will have the opportunity to acquire the knowledge and skills, from basic to highly technical, needed to adapt to emerging new technologies, work methods, and markets through public and private educational, vocational, technical, workplace, and other programs" (National Education Goals Report, 1992, 5). Since then, several states and many school districts have eliminated general, vocational, and/or college preparatory tracks and replaced them with tech-prep programs in areas such as health care, technology, business management, and college preparation. Many of these programs are designed to have students go directly into the workforce; others move students from high school to community and technical colleges, and some move students into four-year colleges and universities. All of them involve apprenticeships that blend classroom learning with workplace experience. According to an article in *Education Week* by reporter Lynn Olsen, in 1991–1992 as many as 100,000 students nationwide participated in tech-prep programs, which could be found in 75 percent of the community colleges, 41 percent of all public school districts, and 82 percent of vocational school districts (1994, 22).

Tech-prep programs may include curriculum in the following areas: sciences, mathematics, applied communication, and principles of technology. In 1993 these courses were taught in as few as thirty-eight states and as many as forty-eight states (Wesson 1993, 197–198). Within tech-prep curriculums, four career clusters are prominent: engineer/industrial, information systems, health/human services, and arts/humanities.

*Benefits of Tech-Prep*    Proponents of tech-prep programs believe they:

- increase students' motivation to learn academic concepts in applied course work or college preparatory courses or both, thus increasing the students' motivation to stay in school.
- increase students' understanding and use of technology helping them to be more successful in school and in the workplace.
- provide students with learning experiences that integrate academic and occupational studying, blending classroom and work-based learning.
- increase the number of students who will pursue postsecondary education at the associate degree level or beyond. (Walter 1992, 7)

*Problems of Tech-Prep*    Many educators have expressed concern that tech-prep programs will lead to the "watering-down" of academic courses and wonder if these technical courses can meet the standards, developed by most professional organizations in education. Will these students be left behind those in regular college preparatory programs in meeting academic standards? How will the articulation between high schools and community colleges be monitored? Will time and funding be available for teachers to cooperate within and between institutions of learning (Olsen 1994, 22–26)?

Others worry that tech-prep programs will be too closely controlled by business and industry (see chapter 5, pp. 174–175 for a discussion of the neo-Marxist, revisionist view). These critics suggest that public schooling is not the domain of business and industry and that if business and industry leaders set curricular standards, they are likely to meet the current needs of the capitalist economy but are unlikely to meet its future needs. They point to the preponderance of the industrial-style high schools, in which students sit in rows and answer questions only when called on, as an example. According to these critics, this type of school might have made sense when a workforce was needed to work on assembly lines, but it no longer makes sense today, and it never provided equal educational opportunity for all students. They ask: Will tech-prep lead us down the same road?

## ROLE OF STANDARDS

Since *A Nation At Risk* proclaimed the need for educational reform in the early 1980s, there has been a constant reexamination of all levels of education, from preschool to teacher education, by almost every segment of society that has led to the setting of educational standards by a multiplicity of boards and commissions. Efforts to set national standards for student learning were begun in 1989 after President George Bush and the nation's governors held an education summit. The nation's political leaders outlined six goals for education, one of which was "world class" standards for what students should know and be able to do in the academic areas of mathematics, science, history, English, and foreign languages. In 1992 Congress enacted the National Education Standards and Assessment Act (P.L. 102–62), establishing the National Education Goals Panel to develop these curricular standards (see chapter 1, pp. 46–47). At approximately the same time, the National Council of Teachers of Mathematics (NCTM) published its own standards for mathematics curriculum. These were lauded by the governors as a model for "world class" standards. In addition to mathematics, by 1993 standards had or were being developed by professional organizations in English, civics, foreign languages, geography, history, physical education, the arts, social studies, science, and economics.

*Benefits of Standards*   The consensus among educators and members of the lay public is that there is a need for standards if we are to reform education. Eighty-one percent of all teachers surveyed by the 1993 Metropolitan Life Insurance Company poll support establishing national standards for what students should know. Proponents believe that standards will provide education with goals and incentives: students will know what they are expected to learn, teachers will know what they are expected to teach, and the public will know how effective the schools have been.

*Problems of Standards* Ironically, there has been considerable criticism of the role of the federal government in developing curricular standards. In 1994 when the federal government asked the states to "set opportunity-to-learn standards" based on national standards, the NGA responded by saying that it was not the federal government's role to assume responsibility for setting standards; it was the states'. Instead, claimed the governors, the federal government should create a "delivery system that enables all students to achieve high standards" (NGA 1994, 9–11).

In addition, educators such as Stanford's Elliot Eisner note that standards are already too pervasive in our culture. According to Eisner, there is a greater need to "celebrate diversity and to cultivate the idiosyncratic aptitudes our students possess" (1993, 23). John O'Neil, contributing editor of *Educational Leadership,* worries that the variability in students' opportunities to learn, students' motivations and interests, and students' learning styles, may make it impossible to design a challenging set of content standards appropriate for all students, including those with special needs (1993, 5). Further, according to Eisner, if we value student work that "displays ingenuity and complexity, we need to look beyond standards" (p. 23). Educator Theodore Sizer agrees with O'Neil and Eisner and further asks if it is possible to set common standards that are consonant with intellectual freedom. He also asks: Who has the right to set common standards for all people and how much control should the state have over the minds of children?

There is no doubt that curriculum is influenced by changes in the society. Likewise, it is clear that there are many definitions of the word *curriculum* and a variety of ways in which curriculum is organized. The importance of the school's curriculum cannot be overemphasized. It affects what is taught, how it is taught, and to whom it is taught.

---

**8-3**

**POINTS TO REMEMBER**

- When the economy of the United States needs a particular set of skills, such as computer literacy, or concepts, the schools generally include these within the curriculum.

- As women entered the U.S. workforce, the curriculum adapted by preparing them in specific skills and by increasing the courses needed for entry into college. The role of minorities was introduced into such courses as history, English, and science. Many critics still contend that the U.S. public school curriculum has not successfully met the needs of either women or minorities.

- Gender-fair, multicultural, and bilingual curriculums have been developed in an attempt to better provide educational equity to diverse student populations.

- In periods when the curriculum is primarily subject-centered, the textbook is the main source of curricular design. The curriculum is strongly influenced by skills and concepts students need to be successful on standardized achievement tests.

- Technology, primarily in the form of computers, has had a major impact on the curriculum and on teaching methodology.

## For Thought/Discussion

1. Is there any way curriculum can combine the best attributes of essentialism and progressivism? How?

2. One might assume, according to Bloom's theory on mastery learning, that anyone can learn to be a neurosurgeon given enough time. Do you believe that is true? If mastery learning is viable in theory, what are its practical drawbacks?

3. Devise a method of testing that would allow the teacher to assess his or her student's progress without causing the student undue stress and that would be fair to all students.

4. Must all students be educated by a similar curriculum to ensure that our nation will be able to compete in the international arena? Why or why not?

## For Further Reading/Reference

Banks, J. A. 1994. *Multiethnic education: Theory and practice* (3rd ed.). Boston, MA: Allyn and Bacon. A discussion of multicultural curricular issues and models based on conceptual and philosophical issues related to culture, race, and ethnicity.

Bloom, B. S. 1981. *All our children learning: A primer for parents, teachers, and other educators.* New York: McGraw-Hill. A discussion of how children can learn at home and at school when mastery learning techniques are implemented.

Holt, J. 1967. *How children learn.* New York: Delacorte. A description of a humanistic approach to learning, relating how easily children learn to read, do mathematics, draw, and paint when those experiences are not forced and are pleasurable.

Jackson, P. W. 1968. *Life in classrooms.* New York: Holt, Rinehart, & Winston. A description of the school's hidden curriculum from firsthand observations in elementary school classrooms.

Sizer, T. R. 1992. *Horace's school: Redesigning the American high school.* Boston, MA: Houghton Mifflin. A discussion of the interrelatedness of standards, curriculum, learning, and testing in individual school communities. Sizer uses fictional characters and schools to make his points.

© 1990 by Sidney Harris in *Phi Delta Kappan*

*"Remember, all these life experiences will someday count as college credit."*

"For Guillienne Audelin, a fifteen-year-old Haitian American who attends a predominantly black high school in Miami, assimilation is a dirty word. It means joining the ranks of the disaffected in her inner-city neighborhood, she said, and being stamped as a 'dummy' by a broader American society that she believes does not see beyond color. It means abandoning her immigrant parents' dreams for her future, and she simply refuses to do that. 'Nothing could stop me from trying to have a better life than we have now,' she said. . . ."

(Sontag 1993, A10)

# Part IV

# STUDENTS IN A MULTICULTURAL SOCIETY

## Chapter 9

### STUDENTS IN A MULTICULTURAL SOCIETY

It is an unusual public school classroom in which most children are the same race, same religion, and same socioeconomic status. In fact, court rulings and federal and state mandates have required heterogeneity in the public schools since the 1960s. The nature of the students and their numbers have a great impact on the school environment, the teacher and method of instruction, the curriculum, and other students. In this chapter, we will examine the nature of some of the special groups that constitute the population in American classrooms.

## Chapter 10

### LEARNING IN A MULTICULTURAL SOCIETY

Our understanding of the concept of learning involves the idea that people will gain new skills, insights, concepts, values, and ideas through some process that may or may not involve a teacher, may or may not require a specialized setting and materials, and may or may not find the learner proceeding through a series of prescribed steps. The assumption that learning has taken place, however, is based on the observation that, in some way, behavior has been changed. This chapter will explore many ways in which researchers from various academic disciplines have attempted to define learning. We will focus on how students learn, what they learn, and what they do not learn.

**CHAPTER OBJECTIVES**

After studying this chapter, you should be able to:

- Discuss the heterogeneity of today's students.
- Describe the various types of students likely to be in your classroom: children with disabilities, children in poverty, and minority children.
- Discuss student motivation and what research suggests about why students are not motivated.
- Describe students' interests, values, and worries.
- Discuss the problems of low graduation rates.
- Explain the likely differences among students you might find in a homogeneously grouped class.

- Define human cognitive development.
- Define developmental needs.
- Explain how psychosocial needs develop.
- Define moral development.
- Discuss how a student's perception of school changes from first grade to high school.
- Explain how a student's skills develop from first grade through high school.

# Chapter 9

# STUDENTS IN A MULTICULTURAL SOCIETY

*I*t is not enough to say that all students are different. It is not enough to try and understand what makes them different. Teachers must somehow reach students from all kinds of backgrounds with varying degrees of limitations and potentials. A few of these students are represented here.

**Manolo.** A recent immigrant to the United States, four-year-old Manolo was immediately enrolled in a comprehensive nursery school. Fortunately, his teacher spoke some Spanish and they were able to communicate. But Manolo, who had previously been popular with peers, suddenly felt excluded. When he proudly wore a pair of red leather sandals to school and was taunted on the playground about wearing "girl's shoes," Manolo responded by pelting his tormentors with sand. To make matters worse, this rejection was followed by the disapproval of his admired teacher.

(Jalengo 1985, 53)

**Jacob.** Three days ago Jacob came to our Open Classroom orientation meeting with nine other new kindergartners and their parents. We all sat together in a circle and began the process of getting to know one another. Except for a brace on his leg and a funny way of walking, Jacob did not seem to be too different from the other children. He was comfortable about sharing his new watch, and he and his mom sang a funny song together that the other children enjoyed. He made comments in response to things the other children said. . . .

Jacob has minimal cerebral palsy and *is* different from the other children. He has difficulty standing up and sitting down, and difficulty walking. His balance is poor, and if a child bumps into him, he topples over. The process of getting up again takes time and effort and involves a kind of struggle that seems strange to the other children.

(Heitz 1989, 11)

**Guilienne.** "For Guilienne Audelin, a fifteen-year-old Haitian American who attends a predominantly black high school in Miami, assimilation is a dirty word. It means joining the ranks of the disaffected in her inner-city neighborhood, she said, and being stamped as a 'dummy' by a broader American society that she believes does not see beyond color. It means abandoning her immigrant parents' dreams for her future, and she simply refuses to do that. 'Nothing could stop me from trying to have a better life than we have now,' she said. . . ."

(Sontag 1993, A10)

**Adam.** When Adam Dang arrived in Kansas City from Vietnam he was put in a special class to learn English. "I was 10 and here I was with 6- and 7-year olds," he said. At first, he felt alone in a school where no one could speak his language, but he persevered, and after two years of the special class, he caught up with his class agemates. He graduated seventh in his high school class and received a $5 thousand Horatio Alger Scholarship, one of seven given nationally. After college, Adam wanted "to give something back." Now nineteen, he plans to study chemical engineering and pursue a career in pollution control while he helps pay for his four younger sisters' college educations.

(Ryan 1994, 32–33)

**Nicholas.** Ten-year-old Nicholas is one of five children of a single mother who is a welfare recipient attending college to become a nurse. They live in the "perilous and virtually all black Englewood section of Chicago." Frequently Nicholas is thrust into an adult role, caring for his younger siblings. One day in the middle of multiplication tables Nicholas was called to the office to account for why his five-year-old sister Ishtar had not been picked up from kindergarten. "How could he begin to explain his reality—that his mother . . . was not home during the day, that Ishtar's father was separated from his mother and in a drug-and-alcohol haze most of the time, that the grandmother with whom he used to live was at work, and that, besides, he could not possibly account for the man who was supposed to take his sister home—his mother's companion, the father of her youngest child?"

Nicholas, caring for his family, often stays up late and goes to school tired. His grades are mediocre. If his report card is bad, he gets a beating. Nicholas and his siblings live with fear. His brother Willie describes the McDonald's playground near his home, "There's a giant hamburger, and you can go inside of it. . . . And it's made out of steel, so no bullets can't get through."

(Wilkerson 1993, A1–A2)

**Kelly.** Sixteen-year-old Kelly Gushue, a student at the urban Boston Latin School, says that she represents one of the many students trying to break the cycle of stereotypes, violence, and substance abuse. According to Kelly, only 2 percent of the teenage population are violent gang members and dropouts. Kelly struggles with at least three hours of homework per night and wants to attend a prestigious college. She takes Latin, trigonometry, honors English, history, and French IV. In addition, Kelly plays varsity volleyball, runs indoor track, and plays varsity softball. She also writes for the school newspaper and literary magazine, is a member of many school clubs, and is active in the Catholic Youth Organization. On weekends, she works fifteen hours as a cashier at a fruit store in her neighborhood. According to Kelly, "Teenagers can be responsible. Too many people believe that being successful is only a dream for lower-income city kids. If one has the desire, drive, and integrity, which so many teenagers do have, that dream becomes a reality."

(Gushue 1994, 50–51)

*7*t is an unusual public school classroom in which most children are the same race, same religion, and same socioeconomic status. In fact, court rulings and federal and state mandates have required heterogeneity in the public schools since the 1960s (see chapter 5). The nature of the students and their numbers have a great impact on the school environment, the teacher and method of instruction, the curriculum, and other students. In this chapter, we will examine the nature of some of the special groups that constitute the population in American classrooms.

## The Diversity of Today's Students

The diversity of today's students can be seen in the chapter opening anecdotes. Public school enrollment in the United States peaked in the fall of 1970, when 45,894,000 attended public elementary and secondary schools. By 1984 the number had decreased to 39,208,000. However, public school enrollment in the 1990s is again increasing (see table 9.1). Students in the United States come from a wide variety of backgrounds, have a broad range of beliefs, are raised under different ethical and religious codes, possess various cultural imperatives, and are taught different approaches to education. The classrooms of the 1990s reflect these differences.

### STUDENTS WITH DISABILITIES

In the fall of 1990 there were 46,450,000 public and private school (K–12) students in the United States. Nearly 12 percent (5.3 million) were classified either as needing special education or having disabilities. They are served under the federally sponsored Chapter I and Individuals with Disabilities Act (IDEA), formerly Education of the Handicapped Act (EHA) programs (amended in 1988) (see chapter 5, p. 191). The number has increased by more than 20 percent since the late 1970s, from 3.7 million in 1977 to 4.9 million in 1991. In the 1992–1993 school year, programs for the disabled spent $2.8 billion, or roughly $8,850 per student. The biggest proportion of that money went to students classified as learning disabled, a group that has grown by 183 percent in less than fifteen years,

**TABLE 9-1**

### Enrollment in Grades K–8[1] and 9–12 of Public Elementary and Secondary Schools, with Projections: 50 States and D.C., Fall 1984 to Fall 2003 (in thousands)

| Year | K–8[1] | 9–12 |
|------|--------|------|
| 1984 | 26,905 | 12,304 |
| 1985 | 27,034 | 12,388 |
| 1986 | 27,420 | 12,333 |
| 1987 | 27,933 | 12,076 |
| 1988 | 28,501 | 11,687 |
| 1989 | 29,152 | 11,390 |
| 1990 | 29,888 | 11,336 |
| 1991[2] | 30,353 | 11,486 |
| **Projected** | | |
| 1992 | 30,895 | 11,691 |
| 1993 | 31,350 | 12,006 |
| 1994 | 31,767 | 12,420 |
| 1995 | 32,285 | 12,786 |
| 1996 | 32,735 | 13,166 |
| 1997 | 33,087 | 13,446 |
| 1998 | 33,396 | 13,599 |
| 1999 | 33,624 | 13,744 |
| 2000 | 33,803 | 13,854 |
| 2001 | 33,944 | 13,951 |
| 2002 | 34,012 | 14,105 |
| 2003 | 33,969 | 14,307 |

[1]Includes most kindergarten and some nursery school enrollment.

[2]Estimate.

Note: Some data have been revised from previously published figures. Projections are based on data through 1990. Because of rounding, details may not add to totals.

From: U.S. Department of Education, National Center for Education Statistics (1993), *Digest of Education Statistics.* (NCES 93-292). Washington, D.C.: U.S. Government Printing Office.

**Student population in public elementary and secondary schools peaked in 1970, and then declined. It is rising again in the 1990s due not only to a rise in births, but also to a growing number of immigrants, and, to some extent, to the mainstreaming of those with disabilities.**

simply because the classifications keep expanding. A **learning disability** is "a disorder in one or more of the basic psychological processes involved in understanding or in using language, spoken or written, which may manifest itself in an imperfect ability to listen, think, speak, read, write, spell, or to do mathematical calculations." The percentage of emotionally disturbed students is up 48 percent since 1977. **Emotional disturbance** is a condition with one or more of the following characteristics over a period of time that adversely affects educational performance: inability to learn that cannot be explained by intellectual, sensory, or health factors; inability to build or maintain interpersonal relationships; inappropriate types of behavior or feelings; a tendency to develop physical symptoms or fears associated with personal or school problems; and schizophrenia. The percentage of students with mental disabilities is down 32 percent from 1980 (Office of Special Education, U.S. Office of Education 1993, 3). A **mental disability** is defined as "significantly subaverage general intellectual functioning existing concurrently with deficits in adaptive behavior and manifested during the developmental period, which adversely affects a child's educational performance" (Office of the Federal Register 1990, 13).

Because more than 40 percent of special education students ages six to eleven and nearly 20 percent of special education students ages twelve to seventeen are mainstreamed into the regular classroom for some part of the school day, it is imperative that classroom teachers learn to work with students with a variety of disabilities (U.S. Department of Education 1991, A–80, A–102). In addition, mainstreaming these students into the regular classroom may require that special education teachers, such as those who can use sign language, attend class with their students. Having a special teacher signing for a deaf student may mean that the regular classroom teacher has to make some adjustment in his or her teaching methodology. If, for instance, some of the terminology is difficult to translate exactly into sign language; it may be necessary for the teacher to write complicated terminology on the chalkboard or overhead transparency so that the student and the special teacher can see it in print. (For additional information about the disabled in school, see chapter 5, p. 191.)

Students with disabilities of all kinds are being mainstreamed wherever possible to a regular classroom. Teachers must be prepared to deal with these students in a sensitive and meaningful way at the same time that they must meet the needs of all other students in the class.

## In the Classroom

Sara Brooks [a first-grade teacher at Blaine Elementary School in North Philadelphia] truly believed that every child could be an A student. If a child was not making As, Sara believed there was a reason and there was a remedy. She even believed it in the case of a boy named Lacy Grissom.

Three weeks after the semester had begun, the special education supervisor came to Blaine to check on our special education students. One student on her list could not be found—a six-year-old trainable mentally retarded boy named Lacy Grissom. He was on the roll of a special education class upstairs, but according to that teacher, he had not reported to school yet that year. The teacher had marked him absent every day. The supervisor came into my office asking where Lacy was and if we had investigated his absence, as school policy required.

I called Lacy's home, and his mother arrived at the school in a matter of minutes, very upset. She said she knew that her son had come to school every day because she had walked him there herself. She had walked him there that morning. She demanded to know where he was that instant.

She got no argument from me. I wanted to know where he was, too.

Liz McCain happened by at that moment, heard the commotion and stepped in as usual to lend a timely hand. "Oh, you're talking about Lacy. He's in 202," she said, leading us all to Sara Brooks's classroom.

I had been in Sara's room several times that year, and I had seen her bending over this particular little boy, poking and prodding him to "Do! Do! Do!" I had seen Sara working with this little boy as he walked down the hallway, his body bent over as if he were in pain. I'd watched Sara urging him to straighten up, to walk erect.

I didn't know his name was Lacy Grissom. I didn't know he had had a heart operation as a baby and several operations after that, and that his mother considered him as fragile as a china doll. I didn't know he was classified TMR—trainable mentally retarded. I didn't know he was supposed to be in that special education classroom down the hall. Special education children were assigned from the district office, and Lacy's record had never arrived in our building. Not knowing he was classified TMR, I had assigned him to Sara's room at the beginning of the year, and he had been there ever since.

Sara didn't know any of this. She could see that Lacy was different, walking as if his limbs were welded together, his body curled up like an arthritic old man's. But she assumed he was part of the challenge I had given her, just another first-grader falling short of his potential.

No one had ever tried to get Lacy to stand up straight. No one had made him sit up at his desk, no one had ever pried his fingers open and put a pencil in there and showed him how to write. No one had imagined Lacy could do these things. But Sara could not imagine that he could *not*.

Now, three weeks into the year, this little boy was sitting up at his desk, writing his name. His mother said she knew he had been going to class and doing well, because he was coming home every night telling and showing her what he was learning.

But the woman from the district office couldn't stand for this. She was a by-the-book supervisor. As far as she was concerned, this situation was outrageous. This little boy did not belong in this room, pure and simple. It didn't matter what he was learning or how he was doing. He had been tested TMR, and that's what he was—TMR.

I said, "Look at the boy. Sara has him sitting and walking straight. He is holding his pencil and writing. He could do none of this when school opened just three weeks ago.

"Look," I said, "this boy is not TMR."

"Mrs. Cartwright," she said, "I know what the laws are. You cannot just move these kids around at your whim."

I said, "Very well. Would you please put Lacy on the list to be reevaluated?"

"I can do that," she said, "but it won't happen right away. He'll have to wait his turn like everyone else. He was just evaluated this summer. He must be placed in his assignment until a qualified evaluator assigns him elsewhere."

Then she took Lacy by the hand and led him to Room 207, the TMR class.

As soon as the supervisor left, I walked right back upstairs, got Lacy out of that classroom, returned him to Sara's room and put him back in his seat. Mrs. Grissom, Sara, and I were delighted. Sara grabbed Lacy and hugged him. Then she hugged his mother and me, as tears streaked all our faces.

Lacy stayed in Sara's room until January, when he was reevaluated and assigned to an EMR—educable mentally retarded—class. He went on through the next five years at Blaine and became one of our most visible and popular students. When break dancing became popular, Lacy went onstage in a school show and brought down the house with a performance the likes of which no one had ever seen. Here was this little boy, whose body Sara had coaxed open like a flower, spinning around that stage like a cyclone.

All I could think of was people telling us what can't be done with children.

(Cartwright with M. D'Orso 1993, 163–166). Madeline Cartwright was past principal of James G. Blaine Elementary School in Philadelphia, Pennsylvania.

## CHILDREN IN POVERTY

In 1980, 17.9 percent of all children under eighteen lived in poverty. By 1991 that number had grown to 21.1 percent (National Center for Education Statistics 1993, 48). Childhood poverty is a problem for all states (see map #4 in atlas, p. 000). In 1991 childhood poverty rates were highest in heavily rural states: Mississippi (33.5 percent), Louisiana (31.2 percent), New Mexico (27.5 percent), West Virginia (25.9 percent), Arkansas (25 percent), Kentucky (24.5 percent), Alabama (24 percent), Texas (24 percent), Arizona (21 percent), and Oklahoma (21 percent). Childhood poverty rates have increased most rapidly, however, in Wyoming (7.7 perent in 1979, 14.1 percent in 1989), Michigan, Wisconsin, West Virginia, and Montana. Likewise, some of the wealthiest states had the highest poverty rates for certain groups of children: Massachusetts, ranked the sixth wealthiest state, had the highest poverty rate for Hispanic children (49 percent), Wisconsin for Asian children (49 percent), and South Dakota for Native American children (63 percent). The highest poverty rate for black children was in Louisiana (56 percent) and for white children was in West Virginia (25 percent) (Children's Defense Fund 1992, 1–2).

Poverty levels vary significantly by race, ethnicity, and family type. In 1991, 16.1 percent of white children under eighteen were in poverty, 45.6 percent of black children, and 39.8 percent of Hispanic children. More children in female headed households, with no husband present, live in poverty than any other group (56 percent) (see figure 9.1).

Children who live in poverty are more likely to experience problems related to low birth weight, inadequate diet, inadequate health care, limited parental education, limited parental supervision, and poor living conditions than children who do not live in poverty. In addition, says sociologist John Cook, a child born into a hopeless situation, like poverty, learns hopelessness very quickly and does things the child would otherwise not do, such as steal for food or sleep in class (1994, 4). What do these problems mean to the classroom teacher? Take, for example, Derek, a ten-year-old child of a single parent. Derek comes to school without breakfast; he is provided breakfast by the school cafeteria. His lunch is also provided by federal free and reduced-cost lunch programs. All these programs require that Derek's teacher complete extensive paperwork. Derek rarely

FIGURE 9-1

## Percent of Children Under 18 Years Old Living in Poverty, by Type of Family: 1960 to 1991

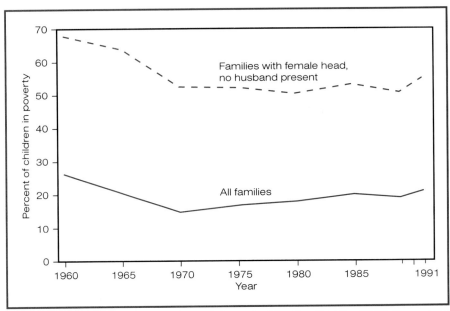

From: U.S. Department of Education, National Center for Education Statistics (1993). Dropout rates in the United States, 1992. Washington, D.C. U.S. Government Printing Office.

The proportion of children living in poverty declined significantly during the 1960s but rose after 1970. In 1991, about 21 percent of all children and 56 percent of children in female-headed families (with no husband present) lived in poverty. Poverty rates were relatively high for minority children. About 46 percent of all black children and 40 percent of Hispanic children lived in poverty in 1991. The proportion of poor children coming from female-headed households has risen dramatically, from 24 percent in 1960 to 59 percent in 1991 for all children, and from 29 percent to 83 percent for black children.

has school supplies such as paper, crayons, and pencils. His teacher tries to provide them when she can, but reduced budgets may make it necessary for her to buy some supplies for needy students out of her own money if she so desires. When the class goes on field trips, Derek can rarely go. Even if the money is available from another source, his mother does not return the required permission slips. Derek misses school often or comes to school sick. He seems to get more colds and ear infections than his classmates and usually comes to school with them. This fall Derek had head lice. His mother could not afford the expensive shampoo, so Derek's teacher arranged for her to pick it up from the community health service. However, since Derek's family does not have a phone, the teacher had to go to his home to give them this information. But Derek's mother had no way to get to the health service and no one to take care of her children when she went. Therefore, Derek's teacher helped arrange transportation through a local church group. Furthermore, Derek rarely does his homework. When his teacher visited his home she better understood why. There is no place for Derek to do his homework; no place for him to escape from his brothers and sisters. All five children sleep in one room, and the only other room in the house is a combination living room, kitchen, and bedroom for his mother. Derek's mother does not encourage him to do schoolwork; instead, she needs him to help with the other children. When the school has activities, Derek's mother cannot attend. Because she herself has problems with reading and mathematics, she is unable to help her own children. Derek has both academic and behavioral problems in school. He is easily distracted from his work, has difficulty reading and computing, and often disturbs the other children. His teacher finds that when she works with Derek individually he can do the work, but as soon as she leaves him to work with other children he is off-task. Consequently Derek's standardized test scores are low. Derek's teacher understands and sympathizes with his problems and is very concerned about him. However, she has twenty-eight children in her classroom and nearly half of them come from homes as poor as Derek's. Thus, subsidizing the poor students from a teacher's salary is not a sustainable solution to a chronic social problem.

## MINORITY STUDENTS

In 1991, 32.6 percent of the school population was classified as minority (nonwhite: black, 16.4 percent; Hispanic, 11.8 percent; Asian or Pacific Islander, 3.4 percent; Native American, 1 percent). The largest concentrations of minority school populations were in the District of Columbia, 96 percent; Hawaii, 76 percent; Mississippi, 61.7 percent; New Mexico, 58.9 percent; California, 55.5 percent; Texas, 50.9 percent; and South Carolina, 42.3 percent. The smallest concentrations of minorities in the school population were in Vermont, 2.1 percent; New Hampshire, 3 percent; West Virginia, 4.5 percent; Iowa, 6 percent; Utah, 8.1 percent; and North Dakota, 8.8 percent.

As the nonwhite population of the United States increases, the definition of the word *minority* is changing. According to Vance Grant, a specialist from the National Center for Education Statistics of the U.S. Department of Education, the federal government's definition of minority now includes all racial and ethnic groups except whites and Hispanics (telephone conversation with the authors, April 19, 1994). Hispanics are an ethnic rather than a racial group and are not, in fact, all members of the same racial group. James Banks suggests that new demographic realities call into question the definition of minority as all nonwhites. According to Banks, by the year 2020, 46 percent of the nation's school children will be children of color (1994, 4). A 1994 report of the Department of Education, Office of Civil Rights (OCR), indicates that many of the largest school districts in the country had high ethnic populations compared to other school districts. The hundred largest districts educate 23 percent of all elementary and secondary students, but just over 40 percent of the nation's 13.1 million minority students. Of the ninety-nine districts for which data about minorities were reported, fifty said that over half of their population was white or non-Hispanic. In twenty-one of those districts, under 25 percent of the students were minorities. In twenty-two of the ninety-nine districts, half or over half of the students were black, non-Hispanic, yet no racial group represented more than half of the student population in twenty-one of the ninety-nine districts. One district reported that most of its students were Asian/Pacific Islanders (Department of Education Reports, June 20, 1994, 8).

The minority population of the public schools is growing because the minority population of the United States is growing. For example, in Los Angeles, California, the Asian American population grew 119.5 percent from 1980 to 1990 (from 434,850 to 954,485). The Hispanic population grew 62.2 percent during the same decade (from 2,066,103 to 3,351,242). In Osceola County, Florida, the Hispanic population grew 1,081.5 percent during the same period (from 1,089 to 12,866). In Marathon County, Wisconsin, the Asian population grew during this decade by 2 percent (from 184 to 2,499). By 2020, the number of whites in the United States is expected to account for 70 percent of the total population and by 2050, 60 percent. The greatest increase in minorities will probably be in the Hispanic population, which is expected to more than double from 6.4 to 15 percent, and Asians, from 1.6 to 10 percent (Bouvier and Agresta 1987).

Within racial and ethnic groups there is also great diversity. Hispanics, for example, include many races. Likewise, according to Moon Lee, a specialist on Asian American affairs for the *Christian Science Monitor,* Asian Americans are not a homogeneous group and "the stereotype of the model majority belies the diversity of Asians in the United States" (1993). For example, says Lee, while it is true that many Asian Americans are successful in school, many others drop out. Schools, she suggests, may not pay attention to the needs of Asian students because they are expected to be academically successful. She further points out that there are many cultural and economic differences in Asians who are Chinese, Japanese, Filipino, and Korean, established groups on the socioeconomic ladder, and those who are Vietnamese, Cambodian, Laotian, or Hmong, more recent immigrants and less socioeconomically established. According to Lee, there are a total of fifty-nine different groups of Asian/Pacific Islanders in the United States.

At Olney High School (Philadelphia, Pennsylvania), dozens of groups of students—some racially mixed, some racially divided—fill the school's long bustling hallways. Spanish, Hindi, and Arabic can be heard echoing off the ornate building's high ceilings. The school is 52 percent African American, 29 percent Hispanic, 12 percent Asian, and 7 percent white.

"There are positives and negatives to having so much diversity," said Sabri "Tony" Ibrahim, a Palestinian student at Olney. "You learn from the other cultures, but you see that every culture has its good and bad traits" (Rhode 1994, 2).

Coupled with the growing minority student population is a decreasing population of minority teachers. Although, according to James Banks, students of color made up the majority of students in twenty-five of the nation's fifty largest school districts in 1991, teachers of color will decline from 12.5 percent of all teachers in 1980 to only 5 percent by the year 2000. According to Martin Haberman in *Preparing Teachers for Urban Schools* (1988), this should not be surprising because by 2000 only 5 percent of college students will be minorities. What are the implications of the growing minority school population and the decreasing percentage of minority teachers? (See chapter 3.) Again, according to Banks, teachers will be working with children who are ethnically different than they are. Students and teachers will be challenged to "construct their own view of reality" from the "multiple voices" they hear. Teachers will have to decide which view of reality should be presented to students through books and classroom materials.

Which authors will appear in literature anthologies? Whose view of history will be presented? Will students learn about the lives of the slaves as well as the slave owners on the plantations of the pre–Civil War South? According to Banks, schools should eliminate "Eurocentrism" from the curriculum and its language. Schools and teachers must establish a clear commitment to provide a diversified school population with what Banks calls "a multicultural literacy" (speech given at the University of North Carolina at Asheville, March 1, 1991). Of course, not everyone agrees with Banks's position on multicultural literacy. E. D. Hirsch, the author of *Cultural Literacy: What Every American Needs to Know,* believes in an "essential, uniform, literate education" for every student and that, regardless of racial or ethnic background, each student should be given similar information so that we can develop a national culture and language (1987).

Another implication of the increase in minority students may be declining standardized test scores, since, generally, minority students do not score as well on standardized tests (see chapter 10, pp. 000–000). The reasons for this result are complicated, but Asa Hilliard (1989) contends that many teachers "teach down" to minority students by making the material much simpler and more superficial than it needs to be. Hilliard, in citing research summarized by Jere Brophy, lists teaching strategies used in teaching down to minorities as:

- less wait time for students to answer questions
- calling on students less often
- criticizing students more frequently
- praising them less frequently
- interacting with them less frequently
- seating them farther away from the teacher
- accepting lower quality work

However, when minority and underprivileged children are treated as if they can achieve, they generally do, and when teachers account for learning styles of minority students and structure their lessons accordingly, the students learn at a high level.

## IMMIGRANTS

Almost one-third of the increase in U.S. population in 1993 was due to immigration when 895 thousand people arrived, the largest number in a single year since 1914. Roughly 48 million people, 19.5 percent of the total population, are estimated to be foreign born (U.S. Bureau of the Census 1994, 3–4).

In 1990 there were 2.6 million immigrant children between five and seventeen years of age in U.S. public schools, a 23.9 percent increase since 1980. The highest concentrations are in California, New York, Texas, Florida, Illinois, New Jersey, Massachusetts, New Mexico, and Pennsylvania (U.S. General Accounting Office 1993, 46). In 1992 the United States spent $8 billion on the education of immigrant children, and a coalition of educators from the most affected states are requesting additional federal funding (Walters 1993, 1–4).

*Effects of Immigration on Students*     Cynthia Coburn in "New Voices," a newsletter of the National Center for Immigrant Students, writes that the stress and trauma of the immigration experience can affect a child's mental health and

# *Cross-Cultural Perspective*

## Immigrant Diversity

*A widely divergent immigrant school population across the United States has led to an astonishing array of social and cultural problems in the classroom. The solutions to these problems have been equally varied. The following excerpt illustrates just one.*

### Creating a Safe Learning Environment: Dearborn, Michigan

Of the 2,700 students in bilingual classes in the Dearborn public school system, 1,800 speak Arabic, according to Wageh Saad, head of the district's bilingual program. New students arrive each year, the majority of whom are Lebanese, Palestinian, Saudi, and Yemeni. But children from Romania, Italy, Greece, Albania, and Spain are also arriving in Dearborn.

The unrest in Lebanon has had an effect on many of the children, notes preschool teacher Maria Ali: "I work with parents a lot, giving them make-and-takes [projects that they can take with them] and showing them techniques for playing with their children. A lot of these parents really don't know how to play. They grew up in war-torn areas and were pressed into adult roles. Everything in this country is so foreign to them—even going to the grocery store, things we take for granted."

Ali recalls one girl who had been in the United States only a short while when school pictures were taken. When the camera flashed, the girl started screaming. The flash seemed like the bombs she remembered from Lebanon.

It's especially important to consider the soul healing involved with kids who are refugees, notes ESL teacher Maura Sedgeman. "You can do that just by giving them the opportunity to talk, to paint, to draw in a safe environment, maybe in their own language. You have to be ready for unexpected triggers, too." The camera flash was such a trigger. "A lot of it is just letting kids talk it out, just listening," she says.

Because many of the immigrant children are Shiite Moslems, cultural adjustments can be especially complex. Dearborn educators who are not Moslems often work with mosques to find solutions when traditional American school practices conflict with religious beliefs, notes Sedgeman. For example, in some schools, girls and boys have separate physical-education classes, pork is not served in the cafeteria, and school activities adjust to kids' low energy levels during *Ramadan,* a month when many Moslems fast from sunup to sundown.

Other adjustments are more individual. Some families' religious beliefs forbid the making of human images, so those children may not have their photos taken; some religions ban singing when there has been a death in the family. Teachers must then find other ways for those children to participate in a class activity.

"You have to take your cues from the child," notes Sedgeman, "and not insist on something until you've found out if the reluctance has a cultural foundation."

From: Harbaugh, 1990, 45–47

ability to learn. Children may contend with: feelings of mourning for the separation from family; conflict between standards and rules in the United States and their native country; the responsibility to translate the language for parents who often do not learn English as quickly as they do and to help manage the household, intergenerational conflict with parents as children attempt to bridge their two worlds; and conflict between the cultures of school and home (1992, 1). In 1993 the National Center for Immigrant Children, founded in 1991 by the National Coalition of Advocates for Children to support the school success of immigrant children, reported on the learning environment and social climate of school for immigrant children. Here is a representative sample of their anecdotal findings:

- "I am sorry to say there are no classes that can teach me about my culture or my native language."
  (Laotian student, Greenfield, Mississippi)
- "My teachers know nothing about Haiti."
  (Haitian student, New York, New York)
- "I can't speak English very well. I have difficulty understanding, if they talk fast. On the first day I went home and cried in the bathroom."
  (Filipino student, Jersey City, New Jersey)
- "At school they see you but they don't notice you."
  (Hmong student, St Paul, Minnesota)
- "Teachers put me down by giving me lower grades and discouraging me from taking certain courses because they doubt my ability."
  (Haitian student, Queens, New York) (NCAS, 22–23, 32–33)

In order for schools to promote the success of immigrant students, the National Center for Immigrant Students, in its 1993 publication *Achieving the Dream: How Communities and Schools Can Improve Education for Immigrant Students,* recommends the following: a mission statement that establishes diversity as a positive factor; a clear disciplinary code providing equitable treatment for all students; hiring, training, and promoting bilingual staff; and providing material that fosters respect for cultural diversity (NCAS, 24–25, 34–35). In California, the state with the largest percentage of immigrant schoolchildren, these suggestions are being implemented through the California Tomorrow Project, which since 1988 has conducted in-service teacher workshops for teachers with immigrant students mainstreamed into their classrooms. This project has communicated the results of its work to schools of education and school-based staff development personnel for use in the training of teachers.

### *Viewpoint*  Hope in a Feather

My life can be compared to an episode from *The Joy Luck Club*. Like Suyuan, one of the mothers in Amy Tan's book, my parents carried a feather from China. This one feather symbolizes all their hopes and good intentions for me in America. From an early age, I discovered that I could succeed at tasks other people did not think I could accomplish. As immigrants, my parents often came home late from work; therefore I had to take care of myself and my sister. This experience was just a little taste of what was to come.

Junior year at Bronx Science, in New York, was the turning point in my life. My parents felt a sense of uselessness, because they knew that they could not support me through college. My parents decided to open a little restaurant in Puerto Rico with the money they had from their life savings and also by borrowing as much as they could from their friends. I had to decide whether I should go with my parents or stay in New York for a better education. And as they departed, the feather was given to me to represent all their hopes and expectations. I remember my parents' telling me that they did not finish elementary school and wanted me to make up for it by going to college. With this in mind, I decided to stay.

The months that I had to live on my own were an experience I will never forget. Every day I had to tackle a new challenge. For the first time, I realized that I was alone and had to do whatever it takes to survive. For myself, I had to balance out everything, whether it was to prepare meals, to shop, or to do homework. I disliked the circumstances I was forced into, because they deprived me of normal childhood experiences, such as the opportunity to make or go out with friends. But as time passed, I learned to survive on my own and to be independent. . . .

Life is difficult for new immigrants. Many have to learn a new language, but there are still some who do not have the opportunity to do so because of other priorities. At the same time, the immigrants have to deal with racism and discrimination. I, too, had gone through many difficulties, but I had never given up on my hopes and dreams. Although my parents may not be here to give me support and guidance, I still hang on to this feather and look forward to the challenges that lie ahead. In life, one must struggle through many hardships before one can succeed.

My life is just one example of the obstacles new immigrants have to face in America. My hope is that others can use their past experiences as stepping stones, the way I have, in order to overcome their present difficulties and not lose sight of their dreams and goals. Although mistakes are made along the way, one should never give up hope. I know I haven't.

> From: Tomen Tse, "In our own words: Special issue by and about urban youth," *The Boston Globe Magazine* (February 6, 1994), pp. 13–14. A version of this article won honorable mention in the English-language category of the 1993 Massachusetts English Plus Coalition's student writing contest. Tomen Tse is a senior at Charlestown High School.

### URBAN vs. RURAL

The percentage of children under the age of fifteen who live in the nation's major urban centers has changed little in the last two decades. However, the number of rural children has declined by 3.2 percent, while the urban population has increased by 1.6 percent and the suburban by 9.2 percent (U.S. Bureau of Census 1993).

Minority school populations tend to be centered in the nation's major urban areas. In the fifteen largest school systems in the United States, the minority population ranges from 70 percent to 96 percent (Council of Urban Boards of Education 1992). A study by the National School Boards Association confirms that the largest percentage of students in urban school districts (those with between 75 hundred and 937 thousand students) were black (40 percent), followed by white (34 percent), Hispanic (21 percent), and Asian (5 percent) (1990). In Philadelphia where there were 201 thousand schoolchildren in 1993, 63 percent were black, 22 percent white, 10 percent Hispanic, and 5 percent Asian (Rhode 1994, 7). It is also important to note that the nonwhite school population is increasing in some suburban districts, as well. For example, in Prince George's County, Maryland (near Washington, DC), from 1967 to 1988, the black school population increased from 13 percent to 64 percent. In Dekalb County, Georgia (near Atlanta), the black school population changed from 5 percent to 54 percent during the same period.

The primary implication for schools and teachers of the decline in rural school-aged population is that there will be fewer jobs for new teachers in many rural school districts, and more in urban schools. Because over 40 percent of all minority schoolchildren are educated in the one hundred largest school districts, a large percentage of new teachers, most of whom will be white (92 percent in

1990), will be teaching students with whom they don't share an identity. Since new urban teachers must learn to successfully interact with the students they will teach, Martin Haberman in *Preparing Teachers for Urban Schools* (1988) suggests that colleges must provide a minimum of at least 2 hundred pre-student-teaching hours in the schools and that at least part of this time should be spent working with minority students who need extra help in regular school subjects. He also suggests that pre-student teachers should conduct after-school activities with urban youngsters. According to Haberman, 95 percent of students entering teaching cite a desire to help students build self-esteem as a reason for teaching; 81 percent say they love children. Haberman suggests that these are not sufficient reasons for teaching in an urban setting. (See chapter 3, pp. 98–101 for information on culturally relevant teaching.)

> Successful urban teachers are able to teach effectively whether their pupils are lovable or not; and they are able to teach students who may not demonstrate gratitude or affection in return. Preservice students and beginning teachers must be disabused of the notion that love is the basis of instruction. . . . [T]here is an extremely strong case to support the contention that how people feel about themselves is a function of the situations in which they find themselves and not in some persisting inner state called the "self-concept." Finally, the cumulated craft wisdom of successful urban teachers supports the premise that how pupils feel about themselves is a *consequence* of successful school experience, not a *prerequisite* condition for learning. . . . Urban schools will chew up and spit out novice teachers who begin with the notion of love as the basis for relating to pupils or who believe that students' lack of achievement or misbehavior is a function of low self-concept. (1988, 29–30)

# Motivation toward School

According to a survey done by Harris and Associates of 1,208 teachers and 2,700 students in grades four through twelve, *How Teachers and Students View Their Schools, the Learning Process, and Each Other,* 92 percent of the students report they want to do as well as they can in school and 58 percent are enthusiastic about what they learn (Metropolitan Life Insurance Company 1988). John Goodlad (1984) found that students in grades four through high school were most interested in the arts, physical education, and vocational education because they had the largest decision-making role in these subjects; "they liked to do activities that involved them actively and in which they worked with others" (p. 115). Students conversely indicated less interest in English, mathematics, social studies, and science. Perhaps this is because when Goodlad visited classrooms he found a great deal of telling, explaining, and questioning as well as a great deal of passive seatwork in these classes. In the arts, physical education, and vocational education, on the other hand, Goodlad observed demonstrations, showing, modeling, acting, constructing, and carrying out of projects (p. 115). He suggests that the students' level of activity may be one reason why they do or do not respond positively to a subject. Allowing them to be more actively involved in all subjects may improve motivation.

A 1993 study that analyzed existing research on student motivation, conducted by professors and researchers Max Thompson and Helen Harrington,

*(continued on p. 360)*

# DOES TRACKING IMPEDE STUDENT SUCCESS?

## PRO Theodore R. Sizer

Tracking—the assigning of students to groups that represent their supposed academic ability and interest—appears to be another self-fulfilling prophecy. To a substantial degree, we all are what we believe we are. And we believe, more often than not, what the teachers or the test scores or our immediate community tells us.

The effects of tracking stare us in the face. Students in schools where the expectations for all are high and the program geared to help youngsters rise to those expectations do so in dramatically greater numbers than in tracked schools. As one Texas middle-schooler put it to her principal, "We did what we were unsupposed to do." In a northeastern senior high school, a student teacher found two "misassigned" students in his Curriculum Two junior English class; they "should have been" in a "lower, slower" Curriculum Four group. His mentor teacher, a maverick, told him just to let it be: the two kids wanted to stay and the guidance office computer would take longer than the term's length to figure out that an "error" had been made. How did the students do? One did fine, a B. The other struggled and passed, though barely. Both seemed to gain much. The youngster with the B had the exquisite pleasure of knowing that he had beaten the system. Both had been treated to the expectation of serious work, which each now knew that he could do, one way or another.

Tracking draws lines by race, class, and sometimes gender, though there is not a shred of evidence that sex or race or economic status prescribes once and for all time one's powers of intellect, imagination, or determination. The stereotypes abound: girls are no good at math. That black kid in Michael Jordan sneakers couldn't be interested in physics or "do" serious science even if he wanted to. Poor kids are shiftless; they lack ambition; they're going nowhere. Asian-American kids achieve. Hispanic kids don't care. Blond kids are cheerleaders and will go to college. . . . The litany is familiar. We decide about children by how they appear and what we have been expected to believe about their appearances. Unwittingly, usually, schools draw the lines, signaling to particular students what they are good for. There are tracks for everyone and anyone.

All too often, the tracking is set early and is made permanent. What a kid can do is decided on, say, when she or he is thirteen, and the youngster is slotted in accordingly. While most American schools allow shifting from track to track, this is usually difficult to do, because the "top" tracks are organized into sequences of courses, each with prerequisites that a student not in the track from the beginning is unlikely to have. More telling, however, is the level of mastery: a student who is not challenged for a period of years, or even months, finds it difficult to catch up with students who have been stretched during the same period. Indeed, the very struggle of trying to catch up often tells the student that she *is* inferior, just as the school said she was. As the academic timetable moves inexorably along—we must get to quadratics by February—no catch-up time allowed. The kid is trapped. The late bloomer flourishes all too rarely. The waste to that student—and to society at large—is prodigious.

From: Theodore R. Sizer. *Horace's School: Redesigning the American High School,* 1992, 35–36.

## Postscript

The changing face of the U.S. school population brings to the forefront the issue of **tracking**, or grouping by likeness, usually ability. Tracking is a common practice in public schools in the 1990s. The questions are: Does tracking work? Do students achieve more or less if they are placed with students of like ability? It is clear that Sizer and Lieberman disagree.

In April 1991 the issue of tracking was brought before the Committee on Labor and Human Resources of the United

# DOES TRACKING IMPEDE STUDENT SUCCESS?

## CON Myron Lieberman

Policies governing assignment to schools are failing to bring about significant improvement in the educational achievement of disadvantaged minorities. Tracking is being perceived as the reason, hence it is also viewed as a civil rights issue. The result is that we can expect more conflict over assignment within schools. . . .

Let me illustrate the rationale that underlies the opposition to tracking. Suppose pupils A and B are of equal ability. Pupil A is placed in the college preparatory track. In this track, pupils are regularly expected to do homework. Pupil B is placed in the general track, in which little homework is assigned. Inasmuch as expectations for B are lower, less is demanded of B, hence B's achievement is correspondingly lower. The expectation of low performance leads to low performance—this is the antitracking argument.

In my opinion, the argument is not persuasive. Of course, schools sometimes underestimate students and assign them to programs on the basis of erroneous assessments. Unfortunately, no system or policy on pupil assignment is free from error. If opposition to tracking means that all students should be enrolled in the same programs, regardless of ability, achievement, or interest, it is unrealistic. Opposition to tracking is not helpful as long as it fails to distinguish acceptable from unacceptable criteria for grouping students for instruction.

Tracking takes place in all-white schools, integrated schools, and all-black schools. Inasmuch as all have "tracks," it is difficult to accept racial explanations for their origins or outcomes. Even if a higher proportion of black students are assigned to the college preparatory track in all-black schools, we do not know whether such students achieve more than comparable black students assigned to other tracks in other schools. Furthermore, we cannot assume that the "college preparatory track," or any track, requires the same level of academic competence in all schools offering the track. . . .

Some critics of tracking distinguish between hierarchical and nonhierarchical courses. Hierarchical courses require a certain level of achievement in the subject: a student should not take advanced French before taking beginning French, or solid geometry before algebra and plane geometry. Other courses, however, do not require previous courses in the same subject. English literature is said to be one example; geography, especially of specific countries, is thought to be another. In nonhierarchical courses, there is supposedly no need to group students by ability or by proficiency in the subject. This reasoning considerably weakens the antitracking argument, especially as it applies to higher grade levels. The opponents of tracking tend to have a narrow view of what subjects are hierarchical, but on any reasonable basis, much of the curriculum falls into this category.

From: Myron Lieberman. *Public Education: An Autopsy,* 1993, 180–182. Lieberman is an educational consultant.

States Senate. The committee attempted to determine whether Title VI was being adequately implemented and enforced by the Office for Civil Rights of the Department of Education, but was unable to come to a conclusion and determined only to improve their monitoring practices. A major question has to do with the possibility that tracking leads to "with-in school discrimination" in that a disproportionate number of minority students are in low-ability tracks. This issue is a complicated and continuing one as we attempt to educate all students in the U.S. melting pot.

found that student motivation for academic achievement correlates with the socioeconomic status (SES) of the family. Students from lower socioeconomic status families have school goals of gaining attention, approval, and rewards. Students from middle to high SES families believe that finding the right answer is their most important school goal. The researchers found the motivational gap between SES groups' achievement levels was smallest in first grade and widened throughout the school years. Thompson and Harrington also concluded that there were no differences based on ethnicity in students' motivation for academic achievement; however, different cultures "have different social norms and cues to signify achievement" (p. 5). They found one interesting exception: sixth- and seventh-grade African American girls "show higher achievement motivation than any other ethnic group for that age" (p. 5). Some of their conclusions may help teachers develop motivation to learn in all children:

- Heterogeneous groups are more likely to have students and teachers with positive expectations for success than are homogeneous groups.
- Younger children are more intrinsically motivated and are willing to engage in achievement activities to satisfy their own needs for mastery.
- Older children are more extrinsically motivated and are more likely to engage in activities to get a good grade.
- Young children, ages four through eight, attend more to social reinforcement and praise than to feedback about performance.
- The age at which grades become important depends on the age at which parents and teachers emphasize the importance of good grades.
- The pleasantness of the learning environment positively correlates with the amount of effort put forth by students.
- More democratic classroom environments promote higher levels of student motivation for achievement.
- Students are more motivated to learn if they perceive value in what they are learning.
- If students connect success to personal effort rather than ability or luck, they are more likely to be motivated to learn.
- Inappropriate or indiscriminate use of extrinsic rewards has a long-term negative effect on student motivation to learn.
- To be intrinsically motivating, activities must give students a feeling of developing or increasing competence.
- More active student learning, more student choice, and more opportunity for students to interact with peers promote increased motivation to learn. (1993, 5–7)

## INTERESTS OF TODAY'S STUDENTS

Susan Mernit, in *Instructor,* states that "today's kids find themselves with more unsupervised time on their hands than their counterparts did a generation ago" (1990, 41). They spend much of this time watching television. According to the 1992 National Assessment of Education Progress survey of students, 61 percent of fourth graders, 65 percent of eighth graders, and 47 percent of twelfth graders spend three or more hours watching television per day. The survey also concluded that 20 percent of fourth graders, 14 percent of eighth graders, and 6 percent of twelfth graders watched six or more hours of televison per day. Almost all students spend less time doing homework than watching television.

The 1994 Gallup Organization for Junior Achievement, Inc., found one-third of adolescents work on the average of ten hours per week after school and on weekends. The implications of the large number of secondary school students who have jobs are both positive and negative. Teachers worry that many students who work put a greater value on their jobs than on their educations since jobs provide immediate gratification, a paycheck. And, since many adolescents have difficulty thinking about long-term goals, the immediate gratification displaces the long-term goals of educational achievement. For example, in 1990, 23.1 percent of high school seniors who worked said they spent all or most of their money on personal items. Similarly, in 1991, 11.9 percent of high school seniors said they spent half of their money on cars, and 7.5 percent saved their money for education (NCES 1993, 96).

On the other hand, many students find a motivation to succeed in school through their work. They see firsthand the kinds of education they need to be successful on the job. They see how adults deal with the problems of the workplace—juggling families and work, negotiating with the boss, and dealing with customers. They learn to deal with people and are trained in the use of equipment. They learn the importance of being on time and doing a good job. They develop a commitment to something beyond themselves. For some students, it's the job that keeps them in school. Others discover new educational and vocational aspirations through the job. Some employers require students to remain in school and get good grades; some even provide scholarships for students who worked during high school and continue during college or technical school.

## VALUES OF TODAY'S STUDENTS

Despite America's many social problems, most of today's young people have traditional values and are concerned about social issues. A 1990 U.S. Department of Labor study revealed that 68 percent of sixteen- to nineteen-year-olds volunteer for an average of 4.3 hours per week in school, church, civic organizations, hospitals, and social organizations (p. 122). Katherine Cress found that 57.7 percent of 1991 high school seniors maintained that religion was important in their lives and 31 percent reported attending church weekly. A 1994 Gallup poll found that teenagers were socially conscious, saying it was important to reduce crime (91 percent); support education (91 percent); and help the homeless (87 percent). Most teenagers consider the role models in their lives to be their parents (94 percent), teachers (78 percent), and religious leaders (50 percent). They also have traditional views on those professions that create a good society: teachers (86 percent), scientists (76 percent), business people (46 percent), politicians (43 percent), artists (37 percent), professional athletes (27 percent), movie personalities (16 percent), and rock musicians (10 percent). The teenagers' aspirations for the future are also quite high: plan to attend college (82 percent), plan to enter a professional career (63 percent), believe they will have a promising future (55 percent), expect to do better than their parents (42 percent), and expect to be as well off as their parents (57 percent). Their goals for their careers include: helping others (85 percent), having people look up to them (74 percent), improving their

**TABLE 9-2**

## Concerns of Today's Youth—Age Nine Through Seventeen

| Concern | Percent of Youth |
|---|---|
| Not being able to get a good job | 61 |
| Not having enough money | 49 |
| Not being able to get into college | 43 |
| Contracting AIDS virus | 42 |
| Family member having drug problem | 38 |
| Being injured in an auto accident | 32 |
| Being beaten or attacked | 28 |
| Having to fight in a war | 24 |
| Having parents lose their jobs | 23 |
| Having a marriage end in divorce | 14 |

From: J. Adler, *Newsweek* (January 10, 1994), based on surveys by Children's Defense Fund and the Yankelovich Youth Monitor Journal.

**Adults generally perceive youth as a carefree time and school to be the best years of one's life. Students, however, have many concerns that affect their daily lives and their ability to accomplish schoolwork.**

community (72 percent), being creative in their work (56 percent), serving the nation (54 percent), and making a lot of money (42 percent).

## WORRIES OF TODAY'S STUDENTS

Despite the adult perception that young people are carefree and have no worries, several studies have proved otherwise. Unfortunately, an increasing number of today's children, particularly those living in urban areas, have fears that relate to personal safety, health, and quality of life. Table 9.2 portrays the concerns of today's youth, ages nine to seventeen, based on surveys conducted by the Children's National Defense Fund and the *Yankelovich Youth Monitor.*

It is also interesting to compare the overall concerns of U.S. students with those of a specific ethnic group. For example, Valerie Ooka Pang has studied the concerns of Asian American immigrants. These students represent highly diverse ethnic groups: Cambodian, Chinese, East Indian, Filipino, Guamanian, Hawaiian, Hmong, Indonesian, Japanese, Korean, Laotian, Samoan, Vietnamese, Bangladeshi, Bhutanese, Bornean, Burmese, Celebesian, Cernan, Indochinese, Iwo-Jiman, Javanese, Malayan, Maldivian, Nepali, Okinawan, Sikkimese, Singaporean, and Sri Lankan. These Asian immigrants make up the fastest growing minority group in the United States. From 1970 to 1980, the Asian population in the United States grew by 143 percent. The concerns of Asian American students focus on conflicts between parental expectations of success and their own desires, worries about the myth of being the "model minority," ethnic prejudice, and taking tests.

The graduation rate for students of all ethnic and racial groups continues to rise, albeit gradually. This rise may be partly due to the implementation of special programs for at-risk students that, among other things, seeks to increase student and teacher interaction and uses many and varied teaching approaches.

Teachers need to understand the problems of immigrant students and to acquire a global view of U.S. society so that myths about ethnic cultures and false generalizations about them are eliminated. Nonminority students should understand that even within an ethnic group there are many differences—such as language, culture, tradition, religion, education, aspirations—that result in differing needs. They must recognize the ethnic students' frustration, depression, and desperation and should consider instituting programs to help Asian American students and their parents deal with conflicting academic values. At the same time, many schools also feel the pressure to help students become a part of the U.S. school community. The theoretical conflict between the melting pot and multiculturalism is not easily resolved.

## GRADUATION RATES

In 1992, 71.2 percent of the school population who entered ninth grade four years earlier graduated with their class. This represented a slight increase from the graduation rate in 1988 (phone conversation with Vance Grant, U.S. Department of Education, April 1994). The highest graduation rates were in Minnesota, 89.2 percent; Iowa, 87.6 percent; North Dakota, 87.5 percent; Nebraska, 87.2 percent; Montana, 85.5 percent; South Dakota, 85.3 percent. The states with the lowest graduation rates were Texas, 56 percent; South Carolina, 58.1 percent; Mississippi,

FIGURE 9-2

### Event Dropout Rates for Grades 10–12, Ages 15–24, By Race–Ethnicity: October 1972 Through October 1992

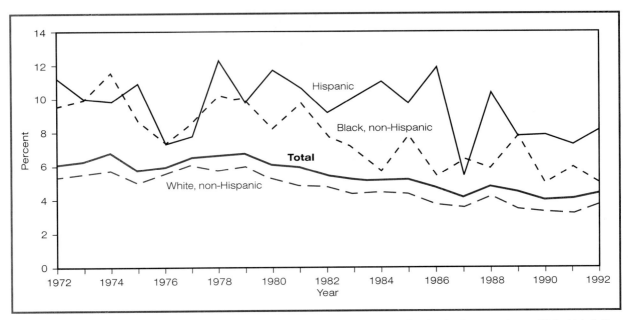

Source: U.S. Department of Commerce, Bureau of the Census, Current Population Survey, October (various years), unpublished tabulations.

**There are many reasons why students drop out of school or finish their education late. Minorities, those living in poverty, and substance abusers are the students most at risk for dropping out of school. Since special programs have been implemented in many schools, their dropout rates have declined significantly.**

62.1 percent; District of Columbia, 69.6 percent; Georgia, 63.7 percent; Florida, 65 percent (U.S. Department of Education 1992, 8).

It is projected by the Western Interstate Commission for Higher Education that the 1995 public high school graduates will come from the following ethnic and racial groups: Anglo American (72.3 percent), African American (13.4 percent), Hispanic (9.2 percent), Asian American (4.3 percent), and Native American (0.8 percent). As the graduation rates increase, the dropout rates for the same groups decrease.

According to the National Center for Education Statistics, the total percentage of nineteen- to twenty-year-olds who had dropped out of school in 1991 by ethnic and racial group was: Anglo Americans (10.7 percent), African Americans (16.9 percent), and Hispanic Americans (35.9 percent). All dropout rates had declined since 1972 when the rate was 13.1 percent for Anglo Americans, 26.8 percent for African Americans, and 38.0 percent for Hispanic Americans (U.S. Department of Education 1993b, 58).

One of the reasons for decreases in the dropout rate is that many programs designed to work with at-risk students have been implemented. According to the National School Boards Association report *A Survey of Public Education in the Nation's Urban School Districts* (1989), half of the urban school districts have programs for at-risk students. At-risk students are defined as those who may be classified as or who are involved with one or more of the following:

- Substance abuse
- Suicide attempt/depression/low self-esteem
- Child abuse (physical, emotional, verbal, or sexual)
- Poverty
- Child of alcohol or substance abuser
- Illiteracy
- A migrant lifestyle
- School dropout
- Sexual activity/pregnancy
- Crime
- Minority
- Student with disability (Helge 1990)

Indications that the dropout rate is declining also can be found in the encouraging statistic that, although 17 percent of sophomores dropped out of school in 1980, almost half returned to receive a high school diploma or equivalency certificate by 1986. See figure 9.2 for a graph of the event dropout rates from grades ten through twelve. An event dropout rate measures the proportion of students who drop out during a twelve-month period (see chapter 12). Special programs for at-risk students must begin as early as the third grade, according to Ernest Boyer in *High School* (1983).

The National Coalition of Advocates for Children (NCAS) recommends several strategies for beginning early dropout prevention.

- Use many and varied teaching approaches.
- Use small cooperative learning groups.

---

**9-1**

**POINTS TO REMEMBER**

- The typical public school is heterogeneous in terms of its student population. The demographic reality of the U.S. population is that it is increasingly minority and immigrant.
- Nearly 11.6 percent of all students in public and private schools are classified as special education, meaning they are learning or physically disabled, emotionally disturbed, or mentally disabled.

- Students from numerous ethnic and racial groups bring a multiplicity of problems into the classroom.
- Although most students are motivated to do well in elementary school, they lose much motivation in high school, except when they are actively involved.
- Although working while attending a school can decrease motivation to learn, research shows that urban, minority teens can gain valuable work and job skills.
- Students at the same age levels have similar interests

based on their development. Today's students watch more television than students of previous generations as well as read less and do less homework. Students' values tend to be rather traditional. Most report a belief in God and value the importance of adults in their lives. Today's students also have many worries about getting good grades, avoiding drugs, and making money.
- Although the dropout rate has declined in the last decade, it is still a problem in many states, particularly where there are large minority populations.

- Stimulate internal motivation.
- Increase student and teacher interaction.
- Integrate language skills across the entire curriculum.
- Monitor student success.
- Provide strong guidance programs. (NCAS 1993, 105)

Other options, suggests N. L. Gage in his summary of programs that work, *Dealing with the Dropout Problem* (1990), include vocational programs that remove potential dropouts from traditional school settings, place them in new environments, and allow them to apply their academic learning to real-life situations. Connecting these programs with paid employment is also helpful. Gage also suggests that low student-teacher ratios are needed so that a bond between teacher and student can form. With this mutual trust it is more likely that at-risk students will stay in school and graduate.

## The Life of a Student

During a single day in the life of a teacher as many as one hundred fifty students may pass through the classroom door. Even though it may be difficult, teachers should know as much about their students as possible.

They can do this by reflecting on what it was like to be a child, a preteen, or a teenager. However, this perspective is limited by time, place, and individual experiences. What it was like to be a child growing up in suburban Connecticut may be different from what it was like growing up in the rural South or the ghettos of a large midwestern city. Although most teachers can empathize with students who are disabled or who do not speak English, they would, of course, find it difficult to understand another's experiences completely.

### SIMILARITIES OF AGEMATES

Teachers frequently comment that despite significant individual differences, students seem similar in many respects. It's not unusual, for example, to hear a teacher say, "If one more student asks how to do that assignment, I'll scream." Frequently, similarities in how students think and act are a result of their age and developmental characteristics. The physical, intellectual, emotional, social, and moral characteristics of early adolescents and later teens have been studied with common developmental patterns seeming to emerge.

In fact, a special-issue cover story in *Newsweek*, "The New Teens: What Makes Them Different" (1990), contends, in a somewhat humorous classification, that teenagers can be divided into four groups: malljammers, house hoppers, video vogues, and neonormals. Although there are differences in terms of the activities and interests of these distinct groups, there are far more similarities. For example, almost all today's teens like movies and television, but the types of programs they select differ. All teens are consumers, buying clothes, records, and videos. However, what they choose to purchase within these categories differs. For example, in 1990, according to *Newsweek*, malljammers favored Paula Abdul, the movie *Pretty Woman,* the television show "America's Funniest Home Videos," cruising, and Dick Tracy T-shirts. The house hoppers selected Technotronic, the movie *House Party,* the television show "The Simpsons," line dancing, and suede Fila hightops. The video vogues liked Madonna, the film *Blue Velvet,* the television show "Twin Peaks," thrift shopping, and nose rings; and the neonormals selected the Grateful Dead, the movie *Driving Miss Daisy,* the television program "Doogie Howser, M.D.," volleyball, and Gap pocket T-shirts (Gelman, 11–17).

## DIFFERENCES OF AGEMATES

Teachers also recognize significant differences in how students of the same age behave and learn. "I can't believe these kids are the same age and the same ability level. The second period students are so enthusiastic, so eager to learn. I hate it when the bell rings and third period arrives. Third period students are so impressed with themselves, so cruel to each other."

Differences occur because each group of students is made up of individuals, and, even if the classroom, teacher, and subject are the same, there are subtle variations in the physical and social environment from one class hour to the next. The personalities of the students are affected by the differing environments, each class acquiring its own individual personality much as each family does.

# How Students Develop

Psychologists have documented the developmental characteristics of human beings that help explain both why agemates are similar and why they are different. First we will discuss the cognitive, needs, psychosocial, and moral development of humans as outlined by Piaget, Maslow, Erikson, and Kohlberg and then present several student diaries. In reading the diaries, see if you can determine which stage of development the student is manifesting.

## COGNITIVE DEVELOPMENT: PIAGET

Jean Piaget, a Swiss psychologist, was the first to document the cognitive growth of humans. He believed that children learn because their developing mental structures are challenged by what they observe and experience in the environment, which in turn results in the development of a more complex mental structure or scheme. He defined **scheme** as an organized pattern of behavior or thought that children formulate as they attempt to interact with their environments, parents, teachers, and agemates. By relating new experiences to an existing scheme through assimilation, a child develops a sense of **equilibrium**, or balance. Or, a child may accommodate for a lack of equilibrium by modifying an existing scheme or developing a new one.

Piaget believed that there are two processes required in cognitive development. The first, **assimilation**, allows the child to integrate a new stimulus into existing schemes. For example, a child learns that there are dogs that look different from his dog but are still dogs. He has assimilated the concept of different breeds of dogs into his scheme of dog.

However, if a new concept cannot be assimilated, a scheme must be changed or a new scheme must be developed. Piaget calls this **accommodation**. For example, a child has learned that dogs and cats are pets. He has a pet dog and plays with him regularly; when he pets the dog, it wags its tail. One day when the child is walking with his mother they see a dog across the street. The child says, "Doggy, doggy," and moves toward the dog. The dog runs to the child, jumps up on him, and knocks him to the ground. The child begins to cry. There is a need to reestablish equilibrium in his cognitive structure; his existing scheme has been challenged, and, therefore, he must accommodate the new experience by developing a new scheme.

Piaget postulated several recognizable stages of development that follow a sequential but uneven or zigzag pattern. These stages begin at birth and continue through adulthood.

*Sensorimotor Period*   According to Piaget, the earliest period in the child's development, between the ages of birth and two years, is the **sensorimotor period**. Marked by the development of reflexes and responses, it involves the practicing and experimentation of motor responses that are increasingly complex. Perception patterns usually begin between eight and twelve months. By the end of this period, the child recognizes that an object may exist even if he can't see it, a skill called **object permanence**.

*Preoperational Period*   The second stage of cognitive development is the **preoperational period**, which occurs between two and seven years of age. At this stage, children acquire language and learn to represent the environment with objects and symbols. At the earliest period of this stage, children infuse their inanimate world with conscious attributes, behavior that Piaget referred to as **animism**. For example, the child plays with dolls and stuffed animals and gives them names and human characteristics. Some children develop imaginary playmates and create an entire world around these imaginary friends. Children at this stage are **egocentric**; they see the world as revolving around themselves. By the latter period of this stage, children can group objects into classes according to their similarities. However, they are frequently unable to discuss the features common to a given class of objects. Hence, they can think intuitively and solve problems, but often they cannot explain the steps they used in solving the problem.

*Concrete Operational Period*   The **concrete operational period**, ages seven to eleven, is characterized by an ability to solve problems through reasoning and thinking symbolically with words and numbers and by grouping into hierarchies by similarities. For example, Piaget suggests in *The Child's Conception of Number* (1952) that if a child at the preoperational stage is given twenty brown and two white wooden beads, the child will agree that all the beads are wooden and that twenty are brown and two are white. If the child is asked, "Are there more wooden beads or more brown beads?" the child is likely to answer that there are more brown beads. This is because the child can compare the classes of brown and white but cannot compare the subclass of brown beads to the larger class of wooden beads. However, at the concrete operational stage, the child will demonstrate the **principle of inclusion** and will respond that the class of brown beads is of necessity smaller than the class of wooden beads. Children at this stage are able to consider differences (nonbrown beads) as well as similarities and can reason about the relationships between classes and subclasses.

Children at the concrete operational stage can also order objects in a series. For example, they can group beads from large to small or small to large. Children at this stage also demonstrate the principle of **conservation**, the ability to recognize the difference between volume and size. If, for example, during the preoperational period you show a child a glass of water in a short, wide glass and pour that water into a tall, narrow glass, it is likely that the child will say that there is more water in the tall glass because she or he does not see the two containers as equivalent in volume. By the concrete operational period, the child recognizes that the amount of water is the same no matter what size container it is in. At this stage, children also show **reversal**, the ability to work a problem backward. In addition, concrete operational children **decenter**; they learn that their perspective is only one of many perspectives. They begin to understand the viewpoints of others.

*Formal Operational Period*    Finally, according to Piaget, humans enter the **formal operational period** between the age of eleven and adulthood. This stage is characterized by abstract, logical, hypothetical reasoning, and systematic experimentation. They can think through the implications and complex relationships of ideas; they can approach problems by thinking through several possible solutions.

Despite the importance of Piaget's work in cognitive development, he is the object of much criticism, primarily that cognitive development is more gradual than he had suggested (Flavel 1982) and that the age levels Piaget placed on the stages tend to be too high (Gelman and Gallistel 1978).

## DEVELOPMENT OF NEEDS: MASLOW

Psychologist Abraham Maslow developed a hierarchy to show graphically how a human meets individual needs; he or she must first meet one level of needs before achieving the next.

The lowest levels of needs are the **physiological** and **safety** needs. The individual must have food, health, warmth, and shelter before working toward the second level, represented by the **belonging or love** needs. The individual must feel wanted and loved before achieving the next level, the **esteem** needs, self-respect, achievement, and status. Once the individual feels personally confident, he or she can begin to seek the higher levels of needs called by Maslow **knowledge or understanding** and **aesthetics**. The need for knowledge is the need to understand one's environment while the need for aesthetics is the need for beauty. Once all these needs have been met, an individual may be able to attain the highest human need of **self-actualization**, reaching one's full human potential.

Generally an individual progresses upward on the needs hierarchy but it is also possible to progress downward. For example, if a child's parents divorce, she or he may feel alone and unwanted, causing the child to withdraw and/or seek attention from others rather than focus on learning.

It is also possible that striving to meet one set of needs may get in the way of meeting a higher set of needs. The adolescent who strives to be part of a peer

**TABLE 9-3**

## Erikson's Theory: Stages of Psychosocial Development

| Psychosocial state | Approximate age | Elements for positive outcomes |
| --- | --- | --- |
| Trust v. mistrust | 0–1 yr. | Infant's needs for nourishment, care, familiarity are met; parental responsiveness and consistency |
| Autonomy v. shame and doubt | Toddler period (1–2 yrs.) | Greater control of self in environment—self-feeding, toileting, dressing; parental reassurance, availability, avoidance of overprotection |
| Initiative v. guilt | Early childhood (2–6 yrs.) | Pursuing activity for its own sake; learning to accept without guilt that certain things are not allowed; imagination, play-acting adult roles |
| Industry v. inferiority | Elementary–Middle school (6–12 yrs.) | Discovery of pleasure in perseverance and productivity; neighborhood, school, and peer interaction becomes increasingly important |
| Identity v. role confusion | Adolescence | Conscious search for identity, built upon outcomes of previous crises |
| Intimacy v. isolation | Young adulthood | Openness and commitment to others in deepening relationships |
| Generativity v. stagnation | Young and middle adulthood | Having and nurturing children and/or involvement with future generations; productivity; creativity |
| Integrity v. despair | Later adulthood; old age | Consolidation of identity; sense of fulfillment; acceptance of death |

From: Erikson, *Childhood and Society* (1963), 272, 273.

> **Erikson believed that human emotional and social development occurred in stages and that conflicts must be resolved for positive relationships to develop. Thus, if adolescents don't successfully find their identity in their teens, they are likely to be confused about their roles throughout their lives.**

group, even if that group violates the values the adolescent has been taught, may find it impossible to meet the higher level, esteem needs. It is difficult to feel good about one's self if behaviors are counter to personal beliefs.

### PSYCHOSOCIAL DEVELOPMENT: ERIKSON

Psychologist Erik Erikson became interested in the relationship between child-rearing and culture as a result of his interest in the work of psychologist Sigmund Freud. Erikson studied child-rearing practices in several societies and concluded that there were recurrent themes in emotional/social development even when the cultures differed. Erikson identified goals, concerns, accomplishments, and dangers that mark each stage from infancy to adulthood. According to Erikson, the stages are interdependent; accomplishments at any stage depend on how conflicts were resolved at earlier stages. If individuals successfully deal with a crisis at one stage, they have the foundation for dealing with a similar crisis at a subsequent stage (see table 9.3). Thus, an infant should learn trust in others in the first stage. If he or she is not loved adequately or cared for appropriately, then mistrust will develop instead and may be a problem for the individual throughout life.

## MORAL DEVELOPMENT: KOHLBERG

Psychologist Lawrence Kohlberg examined the moral development of the individual. He based his theory, in part, on Piaget's stages of cognitive development. Kohlberg believed that individuals develop moral reasoning in a pattern, passing through three levels of development, each with two stages.

The first level, **preconventional moral reasoning**, is characteristic of very young children. At this level, moral judgments are based on expectation of rewards or punishments. In stage I, rules are obeyed to avoid punishment; in stage II, compliance with rules is based on the expectation of reward.

Older children typically employ the second level of moral reasoning, **conventional moral reasoning**, basing their judgments on others' approval, family expectations, traditional values, the laws of society, and loyalty to country. At the first stage, behavior is predicated on the approval of others. At the second stage of this level, moral behavior is based on law and authority in an attempt to avoid guilt and formal censure. It is important to note that many people never move beyond this stage of moral reasoning.

The final level of the development of moral reasoning, is that of **postconventional moral reasoning**. In its first stage, good is determined by socially agreed-upon standards of individual rights and democratically determined laws. In the final stage of postconventional reasoning, the individual possesses a universal ethical principle. "Good and right are matters of individual conscience and involve abstract concepts of justice, human dignity, and equality" (Kohlberg 1981, 409–412). This is a stage of moral development reached by few people.

It is important to note that the work of both Erikson and Kohlberg has been criticized because their research centered on the psychosocial and moral development of males. In "Adolescent Development Reconsidered" (1988), Carol Gilligan attempts to show "an alternative world view . . . [which] called attention to moral judgments that did not fit the definition of 'moral' and to self-descriptions at odds with the concept of 'self' " [in studies of moral development of male subjects only]. Gilligan found "two moral voices [male and female] signaled different ways of thinking about what constitutes a moral problem and how such problems can be addressed or solved" (p. xvii). The males focused primarily on justice, and the females on justice and care and concern for others. She suggests that these two modes of moral judgment develop because of the definition of self based on gender (p. 23).

## School from the Perspective of Students

Although teachers can know a great deal about their students, they rarely have the opportunity to see the school day from the students' perspective. To give you some insight into the lives of students, we asked several, at various grade levels from different geographic regions, to keep diaries.

## A FIRST GRADER: SARAH

Sarah Bachinski is a first grader in a small Vermont city. Sarah's account of each school day is primarily factual. She provides us with few details, particularly in the earlier entries. This may be because Sarah's written vocabulary is limited. Sarah wrote the diary entries herself; the "creative" spelling has not been changed.

> Jan. 16: Monring—We wrote to are pen pels in North Carolina today. We wrote in our fun book. Thaey are books waht you wraht in and dare dare in.
> Affotarnon—We went to Sing a long. My clas Sang the Soing WaSh WaSh WaSh your handS. We did manth waht mrss. mory.
> Jan. 20: Friday—I red to radenise Conagrdn. Wan I got bake I wark on our garnd.
> Aftrnoon—Mr. Schwarz red a book to us. We did the math Bard.

By May, Sarah's descriptions give us a lot more information. Sarah is developing, growing intellectually, socially, and emotionally. She is learning many things and writing more fluently. It's also interesting to note that, with the exception of Mr. Schwarz's oral reading, all Sarah's comments relate to activities in which she is actively engaged.

> May 25: We fond a letter from Mr. Schwarz it siad I wold liKe you to write story problems. We Sang Down By the Bay. Mr. Schwarz riad The Trip by Ezra Jack Keats. Sh word. We made shadow boxs. We hade SSR Silent reading. One grop The Monster Pals Shared their flannel board Stories. 2nd graade came in to read to us. We hade library. We hade Gim. We had Math adding Two numbers. We used the blacklight and the numbers glowed.
> May 31: We made cards for Mrs. Dodd becass She is on crcs. We read books by Ezra Jack Keats and collages. We hade SSr. Mr. Schwarz did reading tests. We got ready for the field trip. We had storyproblems written by the class.
> June 1: We went to our filed trip. We hade fun. We huged trees. We went on trals. We hade lanh ther too. We iesprmt woder. We want on a nahtr hike togatter. We saw tepes. Thay were neht. We sow a Indin boat.

## A SECOND GRADER: JULIE

Second-grader Julie Harvell kept her own diary. Julie goes to school in a suburban community in North Carolina. The details that Julie writes about school and how she reacts to it, compared to the lack of details and limited reactions in the early entries of Sarah's diary, show some interesting developmental changes that usually occur during the early elementary grades. Piaget identified this as a preoperational stage and Erikson called this stage manipulation of objects. In addition, note how much more concerned Julie is about her relationship to her friends than is Sarah, who never mentions a friend. This, too, is developmentally appropriate. Julie's "creative" spelling has been left as she wrote it. Notice how her spelling develops throughout the diary.

> Sept. 12: Today was a good day because we hade art. We leard a bought secondary colors. We had Math and did problems. In reading we sumerrized. In social studies we leard abought maps.

Sept. 13: Today was sort of sort of day. Becaus at playtime me an Rachel wanted to talk privtley. And Rebecc and Amee wien't leave us alone. We hade music today. With therd grdrs. Brodon and Mike gote ther nams on the bord. You are nice Techs Ms. Galeason and Mrs. Denon.

Sept. 14: I was sapos to read today but Kean took to long I do not mind. We hade putis made. We hade math abought ghfsi bacly.

We sarted a studd of dnoaisors. Today was a good day. Becas of picis. [The class had school pictures taken.]

Feb. 13: Today we sewed up harts. Tomorrow is Valentine's Day. In writing we learned how to make the captil D and S. At lunch I sat next to John and Brooke. After math the people that brought their valentines delivered them. Today is great.

Feb. 14: Today was great! We have no homework. In math all we had to do was eight problems. I got alot of valentines. It's my sisters birthday. In hand-writing we learned the cusive captil S and G. [Julie wrote her "S" and "G" in cursive lettering.]

May 22: Today was an O.K. day. I wore some sandles to school and people kept stepping on my feet! What was good is that we got our year books and I got to go to the computer.

## A FIFTH GRADER: JESSICA

Jessica Condits is a fifth-grade student in a growing community on the east coast of Florida. Jessica's diary is filled with details, a concern about time, and the things she likes about school. Jessica, like Sarah and Julie, responds most favorably to learning in which she is actively involved. Her exact, vivid description of the fifth-grade field trip is particularly revealing in that it corresponds to Piaget's concrete stage. It is interesting to compare her report to Sarah's description of her first-grade field trip. Also, notice that Jessica is concerned about her friends and how they are feeling. However, when one gets hurt, she is more concerned about celebrating her own birthday than about her friend's injury. This, of course, is developmentally appropriate for a ten-year-old.

Jan. 23: Everyday before school I work in the Library as an aide. I put books away and straighten them. At 8:40 the bell rings and I go to class. At 8:55 we listen to announcements on the intercom. Then at 9:00 we go to a special class (on Monday we have music). We played the sticks and the two tambourines. Music was fun.

After Music we go to the Computer Lab from 9:40 to 10:00. When we get back to class we work on spelling.

At 10:15–11:05 we change classes for reading. Then my class goes to science from 11:05–11:35. The other two classes—one goes to English and the other goes to Social Studies.

From 11:35–12:05 my class goes to English. Then we go back to class. I think it's fun to change classes because in reading I can see my other friends.

When we go back to the classroom we put our books down and get ready for lunch. We have lunch from 12:20–12:45. I like lunch because it's one of the times I can talk to my friends in my class.

On Monday we go to art from 12:50–1:25. Then we go back to our class to work on Social Studies and Math.

At 2:50 the bell rings and I go to the Library and put my books away. I can't wait until tomorrow because we will get our pen pal letters.

In order to help them preserve their culture, these Chippewa Indian high school students are attending summer courses at Bemidji State University in northern Minnesota. Here they practice a four-man carry that teaches them how to carry game for long distances. Among the usual classes in biology, computer science, and algebra, they also take classes in traditional woodland pottery and native medicine.

Jan. 26: Today was my birthday and we went to P.E. and my best friend hurt her ankle and she had to go home. My mom made a cake and I brought it to school and it was delicious. I had a fun day.

In social studies we did a play.

Jan. 27: Today our class didn't have a special class at 9:00.

After Computer Lab we went to an assembly on lungs. He had a laryngectomy. I got to use the devise they use to talk. I thought the assembly was interesting.

May 24: On Wednesday the whole fifth grade went on a river trip. There were 6 different stations. The first station my group went to was canoeing. We Canoed on part of the Indian River. At station 2 we tried to catch different creatures with a net. Next at station 3 we dug up sand and put it through a sifter to see what different creatures live in the sand. Then we went to station 4. We walked up into some water to see the 3 different kinds of mangroves. Some parts of the sand were squishy and we almost lost our shoes! At station 5 we went out on boats and saw different islands. At station 6 we learned how to clean fish and got to try crab. I didn't try any.

It was a fun day but my best friend and I were split up so one was in one group and one in the other.

That afternoon I didn't feel good so my mom took me to the doctor and I had a strep infection.

## NATIVE AMERICAN CHILDREN

Native American children in Cherokee, North Carolina, have similar concerns about school, but also see it in another light; they emphasize the role of the teacher and transmittal of culture.

"School is wonderful to me. It is big, pretty, roomy, and it is my teacher."
(Nikki Labrado, age ten, fifth grade)

"School is learning from your teacher about your culture. You learn things you have not been taught to do at home. You learn to make friends at school."
(Lechay Arch, age ten, fifth grade)

"School is a teacher who gets you to be curious."
(Steven Brady, age twelve, fifth grade)

"School is fun and full of learning. It is preparing for college. It is getting an education and recess."
(Jamie Kirkland, age eleven, fifth grade)

## TWO IMMIGRANT STUDENTS

Jose Ernesto Sanchez, 12 years old, is typical of the immigrants, who increasingly come from small, rural villages, school administrators said. A month ago, he immigrated to Queens from the El Salvadoran village of Santana, where the school had a dirt floor and only 15 students.

Though he speaks no English, he has already made several new friends at P.S. 19, including some from El Salvador, and is learning to cope with the hustle-bustle of a school that is considerably more populous than his entire hometown.

"I like it here because it's so big," he said of the school, tugging shyly at a T-shirt that reads, "New York State of Mind."

Randy Batista vividly recalls the hardships he encountered when he arrived from the Dominican Republic two years ago, his eyes filling with tears as he describes his first homework assignments in English.

In fluent English, the 10-year-old talks longingly of his native village, where cows roamed through the tomato plants and banana trees in his family's large yard. "Sometimes I wish I could go back," he said. (Dao, May 25, 1992, B22)

## A TWELVE-YEAR-OLD IN A RESOURCE ROOM

At school, some teachers are trying to help. But sitting in one class, a "resource room" tailored to give troubled students individual attention, Crystal slumped on her desk. "We just sit there," she said later. "They are supposed to help you with stuff you don't understand. But I understand everything so I just sit there."

"Kids who study are all nerds," she said dismissively. "Who'd want to be like that? Everybody makes fun of them."

But the kids make fun of one another for failing, too.

"Stooopid," Crystal taunted a friend in the resource room one morning.

"No, you're stupid, stupid," the girl retorted.

"No. You. You're stupid," Crystal shot back, her head resting on her desk top.

Most days, Crystal says, she is usually happy only at lunch, when she and her friends bend over pizza and sandwiches "just talking." The time brings them together, jostling and punching and trading stories of their day. Sometimes they vanish into a bathroom and plant thick lipstick kisses—perfect O's—on one another's foreheads. Their mark of solidarity against a world too often hostile. (Mangold, April 8, 1993, B7)

## AN EIGHTH GRADER: SANDEE

Sandee Cramer is an eighth grader in an independent school in Massachusetts. According to Sandee's homeroom teacher, she is a good, not outstanding, but enthusiastic student. Sandee writes only about her science class in this diary. Notice the reasons that she does not enjoy the class. She shows more discontent with school than the younger students. She is less accepting of what the teacher asks her to do. She tends to be more negative about school and places the blame for her lack of interest on her teacher. This is not only because the inactivity in the class bores her, but also because young adolescents are not yet developmentally aware of how their own behavior affects them and others. However, she is beginning to recognize that errors she makes are a result of her own effort. Sandee is developmentally typical. The names in this diary have been changed.

> Feb. 13: Science Class 1:40–2:18
> I am so bored, why doesn't Mr. Bridgers actually try to do something exciting. I am sick of the regular note taking and lectures. This class is so boring. I could fall asleep any time. Abby is sitting next to me, she looks as bored as I do. 2:10 only 8 more minutes. I'm starting to fall asleep. I hate Mr. Bridgers, he is so boring.
> Feb. 14: Science—2:10–2:42

It is the last class of the day, thank God. I can't wait until it is over. Mr. Bridgers is so boring. This class might actually be fun if we did something. All we ever do is sit and build up our finger muscles by taking notes. Genes how exciting can they be, more than this. Finally the bell. I hate this class.

Feb. 16: Science, 8:55–9:36

First period, what a way to start the day, a test. We have our genetics test today, wonderful, just what I need. It isn't that long but each question counts for 20 points. I think I got a 60 or 80, mostly because of stupid mistakes. At least tests make the day go by faster.

## INNER-CITY STUDENTS

Wilkerson Middle School in Birmingham, Alabama, is an inner-city school of 475, mostly poor, African American students. They shared their ideas about school and education with us. Notice their emphasis on the environment of the school.

"School is a place were [sic] learning takes place. School is place were talent is born. School is not something that should be taken lightly. But most of all school is fun." (April Harris, age eleven, sixth grade)

"School is a place of fundamental opportunities in which people are taught different subjects and skills. It is a place where people learn to communicate with others and share ideas. It's a place where people prepare for the future and get a headstart for what they want to do and be, so they can lead successful and meaningful lives . . ." (Kimberly Ogletree, age twelve, seventh grade)

"School is an institution with a body of teachers and learners and a place to be disciplined." (Ronesial Moye, age thirteen, seventh grade)

"School is a large family house. It is also a large brain for ideas. School is the place where young minds can be creative. All great minds started out in school. This large housing brain encloses a family. It houses many people of different backgrounds, shapes, sizes, colors, and ideas. Despite the differences, all are the same. They all start as inputs, working daily to be great outputs, learning to lead and challenge the world and trying to build a new beginning. THE SCHOOL—A FAMILY HOUSE." (Phaedra L. Riley, age fourteen, eighth grade)

## A NINTH GRADER: DARIUS

Darius Baker is a ninth-grade student in a magnet school in South Miami, Florida. He is more concerned with what he is doing in school than Sandee is. He tells us that he is "task person" and is going on a field trip to a TV station. Although he seems to be interested in much of what is going on in school, particularly as it relates to his magnet program, he, like the other early adolescents, is bored with traditional subjects such as geography. It is interesting to compare how much he writes about the field trip and how little he writes about geography and math. Darius is proud of his accomplishments. He takes his job as "task person" seriously and tells us that their broadcast is on now, "5–4–3–2–1 !!!!" He uses the slang of his generation, but is able to write quite well. However, at times he becomes careless and writes "to" for two and "there" for they are. This is typical of students of Darius's age.

Class 1, October 1, 1991

8:45 class started. I am task person for the week. They think I'm playing but I'm serious! I told them to be quiet, they keep talking, their names go down. The day's going by smooth, It seems as if it'll be a perfect day.

Class 2, October 1, 1991

9:40 class started second half of class one. I have to work on my group project. I like doing it because it contains music videos, I like rap videos.

Class 3, October 1, 1991

10:45 the 3rd class has started. Its a little dull now. Were about to color a map—of Egypt.—Mr. Parker's telling us the four directions N.S.E.W.

Class One/Two, Oct. 2–91

Its another beautiful day first period. I'm in broadcastin' now—It's quiet that's cool.

Class Three, Oct 2–91

Its alright today, better than yesterday. I think I'll go to the Afro Club meeting or library, if he let's me go—I know he will! He's nice!

Class 4, Oct 2

I'm chillin' in math—I had to assignment that cool there easy. Becide I'm workin' with someone I can associate with.

Class 1, Oct. 3

8:45 I'm still task person. Were doing newsroom, setting up for our broadcast. We are eating lunch, at ten thirty today. Due to a field trip. What kind of trip? To channel 23, its a spanish station. I don't know too much spanish—I dont know any spanish. We're gonna be an audience anyway—They're going to do a broadcast for us. Their camera, computers and newsrooms are busting! They make our school, want to do undercover work! We're back!!!!! Its sixth period now—Im in science our broadcast goes on now! 5 4 3 2 1 !!!!

*Viewpoint*  Finding a Way: The Quest of Derrick, 19

From his mother, Shirley White, his stepfather, Wardell Horton, and his high school counselors and neighbors who have heaped their own hopes upon him, he [Derrick White] has soaked up the message that the safest and surest route out of welfare and the project is a good job.

Yet to go much beyond McDonald's, Derrick, who is 19, needs college. And his prospects have blurred since his dashing performance at Northside High. In September he fulfilled a dream, going to the other end of the state to attend the University of Tennessee in Chattanooga on a full scholarship. But in January, worried about fees and troubles at home, he dropped out.

A Northside counselor then steered him to a college in Memphis. But for lack of financial aid, he left in February. He says he will enroll in still another college in June. Even if he does, he will have lost a semester of his freshman year and sidetracked his progress toward a career. . . .

Derrick says he wants to be a doctor, an obstetrician. On a school trip last year to colleges and medical schools, he met a black pediatric neurosurgeon in Baltimore named Ben Carson. After a childhood of poverty and delinquency, Dr. Carson won renown six years ago for successfully separating Siamese twins joined at the head. . . .

While he waits to return to school, he scrounges for work. In March, he earned $276 working for a radio station that put a temporary studio in Hurt Village. Since then he has been tutoring the 16-year-old granddaughter of a prominent black Memphis woman in math and science, and is paid $10 a visit. . . .

He says he just barely avoided one form of employment that entraps many young men. The summer before he started the 11th grade and his job at McDonald's, he considered quitting school to sell drugs.

"I wanted some things my friends had," he said. "I knew what they were doing to get them." . . .

Since McDonald's, he has had four jobs—the two this winter, one the summer of his junior year cleaning public parks and roadsides, and one last summer as a clerk at the Memphis Health Center.

Derrick White doesn't have a real role model nearby, but Hurt Village might have one in him. He will get past his unsettled debut in college, he said.

"I know what I got to do," Derrick said. "There's so much I want, that my family wants. They see me giving up, then they think they should give up."

Obstacles are just part of the game. "It's like a hand being dealt you," he said. "You just got to play it. Get people behind me. I know I'm going to make it."

From: Kilborn, April 22, 1993, A1.

## ARE THESE STUDENTS TYPICAL?

If you look back at the earlier developmental characteristics of today's students, (pp. 367–371), you will see many of them reflected in these diaries and in the In the Classroom and Viewpoints features that appear throughout this chapter. Most of these students want to do well in school and are, for the most part, enthusiastic about what they do. They enjoy participating in schoolwork and are less enthusiastic about subjects in which they must sit and listen. Some are bored and frustrated by school, but most are doing their best.

The students are not particularly interested in doing homework. Second-grader Julie says, "Today was great! We have no homework." However, several of the students, including Julie, mention specific books they are reading. In addition, the adults in their lives are important; the students are concerned about what their parents and teachers think of them. They are concerned about doing well in school and getting good grades. Derrick, for example, credits his mother's work ethic with his success in school.

All of the students, particularly by late elementary school, want to fit in. For them, that means being a part of their peer group. This is of particular concern for the newest immigrants like Jose and Randy. It is also a concern for students like Martha Florence Vedrine who was born in the United States of Haitian parents who taught her to speak Creole. She wonders if she is Haitian or American and is searching for her own identity as a citizen of two cultures.

## ARE THE STUDENTS DEVELOPING?

It is clear that the students cited in this chapter are learning and developing in ways representative of students their age and opportunities.

First-grader Sarah's language makes remarkable gains in five months. By May she doesn't just tell us that Mr. Schwarz read us a book today, as she did in January, she tells us the book is by Ezra Jack Keats. Although Sarah may have hugged a tree in September, she wouldn't have told us so. However, by May she is telling us that she "hugged trees" and made a card for Mrs. Dodd because she is

Derrick White is a young man in search of a dream that will carry him and his family out of the Hurt Village housing project where they live. Fifteenth in a class of 299, Derrick has won awards for outstanding band member, for the highest grade point average on the football team, and for king of the senior prom. Yet even with a scholarship, he couldn't pay all the fees required at the University of Tennessee, so dropped out after one semester. He is struggling to save money to attend a different school.

on crutches. In spite of the fact that Sarah spells crutches "crcs," she is willing to attempt the word in order to put more detail into her writing. She is gaining confidence in herself. Sarah is also learning how to tell stories. Her May entries frequently cover an entire page and tell things like what the children did after Mr. Schwarz read to them.

We can also see Sarah's growth and development exhibited through her diary. For example, Sarah's success in learning how to use language allows her to write a word even when she knows she cannot spell it. Her language learning is helping her become more confident and independent. Sarah is growing developmentally as the first-grade year progresses.

Perhaps the most remarkable development can be seen in Lacy Grissom, the six-year-old boy we meet in the feature In the Classroom (see pp. 347–349). What makes Lacy's development so impressive is that no one really expected him to grow. He was both physically and mentally disabled. His mother had coddled him and the school had labeled him. A remarkable teacher, however, knew that hidden beneath his bent back were a mind and a body that with nurturing could grow and develop. And, as Madeline Cartwright tells us, Lacy not only grew in the first grade, but continued his growth for the five years he spent in Blaine Elementary School.

Julie Harvell, who is in the second grade, is also learning what she has been taught. In September she spells "had" "hade" and "learned" "leard," but she knows how to spell "social studies" and "secondary colors." She has been taught to spell these words. And she has also been taught to spell words the way they sound. That's why she spells "summarized" "sumerrized," a very intelligent misspelling. By May she has learned to spell "had" and "learned." Julie is learning the conventions of the English language.

By second grade, Julie's diary is more descriptive. She, like Sarah, still enjoys school most when she can be active. She is concerned about her relationships with her friends. She talks frequently of her friends and comments on her classmates who get their names on the "bord," presumably because they have misbehaved. She talks about school in terms of good or bad days. Good days are when learning is active, when there is no homework, and when she can be with her friends. Children of Julie's age frequently see situations as good or bad, black or white.

Fifth-grader Jessica is learning how she learns. She tells us in detail about the assembly on lungs and the field trip to the river. Jessica doesn't tell us much about what she is learning in English, but we observe what she has learned as we compare her January diary entries, where she mostly lists, to her May entries, where she describes in detail.

In the fifth grade Jessica is increasingly concerned with her friends. She has a best friend who hurts her ankle on Jessica's birthday and is in a different group than she is on the field trip. The idea of a best friend is very important to Jessica, and she looks forward to times when she can talk to her friends at school. In fact, she is more concerned with her friends than she is with what she is doing in school. Jessica, too, is meeting the developmental tasks of her age group. By the time students reach the age of ten, they are increasingly concerned with having friends and becoming part of a peer group. Preteenagers are also becoming increasingly concerned with helping others and are willing to accept more responsibility than the younger students. Jessica, for example, works in the school library each morning as a volunteer. However, although students of Jessica's age have a broader world view than students of Julie's age, they are still more concerned about their own social needs than the welfare of a friend. Although Jessica expresses concern that her friend hurt her ankle, her primary thoughts center on her own birthday party.

But, what of Jose, Randy, and Crystal? Are they developing and growing? We know that both Jose and Randy feel isolated. They are new to the country and new to their school. It is difficult for immigrant children who often do not speak English to become a part of a school. And, for many of these children, even the concept and culture of school is new. Children who come from underdeveloped nations may never have attended school, or may have only been in a poor school lacking equipment and trained teachers for only a few years. So, for many of these students, English is not their only problem. Many of them cannot read and compute in their native language. For those who grow socially and academically, their development may appear delayed, but when the obstacles they have overcome are taken into account, their development is frequently remarkable.

Sandee is in the eighth grade and in the midst of adolescence. Like most students her age, she is less satisfied with school than younger students. Although she is still concerned with how her teachers perceive her, she blames her lack of success on her teachers. She is egocentric. However, toward the end of the eighth-grade year, Sandee is beginning to realize that her mistakes may be her own. She complains about how boring her science class is, how dull the teacher makes it, but, after the test, she acknowledges, "I think I got a 60 or 80, mostly because of stupid mistakes." Sandee, like most students her age, is beginning to accept some responsibility for her own actions. If she continues to develop normally, what her teachers do will matter less and less. She will learn because she knows that only she is responsible for her own learning.

Darius, who is in ninth grade, is more contented with school than Sandee is. He is maturing and displays an interest in broadcasting and in his accomplishments. He uses the slang of his peers, but doesn't focus on his interaction with them. Like the other adolescents, he finds some of his academic subjects boring and likes it when he finds them easy. He does not yet focus on the world beyond high school; he is still consumed with his day-to-day activities.

Derrick is a student who developed despite the difficulties inherent in his life of poverty. He managed to succeed in school while others took to the streets. His mother was his inspiration—she believed in him. Now, Derrick has new challenges. Can he continue to develop outside of his nurturing home and caring school? College not only is expensive, but places new demands on his life. There is no doubt he has the motivation to succeed and has seen that success is possible, but he must move beyond his surroundings in order to grow beyond the limited opportunities of his high school and community.

---

**9-2**

**POINTS TO REMEMBER**

- In homogeneously grouped classrooms, there are numerous differences: ability levels, parental background, home environment, behavior, or health problems.

- Humans develop cognitively, from the sensorimotor period of reflexes and responses, to the preoperational period of egocentric thinking, to the concrete operational period of thought and logic, and, finally, to the formal observational period of logic and reasoning. (Piaget)

- Needs are developed, in hierarchical order, from the basic human physiological and safety needs to those of belonging and esteem, understanding and knowledge, and, finally, self-actualization. (Maslow)

- Early psychosocial development is marked by trust or mistrust. By the time the student is an adolescent, psychosocial development is marked by identity or role confusion. (Erikson)

- Humans also develop morals through stages. The preconventional stage of moral reasoning is based on the rules of others, the conventional stage on expectations and approval, and the postconventional stage on socially agreed standards and individual rights. (Kohlberg)

- In the early years, students tend to like school and teachers. By the middle of elementary school, they are more interested in their peers than schoolwork. By junior high school, students are likely to blame their failure on others. In high school, they see how their own actions affect their performance.

- In the early years students have limited language skills but as they develop, they can express thoughts, analyze, and interpret.

Today's student population represents numerous ethnic and racial groups and comes from a wide range of economic and social backgrounds. A large percentage have disabilities. Although their values tend to be traditional, students today have additional concerns about social problems such as drugs and AIDS. Differences in background and gender may affect cognitive and psychosocial development in ways that were not imagined by early theorists. Even in classrooms in which students are more similar than they are different, the differences are vast. Some children read well above grade level; others read below grade level. Some children have parents who are actively involved in the schools; other parents never cross the school threshold.

The teachers of today must learn to work with all these children. Teaching them a common set of skills and concepts is no longer possible. Helping a diverse group of children develop a global, multicultural view of their world is the challenge and may be the reward of teaching in the twenty-first century.

## For Thought/Discussion

1. How can understanding a student's interests, values, and worries help a teacher prepare a class that will be meaningful and interesting to students?

2. If Maslow's development of needs theory is correct, how can children of poverty be expected to learn if they come to school hungry and tired? What would you do, if such children appeared in your class, to help them learn effectively?

3. If you have a homogeneously grouped classroom, is it reasonable to expect that everyone will achieve at the same level? Why or why not?

4. If several eighth-grade students, recently immigrated from Haiti, entered your classroom and could speak only a little English, how would you introduce the lessons and answer their questions?

## For Further Reading/Reference

Bennett, W. J. 1993. *The book of virtues.* New York: Simon and Schuster. A collection of moral stories from fables, folktales, fiction, and drama with commentary from this well-known politician and educational reformer.

Gay, G. 1990. Ethnic minorities and educational equality. In *Multicultural education: Issues and perspectives,* ed. J. A. Banks and C. A. M. Banks, 167–188. Boston, MA: Allyn and Bacon. A discussion of educational inequality and comparison of access of blacks, Hispanics, Asians, and Native Americans in the same school and instructional programs to that of middle-class white students.

Oakes, J. 1985. *Keeping track.* New Haven, CT: Yale University Press. Firsthand information regarding tracking practices taken from observation and surveys; results of tracking and grouping; grouping recommendations for school personnel.

Reed, S., and Sautter, R. C. 1990. Children of poverty: The status of 12 million young Americans [special report]. *Phi Delta Kappan,* 71 (10), K1–K12. Discussions of the children of poverty, what child advocates say should be done about them, and whether schools can realistically improve their lives.

Sachar, E. 1991. *Shut up and let the lady teach.* New York: Random House. Experiences of a journalist/author who spent a year teaching in an urban middle school. Discussed are physical facilities, racism, urbanism, tracking, and literacy.

Wirths, C. G., and Bowman-Kruhm, M. 1987. *I hate school: How to hang in and when to drop out.* New York: Thomas Y. Crowell. A discussion of how it is possible for students to take control of their school life rather than dropping out; suggestions for helping with social problems.

*Sources of current demographic data*

Because the demographics of schools and society change so rapidly, we are including in this list of further readings two sources that provide periodic updating of statistical information.

National Center for Education Statistics, U.S. Department of Education (annual). *Digest of education statistics.* Washington, DC: Author. An annual publication providing a compilation of statistical information covering the broad fields of American education, including enrollment, graduates, dropouts, the disabled, teacher salaries, and educational achievements.

U.S. Department of Commerce, Bureau of the Census (annual). *Statistical abstract of the United States.* Washington, DC: Author. Published since 1878, this annual statistical abstract is the standard summary of statistics on the social, political, and economic organization of the United States. Presents demographics such as population trends, education statistics, poverty, racial and ethnic population, employment, and families.

Stan Fine in *Phi Delta Kappan*

*"You'll never get away with it. She's bound to know it was* **you,** *Pablo!"*

After studying this chapter, you should be able to:

- Define learning.
- Define the behavioral view of learning.
- Explain how the neobehaviorist view of learning is built on the behaviorist view.
- Discuss the cognitive view of learning.
- Understand the neurological concept of hemisphericity.
- Explain how sociologists examine learning.
- Discuss how learning styles differ.
- Describe the relationship between gender, race, culture, and learning style.
- Identify the results of the National Assessment of Educational Progress in reference to the reading and writing progress of U.S. students.
- Identify the results of the National Assessment of Educational Progress in reference to the mathematics and science performance of U.S. students.
- Identify the results of the National Assessment of Educational Progress in reference to the history performance of U.S. students.
- Compare the achievement of U.S. students with that of students in other countries.
- Assess SAT and ACT scores over the last three decades.
- Explain why U.S. students do not do well on standardized tests.

# Chapter 10

# LEARNING IN A MULTICULTURAL SOCIETY

$\mathcal{J}$amel Oeser-Sweat walks home at night from the subway, a 17-year-old in big black sneakers and a baseball cap, passing drug dealers asking "What do you want? What do you want?" and young ladies making eyes at him.

At his housing project on the Lower East Side of Manhattan, he sometimes has to stand on his toes in the elevator to avoid the urine puddles. Upstairs, the apartment is frayed and spare. His family only recently acquired a telephone. A good thing, too. Opportunity is suddenly on the line.

"Harvard called last night," he said on Thursday. "The first thing I thought is, does this woman know she's calling the projects?"

On Monday, [January 24, 1994] Mr. Oeser-Sweat was named one of 40 finalists in the nationwide Westinghouse Science Talent Search scholarship out of 1,645 entrants, all competing for $204,000 to be awarded in March. It is a remarkable achievement for even the most fortunate high school student from the best of schools, which he is not.

Out of a fatherless, somewhat chaotic existence in the inner city, Mr. Oeser-Sweat has cobbled together an impressive life. He tutors elementary-school children in Harlem two afternoons a week and runs activities and field trips for them on Saturdays. He has completed his requirements to become an Eagle Scout. He is the president of a youth advisory council for Supportive Children's Advocacy Network, a social services agency. The Westinghouse honor has raised his accomplishments to a new level.

For his project, Mr. Oeser-Sweat, a senior at Martin Luther King High School, near Lincoln Center, traced bacteria to luffa sponges and other materials used for scrubbing away dead skin. Working for two years in a program for high school students at Mount Sinai Medical Center, he showed that the materials could cause skin lesions and other diseases if not decontaminated regularly.

"The judges saw the value of the project because it has tremendous public health significance," said Dr. Edward J. Bottone, a microbiologist who became a mentor and friend to Mr. Oeser-Sweat, and who recommended the project after a hospital employee developed mysterious lesions.

Mr. Oeser-Sweat's selection is made sweeter because King, unlike the Bronx High School of Science and other competitive schools, is not known for producing Westinghouse finalists. In fact, he was the first King student to enter. . . .

Mr. Oeser-Sweat's family has lived in poverty since his father became ill with cancer when Mr. Oeser-Sweat was a year old and died three years later. Threatened by a social worker with losing her three sons to foster care if she did not leave the family's rundown South Bronx apartment, Mr. Oeser-Sweat's mother moved her family to the Prince George Hotel, a Manhattan hotel for the homeless that was infamous for its squalor and rampant drug-dealing. He remembers shootings in the lobby and drug addicts trying to sell their underwear.

Five years ago, after years on the public housing waiting list, the family moved to the Baruch Houses. Mr. Oeser-Sweat's mother, Jeanieclai Sweat, said that when her sons saw their new home they asked her, "Mommy, did you strike it rich?"

But within months of moving, Mrs. Sweat, who had been a foster child and has a chronic psychological illness, was taken from their apartment to the hospital. Mr. Oeser-Sweat was put in a group home for boys and his two younger brothers were placed in foster care. "The ambulance took her and the police took us," Mr. Oeser-Sweat said. "It was two nights before Thanksgiving."

Mrs. Sweat's hospitalization was brief, but it took her a year to convince the authorities that she was competent to care for her children and to reunite the family. In that period, Mr. Oeser-Sweat was in the eighth grade and began attending school regularly for the first time, he said.

Although Mr. Oeser-Sweat began reading at 5 and could write letters and numbers before kindergarten, Mrs. Sweat said she was unable to make him go to school regularly. But he said that while he was in the eighth grade, living in group homes in Brooklyn and Queens and separated from his mother and his friends, going to school in his neighborhood in lower Manhattan was the only connection to the life that he missed.

"For the first time, school was the only anchor for my life," he said. . . .

"For me, it's the whole confidence thing," Mr. Oeser-Sweat said. "If you see bad, you'll be bad. Dr. Bottone says you can't visualize yourself hitting a home run until you see one hit."

Now, Mr. Oeser-Sweat can visualize hitting another one. When Harvard called, he had been favoring Yale, but he demurred and will be at the Harvard Club for an interview in two weeks.

He said he knows that his grades and achievement-test scores are below those of the average Ivy League student, but added, "I think my biggest selling point is that I can endure through things."

"I was looking at the stuff from Harvard and it said a lot of kids don't make it through the first year because of too much pressure," he said. Then he chuckled at the thought of college life being too much to bear, and said, "What could stop me now?"

From: M. Purdy, "Budding Scientist's Success Breaks the Mold," the *New York Times* (January 30, 1994), 1, 17.

While a senior at Martin Luther King High School in New York City, Jamel Oeser-Sweat, left, was named a finalist in the nationwide Westinghouse Science Talent Search. One of his many activities included tutoring students like Janaya Rivas in an elementary school in Harlem. In March 1994, the Westinghouse Science Talent Search awarded him a $10 thousand scholarship as one of the top ten outstanding students. He plans to attend Harvard.

*A* social scientist who looked at Jamel Oeser-Sweat's history would have predicted a future filled with despair, little education, menial work, possibly drugs, crime, and an early death. What had made the difference in his life? Adults, like his science teacher Michael Schonberg and his Mt. Sinai mentor Dr. Edward J. Bottone, recognized in Jamel not only a budding genius, but also the difficulties he was facing. They believed in him and encouraged him by being models, providing him with opportunities, and expecting the best from him.

Young African American males from housing projects are particularly vulnerable to society's ills. As Jamel tells us, he passes drug dealers on the way home from school and returns to a apartment in which the halls smell of urine and a telephone is a recent luxury. And, even more than many young project dwellers, Jamel has faced the harshness of a life of poverty. When his mother was hospitalized for a psychological disorder, he was separated from his family and placed in a group home. But, in spite of all this, or perhaps because of it, as he suggests, he has endured. Why has he succeeded when others have failed? Is his success from personal drive and intelligence, or can it be attributed to luck? In this chapter, we will attempt to answer some of these questions.

# What Is Learning?

Psychologists, neurologists, sociologists, and educators have attempted to describe how and why human learning occurs and, thereby, define learning. They have established that there is no single way in which all humans learn, but many ways, perhaps as many as there are human beings. In addition, since researchers bring to their observations their own individual perceptions of learning, there are nearly as many different definitions as there are researchers. The one common denominator, however, is a change in behavior.

Definitions of learning and descriptions of how people learn differ, in part, because researchers from different academic disciplines attempt to examine the process using different research methodologies. Psychologists, for example, observe behavior, frequently in a laboratory setting, sometimes in the actual learning environment, attempting to determine how the organism's actions, traits, attitudes, and thoughts develop.

Neurologists study ways in which the brain functions. Recent neurological studies of the hemispheres of the brain have produced new interpretations of learning and new descriptions of how we learn.

Sociologists examine the learning environment. Sociological research on effective schools has given us descriptions of common environmental factors that appear to contribute to learning.

Educational researchers attempt to describe different "learning styles" and the effects of gender and race on how students learn. They attempt to translate learning styles into teaching strategies that work most effectively for different learners. Likewise, they explore ways to match individual teaching styles to individual learning styles.

## LEARNING: A PSYCHOLOGICAL PERSPECTIVE

Within a single academic discipline there are various ways of examining how students learn. In psychology, for example, there are two major schools of learning theories: behavioral and cognitive. In addition, a neobehaviorist theory, also referred to as the social cognitive theory, has expanded the behavioral view of learning.

*Behavioral View*   Behavioral psychologists define learning as "a change in behavior, in the way a person acts in a particular situation" (Woolfolk 1987, 165).

Four of the most important proponents of the behavioral point of view were Ivan Pavlov (Russian physiologist and pharmacology researcher at St. Petersburg Institute of Experimental Medicine), J. B. Watson (psychologist and researcher at Johns Hopkins University), Edward L. Thorndike (educational psychologist and researcher at Teacher's College, Columbia University), and B. F. Skinner (psychologist and researcher at Harvard University). These men focused their research on observable behavior and behavioral change in learners. Consequently, they rarely discussed thinking or emotions as part of learning. Behavioral learning studies are usually conducted in laboratories using animals to identify some general laws of learning that are then applied to humans.

*Ivan Pavlov*    In the late nineteenth and early twentieth centuries Ivan Pavlov (1849–1936) developed the concept of classical conditioning while studying the digestive process of dogs. Pavlov and his colleagues recognized that if a piece of meat were placed near a dog, the dog would salivate. Because the meat automatically provoked the salivation, Pavlov called it an **unconditioned stimulus**. Likewise, because the salivation response was not taught, he called it an **unconditioned response**.

Pavlov experimented by introducing the dog to the stimulus of a bell. Since the dog did not respond, he called the bell a **neutral stimulus**. However, when he paired the neutral stimulus (the bell) with the unconditioned stimulus (the meat), the dog salivated. When the meat was removed, the dog still salivated when the bell was rung. Hence, the neutral stimulus became what Pavlov called a **conditioned stimulus**. He referred to this process as **classical conditioning**. Pavlov further learned that from time to time it was necessary to **reinforce** the conditioned response by presenting the dog with meat after the bell had been rung or the response would disappear or **extinguish**.

*J. B. Watson*    John B. Watson (1878–1958) believed that scientists should base their conclusions exclusively on the observation of behavior and coined the term **behaviorist** to emphasize this point. Believing that Pavlov's experiments provided the key to behavior manipulation in humans, he continued investigating behavior by experimenting with an eleven-month-old boy and a white rat. As the boy began to enjoy the activity of playing with the white rat, Watson introduced a sudden, loud sound that he had observed frightened most children. When the boy began to associate the rat with the frightening stimulus, he responded with fear and later generalized his fear to anything white and fuzzy.

*Viewpoint*   Learning—Second Graders' Perspective

When Sue Morrison, a second-grade teacher, asked her class, "What is learning?," this is what they told her. Ms. Morrison wrote down their responses on chart paper for all to read.

—If you didn't learn your friend would have to help you all through life and you couldn't help yourself or anyone else.

—When you learn you think about things . . . lots of things.

—Learning is like when you go to school and find out what something is.

—If you had no education you would have a hard time surviving.

—You wouldn't know anything if you didn't learn.

—If our country wasn't as well educated as another country then that country might make fun of our country and might even try to challenge our country and take all we had. Then we'd lose.

—A person needs an education to apply for a job.

—It would be horrid not to learn . . . maybe even harmful. I mean . . . if I had a baby and couldn't read or learn then I couldn't feed my baby and we would both die.

—If you want to be educated and learn, you have to put your mind on it and really try to learn to live.

—If you don't know anything you get all mixed up and you feel like you want to learn but you don't know how to express what you want to know. . . .

From: Sue Morrison, Ira B. Jones Elementary School, Asheville, North Carolina

*E. L. Thorndike* Edward L. Thorndike (1874–1949) believed that stimuli in the environment could prompt behavioral responses. His theory was the forerunner of what has come to be known as stimulus-response, or S-R, theory. Thorndike linked behavior to certain physical reflexes that occur without conscious or unconscious thought, such as the reflexive jerking of the tapped knee. Thorndike experimented by placing cats in boxes from which they had to escape in order to get food. He found that over time the cats escaped from the boxes more and more rapidly by repeating those behaviors that led to escape and eliminating those that did not. He named this the **law of effect**, which states that if an act leads to a satisfying change in the environment, the likelihood that it will be repeated in similar situations increases. However, if the act does not lead to a satisfying change, the likelihood that it will be repeated decreases.

*B. F. Skinner* Burrhus F. Skinner (1904–1990), the best-known of the behavioral psychologists, coined the term **operant conditioning** to stress that an organism "operates" on the environment when it learns. He also referred to this as **instrumental learning** because the organism is "instrumental" in securing a response that may be repeated if the organism receives **reinforcement**, a reward of some type such as food, money, or praise. Skinner believed human behavior is caused by experiences over which the individual has incomplete control. Therefore, students can learn if they are presented with stimuli designed to produce a predetermined, desired result. To this end, teachers should construct a methodology providing either positive or negative reinforcement so that students will actively learn.

For example, if the student does well on a quiz, using positive reinforcements, such as praise, a high grade, or a sticker, would likely cause the behavior to continue.

Negative reinforcement strengthens a behavior if an unpleasant situation or incident is removed. For example, if a student has done well on a quiz, he or she may be exempt from taking the next quiz. This should then reinforce behavior that produced learning, for subsequent quizzes.

In 1968 Skinner outlined four behavioral learning principles based on his research: (1) Students will learn better if they know exactly what they are expected to learn—in other words, what learning will be reinforced. (2) Students must master basic/simpler skills before they can master complex skills. (3) All students do not learn at the same rate. (4) Subject matter should be programmed into small bits, with immediate positive feedback. Based on Skinner's principles, computer-programmed instruction was developed. **Computer-assisted instruction** allows students to progress at their own rate by completing a series of complex tasks, each of which receives immediate feedback in the form of a corrected response.

*Viewpoint* Definitions of Learning

**Students at Cherokee Elementary School, Qualla Cherokee Reservation, Cherokee, North Carolina:**

Learning is fun and you can use it when you are older.

Hannah Johnson, Age 10

Learning is knowing how to do stuff like math, language, and reading. It is to know about prehistoric times and about education.

Preston Bark, Age 11

Learning is making good grades, doing homework every night, doing classroom work, and turning it in on time. Learning is easy if your teacher is creative.

Stefanie West, Age 10

Learning is helpful. It is fun. To learn you must be teachable.

Mindy Larch, Age 11

**Students at Wilkerson Middle School, Birmingham, Alabama. Wilkerson Middle School has a population that is over 90 percent African American:**

Learning is the ability to let your mind be educated.

Stacie Sturdivant, Age 12

Learning is a possession of knowledge gained by studying.

Tamika Terriel, Age 12

Learning is a long process that never stops and enhances the minds of people.

LaChaune Slater, Age 11

Learning is the discovery of what you didn't already know.

Tameca Moss, Age 12

Learning is to obtain knowledge. To obtain knowledge is to obtain wisdom. Learning is the wisdom to obtain knowledge.

Keithon Terry, Age 13

Learning is the ability of taking in knowledge and keeping it in storage for good usage.

Jermaine Wilson, Age 14

Learning is something we do every day. We don't just learn in school, we learn from the people who we live around.

Marcus Laister, Age 14

**Students at Gretchen Whitney High School, Cerritus, California:**

Learning is finding out new things, grasping concepts that are new to you.

Barbara Vuu, Age 17

Learning is the only thing one can do that no one can take away.

Claudia Park, Age 17

Learning is a journey, not a destination. Through education we can find the meaning of life.

Scott Kim, Age 17

**Students at New Trier High School, Winnetka, Illinois:**

Learning is the never-ending pursuit of knowledge. It extends far beyond the acquisition of factual information. It consists of the exploration of unchartered territory. Learning demands questioning and probing into realms—known and unknown.

Kimberly Vender, Senior

Learning is more than just an organized activity. It is a living, breathing experience which touches every part of your body. Learning is not confined to a classroom or school; rather, it is omnipresent. It is in your relationship to everything you touch, see, hear, smell, taste, and feel. Finally, learning is never ending. The day you stop learning is the day you die because learning is the very essence of life.

Polly Cline, Junior

*Neobehaviorist View*    Neobehaviorists, such as Albert Bandura (social psychologist, author, and researcher), expanded the behaviorists' view of learning into a social cognitive theory that includes such internal, unobservable behaviors as intentions, expectations, beliefs, and thoughts. Bandura determined, as well, that children learned as much by imitation and observation as they did by reinforcement of specific behaviors. In one famous experiment with a punching toy, called Bobo, he determined that children were more aggressive after watching an adult punch the toy or after viewing an aggressive film or cartoon than after viewing a nonaggressive one. This theory became known as **modeling** or observational learning. According to Bandura, there are four elements to observational learning: (1) The learner must pay attention to the role model. (2) The learner needs clear explanations. (3) The learner produces the desired behavior with practice and receives feedback. (4) The behavior needs to be reinforced in order for it to continue.

The concept of modeling is still a very important one for teachers. Teachers model behavior for students in many ways: through their own actions, through demonstrations, through guided practice leading the student step-by-step through a process, and through the selection of materials and activities.

*Cognitive View*    The cognitive psychologists view learning as an internal process that cannot be observed directly and involves such complex tasks as problem solving, concept learning, perception, and remembering. Cognitive psychologists, such as Jean Piaget, Jerome Bruner, David Ausubel, and Robert Gagne, usually conduct their research in schools with human learners. Although all cognitive theorists define learning in similar ways, they do not agree upon a learning model in which all people learn in a similar way, as the behaviorists do. These theorists agree that "learning is the result of our attempts to make sense out of the world" (Woolfolk, 234). To do this, according to the cognitive theorists, learners use the various mental tools at their disposal. The learners' thoughts about the situation, along with beliefs, expectations, and feelings, make them actively seek out information to solve problems and reorganize what they know in order to achieve new learning (Woolfolk, 235). Piaget, discussed in chapter 9 (pp. 367–369), developed a hierarchy of how learners learn. The theories of Bruner, Ausubel, and Gagne will be introduced here.

*Jerome Bruner*    Jerome Bruner (b. 1915; Harvard University psychologist, founder of Harvard Center for Cognitive Studies) contends that we learn by actively being involved in problem solving through the use of inductive reasoning and intuitive thinking—making guesses, confirming, disproving, and discovering solutions.

Bruner believes that the best way for students to learn is for teachers to confront them with problems so that they can seek solutions. According to Bruner, this is important because "conceptions that children arrive at on their own are usually more meaningful than those proposed by others and . . . students do not need to be motivated or rewarded when they seek to make sense of things that puzzle them" (Biehler and Snowman 1986, 254). In addition, according to Bruner, when children are given practice finding solutions to problems they acquire the skills necessary to solve other problems.

Bruner's instructional model has become known as **discovery learning**. In this model, teachers create situations where children learn through discovery rather than through prepared and teacher-presented information. For example, children can discover phonetic coding skills by noting similarities and differences in consonant/vowel sequences rather than by memorizing phonetic rules. And by using concrete rectangles and squares, students can discover differences in length, width, and weight.

*David Ausubel*   David Ausubel (b. 1918; professor and researcher at City University of New York) contends that children learn through reception and listening rather than through discovery. The key to this theory, however, is that all new learning must be linked to what the student already knows and that facts, principles, and concepts should be presented in meaningful ways and in a sequential and organized manner.

Since Ausubel believed that children learn deductively, from the general to the specific, from rule to example, he developed a concept of expository teaching. The teacher provides external motivation for learning by beginning a lesson with overall aims, giving examples, relating the learning to past learning and experiences (what he called **advanced organizers**), and presenting the lesson in an organized sequence from the general to the specific. His theory has come to be called **expository learning**, or **deductive teaching**.

Ausubel's theory has many applications in the classroom. For example, a teacher might begin a unit on the Civil War by telling students that the goal of the unit is to help them better understand how that war affected various groups of people. Using Ausubel's approach, the teacher would use a series of increasingly specific advanced organizers. The teacher might begin with a film such as *Gone With the Wind* to help students tie the Civil War to their own experience. Next, the students and teacher might discuss how the Civil War affected plantation owners in general and the South specifically. This might lead to readings on the causes and effects of the war. The teacher might then provide another advanced organizer to examine the Civil War through the eyes of slaves. For example, the teacher might read aloud selections from Toni Morrison's *Beloved* and Julius Lester's *To Be a Slave,* which focus on the life of slaves and the implications of slavery. Irene Hunt's *Across Five Aprils,* about a family in which one son fights for the Union and the other for the Confederacy, might then be read. The students might then investigate how different individuals reacted to the causes of the war. Perhaps, after several more advanced organizers, the students would work in groups to develop class presentations related to how different populations reacted to and were affected by the war. As a culminating activity, the students and the teacher might develop an interconnected learning web, diagrammed on the chalkboard, in an attempt to connect the various populations of the Civil War to its effects. The unit would continue in this manner until the original aims were reached. Expository teaching, such as that described by Ausubel, requires a great deal of interaction between students and teacher.

*Robert Gagne*   According to Robert Gagne (b. 1916; director of research, American Institute of Research; professor and researcher at Stanford University and Florida State University), learning skills, which he calls **learning outcomes**, can be categorized into five types: (1) attitudes—learned through positive/negative experiences and modeling, (2) motor skills—learned through observation and practice, (3) verbal data—learned in almost every lesson, (4) intellectual skills—learned as symbols for communicating and solving problems, and (5) cognitive strategies—learned to assist in selecting, processing, and retrieving information. The more complicated skills are discussed below.

An attitude (a reaction toward or against a solution, person, or thing, learned through positive or negative experiences and modeling) intensifies a person's reaction toward something. For example, if a person has a positive attitude toward music, she or he will frequently choose to listen to it. The more positive the attitude, the greater the frequency with which the individual chooses to pursue the activity. The opposite is also true: a negative attitude decreases the frequency with which the activity is pursued. The relationship between attitude and performance is very strong. Hence, a positive attitude toward music, for example, may result in playing an instrument.

Intellectual skills are those capabilities that make individuals competent. They enable people to respond successfully to their environment and range from simple skills, such as arranging a sentence, to technical ones involved in the sciences and mathematics. They allow students to think, analyze, and create at high levels. For example, those who possess intellectual skills not only know the meaning of the term *metaphor* but can also think metaphorically and use metaphorical language in speech and writing. This intellectual skill then becomes the basis for future learning—developing more sophisticated writing techniques; comparing unlike elements in literature or the sciences; or conducting sophisticated scientific experiments such as determining how a specific insect might affect a specific plant were it to be introduced to the plant's environment.

Cognitive strategies govern the individual's learning, remembering, and thinking abilities. They allow students to read a passage and determine what is most important, to analyze information that is learned, and to solve problems. These skills are gained over a long period of time through active studying, learning, and thinking.

To assist students in developing these capabilities, Gagne suggested that there are eight essential events of instruction that directly influence the process of learning. These include the following:

- motivation (teacher-provided stimulus and lesson objective)
- apprehending (directing student's attention/focusing on particulars)
- acquisition (recalling past, related information/presenting new material/giving examples)
- retention (practicing new skill)
- recall (review over several days)
- generalization (transfer of new information to other situations)
- performance (demonstration of knowledge: tests, written papers, experiments)
- feedback (grades, praise, and correction)

These events are external to the learner and can be structured by either the learner or the teacher. In an authoritarian or subject-centered classroom, for example, the teacher will organize the events of instruction, and in a student-centered classroom, the students will largely determine the method or pattern of learning.

***Multiple Intelligence*** Since 1979, Howard Gardner (professor of neurology at Boston University School of Medicine) has headed a team of researchers at Harvard Graduate School studying the nature and realization of human potential. Their research involves that which is known concerning the development of skills in normal children and extends to an examination of how the development of skills breaks down when the brain is damaged. Populations such as stroke victims, prodigies, idiot savants, autistic children, and children with learning disabilities all have been studied. The research has resulted in Gardner's preliminary list of **multiple intelligences**, a theory of plurality of intellect that suggests that each of seven intelligences has equal claim to priority.

According to Gardner, the seven intelligences are: (1) linguistic intelligence, exhibited in its fullest form in poets; (2) logical-mathematical intelligence and scientific ability; (3) spatial intelligence, or the ability to form a mental model of a spatial world and operate according to that model, exhibited in sailors, engineers, surgeons, sculptors, and painters; (4) musical intelligence, exhibited in its highest form in such artists as Mozart; (5) bodily-kinesthetic intelligence, ability to solve problems or fashion products using one's whole body or parts of the body, exhibited by surgeons, dancers, athletes, and craftspeople; (6) interpersonal intelligence, ability to understand other people, what motivates them, and how to work cooperatively with them, exhibited by salespeople, politicians, teachers, clinicians, and religious leaders among others; (7) intrapersonal intelligence, the capacity to form an accurate model of oneself and be able to use the model to operate effectively in life (1993, 8–9).

According to Gardner, none of these intelligences is more important than any other. He suggests that theorists such as Piaget (see chapter 9, p. 367–369) studied only the development of logical-mathematical intelligence rather than multiple intelligences and that adherence to theories such as Piaget's has created a myopic view of how we learn.

Individuals, says Gardner, differ in the particular intelligence profiles with which they are born and those they develop. Intelligences are raw, biological potentials that work together, in most individuals, to solve problems and develop various vocations and avocations. Therefore, suggests Gardner, "It is of the utmost importance that we recognize and nurture all of the varied human intelligences, and all of the combinations of intelligences" (p. 12).

Gardner suggests that educators must consider multiple intelligences in the design of schools and instruction.

> The design of my ideal school of the future is based upon two assumptions. The first is that not all people have the same interests and abilities; not all of us learn in the same way. (And we now have the tools to begin to address these individual differences in school.) The second assumption is one that hurts: it is the assumption that nowadays no one person can learn everything there is to learn. We would all like, as Renaissance men and women, to know everything, or at least to believe in the potential of knowing everything, but that ideal clearly is not possible anymore. Choice is therefore inevitable, and one of the things that I want to argue is that the choices that we make for ourselves, and for the people who are under our charge, might as well be informed choices. An individual-centered school would be rich in assessment of individual abilities and proclivities. It would seek to match individuals not only to curricular areas, but also to particular ways of teaching those subjects. And after the first few grades, the school would also seek to match individuals with the various kinds of life and work options that are available in their culture. (p. 10)

## LEARNING: A NEUROLOGICAL PERSPECTIVE

In the late 1970s, studies by neurologists who had researched the function of each of the brain's hemispheres began to appear. They have determined that each hemisphere has a specialized, but not exclusive, function. Both hemispheres in normal individuals receive the same information but process it differently. There is a combination of specialization and integration of functions between and within the hemispheres, both of which are necessary to learning (Fadely and Hosler 1983).

Each hemisphere controls the opposite side of the body. Researchers believe that the left hemisphere is the more logical, analytical, and verbal; it controls manual dexterity, reading, language, and understanding speech. The right hemisphere processes nonverbal information and organizes a human's artistic aptitudes and emotions. The primary functions of each hemisphere have been studied and outlined by such researchers as Roger Sperry, Ronald Myers, and Michael Gazzaniga in the 1950s (see table 10.1).

We can understand how the hemispheres work, both together and separately, primarily because of the work of Roger Sperry, who studied epileptic individuals in whom the corpus callosum, the nerve bundle connecting the two hemispheres, had been cut to attempt to reduce the frequency of seizures. He found subtle dysfunctions in these individuals. In a normal individual without a split brain, the eye's left field of vision is initially received only by the right hemisphere, and the right field of vision is received only by the left hemisphere. The information is quickly transmitted to both hemispheres, and the left hemisphere, the center of language production, names it. Sperry found that this was not true in split-brained patients. If an object was placed in the right hand of a split-brained patient, the information was received by the left hemisphere and the patient named the object. However, if it was placed in the left hand and received by the right hemisphere, the patient could not name the object. Why? According to Sperry, the right hemisphere, which had received the information, could not transfer it to the left, the center for language production, because of the cut corpus callosum.

Researchers contend that some people are whole brained; others have dominant left or right hemispheres. According to Bernice McCarthy (president of Excel, Inc., Barrington, Illinois), "the two halves of the brain process information differently; both hemispheres are equally important in terms of whole-brain functioning; and individuals rely more on one information processing mode than the other, especially when they approach new learning" (1990, 32). Most, according to researchers, have dominant left hemispheres. However, no matter which hemisphere is dominant, all individuals use both sides of the brain. As McCarthy states, "The goal of education should be to help develop a whole brain . . . intellectual and intuitive, mind and heart, content-centered and student-centered" (1990, 77).

## LEARNING: A SOCIOLOGICAL PERSPECTIVE

Sociological research on effective schools examines those elements of the instructional environment that promote academic achievement (see chapter 7 for more information). It is important to note that effective schools research does not

(continued on p. 398)

**TABLE 10-1**

## Summary of Hemisphericity: Left- and Right-Brained Functions

| Left hemisphere | Right hemisphere |
|---|---|
| • Has Intellectual Focus<br>• Recognizes and Controls Speech; Relies on Language; Prefers Talking and Writing<br>• Rarely Uses Metaphors and Analogies<br>• Receives, Stores and Synthesizes Verbal-Auditory Data<br>• Responds Best to Auditory, Visual Stimuli<br>• Serializes and Sequentially Organizes Verbal Data<br>• Remembers Names<br>• Responds to Verbal Instructions and Explanations<br>• Focuses on Temporal (Time) Memory and Behavior<br>• Has Logical, Rational Problem-Solving Behavior<br>• Plans and Structures<br>• Analyzes Reading<br>• Prefers Multiple-Choice Tests and Research with Single Variable<br>• Socializes Values; Establishes Information<br>• Prefers Hierarchical Authority Structures; Likes Structured Environment<br>• Makes Objective Judgments<br>• Is Not Facile in Interpreting Body Language<br>• Controls Feelings<br>• Prefers Higher Math Skills Involving Formulation and Time-Space Concepts<br>• Systematically Controls Experimentation | • Is Intuitive; Insightful<br>• Is Fluid and Spontaneous<br>• Relies on Images in Thinking and Remembering<br>• Frequently Uses Metaphors and Analogies<br>• Prefers Nonverbal Auditory Information; Minor Comprehension of Language<br>• Is Creative and Artistic<br>• Recognizes and Synthesizes Musical Perception, Rhythm, and Movement Patterns in Music<br>• Prefers Drawing and Manipulating Objects<br>• Easily Manipulates Forms, Shapes, Form-Space Relationships<br>• Develops Complex and Fine Motor Skills<br>• Responds Best to Kinetic Stimuli<br>• Remembers Faces<br>• Interprets Nonverbal Information; Good at Interpreting Body Language<br>• Responds to Demonstrated, Illustrated, Symbolic Instructions<br>• Synthesizes Reading<br>• Prefers Open-Ended Questions, Work and Study, and Multivariable Research<br>• Prefers Collegial (Participative) Authority Structures<br>• Is Self-Acting<br>• Sees the Whole; Solves Problems Intuitively by Examining the Whole<br>• Makes Subjective Judgments<br>• Experiments Randomly With Little Restraint<br>• Is Free With Feeling<br>• Prefers Concrete Math Functions; Simple Calculations |

Adapted from: J. L. Fadely and V. N. Hosler, *Case Studies in Left and Right Hemispheric Functioning* (Charles C. Thomas, 1983) and B. McCarthy, *The 4 MAT System: Teaching to Learning Styles With Right/Left Mode Techniques* (EXCEL, 1987).

**Researchers have found that both hemispheres of the brain have different but not mutually exclusive functions. The left side is primarily verbal, logical, and analytical; the right side is primarily nonverbal and emotional. This table summarizes the functions of each hemisphere.**

attempt to define learning, nor does it attempt to determine why and how the best students learn. Instead, it attempts to describe which specific environments help children learn most effectively. The results of this research are summarized below.

*Reading*

- Children get more out of a reading assignment when the teacher precedes the lesson with background information and follows it with discussion.
- Students in cooperative learning teams work toward a common goal, help one another learn, gain self-esteem, take more responsibility for their own learning, and come to respect and like their classmates.
- Telling young children stories can motivate them to read. Storytelling also introduces them to cultural values and literacy traditions before they can read, write, and talk about stories by themselves.
- Hearing good readers read and encouraging students repeatedly to read a passage aloud helps them become good readers.

*Science and Mathematics*

- Children learn science best when they are able to do experiments, so they can witness "science in action."
- Although students need to learn how to find exact answers to arithmetic problems, good math students also learn how to estimate answers.
- Children in early grades learn mathematics more effectively when they use physical objects in their lessons.
- Students will become more adept at solving math problems if teachers encourage them to think through a problem before they begin working on it, guide them through the thinking process, and give them regular and frequent practice in solving problems.

*Writing*

- The most effective way to teach writing is to teach it as a process of brainstorming, composing, revising, and editing.
- Students become more interested in writing and the quality of their writing improves when there are significant learning goals and a clear sense of purpose for the assignments.
- Children learn vocabulary better when the words they study are related to familiar experiences and to knowledge they already possess.

*Understanding Student Development*

- Children's understanding of the relationship between being smart and hard work changes as they grow.
- As students acquire knowledge and skill, their thinking and reasoning take on distinct characteristics. Teachers who are alert to these changes can determine how well their students are progressing toward becoming competent thinkers and problem solvers.

*Classroom Management*

- How much time students are actively engaged in learning contributes strongly to their achievement. The amount of time available for learning is determined by the instructional and management skills of the teacher and the priorities set by the school administration.
- Good classroom management is essential for teachers to deal with students who chronically misbehave.
- Specific suggestions from teachers on how to cope with their conflicts and frustrations help students gain insights into their behavior and learn control.

*Motivation of Students*

- When teachers explain exactly what students are expected to learn and demonstrate the steps needed to accomplish a particular academic task, students learn more.
- Constructive feedback from teachers, including deserved praise and specific suggestions, helps students learn, as well as develop positive self-esteem.
- Teachers who set and communicate high expectations to all their students obtain greater academic performance from those students than teachers who set low expectations.
- Students tutoring other students can lead to improved academic achievement for both student and tutor, and to positive attitudes toward coursework.
- Memorizing can help students absorb and retain the factual information on which understanding and critical thought are based.
- Frequent and systematic monitoring of students' progress helps students, parents, teachers, administrators, and policymakers identify strengths and weaknesses in learning and instruction.
- When teachers introduce new subject matter, they need to help students grasp its relationship to facts and concepts they have previously learned.
- Student achievement rises when teachers ask questions that require students to apply, analyze, synthesize, and evaluate information in addition to simply recalling facts.
- Well-chosen diagrams, graphs, photos, and illustrations can enhance students' learning.

*Homework*

- The ways in which children study influence strongly how much they learn. Teachers can often help children develop better study skills.
- Student achievement rises significantly when teachers regularly assign homework and students conscientiously do it.
- Well-designed homework assignments relate directly to classroom work and extend students' learning beyond the classroom. Homework is most useful when teachers carefully prepare the assignment, thoroughly explain it, and give prompt comments and criticism when the work is completed. (U.S. Department of Education 1987)

*(continued on p. 401)*

**TABLE 10-2**

## Twenty-Eight Categories of Influence on School Learning

| Categories | Examples of One Variable in Category |
|---|---|

**Student Aptitude** includes gender; academic history; and a variety of social, behavioral, motivational, cognitive, and affective characteristics.

| | |
|---|---|
| 1. Metacognitive Processes | *Comprehension monitoring (planning; monitoring effectiveness of attempted actions and outcomes of actions; testing, revising, and evaluating learning strategies)* |
| 2. Cognitive Processes | *Level of specific academic knowledge in subject area* |
| 3. Social and Behavioral Attributes | *Positive, nondisruptive behavior* |
| 4. Motivational and Affective Attributes | *Attitude toward subject matter instructed* |
| 5. Psychomotor Skills | *Psychomotor skills specific to area instructed* |
| 6. Student Demographics | *Gender and socioeconomic status* |

**Classroom Instruction and Climate** includes classroom routines and practices, characteristics of instruction as delivered, classroom management, monitoring of student progress, quality and quantity of instruction provided, student-teacher interactions, and classroom atmosphere.

| | |
|---|---|
| 7. Classroom Management | *Group alerting (teacher uses questioning/recitation strategies that maintain active participation by all students)* |
| 8. Student and Teacher Social Interactions | *Positive student response to questions from teacher and other students* |
| 9. Quantity of Instruction | *Active engagement in learning* |
| 10. Classroom Climate | *Cohesiveness (class members share common interests and values and emphasize cooperative goals)* |
| 11. Classroom Instruction | *Clear and organized direct instruction* |
| 12. Academic Interactions | *Frequent calls for substantive oral and written response* |
| 13. Classroom Assessment | *Assessment used as a frequent, integral component of instruction* |
| 14. Classroom Implementation and Support | *Establishing efficient classroom routines and communicating rules and procedures* |

**Context** includes community demographics, peer culture, parental support and involvement, and amount of time students spend out of class on such activities as television viewing, leisure reading, and homework.

| | |
|---|---|
| 15. Home Environment/Parental Support | *Parental involvement in ensuring completion of homework* |
| 16. Peer Group | *Level of peers' academic aspirations* |
| 17. Community Influences | *Socioeconomic level of community* |
| 18. Out-of-Class Time | *Student participation in clubs and extracurricular school activities* |

**Program Design** refers to the physical and organizational arrangements for instructional delivery and includes strategies specified by the curriculum and characteristics of instructional materials.

| | |
|---|---|
| 19. Curriculum Design | *Instructional materials employ advance organizers* |
| 20. Curriculum and Instruction | *Alignment among goals, content, instruction, students assignments, and evaluation* |
| 21. Program Demographics | *Size of instructional group (whole class, small group, one-on-one instruction)* |

**School Organization** refers to culture, climate, policies, and practices; includes demographics of the student body, whether the school is public or private, funding for categorical programs, school-level decision-making variables, and school-level policies and practices.

| | |
|---|---|
| 22. School Culture | *Schoolwide emphasis on and recognition of academic achievement* |
| 23. Teacher/Administrator Decision Making | *Principal actively concerned with instructional program* |

| Categories | Examples of One Variable in Category |
|---|---|
| 24. Parental Involvement Policy | *Parental involvement in improvement and operation of instructional program* |
| 25. School Demographics | *Size of school* |
| 26. School Policies | *Explicit schoolwide discipline policy* |

**State and District Characteristics** refers to governance and administration, state curriculum and textbook policies, testing and graduation requirements, teacher licensure provisions in teacher contracts, and district-level administrative and fiscal variables.

| | |
|---|---|
| 27. State-Level Policies | *Teacher licensure requirements* |
| 28. District Demographics | *School district size* |

---

From: M. C. Wang, G. Haertel, and H. J. Wolberg, "What Helps Students Learn? Synthesis of Research," *Educational Leadership* (December/January 1994), 76, 77.

> **Researchers have found that direct influences on learning, such as the amount of time a teacher spends on a subject, have a greater impact than indirect influences, such as state-level policies.**

*Direct vs. Indirect Influences on Learning*   Researchers Margaret C. Wang, Geneva D. Haertel, and Herbert J. Walberg synthesized research on the environmental factors that influence learning. After creating a knowledge base of 11 thousand statistical findings that showed "reasonable consensus on the most significant influences on learning," they grouped them into twenty-eight categories of influence on school learning (see table 10.2). They concluded that direct influences, including such things as amount of time a teacher spends on a topic and the quality of social interactions between teacher and students, had a greater impact on learning than indirect influences, including such things as school policies and the organizational structure of the school. Their research also found that the most important broad type of influence on school learning was student aptitude, followed closely by classroom instruction and climate.

## LEARNING: AN EDUCATIONAL PERSPECTIVE

Despite research that attempts to identify common elements of learning, many educators contend that everyone learns differently. Rita Dunn and Kenneth Dunn in *Learning Styles/Teaching Styles: Should They . . . Can They . . . Be Matched?* (1979) claim that **learning style** is the manner in which various elements in one's environment affect learning. Judith C. Reiff in her book *Learning Styles* (1992) takes this definition a step further. According to Reiff, "Learning style can be described as a set of factors, behaviors, and attitudes that facilitate learning for an individual in a given situation" (p. 7). According to Reiff, although each person is born with certain tendencies toward particular styles, these biological or inherited characteristics are influenced by culture, personal experience, maturation, and development.

Barbara Bree Fischer, director of Smith College Campus school, and Louis Fischer, professor at the University of Massachusetts, in *Styles in Teaching and Learning* (1979) say that "style" refers to a "pervasive quality in the behavior of

**TABLE 10-3**

## Learning Styles: Research Findings

| Fischer and Fischer | Castaneda and Gray | Grasha | Dunn and Dunn | Reiff |
|---|---|---|---|---|
| Incremental Learner: step-by-step | Field-Dependent: group interaction with teacher, motivated by praise, needs explicit instruction, defined outcomes, prefers humanities, extrinsically motivated | Dependent: little intellectual curiosity, needs structure and support, looks to authority | Environmental Stimuli: sound, light, temperature, design of room | Reflective Learners: analyze, concentrate, perform solitary work, avoid errors, emotionally controlled, good problem solvers, inductive thinkers |
| Intuitive Learner: unsystematic | | | Emotional Stimuli: motivation, persistence, responsibility, structure | |
| Sensory Specialist: relies on one sense | | Independent: self-thinking, works on own, listens to others, self-confident | | |
| Sensory Generalist: all or many senses | Field-Independent: independent, individualized, prefers to structure own tasks, prefers math/science, intrinsically motivated | Participant: wants to learn course content, likes school, works with others, responsible, does little beyond what is required | Sociological Stimuli: peers, self, pairs, team, adults, varied combinations | Impulsive Learners: quick to respond, less able to concentrate, risk takers, curious, easily frustrated, bored, distractible, difficulty considering quick decisions and alternatives |
| Emotionally Involved | | | | |
| Emotionally Neutral | | Avoidant: doesn't want to learn, doesn't participate, uninterested, overwhelmed | Physical-Perceptual-Strength Stimuli: time of day, mobility, intake | |
| Explicitly Structured: unambiguous structure | | | Psychological Stimuli: global/analytical, hemisphericity, impulsive, reflective | |
| Open-Ended Structure: open environment | | Collaborative: learns most by sharing, sees class as social interaction | | |
| Damaged Learner: negative learning style | | Competitive: learns to perform better than others, sees class as win-lose situation, must always win | | |
| Eclectic Learner: shifting style | | | | |

**Each researcher listed in this table has identified individual learning styles. While the terminology might be different for each researcher, all learning styles are influenced by four major stimuli: environmental, emotional, sociological, and physical-perceptual.**

an individual, *a quality that persists though the content may change*" (1979, 245). They illustrate this point by discussing speaking styles. According to Fischer and Fischer, John F. Kennedy and Martin Luther King, Jr., each had persistent, identifiable speaking styles that did not change even when the content of the speech changed. They suggest the same is true of artists such as Monet and Picasso. And, they conclude, the same is true in learning. Christine I. Bennett, a professor and researcher in multicultural education, agrees with Fischer and Fischer and suggests in her book *Comprehensive Multicultural Education* (1990) that "learning style is that consistent pattern of behavior and performance by which an individual approaches educational experiences. It is the composite of characteristic cognitive, affective, and physiological behaviors that serve as relatively stable indicators of how a learner perceives, interacts with, and responds to the learning environment." She further suggests that learning is "formed in the deep structure of neural organization and personality and is molded by human development and the cultural experiences of home, school and society" (p. 140).

A ten-year study on how individuals learn resulted in the identification of four stimuli and eighteen environmental variables that affect an individual's learning. Dunn and Dunn point out that, "Regardless of their age, ability, socioeconomic status, or achievement level, individuals respond uniquely to their immediate environment. Some require absolute silence when they are concentrating, while others can 'block out' sound. In addition, there is a segment of the population who actually *require* sound when they are trying to learn" (1979, 239). Table 10.3 identifies how several researchers described differences in individuals' learning styles.

*In the Classroom*

Long seen as a powerful tool for teachers, knowledge of learning styles is equally valuable to students. Teaching my 8th grade students about style has become my most important learning styles application. I don't emphasize the diagnosis of student style; my purpose is to help students become more aware of their own styles and to help them develop strategies for dealing with the diverse demands of school and of life in general.

Several times each week we take a few minutes to talk about the ways that our own styles show in class. For example, after students finish a task, we might discuss the various ways in which they approached it and the successes and frustrations they experienced. When we begin a task, especially an unfamiliar one, I talk about the kinds of thinking that the task requires; and we brainstorm ways to confront it. Frequently we see that very different approaches can produce equally successful results, thus reinforcing my constant refrain that there is seldom only "one right way."

Besides helping students become more aware of their own styles, these informal sessions have an added benefit: by hearing how other students attack particular problems or assignments, students can add many new strategies to their repertoires. This means that they are better equipped to deal with assignments that do not match their strengths: style is a tool, never an excuse.

This style debriefing has been especially useful when students work cooperatively. We can use style to understand why it's easier to work with some people than with others. Style also helps us understand many of the conflicts that arise in groups; seeing behaviors as "different" rather than as "good" or "bad" helps the group concentrate on finding productive solutions. Debriefing cooperative activities also allows me to reinforce students whose styles make them good at facilitating the group, or keeping it on task, or seeing new ways to solve problems that arise. Taking these few minutes during the school day to look at style issues keeps style in the front of everyone's mind and gives me repeated opportunities to reinforce the values that I find in style diversity.

From: Kathi L. Hand. "Style is a Tool for Students, Too!" *Educational Leadership* (October 1990), 13–14.

---

*Teaching and Learning Styles*   Dunn and Dunn and Fischer and Fischer suggest that not only do individuals have specific learning styles, but teachers have different teaching styles that are related to their own individual learning styles. Dunn and Dunn feel it is accurate to say, "Teachers teach the way they learned" (1979, 241). Just as learners can expand their dominant learning styles, however, teachers can modify and expand their teaching styles. No single teaching style is effective with all learners; hence, it is important for teachers to adapt their teaching styles to the various learning styles of their students.

Fischer and Fischer suggest that there may not be sufficient research in learning styles to adequately guide the teacher (1979, 246). They also caution that not all teaching styles are acceptable in the classroom. Fischer and Fischer believe that "Well, that's my style" is not an excuse for poor teaching. In addition, some educators worry that focusing on individual learning style may encourage the same kind of self-indulgence in students as observed in some teachers. There is a danger, they contend, that students may begin to think they can do everything just the way they want to in the name of "style."

*Females and Learning Style*   Most researchers agree that gender makes a difference in how students learn and point out that earlier learning style research tended to focus only on how male students learn. *Failing at Fairness: How America's Schools Cheat Girls* (1994) by Myra Sadker and David Sadker is a synthesis of their research on male/female learners in over one hundred U.S. classrooms. They found that girls tend to be passive and independent learners and, therefore, are not called upon as often as boys. Similarly, girls do not receive as much praise, help, and correction as boys. However, when girls were called on and received praise they became more participatory learners. Most teachers make "it clear that relying on noisy students, the ones who volunteer, is a direct path to a classroom controlled by boys. Girls who know the answer are more likely to wait to be called on, while males are more apt to shout out" (p. 269).

Diane S. Pollard (1993), a professor of educational psychology, reviewed the research on female learning styles and found that their gender-related styles of perceiving, interpreting, and processing information from the environment seem to fall into three broad categories: (1) Some are independent learners, gathering information from the written word and believing that knowledge comes from recognized authorities whom they expect to be valid and correct; (2) Some are problem solvers, believing that true knowledge comes from within and is subjective; (3) Some are incremental learners (Fischer and Fischer's terminology) who see knowledge as acquiring specific procedures and skills and using them in a reasoned manner. Pollard suggests that when females are provided opportunities to learn in a variety of ways, their academic achievement improves.

Meg Milne Moulton and Whitney Ransome (1993), executive directors of the National Coalition of Girls' Schools, have studied and observed how girls learn and agree with Pollard's findings. According to Moulton and Ransome, girls learn better when they have hands-on experiences, small group discussions, have time to reflect before responding, and are in cooperative rather than competitive environments. Sadker and Sadker confirm this stating that "many teachers have . . . said that using wait time works well. In classrooms where discussion moves rapidly and less than one second goes by between the teacher's question and a student's answer, girls may be left out" (p. 269).

Moulton and Ransome point to a potential problem in making generalizations about how females learn, however. As Pollard suggests, more research needs to be done on the intersections of gender, race, and class when studying learning styles of various groups. For example, Moulton and Ransome found that Asian American females worked better in competitive environments and were more persistent learners than Anglo-American girls because they have not been overprotected by their parents.

Carol Gilligan in her studies of the moral development of females (see chapter 9, p. 371) concludes that girls and women are more likely to possess what she calls the ethic of care. Those rooted in this ethic, says Gilligan, learn through making connections, personal experience, and caring for others. They also take responsibility for their own learning. Sadker and Sadker point to research that seems to illustrate this ethic of care. "In a study of junior high school math groups, observers found that females were generally helpful to all other group members, but males were more likely to help other males." This tends to make boys the center of attention. "Even in groups with more girls, boys became the focus of attention" (p. 270). Teachers can make cooperative learning more productive for girls by setting up rules that require the involvement of all group members.

*Culture and Learning Styles*   According to Christine I. Bennett, because there is a relationship between culture and learning style, teachers should provide students with a variety of ways to learn. Bennett identifies four cultural factors that affect learning styles:

- Learners from societies that exercise authoritative control over the young rather than being laissez-faire, will be field-dependent.
- Learners from societies that depend on unspoken observations for survival will be visual.
- Learners from societies/cultures that have poor nutrition, and learners lacking protein tend to be field-dependent.
- Learners from contemporary, literate societies will learn from the written word; learners from traditional, preliterate societies will learn from direct experiences. (1990, 157)

According to Bennett, "The notion that certain learning styles are associated with different ethnic groups is both promising and dangerous" (1990, 70). She suggests that it is promising because it helps educators realize that low academic

Studies on the learning styles of females are inconclusive but generally point to the fact that girls tend to be more independent than boys, gathering information from written sources rather than waiting to be told. In the classroom, this independence may result in the teacher's giving them less help and attention than boys.

*(continued on p. 408)*

# HOW VALID IS THE RESEARCH ON LEARNING STYLES?

## PRO  Rita Dunn

**Q: Aren't we labeling children when we say they have one style or another?**

A: No more than categorizing them as "students" or as "humans." *Everybody* has a learning style, and everybody has learning style strengths. Different people just have different strengths.

**Q: Why do you call students' preferences their "strengths"?**

A: Because many researchers have repeatedly documented that, when students are taught with approaches that match their preferences as identified by the *Learning Style Inventory* (LSI) (Dunn, Dunn, and Price 1975, 1979, 1981, 1985, 1989), they demonstrate statistically higher achievement and attitude test scores—even on standardized tests—than when they are taught with approaches that mismatch their preferences. If learning through your preference consistently produces significantly better test scores and grades, then your preference *is* your strength.

**Q: Why should students be "matched" with complementary resources? Shouldn't they learn to flex?**

A: It is important to note that three-fifths of learning style is biologically imposed. Thus, those students with strong preferences for specific learning style conditions/environments/approaches cannot flex; if they could, they would not be failing. Only those for whom a specific characteristic is relatively unimportant have the luxury of flexing. . . .

**Q: How strong is the instrumentation to identify individual styles?**

A: Two separate reports agree on the reliability and validity of various instruments (Curry 1987, DeBello 1990). These help educators decide which should—and should not—be used with K-12 students. Because it is crucial to use a reliable and valid diagnostic assessment, people should become familiar with those studies.

Another alternative is to request the research manual of any instrument you are considering. Read its reliability and validity data carefully, and be certain that the instrument has been widely used with the age group you are planning to test.

**Q: How well does learning styles-based instruction really work in the schools?**

A: After having been shown how to study and do homework through their learning style strengths, students at many institutions and at varying academic levels have demonstrated statistically significant increases in academic achievement and improved attitudes toward school, less tension in classes, and significantly increased school retention. And that progress continues over years.

From: L. Curry. "Rita Dunn Answers Questions on Learning Styles," *Educational Leadership* (October 1990), 15–16. Rita Dunn is codirector with Kenneth Dunn of St. John's University Center for the Study of Learning and Teaching Styles and the author of numerous learning-style inventories. She was interviewed by Lynn Curry.

# Postscript

Vicki Snider bases her argument about the potential dangers of learning-style inventories and using their results to select methods for teaching students on both research and personal experience. Rita Dunn, the author of the inventory Snider cites and several others, points to other research to show that the inventories have effectiveness and validity. She also suggests that the results of these inventories pro-

# HOW VALID IS THE RESEARCH ON LEARNING STYLES?

## CON  Vicki E. Snider

The notion that individual differences can and must be accommodated by modifying instructional methods is a central tenet of special education. When I was a special education teacher, I advocated an eclectic approach, meaning that each student needed to be taught in a different way depending on his or her individual characteristics. Over the course of 10 years, however, I realized that, regardless of student characteristics, some approaches worked, and some didn't. I now have a better understanding of the problems that troubled me as a teacher. With the use of learning styles gaining popularity in general education, I fear that the mistakes made in special education will be repeated and learners, especially low-performing students, will suffer.

Learning styles is a type of aptitude-treatment interaction. Aptitude-treatment interactions suggest that a person's distinctive characteristics or aptitudes (in this case, learning style) can be matched to a specific treatment (instructional method) resulting in a statistical interaction (a more effective outcome than could otherwise have been achieved). But numerous reviews of the literature have failed to find support for aptitude-treatment interactions. They have not been supported by research in educational psychology.

People are different, and it is good practice to recognize and accommodate individual differences. It is also good practice to present information in a variety of ways through more than one modality, but it is *not* wise to categorize learners and prescribe methods solely on the basis of tests with questionable technical qualities. For example, the Carbo, Dunn, and Dunn (1986) model of learning styles, which currently seems to be gaining the most momentum in general education, promotes two assessment instruments: the *Learning Style Inventory* (Dunn et al. 1985) and the *Reading Style Inventory* (Carbo 1983). Both instruments suffer from inadequate reliability and validity. The idea of learning styles is appealing, but a critical examination of this approach should cause educators to be skeptical.

From: V. E. Snider, "What We Know about Learning Styles from Research in Special Education," *Educational Leadership* (October 1990), 53. Vicki E. Snider is currently an associate professor, Department of Special Education, University of Wisconsin-Eau Clair. She taught special children for ten years.

vide effective indicators for selecting a teaching methodology for individual students. Snider does not negate the importance of viewing each learner as an individual who learns differently from others, but rather suggests that using learning-style inventories to determine how students learn and basing instruction on the results of these inventories may be counterproductive.

achievement among some ethnic groups may sometimes be attributed to differences or conflicts between teaching and learning styles rather than low intelligence that could, in turn, lead to teachers altering their teaching styles so that they better match the learning styles of their students. It is dangerous in that "new stereotypes will develop while old ones are reinforced." In addition to cautioning about the need to study the intersections of gender, race, and class, Bennett reminds researchers that there are many different cultural groups within an ethnic group. Gloria Ladson-Billings, a professor and researcher in multicultural education, suggests another caution: more research is needed to know whether focusing on individual learning styles makes a significant difference in academic performance. Ladson-Billings suggests that "culturally-relevant teaching" is one way of (see chapter 3, p. 98) "using the students' culture to help them create meaning and understand the world" (1992, 110). According to Bennett, knowledge of learning style is a "value-neutral approach for understanding individual differences among ethnically diverse students" (p. 141).

*African Americans and Learning Style*   According to Asa Hilliard, a noted authority on race and IQ, African American students tend to learn better in wholes than parts. Barbara A. Shade and Clara A. New, both professors of education, call this a synergetic style and suggest it is more appropriate for African American students than an analytical style. In the synergetic style, information processing moves from the whole to the part, rather than the other way around. Further, says Hilliard, African American learners generally prefer inferential reasoning to deductive or inductive reasoning; active involvement and nonverbal communication rather than verbal fluency. James Banks has also indicated that African American students typically have learning styles that are more action oriented and expressive (quoted in Bennett 1994, 253).

According to Bennett, African American students learn better in cooperative rather than competitive settings. Ladson-Billings agrees that African American learners favor group work over individual work and respond more to a relaxed teaching/learning pace. She further states that they need flexibility in rules of behavior and are very emotionally expressive.

*Native Americans and Learning Style*   Karen Swisher and Donna Deyhle have researched the learning styles of Native American and Native Alaskan learners by interviewing both their Anglo- and Native American teachers. According to Swisher and Deyhle, Native American students are field-dependent learners, motivated by praise. Navajos tend to learn by repeated observation, practice, and review before performing. They are primarily visual and learn best through watching and modeling. Their most effective learning environment is to have an experience in a natural setting. Bennett's research agrees. She cites J. C. Phillips's article "College of, by and for Navajo Indians" to illustrate the Navajo's need to imitate skilled performers.

> [Native] American students customarily acquire the various skills of their culture (i.e., hunting, tanning, beadwork) in a sequence of three steps. First, the child over a period of time watches and listens to a competent adult who is performing the skill. Secondly, the child takes over small portions of the task and completes them in cooperation with and under the supervision of the adult, in this way gradually learning all of the component skills involved. Finally, the child goes off and privately

tests himself or herself to see whether the skill has been fully learned: a failure is not seen by others and causes no embarrassment, but a success is brought back and exhibited to the teacher and others. The use of speech in this three-step process is minimal.

When these same children go to school they find themselves in a situation where the high value placed on verbal performance is only the first of their cross-cultural hurdles. . . . Acquisition and demonstration of knowledge are no longer separate steps but are expected to occur simultaneously. Furthermore, this single-step process takes place via public recitations, the assumption apparently being that one learns best by making verbal mistakes in front of one's peers and teachers. Finally, the children have little opportunity to observe skilled performers carrying out these tasks, for the other children who perform are as ignorant and unskilled as they. Under these circumstances, it is small wonder that these [Native] American students demonstrate a propensity for silence. (Phillips 1978, 10–12)

Cherokee Indian learners, according to Swisher and Deyhle, learn more effectively when they can make choices of when and how to participate in small, student-directed groups. They also prefer cooperative rather than competitive environments. The authors warn that, while Native American children tend to learn better in cooperative ways, they still need to experience competition so they can succeed in the competitive world (1989, 12).

*Asian Americans and Learning Style*   Christine I. Bennett claims that very little research has been conducted on Asian American learning styles. She suggests that this may be because there are so many subgroups and so many languages making it almost impossible to make generalizations. Geneva Gay, a professor and researcher in multicultural education, agrees. Even though Japanese, Chinese, Filipino, and Korean American students tend to be persistent learners, are high achievers, and equal or surpass Anglo-American students in median number of years of school completed, a high percentage of the Asian American adult population also has less than five years of formal education and usually holds low-paying jobs. Gay claims that Asian American high academic achievers are not necessarily socially and emotionally well adjusted. They do not express the same positive feelings for their physical features as their Anglo-American counterparts and often experience stress associated with pressure for high performance and high expectations teachers and students have for the "model minority" (1993, 176).

Often considered the model minority, this positive stereotype overlooks the immense diversity of the Asian American subgroups, the serious language and adjustment problems that recent Southeast Asian refugees and new immigrants encounter, the disparity that exists between educational attainment and income, and the special educational needs of individual Asian students (Gay, 176).

Bennett found that Japanese American learners, in particular, are persistent, committed, docile, and hard working. They are field-independent, expressing themselves more in technical and scientific fields rather than verbally. According to Bennett, Hmong students are field-dependent and are global learners (called synergetic by Shade and New) rather than analytical problem solvers. They tend to be passive rather than active learners, prefer memorization, closely identify with the teacher, seek group support, and learn better in a cooperative rather than competitive environment. Gay's findings agree with Bennett's suggesting that Asian American students prefer memorization and rarely challenge authority, hence they tend to do well in school and on standardized tests.

*(continued on p. 411)*

*Cross-Cultural Perspective*

## The Asian Connection: Popular Stereotype Blown Out of the Waters: Critical Thinking Is Valued in Asia

*[James] Stigler and [Harold] Stevenson logged over 6000 observation hours in Japan and China. Here is a small sampling of what they found (as recorded in "Polishing the Stone,"* American Educator, *Spring 1991).*

"If we were asked briefly to characterize classes in Japan and China, we would say that they consist of coherent lessons that are presented in a thoughtful, relaxed, and nonauthoritarian manner. Teachers frequently rely on students as sources of information. Lessons are oriented toward problem solving rather than rote mastery of facts and procedures and utilize many different types of representational materials. The role assumed by the teacher is that of knowledgeable guide, rather than that of prime dispenser of information and arbiter of what is correct. There is frequent verbal interaction in the classroom as the teacher attempts to stimulate students to produce, explain, and evaluate solutions to problems. These characteristics contradict stereotypes held by most Westerners about Asian teaching practices. Lessons are not rote: they are not filled with drill. Teachers do not spend large amounts of time lecturing but attempt to lead the children in productive interactions and discussions. And the children are not the passive automata depicted in Western descriptions but active participants in the learning process."

"Asian lessons almost always begin with a practical problem . . . or with a word problem written on the blackboard. Asian teachers, to a much greater degree than American teachers, give coherence to their lessons by introducing the lesson with a word problem.

It is not uncommon for the Asian teacher to organize the entire lesson around the solution to this single problem. The teacher leads the children to recognize what is known and what is unknown and directs the students' attention to the critical parts of the problem. Teachers are careful to see that the problem is understood by all of the children, and even mechanics, such as mathematical computation, are presented in the context of solving a problem.

Before ending the lesson, the teacher reviews what has been learned and relates it to the problem she posed at the beginning of the lesson."

"In the United States, the purpose of a question is to get an answer. In Japan, teachers pose questions to stimulate thought. A Japanese teacher considers a question to be a poor one if it elicits an immediate answer, for this indicates that students were not challenged to think. One teacher we interviewed told us of discussions she had with her fellow teachers on how to improve teaching practices. "What do you talk about?" we wondered. "A great deal of time," she reported, "is spent talking about questions we can pose to the class—which wordings work best to get students involved in thinking and discussing the material. One good question can keep a whole class going for a long time; a bad one produces little more than a simple answer.""

"Chinese and Japanese teachers rely on students to generate ideas and evaluate the correctness of the ideas. The possibility that they will be called upon to state their own solution as well as to evaluate what another student has proposed keeps Asian students alert, but this technique has two other important functions. First, it engages students in the lesson, increasing their motivation by making them feel they are participants in a group process. Second, it conveys a more realistic impression of how knowledge is acquired."

Note: The research described in this article has been funded by grants from the National Institute of Mental Health, the National Science Foundation, and the W. T. Grant Foundation.

From: Report on Research of James Stigler and Harold Stevenson, *Educational Vision: The Magazine for Critical Thinking* (1994), 2 (2), 19. James Stigler is associate professor of psychology at the University of Chicago. Harold Stevenson is professor of psychology at the University of Michigan. Their research is being published by Summit Books (*Cultural Lessons: A New Look at the Education of American Children*).

*Mexican Americans and Learning Style*   Christine I. Bennett has found in her research that Mexican American students tend to be field-dependent and global in their orientation toward learning. Because many of these students are bilingual they also tend to be bicognitive, thereby having greater cognitive flexibility than monolinguists, including the ability to move back and forth between global and analytical styles as needed. According to James Banks (1991), Mexican American learners usually are field-sensitive preferring to work with other people rather than individually to achieve goals. As a group, according to Banks, Mexican American students prefer cooperative learning to competition.

Professors of education Barry L. Bull, Royal L. Fruehling, and Virgie Chattergy write in their book *The Ethics of Multicultural and Bilingual Groups* (1992) that Mexican American females are more attentive and structured in their learning than are their male peers. This may be part of the reason why more Mexican American females graduate from high school than males. In addition Mexican American males traditionally are expected to develop independence from their families and prefer to be in clubs and gangs with their male friends, thus alienating them from school. Mexican American males, therefore, benefit from tutoring, counseling, small group instruction, and much praise.

---

**10-1**

**Points to Remember**

- Learning is defined differently by different disciplines but always indicates a change in behavior.
- The behaviorists define learning as an observable change in a student's behavior. They study how laboratory animals learn and apply their results to humans.
- Neobehaviorists examine internal and unobservable behaviors as well as those that can be observed. They examine such aspects of learning as attitudes and beliefs.
- Cognitive psychologists look at learning as an internal process that cannot be directly observed. They examine problem solving, concept learning, perception, and remembering.
- Researcher Howard Gardner has identified multiple intelligences, maintaining that each has an equal claim to priority.
- The brain has two hemispheres, which, according to many neurologists, receive stimuli at the same time but process them differently. The left hemisphere processes verbal stimuli; the right, spatial stimuli.
- Sociologists observe learning environments and conduct teacher effectiveness research to determine successful learning.
- Students have different learning styles. Some learn better in groups, others individually.
- Educators are examining differences in gender, ethnic, and cultural learning styles to better understand and respond to how different groups of students learn.

---

## How Well Are Students Learning?

The only measures we have of students' learning are scores on standardized tests based only on easy-to-test bits of information in any given subject area. Test results tell us little about whether students have developed the ability to solve sophisticated problems. Neither do they tell us about students' appreciation of art or reading or mathematics. Tests tell us, instead, the level at which the students can succeed on the particular tests.

### NATIONAL ASSESSMENT Of EDUCATIONAL PROGRESS

In an attempt to determine the level of student learning, the **National Assessment of Educational Progress (NAEP)** was begun in 1969. Since that date, this test has been given periodically to students in grades four (age nine), eight (age thirteen), and twelve (age seventeen) across the United States to sample educational progress by race, ethnicity, gender, and geographic region. This congressionally mandated test is a project of the National Center for Education Statistics of the U.S. Department of Education and is the only ongoing, comparable, and representative assessments of what American students know and can do in various content areas. The results have been called *The Nation's Report Card.*

In 1992 NAEP changed the test, based on new national standards of achievement developed by professional organizations, and new methods of reporting test scores. Five proficiency levels have been revised to three levels: Basic, Proficient, and Advanced. Basic denotes "partial mastery of the knowledge and skills fundamental for proficient work at each grade. . . . Proficient, the central level, represents solid academic performance and demonstrated competence over challenging subject matter. . . . The Advanced level signifies superior performance beyond proficient" (NAEP, *Reading Report Card,* 1993, 12). The operational definition of each proficiency level changes for each grade level. Therefore, what is meant by proficient at grade four is different from what is meant by proficient at grade twelve. In addition, NAEP changed how they identify test takers from age level (prior to 1992) to grade level. Grade levels on the 1992 test can be viewed as parallel to age levels on previous tests: age nine = grade four, age thirteen = grade eight, age seventeen = grade twelve. When reporting results in this chapter, age levels will be used if results are for tests prior to 1992, and grade levels when results are for the 1992 tests.

*Reading Assessment*   From 1971 to 1992, NAEP reading test results indicate improvement at all three age and grade levels for whites, blacks, and Hispanics, particularly those at the lower end of the scale. Test results for whites were higher than for either blacks or Hispanics on each of the tests. Reading scores of blacks had risen significantly, but have leveled off in more recent assessments, while scores for whites and Hispanics (except for seventeen-year-olds) have shown limited improvement since 1971, tending to decrease the performance gaps at all three age levels. Females outperformed males at all three age levels. Reading achievement changed little in the Northeast for nine- and thirteen-year-olds from 1971 to 1990, but fell initially and then improved significantly for seventeen-year-olds. Students in the Southeast scored markedly better at all three age levels in 1988 than in 1971, but dropped in 1990. In the central region of the country, the reading performance for nine- and seventeen-year-olds remained relatively constant from 1971 to 1990. However, the proficiency of thirteen-year-olds in the central region rose from 1971 until 1980 and then dropped significantly from 1980 to 1990. (See table 10.4 for an interpretation of each score level on the 1971 to 1990 tests and the percentages of students at or above each level of reading proficiency.)

As in previous administrations of the NAEP test, "substantial proportions of students [on the 1992 test] demonstrated understanding of reading materials considered straightforward for their grade. However, very few, at any grade, were able to examine more complex materials and extend their thinking beyond the

**TABLE 10-4**

## Trends in Percentages of Students Performing At or Above Reading Proficiency Levels

| Level | AGE 9 | | AGE 13 | | AGE 17 | |
|---|---|---|---|---|---|---|
| | Percent in 1990 | Difference from 1971 | Percent in 1990 | Difference from 1971 | Percent in 1990 | Difference from 1971 |
| 350 Can synthesize and learn from specialized reading materials | 0 (0.1) | 0 (0.1) | 0 (0.1) | 0 (0.1) | 7 (0.5) | 0 (0.6) |
| 300 Can find, understand, summarize, and explain relatively complicated information | 2 (0.3) | 1 (0.3) | 11 (0.6) | 1 (0.8) | 41 (1.0) | 2 (1.4) |
| 250 Can search for specific information, interrelate ideas, and make generalizations | 18 (1.0) | 3 (1.2) | 59 (1.0) | 1 (1.5) | 84 (1.0) | 6 (1.3)* |
| 200 Can comprehend specific or sequentially related information | 59 (1.3) | 0 (1.6) | 94 (0.6) | 1 (0.8) | 98 (0.3) | 2 (0.4) |
| 150 Can carry out simple, discrete reading tasks | 90 (0.9) | −1 (1.0) | 100 (0.1) | 0 (0.3) | 100 (0.1) | 0 (0.1) |

* The standard errors of the estimated percentages appear in parentheses. It can be said with 95 percent certainty that for each population of interest, the value for the whole population is within plus or minus two standard errors of the estimate for the sample. (No significance test is reported when the proportion of students is either > 95.0 or < 5.0.) When the proportion of students is either 0 or 100 percent, the standard error is inestimable. However, percentages 99.5 percent and greater were rounded to 100 percent, and percentages less than 0.5 percent were rounded to 0.

From: U.S. Department of Education, National Center for Education Statistics, *Trends in Academic Progress: Achievement of U.S. Students in Science, 1969–70 to 1990; Mathematics, 1973–1990; Reading, 1971–1990; Writing, 1984–1990* (1991), 7.

---

The National Assessment of Educational Progress (NAEP) has tested students at ages nine, thirteen, and seventeen in reading proficiency. The levels as of 1990 ranged from rudimentary (level 150) to advanced (level 350). In 1992 the levels were simplified to three: Basic, Proficient, and Advanced. Progress has been steady at all age levels at all levels of reading except for those here characterized as adept (level 300) and advanced.

information presented as defined at the Advanced level. Only a handful of students at this top level were able to provide the thorough, thoughtful, and extensive answers expected by the standards setting panelists" (NAEP 1993, 13). (See table 10.5 for an interesting comparison of proficiency scores by race and ethnicity.) In fact, the percentage of students scoring at the highest levels has declined since 1971 when 6.6 percent of seventeen-year-olds scored at the Advanced level. In 1992 only 3 percent scored at the newly defined Advanced level. It is possible that this decline is the result of changes in the scoring, since the only year of increase at the Advanced level was in 1990 when 7 percent scored at that level, or it may be that the 1990 score was an anomaly and the decreasing percentage of students scoring at higher levels is related to the instructional and curricular interventions of recent years that have succeeded in strengthening students' basic and proficient reading skills, but not their higher level reading abilities.

**TABLE 10-5**

## Average Reading Proficiency and Achievement Levels by Race/Ethnicity, Grades 4, 8, and 12, 1992 Reading Assessment

| | Percentage of Students | Average Proficiency | Percentage of Students At or Above | | | |
| --- | --- | --- | --- | --- | --- | --- |
| | | | Advanced | Proficient | Basic | Below Basic |
| *Grade 4* | | | | | | |
| White | 71 (0.2) | 226 (1.2) | 6 (0.7) | 31 (1.6) | 68 (1.4) | 32 (1.4) |
| Black | 16 (0.1) | 193 (1.7) | 0 (0.2) | 7 (1.4) | 31 (2.3) | 69 (2.3) |
| Hispanic | 9 (0.1) | 202 (2.2) | 2 (0.6) | 13 (1.8) | 41 (2.2) | 59 (2.2) |
| Asian/Pacific Islander | 2 (0.3) | 216 (3.3) | 2 (1.3) | 21 (4.8) | 55 (5.9) | 45 (5.9) |
| American Indian | 2 (0.2) | 208 (4.7) | 2 (1.9) | 15 (4.7) | 50 (6.1) | 50 (6.1) |
| *Grade 8* | | | | | | |
| White | 70 (0.2) | 268 (1.2) | 3 (0.4) | 34 (1.5) | 77 (1.1) | 23 (1.1) |
| Black | 16 (0.2) | 238 (1.6) | 0 (0.2) | 8 (1.0) | 44 (1.9) | 56 (1.9) |
| Hispanic | 10 (0.2) | 242 (1.4) | 1 (0.3) | 13 (1.1) | 49 (2.1) | 51 (2.1) |
| Asian/Pacific Islander | 3 (0.2) | 270 (3.1) | 6 (2.6) | 38 (4.1) | 77 (3.2) | 23 (3.2) |
| American Indian | 1 (0.2) | 251 (3.7) | 1 (0.9) | 18 (7.2) | 60 (5.0) | 40 (5.0) |
| *Grade 12* | | | | | | |
| White | 72 (0.4) | 297 (0.6) | 4 (0.3) | 43 (0.9) | 82 (0.8) | 18 (0.8) |
| Black | 15 (0.4) | 272 (1.5) | 0 (0.2) | 16 (1.5) | 54 (2.5) | 46 (2.5) |
| Hispanic | 9 (0.4) | 277 (2.4) | 1 (0.7) | 21 (2.8) | 61 (3.2) | 39 (3.2) |
| Asian/Pacific Islander | 4 (0.2) | 291 (3.2) | 4 (1.8) | 39 (3.8) | 74 (4.1) | 26 (4.1) |
| American Indian | 0 (0.1) | 272 (5.3) | 1 (1.2) | 24 (6.9) | 52 (7.7) | 48 (7.7) |

The standard errors of the estimated percentages and proficiencies appear in parentheses. It can be said with 95 percent certainty for each population of interest that the value for the whole population is within plus or minus two standard errors of the estimate for the sample. In comparing two estimates, one must use the standard error of the difference. When the proportion of students is either 0 percent or 100 percent, the standard error is inestimable. However, percentages 99.5 percent and greater were rounded to 100 percent and percentages less than 0.5 percent were rounded to 0 percent. Percentages may not add to 100 percent due to rounding error or because some students categorized themselves as "others."

From: U.S. Department of Education, National Assessment of Educational Progress (NAEP), *Reading Report Card for the Nation and the States* (1992), 101.

In a Reading Assessment conducted by the National Assessment of Educational Progress (NAEP) for the U.S. Department of Education, it was found that, at all grade levels, all races and ethnic groups scored very poorly at the Advanced level. At the Basic and Proficient levels each group improved from grade 4 to grade 12, with Asian/Pacific Islanders and whites showing the most progress.

In fact, in 1990 NAEP indicated concern that not more progress was being made at Advanced levels saying that curricular reform efforts must continue to be pursued, reevaluated, and redirected in the years ahead to provide for more substantial gains, especially at the Advanced level where test reading passages contain "challenging syntactic and rhetorical elements" and test questions are more open-ended, "asking students to articulate their views and ideas based on the selection presented" (Educational Testing Service 1990, 33–35).

*Lack of Homework*   The NAEP found that students who spend more time on homework test at a higher level of reading proficiency than those who spend less time. Similarly, students at all three grade levels who read books, newspapers, and magazines more often receive higher proficiency scores in reading.

Of course, it is not only the amount but the kind of homework that is important. In addition, research suggests that assignments that encourage students to think are more effective in motivating them to learn and helping them become independent learners, resulting in higher scores on standardized tests that require high-level thinking skills.

According to Bennett, high school teachers report giving an average of ten hours of homework per week, while high school seniors report doing only four to five hours per week (p. 51). This may be because the students complete the homework more quickly than the teachers expect, do it incompletely or poorly, or do not do it at all. In any case, it may help explain why students who do more homework generally do better on standardized tests. In the past six years, according to NAEP, a higher percentage of seventeen-year-olds report NOT doing their homework than students at ages thirteen or nine.

A similar positive relationship was found between the amount read per day and achievement as measured by the NAEP. Students who read more per day tended to score at a higher level of proficiency than students who read less. A negative relationship was found at all three levels for the amount of time spent watching television and achievement on the NAEP.

- In all three grades, students who reported watching six or more hours of television each night had substantially lower proficiency scores than their counterparts who reported less viewing.
- Twenty percent of the fourth graders, 14 percent of the eighth graders, and 6 percent of twelfth graders reported watching six or more hours of television per day.
- Sixty-one percent of the fourth graders, 65 percent of the eighth graders, and 47 percent of the twelfth graders reported watching three or more hours of television per day. At grades eight and twelve, students watching this much television had lower average proficiency than their classmates. At grade four, those watching four or more hours had lower average proficiency than less frequent viewers. (NAEP 1993, 12)

In addition, NAEP researchers found that children's television viewing patterns tend to follow the example set by their parents (NAEP 1993, 17). Therefore, it is likely that fourth graders will continue the viewing patterns they have set.

*Writing Assessment*   Levels of writing performance, based on two national assessments of writing proficiency conducted by the NAEP, changed little from 1984 to 1990 (only two administrations of the test were given). In fact, they have remained relatively constant since 1974. Whites continued to outscore blacks and Hispanics at all three age levels. However, at all three levels, black and Hispanic students appear to show consistent, if not statistically significant, improvement.

Females at all grade levels scored noticeably higher than males in overall writing proficiency between 1984 and 1990. The NAEP analyzed scores using the average response method, which estimates how well students in each grade would have done if they had taken eleven of the twelve writing tasks tested. Fourth-grade girls' writing scores on a scale of 0–400, for example, increased significantly, from 184 in 1984 to 193 in 1990, whereas boys' scores remained essentially the same. At grade eight, boys' writing proficiency decreased from 199 in 1984 to 187 in 1990, whereas girls' scores increased slightly. As with reading scores, in 1990 "many students continued to perform at minimal levels on the NAEP writing assessment tasks, and relatively few performed at adequate or better levels" (Educational Testing Service 1990c, 6). At the "minimal" level on writing samples, students "recognized some or all of the elements needed to complete the task but did not manage these elements well enough to assure that the purpose of the task would be achieved," whereas students scoring at what NAEP calls the "adequate" level provided "adequate responses [including] the information and ideas necessary to accomplish the underlying task and were considered likely to be effective in achieving the desired purpose" and, at the "elaborated" level of writing proficiency, students "elaborated responses [that] went beyond the essential, reflecting a higher level of coherence and providing more detail to support the points made" (p. 7). According to an NAEP summary of the results of the writing assessments, students scored best on "informative writing tasks that required straightforward reports or letters" (p. 8). We must ask ourselves why students are able to perform at basic, rudimentary levels in both reading and writing but rarely achieve higher levels of performance. Are U.S. schools adequately challenging students? Are schools spending too much time emphasizing basic skills and not enough time requiring students to think and perform at the higher cognitive levels of analysis, synthesis, and evaluation? Are current instructional strategies appropriate to help students meet the new proficiency levels required by the tests? Are the learning styles of ethnically, culturally, and racially diverse students being acknowledged in how they are taught?

***Mathematics and Science Assessment*** Between 1990 and 1992, mathematics proficiency, measured by the NAEP, improved slightly for all groups. Science proficiency for these groups changed little from 1977 to 1990 (the last administration of the science test; see table 10.6), however, this limited change reflected a significant increase in proficiency at all grade levels between 1986 and 1990, perhaps indicating a reversal of a downward trend. Levels of mathematics and science proficiency still remain low. Most U.S. students, even at age seventeen, are unable to perform at the upper levels of the NAEP mathematics and science proficiency scale.

As in reading and writing, results of NAEP tests in mathematics showed that students' performance on basic skills improved between 1978 and 1992; however, performance on more advanced operations remained the same with a slight increase in 1992. Because the 1992 test was based on new standards set by the National Council of Teachers of Mathematics (NCTM) and new NAEP proficiency levels, it is difficult to compare results with earlier tests. However, NAEP reports that in 1990, 58 percent of eighth-grade students performed at or above the Basic level and 63 percent at or above this level in 1992. A similar small increase can be seen at the Proficient level (20 percent in 1990 and 25 percent in 1992) and a less significant increase at the Advanced level (2 percent in 1990 and 4 percent in 1992). The proportion of thirteen-year-olds (eighth graders) who could perform

**TABLE 10-6**

## Trends in Percentages of Students Performing At or Above Science Proficiency Levels

| Level | AGE 9 | | AGE 13 | | AGE 17 | |
|---|---|---|---|---|---|---|
| | Percent in 1990 | Difference from 1977 | Percent in 1990 | Difference from 1977 | Percent in 1990 | Difference from 1977 |
| 350 Can infer relationships and draw conclusions using detailed scientific knowledge | 0 (0.0) | 0 (0.0) | 0 (0.1) | 0 (0.1) | 9 (0.5) | 1 (0.6) |
| 300 Has some detailed scientific knowledge and can evaluate the appropriateness of scientific procedures | 3 (0.3) | 0 (0.4) | 11 (0.6) | 0 (0.8) | 43 (1.3) | 2 (1.6) |
| 250 Understands and applies general information from the life and physical sciences | 31 (0.8) | 5 (1.1)* | 57 (1.0) | 8 (1.5)* | 81 (0.9) | 0 (1.2) |
| 200 Understands some simple principles and has some knowledge, for example, about plants and animals | 76 (0.9) | 8 (1.4)* | 92 (0.7) | 6 (1.0)* | 97 (0.3) | 0 (0.4) |
| 150 Knows everyday science facts | 97 (0.3) | 3 (0.7) | 100 (0.1) | 1 (0.2) | 100 (0.2) | 0 (0.2) |

* Statistically significant difference at the .05 level. The standard errors of the estimated percentages appear in parentheses. It can be said with 95 percent certainty that for each population of interest, the value for the whole population is within plus or minus two standard errors of the estimate for the sample. (No significance test is reported when the proportion of students is either > 95.0 or < 5.0.) When the proportion of students is either 0 or 100 percent, the standard error is inestimable. However, percentages 99.5 percent and greater were rounded to 100 percent, and percentages less than 0.5 percent were rounded to 0.

From: U.S. Department of Education, National Center for Education Statistics, *Trends in Academic Progress: Achievement of U.S. Students in Science, 1969–70 to 1990; Mathematics, 1973–1990; Reading, 1971–1990; Writing, 1984–1990* (1991), 5.

---

**Analysis of the NAEP (National Assessment of Educational Progress) tests of science proficiency (1977–1990) indicates that at lower levels of factual knowledge, most students perform very well, but that at higher levels of analysis and interpretation very few do.**

basic numerical operations rose from 65 percent in 1978 to 75 percent in 1990, but the proportion of these students who could perform moderately complex mathematical procedures declined from 18 percent in 1978 to 17 percent in 1990. Since no similar proficiency level existed in 1992, a comparison cannot be made. The proportion of seventeen-year-olds (twelfth graders) who could perform basic numerical operations rose from 92 percent in 1978 to 96 percent in 1990, but the proportion of those who could perform multistep problems remained at the same 7 percent level for the same time period. Only subsequent tests utilizing the new standards and proficiency levels will show if these trends are continuing or are reversing (see table 10.7).

According to the NAEP's assessment of 1992 test results, performance improved especially among black and Hispanic students and students in the Southeast. However, these positive changes must be tempered with a concern

**TABLE 10-7**

### Trends in Percentages of Students Performing At or Above Mathematics Proficiency Levels

| | AGE 9 | | AGE 13 | | AGE 17 | |
|---|---|---|---|---|---|---|
| Level | Percent in 1990 | Difference from 1978 | Percent in 1990 | Difference from 1978 | Percent in 1990 | Difference from 1978 |
| 350 Can solve multi-step problems and use beginning algebra | 0 (0.0) | 0 (0.0) | 0 (0.1) | −1 (0.2) | 7 (0.6) | 0 (0.8) |
| 300 Can compute with decimals, fractions, and percents; recognize geometric figures; solve simple equations; and use moderately complex reasoning | 1 (0.3) | 0 (0.3) | 17 (1.0) | −1 (1.2) | 56 (1.4) | 5 (1.8)* |
| 250 Can add, subtract, multiply, and divide using whole numbers, and solve one-step problems | 28 (0.9) | 8 (1.1)* | 75 (1.0) | 10 (1.6)* | 96 (0.5) | 4 (0.7) |
| 200 Can add and subtract two-digit numbers and recognize relationships among coins | 82 (1.0) | 11 (1.3)* | 99 (0.2) | 4 (0.5) | 100 (0.1) | 0 (0.1) |
| 150 Knows some addition and subtraction facts | 99 (0.2) | 2 (0.3) | 100 (0.0) | 0 (0.1) | 100 (0.0) | 0 (0.0) |

\* Statistically significant difference at the .05 level. The standard errors of the estimated percentages appear in parentheses. It can be said with 95 percent certainty that for each population of interest, the value for the whole population is within plus or minus two standard errors of the estimate for the sample. (No significance test is reported when the proportion of students is either > 95.0 or < 5.0.) When the proportion of students is either 0 or 100 percent, the standard error is inestimable. However, percentages 99.5 percent and greater were rounded to 100 percent, and percentages less than 0.5 percent were rounded to 0.

From: U.S. Department of Education, National Center for Education Statistics, *Trends in Academic Progress: Achievement of U.S. Students in Science, 1969-70 to 1990; Mathematics, 1973-1990; Reading, 1971-1990; Writing, 1984-1990* (1991), 6.

---

As measured on the NAEP (National Assessment of Educational Progress), students have improved mathematical skills from 1978 to 1990, but only at the low skill levels. At moderately complex levels (level 300), little more than half of all seventeen-year-olds were able to perform adequately, and at the highest level (level 350), only 7 percent of all seventeen-year-olds were able to solve the problems.

about the fact that the improvement is at low levels of skill performance and limited improvement or no improvement is seen between the 1990 and 1992 administrations of the mathematics test (see table 10.7). According to NAEP, this suggests that schools are more concerned with "students' rote use of procedures than with their understanding of concepts and development of higher-order thinking skills" (Educational Testing Service 1988a, 12). It also suggests that the improvement seen in earlier years has leveled off and, perhaps, is beginning to decline. Possibly, changes in the content of the 1992 mathematics tests, based on standards set by the National Council of Teachers of Mathematics (NCTM), led to this decrease in minority test scores although it did not lead to a similar decrease in the white students' scores on the 1992 tests.

Science achievement, as measured on the National Assessment of Education Progress (NAEP), has been moderate at best for high school students in the United States. At the higher levels of analysis, roughly one-half of the boys and only one-third of the girls were able to deal with scientific procedures and data. These students are using scales to weigh metals.

Positive results are seen on the NAEP science assessment. Students' achievement scores in science rose between 1977 and 1990 for nine- and thirteen-year-olds but showed no significant change for seventeen-year-olds. In fact, from 1989 to 1990 there was a significant decline in science achievement scores. Although blacks and Hispanics have made substantial gains in recent years, the average proficiency for thirteen- and seventeen-year-old blacks and Hispanics is considerably lower than their white peers. NAEP's analysis of scores suggested that the differential in scores between races may relate to parents' socioeconomic status and level of education rather than race.

The greatest improvement in science achievement is among nine-year-olds, to the levels they had achieved in 1969. In 1990, 76 percent, up from 68 percent in 1977, could understand simple scientific principles. At age nine, the proficiency of boys and girls was relatively the same, but by ages thirteen and seventeen, roughly one-half of the boys and only one-third of the girls could analyze scientific procedures and data. According to the NAEP, the difference in scientific achievement by gender cannot be explained by course-taking patterns. Citing a study by Marsha Matyas and Jane Kahle, *Equitable Precollege Science and Mathematics: A Discrepancy Model* (1986), NAEP suggested that the differential may stem from teachers' higher expectations of boys than girls: asking boys higher-level questions than girls and providing different treatment and opportunities in science instruction. In addition, NAEP suggested that textbooks that show that most scientific accomplishments are made by white males might contribute subtly to this gender discrepancy (Educational Testing Service 1988b, 8).

More than in any other content areas, U.S. students' achievement in mathematics and science has been compared with students' achievement in other countries. In both disciplines, the achievement of U.S. students is relatively low when considering the scientific contributions of U.S. scientists. In 1991, in mathematics, students ranked last on the second International Assessment of Educational Progress (IAEP) when compared to students in five other developed nations; in science they ranked second to last. In the United States, thirteen-year-olds, for example, could compute only at the basic operational and problem-solving level in mathematics, whereas Korean students could operate at the intermediate level and solve two-step problems. The same contrast can be seen in science, where thirteen-year-olds in the United States could work only marginally at the basic level, understanding simple scientific information. Korean students, operating a level above U.S. students, could use scientific procedures and analyze scientific data.

Again, we must question why this is so. According to the 1990 NAEP science assessment, Americans are relatively unscientific. Use of scientific equipment by third graders and seventh graders is relatively low. Only 68.1 percent of U.S. third graders, for instance, had used a yardstick. Similarly, only 25.1 percent of U.S. seventh graders had used a barometer. However, 91 percent had used a microscope. The NAEP also asked students about their independent science activities. According to the study, only 39 percent of high school students read books or articles about science, and fewer engaged in scientific discussions with friends, took trips to museums, or had science hobbies. A surprisingly small percentage of U.S. eleventh graders report applying scientific knowledge to practical situations. Only 27 percent reported fixing anything mechanical, and only 10 percent reported figuring out what was wrong with an unhealthy plant.

*History Assessment*   In 1988 the NAEP assessed student progress in history for the first and only time to date. Students were tested in the fourth, eighth, and twelfth grades. According to the test results, most students, at all three grade levels, have a limited grasp of U.S. history.

Because this was the first history assessment of U.S. students, it is not possible to make comparisons across years. It is possible, however, to examine the results of this test. NAEP concludes that "a large percentage of students approaching high school graduation—and a disproportionally large percentage of minority students—lack a sense of the national heritage" (Educational Testing Service 1990b, 6). At grade four, approximately three-quarters of students tested performed at or above level 200, the lowest proficiency level. Approximately two-thirds of eighth graders performed at or above level 250 and could identify more events and personalities of U.S. history. However, only 13 percent scored at level 300 and could understand historical terms and relationships. Eighty-nine percent of high school students displayed an understanding of beginning historical information, and 46 percent understood historical terms, texts, and relationships. However, only 5 percent of high school seniors performed at the highest level and could interpret historical information and ideas. Only 38 percent of high school seniors, for example, recognized the opening statement of the Declaration of Independence and had more than a rudimentary understanding of U.S. historical policies on civil rights. Hence, this assessment, like the other NAEP assessments, seems to reveal that U.S. students have basic and rudimentary

**TABLE 10-8**

## SAT Scores by Ethnic Group 1993–1994

|  | 1993 | | 1994 | |
|---|---|---|---|---|
|  | **Verbal** | **Math** | **Verbal** | **Math** |
| American Indian | 400 | 447 | 396 | 441 |
| Asian American | 415 | 535 | 416 | 535 |
| African American | 353 | 388 | 352 | 388 |
| Mexican American | 374 | 428 | 372 | 427 |
| Puerto Rican | 367 | 409 | 367 | 411 |
| Other Hispanic/Latino | 384 | 433 | 383 | 435 |
| White | 444 | 484 | 443 | 495 |
| Other | 422 | 477 | 425 | 480 |

Note: The question on ethnic background was changed in 1987 to include the "Other Hispanic" category.

Adapted from: The College Entrance Examination Board, *1994 Profile of SAT and Achievement Test Takers* (1994), 6 and *1993 Profile of SAT and Achievement Test Takers* (1993), v.

**With the more analytical form of the SAT test taken in 1994, scores for almost all ethnic groups remained the same or declined slightly from the 1993 scores.**

knowledge of a subject, but few possess knowledge at advanced levels (Educational Testing Service 1990b).

## COLLEGE ENTRANCE EXAMS

The single most quoted measure of student progress through high school is the Scholastic Aptitude Test (SAT), used primarily to assess students' likely success in college. The American College Testing Program (ACT) is also used by college admissions staffs to predict student success in college.

From 1982 until 1986, SAT and ACT scores increased after a nearly twenty-year decline. However, from 1986 through 1990, the scores again fell with a slight rise in 1992 and 1993. From 1976 to 1993, average SAT verbal and mathematics scores of black students increased by 21 and 34 points respectively, on an 800-point scale. Other minority students' scores increased only slightly (see table 10.8). Although minority students are making progress, the gap between minority and white students is still large. In 1993, white students had a composite (combined verbal and mathematics) score of 938 on the SAT, and black students had a composite score of 741; Native Americans of 887; Mexican Americans of 802; Puerto Ricans of 776; and other Hispanics of 817. The only minority students who scored higher than whites were Asian Americans, who had a composite score of 950 in 1993.

Since the SAT does not test specific knowledge but rather tests aptitude to learn, the decline in its scores may be related to the low level of proficiency held by the majority of high school students in all subjects, as revealed by the NAEP.

The SAT tests a student's ability to analyze, synthesize, evaluate, and solve multistep problems. NAEP results indicate that the vast majority of U.S. students do not function well on these high-level skills probably because most school time is used in learning basic skills. In 1994, students took a newly revised version of the SAT that, according to the College Board, sponsors of the test, required even higher level thinking skills than earlier versions of the test. (Students had to solve ten mathematics problems using calculators; multiple-choice answers were not provided. Reading comprehension questions included questions on vocabulary that appeared in the passages.) As expected, scores from the 1994 SATs indicated a slight decline in both math and verbal areas for all ethnic groups.

As the test results show, many of the students who do not progress at expected levels as measured by standardized tests are nonwhite, poor, urban, and male. Is the public school system failing these students? In addition, test results reveal that few students are performing successfully at high cognitive levels. Are the public schools failing to challenge students to reach their highest level of potential? And what of society? Are the values of society militating against the academic achievement of U.S. students? We will deal with these questions in chapters 11 and 12.

---

**10-2**

**Points to Remember**

- The NAEP indicates that most students in the United States are not doing as well on standardized achievement tests as might be hoped. In both reading and writing, students score better in areas of basic skills than on test items that require critical and creative thinking.
- In mathematics and science, students function more successfully in areas of rudimentary knowledge and basic, simple functions. There is a significant gap between the achievement of males and females, particularly at the higher levels.

- Students are able to identify important historical personalities and events but are unable to relate these to each other. Students are unable to think at the higher levels of synthesis, analysis, and evaluation.
- The NAEP is redesigning its tests based on standards set by national professional organizations.
- Students who spend more time on carefully prepared homework, read more daily, and spend minimal time watching television receive higher proficiency scores on NAEP tests.
- Students in the United States score lower on standardized tests than students in many other developed nations.

- SAT and ACT scores declined significantly from the early 1960s through the early 1980s, when there was a slight increase. However, the scores declined again in the late 1980s and early 1990s—with a slight increase in the 1992 and 1993 scores.
- Theories about why U.S. students do not do well on standardized tests include: U.S. schools teach students to think rather than to take tests; U.S. values do not encourage students to do well on standardized tests; U.S. students do not do as much homework and are not willing to work as hard as students in other countries.

---

## For Thought/Discussion

1. What are the differences between the behaviorist and neobehaviorist definitions of learning? How can these differences be reconciled in a practical way in the classroom?

2. From the sociological perspective of learning environment, what are some things teachers can do to motivate students to learn?

3. How do the learning styles of females differ from those of males? How would you structure a class lesson so that both boys and girls benefitted equally from the information given?

4. What are the relationships among television, homework, and students' test scores? If you were a parent, how would you balance the time your child spends watching television, reading, and doing homework without causing negative psychological attitudes?

## For Further Reading/Reference

Brown, R. C. 1991. *Schools of thought.* San Francisco: Jossey-Bass. A discussion of the definition of literacy as the ability to think critically and creatively and to become a lifetime learner. The author contends that many of the methods used in today's schools discourage critical and creative thinking.

*Educational Leadership.* 1990. 48 (2), complete issue. "Learning styles and the brain." Discussions by various authors on learning styles. Articles include student awareness of learning styles, left brain/right brain, how learning styles should influence teaching and curriculum, and a private school that implements learning styles research.

Gardner, H. 1993. *Multiple intelligence: The theory and practice.* New York: Basic Books. A discussion of the author's thesis that humans have seven intelligences. Applications of his theory to all levels of schooling from kindergarten through college.

Holt, J. 1989. *Learning all the time.* Reading, MA: Addison-Wesley. A discussion of how children learn from those things that are significant for them in the real world rather than from special learning materials.

Sadker, M., and D. Sadker. 1994. *Failing at fairness: How America's schools cheat girls.* New York: Charles Scribner's Sons. A detailed discussion and analysis of the authors' twenty years of research on gender bias in the educational system.

Stan Fine in *Phi Delta Kappan*

Like high school students everywhere, seventeen-year-old Danielle Schuler of New Britain [Connecticut] tumbles out of bed each weekday at dawn and rushes to get ready for class.

But these days she adds an extra ritual: rousing her seven-week-old son, Kreyshon, who will join her at school. While Ms. Schuler toils at English and math, Kreyshon is put in the care of the nursery down the hall where he is bathed, played with, and cuddled.

"I'm tired a lot and have no time to myself, so this place gives me the space to learn. . . . Before I got pregnant . . . I had two girlfriends and we had this dream: None of us would get pregnant and we would get jobs and share an apartment together. Now I have a baby and both of my girlfriends are pregnant. I stay in the house a lot and don't go around with anybody."

From: Rierden, "The Age of School and Motherhood" (1994), 1, 7.

# *Part V*

# SOCIETY
# AND SCHOOLS

## Chapter 11

### SOCIETY'S EFFECT ON THE SCHOOLS

In this chapter we discuss some of the major issues facing U.S. society and how they affect children and the school. These include the changing family, teenage sexual activity, AIDS, chemical abuse, crime, and suicide. Many of the statistics presented in this chapter are grim. However, because society's problems have such a major impact on today's children, teachers must be aware of them. Here and in chapter 12 we will talk about some of the ways in which contemporary schools are attempting to meet the needs of children and, thereby, help solve some of society's problems.

## Chapter 12

### SCHOOLS RESPOND TO SOCIAL CHANGE

Although schools do not change rapidly and many argue that they should conserve rather than change society, they do attempt to deal with social changes and to meet the needs of society through direct and indirect measures. This chapter will examine some of the ways in which schools are affected by social change and how schools attempt to meet the needs of today's children and families.

**CHAPTER OBJECTIVES**

After studying this chapter, you should be able to:

- Analyze the diversity of contemporary U.S. families.
- Discuss the single-parent family.
- Understand the problems of working mothers.
- Discuss the implications of homelessness for school-aged children.
- Discuss problems related to teenage parents.
- Compare and contrast characteristics of minority families with similarly configured white families.
- Discuss how schools can respond to the needs of families.
- Define and discuss child abuse and its impact on children and schools.
- Discuss the problems of children in poverty.

- Understand how crime affects the schools.
- Discuss how sexism affects students and the schools.
- Discuss how racism affects students and school personnel.
- Discuss how substance abuse education attempts to deal with society's needs.
- Analyze the problems of students who are chemically dependent.
- Discuss problems related to teenage sexual activity.
- Define and discuss sexual harassment.
- Explain how sex education attempts to deal with students' needs.
- Discuss AIDS education.
- Define teenage suicide.

## Chapter 11

# SOCIETY'S EFFECT ON THE SCHOOLS

*S*ingle Mothers—Long before morning light has dimmed the street lamp outside her window, Pauline Britton smooths her hair one last time. She steps into two tiny bedrooms and touches the sleep-warm heads of her four children. Hurrying downstairs, she sips the last of her hot tea and pulls the door shut as she leaves, the clunk of the deadbolt loud in the deserted street at 5 a.m.

From the bus, Pauline looks out at the broken streets and thinks maybe, with a few more years of saving, her kids could wake up in a house on a good street. But if she paid someone to stay with them while she worked, she could not keep the dream alive. So, for the last three years, fourteen-year-old Hope has been part-time mother to the three younger children.

By 6:30, Pauline is at the nursing home where, for $7.10 an hour, she spoon-feeds breakfasts and combs thinning scalps. She waits until exactly 7 a.m. to dial home. "Hope, it's Mom. Time to get up. Breakfast is on the counter, and make sure the others wear their coats to school. Love you." At 7:20, Pauline phones again: "Just wanted to make sure you were all up. Love you." At 8:15, she dials again. No answer. Just as it should be, since the children should have left for school; a quick call to a neighbor confirms it. Now, knowing she has done all she can, Pauline must trust in Hope and God that things will be OK until she gets home.

From: Creighton, "Kids Taking Care of Kids" (1993), 26, 31.

**Teenage Mothers**—Like high school students everywhere, seventeen-year-old Danielle Schuler of New Britain [Connecticut] tumbles out of bed each weekday at dawn and rushes to get ready for class.

But these days she adds an extra ritual: rousing her seven-week-old son, Kreyshon, who will join her at school. While Ms. Schuler toils at English and math, Kreyshon is put in the care of the nursery down the hall where he is bathed, played with, and cuddled.

"I'm tired a lot and have no time to myself, so this place gives me the space to learn. . . . Before I got pregnant . . . I had two girlfriends and we had this dream: None of us would get pregnant and we would get jobs and share an apartment together. Now I have a baby and both of my girlfriends are pregnant. I stay in the house a lot and don't go around with anybody."

> From: Rierden, "The Age of School and Motherhood" (1994), 1, 7.

**Teenage Fathers**—"Guess what? I'm pregnant," Amy Lister said to Efrain Talavera when he was sixteen and she was fifteen. "Oh yeah?" Efrain recalls responding with all the nonchalance he could muster. "Guess what? I'm hungry. Let's go to McDonald's." He spent the next several months being cruel to her in hopes she would leave him. "She would call and I'd tell [whoever answered the phone] 'I'm not here'—but I'd say it loud enough so she heard." He was terrified and angry about the prospect of fatherhood. . . . Amy had not wanted to get pregnant, but she desperately wanted to keep the baby. . . . As the delivery date approached, Efrain decided he couldn't abandon his child. "I want to live long enough to see her grow up," he says. He stood by Amy's side when Lillyana was born. . . . Amy received welfare after the birth but now lives with Efrain and his mother. . . . Efrain just got a job as a janitor to help pay the bills.

> From: Waldman, "Taking on the Welfare Dads: Teen Parenthood" (1994), 34–38.

**Abused Children**—My first impression of Robbie was of the dull appearance of his hair and eyes. Somehow this was even more striking than the odor emanating from his corner desk. Sullen and quiet, Robbie drifted through my first grade lessons, barely able to find a pencil in his disorganized desk. His lunch usually consisted of Twinkies, which he said he bought on his walk to school. Later I learned that he more frequently stole them from the corner store. He eyed the other children's lunches covetously, and once I saw him steal an apple when a classmate turned her back. Quickly, like a furtive animal, he thrust the apple into the pocket of his dirty, faded, tattered pants.

Notes and phone calls to his parents met with no response. Robbie was a sad little nomad, drifting into school and listlessly returning home, reportedly to take care of his younger brother and sister.

> From: C. C. Tower, *How Schools Can Help Combat Child Abuse and Neglect* (1987), 29.

**Homeless Families**—Carmen Ramos is twenty-six and has five children, the eldest nine, the youngest an infant. She has lived in four or five New York City welfare hotels, including the infamous Martinique. Conditions there were crowded. There was a lot of thievery and drugs, she says, "lots of chaos, a lot of trouble." She says her children were "acting like savages because they had been living at the hotel for a long time."

Before the hotels, she had been living with the father of one of her children. He beat her. . . . She says her mother used to hit her with extension cords for coming home late from school. She once had a job for two months at a Jack-in-the-Box.

She plans to avoid living with any more men. . . .

"If I find the right job that pays more money than welfare," she says, "I might stop welfare. . . ."

Carmen was living in a hotel when she became pregnant with her last child. "I wanted another child," she says. "I planned for the pregnancy to take place. I love children."

From: C. Lockhead, "Homeless in America, All Alone With No Home" *Insight* (May 1988), 11.

---

*I*n this chapter we discuss some of the major issues facing U.S. society and how they affect children and the school. These include the changing family, teenage sexual activity, chemical abuse, crime, and suicide. Many of the statistics presented in this chapter are grim. However, because society's problems have such a major impact on today's children, teachers must be aware of them. Here and in chapter 12 we will talk about some of the ways in which contemporary schools are attempting to meet the needs of children and, thereby, help solve some of society's problems.

## The Family and the School

Families in the United States are diverse; they have different needs and problems. In fact, the sociologist L. P. Howe, in *The Future and the Family,* wrote, "The first thing to remember about the American family is that it doesn't exist. Families exist. All kinds of families in all kinds of economic and marital situations . . ." (1972, 11). In actuality, says Richard Louv, there is a widening variety of family definitions that have become the norm, rather than departures from the norm (1990). William Hass, United Nations spokesman for the "1994 United Nations International Year of the Family (IYF)" points out that the UN avoided defining the family or singling out any type of family as a model. According to Hass, "It's a diversified world and we have to stress the respect for human rights and encourage the stability that families give" (Mouat 1994, 16).

Barbara Lindner in *Drawing in the Family: Family Involvement in the Schools* identified eight family types, six of which we will discuss here: single-parent families, families with two wage earners, two-parent families with one wage earner, joined or blended families, homeless parents, and teenage parents. Within these groups there are numerous variations related to age, family size, culture, race, religion, socioeconomic level, education, and experience. There are almost as many variations as there are families.

**Table 11.1**

## Living Arrangements of Children Under 18 Years, by Race and Hispanic Origin: 1992, 1980, and 1970

| | | | | Percent distribution | | |
|---|---|---|---|---|---|---|
| Living arrangement | 1992 | 1980 | 1970 | 1992 | 1980 | 1970 |
| ALL RACES | | | | | | |
| *Children under 18 years* | 65,965 | 63,427 | 69,162 | 100.0 | 100.0 | 100.0 |
| Living with— | | | | | | |
| Two parents | 46,638 | 48,624 | 58,939 | 70.7 | 76.7 | 85.2 |
| One parent | 17,578 | 12,466 | 8,199 | 26.6 | 19.7 | 11.9 |
| Mother only | 15,396 | 11,406 | 7,452 | 23.3 | 18.0 | 10.8 |
| Father only | 2,182 | 1,060 | 748 | 3.3 | 1.7 | 1.1 |
| Other relatives | 1,334 | 1,949 | 1,547 | 2.0 | 3.1 | 2.2 |
| Nonrelatives only | 415 | 388 | 477 | 0.6 | 0.6 | 0.7 |
| | | | | | | |
| WHITE | | | | | | |
| *Children under 18 years* | 52,493 | 52,242 | 58,790 | 100.0 | 100.0 | 100.0 |
| Living with— | | | | | | |
| Two parents | 40,635 | 43,200 | 52,624 | 77.4 | 82.7 | 89.5 |
| One parent | 10,971 | 7,901 | 5,109 | 20.9 | 15.1 | 8.7 |
| Mother only | 9,250 | 7,059 | 4,581 | 17.6 | 13.5 | 7.8 |
| Father only | 1,721 | 842 | 528 | 3.3 | 1.6 | 0.9 |
| Other relatives | 643 | 887 | 696 | 1.2 | 1.7 | 1.2 |
| Nonrelatives only | 243 | 254 | 362 | 0.5 | 0.5 | 0.6 |

Note: Excludes persons under 18 years old who were maintaining households or family groups. Numbers in thousands.

The numbers of children living in families headed by a single parent has risen dramatically in recent years. This has serious implications for the students and the schools, which need to accommodate single working parents and noncustodial parents in their schedules.

### SINGLE-PARENT FAMILIES

In 1992, 17.6 million (or 26.6 percent) of the 65.9 million children under the age of eighteen in the United States lived in **single-parent families** (see table 11.1). By 1992, 10.5 million (or 29.7 percent) of the 35.3 million family groups were headed by a single parent, according to the 1992 U.S. Bureau of Census Current Population Report.

Of children who lived with a single parent, 15.4 million lived with their mothers and 2.2 million with their fathers. In the past twenty-five years, the number of families headed by women has increased significantly. In 1970, only 10.8 percent of all families were headed by women; by 1992, the figure had grown to more than 23.3 percent.

Ninety percent of U.S. children whose parents divorce are placed in the sole custody of their mothers. Hence, most noncustodial parents are male. However, the number of children living with fathers almost tripled from 1970 through 1992.

| Living arrangement | 1992 | 1980 | 1970 | Percent distribution | | |
| --- | --- | --- | --- | --- | --- | --- |
| | | | | 1992 | 1980 | 1970 |
| BLACK | | | | | | |
| *Children under 18 years* | 10,427 | 9,375 | 9,422 | 100.0 | 100.0 | 100.0 |
| Living with— | | | | | | |
| Two parents | 3,714 | 3,956 | 5,508 | 35.6 | 42.2 | 58.5 |
| One parent | 5,934 | 4,297 | 2,996 | 56.9 | 45.8 | 31.8 |
| Mother only | 5,607 | 4,117 | 2,783 | 53.8 | 43.9 | 29.5 |
| Father only | 327 | 180 | 213 | 3.1 | 1.9 | 2.3 |
| Other relatives | 625 | 999 | 820 | 6.0 | 10.7 | 8.7 |
| Nonrelatives only | 154 | 123 | 97 | 1.5 | 1.3 | 1.0 |
| HISPANIC ORIGIN* | | | | | | |
| *Children under 18 years* | 7,619 | 5,459 | **4,006 | 100.0 | 100.0 | 100.0 |
| Living with— | | | | | | |
| Two parents | 4,935 | 4,116 | 3,111 | 64.8 | 75.4 | 77.7 |
| One parent | 2,447 | 1,152 | (NA) | 32.1 | 21.1 | (NA) |
| Mother only | 2,168 | 1,069 | (NA) | 28.5 | 19.6 | (NA) |
| Father only | 279 | 83 | (NA) | 3.7 | 1.5 | (NA) |
| Other relatives | 196 | 183 | (NA) | 2.6 | 3.4 | (NA) |
| Nonrelatives only | 41 | 8 | (NA) | 0.5 | 0.1 | (NA) |

NA Not available.

 * Persons of Hispanic origin may be of any race.

**All persons under 18 years.

Source of Hispanic data for 1970: 1970 Census, of Population, PC(2)-1C, *Persons of Spanish Origin*.

From: U.S. Bureau of Census, Current Population Reports. (1992). *Marital Status and Living Arrangements: March 1992* (Series P-20, No. 468), Washington, DC: U.S. Government Printing Office, p. xii.

*Marriage and Divorce*   Most single parents are either divorced or have never been married. In 1992, about 38 percent (down from 44 percent in 1980) of single parents were divorced; 35 percent (up from 16 percent in 1980) had never been married; 22 percent (down from 28 percent in 1980) were married but not living with their spouse; 5 percent (down from 12 percent in 1980) were widowed. The number of married-couple families decreased from 71.7 percent in 1970 to 55 percent in 1992. Although married-couple families constituted the majority of all families in 1992 (55 percent), most of them did not have children under the age of eighteen in the home. In 1992, 11 percent (16.3 million) of all adults over fifteen years of age who had ever been married were divorced (up from 4 percent or 4.3 million in 1970) (U.S. Bureau of Census 1992).

If predictions based on population demographics hold true, half of the newly married couples will eventually divorce. Therefore, one-third or more of all children will be living with a divorced parent at some point in their lives.

*Problems of Single-Parent Families*   This change in the structure of U.S. families puts significant pressure on the single parents, the children, and the school. In 1992, of the 17.4 million children who lived in single-parent homes, 11.2 million had custodial parents who were in the labor force; 1.5 million had parents who were unemployed and 6.3 million had parents not in the labor force. Nearly 8 million children lived in single-parent homes in which the custodial parent was neither employed nor in the labor force. In 1992, 86 percent (9.0 million) of single parents were mothers.

Children growing up in single-parent families typically do not have the same economic, housing, or human resources available as those growing up in two-parent households. Among families with children, the poverty rate for single-parent families is 42 percent compared to 8 percent for two-parent families (The Annie E. Casey Foundation 1994, 16).

In addition to having to find reliable, affordable day care, single parents who work are frequently frustrated by the constraints and demands of the school, which functions during the same basic hours that most people work, thus preventing most of them from attending school meetings and events. In order to meet the needs of the child in single-parent homes, the school day might be structured to allow for varied activities before and after classtime so that children, like Pauline's, not only can be cared for but also can participate in motivational and enjoyable activities. After-school programs should also allow time for study and instruction (see chapter 12).

## FAMILIES WITH TWO WAGE EARNERS

Although the percentage of children in two-parent households has decreased from 85.2 percent in 1970 to 73.1 percent in 1992, they are still in the majority. However, only 35.6 percent of black children in 1992 came from two-parent households, whereas 64 percent of Hispanic children did (see table 11.1 on p. 430).

*Working Mothers*   More and more children live in homes in which their mothers are in the labor force. By 1991, 59.7 percent of women with children under five and 75 percent of women with children between six and seventeen worked part- or full-time (The Annie E. Casey Foundation 1994, 18). In every state except West Virginia and in every ethnic group and race, a majority of mothers work (Population Reference Bureau 1993, 10–11).

White married mothers with school-aged children are less likely to be working outside the home than white single-parent mothers. For black women, the reverse is true. The U.S. Department of Labor, Bureau of Labor Statistics, reports that the overall proportion of children with mothers working full-time for part of the year more than doubled between 1975 and 1992, from 29 percent to 59.7 percent. Likewise, the proportion of children with mothers who work full-time throughout the year has nearly doubled since 1971, from 17 percent to 30 percent in 1988.

Most women who work generally do so out of necessity rather than choice, mainly for economic reasons. The greatest growth in the number of women workers during the past few years has been among the well-educated from families with moderate incomes that are insufficient to maintain established and expected patterns of consumption. Before World War II, those married women

---

## *Cross-Cultural Perspective*

## Political Power Is Only Half the Battle

Norway is the only country where children ask their parents if a boy can grow up to be prime minister and get told that at present, the answer is "no way."

Nowhere else in the world do women have more political clout. In last fall's national election, Prime Minister Gro Harlem Brundtland and the leaders of the nation's two main opposition political parties were women. Helped by a quota system that recommends women make up at least 40 percent of every political party's list of candidates for Parliament, women hold almost half the seats in the cabinet and in Parliament. Norway has even changed its Constitution to allow the first-born daughter—rather than just the eldest son—to succeed to the throne upon the death of the monarch. "Norway is a leading country in the field of equal rights," says Brundtland, a physician, a mother of four and the daughter of a doctor and former cabinet minister.

She is only half right. Despite their political gains, Norwegian women remain second-class citizens in the job market. They are hired last, fired first, denied equal pay for the same work as men and held back from promotions to top executive jobs. New laws pushed through by women politicians were supposed to end all that. But Norway's experience suggests that reforming the law is not enough to guarantee women a fair shake.

**Where men still rule.** Others think the real reason is that legislation can only do so much. New laws have not changed the realities of private industry, where men still rule—and do the hiring and promoting. "Put crudely," says sociologist Oystein Holter, "that means men inject male values into personnel decisions. Perhaps a man gets the job because his military service is regarded as a better qualification than a woman rival's child-care experience. No sex-ual discrimination is involved, just a value judgment, and you cannot legislate against that. Instead, you have to change attitudes."

A Norwegian woman's place has traditionally been in the home, as in Henrik Ibsen's classic play *A Doll's House.* Wives stayed away from business; husbands never put the teakettle on. Inflation and economic necessity have now pushed wives into the work force but largely in lower-paying positions, such as nurses or secretaries.

**Catching up.** That is changing, but slowly. Women now outnumber men in Norway's law and medical schools but trail significantly in business schools. Meanwhile, Norway's legislative reforms have produced some surprising results. Women now get 52 weeks of paid maternity leave, but only if the husband takes off the first month, too. If he doesn't, the wife's paid leave is cut in half. The idea is to encourage fathers to help with a baby from the beginning, in the belief that once they start, they will stay engaged in child rearing. But the policy has led to unexpected results: In many divorce cases, Norwegian fathers are now fighting for child custody.

For all the advances in women's rights, Norwegians are not sure that they ultimately will be more successful than other nations in creating a society in which women can be equally fulfilled as wives, mothers and professionals. For now, they are counting on improvements in child care and job rights to allow women to put families first at some stages of their lives, and to focus on their careers at others.

From: Fred Coleman, "Political Power Is Only Half the Battle," *US News & World Report* (June 13, 1994), 58.

---

who worked were primarily from low-income families; today, they are just as commonly from middle-class families. M. L. Usdansky found that more women in midsized cities in the Midwest worked than in other types of communities in other regions of the country (1994, 2A).

According to a 1994 study conducted by sociologists Toby L. Purcel and Elizabeth C. Menaghan, mothers with complex, autonomous jobs were found to be less restrictive with their children, showed greater involvement with them and warmth toward them, and reported less use of physical punishment than mothers with routine jobs. Their children scored higher on the Peabody Test of Verbal Ability and had equal or better verbal facility than children whose mothers did not work. Conversely, working mothers with routine jobs with little autonomy were more restrictive with their children and reported more physical punishment. Their children did not score as well on verbal ability tests as children of mothers in complex jobs. However, in many instances other factors such as siblings and formal or informal child care positively influenced these children's verbal facility, a strong indicator at this age of mental, social, and emotional maturity (1994, 972, 1002).

A Gallup poll of one thousand working mothers commissioned by *Working Mother Magazine* found that most were "extremely" or "very satisfied" with the balance between their jobs and families. The survey found that 80 percent of working mothers are pleased with how their children are doing and with the job they are doing as mothers; 90 percent reported that their children are happy. This contradicts popular beliefs that mothers feel guilty about working (Rubenstein 1994, 38–47).

***Problems of Families in Which Both Parents Work***   Although families with two wage earners may avoid the financial problems of single-parent families, they frequently do not avoid many other problems. Like single-parent families, they are usually not available during the school day; therefore, parent-teacher conferences and other programs held during the day are difficult for working parents to attend. Like single parents, working parents are also concerned with child care. Many have to shuttle their children from a child-care facility to school and back to the child-care facility. Often the transportation has to be handled by someone other than the parent.

Because of the large number of parents who work, schools must attempt to accommodate the needs of these families. This might mean scheduling such things as parent-teacher conferences in the evenings and arranging for extended child care before, during, and after school hours and while parents attend special school events.

## TWO-PARENT FAMILIES WITH ONE WAGE EARNER

Two-parent families with one wage earner were most common in the mid-1960s. Today only 7 percent of children come from such families. The increased numbers of single-parent families and working mothers have shifted family structures away from this model.

***Problems of Two Parents, One Wage Earner***   Many families with single wage earners experience financial difficulties. According to the U.S. Department of Labor, Bureau of Labor Statistics, the median family income for a white family where both parents were employed was $43,179 in 1991, for a black family $35,358, and for a Hispanic family $27,296. In a white family where only the male wage earner was employed, the average 1991 income was $24,509, for a black family $20,920, and for a Hispanic family $19,192. In a white family with only the female wage earner employed in 1991, the average income was $15,513, for a black family $9,413, and for a Hispanic family $10,216.

In terms of accommodating school schedules, families of this type have fewer problems than families where both parents work. Volunteerism, daytime parent-teacher conferences, and parent involvement in school activities are relatively easy. In fact, despite the modest numbers of this type of family, most schools still operate as if it were the norm.

## JOINED OR BLENDED FAMILIES

Within five years of their parents' divorce, four of every seven children become part of new **blended families**, in which one or both adults in a new marriage or living arrangement have children from a previous marriage.

*Problems of Blended Families*　Of course, the blended family can have many problems. The increased number of children may place demands on parents accustomed to having fewer children. Frequently, the children do not accept the authority of the new parent; they are confused about which parent makes the final decision. They are unsure of the role of the noncustodial parent in this new relationship, and if the noncustodial parent also lives in a blended household, the children may wonder, Who are my parents anyway? Visitation with these children can cause stress among the children who normally live in the household, and the noncustodial parent may experience anger or guilt because he or she spends more time with the children who live in his or her home than with his or her own children.

For children from blended families, sibling rivalries can also occur in school. For example, the Rosman family has six children: two are hers and two are his and two are theirs. All four oldest children are girls: two are named Jennifer and two Stephanie. Both Jennifers are in the same class at school. The Jennifers, one named Rosman and the other Smythe, have different biological parents but share a stepparent. They do not live in the same household. The school did not realize when they placed the Jennifers in the same class that they were children of a blended family. Nor did they know that there were many conflicts between them that carried over into the schoolroom, and it is the teacher who must deal with the consequences.

## HOMELESS FAMILIES

The image of the homeless as a collection of alcoholics, drug addicts, and those with mental disabilities is incorrect. In fact, fewer than half of the homeless fall into that group. In 1992 the homeless were located in rural and suburban communities as well as inner cities and includes families with children, people working at least part-time, men and women suffering from severe mental illness or substance abuse, veterans of military service, and those who are homeless only part of the time (National Coalition of Homeless 1993).

The 1980s and 1990s have witnessed an explosion in the size and scope of the nation's homeless. Although it is difficult to get accurate counts of the number, it is possible to examine the number living in shelters. In one week of 1988, for example, 500 thousand to 600 thousand were living in shelters across the country as compared to one week in 1993 when 1.8 million were. In 1993 every state reported both an increase in the number of people seeking shelter and the number denied shelter, particularly families with children (National Coalition of Homeless 1994A). Thirty percent of homeless people in 1992 were children under the age of eighteen; 50 percent of those were under five years of age; 40 percent were members of families and 30 percent were single parents with children; 44 percent of the homeless were African American and 42 percent white. The fastest growing homeless groups are families with children and mothers with children, 50 percent of whom are escaping abuse (National Coalition of Homeless 1993).

***Problems of the Homeless Family***   The problems of homeless families are numerous. Besides lacking security, they are frequently in physical danger, have numerous health problems without appropriate care, are unable to obtain child care, often do not have enough to eat, and are ostracized by the rest of society and thus have poor self-esteem.

Bonny F. Ford, professor of education at the University of Central Oklahoma, found that in 1991 of 500 thousand school-aged homeless children, between 28 percent and 57 percent did not attend school regularly. In some instances, homeless children were denied admittance to school because of lack of a permanent address. Fortunately, recent court decisions and the Stewart B. McKinney Homeless Assistance Act, enacted by Congress in 1987 requiring schools to provide services to homeless children comparable to those provided others, have significantly limited this practice. However, even when homeless children are admitted to school, they frequently do not have records of immunization, school attendance, and even guardianship. Although under the McKinney Act schools are required to keep records, the act relies on the compliance of the states and local education agencies, which are not penalized for noncompliance (Ford 1992). In addition, many homeless schoolchildren have no transportation and lack proper clothing and money for school supplies. In 1990 the McKinney Act was amended by Congress to remove these barriers for homeless children by increasing funding levels to states and providing competitive grants to Local Education Agencies. In school many homeless children act out, fight, are restless or depressed; others are well-adjusted. However, as a group, homeless children experience more educational problems than others. For example, in Boston 43 percent of homeless children living in shelters repeated a grade, double the rate of low-income children living at home (Ford 1992).

While homeless children's frequent school failures make them vulnerable to peer pressure that may encourage involvement in gangs, crime, and drugs, many schools are working to help them succeed. In City Park School in Dallas, Texas, for example, "the school emphasizes an atmosphere in which the staff does not differentiate between the permanent population and [the twenty or so] students from shelters. The staff holds the belief that all children will learn regardless of the length of their stay at the school" (Ford, 14). When new homeless children enter City Park School, they and their parents are met by the principal, given an orientation to the school, provided with school supplies, and warmly greeted by classroom teachers. A special friend is provided each child who also meets with a counselor twice a week. The children's medical concerns are reviewed by a school nurse and needed clothing is provided out of the school clothing closet. The curriculum focuses on basic skills, and every week administrators and psychologists from the school meet with a community liaison agent to discuss at-risk children. Parents are referred to appropriate agencies for medical and social help. Additional grants from private agencies provide textbooks, library books, school supplies, and classroom games. Volunteers supply before-and-after-school tutoring, recreational activities, field trips, toys, and clothing. The Dallas police visit the school, have lunch with the children, and help them attend special events.

## TEENAGE PARENTS

In 1991, 519 thousand women between fifteen and nineteen years of age gave birth, representing 12.5 percent of all U.S. births (Children's Defense Fund 1994, 53). About half of all teenage pregnancies result in birth (more likely in older than in younger teens), over one-third in abortion, and the rest in miscarriage. According to data reported by the National Education Association in *How Schools Can Help Combat Student Pregnancy* (Compton, Duncan, and Hruska 1987), approximately 12 percent of teenagers having babies have not yet completed ninth grade. The Alan Guttmacher Institute reported that of the 70 percent of adolescent mothers who stay in school, 77 percent will graduate, almost as many as those who do not have babies while in high school; however, many will graduate much later than at age seventeen or eighteen. Only about 30 percent of those who drop out of high school either before or after the baby's birth will eventually graduate (1994, 59).

Although 85 percent of teenage pregnancies are unintended, about 90 percent of white teenage mothers and 97 percent of black teenage mothers keep their babies. According to a 1993 study by Diane Scott-Jones, a psychology professor at Temple University, many adolescent mothers are emotionally attached to their babies and are unable to give them to someone outside the family. Many babies of teenage mothers, particularly African Americans, become part of extended, multigenerational families. This, according to Steven Ruggles, professor of history at the University of Minnesota, is not a recent phenomenon in African American families. Following the Civil War, extreme poverty destabilized and disrupted many free black families and required the establishment of an extended, multigenerational family, a social norm that differed from that of white families. In many African American families, women were the heads of households because they were more able to obtain employment than males. Thus, African American children have lived in extended families for more than a century (1994, 136–147). Teenage mothers who live with their own parents or other relatives generally are better parents themselves, frequently continue in school, and are more emotionally stable than those who live alone. In the long run, their children benefit from this stability and from social interaction with adults.

Teenage fathers have backgrounds similar to those of teenage mothers. Although there were 553 thousand babies born in 1990 to teenage mothers, only 129 thousand teenage males were reported as being fathers (U.S. Bureau of Census 1993, 74). Richard Louv in his book *Father Love* interviewed teenage fathers participating in a Teen Fathers Program in Cleveland, Ohio. When he asked the fifteen boys how many were fathers, two raised their hands. When he asked how many had babies, twelve hands were raised (1993, 237). Charles Ballard, director of the Teen Fathers Program, explains that teen fathers do not think like fathers. According to Ballard, "They don't connect pregnancy with marriage or husband-

Teenage parents not only have to continue their own education but also have to care for their infants, placing the parent-student in a difficult situation. Several school districts acknowledge the reality of teen parenthood and have begun to provide some type of state-financed child care for the student who remains in school. The Young Parents Program in New Britain, Connecticut, provides such a nursery so that Brenda Lockery, left, Lourdes Rivera, center, and Danielle Schuler can attend high school classes.

ing or fatherhood." This may be due to the fact that 65 percent of the teenage fathers in the Cleveland program never knew their own fathers (Louv, 237). One of the difficulties for them, reports Deborah L. Cohen, an education reporter for *Education Week,* is that there are few programs directed at teen fathers. Yet these programs are essential because teenage fathers, like teenage mothers, tend to be low academic achievers, naive, are incorrectly informed about sex and parenthood, and want babies as an antidote for loneliness. In addition, they believe that getting a girl pregnant proves they have been successful.

The Alan Guttmacher Institute suggests that the discrepancy between the numbers of teenage mothers and fathers comes in part from how births are reported. In 1988, for example, there were 96 thousand births to mothers between fourteen and sixteen years of age, but only 9 thousand teenage fathers were listed that same year (1994, 52). In addition, it is estimated that only 26 percent of the men fathering babies of teenagers under eighteen are teenagers themselves. Similarly, data suggest that, while 18 percent of fifteen- to seventeen-year-old women become pregnant each year, only 4 percent of sexually experienced men of that age impregnate their partners (1994, 42).

*In the Classroom*

The homes in Strawberry Mansion [section of North Philadelphia] were largely decrepit leftovers from the last century, chopped up inside by slumlords who would nail up a couple of walls of plywood, screw a sink to one wall, run some water into it, nail a board next to it, set a hot plate on that and call the room a kitchen.

The slumlords sectioned small houses into "apartments," with one bathroom in each building for three families to share. There were better homes than these, and there were many that were worse.

City records showed that the average family income in Strawberry Mansion was $450 a month, and that 95 percent of those households were on welfare. Our school records showed that fewer than ten of the nearly six hundred children attending Blaine by my second year there did not qualify for the free or reduced-price lunch program.

Our records also showed that fewer than twenty of our children went home to both a mother and a father. The others lived with a single parent, foster parents, grandparents or relatives.

A check of lunch applications revealed that the average age at which the mothers of our students had their first child was sixteen. Many were barely thirty when they became grandparents.

Children in homes like these learn early to be caretakers. It is not strange for them to see their mother and their sister each having a baby at the same time. The mother might be only thirty and the sister thirteen, and both might have a year-old infant who needs care. The mother in such a situation sees her thirteen-year-old daughter with a child and says, "For God's sake, I have my *own* baby. I can't take care of another one." The daughter, who has been helping raise the other children until now, is suddenly occupied with her own baby.

So the other household duties fall into the laps of the little siblings, the children from ages six through twelve whom I greeted as students every morning at Blaine.

Sometimes we had children who didn't come to school because they were home caring for their brothers and sisters. Regularly I would have several third- and fourth-graders absent because they were home watching babies. That was very, very common, a fact of life.

A child grows up fast when he is changing diapers and putting food on the table before he has even begun the first grade. A child sees the world a certain way when his house is wall to wall with babies and children and mothers, and there's no man living there because the father is living with his own mother or is off in prison.

From: Madeline Cartwright and Michael D'Orso, *For the Children: Lessons from a Visionary Principal* (1993), New York: Doubleday.

***Problems of Teenage Parents***    According to a 1994 report of the Children's Defense Fund, the majority of teen parents, particularly those living on their own, do not have the resources, support systems, or opportunities essential for raising children to adulthood. Consequently, children of teenage parents are more likely to be developmentally impaired. Children of teenage mothers consistently score lower than children of older mothers on measures of cognitive development. This, according to the Guttmacher report, may not be a direct consequence of the mother's age, but rather may be the result of the increased likelihood that she would be a single parent (30 percent of those who marry as teenagers divorce within five years compared to 15 percent who delay marriage until their twenties), have a larger family, have low educational attainment (only 5 percent get a college diploma compared to 47 percent of women who do not have babies as teenagers), and have a lower socioeconomic status. According to the report, "The educational deficits of children born to adolescent mothers appear to accumulate, causing the child to fall farther behind in school as he/she grows older" (1994, 63). This has important implications for the schools not only in terms of educating the teenagers, many of whom have not yet completed high school, but also in terms of educating their children.

The health risk to children of teenage parents is also very high. Not only are they more likely to be born with birth defects and mental disabilities, but they are also more likely to be victims of childhood illness and to die in infancy. Those who live beyond infancy are also at risk primarily because of the threat of abuse and neglect, the impairment of cognitive development because of limited interaction with caregivers, and social and emotional problems and subsequent low self-esteem (Compton, Duncan, and Hruska, 15–16).

Teenage mothers, according to a study conducted for the National Educational Association by Compton, Duncan, and Hruska, are lonely, feel resentment toward the child's father, and are jealous of peers and friends not burdened with responsibility (1987, 114). Teenage fathers frequently express concern for the teen mother but feel overwhelmed, burdened, angry, and confused. Counseling is rarely available to young fathers, and when it is, it is often not utilized. Few pregnant teenagers or teenagers with children marry, but those who do are likely, eventually, to separate and divorce. Seventy percent of children born to mothers seventeen and under have spent part of their childhood in a single-parent home.

## What Schools Can Do

Most schools have not changed how they interact with families since the early 1950s; however, family structures have changed significantly. If the schools are to involve parents in the education of their children, they must seek new ways to interact with the parents such as providing alternative schedules for meetings and conferences and designing programs that all parents can attend. They must consider spending more time in the neighborhoods and homes of the students they teach. They must find ways for parents to volunteer their services after school and in the evenings and must hire additional support staff such as social service workers and counselors to assist in some of the programs conducted after regular hours.

According to Richard Louv in *Childhood's Future,* some visionary educators are coming to believe that school reform has more to do with strengthening the invisible web that connects families with their schools than with curriculum. Louv contends that schools should be reshaped to reduce their isolation from families. Schools should augment the family rather than replace it. Families need help, but they do not need to be replaced. "Public schools could become the most important community hubs for families, complete with large counseling centers, day care facilities, and in-house and out-reach parenting programs. Schools could increasingly serve as part of the child's extended family" (1990, 333).

# Societal Changes That Affect Families

Some of the other societal changes in the United States that affect families include the aging of the population, changes in the birth rate, and child abuse.

## THE AGING U.S. FAMILY

From 1980 to 1991 the population of adults over the age of sixty-five increased by 6.2 million. By the year 2050, the U.S. Department of Health and Human Services predicts that the number of people over sixty-five years of age will exceed the number of people between the ages of birth and seventeen.

The aging of U.S. society will have a significant impact on the American family; longer life expectancy and more divorces and remarriages will likely result in a great many extended families. In 1991, 25 percent of adults between the ages of sixty-five and seventy-four lived alone; 10 percent lived with married children or other relatives. Of adults seventy-five and over, 41 percent lived alone, and 16 percent lived with children or other relatives. According to John Macionis (1991), professor of sociology at Kenyon College, approximately 25 percent of adults spend four to five hours daily caring for aged parents or grandparents.

> Long life expectancy plus more divorces yields the multiple-dependent family. Think of a married couple, the Smiths, sixty and sixty-two years old. The husband has had a stroke and cannot care for himself. The wife's eighty-five-year-old mother has come to live with them. They have two daughters; the first has been divorced and has a child with partial paralysis who cannot go to school. The second daughter has two children; she and her husband live in the same house with all the others. The sixty-year-old wife is responsible for the care of her mother, her husband, the partially paralyzed son of her first daughter when she is working, and the four-year-old child of her second daughter, who is too young to go to school. This type of multiple-dependent family is rapidly becoming more common in the United States. (Hodgkinson 1989, 5)

This type of family will have a significant impact on the children when they reach school age. Who will go to the school to attend parent-teacher conferences and school events? Who will the school contact if one of the children becomes ill? Who is ultimately responsible for the education of the children?

## BIRTH RATE

Since World War II the birth rate has dramatically dropped, especially among whites. In 1950 there were 47 million children under the age of eighteen. By 1970, as a result of the baby boom following World War II, there were 70 million.

However, despite the increase in number of women of childbearing age, the birth rate began to fall. By 1992, there were only 66 million children under the age of eighteen. It is expected that the birth rate will increase slightly in the next few decades, and by 2000 there will be approximately 69 million children in the United States.

On the other hand, the black and Hispanic birth rates have not declined. In 1970 there were 9.4 million black children under the age of eighteen. By 1992, the number had grown to 10.4 million and is expected to grow to 12.5 million by 2021. The number of Hispanic children has grown from 5.5 million in 1980 to 7.6 million in 1992. It is expected to grow to 9.7 million by 2010.

These fluctuations in birth rate affect the schools. The number of preschool children increased by more than 3 million from 1980 to 1992. It is, however, expected to decrease before the turn of the century. (The increase in preschool children relates not only to the birth rate but also to the fact that more mothers are working and leaving their children in preschool.) The number of elementary school children has remained relatively low when compared to 1970. Nevertheless, it is predicted that this number will increase through the year 2000 and then drop off again.

Because the birth rate affects school enrollment, the school must continually project changes in its structure. It is possible that one year a school's enrollment will be high, requiring new teachers and even new classrooms. But in two or three years the enrollment may decrease significantly, requiring the school to transfer teachers and close unused classrooms. Because schools recognize these demographic changes, they adapt by hiring districtwide teachers who move from school to school based on need, using temporary classrooms such as trailers rather than building new schools, and combining grade levels to make a complete class or sectioning grade levels to make several classes.

## CHILD ABUSE

Although child abuse and neglect are not new problems (definitions of child abuse and the role of child welfare agencies have been part of states' statutes for over 2 hundred years), they have been given increased attention in recent years. In 1974, Congress enacted The Child Abuse and Treatment Act (P.L. 93–237). Although the act set standards for the identification and management of child abuse cases, states continue to determine their own definitions, investigative procedures, and child abuse reporting procedures. In most definitions, **child abuse** includes physical abuse, sexual abuse, physical neglect, and/or emotional maltreatment (see table 11.2). Hence, cases of abuse or neglect are varied in terms of type and intensity and may be difficult to prove. However, there is no doubt that the number of reported cases of child abuse and neglect is increasing. In 1983, 828,417 child abuse and neglect cases were reported in the United States and in 1993, 2,989,000 cases were reported.

It is difficult to tell how many cases of child abuse and neglect there actually are, but in 1992, more than 1,299 children died from abuse-related incidents. From 1990 to 1993, the death rate in abuse cases rose by 14 percent. Many cases still go unreported, however; frequently people do not want to get involved or fear lawsuits. According to a 1993 poll of the states conducted by the National Committee to Prevent Child Abuse, the number of substantiated, investigated

**TABLE 11-2**

## Physical Indicators of Child Abuse and Neglect

---

**Physical Abuse**
– Unexplained fractures, burns, bruises, cuts, welts, or bite marks
– Explanation for an injury that is inconsistent with the injury
– Child's report of injury by parents

**Sexual Abuse**
– Bizarre, sophisticated, or unusual sexual behavior or knowledge relative to child's age
– Pain or itching, bleeding or bruises in or around the genitals
– Child's report of sexual abuse by parent or other adult

**Neglect**
– Constant hunger or fatigue, inappropriate dress or poor hygiene (matted hair, dirty skin)
– Lack of supervision over long periods of time
– Unattended physical or dental problems
– Evidence of alcohol or drug use

**Emotional Abuse**
– Impaired sense of self-worth
– Delayed physical, emotional, or intellectual development or failure to thrive
– Extremes in behavior, such as overly aggressive or overly passive

---

From: National Committee to Prevent Child Abuse (1994). *Scared and Silent: Ways to Save our Children from Abuse and Neglect.*

**Most teachers are not given training in recognizing child abuse and neglect. The school should ideally have a team of counselor, social worker, nurse, teacher, and administrator that can correctly evaluate a situation and report it to officials.**

cases of child abuse and neglect closely approximates the number of cases reported. The National Committee points to the increased number of well-trained case workers who report and investigate cases as one of the major reasons for the substantiation of reported cases. In addition, teachers and other school personnel have been trained in recognizing child abuse and neglect from both the physical signs and also from a child's behavior, the public is more aware of the problems, and the reporting of these cases has been simplified through computerization.

Teachers are legally responsible for reporting suspected child abuse and neglect cases to local child protection agencies. The NEA recommends that each school develop a team consisting of a counselor or social worker, nurse, administrator, and teacher to discuss these cases. This team approach in the long run is the most efficient and most just method of deciding which of them should be reported to authorities. When a suspected case is not reported, everyone may be culpable: the state education agency that did not provide sufficient funds for training, the school district that did not provide adequate training for all personnel, the school administrator who was unwilling to report the case to the appropriate agency for fear of community retribution, and the teacher who either didn't recognize the signs or was afraid to report them.

**11-1**

**Points to Remember**

- U.S. families are very diverse. They include eight basic family types: single-parent families, noncustodial parents, families with two wage earners, two-parent families with one wage earner, joined or blended families, homeless families, teenage parents, and minority families.
- Single-parent families, most often headed by women, are among the families most likely to be poor. Child care is often a problem, as is cooperating with schools.
- Nearly three-fourths of U.S. mothers work part- or full-time and must arrange for child care and before- and after-school care.
- Homeless children face a lack of security, poor diet, health problems, and ostracism, all of which affect their ability to perform in school.
- Teenage parents are likely to be poor and poorly educated and their children are likely to experience health and other related problems.
- Children of teenage mothers are likely to experience low birth weight, poor health, and developmental delays.
- Schools can respond to the needs of families by adapting their schedules to those of parents for such events as meetings and conferences.
- Physical, sexual, and emotional abuse or neglect of a child affects the child not only in the home but also at school. Teachers are responsible for reporting suspected cases of child abuse.

## The Community and the School

In addition to changes in the structure of the U.S. family, other societal changes put pressure on the schools. This section of the chapter will discuss some of these community problems challenging the public schools.

> It is 9 A.M. on a November morning, and Terrence Quinn, principal of Public School 225 in Rockaway, Queens, New York, is serving breakfast. But he's not in the school cafeteria. He's in the lobby of a ramshackle welfare hotel where homeless parents and their children come to seek shelter.
>
> With a social worker in tow, Quinn has cruised the hotel corridors, knocking on doors, inviting what is an ever-changing group of parents to share coffee and break bagels and doughnuts with him while he tries to persuade them to send their children to his elementary school six blocks—and a world—away. (Reed and Sautter 1990, K2)

This is a poignant example of how society affects the schools. Contemporary teachers and administrators can no longer simply teach and administer. In many communities, they must first reach out to the children if they are to educate them. The problems of poverty, crime, sexism, racism, and ethnocentricity paint a bleak picture. Although many schools are relatively free of overt examples of these problems, most are not. It is important that today's teachers understand these problems, so they are not shocked and surprised by the impact they have on their students and their classrooms.

### POVERTY

We will begin by discussing poverty because it is the direct or indirect cause of many of the problems children experience in or out of school (see table 11.3).

**TABLE 11-3**

## One Year in the Life of American Children

| | |
|---|---|
| 208 | children under 10 are killed by firearms. |
| 560 | children 10–14 are killed by firearms. |
| 2,243 | children and youths under 20 commit suicide. |
| 4,173 | children 15–19 are killed by firearms. |
| 4,941 | children and youths under 20 are killed by firearms. |
| 73,886 | children under 18 are arrested for drug abuse. |
| 112,230 | children under 18 are arrested for violent crimes. |
| 124,238 | children under 18 are arrested for drinking or drunken driving. |
| 232,093 | babies are born to women who received late or no prenatal care. |
| 531,591 | babies are born to teen mothers. |
| 613,514 | students are corporally punished in public schools. |
| 928,205 | babies are born to mothers without high school degrees. |
| 1,047,000 | babies are born into poverty. |
| 1,200,000 | latchkey children come home to houses where there is a gun. |
| 1,213,769 | babies are born to unmarried mothers. |
| 1,939,456 | children under 18 are arrested for all offenses. |
| 1,977,862 | students are suspended from public schools. |
| 2,695,010 | children are reported abused or neglected. |

From: Children's Defense Fund, *State of America's Children Yearbook* (Washington, DC: Author, 1994).

**Violence. Neglect. Abuse. America's children are constantly subjected to a reality that threatens their security, their peace of mind, and their ability to learn. We must find a way to reverse the trend as one way of preserving the integrity of our nation.**

Children are more likely to live in poverty, as defined by the federal government, than any other age group. While the poverty rate for the nation as a whole was 14.2 percent in 1991, nearly 21.2 percent of all children under the age of eighteen and 23 percent of preschoolers lived in poverty. In 1991, the percentage of minority children under eighteen living in poverty was significantly higher than white children. Forty-six percent of African American children and 40 percent of Hispanic children lived in poverty compared to 16 percent of white children. In female-headed households, 47.4 percent of white children, 83.1 percent of African American children, and 47 percent of Hispanic children live in poverty (U.S. Bureau of the Census, Statistical Abstract 1993, 469–471).

By 1991, according to the Children's Defense Fund, 13.7 million children, or more than one in five, were living in families with incomes below the poverty threshold. Between 1973 and 1989, the years when the U.S. business cycle reached its peak, families headed by persons younger than thirty years of age and with children suffered terribly. The family's median income (adjusted for inflation) plunged by 32 percent from 1973 to 1990. In addition, the period of economic growth that occurred between 1982 and 1989 bypassed these families who continued to suffer losses in the recession of the early 1990s. For the one-half of children who start their lives in young families, the picture is bleak as these families get poorer and poorer. As a result of loss of income, the poverty rate for children in young families doubled, from 20 percent in 1973 to 40 percent in 1990 (Children's Defense Fund and Northeastern University's Center for Labor Market Studies 1992).

The growing number of poor and at-risk children could mean a grim future for America and its children. Policymakers and school officials will have to develop new strategies to help these children achieve at the high levels that will be demanded by new education standards. For example, schools will have to develop new ways to address the educational disruption experienced by children who change schools frequently, as well as the needs of children from varying languages and backgrounds (U.S. General Accounting Office 1994, 13).

The Children's Defense Fund in their 1992 annual report on child poverty in the United States identified which children are poor, dispelling the stereotype.

- In 1991 only one in ten poor children in America was black and living in a female-headed family on welfare in a central city.
- The youngest, most defenseless Americans suffer most of all. Younger children are more vulnerable to developmental delay and damage caused by inadequate nutrition or health care. One in four infants and toddlers is poor. The bulk of the growth in child poverty during the 1980s was among children younger than six.
- Two in three poor children are white, Latino, Asian, or Native American. One-third of poor children are black. A black child is more likely to be poor than is a white or Latino child. But because a relatively small share of the total population is black, blacks make up only a minority of poor children. During the 1980s Latino poverty rates grew fastest, and roughly half of all children who joined the ranks of the poor between 1979 and 1991 were Latino.
- Children in female-headed families are far more likely than others to be poor. Yet nearly one-half of poor children live in families where the father is present. Even if there were no families headed by women in this country, we still would have one of the highest child poverty rates among all industrialized societies.
- There are more poor American children living outside central cities (7.2 million in 1991) than inside them (6.2 million). The child poverty rate is higher in rural areas than in the rest of the nation (37 percent versus 20 percent). In 1991, eighty-six rural counties had a higher percentage of children living in poverty than in the nation's poorest city—Detroit.
- Most poor families with children are working families. Nearly two out of three poor families with children had one or more workers in 1991. Nearly one in every five poor families with children had a household head who worked full-time throughout the year but still could not earn enough to lift the family out of poverty.

- Earnings from employment are the largest source of income for poor families with children. Total earned income for such families in 1991 was more than twice as great as the total amount of income they received through public assistance programs.
- The inflation-adjusted median income for young families (those headed by persons younger than thirty) with children dropped by nearly one-third between 1973 and 1990. As a result, more than one in three children living in young families is poor. (Children's Defense Fund 1992, 25–30)

## CRIME

One of the results of poverty is crime. Violent crimes such as murders, rapes, and robberies continue to grow. From 1960 to 1991, the murder rate increased 4.7 percent; rape 32.7 percent, and aggravated assault 347.2 percent. Teenagers are frequently both the victims and perpetrators of violent crimes. The Children's Defense Fund reported in 1991 that the teen violent death rate of 71.1 in 100 thousand represented an increase of 13 percent since 1985. Although property crimes such as burglaries and larcenies decreased in 1991 (3.5 percent), increases in recent years continue to make these crimes a major threat. In 1991, the total number of reported crimes in the United States was 14.9 million. In 1952, for example, New York City had 8,757 robberies; in 1989, it had 93,387, one every six minutes. In the fifty-nine days of the Persian Gulf War in 1990 and 1991, 281 Americans were killed in the war; during that same period, 295 were killed, as a result of crime, in New York City (ABC Morning News, June 10, 1991).

The U.S. Bureau of Justice Statistics estimates that 83 percent of children now twelve years old will become victims of actual or attempted violence, if crime continues to grow at current rates. According to a 1993 study (Toch) reported by *U.S. News & World Report,* more than 3 million crimes a year are committed in or near schools. In 1992, there were 5,761 violent incidents in New York City schools, up 16 percent in one year. Sixty-four percent of urban principals reported that violence in their schools had increased in the last five years; 54 percent of suburban principals and 43 percent of rural principals also reported an increase in crime. A 1993 Metropolitan Life Insurance Company poll of third through twelfth grade teachers found that 11 percent had been victims of acts of violence in or around school; 95 percent of these incidents involved students. The poll also revealed that 23 percent of the students had been victims of crime and that they are not likely to report these incidents to authorities. Fifty percent of the students and 23 percent of the teachers surveyed said they did not feel safe in school.

## HOW CRIME AFFECTS THE SCHOOLS

In 1989, researchers Julius Menacker, Ward Weldon, and Emanuel Hurwitz studied teachers and sixth- and eighth-grade students in four Chicago inner-city schools that serve low-income and minority children in some of the most crime-ridden sections of the city. They reported that the following crimes occurred within the school:

- More than 50 percent of students reported that money, clothing, or property was stolen from them at least once during the school year, and 35 percent indicated that thefts occurred more than once
- Eight percent of students reported being threatened by someone with a gun or knife who wanted money or drugs, and 3 percent reported that they had been threatened more than once
- Four percent of students reported being beaten so badly during the school year that they required medical attention
- Seven percent of students reported coming to school high on drugs or alcohol at least once during the year
- Thirty-two percent reported that they had carried a weapon to school at least once, and 14 percent said that they had done so more than once. (p. 40)

*What Schools Are Doing about Crime*   Many schools and communities have developed programs designed to make students more aware of crime and to prevent it. The passage of the Safe School Act by Congress in 1994 provides federal allocations to states for school-based programs to prevent crime, violence, and drug and alcohol abuse. Some of these funds are targeted for after-school programs, summer recreation programs, and counseling programs about the use of weapons. For example, in Boston a program developed by Deborah Prothrow-Stith of the Harvard School of Public Health is designed to reduce the allure of violence by making students aware of the consequences and giving them alternative means for dealing with anger. In addition, every Boston public school student caught with a weapon is sent to the Barron Assessment and Counseling Center for a five- to ten-day stay. Students undergo psychological and educational assessments. A plan is developed for working with the student once he or she returns to school or an alternative setting. Students also participate in counseling, academic work, violence-prevention classes, and trips to detention facilities.

Many schools, particularly in urban areas, have installed metal detectors. At Sam Houston High School in Houston, Texas, for example, students can carry only see-through back packs and purses no larger than five by eight inches.

In Dade County, Florida, schools have initiated a gun-safety program in cooperation with the Center to Prevent Handgun Violence. Through books, videos, and role-playing, the program attempts to "deglamorize and deglorify the possession and use of guns" (*U.S. News and World Report,* April 8, 1991, 32). In Oakland, California, in a program called Teens on Target, student volunteers are trained as violence-prevention "advocates." As such they learn about guns, drugs, and family violence. They are then sent into schools to teach other teens about preventing violence.

Many school districts are attempting to educate young children about violence and how to prevent it. Some school-based programs use private rather than public funds. For example, philanthropist Walter Annenberg donated $500 million, the largest private education grant ever given, to several educational institutions in 1994 to develop antiviolence programs for children.

- Schools in New York, California, New Jersey, and Florida instruct kindergarten children about the danger of guns.
- Duvall High School in Greenbelt, Maryland, is one of numerous high schools with a student mediation program.

**TABLE 11-4**

## Laws Against Weapons Possession in School

Tough new laws are being enacted by states imposing new penalties for weapons possession on or near school grounds.

**These new laws include the following:**
• Gun-free school zone laws, modeled on the federal Gun-Free School Zone Act of 1990 that prohibits the possession or discharge of a firearm at or within 1,000 feet of a public or private school.
• Drug-free school zone laws, which impose criminal sanctions for dealing drugs at or near a school. Minnesota has extended the zone to cover parks, housing projects, and school buses.
• Automatic suspension/expulsion laws for students caught with firearms or other weapons. In 1993 California provided for automatic suspension leading to expulsion for students carrying guns on school grounds or to off-campus school activities, with backup provisions permitting education to continue in another setting.

**Other school violence prevention strategies include:**
• safe passage plans to provide protection to students going to and from school, and safe haven projects establishing protected areas for youth activities
• anonymous tip lines so students can report other students carrying weapons without fear of recrimination
• school dress codes prohibiting gang colors or styles
• detection and search strategies such as metal detectors, security guards, and unannounced searches of students and their lockers
• recreation and after-school programs.

From: L. McCart, *Kids and Violence* (Washington, DC: National Governors' Association, 1994), 34.

> **In an effort to help communities and schools deal with crime, a number of laws were recently passed and strategies developed that focused specifically on preventing violence.**

• In North Carolina a statewide program called N.C. Star sends college students into local high schools to help teenagers deal with frustrations before they turn to violence.
• A violence prevention program in New York City high schools is credited with reducing classroom fights in one hundred high schools by 71 percent since 1992.

Despite these efforts at controlling crime, the problem remains in many cities and their schools. Ultimately, schools and communities must work together to break the cycle of inadequate housing, poor-paying jobs, poverty, crime, and substandard education. A good example of a community-based, school violence prevention program is the Salt Lake County Service and Conservation Corps Youth Force. It offers alternatives to gang membership through the formation of community problem-solving teams. Funded by the Job Training Partnership Act, the Community Development Block grant, and the county, three pilot projects in four Salt Lake County school districts involving fifty students each were started in June 1993. Youth Force members have renovated two Head Start centers and constructed a park and a 1.5-mile stretch of trail along the Jordan River. Other activities include creating a mural by rival gang members in a multiracial school, redesigning a city park to reduce crime, developing a community gardening program, and devising a highly supervised tutoring and mentoring program for elementary school children (McCart 1994). New laws are being enacted in many states to help communities and the schools deal with the problem of crime and develop solutions to it (see table 11.4).

## SEXISM

Despite nearly three decades of the women's movement in the United States, women still lag behind men in professional and economic status, which affects the schools in many direct and indirect ways. There are still, for example, a greater number of men in higher paying administrative positions than there are women. Indirectly, students are influenced by the messages they receive from this discrimination.

Although an increasingly large percentage of women are in the labor force, they rarely hold positions of power. Women are vastly overrepresented in nonleadership positions with limited mobility. For example, 98.2 percent of secretaries are women, as are 96.8 percent of receptionists, 91 percent of bank tellers, 98.1 percent of dental assistants, and 95.8 percent of nurses (U.S. Department of Commerce 1993, 405–406).

Although legislation has been passed by Congress (1963 and 1972 Equal Pay Acts; the 1964 Civil Rights Act and 1972 amendment prohibiting discrimination in employment based on sex), local and state government salaries for men and women are still unequal. Men in executive, administrative, and managerial positions, for example, made an average of $38,622 per year, and women made $26,928 per year in 1992. Even among office and clerical workers where women dominate, men are paid more. Male office workers are paid an average of $21,335 and women are paid an average of $19,444 (U.S. Bureau of Census 1993, 428).

According to a 1990 survey by *Working Woman,* male professors at public colleges and universities earned an average of $53,890 and women professors $48,490. The same was true at lower ranks; at the assistant professor rank, males earned $34,620 and women earned $31,830 (Russell 1991, 68). In 1992, according to the U.S. Bureau of Census, fully employed women earned $21,245 and fully employed men earned $30,322. Although this was an increase for both men and women, fully employed women in 1992 earned considerably less than fully employed men in 1985 and only slightly more than fully employed men in 1980.

*Women in Education*    Women make up the majority of professionals in education. In 1992, for example, 72 percent of teachers in public school were women. Despite this, women teachers are paid less than their male counterparts. In 1991–1992, the base salary of male teachers was $33,702 and that of women teachers was $30,501 (U.S. Bureau of Census 1993, 160).

Moreover, women make up a declining percentage of the professionals in education as one ascends the professional ladder. In 1973, 35 percent of public school administrators were women. In 1974, the number had declined to 14 percent, rising slowly to 20 percent in 1979, 25 percent in 1980, 26 percent in 1985, 30 percent in 1988, and 38 percent in 1993. In 1993 the percentage of women in administrative positions had only barely surpassed what it had been in 1974. Why? The major shift in the percentage of women administrators occurred in the late 1960s, when schools were integrated. Most black schools were headed by

While the majority of professionals in education are women, they have in the past filled very few administrative positions. In the 1990s, however, their numbers have begun to increase on committees, school boards, as principals, assistant superintendents, and superintendents.

women principals; when the schools were integrated, most of them lost their positions.

In the late 1980s and early 1990s, the number of women in high-level positions in education was beginning to increase. During the period from 1982 to 1992, women's school board membership increased from 28 to 43 percent. In 1993, eleven of the chief state officers of education and 7 percent of school district superintendents were women, up from 0.6 percent in 1971. However, in terms of numbers the 1993 figure translates to a total of 12,513 superintendents, 11,625 males and only 888 females. The percentage of assistant superintendents who are women is significantly larger, 24.3 percent in 1993. This compares to a meager 3 percent in 1971 (Montenegro 1993, 3, 7).

## RACISM

Although the percentage of minorities in positions of power has increased since the early 1960s, it is still relatively low. The higher up the socioeconomic and prestige ladder the position, the less likely minority members are to occupy it.

For example, in state and local governments in 1991 there were 1,011,000 African Americans and 340,000 Hispanics out of 5,459,000 employed. In administrative positions in government in 1991 there were only 28,000 African Americans and 10,000 Hispanics out of the total 304,000 administrators. Of the total 679,000 service and maintenance workers, 213,000 were African American and 62,000 Hispanic (U.S. Bureau of Census 1993, 318).

Analysis of the 1993 Bureau of Census statistics confirms that African Americans and Hispanics, particularly women, are clustered in service jobs such as cooks, dishwashers, cleaning service employees, nurses' aides, and child-care workers. In addition to low salaries, these positions have few fringe benefits and poor working conditions. Paul Johnson, a North Carolina newspaper reporter, in an analysis of Bureau of Census data concluded that lower educational levels leading to limited job opportunities is one of the major problems facing African Americans in the 1990s. Other reasons for what he called the "crisis facing blacks," according to Johnson's analysis, "are probably due to intangible forces, such as racism" (1992, 8a). A 1993 survey of racial attitudes in North Carolina revealed that 52 percent of blacks and 13 percent of whites surveyed believed that local governments favored hiring whites over blacks, and 70 percent of blacks and 19 percent of whites responded that blacks did not have as good a chance as whites of getting any job for which they were qualified in their community (Howard, Merrell and Partners 1993).

*Minority Leadership in the Schools*   Racial minorities have fared even less well than women in educational leadership positions. Between 1982 and 1993, the percentage of minority school board members remained at 7 percent across the nation. The percentage is slightly larger in the South, where 11 percent of school board members are black and 3 percent Hispanic.

In 1982, 12.9 percent of public school administrators were minorities. By 1988 that figure had increased to only 16.3 percent, and in 1993 the figure was only 16.4. In 1993, 83.6 percent were white, 10.3 percent black, 4.9 percent Hispanic, 0.8 percent Asian-Pacific, and 0.4 percent Native American.

The percentage of minority superintendents has increased very slowly. In 1982, 2.2 percent of the superintendents in the thirty states reporting were minorities. By 1988, 3.1 percent were, and in 1993, 3.7 percent. The percentage of assistant superintendents who are members of minority groups has risen equally slowly. In 1982, 10.8 percent of assistant superintendents were minorities in the twenty-three states reporting. In 1988, the number had grown to 12 percent and in 1993 to 14.1 percent. The percentage increase in minority principals has been equally slow. In 1982, 12.1 percent of principals in the twenty-three states reporting were minorities. In 1988, the figure had increased to 15 percent. In 1993, 16.4 percent of principals in thirty-five states were minorities.

*How Do Racism and Sexism Affect Students?*   Racism and sexism affect students both directly and indirectly. The majority of students will be taught by female teachers and administered by male administrators; few students will have minority teachers or administrators. Similarly, few students will be in school districts with a large number of board of education members who are either women or minorities. Decisions thus made, in many cases, will not consider women or minorities as priorities. These are the direct results.

The indirect results lie in the message this gives to U.S. students. For example, are female and minority students likely to set goals to become school administrators and leaders in government and industry when they see few models in the schools? Are minority students likely to strive to become teachers when most of the teachers they know are white? Are male students likely to want to become teachers when all their teachers are female?

There may be another indirect result. If studies are correct and many white, middle-class teachers have difficulty dealing with minority students, these students may not be receiving the education they need in order to succeed. Similarly, if teachers tend to have lower expectations for minority students, these students may be given instruction that provides little challenge. (For what schools can do to improve the achievement and self-concept of minority students, see chapter 12, pp. 491–495.)

## The Individual and the School

While society and the family struggle with ethical, structural, and emotional changes thrust upon them, many students have problems of their own that interfere with their schooling. We will address several of these problems in this section: chemical dependency, crack babies, sexual activity and AIDS, sexual harassment, and suicide.

### CHEMICAL DEPENDENCY

In the 1990 Metropolitan Life Survey of the American Teacher, conducted by Louis Harris and Associates, Inc., 70 percent of teachers thought the use of drugs was a serious problem; this was up from 58 percent in 1985. Drinking was considered a problem by 81 percent of the teachers in 1989; this was up from 66 percent in 1985. The 1992 Gallup poll of the American public's opinions about education revealed that drug abuse was viewed as the second leading problem facing the schools.

The National Survey Results on Drug Use from Monitoring the Future Study, 1975–1992 (Johnston, 1993), in which 17 thousand high school seniors were interviewed on drug abuse, revealed that there is a continuing decline among those using illicit drugs. The percentage of high school seniors using any illicit drug one or more times in the prior twelve months fell to 27 percent in 1992, exactly half the peak of 54 percent in 1970, and those using any illicit drug once in their lives also fell to 41 percent in 1992. However, this poll and the third annual drug abuse poll of eighth and tenth graders found a sharp rise at all three grade levels in the use of marijuana (4 percent for seniors, 6.2 to 7.2 percent for eighth graders). Since 1987 there has been a decline in the use of cocaine and since 1988 a decline in the use of crack. Sixty-nine percent of eighth graders, however, reported having tried alcohol, and 27 percent said they had been drunk at least once; 45 percent have tried cigarettes, and 16 percent smoked during the prior month; 49 percent said there was not a great risk unless a pack per day is smoked. Researchers fear that although there has been a general decrease in the use of drugs, younger students seem to be more vulnerable. They suggest that this may be because they have not seen the dangers of drug use older students have seen.

The percentage of high school seniors drinking at least once a month declined from 72 percent in 1980 to 51 percent in 1992. Fewer students reported binge drinking in the 1992 survey, but 28 percent reported having at least five drinks in one sitting within the two weeks prior to the survey. Today's teenagers are more aware of the range of substances they can use to alter mood and consciousness than were young people of earlier generations. Likewise, they have access to highly elaborate supply systems. Richard Towers indicates that teens drink and take drugs for many reasons: pleasure, peer pressure, life stress and pain, experimentation, rebellion, societal influence, low self-esteem, poor life attitude, family influences, and school factors. All of this means that educators must be vigilant in order to avoid a burgeoning new epidemic.

*How Does Drug and Alcohol Abuse Affect the School?*  "Teenage pregnancy, suicide, low self-esteem, poor nutrition, and drug abuse may indeed be different facets of the same set of problems [poverty, poor home life, home and school pressures] that are closely related to each other and to such other problems as class cutting, truancy, and disruptive behavior" (Towers, 51). Students who abuse drugs and alcohol are more likely to have academic, social, and behavioral problems in school. It is not clear whether these problems tend to cause chemical abuse, but it is clear that chemical abuse causes additional school-related problems. Similarly, drug and alcohol abuse can cause serious classroom problems for the teacher. Consider the difficulties in teaching a class if one or several of the students are drunk or high. Students who are unruly, sleepy, or boisterous will not be ready for learning and will adversely affect the learning of the other students in the classroom.

One of the educational goals outlined by President George Bush and endorsed by President Bill Clinton is that "by the year 2000, every school in America will be free of drugs and violence and will offer a disciplined environment conducive to learning" (National Governors' Association, *Educating America: State Strategies for Achieving the National Education Goals,* 15).

In order to reach this goal, Towers suggests that teachers and parents must know how to recognize the symptoms and signs of drug and alcohol abuse.

1. Drastic physical changes—in skin coloring, weight fluctuation, over-susceptibility to illness
2. Eye, nose, and throat problems—red, watery eyes with unusual pupil size, frequent runny nose, bad breath
3. Change in appetite and activity level—cravings for sweets or liquids, decreased activity
4. Change in sleeping patterns—marked change from normal habits in amount and time of sleep
5. Change in affect [emotions]—extreme mood swings, withdrawn and sullen
6. Change in school performance—drop in achievement and grades, truancy, loss of interest in academic and extracurricular activities
7. Change in friends—sudden new peer group
8. Departure from value system—disregard for laws and rules
9. Problems at home—disobedience, inability to carry on a conversation without expressing anger, defiance, secretive behavior
10. Change in financial resources—sudden appearance of more money or less money with no explanation
11. Dramatic attention-seeking behavior—tantrums, hyperactivity, hostility, destructiveness (Fox and Forbing 1992, 29)

Towers recommends that when confronted with a drug or alcohol problem, teachers do the following:

1. Express their concern to the student.
2. Notify the parents of their concerns.
3. Consult with and/or refer to appropriate staff.
4. Participate as appropriate in the intervention plan.

This, of course, means that each school must have a plan for dealing with drug and alcohol problems and an awareness of what resources are already available to help. In addition to developing educational programs to help students avoid drug and alcohol abuse, schools should be part of school-community action teams in which the entire school population and members of the community assume ownership of the problem, take part in the solutions, and help create a positive school climate.

## CRACK BABIES

The crack baby syndrome is caused by the mother's use of drugs, particularly crack and cocaine, during pregancy. Of the children who were prenatally exposed, 55 percent were exposed to cocaine and 24 percent were exposed to more than one drug during the prenatal period. In 1991, 62 percent of the 429 thousand children in foster care were crack babies, representing a 19 percent increase since 1986, according to the U.S. General Accounting Office. According to Linda Stevens, a newspaper reporter, and Marianne Price, an administrator in the Radnor Township School District in Wayne, Pennsylvania, 350 thousand newborns each year have been exposed to prenatal drugs. Their research in eleven Florida hospitals revealed that the mothers of these infants were equally likely to be black or white, rich or poor. According to Stevens and Price, as crack babies develop, they may demonstrate some of these behaviors: hyperactivity, screaming, poor communication skills, poor attention span, poor social relationships, and difficulty making judgments and decisions. In addition, these children frequently experience an overall developmental delay.

Under the Individuals with Disabilities Education Act of 1991 (P.L. 102–119), these children and their parents are guaranteed special health and education services. The U.S. General Accounting Office recommends that school drug programs focus on the effects of drug use during pregnancy. This is particularly important given the number of teenage pregnancies and the number of teenagers who use drugs. Further, according to the GAO, communities should provide drug abuse treatment programs that target pregnant women to prevent further risks to children prenatally exposed to drugs.

*Viewpoint* Crack-Infected Child

The few days that I observed the year-old crack-infected daughter of Cassandra, she was super-hyperactive. She resisted cuddling. She was civil to even her siblings only when she was hungry. Once fed, she struggled to be "free," staying in constant motion until she was exhausted and literally fell over to sleep. Extreme efforts must be made early to nurture such children into cooperative, trusting little people. I would suggest keeping them still for short periods of time, to be gradually extended until they can attend normally. They should be encouraged to sit in a chair. They could be read a story, or they could play with a desk game or watch a television story or observe fish in a tank.

Schools must plan individual education programs designed to meet the needs of these children. Their constant movements suggest to me that there should be some well-defined rigorous physical activity before and after their forced attentive periods. I would suggest that a time-out place be set up for these children so that they are not allowed to impede the progress of the class, while at the same time their needs can be addressed.

> From: Madeline Cartwright and Michael D'Orso, *For the Children: Lessons from a Visionary Principal,* 231.

## DRUG AND ALCOHOL ABUSE PREVENTION PROGRAMS

Most middle and secondary schools are actively involved in helping students avoid the pressure to begin taking drugs or start drinking. The objectives of the National Institute on Alcohol Abuse and Alcoholism (NIAAA) kindergarten through twelfth grade curriculum *Here's Looking At You, 2000* are typical.

1. *Information*—to expose youth to the basic facts about the physiological, psychological, and sociological implications of drug and alcohol use, and to teach them how to gather information about alcohol and drugs; to distinguish between reliable and unreliable, and relevant and irrelevant information.
2. *Analysis*—to help youngsters identify and define problems; gather information; brainstorm alternatives; predict consequences associated with different choices and behaviors; identify analysis factors such as attitudes, values, feelings, emotions, pressures from peers and families, risk levels, and habits; develop action plans on the basis of these analyses and evaluate the appropriateness of their actions.
3. *Coping skills*—to help students gain skills in identifying sources of stress in their lives; to recognize when they are stressed and its effects on them; to identify mechanisms for coping with the stress and determining consequences of the coping behaviors.
4. *Self-concept*—to help young people increase their self-awareness by helping them identify what is important to them in their lives; to help them recognize their feelings and know how to express them by explaining how they feel about themselves and identifying their various roles and activities, as well as increasing positive self-concepts so that students can identify their own personal strengths and weaknesses and develop skills in selecting and practicing changed behaviors. (National Institute of Alcohol Abuse and Alcoholism, *Here's Looking at You, 2000: A K–12 Drug and Alcohol Curriculum,* available from Comprehensive Health Education Foundation, Seattle, WA) (Fox and Forbing, 1992)

## SEXUAL ACTIVITY

According to a 1990 survey conducted by the Centers for Disease Control of 11,631 high school students nationwide, a large proportion of today's teenagers are sexually active: 40 percent of ninth graders reported they had had intercourse, 47 percent of tenth graders, 57 percent of eleventh graders, and 72 percent of twelfth graders. Teenagers in the 1990s are more sexually experienced than teenagers were in the 1970s when 10 percent of ninth graders and 57 percent of twelfth graders reported having had intercourse. By comparison, a 1994 study, conducted by Michael Benson of Northwestern University, of one thousand Chicago junior high school students, found that 26 percent of sixth through eighth graders reported having had sex. Eighty percent of black eighth-grade boys and 40 percent of white and Hispanic eighth-grade boys reported having had sex. Of the girls, 30 percent of black eighth graders and 10 percent of white and Hispanic eighth graders reported having had sex. According to Benson, church attendance, high grade point averages, high self-esteem, and sex education courses did not halt early sexual initiation (reported in Painter 1994, 1a). In addition, a 1990 survey asked high school students if they had had intercourse with four or more partners. Seven percent of ninth-grade girls, 19 percent of ninth-grade boys, 18 percent of twelfth-grade girls, and 39 percent of twelfth-grade boys reported that they had had at least four sexual partners (CDC, 1990 Youth Risk Behavior Study 1991, 4–8).

Condom distribution in schools continues to be a controversial issue. Those who approve believe that easy availability of condoms saves lives by making their use common and acceptable. Those who disapprove believe that availability implicitly condones sexual behavior and thus promotes promiscuity and disease.

The Alan Guttmacher Institute reports that low economic level teenagers are more likely than high economic level teenagers to be sexually experienced as are those teens who use drugs and alcohol (1994, 21). The Planned Parenthood Federation reports that teenagers tend to begin sexual activity younger if they have below-average grades in school or do not go to school at all, are unemployed, and live with only one parent or have parents who are not college graduates. This group of teenagers is also less likely to use contraceptives. A *Time Magazine* poll of 5 hundred thirteen- to seventeen-year-olds reported that teenagers have sex for the following reasons: curious and wanted to experiment (80 percent of females, 76 percent of males); under pressure from dating partner (65 percent of females, 35 percent of males); wanted to be more popular and impress friends (58 percent of males and females); and were in love (63 percent of females, 50 percent of males) (Gibbs 1993, 63).

Contraceptive use, particularly condoms, has increased since 1982. Of the 4,484,000 teenagers between fifteen and nineteen years of age interviewed by the Guttmacher Institute from 1982 to 1992, 23 percent of females used condoms at first intercourse in 1988, 42 percent in 1992. In 1992, 65 percent of females and 55 percent of males reported using some form of contraception at first intercourse. Many teenagers report they use two methods (50 percent of females and 55 percent of males) to protect themselves and their partners against pregnancy and sexually transmitted diseases. The distribution of condoms in public schools is very controversial. In a 1992 Gallup poll, 60 percent of the general public approve (19 percent with parental approval) of condom distribution and 38 percent disapprove.

***Diseases Related to Teenage Sexual Activity*** Pregnancy is not the only possible result of teenage sexual activity; sexually transmitted diseases such as syphilis, gonorrhea, and AIDS are also. According to the Alan Guttmacher

*(continued on p. 460)*

# SHOULD CONDOMS BE DISTRIBUTED IN PUBLIC SCHOOLS?

## PRO  Center for Population Options

Condoms are currently available to teens from a variety of sources: drugstores, family planning clinics, health clinics, supermarkets, convenience stores and vending machines. Making condoms available within schools does not introduce an otherwise unobtainable commodity to students. Rather, it expands the range of sources and facilitates teens' access to an important health aid. Adults understand that social endorsement by adults and society is a critical factor in normalizing condom use, and large majorities support giving teens access to condoms in school.

By making condoms available to students who choose to engage in sexual activity, schools let students know the community cares about their health and well-being. School programs reinforce that there are adults who will address adolescent sexual behavior, rather than deny it is a reality. While adults may prefer that young people refrain from sexual intercourse, it is important to help those teens who do not to avoid the negative consequences of HIV and other STDs, as well as unplanned pregnancy. . . .

Several studies have shown that sexually active teens are more likely to use condoms if they believe their peers are using them. Condom availability in schools promotes positive and open attitudes toward condoms, increasing the likelihood that teens not only will acquire the condoms they need to protect themselves, but will also use them.

Schools are in a unique position to help teens address issues that are clearly associated with inappropriate risk-taking behaviors. Schools can provide opportunities for students to increase self-esteem and to practice decision-making, negotiation and conflict-resolution skills. Thus, school condom availability programs supported by comprehensive life skills training are uniquely able to help students gain and practice the skills necessary for successful condom use.

Despite fears to the contrary, research clearly demonstrates that students in schools which make condoms and other contraceptives available through school-based health centers are no more likely to be sexually experienced than students in schools without these services available. In fact, at some schools with centers making contraception available, teens' mean age at first intercourse was older—and already sexually active teens' frequency of intercourse was lower—than at schools without contraception availability.

From: Center for Population Options. *Condom Availability in Schools: A Guide for Programs* (Washington, DC: Author, 1992), 5–6.

## Postscript

The Center for Population Options bases its argument on statistics about teenage parenthood and sexually transmitted diseases. When you view the argument in terms of the statistics presented on the earlier pages of this chapter, it is hard to deny that we must do something to prevent teen pregnancy and the risk of STDs and HIV. Perhaps, condom distribution in the schools will move us closer to a solution. On the other hand, the argument delivered by Edwin

# SHOULD CONDOMS BE DISTRIBUTED IN PUBLIC SCHOOLS?

## CON  Edwin J. Delattre

Even if saving lives were our only moral concern, there is no reason to believe that distributing condoms in schools is the best way to save lives. Certainly, the distribution of condoms is an unreliable substitute for the creation of a school environment that conveys the unequivocal message that abstinence has greater life-saving power than any piece of latex can have.

Furthermore, even if condoms were the best means of saving lives, there would be no compelling reason for schools rather than parents to distribute condoms; no reason for schools to be implicated in the distribution of condoms when others are willing and eager to do so; no reason for schools to assent to the highly questionable claim that *if* they distribute condoms, they will, in fact, save lives.

We have a duty to make clear to our students . . . the implications of sexual involvement with other people who are ignorant of the dangers of sexual transmission of diseases or uncaring about any threat they may pose to the safety of the innocent. Our students need to grasp that if any one of us becomes sexually involved with someone and truly needs a condom or a dental dam because neither we nor the other person knows how much danger of exposure to AIDS that person may be subjecting us to, then we are sleeping with a person who is either staggeringly ignorant of the dangers involved or else is, in principle, willing to kill us. Such a person has not even the decency to wait long enough for informative medical tests to be conducted that would have a chance of disclosing an HIV positive condition; not even the decency to place saving our lives,

or anyone else's, above personal gratification. Obviously, if we behave in this way, we, too, are guilty of profound wrongdoing. . . .

We also have a duty to describe to our students the very real dangers of promiscuity even with condoms. According to research conducted by Planned Parenthood, condoms have a vastly greater rate of failure in preventing pregnancy when used by young unmarried women—36.3 percent—than has been reported by condom distribution advocates. The Family Research Council stresses that this figure is probably low where condom failure may involve possible exposure to AIDS, since the HIV virus is $\frac{1}{450}$ the size of a sperm and is less than $\frac{1}{10}$ the size of open channels that routinely pass entirely through latex products such as gloves.

In being forced to distribute condoms . . . —to children and adolescents whose emotional and intellectual maturity remain, for the most part, in the balance—we are made to convey to the young the false message that we do not know these things about basic decency, about safety, about the high price of putting everything at risk for instant pleasure. And we are also giving youths whose judgment is still being formed the impression that we do not particularly care about the moral dimensions of sexual life, and that there is no particular reason for them to do so either.

From: E. J. Delattre. "Condoms and Coercion: The Maturity of Self Determination," *Vital Speeches of the Day* (April 15, 1992), 58 (13), 412–416. Edwin J. Delattre is the Dean Ad Interim of the Boston University School of Education. This article is based on a speech he delivered to the Chelsea Management Team, the administrative team of the Chelsea, Massachusetts, Schools on January 14, 1992.

---

Delattre relates to the moral responsibility of the school. If educators believe that teens should not be sexually active, aren't we condoning this promiscuity by distributing condoms in schools? Indeed, the statistics presented here must lead to the conclusion that the sexual activity of teens results in many of society's problems. How can we argue with Delattre that when educators hand a student a contraceptive we are saying, "Here, we approve of your sexual activity"?

459

Institute, 3 million teens are infected by sexually transmitted diseases each year, representing one-fifth of all STD cases. Because of their physiological development, adolescent women are more susceptible to contracting STDs than adult women. The rate of reported cases of infectious syphilis among adolescent women more than doubled from 1980 to 1990 (1993, 38). The American Medical Association estimates that by the year 2000 one out of four teenagers will have an STD before high school graduation.

AIDS, which is caused by the human immunodeficiency virus (HIV), is the seventh leading cause of death among fifteen- to twenty-four-year-olds, according to a report in *Medical Clinics of North America*. The Center for Population Options reports that between 1990 and 1992 there was a 43 percent increase in AIDS cases among thirteen- to twenty-four-year-olds. Although most of the reported AIDS cases were for nineteen- to twenty-four-year-olds, the disease in these individuals was probably contracted between thirteen and nineteen years of age because of its long incubation period (up to seven years). In 1985, thirty-five teenagers between ages thirteen and nineteen died of the incurable AIDS virus. By 1992, 142 teens in the same age group had died of the disease.

The two major causes of AIDS among young adults are sexual intercourse and drug abuse with shared needles contaminated with the AIDS virus. Sixteen percent of all teenage females who have had sexual intercourse report that they have had four or more partners. Over 12 million high school students used drugs such as heroin, cocaine, and other substances that can be injected intravenously. The large percentage of students who are sexually active and the problem of drug dependency among teenagers have both contributed to the increase in cases of AIDS among young adults.

*Teenage Pregnancy*   The U.S. teenage birth rate, at approximately 53 percent of the teenage pregnancy rate, is higher than in any other developed country. It cuts across all races and all classes. According to the Alan Guttmacher Institute, U.S. teenage pregnancy rates are thirteen times higher than those in Japan, nine times higher than in the Netherlands, six times higher than in Denmark and Finland, and more than twice as high as those in Canada, Norway, New Zealand, England, and Wales. Most teenagers try to prevent pregnancies by using contraceptives; however, one million teenage women between fifteen and nineteen years of age become pregnant each year at a rate that has increased 23 percent from 1972 to 1990 and is now at the highest level in twenty years.

Each year 300 thousand babies are born to teenage mothers who have not yet completed high school. Of these mothers, 36 thousand have not yet completed ninth grade.

According to the Center for Population Options, each year over 40 thousand adolescent women drop out of school due to pregnancy. Thus, teenage mothers get less education than their peers who postpone childbearing. Ninety-six percent of those who become pregnant do not complete high school on time, many waiting until their late thirties to do so.

## SEXUAL HARASSMENT

Although not a new problem, recent news events have encouraged schools to focus on the issue of sexual harassment. According to a 1993 survey of 1,632 eighth- to eleventh-grade public school students conducted by the American Association of University Women (AAUW), **sexual harassment** is widespread. Defined as an unwanted and unwelcomed sexual behavior that interferes with the life of the student, sexual harassment is clearly different from behaviors the student might like or want such as kissing, touching, or flirting. According to the AAUW survey, 81 percent of students (85 percent of the girls and 76 percent of the boys) have experienced one or more sexual harassment incidents but frequently do not report them. Only 7 percent of those polled told a teacher and 23 percent a parent. However, sexual harassment affects students educationally, emotionally, and behaviorally. After such an incident, for example, 23 percent stayed home or cut class, 21 percent said they could not attend or could not participate in class, 64 percent said they were embarrassed and felt less confident than they had, and 69 percent said they avoided the person who had harassed them. In 1992 the U.S. Supreme Court ruled that students could sue and collect damages for harassment under Title IX of the Education Act of 1972 (see figure 11.1).

*What Schools Can Do about Sexual Harassment*   According to Edward J. Mentell, assistant principal in the Green Bay Area School District in Wisconsin, schools have a responsibility to ensure that each student can attend in a safe environment; sexual harassment constitutes an unsafe environment for many students. The AAUW report concluded, "Schools must develop sexual harassment policies that are clearly communicated and routinely enforced" (1993, 21).

- The school must make the elimination of sexual harassment a top priority.
- Students must be educated about sexual harassment.
- Schools should get parents involved.
- Schools should teach students how to deal with incidents of sexual harassment. (Mentell 1993, 97)

## SEXUALITY EDUCATION PROGRAMS

Sexuality education programs have objectives similar to those of drug and alcohol education programs. They were traditionally subsumed under health education and, therefore, had a biological and psychological focus. But they have become far more comprehensive and now cover the topics of "family relations; gender identity/roles/socialization; dating and marriage; reproduction, pregnancy, and childbirth; parenthood; growth and development; family planning; sexual values; attitudes and behaviors; and rape and sexual abuse. . . . [S]exuality education . . . programs often extend the range of subject matter to include the historical, ethical, and cultural aspects of human sexuality, human sexual behaviors, and sexual functioning" (de Mauro, *SIECUS Report,* Dec. 1989/Jan. 1990, 2). And today, according to the 1989–1990 *SIECUS Report* (Sex Information and Education Council of the U.S.), most sexuality education programs also deal with AIDS and other sexually transmitted diseases.

*Who Takes Sexuality Education?*   Because teenage pregnancy, venereal disease, and AIDS have increasingly become problems, many school and governmental officials agree that the schools must assume responsibility for sexuality education. As of 1993, forty-seven states have laws or policies recommending or

*(continued on p. 463)*

**FIGURE 11-1**

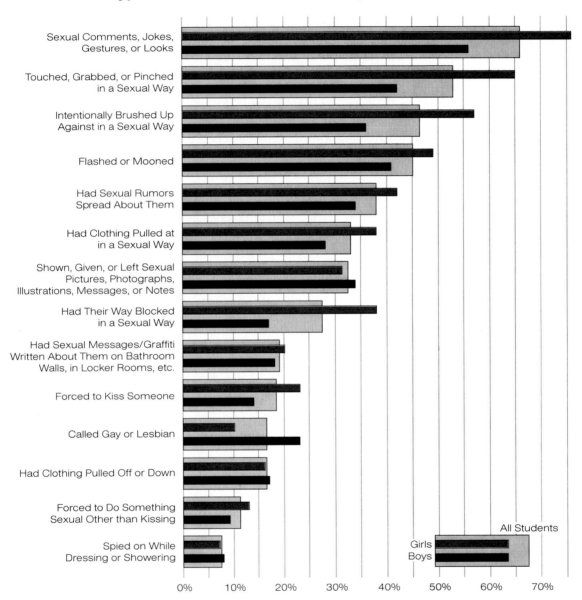

## Types of Sexual Harassment Experienced in School

From: Louis Harris and Associates, *Hostile Hallways: The AAUW Survey on Sexual Harassment in America's Schools* (AAUW Education Foundation, 1993), 2.

Many students experience some type of sexual harassment in school, but few of them report the incident to authorities or their parents. Since this behavior can affect a student's emotional state and his or her ability to learn, the schools clearly need to develop sexual harassment policies and enforce them.

requiring sexuality education: seventeen states require it and thirty states encourage schools to adopt programs. By contrast, in 1986, only three states required sexuality education. In 1993, thirty-eight states, the District of Columbia, and Puerto Rico had actually developed curriculums and guidelines for topics.

*The Controversy*    According to SIECUS, almost all states include abstinence messages as well as positive and affirming statements about human sexuality in their curriculums. In 1992 there were still "huge information gaps" because many state curriculum guides leave out controversial topics such as sexual behavior, contraception, and sexual identity; thus only 10 percent of schoolchildren are receiving what SIECUS considers comprehensive sexuality education. In addition, the Alan Guttmacher Institute claims that sexuality education does not change student behavior or increase the use of contraceptives.

## AIDS EDUCATION

There has been a dramatic increase in the number of states mandating or recommending HIV/AIDS education. The federal *Objectives for the Nation* (U.S. Department of Health and Human Services, Division of HIV/AIDS 1986) outlined preventative measures for the spread of AIDS including education about sexually transmitted diseases (STD) for all schoolchildren before and during high-risk periods (middle school through high school years). The Centers for Disease Control (CDC), the President's Domestic Policy Council, and the Institute of Medicine/National Academy of Sciences also support these educational programs. In 1988 only eighteen states and the District of Columbia required HIV/AIDS education and fourteen additional states recommended it. By 1992, according to Debra Haffner, executive director of SIECUS, almost all states provided teacher training including guidelines or in-service instruction, and almost all placed HIV/AIDS instruction within the framework of the health education curriculum. In addition, parental support for HIV/AIDS instruction was strong.

The CDC has adopted specific guidelines for AIDS education, which have as their major goal the prevention of the transmission of the HIV virus. The guidelines suggest specific facts appropriate for different grade levels. For example, early elementary school children should be told that AIDS is a disease that cannot be transmitted by casual contact. By later elementary and middle school, students should be given information on viruses, transmission routes, and behavioral aspects of the disease. In junior and senior high school, students should receive explicit information about transmission, protective behaviors, testing, and where to get additional information. Although AIDS education programs differ, most schools today follow the CDC guidelines. However, according to Haffner, there are many gaps in the students' knowledge, primarily in the areas considered controversial such as safer sex, condom use, sexual responsibility and decision making, sexual orientation, and compassion for people with AIDS.

## SUICIDE

According to the Centers for Disease Control (1992), the percentage of young people who actually commit suicide has tripled in the last thirty years (from 2.7

Problems of self-identity, self-worth, success in school, and depression all contribute to the rising incidence of teenage suicide. These friends and schoolmates of Cheryl and Lisa Burress, sisters, and two of the four youths who killed themselves in a Bergenfield, New Jersey, garage, console themselves outside the funeral home where the girls are being waked.

per 100 thousand in 1960 to 8.5 in 1990). Every four hours in the United States a child commits suicide (Children's Defense Fund 1994, xii). In a survey of 12 thousand ninth to twelfth graders in twenty-three states conducted by CDC, 29 percent said they had thought about committing suicide within the previous twelve months; 19 percent had made plans to commit suicide; 7 percent had actually attempted it (1992, 21). Teenage suicide is a problem related to drug dependency, pregnancy, parenthood, and other issues of adolescent development that cause depression and low self-esteem.

In the 1991 Gallup Teenage Suicide Study, teenagers were asked if they knew someone who had attempted to commit suicide. If they did, they were asked what signs there were prior to the suicide attempt. More than nine out of ten teens reported depression as the number one sign. Other signs of teenage suicide were problems that may have moved the teen toward depression. These included feeling worthless, not getting along with parents, trouble at school, dating problems, and alcohol and drugs (see figure 11.2).

Males are much more likely to commit suicide than females, even though females are more likely than males to attempt it. This may be because girls are more likely than boys to admit they are depressed and seek help for it. Significantly more white than black teens will commit suicide. Native American males kill themselves ten times more often than white males (CDC 1992, 2).

***Why Are Teenage Suicides Increasing?***   Although a suicidal teenage personality has not been defined, numerous studies have been conducted to determine the causes of teenage suicide. Many of the problems discussed in this chapter may cause teenage suicide: troubled families, increased use of alcohol and drugs, child abuse, teenage pregnancy, and availability of firearms. Compton, Duncan, and Hruska cite teenage parenthood and its overwhelming responsibilities, particularly among females, as an important cause. Richard Towers points to abuse of alcohol and drugs. Levine and Havighurst suggest that suicide relates to people's uncertainty about the future, lack of external rules and expectations on which they can depend, glorification of suicide by the media, the diminishing role of religion, family disruptions, failure in sports and in academics, and inability to find employment. When adolescents are unable to reach their goals or the goals of their families and schools, they may lose their sense of self-worth. Similarly, if they do not have supportive friends and family or if they attend large impersonal schools, they may become so depressed that suicide becomes an attractive alternative to coping with life's problems (Levine and Havighurst 1989, 187–188).

***What Can Schools Do?***   The primary role of the school must be in attempting to prevent teenage suicide. Superintendents must serve in a leadership role to raise the level of awareness of the staff and provide appropriate resources. Large schools should work toward becoming less impersonal and providing counselors and psychiatric services for students who are at risk. Students must be taught coping skills; they should understand that abuse of drugs, alcohol, and sexual promiscuity lead to school failure and more stress. In addition, the CDC suggests that schools should establish peer-support groups in which students can talk about their problems. The focus of a suicide prevention, peer-group program in St. Paul, Minnesota, for example, is to help others and provide them with friendship. Through the program, students identify resources that are available

*(continued on p. 466)*

**FIGURE 11-2**

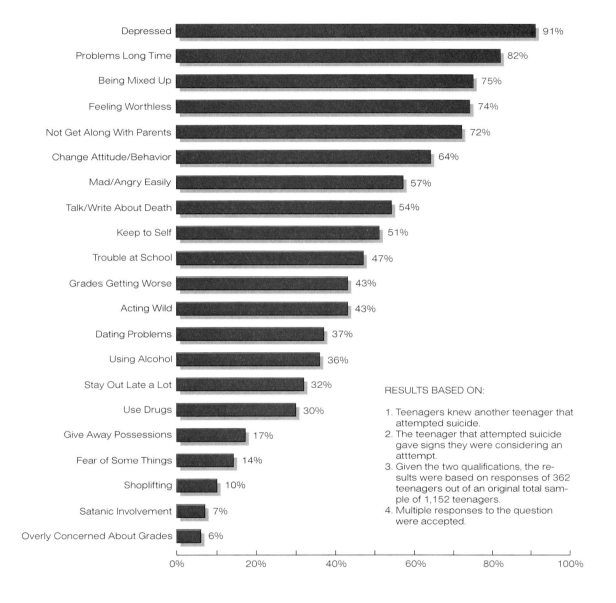

## Signs Teenager Might Attempt Suicide

| Sign | Percentage |
|------|-----------|
| Depressed | 91% |
| Problems Long Time | 82% |
| Being Mixed Up | 75% |
| Feeling Worthless | 74% |
| Not Get Along With Parents | 72% |
| Change Attitude/Behavior | 64% |
| Mad/Angry Easily | 57% |
| Talk/Write About Death | 54% |
| Keep to Self | 51% |
| Trouble at School | 47% |
| Grades Getting Worse | 43% |
| Acting Wild | 43% |
| Dating Problems | 37% |
| Using Alcohol | 36% |
| Stay Out Late a Lot | 32% |
| Use Drugs | 30% |
| Give Away Possessions | 17% |
| Fear of Some Things | 14% |
| Shoplifting | 10% |
| Satanic Involvement | 7% |
| Overly Concerned About Grades | 6% |

RESULTS BASED ON:

1. Teenagers knew another teenager that attempted suicide.
2. The teenager that attempted suicide gave signs they were considering an atttempt.
3. Given the two qualifications, the results were based on responses of 362 teenagers out of an original total sample of 1,152 teenagers.
4. Multiple responses to the question were accepted.

From: The Gallup Organization, Inc., *Narrative Summary Teenage Suicide Study,* January 1991, p. 57.

Teenagers are committing suicide at an alarming rate. Depression is the most common indicator in a suicidal personality, but feelings of worthlessness and confusion also contribute to the attitude that self-destruction is a viable alternative.

when a friend needs help or has problems that require intervention. This program, Link-Up, builds skills in three areas commonly lacking among students at high risk for suicide: peer support, coping skills, and self-esteem.

Teachers and students must be taught warning signs. These might include trouble complying with school rules, deteriorating academic performance, isolation from peer group, increased irritability, pushing others away who want to help, and increased aggression. Teens who are prone to suicide may become involved in crime, vandalism, drugs and alcohol, and sexual promiscuity in an attempt to solve their problems.

Although the percentage of teenagers committing suicide is relatively low, it is increasing at an alarming rate. When a teenager dies for whatever reason, school is disrupted and students must be helped to understand and deal with the tragedy.

Many of society's problems affect children and the schools. In order to combat these problems, educators must reach out to parents to help them become involved in the education of their children; they must work with children and their families to help them overcome the problems of homelessness, poverty, child abuse, teenage sexuality, drug and alcohol abuse, sexism, racism, and suicide. Although the problems of society that affect children and the schools often seem overwhelming, school-based programs that involve other community agencies and business can often help children and families rise above these problems.

---

**11-2**

### Points to Remember

- The number of children across all racial and ethnic groups who live in poverty is growing. Health and other poverty-related problems can affect a child's performance in school.

- Violence and crime infiltrate the schools and severely affect the learning environment.

- Women are less likely than men to attain high-prestige, high-paying positions in education.

- Minorities are even less likely than women to hold high-level administrative positions, thus do not have role models in the schools.

- Many middle and high school students abuse drugs and al-cohol, affecting performance in the classroom.

- Substance abuse education is designed to prevent students from abusing alcohol and drugs and to help them cope with abuse problems.

- Crack babies are born to mothers who have taken drugs during pregnancy. They are likely to be hyperactive and ex-perience developmental and cognitive delays.

- A large percentage of teenag-ers are sexually active, which can lead to pregnancy and sexually transmitted diseases, including AIDS. Programs help students deal with these prob-lems.

- Over 80 percent of middle and high school students say they have experienced sexual ha-rassment in school, defined as unwanted and unwelcomed sexual behavior that interferes with their school life.

- Sexuality education helps stu-dents deal with problems such as family relations, gender identity, dating and marriage, reproduction, family planning, sexual values, attitudes, and behaviors, and rape and sex-ual abuse.

- AIDS education is required in almost all states and is de-signed to make students aware of how one can contract the AIDS virus, how to deal with AIDS victims, and how to pre-vent AIDS.

- The number of teenage sui-cides is increasing at an alarm-ing rate. The most likely suicide victim is a white male who is depressed.

## For Thought/Discussion

1. What specific things can schools do to accommodate the changing nature of the American family?
2. For what reasons are minority children more likely than whites to be poor and ineffectively educated?
3. What are some signs in the child of physical and/or emotional abuse? If such a child appeared in your classroom, what should you do?
4. Do you believe schools have a responsibility to teach sexuality education? If not, why not? If so, how would you deal first with a parent, and second with a school system, that opposed it?

## For Further Reading/Reference

Besharov, D. J. 1988. *Protecting children from abuse and neglect.* Springfield, IL: Charles C. Thomas. A collection of articles on physical, sexual, and emotional child abuse cases; problems related to reporting child abuse are discussed.

Blankenhorn, D., Bayme, S., and Elshtain, J. B. 1991. *Rebuilding the nest: A new commitment to the American family.* Milwaukee, WI: Family Services of America. A series of essays on the current state of the American family, including articles on the quality of life for children and family values.

Fox, C. L., and Forbing, S. E. 1992. *Creating drug-free schools and communities.* New York: Harper & Row. A comprehensive discussion of drug abuse, prevention, intervention, and treatment in schools and communities.

Klein, T., Bittel, C., and Molnar, J. 1993. No place to call home: Supporting the needs of homeless children in the early childhood classroom. *Young Children,* 48 (6), 22–31. The authors discuss their experiences with homeless children and offer suggestions for other educators.

Popham, W. J. 1993. Wanted: AIDS education that works. *Phi Delta Kappan,* 74 (7), 559–562. The author discusses five obstacles to AIDS education and makes recommendations to overcoming them.

Sautter, R. C. 1992. Crack: Healing the children. *Phi Delta Kappan* 74 (3), K1–K12 (Kappan Special Report). Author discusses the problems of children born to drug users, and programs that can help them.

Scott-Jones, D. 1993. Adolescent childbearing: Whose problems? *Phi Delta Kappan,* 75 (3) (Special Report K1–K12). This special report examines childbearing in the United States and compares sexually active American teens with those in other countries.

Tower, C. C. 1992. *The role of educators in the prevention and treatment of child abuse and neglect.* National Education Association. This is a comprehensive revision of guides published in 1979, 1984, and 1987. The author provides educators with signs to look for and what to do when child abuse or neglect is suspected.

Mike Streff

*"Do you have a system designed to keep teenagers in?"*

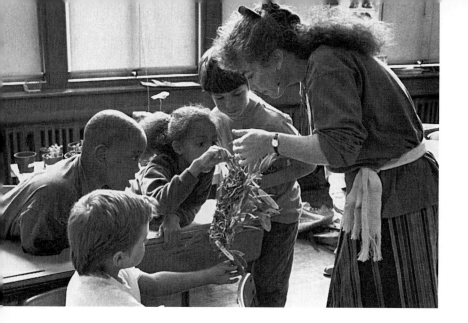

## CHAPTER OBJECTIVES

After studying this chapter, you should be able to:

- Identify how schools deal with society's problems.
- Discuss how preschools are attempting to meet the needs of society.
- Discuss how the middle school attempts to deal with the needs of early adolescents.
- Analyze the issue of school choice.
- Discuss different models for school choice.
- Describe the reasons for home schooling.
- Assess the role of before- and after-school programs in the changing society.
- Discuss the reasons for the federal free meals program.
- Describe the hurdles that students overcome with the help of dropout prevention programs.
- Describe programs for gifted and talented students.
- Discuss the various roles of parents in education.

*Chapter 12*

# SCHOOLS RESPOND TO SOCIAL CHANGE

*C*hoice in education? Can it happen? Would it be valuable? As parent *and professional, I can't imagine another way.*

When I sent my oldest child, now 21, off to kindergarten, the Minneapolis Public Schools' federally funded "Southeast Alternatives" program was in its fledgling years. I had the choice of four schools, each with a different philosophy. The school I chose fit with my philosophy of child development; my child's education complemented our family's values. At one point I had seriously considered moving out of the city, but, in the end, I just couldn't imagine buying into a suburban school system that believed there was only one way to educate all children. One system can't meet all of the diversity of our human interests and multi-intelligences.

As my last child prepares to enter high school, her choices are even broader—the Open Magnet, the International Baccalaureate, the Arts School, the Technology Magnet, the Liberal Arts Magnet—and, if none of these fully meets her needs, she has the right to enroll in classes at the University of Minnesota.

I am also an elementary teacher in a K–8 Minneapolis public alternative school, where parents, students, and teachers all have choices. Parents choose to send their children to our school and we have been overenrolled for years. Every spring parents visit our classrooms and give their input on choice of teacher for their child's next school year. For 10 years, we've held "Goal-Setting Conferences" each September, during which parents, teacher, and student discuss the student's strengths, interests, and needs, including academic, physical, interpersonal, and artistic goals. Together, they choose specific goals for the student, going beyond traditional curriculum. Our school's "whole child" emphasis includes interdisciplinary thematic

469

curriculum, experiential curriculum, hands-on manipulatives, the direct teaching of social skills, and attention to each learner's distinct style.

In my multi-age classroom, students have many choices. They may elect to sit in the pillow corner or at the tables; they may decide to interact with peers for "teaching"; and they may choose what mini-courses to take or teach, how to organize their work time, what topics they believe are most meaningful to investigate within a theme, and when to eat a healthy snack. Our staff believes it is important for students to make choices and evaluate the results of their choices. We give students the opportunity to make many choices in order to help them learn how to make good choices.

As a teacher in this site-based managed school, I also make many choices each day. Some choices involve next year's budget, the staff development focus, and the day-to-day operations of our school. Most important, however, I choose how to facilitate the growth of my students. I determine the interdisciplinary themes that incorporate our district's curriculum guidelines, and I select the wide variety of materials for teaching each theme rather than relying on standard textbooks. I also choose the math manipulatives, the problem-solving situations, and the novels for my literature-based approach to reading. I am accountable for the success of each of my students; therefore, I choose the strategies that nurture each child's learning based on my understanding of his or her learning style, interests, skills, and deficits. I am the professional educator who determines—who chooses—how to help them focus their energies.

Over the years, my opportunity to make educational decisions has increased my commitment to excellence, to success for every student. Over time, increasing student choices has also significantly decreased my discipline problems. Maybe William Glasser, a noted psychiatrist, has been right all along. After basic physical needs, we seek to have power, freedom, and fun. It certainly is a lot more fun to have the power and freedom to make choices than to have them made for us.

From: L. Ellison, 1990–1991, "The Many Facets of School Choice," *Educational Leadership* 48 (4), 37.

*In the school district that is probably the most celebrated example of choice in the country, the students of the East Harlem Maritime School practice rowing and sea chanties. The students tug at the large oars under a hot sun, largely oblivious to the drama that has unfolded at their school over the last few years.*

The Maritime School is one of 24 junior high schools that students in East Harlem's District 4 can choose as they leave sixth grade. Like many other schools in the district, in addition to regular course offerings the maritime school adopted a special theme to define its educational vision and appeal to students. . . .

The school now offers courses in navigation, oceanography, and marine biology. Students took first and third prizes in a recent model boat regatta in Central Park. Once a week, they travel from East Harlem to the campus of the New York Maritime Academy at the base of the Throgs Neck Bridge in the Bronx. There they row, drill, and file into classrooms on a ship, the Ernestina. . . .

Fred Hornedo Jr., a dental technician and Navy veteran, visited several schools with his son, Freddy, who had done well at an alternative elementary school but was having trouble, as his father put it, "being able to sit down.". . .

"I was looking for a place where Fred could fit in," said Mr. Hornedo, an advocate of choice. "This is my first experience with this. I just went to school in my district. I find this to be great." Mr. Hornedo has been emboldened to send his son next year to a Staten Island high school with an even more extensive maritime program.

From: S. Chira, "The Rules of the Marketplace Are Applied to the Classroom," *New York Times* (June 12, 1991), A1, B5.

---

*A*lthough schools do not change rapidly and many argue that they should conserve rather than change society, they do attempt to deal with social changes and to meet the needs of society through direct and indirect measures. This chapter will examine some of the ways in which schools are affected by social change and how they attempt to meet the needs of today's children and families.

## Structural Changes in the Schools

We must first, however, understand the problems of society that affect children, families, and schools. Historian Lawrence A. Cremin in *Popular Education and Its Discontents* (1990) argued that "our recent assessments of how far [education has] come, especially as those assessments have been expressed in the policy literature of the 1980s and 1990s, have been seriously flawed by a failure to understand the extraordinary complexity of education—a failure to grasp the impossibility of defining a good school apart from its societal and intellectual context" (p. viii). In other words, we really cannot understand schools unless we understand the society of which they are a part. And, according to Cremin, we have frequently failed to recognize the importance of the interrelatedness of society and the schools and how each affects the other. In chapter 11 we examined some of the problems that face today's children, families, and schools. In this chapter we will examine some of the ways in which the schools are attempting to deal with these problems.

A preschool not only cares for the daily needs of children but also prepares them for school. Without any federal or state regulation in terms of teacher preparation or curriculum, preschools vary in their quality and effectiveness. Parents, therefore, need to select carefully the preschool that best meets the needs of their child.

## Preschools

One of the ways in which schools are meeting the needs of single-parent families, working parents, and underprivileged or disabled children is through the establishment of preschools. Certainly, the concept of preschool is not new. You may have attended a preschool. Perhaps it was called a nursery school. What is new is the emphasis on early childhood education, specifically for three- and four-year-olds, including disabled children, in public schools.

Early childhood education differs from child care in that it prepares children for school. According to the Committee for Economic Development (CED), a research and policy organization of 250 corporate and university leaders, in *The Unfinished Agenda: A New Vision for Child Development and Education* (1991), child care is seen more as a benefit to parents than to children since it allows parents to work (p. 27). However, the CED suggests that attempting to separate the education and care of young children is counterproductive because all children need both. In their 1994 research report on young children, *Starting Points: Meeting the Needs of our Youngest Children,* the Carnegie Corporation confirmed the educational importance of quality child care that "enables a young child to become emotionally secure, socially competent, and intellectually capable."

The National Governors' Association recognized this link between quality child care and future schooling when they set as their first national education goal that by the year 2000 all children in America will start school ready to learn (see chapter 5, pp. 210–212). As a part of this goal, the governors went a step further setting the objective that "all disadvantaged and disabled children will have access to high quality and developmentally appropriate preschool programs that help prepare {them} for school" (National Governors' Association 1992, 8). The Carnegie Corporation supports the governors' commitment to quality child care as the best route to ensuring children are ready for school.

> Children who receive warm and sensitive caregiving are more likely to trust caregivers, to enter school ready and eager to learn, and to get along well with other children. . . . Children who receive inadequate or barely adequate care are more likely later to feel insecure with teachers, to distrust other children, and to face possible later rejection by other children. Rejection by other children appears to be a powerful predictor of unhappy results, including dropping out of school and delinquency. (p. 49)

## In the Classroom

Kai Ming Head Start in San Francisco was created in 1975 because the federal government wanted to identify a local agency that could meet the early childhood education needs of the Chinese community. The Clay/Larkin Street branch of Kai Ming is housed in a grey limestone church along the border between Chinatown and North Beach. The brightly lit facility has been divided into a small section for offices and two spacious, open classrooms. English and Chinese signs appear throughout, and the walls are liberally covered with art work made by the children. The cheerful sounds of pre-schoolers using both Chinese and English words greet the ears of visitors as they enter.

The children enrolled are at the center for 4 hours every day during which they are provided with comprehensive services designed to foster the whole child, including physical, emotional and intellectual development. Half come in the morning and half in the afternoon. A typical day includes a meal, an hour of free play followed by a "recall" exercise where children describe how they spent that time, small group activities, music, outdoor play, story time and another snack.

Kai Ming strives to promote language development in both English and Chinese. Their policy is to emphasize development in Chinese among three year olds. Then as children near kindergarten, teachers increase emphasis on English. Staff would like children to start school already having some basic English.

Language development occurs throughout the day through a variety of activities rather than during a set period of time. For example, it occurs by teaching children Chinese and English songs and encouraging them to use their language skills during recall time.

At Kai Ming, language development is fostered through exposure to appropriate role models. Staff takes particular care to avoid code switching (e.g. switching from Chinese to English in one sentence) and always makes clear distinctions between the two languages. In addition, Kai Ming has intentionally recruited native English speaking teachers to provide students with appropriate language models.

From: Hedy Nai-Lin Chang (1993). *Affirming children's roots: Cultural and linguistic diversity in early care and education.* San Francisco, CA: California Tomorrow.

Child care has become even more important since the passage of the Family Support Act of 1990 (P.L. 101–239), which requires states to develop special education and employment/training programs for many, if not most, teenage parents on welfare. For these programs to succeed, child care must also be provided. In 1990 Congress passed the Child Care and Development Block Grant (P.L. 101–508) creating two child-care programs as well as tax credit and income support for low-income families at risk of going on welfare without child-care assistance. In addition, all states must supply child care to AFDC [Aid to Families with Dependent Children]-supported parents who are enrolled in education and/or employment training programs, as required under the Family Support Act (1990, 19). This increasing emphasis on both early education and child care is related to society's changing needs, particularly the changing structure of the American family.

## PRESCHOOL ENROLLMENT

In the decade of the 1970s, preschool enrollment (three–five-year-olds) increased 19 percent. Between 1980 and 1993 preschool enrollment increased another 27 percent (U.S. Department of Education, National Center for Education Statistics 1994, 62). In 1970, 17 percent of preschool youngsters attended full-day school programs; in 1993, 40 percent did. These figures include only children enrolled in preschool programs that are monitored by governmental agencies; they do not include those who are cared for by unlicensed child-care givers.

The Children's Defense Fund estimates the child-care acts of the early 1990s have helped the parents of as many as 400 thousand children pay for child-care services. In Alabama, for example, twice as many low-income children receive child-care assistance as before the legislation. Between 1990 and 1991 in Ohio the number of children served in subsidized child care increased from 25 thousand to 41 thousand (CDF 1995, 15–18).

This dramatic increase in the number of children enrolled in preschool programs illustrates a social need for more and better preschools—more, because many mothers are entering the workforce; better, so that those underprivileged and disabled children who previously entered school developmentally behind their peers can improve their learning skills and function more successfully. According to a report of the National Governors' Association, preschool programs should be "preventative, compensatory, and preparatory efforts" (1992, 12).

## FUNDING OF PRESCHOOLS

By 1970 only seven states had appropriated funds for preschool programs in their public schools, and only four states had contributed funds to Head Start, a federally funded preschool program for underprivileged children (see chapter 5, pp. 185–188). However, by 1993 thirty-nine states had appropriated funds for state-initiated preschool programs and/or made direct contributions to Head Start (telephone interview with Ruth Massie, administrative director, Child Care/Preschool, Children's Defense Fund, July 6, 1994). Most of the funded programs are all-day, year-round programs for at-risk children in local public school districts and are administered by state departments of education.

Since 1990, the federal government has significantly increased funding for Head Start. The federal authorization for Head Start in 1995 is $4 billion, up from $2.5 billion in 1993. In addition, $4 billion has been authorized to the states to provide preschool and child-care programs through the Developmental Block Grant.

States have used these funds in different ways. Twenty states, according to Helen Block of the Children's Defense Fund, have used the funds to supplement Head Start programs for three- to five-year-olds, providing extended child-care hours for working mothers. Two states have started preschool programs for four- and five-year-olds. Forty-six states have used grant money to develop school-age programs or train child-care providers for school-age children, and nineteen have expanded child-care services for teenage parents, many of whom are in school (1993, 32–34).

Although both state and federal funds have been invested in Head Start programs for low-income children, only limited funds have been invested in state-initiated and -governed preschool programs. In 1992 forty-eight states funded public school programs for five-year-olds, but only six states funded similar programs for three- and four-year-olds and none reported funding programs for two-year-olds (Robinson and Lyon, 776). A 1993 Phi Delta Kappan education poll revealed that 59 percent of taxpayers would be willing to pay for child-care centers within the public school system for all preschool children, up from 35 percent in 1992. Similarly, 61 percent of taxpayers, according to the poll, would be willing to pay higher taxes for funding free preschool programs for disadvantaged children (Elam, Rose, Gallup 1993, 143–144).

Many people, including those on the Committee on Economic Development, believe that the funding of preschools must come from a combination of sources: foundations, corporations, and federal, state, and local governments. In 1990 the CED estimated that $11.5 billion were needed during the first five years of the 1990s—7 percent of what was spent on all education in 1988.

The CED suggests that preschool programs, although expensive, are cost effective for dealing with long-term problems such as the dropout rate and helping at-risk students become more productive learners. The National Governors' Association estimates that each dollar spent on preschool education will prevent educational failure and produce long-term savings to society. In 1992, according to NGA, the average annual cost to maintain each prisoner was $20 thousand in comparison to the $48 hundred cost of a year of quality preschool, which has been shown to decrease teen arrest by 40 percent (1992, 12).

## INCREASED STATE INVOLVEMENT

Anne Mitchell, dean of the Division of Research, Demonstration, and Policy at Bank Street College, says the increased state concern for preschool programs comes from five sources: (1) demand from working mothers in all income groups; (2) concern for present and future economic productivity, international com-

*(continued on p. 477)*

# *Cross-Cultural Perspective*

## If the French Can Do It, Why Can't We?

Pascal Favre-Rochex is in the midst of that morning tightrope walk parents know so well—settling his son in preschool. His knees are scrunched up against the pint-size table as he hams it up, reading "Monsieur Rigolo" to 3-year-old Clément. A moment later he gives his son a hug and is out the door. The teacher, Maryse Corne, invites Clément, Antoine, Inès, Mehdi, Stanislas and 16 other toddlers to sit on the gray rug at her feet. First they recite rhymes about escargots and bumblebees, and then they sing "Frère Jacques," pumping their right arms up and down to ring imaginary church bells.

By French standards it's just another day in preschool. But through American eyes what's going on in this Parisian preschool is extraordinary. This class is part of a free, full-day, public preschool, or école maternelle. Many New Yorkers, Washingtonians and Californians pay $8,000 to $14,000 a year to send a child to preschool or a day-care center, if they are lucky enough to find a place. In France, 99 percent of 3-, 4- and 5-year-olds attend preschool at no or minimal charge.

In sharp contrast, just one-third of American 3- and 4-year-olds attend preschools or day-care centers, and in many communities the nonaffluent need not apply. But with the strong backing of left and right, the French spend $7 billion a year to make sure every child—rich, middle class or poor—gets off to a good start. They feel the benefits outweigh the cost.

Comparing the French system with the American system—if that word can be used to describe a jigsaw puzzle missing half its pieces—is like comparing a vintage bottle of Château Margaux with a $4 bottle of American wine. The first child-care centers were built in the early 1800's to protect the children of women who took jobs in rapidly industrializing Paris. But it was only after World War II that the system exploded in size as the battle-scarred nation sought to protect its young from starvation and disease. Today, for France's 4.5 million children under the age of 6, the constellation of child-care offerings is vast and all of them are linked to health care. The three major categories are day-care centers and day-care homes, for children 3 months to 3 years of age, and preschools, for children 2½ to 5 years old.

Day-care centers, or crèches, and day-care homes charge fees on a sliding scale. Public preschools, or écoles maternelles, are free; parochial preschools are heavily subsidized.

"Our objective is to be both a place of learning and a place that stimulates children," says Josiane Mattei, the director of the preschool Clément attends, off Avenue du Général Leclerc. Mattei coordinates the curriculum for 210 children and, since this is France, sees to it that the children use proper table manners.

"We don't want parents to feel that they're leaving their kids at a baggage claim," she says.

Preschools run from 8:30 A.M. to 4:30 P.M.; parents can pay $300 a year for wraparound programs that provide supervised activities from 7:30 to 8:30 A.M. and 4:30 to 6 P.M.

Local government supports the day-care centers, which are normally open from 7 A.M. to 7 P.M. The overall cost of sending a child to a Parisian day-care center is $10,000 a year. Poor families pay $390 per year, middle-class families pay about $3,200, and the rich pay $5,300. When we lived in France, our son, Jeremy, attended a crèche in the Latin Quarter. The fee was $3,850 a year.

The staff of 19 was responsible for 72 children. The director, Odile Caplier, is a registered nurse who spent two years studying child development. Like all municipal crèche directors, she has an apartment in the same building, enabling her to keep a child past 7 P.M. in an emergency. The staff includes a deputy director (also a registered nurse) and two teachers (each with the equivalent of four years of college). The 12 child-care aides are high-school graduates who have taken a one-year course in child development.

What wowed my wife, Miriam, was the food. She often mailed copies of the crèche's weekly menu to friends in the United States so they could salivate over the poached fish, cauliflower mousse, parsleyed potatoes and Camembert cheese—not bad compared with the peanut butter sandwiches served at so many American preschools.

From: S. Greenhouse, "If the French Can Do It, Why Can't We?" *The New York Times Magazine* (Nov. 14, 1993), 59.

petitiveness, and the changing nature of the workforce; (3) efforts to get mothers with Aid to Families with Dependent Children (AFDC) funds into the workforce; (4) desire to provide a better educational start for poor children; and (5) evidence that high quality early childhood programs have a long-term positive effect for disadvantaged children (p. 667). In addition, many groups, including the Carnegie Foundation for the Advancement of Teaching, the National Association for the Education of Young Children, the Task Force on Early Childhood Education for the National Association of State Boards of Education, the Committee for Economic Development, and the National Governors' Association, have taken an active role in promoting preschool funding initiatives.

## REGULATION OF PRESCHOOLS

Since nearly twice as many preschool programs in the late 1980s were private rather than public, regulation was a problem. However, increased federal and state funding of preschools means more and more are public. Even today, however, the vast majority of preschool teachers lack the training required of public school teachers. In fact, the majority of preschool teachers are caregivers rather than educators.

In 1994 there were three kinds of licenses available to child-care educators. The National Association of Education of Young Children (NAEYC), the accrediting agency for programs that train teachers to work with young children, is developing birth to kindergarten (B-K) college and university four-year programs leading to a B-K teaching certificate and two-year college programs leading to a certificate as a Child Development Associate (CDA). Another credential established for child-care workers is the Child-Care Credential, designed for anyone (teachers, aides, parents, or volunteers) who want to work in day-care centers. This nonprofessional credential requires the completion of thirty-three clock-hours of course work at a community college. NAEYC estimates that there are nearly 18 hundred early childhood teacher or associate training programs with established standards and guidelines for developmentally appropriate training (telephone interview, July 7, 1994).

In North Carolina, for example, a B-K teaching certificate requires a four-year baccalaureate degree. Although this is a big step toward professionalizing the teaching of young children, the certificate is not required for work in most preschools in the state since they are private. Likewise, only twenty accredited teaching or associate training programs exist in North Carolina, far fewer than the number needed to train all early childhood educators.

North Carolina's early childhood teaching certificate responds, in part, to P.L. 99–457 (1987; reauthorized in 1993) mandating that the states provide early intervention services to special-needs children under the age of five, including those who are mainstreamed. These services include preschool care and education, physical and occupational therapy, and home-based family support.

## PRESCHOOL CURRICULUM

The curriculum of preschools in the 1990s is changing to one focusing on early childhood education and school readiness. Sue Bredekamp, director of NAEYC's professional development for early childhood educators, says that professionals and providers are attempting to determine what is meant by developmentally appropriate in light of new knowledge and to relate this information to a curriculum that can best serve the diverse young children in the classrooms. NAEYC reports that a growing number of states and local communities are employing curriculums that have holistic approaches to meeting the needs of children and their families and stress collaborative planning and integration of child care, education, health, and social-service programs (1994, 68). Bredekamp suggests that the elements of this curriculum go beyond the Piagetian perspective of construction of knowledge (see chapter 9, pp. 367–369) and include the children's potential, curiosity, interest in constructing their own learning, dramatic and creative play, and hands-on activities (1993, 13).

Two research projects that seem likely to influence the preschool curriculum are Carolina Abecedarian housed at the Frank Porter Graham Child Development Center in Chapel Hill, North Carolina, and Project Spectrum at Harvard and Tufts Universities. The Carolina Abecedarian project focuses on "center activities" such as housekeeping, tools, art, music, dramatic play, language development, number concepts, and for four- and five-year-olds phonics training. Parents are provided with curriculum packets so that they can follow up on the concepts and skills taught in the school. Researchers followed a group of ninety-three Abecedarian children and ninety-three other children who had not been through the curriculum but were given extra help beginning at age six through sixteen (grades kindergarten through ten). The Abecedarian children surpassed the control group at all age levels and kept their academic advantage throughout the ten years.

Project Spectrum focuses on curricular materials in theme-related kits such as "night and day" and "you and me." Based on Howard Gardner's multiple intelligences theory (see chapter 10, pp. 394–395), the curriculum is exploratory with younger children and begins to develop skills in reading, writing, and calculating, in the context of theme areas in which four- and five-year-olds have demonstrated interest. The curriculum has been used for a decade with at-risk, gifted, disabled, and average students in several regions of the United States.

## Middle Schools

The concept of middle school, a transitional institution between elementary and high schools, is not new. It is, however, evolving, with a new emphasis on what has been called the middle school philosophy, an approach that focuses on the early adolescent rather than on the subject matter. A 1992 report of the National Middle Schools Association (NMSA), *This We Believe,* defines the middle school as "an educational response to the needs and characteristics of youngsters during transescence [a coined term referring to ages ten through fourteen or early adolescence], and, as such, deals with the full range of intellectual and developmental needs" (p. 9). Middle schools create a learning environment for early adolescents that bridges the gap between elementary school, where the child spends most of the day in a single classroom with a single teacher, and high school, where the adolescent moves from class to class and has as many as eight teachers per day. In addition, the middle school is intended to redefine not only the organizational structure of the school but also its educational methods. It not only meets the cognitive needs of the students but tries to meet their psychological and social developmental needs as well. Proponents of this student-centered middle school philosophy believe that it has the potential to deal with some of society's major problems, including drug abuse, teenage pregnancy, and dropping out of school, thereby improving the lives of adolescents.

By the late 1960s schools that had previously been called junior high schools were becoming middle schools. This restructuring involved a change in the ages within each school's population from grades seven through nine to grades six through eight. But most of these middle schools did not immediately change their organizational structure. Deborah L. Cohen, an education reporter for *Education Week,* found that most still used the secondary school schedule of uniform periods. She also found that the majority of middle school teachers lacked special training to work with these students (1989).

However, by the early 1990s most middle schools were restructuring. A research study of twelve middle schools in five cities funded by the Edna McConnell Clark Foundation found that the first two years of middle school reform, from 1989 to 1991, were full of frustration and confusion at these schools, but from 1991 to 1993 the reforms began to bear fruit. Anne C. Lewis, the author of this report entitled *Changing the Odds,* suggests that as a result of intensive and high quality staff development, more of the middle school teachers in these schools believed that students could perform at high levels and were more confident that they could help them do so; the curriculum was more active, student centered, and challenging; retention and suspensions were reduced while attendance and performance improved (1993, 12). According to NMSA, true middle schools, like those reported on by Lewis, share ten essential elements.

- Educators knowledgeable about 10- to 14-year-olds.
- A balanced curriculum based on developmental needs.
- A range of organizational strategies.
- An exploratory program.
- Comprehensive advisory and counseling programs.
- Cooperative planning.
- A positive school climate.
- Appropriate evaluation procedures.
- Varied instructional procedures.
- Continuous progress. (1992, 9)

## ADOLESCENT DEVELOPMENT

In June 1989 the Carnegie Council on Adolescent Development issued what has become a pivotal report in middle school reform, *Turning Points: Preparing American Youth for the 21st Century,* in which it criticized middle-grade education as not focusing on the needs of early adolescents. This report, supported by developmental psychological research, stated that young adolescents, ages ten to fifteen, face more significant turning points—growth and changes—than any age group other than infants.

The report further contended that social conditions have changed dramatically from past generations. Although early adolescents today may have a better sense of self and more opportunities for intimate relationships, they also face unprecedented choices and pressures. They do not have the dependent needs of childhood but haven't found their own path to adulthood. They feel isolated while surrounded by peers. They are confused by all these changes and frequently make harmful decisions with harmful consequences. The report cited statistics about increased numbers of young adolescents who have alcohol and drug problems, who are pregnant, and who exhibit high risk behaviors and school failure (see chapter 11).

Although there have been significant changes in middle school education since the 1989 report, the Carnegie Council in a 1992 report, *Fateful Choices: Healthy Youth for the 21st Century,* by Fred M. Hechinger, found that in the 1990s poor health among adolescents was reaching crisis proportions with large numbers of suicides, abuse of drugs and smoking, significant sexual activity, and adolescents as the victims or perpetrators of violence. To help counteract this, the report suggested that all upper elementary and middle schools offer two years of health or life science education including human biology. Although the 1992 Carnegie Council report sees many things that must be accomplished in the education of young adolescents, the report focuses not only on what schools need to do, but also what society must do.

Fateful choices are ours as a society: if we give young adolescents sufficient attention and support, they may have the chance to grow up healthy and whole in body and in mind. At stake are not only individual young lives, but our future as a nation (Hechinger 1992, 4).

## MIDDLE SCHOOL INSTRUCTION

The difference between how students are taught in the traditional secondary school and the contemporary middle school is the difference between subject-centered instruction and child-centered instruction (see chapter 8, pp. 302 and 316). This difference is made clear by Terry Weeks's experience.

> When Terry M. Weeks, former Teacher of the Year, set out in the mid-1970s to teach his Murfreesboro, Tennessee, 7th graders a lesson on the Middle East, the approach he chose was the lecture.
>
> He told his class the story of the Arab-Israeli conflict, hoping that they "would imagine it through my words."
>
> But [in the late 1980s] when the topic came up, he let students offer their own solutions to the conflict. And when one suggested that the United States find a new homeland for Israelis, that became the inspiration for an exercise in which pupils assumed the roles of politicians, Jews, Arabs—and even American Indians.
>
> That lesson allowed the class to "see the solution through different eyes," Mr. Weeks says, to "play it through" to discover the problem's full complexity.
>
> He attributes the change in approach to his school's transition to the philosophy of what is known as the middle school movement. It was a shift, he says, that transformed "the heart and soul of what I do."
>
> "Students became my main focus," he explains, "rather than my subject." (Cohen 1989, 1, 20)

## IMPROVING MIDDLE SCHOOLS

To help alleviate the problem of disenfranchised youth in the middle grades, the Carnegie Council on Adolescent Development proposed a series of recommenda-

**TABLE 12-1**

### Recommendations for Middle Schools

---

1. Create small communities for learning
2. Teach an academic core
3. Ensure success for all students
4. Empower teachers and administrators to make decisions regarding educational experiences
5. Staff middle schools with teachers who are expert at teaching 10- to 14-year-olds
6. Improve academic performance through fostering health and fitness
7. Re-engage families in the education of learners
8. Connect schools with communities

---

Adapted from *Turning Points: Preparing American Youth for the 21st Century.* (1989). Washington, DC: Carnegie Council on Adolescent Development. This report was prepared by the Carnegie Council on Adolescent Development's Task Force on Education of Young Adolescents. The Carnegie Council is a program of Carnegie Corporation of New York.

**The middle school has long been considered simply a phase between elementary and high school. Recently, however, several reports have recommended that the middle school should have its own philosophy and specific teaching practices appropriate to students in early adolescence.**

tions intended to develop a teaching staff trained in the psychology of the middle school student and a curriculum and approach to learning appropriate to that age level (see table 12.1). M. Lee Manning in *Developmentally Appropriate Middle Level Schools* (1993) suggested appropriate practices to help achieve those recommendations such as elimination of tracking by achievement level, developing thinking skills, cooperative learning, and flexibility in instructional time.

In order best to implement these recommendations, the Carnegie Council on Adolescent Development suggested that the schools take some immediate steps: change the focus of middle-grades education immediately, prepare teachers specifically for middle school, collaborating with middle schools in the process, and provide better access to health-care services. In addition the council suggested that statewide task forces should examine the implications for their schools, youth organizations should form partnerships with schools, the president and other national leaders should establish federal policy for funding youth development research, and parents should help their children define their goals, monitor their studies, and bring pressure on the schools for change. As reports such as Lewis's and Manning's show, many of these reforms have been adopted by contemporary middle schools.

## School Choice

Perhaps the most controversial concept in public education in the United States is parental choice of educational institutions at the elementary and secondary levels. Many parents believe that they should have the right to determine the school that is most suited to the needs of their child.

There has always been some degree of choice in education; parents could elect to move or send their children to independent, private, or parochial schools. However, the degree of choice has been historically limited to people of means, either economic or educational. Many educators believe that allowing *all* parents to choose the educational institution to which they send their children will promote better education for all children.

## FREE MARKET SYSTEM IN EDUCATION

The concept of choice is built on the concept of competition in the free market system. Proponents of choice contend that if parents have the right to select their children's schools, they will select only the best schools; the others will have to close their doors or improve their methods of operation. Opponents, however, contend that parental school choice is "a surreptitious plan that gradually puts the functions of public education into private hands. In the end, public funds will support private education institutions" (Frick 1994, 1995). Others studying current school choice plans are also skeptical of their results. The Carnegie Foundation for the Advancement of Teaching in a 1992 survey of school choice plans suggests that "it is difficult to conclude that choice itself will drive academic improvement through competition" (p. 14).

Many educators warn that if school choice is widely employed, some schools will attract not only the better students but also the better teachers and, perhaps, more of the resources. What does this leave for other schools—poorer students and teachers, fewer resources? In fact, many critics contend that "open enroll- ment is elitist—at least in the sense that only those who have the means to do the driving will be able to choose. Choice will not be available to many low-income or single-parent families. Distance and geography will also determine who can choose, especially when extracurricular activities are added to the schedule" (Pearson 1989, 821). In addition, education critic Jonathan Kozol suggests that many poor parents are only semiliterate and have neither the ability nor the opportunity to read materials school systems distribute, even announcements calling them to meetings where school choice might be explained. According to Kozol, "the myth here is that choices will be equal, and that everybody will be equally informed about the choices available" (Kemper 1993, 26). Therefore, critics of school choice worry that it will do little to help meet the needs of society. In fact, it may exacerbate the situation further for those students who most need the best schools.

Despite these concerns, there is no doubt that some level of choice will continue in public schools. Sixty-five percent of parents surveyed in a 1993 Phi Delta Kappan/Gallup Poll favored choice for parents and students (Elam 1993). However, according to a survey conducted by the Carnegie Foundation for the Advancement of Teaching, 70 percent of parents said they would not transfer their children to another school if given the choice (1992, 11).

There are two different models of school choice: districtwide choice and statewide choice. The district model permits parents and students to select a public school within their home district and, according to a Carnegie Foundation report, scores of districts have introduced a variety of these arrangements. One particularly successful model is in East Harlem, New York (see opening anecdote), proving, the Carnegie Foundation suggests, that school choice plans can be successful in poor, urban settings. Because of the success of the East Harlem plan, in 1993 New York City adopted a systemwide plan allowing parents to send their children to any school outside their district throughout New York City's five boroughs, making this one of the largest choice plans in the nation. The Carnegie Foundation report concludes that although choice is not a panacea, districtwide plans can stimulate school renewal by empowering teachers, engaging parents, and improving the academic performance of students. (Other districtwide school choice plans are described in table 12.2, p. 487.)

Statewide choice is a less common model and, perhaps, the most controversial. By 1992 seventeen state legislatures, led by Minnesota, had adopted statewide plans. The state of Minnesota has an open enrollment plan that allows for parental choice in all districts with more than one thousand students. However, the Carnegie Foundation reports that participation in these plans is very small since parents are reluctant to enroll their children in schools outside of their communities, thus limiting the potential for school reform. Most parents who do choose schools outside of their districts do so because of proximity to work or child care, or for other personal reasons (65 percent); a much smaller percentage selects schools for academic reasons (33 percent). In Minnesota, the Carnegie Foundation reports, only 1.8 percent of the total student population participates in the choice plan. The report found numerous other problems in statewide plans: few states had dealt with the problem of funding disparities across districts before initiating the plan; few had adequately informed parents about choice programs; few had helped students get transportation to their chosen districts. The Carnegie Foundation concludes, unless states address these crucial issues "the promises of statewide choice cannot . . . be realized" (p. xvi).

## MAGNET SCHOOLS

The single most frequently proposed type of school for parental choice is the magnet school.

Magnet schools are alternatives to traditionally structured schools usually organized by academic or vocational theme and are generally open to all applicants based on availability. The term *magnet* assumes that the students will be attracted to the school because of the theme or special opportunities the school provides. Steuben Middle School in Milwaukee, Wisconsin, for example, has developed a computer specialty program. Students can become familiar with computer operation, robotics, and videodisc technology.

Since one of the goals of the magnet school concept is to attract students from all socioeconomic, ethnic, and racial backgrounds, a broad range of students is usually selected in an attempt to help integrate the public schools. LaGuardia High School of Music and the Arts in New York City and Thomas Jefferson High School for Science and Technology in Alexandria, Virginia, for example, have been able to balance their populations racially and socioeconomically by reattracting white students into urban schools that had been largely populated by black students. Proponents of school choice believe that this integration will lead to superior education for all students.

In 1991–1992, 1.2 million U.S. students were enrolled in either a separate local magnet school or in a magnet school program; this represents a 300 percent growth in one decade. Likewise, the number of magnet school programs had more than doubled in a decade. By 1991 there were 230 local school districts with magnet school programs, 2,400 individual magnet schools, and 3,200 magnet programs. More than half were in urban districts. More than 60 percent of magnet school programs cannot accommodate all parents' requests for student enroll-ment, thereby the demand is greater than the supply, another problem that many say limits the potential of choice to transform the public schools.

The graduates of a large proportion of magnet schools have been very successful. Average achievement scores at Thomas Jefferson High School, for example, were in the 98th percentile in science and mathematics and the 94th in reading. Fifty-nine of approximately 4 hundred seniors at Thomas Jefferson won National Merit Scholarships; fifteen were in the Westinghouse Talent Search. John E. Chubb and Terry Moe of the Brookings Institute concluded from their research on magnet schools that dropout and absenteeism rates were down and parents were better informed and participated more fully in their child's education. Similarly, they found that teachers in magnet schools were more autonomous, more satisfied with their work, and more influential in decision making (1990, 209).

## *Viewpoint* City Magnet School: A Microsociety

The Lowell Public Schools established the City Magnet School (K–8) in the downtown business district. The school was designed to engage students, par-ents, and teachers in the building of a miniature society. It was the first microsociety school in the nation.

The effort began with the introduction of money, markets, and property into the school. The students, advised by their teachers, used these ingredients to create a microeconomy. The microeconomy, in turn, has led to the creation of numerous organizations and jobs in them. Students fill these positions. Some of the work opportunities have arisen in the business sector; others have developed in government agencies, in the miniature society's fledgling legal system, and in a variety of cultural organizations. As these institutions evolve, so do markets for land, labor, and capital. Interacting with these markets has become a dynamic part of each student's school experience.

Beginning in kindergarten, children attending the microsociety school play with the fundamental building blocks of modern society. As they grow and mature, their miniature society matures with them. Apart from gaining insight into adult experience and adult society, there is no prescribed ideological path that the students must follow. With the assistance of parents and teachers, they fashion their own.

The Lowell microsociety school is a living experiment in applied moral development. Children and adults constantly face moral dilemmas that they must solve as they strive to build a "good" society. Do you want a microsociety with the extremes of poverty and wealth? Do you want a state based on law or one based on fear and violence? Should the microsociety's government assist or ignore children who may not be succeeding? Do you want a democracy or a totalitarian state? What liberties should students have? And what responsibilities should they shoulder? What kinds of activities should be taxed? When does one put the community's welfare ahead of the rights of the individual? What civil rights should children enjoy in their microsociety? When has justice been done?

Magnet schools are organized around a particular theme or topic and attract those students who are motivated to study those subjects. These students of East Harlem Maritime School practice rowing and navigational skills. They also study such related topics as oceanography and marine biology.

Children attending the City Magnet School face these dilemmas under the guidance of parents and teachers, many of whom may be struggling with similar issues in the real world.

The City Magnet School provides students with a strong, traditional program in the basic skills. Teaching the basic skills effectively is a goal of virtually every school in the nation. In this magnet school, however, the students learn basic skills as they legislate, adopt budgets, pass tax measures, administer justice, govern, or simply communicate with one another regarding commercial and legal matters. They read, write, and use mathematics with purpose. In other words, the basic skills have utility. In the tradition of John Dewey, *doing* reinforces *learning. . . .*

The microsociety school has produced dramatic changes in the curriculum. For example, publishing—generally known as "English" in the traditional curriculum—has evolved into the most important industry group. Children now write to be published, publish to be read, read to be informed, and use information to make intelligent decisions. The rewards for literacy are significant: recognition, influence, other writing opportunities, and payment in "mogans" (the microeconomic currency).

Arithmetic, once taught as a string of abstract concepts that might be useful in the future, now has immediate and practical application. Students bank, keep books, write checks, bill customers, prepare tax returns, prepare budgets, and perform financial audits. . . .

The typical graduate of City Magnet School has had a host of socialization experiences and has been exposed to a variety of occupations. (One recent graduate wrote that she had served as a judge, a legislator, a lawyer, an entrepreneur, a writer, an editor, an accountant, and a tax collector—all in the same year.) Graduates leave, we hope, with a better sense of their own skills and interests and of the direction in which they are heading. They have also come to realize what organizations can and cannot accomplish and to understand the need for both cooperation and healthy competition.

From: Richmond, 1989

*Funding of Magnet Schools*   Magnet schools are funded like all public schools. Frequently, however, special state or federal grants are available for specialized programs in these schools. Since 1985 the federal government has provided $739 million to 117 school districts for magnet programs aimed at desegregation (most magnet programs are associated with formal, court-ordered desegregation plans), with 80 percent of the funding going to urban, low-income districts with large percentages of minority students. In 1994 the Improving America's Schools Act provided $120 million in federal funds for developing magnet schools. In addition, magnet schools have attracted significant private funding from business and industry. Thomas Jefferson High School, for example, received over $4 million worth of high-tech equipment from four large companies in one year. Proponents of magnet schools contend that the increased involvement of business and industry in public education will not only provide needed funds, but also will lead to community awareness of social issues and, hence, involvement in helping to remedy these problems.

## TUITION TAX CREDITS AND VOUCHERS

To make a wide range of choice possible for all parents, some propose a system of tax credits and/or vouchers. A **tax credit** would allow parents to subtract from their state or federal income taxes an amount equal to a percentage of school tuition, up to a predetermined limit. In Minnesota, whose open enrollment program was upheld by the U.S. Supreme Court in 1983, parents can deduct up to $650 for elementary school tuition and school-related expenses and up to $1 thousand for secondary school tuition from state income taxes whether their child attends public or private school.

Typically, **vouchers**, equal to the average per-pupil cost for educating a child in that specific area's public schools, are provided to all parents by their local governments. Parents then select their child's school, public or private, and the school redeems the voucher for cash from the government. The Wisconsin legislature passed the first voucher plan in the country in 1987. The Milwaukee Choice Plan (the only fully implemented voucher plan in operation in 1994) allows parents to select private schools if their children meet low-income guidelines. These schools are then given $25 hundred for each student admitted; up

*(continued on p. 490)*

**TABLE 12-2**

## A Comparison of School Choice Plans

**California (Cupertino):** The Cupertino Union School District near San Jose subsidizes home schooling. Parents who choose to educate their children at home can receive an annual $1,000 subsidy that can be used to purchase products or services available to public school students. It may not be used for private school tuition.

**Massachusetts (Cambridge):** The Cambridge School District has had a choice plan since 1981 that has served as a model for others in the state and around the nation. The district abolished school attendance zones, and parents may send their children to any of the district's 13 elementary schools. Assignments are made on a first-come, first-served basis, providing space is available and subject to desegregation constraints. According to the U.S. Department of Education, the proportion of students attending public schools in the district rose from 74 to 82 percent after the introduction of the choice plan.

**Minnesota:** Students in all parts of the state may attend public schools outside their district if the receiving district has space available and racial balance is not adversely affected. Parents may deduct from their taxable income up to $650 for elementary school students and up to $1,000 for secondary school expenses.

**New Hampshire (Epsom):** The small town of Epsom has enacted a controversial choice plan that allows parents who educate their children outside the public school system to receive a $1,000 property tax abatement.

**New York (East Harlem):** Students can choose among twenty-four public junior high schools offering specialties from maritime skills to performing arts. These magnet schools are available only to students in the district.

**Vermont:** Since 1969, Vermont has had a plan that allows parents in areas without public high schools to have the school district pay to send their children to public or private secondary schools (excluding parochial schools) in or out of the state. The plan covers the full tuition to a public high school and provides a capped tuition payment equal to the average tuition of the state's high schools to private schools. The plan was modified in 1990 to allow parents in areas that do have public high schools to participate. The 1990 law also extended the plan to elementary school students.

**Washington:** The legislature passed a new choice law during the 1990 session. It expanded the old choice law and widened the reasons a parent could give for requesting a transfer, such as proximity to day care or the parent's place of employment. It also provided that every school district have a policy on interdistrict transfers.

**Wisconsin (Milwaukee):** Initially, 24 of 144 schools were set aside as specialty schools, and the remainder were opened for students on the availability of space and racial guidelines in an attempt to desegregate the city schools. The Milwaukee Choice Plan, passed by the state legislature in 1990, allows parents to select private schools, to be funded by state aid reimbursements of $2,500 for each student accepted. Based on low-income guidelines, approximately 1 percent of students are eligible, making Milwaukee's plan the first voucher plan in the country.

From: R. Worsnop, "How Choice Plans Operate in the States," *CQ Researcher* (May 10, 1991), 269. Adapted, revised, and updated.

Parents have had the opportunity to select a school for their children for many years. Each plan is different and may involve private as well as public schools. This table describes some of the more common plans.

# CAN SCHOOL CHOICE REFORM PUBLIC EDUCATION?

## PRO  John E. Chubb and Terry M. Moe

The most innovative and promising reforms to have gained momentum . . . fall under the heading of "choice." In the past, educators tended to associate this concept with the privatization of public education, aid to religious schools, and racial segregation, portraying it as a subversive notion that threatened the common school ideal and virtually everything else the public system had traditionally stood for. In recent years, however, choice has come to be viewed very differently, even by many in the educational establishment.

This new movement puts choice to use as part of a larger set of strategies for reform *within* the public sector. It is not about privatizing the public schools, nor is it a surreptitious way of giving aid to religious schools. Choice is being embraced by liberals and conservatives alike as a powerful means of transforming the structure and performance of public education—while keeping the public schools public. In the process, it is being used to combat racial segregation; indeed, it has become the preferred approach to desegregation in districts throughout the country—in Rochester and Buffalo (New York), Cambridge (Massachusetts), and Prince George's County (Maryland), to name a few.

Support for public sector choice is widespread. Surveys reveal that the vast majority of public school parents want to choose the schools their children attend—and that, when choice plans are implemented and people have a chance to exercise their newfound freedom, popular support for choice grows. Not surprisingly, many public officials are also singing the praises of choice. . . . Respected groups of academics and reformers, less satisfied than before with the intellectual mainstream, are increasingly arguing the advantages of choice. So are business groups, which have been disappointed in past reforms and are increasingly calling for more innovative approaches that take greater advantage of market-based incentives. And many groups speaking for minorities and the poor have become supporters as well, embracing choice as a crucial means of escaping from the intolerably bad urban schools that the traditional system of fixed boundaries and assignments forces on them. . . .

Yet all this enthusiasm has not translated into truly successful reform, and it may never do so, at least if current efforts are projected into the future. . . . Virtually all choice plans are entirely demand focused: they offer parents and students a measure of choice among schools. Period. Rarely do these plans take any steps to free up the supply side by decontrolling—or, at least, encouraging and promoting through official actions—the emergence of new and different types of schools, so that people really have an attractive and dynamically responsive set of alternatives from which to choose. Instead, choice is usually restricted to a fixed set of existing schools, which reformers hope to improve through the "competition" that choice will presumably stimulate. . . .

Without being too literal about it, we think reformers would do well to entertain the notion that choice *is* a panacea. This is our way of saying that choice is not like the other reforms and should not be combined with them as part of a reformist strategy for improving America's public schools. Choice is a self-contained reform with its own rationale and justification. It has the capacity *all by itself* to bring about the kind of transformation that, for years, reformers have been seeking to engineer in myriad other ways.

From: J. E. Chubb and T. M. Moe. *Politics, Markets and America's Schools* (1990). Washington, DC: The Brookings Institute. In their report from the Brookings Institute, Chubb and Moe examine changes in the political and economic structure of America's public schools.

## Postscript

John E. Chubb and Terry M. Moe maintain that school choice can be a panacea for reforming education if educators allow it to work on its own without muddying the waters with other types of educational reforms. They recognize that there are problems with school choice, including that it is demand rather than supply and demand driven. However, they suggest that school choice is the only reform that will totally transform public education.

# CAN SCHOOL CHOICE REFORM PUBLIC EDUCATION?

## CON  Lewis J. Perelman

"School choice" is the wrong kind of choice needed to reverse educational waste and obsolescence. While choice and competition are prerequisites to the market systems needed to replace unproductive education systems, school choice does not provide real consumer choice and does not lead to genuine competitive markets for learning.

*Elasticity* is the key. This somewhat arcane economist's term identifies the foremost in a list of reasons why school choice has not and cannot lead to true restructuring and improved productivity in education.

School choice seems reasonable—in fact, to *deny* families the right to choose what schools their children will attend is eminently unreasonable, as [former] Education Secretary Lamar Alexander often points out. But rights and reason are not the same as competition and efficiency. Those who expect school choice to unleash "market forces" that lead to better, more efficient education face inevitable disappointment.

Efficiency in markets depends directly on the "elasticity" of supply and demand—that is, the ease with which supply stretches and shrinks to match changing demands, and vice versa. "Inelastic" supply or demand tends to get stubbornly stuck, and inefficiently out of sync with the other.

School choice has not and will not lead to more productive education because the obsolete technology called "school" is inherently *inelastic*—it cannot significantly respond to changes in the size or direction of demand. As long as "school" refers to the traditional structure of buildings and grounds with services delivered in boxes called classrooms to which customers must be transported by car or bus, "school choice" will be unable to meaningfully alter the quality or efficiency of education.

So-called "good schools," whether public or private, have not and will not expand or relocate to satisfy all the demand for their services. And "bad schools," especially public but often even private ones, are difficult to shrink or shut down, much less move, when demand falls or disappears. This genetic inelasticity of schools-as-buildings lies at the heart of many of the objections to and problems with school choice. . . .

The choice that really matters is not a family's annual choice among a few school buildings but the individual learner's minute-to-minute choice among a wide array of specific media, programs, services, products, and sources of knowledge available to nurture the learner's brain—whether the individual makes that choice alone or in cooperation with other members of a team. That's the "point of sale" that the true market for learning rotates around. And school choice does almost nothing to alter the efficiency of that transaction compared to the status quo.

From: L. J. Perelman. *School's Out: Hyperlearning, the New Technology, and the End of Education* (1992). New York: William Morrow. Perelman, director of Project Learning 2001 at the Hudson Institute, writes of the educational reform movements of the 1980s.

Lewis J. Perelman, on the other hand, contends that choice is not the panacea for school reform. Schools can never be totally free in the free market sense because that requires elasticity and schools are inherently inelastic. The traditional structure of schools, including the school buildings, will keep reform from occurring. The only kind of choice that really matters is the student's choice among the sources of knowledge available.

to 49 percent of the school's population may participate in this plan. Not all states agree, however, that these plans are legal. In the summer of 1990 the Dane County (Wisconsin) Circuit Court ruled that the Milwaukee Choice Plan did not violate the Wisconsin constitution, in a case brought by the Wisconsin Educators Association Council, the state's largest teachers union, and the National Association for the Advancement of Colored People and others. In 1992 following an appeal from these organizations, the Wisconsin Supreme Court upheld by a vote of four to three the Milwaukee Choice Plan as authorized by the Wisconsin legislature.

## HOW WILL SCHOOL CHOICE AFFECT PUBLIC EDUCATION?

If and how the school choice movement will change public education is still not clear. Initially, it has meant more variety in curricular and extracurricular programs, and as the Carnegie Foundation reported, increased enthusiasm for school renewal in districts that have magnet schools. However, research shows that most parents are likely to select schools for their children like the schools they themselves attended. If this is true, increased variety may not be an ultimate outcome of school choice.

It appears that magnet schools are affecting the racial balance in some school districts. Where minority students are a majority enrolled in the school district where magnet schools are not available, white students comprise an average of only 20 percent of the students. However, when magnet school programs are available, white students constitute an average of 32 percent. In school districts in which white students comprise the majority of students enrolled, minority students equal an average of 31 percent of the students when magnet schools are not available. However, when magnet schools are available, minority students represent 46 percent of the total student population (Planning and Evaluation Service, U.S. Department of Education 1994, 9).

---

**12-1**

### POINTS TO REMEMBER

- Schools deal with social problems in a variety of ways; there is disagreement about how involved schools should be.
- Preschools attempt to meet the needs of families and children through child care and early childhood education. Proponents of public preschools point to the amount of money that may be saved in the long run.
- Middle schools meet the needs of early adolescents by designing instructional programs that focus on the developmental strengths of the middle-grade child.
- School choice is a controversial issue that allows parents to select the schools their children will attend.
- Some school choice programs allow parents to choose among a variety of public magnet schools or private schools. Tax credits or vouchers are two methods of financing school choice.

# Home Schooling

The number of school-aged children being educated at home is growing. In 1993–1994 there were 750 thousand to one million home schoolers. This number is up from approximately 250 thousand in the late 1980s (Thomas 1994, 5D). Parents choose to educate their children at home for a variety of reasons. Some parents suggest that through home school they can detect their children's educational problems and remedy them before they snowball. Others cite reasons of school violence, poor school curriculum, incongruence of religious and family values with the school's curriculum, and a need to spend more time together as a family, for choosing to school their children at home.

Many educators worry that not all parents teaching their children at home have an appropriate educational background in subject areas, child development, and teaching methods. Likewise, some educators are concerned about lack of interaction of home-schooled children with children outside their immediate families.

States differ in what they require of parents or other adults who teach children at home. Some require that home-schooled children pass the same tests as public school students; others that the curriculum used in the home be approved by the state. Some states require that home-school teachers be certified, while others require only that the teacher has completed the grade being taught. In 1994 the National Home Schoolers Association was able to lobby to defeat a House Bill (HR-6) that would have required all teachers, including home teachers, to be licensed in order to receive federal funding under the Elementary and Secondary School Act. As of 1994 the bill, which has been voted on in the House but not the Senate, has been amended to read: "Nothing in this bill should be construed to affect home-school teachers." According to Sharon Daly, director of government and community affairs, Children's Defense Fund, this can be interpreted to mean that at this time the federal government will not interfere with home-school standards, including licensing of teachers (telephone interview, July 8, 1994).

# Special Needs Programs

Because there are so many needs of today's schoolchildren that are not being met at home or by other institutions, the schools have adopted many special programs. In this section of the chapter, we will discuss before- and after-school programs, free meal programs, dropout prevention programs, programs for gifted and talented students, and special programs to involve parents in the schools.

## BEFORE- AND AFTER-SCHOOL PROGRAMS

Another important development in American society is the proliferation of families in which both parents work outside the home. According to a report of the U.S. Bureau of Census, in 1991, 7.6 percent (1.6 million) of the 21.2 million

Many schools have adopted before- and after-school programs so that children would have adult supervision while their parents are at work. At Public School 70 in the South Bronx, New York, Jonathan Alejandro teaches second graders how to play chess as one way of helping the students develop positive attitudes about themselves. Chess is a popular activity in many after-school programs.

children of employed women were **latchkey children**, children who are left unsupervised during the day or with no one at home when they arrive home from school. More latchkey children are between the ages of twelve and fourteen (16.8 percent of all twelve- to fourteen-year-olds) than between five and eleven (3.7 percent of all five- to eleven-year-olds).

Children of single parents are twice as likely to be latchkey children as those in two-parent households, and more of them live in urban and suburban communities than in rural communities. The Census Bureau report cited that 35 percent of employed women reported spending about 7.1 percent of their monthly income on child care so that their children would not face the home-alone syndrome.

As a result of a growing need for affordable, accessible, supervised care for school-aged children, the length of the school day has been extended. Large numbers of children begin the school day in before-school programs, frequently beginning as early as 7 A.M., and end the day in after-school programs, frequently continuing to 6 P.M. Many such programs range from babysitting to formal activities for children and young adolescents. They are sponsored by public schools, social service agencies, libraries, YMCAs, YWCAs, Boys' and Girls' Clubs, churches, and a variety of independent groups. Although some states have regulations and the National Association for the Education of Young Children (NAEYC) has adopted guidelines, most of these programs are unregulated and rarely monitored. The care and services range from excellent to poor.

Many questions remain to be answered about before- and after-school programs:

- Is it the school's role to provide care, in addition to education, for the child?
- If it is, who will give the care and for how long?
- Will the care be supervised play or formal activity programs?
- Who will pay?
- Will there be academic/professional requirements for licensing of caregivers and programs?
- Who will license and who will monitor?
- How will the increased length of in-school time affect the curriculum during the regular school day?
- How will before- and after-school programs affect the giving of home-work?
- Will the length of the teacher's and administrator's day change?
- How will discipline be handled? By whom?
- Will before- and after-school programs affect the extracurricular program of the school?

There is little doubt that we will see a rapid increase in school-based before- and after-school programs; however, until the above questions are answered, their impact on the public schools remains unclear.

## FREE MEALS PROGRAMS

Federal funding for free meals during the school year, provided by the National School Lunch Child Nutrition Acts administered by the U.S. Department of Agriculture (USDA), is guaranteed for all children whose family income is below 130 percent of the federal poverty level; reduced-price lunches are available to all students whose family income is below 185 percent of the poverty level. (Federal poverty levels are based on a complicated formula involving the number of children in the family, number of adults, number of adults working, and salary.) In 1993, 13 million schoolchildren received free or reduced-price lunches and 4.6 million received free or reduced-price breakfasts in their schools. The cost to the federal government of the free meals programs in 1994 was $4.7 billion. Ninety-five percent of public schools offered free lunch programs in 1993, but only 58 percent offered free breakfast programs.

Although some child advocates have been arguing to provide free rather than reduced-price lunches to all elementary students whose families are at 185 percent of the federal poverty level at a cost of $2 hundred per year per child, there is significant support for current meal programs. In a 1993 poll, 87 percent of parents surveyed said that schools should provide free or low-cost lunches, and 74 percent said schools should provide free or low-cost breakfasts (Elam, Rose, Gallup, 144).

School lunch food has been under attack by students for probably as long as there have been school lunches. School cafeteria workers have added such things as hot dogs, hamburgers, and ice cream to the menu in order to make it more appealing to the students. However, in 1993 the attack on school lunches came not from students, but from USDA hearings on the nutritional value of school meals, which were criticized by nutritionists, educators, and child advocates for their high fat and sugar content. In 1994 the USDA released new dietary requirements to go into effect during the 1998–1999 school year that will limit the amount of fat, sugar, and salt allowable in school meals.

## DROPOUT PREVENTION PROGRAMS

Many schools are developing programs with the specific goal of preventing students from dropping out. These programs are varied, but all of them attempt to make school a more hospitable place for students to learn and education more meaningful with a combination of course work, tutoring, and counseling. Many dropout prevention programs begin in late elementary school or in middle school.

Most dropout prevention programs are local; however, some are statewide. Most provide positive incentives for students to stay in school, but two very controversial statewide programs punish students for poor attendance and dropping out. In West Virginia, students who drop out of school cannot drive. No School/No Drive, begun in 1988, gives the Department of Motor Vehicles the authority to revoke the driver's licenses of sixteen- to eighteen-year-olds who accumulate ten consecutive unexcused absences or miss more than fifteen unexcused days in a semester. Students cannot get their licenses reissued until they pay a $15 fee and reduce the number of unexcused absences. Another statewide program penalizes families whose children do not attend school. In Wisconsin, Learnfare requires all children between thirteen and nineteen years of age whose families receive Aid to Families with Dependent Children (AFDC) to be enrolled in and attending school. If attendance guidelines are not met or the student drops out of school, the family is subject to a reduction in monthly AFDC benefits until compliance is documented. Minnesota, on the other hand, has a statewide incentive program for at-risk students that includes earning college credit for courses not offered in the traditional high school curriculum, the ability to transfer out of an unsatisfactory school (this can occur because of Minnesota's statewide choice program), and reimbursement for tutorial and transportation costs. Students in eleventh and twelfth grade can also enroll full- or part-time in universities, colleges, or vocational schools.

***Dropout Prevention Curriculum***   Jerry Downing and Thomas C. Harrison, Jr., believe that dropout prevention programs must be more positive than negative, and help students overcome specific hurdles that include completing high school graduation requirements, adapting to a teaching approach that is aimed at college-bound students, passing competency and proficiency examinations, understanding that it's a myth that a good job requires a college degree, following school rules, and fighting student isolation and bigotry (1990).

Although the goals of these curriculums are similar and all try to help the students overcome academic, social, and personal problems, the programs vary depending on the location. Some are "school-within-a-school" programs in which potential dropouts participate in activities that are parallel to the regular school curriculum but are designed specifically for them. For example, in Amityville, New York, teachers learn teaching styles compatible with the learning styles of their ninth graders who are potential dropouts.

Some programs feature tutoring as their primary objective. For example, a program in Asheville, North Carolina, matches each of approximately thirty-five University of North Carolina undergraduate students with two middle school students with whom they work three times per week during the school year. After school hours, the university students take the middle school children to athletic events, movies, and other events. Several parties are held to establish a social camaraderie. Finally, the undergraduates publish a journal of writing completed during the school year by the middle school students. The program emphasizes that each group learns from the other: the middle school students develop language and reading skills, and the university students develop teaching skills.

The Cities in Schools program in the Charlotte-Mecklenburg public schools in North Carolina unites the community with the schools. CIS acts as a resource broker bringing into the schools social services and volunteers for tutoring, mentoring, and recreational activities from virtually every aspect of the community including business and civic organizations, colleges, local government, and private foundations. More than 5 hundred volunteers meet weekly with CIS students. In 1994, 96 percent of these students stayed in school and 96 percent were promoted.

***Funding Dropout Prevention Programs*** Because many dropout prevention programs also meet the goals of other educational reforms, most of the programs are funded through regular state and local channels. However, under the Equity and Excellence Act of 1990, Congress allocated $1.95 billion for federally funded dropout prevention programs. Some of these funds have been used to improve school counseling programs, enrich curriculums, and develop schools within schools, such as the one developed by Charles Mingo at DuSable High School.

Funding for dropout prevention programs also comes from businesses, industries, private foundations, and individual contributors. In the Charlotte-Mecklenburg Cities in Schools program, for example, all of the $200 thousand it costs to run the program yearly comes from contributions. CIS negotiates with businesses and local agencies serving children and families, asking them to realign their services and work in the schools, thereby cutting costs of the services. Businesses also donate merchandise, gift certificates, and tickets to special events to use as student incentive awards for academic and attendance achievements.

## GIFTED AND TALENTED PROGRAMS

Programs for students classified as "gifted and talented" have increased in recent years in part as a response to declining Scholastic Aptitude Test (SAT) scores (see chapter 10, p. 421). In 1970, Section 806, Provisions Related to Gifted and Talented Children (P.L. 91-230), was added to the Elementary and Secondary Education Act (ESEA) Amendments of 1969. This law required the U.S. commissioner of education, Sidney P. Marland, Jr., to determine (1) the extent to which programs for the gifted and talented were necessary, (2) which federal assistance programs were used to meet the needs of the gifted, (3) how existing federal programs could be used to meet these needs, and (4) which new programs to recommend, if necessary.

*Identifying the Gifted*   In 1972 Marland reported his findings to Congress. Only 4 percent of an estimated 1.5–2.5 million gifted children were benefiting from existing programs and these were considered low priority in the schools. Guided by Marland's report, an increasing number of states funded programs for the gifted and talented. In 1977 Jeffrey Zettel determined that (1) nearly 75 percent of the states had identified gifted and talented students, (2) thirty-three states served 25 percent more gifted students than in the previous year, (3) thirty-one states increased appropriations to gifted and talented students by 50 percent, and (4) forty-two states reported sponsoring in-service training for teachers interested in working with gifted and talented students. By 1990 twenty-five states had mandated programs for gifted and talented students and nineteen other states had discretionary, state-supported programs (U.S. Department of Education, National Center for Education Statistics 1993, 67). According to Pat O'Connell Ross, director of the Javits Gifted and Talented Education Program, U.S. Department of Education, gifted and talented programs exist in every state. In 1990 thirty-eight states served more than 2 million gifted students in all grades (1993, 16). However, this number probably represents fewer students than are actually served since the states do not report the number of students in various programs.

Gifted and talented students were broadly defined by Marland in 1972 as "children . . . identified by professionally qualified persons, who by virtue of outstanding abilities are capable of high performance," meaning those with demonstrated achievement and/or potential ability in any of the following, singly or in combination: general intellectual ability, specific academic aptitude, creative or productive thinking, leadership ability, talent in the visual and performing arts, and psychomotor ability (Ross 1993, 16).

Because of the broad Marland definition of gifted and talented students that is used by the federal government, state laws and guidelines for selecting gifted and talented students differ. According to Ross, some states require that, in order to receive funding for their programs, local districts must use state-specified IQ test cutoff scores or specified levels of performance on standardized tests to identify students, while others do not require specified test scores or even that students take tests. Therefore, the percentage and number of students identified in each state vary significantly. For example, four states identify more than 10 percent of their students as gifted and talented, while twenty-one states identify less than 5 percent. Likewise, how the local districts identify the gifted also affects the number of students in the programs. Ross reported that, according to a national survey, 73 percent of school districts had adopted the Marland definition, but only a few used it to identify and serve all areas of giftedness. Most used primarily test scores and teacher recommendations. Therefore, most local programs focus on the academically or intellectually gifted and the other areas of giftedness are neglected. Culturally different students who don't score well on standardized tests are underserved and females are underrepresented in the mathematics and science gifted and talented programs.

*(continued on p. 498)*

*In the Classroom*

SELLS, ARIZ.—As June Maker and her assistants drove through the Sonoran Desert in a van loaded with toys one day last month, their intent was not to bear gifts, but to find them.

Here on the Tohono O'Odham Indian Reservation, where most of the children live in poverty, speak a combination of O'Odham, English, and Spanish, and stand a good chance of dropping out of school, Ms. Maker and her colleagues hoped to identify children with potential for great academic success.

At Indian Oasis Primary School, the educators distributed the toys to small groups of 2nd graders and asked them to perform a number of tasks, including building objects and telling stories.

"We are watching children solve problems," Ms. Maker, an associate professor of special education at the University of Arizona, said as she observed one group.

She and her assistants later talked excitedly about one boy who used plastic shapes to solve a geometric puzzle in a way they had never seen. They were enthusiastic, too, about a girl who seemed to take charge of her group and lead it in using pieces of cardboard to build farm animals. And they spoke animatedly about another girl who manipulated little plastic people to weave a detailed story of a family doing chores.

By watching the children solve problems, Ms. Maker and her assistants were themselves attempting to solve a vexing problem—the widely acknowledged failure of many educators to recognize and develop the intellectual potential of language-minority students.

Ms. Maker has largely abandoned hope of identifying gifted L.E.P. students using standard intelligence tests, which she describes as fraught with bias and limited in their views of intelligence. . . .

Ms. Maker has based her test largely on the writings of Howard Gardner, a professor of education at Harvard University. Mr. Gardner's theory of giftedness posits that intelligence is not just verbal and mathematical, as is commonly assumed, but can also be spatial, musical, or kinesthetic, or reflected in one's self-knowledge or understanding of others.

In her screening, Ms. Maker provides children with plastic and cardboard shapes and toys and asks them to perform such tasks as matching pieces, building certain geometric shapes, creating animals, or telling stories.

In keeping with Mr. Gardner's theories, the children progress from trying to solve problems with one known answer, to attempting to solve problems with several possible answers, to working to create and solve open-ended problems of their own.

"What we are looking for is not intelligence or creativity alone, but the ability to solve a variety of problem types," Ms. Maker said.

From: Peter Schmidt, "Seeking to Identify the Gifted Among L.E.P. Students," *Education Week* (May 26, 1993) 1, 12–13.

Because of the Javits Gifted and Talented Program's concern that current ways of identifying the gifted ignore what we know about multiple intelligences and many groups of students are underrepresented, the U.S. Department of Education has developed a new definition, based on the original but reflecting new knowledge:

- Children and youth with outstanding talent perform or show potential for performing at remarkably high levels of accomplishment when compared with others of their age, experience, or environment.
- These children and youth exhibit high performance capability in intellectual, creative, and/or artistic areas, possess an unusual leadership capacity, or excel in specific academic fields.
- They require services or activities not ordinarily provided by the schools.
- Outstanding talents are present in children and youth from all cultural groups, across all economic strata, and in all areas of human endeavor. (Ross 1993, 26)

In addition, the Department has designated criteria that schools must use to identify gifted students:

- Seeks variety—looks throughout a range of disciplines for students with diverse talents;
- Uses many assessment measures—uses a variety of appraisals so that schools can find students in different talent areas and at different ages;
- Is free of bias—provides students of all backgrounds with equal access to appropriate opportunities;
- Is fluid—uses assessment procedures that can accommodate students who develop at different rates and whose interests may change as they mature;
- Identifies potential—discovers talents that are not readily apparent in students, as well as those that are obvious; and
- Assesses motivation—takes into account the drive and passion that play a key role in accomplishment.

***Funding Gifted and Talented Programs*** In 1988 Title IV, Part B, of the Hawkins-Stafford Elementary and Secondary Amendments to the ESEA (P.L. 100–197) was passed by Congress. This law, referred to as the Jacob K. Javits Gifted and Talented Students Act, provided $10 million in financial assistance to the states, local education agencies, and institutions of higher education for research, demonstration model projects, and personnel training to identify and meet the special needs of gifted and talented students. In 1994 the allocation was doubled to $20 million.

## CURRICULUM FOR THE GIFTED AND TALENTED

In 1977 Joseph S. Renzulli suggested a curriculum consisting of an "enrichment triad" for the gifted that is still widely used. The basis of this triad is a self-designed and self-directed student learning program incorporating general exploratory activities, group training activities, and individual and small group investigations of problems.

Another enrichment approach to the education of gifted and talented students is **synectics**, which was first designed for industry by William J. Gordon in 1971. In education it is a process of thinking in which the strange is made to appear familiar and the familiar to appear strange by using metaphors to link various areas of substantive knowledge. For example, students might be asked to compare an automobile wheel to other things that rotate: the cutter on a can opener, the rotor of a helicopter, the orbit of Mars, a spinning seed pod, or a hoop snake (Joyce and Weil 1972, 238). Synectics also teaches problem solving because it requires creating something new or acquiring a new perspective of the familiar. The technique moves through several stages: phase one—the students describe the problem; phase two—the students state the problem and clearly define their task; phase three—the students then make direct analogies; phase four—the students make personal analogies; phase five—the students look for conflict; phase six—the conflict serves as the basis for the next analogies; and phase seven—the students examine the process and eventually return to the original problem.

Despite the development of several innovative strategies, a study of gifted and talented programs conducted by the U.S. Department of Education revealed that current curricular practices do little to challenge gifted students. They spend most of the school day in the regular classroom where little is done to adapt the curriculum to their needs (84 percent of all assignments are the same as those made to the whole class, with the exception of mathematics where more advanced content is pursued by gifted students). Seventy-two percent of school districts use a "pull out" approach where gifted students are given a few hours of special project work each week. A few districts, according to the survey, have special arts programs for gifted elementary and middle school students in magnet schools, but these are not widely available. Even the high school college preparatory curriculums do little in terms of providing difficult and challenging work for gifted students. According to the survey, some specialized magnet schools and intensive summer programs are effective in challenging students, but these are small in number. However, despite these dismal results, the survey revealed many effective gifted and talented programs that could be used as models. The Urban Scholars Middle School Program is one such model.

It provides a family of friends and caring adults for gifted and talented middle school students selected to participate from three of Boston's toughest neighborhoods. In an environment where one infamous principal declared, "There are no talented and gifted students in this school," these youngsters voluntarily compete for the opportunity to attend two hours of advanced math and science classes twice a week after their regular school day has ended. They also meet other rigorous standards, which include improving their regular grades.

Founded in 1983 by the University of Massachusetts, Boston, Urban Scholars has since evolved into a panoply of year-round programs for both middle and high school students. It combines classes, projects, internships, mentorships, volunteer work, discussions, workshops, and trips. The program has been very successful in helping disadvantaged students succeed in school and go to college (Ross 1993, 21).

## PARENTS AND THE SCHOOLS

Recent educational initiatives for dealing with social problems have recognized that parents must be part of the solution. In *Educating America: State Strategies for Achieving the National Education Goals* (1990), a report of the National Governors' Association, the following ideas were suggested for encouraging parental involvement in the education of their children: (1) welcoming parents as equal partners in the learning and schooling of their children, (2) challenging parents to assume more responsibility for their children's learning, (3) helping parents and students to understand and take advantage of educational choices, and (4) engaging and supporting parents far more extensively in their children's learning at school (pp. 15–21). The 1993 Family and Medical Leave Act makes it possible for more parents to be involved in their children's education. It requires that businesses provide parents more time to participate in the schools. In a 1993 education poll, 96 percent said they think it is very important that they be encouraged to take a more active part in educating their children (Elam, Rose, Gallup, 149).

### *Viewpoint*   A New Road to Learning: Teaching the Whole Child

New Haven, [CT]—For more than 20 years in this city of scholars and elms, schoolchildren and their parents have been studying a basic axiom: students in troubled schools learn better when families and educators work together.

In the process, these children of troubled schools and their parents, most of them poor and black, are discovering that schools need not be rigid institutions concerned only with academic performance, but can also be places that tend to a child's psychological and social growth. And when those two sides of a child's life are entwined, the child feels better about himself and learns more.

This is the essence of a program developed by Dr. James P. Comer, a Yale University psychiatrist, and carried out in New Haven. The results have been higher attendance, fewer behavior problems and improved academic performance. School systems around the country are eager to replicate it, and the Rockefeller Foundation has committed $15 million to that end.

The process turns on a seemingly simple insight: that a child's home life affects his performance in school, and that if schools pay attention to all the influences on a child, most problems can be solved before they get out of control. The Comer process, as it is called, encourages a flexible, almost custom-tailored approach to each child.

Take the case of Ramon Cato. Ramon, a chubby, bright-eyed boy with a chipped front tooth, has known extreme family stress. For much of the last two years, Ramon has lived with his mother, described by relatives as a drug substance abuser, and her boyfriend in one room in a condemned house known as a haven for drug users. He struggled in school and behaved badly when he was there. He missed 57 of 180 days in the term that ended a year ago.

Educators at Grant Elementary School did not throw up their hands and write him off. When they could not get his mother involved, they found a great-uncle who cared. Now the uncle is a regular visitor to Ramon's classroom, and the boy is living with a foster family, doing well in school. He will graduate from fourth grade with his classmates. . . .

Not every child has problems as severe as Ramon's. But whatever the pressures on a family may be, a school using the Comer process will be alert to discovering those problems and helping solve them, supporters say.

The method of instruction developed by Dr. Comer in the New Haven, Connecticut, school system combines a child's psychological, social, and intellectual needs. Its success hinges on the involvement of a parent or close relative in a child's education. Here, Jacqueline Lecraft helps her godson Jeffery Gilmore at Grant Elementary School.

This common-sense melding of home life, school life and social service aid is what attracted the Rockefeller Foundation's attention and led it earlier this year [1990] to make a five-year, $15 million commitment to replicate the methods of Dr. Comer, the coolly charismatic father of the approach.

The Comer process has already been adopted by more than 100 schools in nine districts in eight states. In the last three years, the New Haven school system has expanded it to include all 42 schools in the 18,000-pupil system.

"There's a difference one can see almost right away once his principles are applied," said Priscilla Hilliard of Howard University in Washington, D.C., who heads a partnership between the college and that city's public schools to carry out the program.

For low-income students in troubled inner cities, and especially for black and Hispanic students, whose achievement-test scores badly trail the national average, Dr. Comer's program offers one of the greatest hopes, many educators say. . . .

The Comer process, which Dr. Comer himself calls the School Development Program . . . concentrates on the emotional, social, and psychological needs. His clearly-structured programs establish three goals: to induce parents to participate in the school's life; to force school administration, teachers, and other staff to share authority in managing the school; and to bring guidance counselors, mental health professionals and teachers into a team that meets regularly to combat behavior problems.

Parents, for example, are encouraged to become classroom assistants, tutors or aides. Some are encouraged, as are some teachers, to join their school's governance committee, which meets bi-weekly and includes the principal. The mental health and guidance professionals are part of the process of school management.

According to Dr. Comer, most administrators and teachers are not trained to recognize that a student's academic and behavioral lapses may be linked to the cultural and social gap between home and school.

"Some of these children come from families that cannot give them often the elementary things they need, like how to say 'Good morning,' 'Thank you,' 'Sit still' and all kinds of stuff," said the 55-year-old psychiatrist. "On the other hand, you have staff that often doesn't understand that that is the problem." . . .

There are some, albeit only a few, detractors of the Comer program.

A professor of social work at a prestigious Southern university said Dr. Comer's program raises nearly as many questions as it answers. "A crucial question is whether Comer's model can be replicated in any school district," said the professor, who asked not to be identified. "Are there some school systems that are simply too large, such as New York City's?" The professor also wondered if Dr. Comer's program can cope with fragmenting families, whose members may be unable to participate in school life because of poverty.

Dr. Comer maintains that with careful application his program can be adapted to the needs of any school system, although neither he nor his Rockefeller Foundation supporters are yet prepared to tackle New York.

And Dr. Comer agrees with his critics to a degree in acknowledging that the social deterioration in many major cities will force educators and parents to work even harder.

"We are beginning to see the first of our crack babies in our schools," Dr. Comer said, adding that their behavioral problems will present his program with special challenges.

Nonetheless, he said he is not shaken in his long-held belief that child development should be the centerpiece of education. For many black and Hispanic children, whose parents, Dr. Comer says, have had a "traumatic social history," education must do more than teach the basics.

"Those families under stress are least able to give children the kinds of experiences they need to go to school and succeed," Dr. Comer said.

At Katherine Brennan School, one of the New Haven elementary schools where Dr. Comer introduced his approach early on, there is a climate of calm and caring. The sight of parents in the school is almost as commonplace as that of teachers. Halls are quiet and clean. Bulletin boards celebrate black history and achievement in brightly colored posters and hand-cut construction paper.

From: Marriott, 1990

## TYPES OF PARENTAL INVOLVEMENT

A study of over 37 hundred teachers revealed that those who were "leaders in the use of parent involvement" encouraged parents from all kinds of backgrounds to be supportive of their children both in school and at home. Joyce Epstein, a researcher at Johns Hopkins University, identifies some of the areas in which parents need to work.

1. The basic obligations of parents include providing for children's health and safety, child-rearing to prepare children for school, and building positive home conditions that support school learning and behavior.

Schools vary in how actively they assist parents with social services or provide programs to build positive parenting skills.

2.  The basic obligations of schools include communicating with parents about school programs and children's progress. Schools vary the form and frequency of communications and greatly affect whether information sent home can be understood and used by parents.

3.  Parent involvement at school includes parent volunteers who assist teachers, administrators, and children in classrooms or in other areas of the school. It also refers to parents who come to school to support student performances, sports, or other events, or to attend workshops or other programs for their own education or training. Schools vary in the extent to which they successfully recruit and maintain the involvement of many different parents at the school building.

4.  Parent involvement in learning activities at home includes requests and instructions from teachers for parents to assist their own children at home on learning activities that are coordinated with the children's class work. Schools and teachers vary in how frequently and clearly they request parent-child interaction on homework and other learning activities at home.

5.  Parent involvement in governance and advocacy includes parents in decision-making roles in the PTA/PTO, advisory councils, or other committees or groups at the school, district, or state level. It also refers to parents as activists in independent advocacy groups in the community. Schools vary in the extent to which parents have real influence in school policies, programs, and decision-making processes. (Epstein 1990, 6–7)

*Phi Delta Kappan*

**"I'll be taking the day off tomorrow, so I'll probably just fax you my homework."**

***Low-Income Parents*** As Epstein pointed out, all parents can be involved in the school. However, involving low-income parents has not been easy and may take additional effort. Because many low-income parents cannot come to the school, one way to involve them is in home-based programs, which, according to McLaughlin and Shields (1988), yield academic gains for the students involved. To initiate home-based partnership programs, they suggest that teachers must be educated about the value of such programs and that administrators must realize the importance of making it possible for teachers to participate in them. Wolf and Stephens (1989) emphasize the value of teacher home visits, which can build rapport between the parent and the teacher, through which the teacher can obtain information about the child, and through which the parent can obtain information about the school.

At times all educators feel overwhelmed by the problems they face and the problems their students face. There are days when it is difficult to continue teaching knowing that one of their student's brothers was just murdered, several students are physically abused, and another may or may not have slept with a roof over his head last night. However, the innovative programs discussed throughout this chapter and the text should encourage them knowing that some schools, communities, and individuals have found solutions that are working. As teachers, each of us has the opportunity to be a part of these solutions, and, for most of us, that is why we continue to teach even on the bleakest days.

---

**12-2**

**POINTS TO REMEMBER**

- Before- and after-school programs meet the needs of society by providing care for children whose parents work or are not at home during these hours.

- Dropout prevention programs usually provide incentives to keep students in school, and involve the community as well.

- Gifted and talented programs are often funded by the federal government. Although there are many good ones, they are only provided for academically gifted students. Many employ curriculums that are neither challenging nor motivating.

- No one argues that involving parents in their children's educations will go a long way to ensuring the progress of these children. However, it is the schools' responsibility to reach out to parents, particularly low-income parents.

---

## For Thought/Discussion

1. For what reasons are middle schools restructuring? Do you believe this effort will help solve many social problems? Why or why not?

2. What are some of the primary objections to school choice? Do you believe they are valid objections? Why or why not?

3. In what ways can the techniques used to teach gifted and talented students be used to reach the disadvantaged or at-risk students?

4. If the parents of many of your students failed to become involved in their children's schoolwork, what specific activities can you think of that might get them interested and prompt them to participate?

## For Further Reading/Reference

Brandt, R. S. (Ed.). 1990–1991. Schools of choice? [special issue]. *Educational Leadership* 48 (4). Twenty articles on school choice, pros and cons of school choice, specific examples from five states, and choice in private schools.

Fliegel, S., with J. McGuire. 1992. *Miracle in East Harlem: They fought for choice in public education.* New York: Times Books. A discussion of what school choice is and how District Four in East Harlem implemented a choice program and the success story that resulted.

Massachusetts Advocacy Center and the Center for Early Adolescence. 1988. *Before it's too late: Dropout prevention in the middle grades.* Boston, MA, and Carrboro, NC: Authors. Descriptions of two centers that work with the schools and community using such structured activities as counseling, homework, working after school, and parental involvement to prevent dropping out.

National Association for the Education of Young Children. 1994. NAEYC position statement: A conceptual framework for early childhood professional development. *Young Children,* 49 (3), pp. 68–77. NAEYC's recommendations for standards and requirements for professionals working in early childhood education.

Olmstead, P. O., and Weikart, D. P. (Eds.). 1989. *How nations serve young children: Profiles of child care and education in 14 countries.* Ypsilanti, MI: High Scope Press. A discussion of perceptions of and effects of early child care and education in countries in Asia, Africa, and Europe.

As he sat in the living room of his white-frame home on this city's hardscrabble, mostly Hispanic west side, Demetrio P. Rodriguez spoke intensely about how poor schoolchildren have been robbed by the Texas Legislature.

The state doesn't give property-poor school systems enough money, leaving them at a disadvantage, he complained. "We want no more or no less than our fair share," said Mr. Rodriguez, a quiet-spoken 67-year-old retired sheet-metal worker. "But people have been so greedy and uncaring."

It is a lament that Mr. Rodriguez has uttered many times in the more than 25 years that he has been the name and face behind the nation's longest-running lawsuit over state funding for public schools. . . .

From: W. Celis 3d, April 10, 1994, 30.

# Part VI

# SCHOOLS AND GOVERNANCE

## Chapter 13

### THE POLITICAL INFLUENCES ON EDUCATION

In this chapter we will explore the role of the federal, state, and local governments and courts in public education. We will also discuss the influence of businesses and foundations on the public schools, as well as the roles played by religious organizations and nonpublic schools.

## Chapter 14

### FUNDING EDUCATION

While most citizens of this country believe in the democratic ideal of equal education for all, the reality is that the quality of education is hardly equal for all children in all school districts. Because the system of educational funding is so heavily dependent on state and local tax revenues, which in turn are so dependent on the economy in various areas of the country, schools even within the same state receive unequal allotments of money. In this chapter we will examine how funding contributes to quality of education.

## Chapter 15

### LAW AND THE SCHOOLS

Legal issues affect both students and teachers while they are engaged in the process of education. Attendance, censorship, achievement, freedom of expression, and discipline are issues that particularly affect students. Teachers are affected by such legal issues as contracts, sexual harassment, liability, and copyright laws. The chapter concludes with a discussion of ethical decision making.

**CHAPTER OBJECTIVES**

After studying this chapter, you should be able to:

- Explain how the U.S. Constitution gives the states the power to govern education.
- Summarize how U.S. congressional legislation affects the schools.
- Discuss the president's role in education.
- Describe the U.S. Supreme Court's role in education.
- Analyze why the governance of education differs from state to state.
- Compare the role of the states' governors and legislatures in education.
- Describe the relationship among state boards of education, chief state school officers, and state education agencies.
- Describe the hierarchy of the state court system.
- Explain the role of the local education agency, local board, and local superintendent in the governance of schools.
- Describe how businesses and foundations influence public education.
- Describe how religious organizations affect public education.
- Discuss the role of nonpublic schools in U.S. education.

# Chapter 13

# THE POLITICAL INFLUENCES ON EDUCATION

*H*oward L. Hurwitz was a principal of a Long Island, New York, school in 1976 when he was suspended from his post by the New York City Schools chancellor for refusing to readmit a suspended student. These kinds of suspensions still occur in the 1990s, often for similar reasons (see chapter 8, p. 315). The following anecdote helps illustrate how social and political forces working together can influence the public schools.

I was being brought up on charges of insubordination because I had refused to readmit to my school a student with a long record of disruptive behavior. I knew instantly that if I left my office as ordered, I would never again be the principal of Long Island City High School, or any school. I could not live with that thought.

I reached for my phone and called Peter Vallone, a city councilman. Over a ten-year period I had established close links with the community that reflected the composition of our neighborhood high school—Italians, 40 percent; Greeks, 15 percent; Hispanics, 15 percent; blacks, 10 percent; others, 20 percent, including about 2 percent Asians. . . .

"Hello, Pete. I'm calling to let you know that I've been fired."

Pete dismissed such nonsense with a quip.

"Let me read you a letter from Irving Anker that was just hand-delivered to me."

I read the whole letter. . . .

"What do you want me to do, Pete?"

"Stay there."

Within a half hour, six men entered my office. I recognized a few of them as parents of students in the school. Gerald Nozilo, who was to be the field commander of the operation, told me that I was being barricaded in my office. "No children are coming to this school, Doc, unless you're the principal." They placed a long bench outside of my secretary's office and piled chairs on top of it. We had begun three days and nights of 'round the clock defense of discipline in the schools that electrified the nation.

The episode which made me a national symbol of discipline in the schools was triggered by the outburst of a 16-year-old girl. She screamed at a secretary in the general office who had objected when she took a magazine from the librarian's letter box without permission. . . .

I phoned Mrs. Doe [the girl's mother] and told her that I was sending Jane home, directly. . . .

Jane . . . asked for a transfer to Bryant, a neighboring school. . . .

Two days later, after the superintendent had agreed to the suspension and said he would arrange for the transfer, he phoned. . . . It was his decision to return the suspended student to LIC. . . .

I told him that he had not been a principal for 10 tough years. Therefore, he could not understand how a single student could undermine even a strong principal. . . .

Nevertheless, the superintendent insisted that I accept the girl. I told him flat out that I would not permit her to enter the school. . . .

The next morning I found Jane Doe, her mother, and a man and woman from the local federally funded poverty agency seated on a bench outside my office door. They had been placed there by the Dean of Boys who had refused to permit Jane to go to classes. . . .

I explained that I had refused to readmit Jane to the school. . . . I called for the assistance of the police officer assigned to the vicinity of the school. When he arrived, I said: "Officer, I am asking you to persuade these people to leave this school. . . ."

Before noon the superintendent's assistant phoned and read a letter from the superintendent to me. . . . The final paragraph stated: "It is now my judgment that [Jane] be returned to Long Island City High School, effective Friday morning. . . ."

*Dr. Hurwitz continued to refuse to admit Jane Doe. This began a series of confrontations and litigation between Dr. Hurwitz and the school system that lasted more than a year and a half. The superintendent, threatened by a suit from a local poverty lawyer, continued to demand that Jane return to school, but Dr. Hurwitz refused three times, believing that readmitting her would undermine his authority. The chancellor of the New York City Schools then suspended Hurwitz. . . .*

*Dr. Hurwitz and his supporters felt that the superintendent's office was trying to placate the Civil Liberties Union and the federally funded poverty workers who supported Jane's readmission, rather than examine the issues involved in the case.*

*The hearing [of the board of education] concluded with a compromise: Dr. Hurwitz's suspension would be lifted, Jane Doe would return to school accompanied by a full-time security guard, and Hurwitz would appear at a second hearing in civil court.*

*Anxious that boycotting students return to class, Hurwitz agreed with the decision, but called the civil court hearing a "kangaroo court" because the judge refused to hear any witnesses speaking on behalf of Hurwitz's forty years of service or permit Jane Doe's record to be* *used as evidence. The civil court ruled that Hurwitz should pay a $3,500 fine to the board of education.*

*The parents wanted to pay the fine, but Hurwitz refused their support and appealed the decision to the New York Supreme Court. The case was heard almost one year later. The Court handed down a judgment "annulling and vacating" the resolution of the board. Hurwitz did not pay the fine, Jane Doe remained in school with a security guard, and left the school at the end of the term without a diploma.*

From: Howard L. Hurwitz 1988, *The Last Angry Principal.*

$7$he opening anecdote points out the difficulty in determining who controls the school. The local, state, and federal agencies all tried to exert their influence on this case. Not until it reached the state Supreme Court was the case settled. In this chapter we will explore the role of the federal, state, and local governments and courts in public education. We will also discuss the influence of businesses and foundations on the public schools, as well as the roles played by professional organizations, teacher unions, and nonpublic schools.

## Who Controls the Schools?

Despite the fact that the power to run the schools is given to the states by the U.S. Constitution, no single branch or level of government exerts complete control over public education. Instead, there is an interactiveness, involving all branches of government at all levels, the courts, and the offices of chancellors, superintendents, and principals, that is based on legislative statutes. **Formal control** is that power delegated to individuals or groups through statute or law. **Informal influence** is exerted by individuals or groups on those who formally possess power to control the schools. These groups have no legal authority but have a strong interest in, or commitment to, the schools.

Teachers have little formal control but can influence the governance of the public schools through their unions and professional organizations. In addition, a variety of special interest groups, such as the Civil Liberties Union and the poverty workers of the opening anecdote, affects what happens in the schools. In recent years, the business community and charitable foundations have funded special programs in U.S. public schools and have developed partnerships with the schools to implement some of these programs (see figure 13.1 for a diagram of the interactive network of school control).

*(continued on p. 513)*

**FIGURE 13-1**

## Interactive Network of School Control

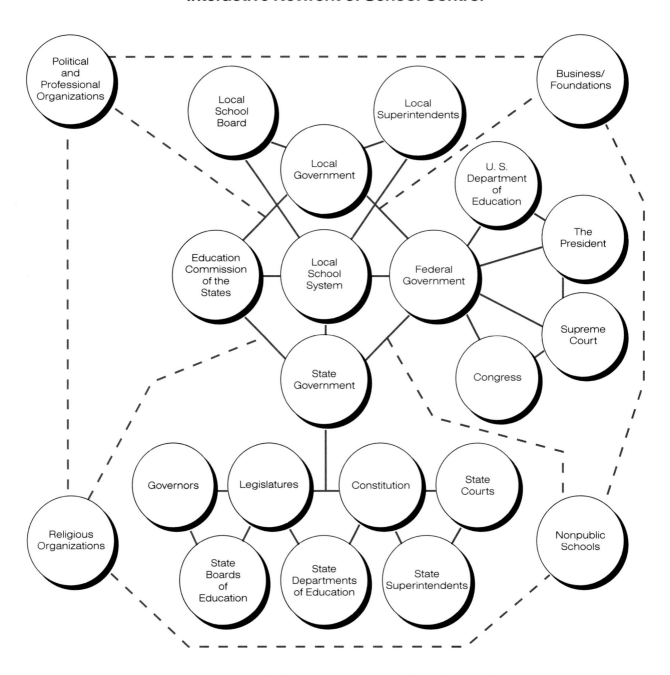

Adapted from: E. Mosher, *Education and American Federalism: Intergovernmental and National Policy Influences* in J. D. Scribner, (Ed.), *The Politics of Education* (National Society for the Study of Education, 1977).

Federal, state, and local agencies all have some jurisdiction over public schools. This chart graphically shows how the various agencies interact with one another to influence policy and procedure in the local public school.

# Role of the Federal Government in Public Education

The U.S. Constitution, the federal courts, Congress, the president, and the U.S. Department of Education are the federal forces that influence public education. The Constitution sets the foundation for state control of the public schools. The Supreme Court is the highest authority for interpreting both the federal and state constitutions, legislation, and court decisions. The president recommends legislation to Congress and has the power to endorse or veto legislation enacted by it.

## U.S. CONSTITUTION AND PUBLIC EDUCATION

Although the U.S. Constitution does *not* mention education specifically, Article I, Section B, states, "The Congress shall have Power to lay and collect Taxes, Duties, Imposts and Excises, to pay the Debts and provide for the common Defense and general Welfare of the United States; but all Duties, Imposts and Excises shall be uniform throughout the United States." The "provide for the general welfare" clause of Article I has been commonly interpreted by the courts to include education.

The Tenth Amendment of the U.S. Constitution defines the states' role in education. "The powers not delegated to the United States by the Constitution, nor prohibited by it to the states, are reserved to the states respectively, or to the people."

## THE U.S. CONGRESS AND EDUCATION

The U.S. Congress passes legislation that affects the public schools. Because of the Tenth Amendment, the federal government's involvement in education is indirect rather than direct. However, when congressional legislation involves significant funding attached to specific criteria, federal control over education is increased. The role of Congress prior to the early years of the twentieth century was limited to providing land grants for schools. The Ordinance of 1785 stated: "There shall be reserved the lot No. 16 of every Township for the maintenance of public schools within said Townships." The Northwest Ordinance of 1787 also awarded land grants for schools.

*Setting Standards*   Congressional legislation in the twentieth century has attempted to ensure equal access to and set standards for public education. The role of the Congress in setting standards can be seen in such acts as the Smith-Hughes Act (1917) that allocated millions of dollars for vocational education; and the National Defense Education Act (P.L. 85–864) in 1958 that gave funds to states, colleges, and universities to improve education in mathematics, sciences, and foreign languages.

*Equal Access*   The role of Congress in promoting equal access can be seen in such acts as the Economic Opportunity Act (P.L. 88–452) of the Civil Rights Act of 1964 that allocated funds for community action programs such as Head Start and provided special assistance to public school districts to implement desegregation, and the Elementary and Secondary Education Act (ESEA) (P.L. 89-10) of 1965 that established a wide range of compensatory programs, particularly for underprivileged youth from low-income families. (See chapter 5, pp. 202–212, for an extensive discussion of these and other acts.) With federal funding came federal regulations for implementing this legislation in the schools.

During the 1980s and early 1990s, the congressional role in public education shifted away from ensuring equal opportunity for all students, although this was still a concern, to suggesting what should be taught and who should teach it. In 1990 President George Bush brought together the fifty governors to set six goals for the nation's schools. These, and one additional, became Goals 2000: Educate America Act (P.L. 103–227), passed during Bill Clinton's administration. The act allocated federal funds to states and professional organizations to develop educational standards, encourage drug free programs, and increase parental involvement in the schools. Similarly, the School-to-Work Opportunities Act of 1994 (P.L. 103–239) provided funds to schools and community colleges to develop programs that provided students access to jobs after school as well as to community colleges. At the same time, Congress reauthorized Head Start (P.L. 103–252) and the Elementary and Secondary Education Amendments of 1993 (P.L. 103–382).

Many worry that the federal government's current role in public education promotes federalization into areas that had been reserved for states and localities. Chester Finn, former assistant secretary of education, suggests that Goals 2000 federalize the public schools by giving "the impression around the country that education is now the federal government's responsibility to lift it off the shoulders of the states and localities" (Walters 1994, 14). Stephen Arons, a professor of legal studies, University of Massachusetts, claims that Goals 2000 will create a national curriculum and "the conflict over whose beliefs will be reflected in {that} curriculum may become so intense that it cripples the entire federal school-reform effort and weakens intellectual freedom and cultural diversity around the country" (1994, 52).

## THE PRESIDENT AND EDUCATION

The U.S. president's effect on public education is more indirect than that of Congress. The president frequently establishes the legislative agenda of Congress and sets the tone for the decisions of the Supreme Court. However, some presidents take more initiative than others in influencing educational policy.

As early as the 1800s, President Thomas Jefferson, highly suspicious of centralized government, claimed that the preservation of democracy required that political power be kept in the hands of the people. He believed that education was the ultimate safeguard of liberty, and that only educated people could maintain and use the institutions designed to protect them from tyranny. Jefferson equated education with democracy: "No other sure foundation can be devised for the preservation of freedom and happiness" (Jefferson 1781–1785).

A century and a half later, John F. Kennedy was responsible for the passage of legislation designed to improve educational opportunities for migrant workers and their families, and to increase funding for classroom construction, teacher salaries, and improvement of instruction in science and mathematics.

Ronald Reagan in the 1980s began to shift congressional concerns away from federally funded compensatory programs for children in poverty that did not appear to improve their achievement levels, to incentive programs for students who achieved and merit pay programs for teachers whose students achieved (State of the Union Address, January 25, 1988). He attempted to return educational control to the states, believing that increased federal spending had not resulted in increased learning as measured by standardized tests. His secretary of education, William Bennett, wrote numerous publications on the need to return to the basics, the importance of homework, and the value of hard work.

In the late 1980s and early 1990s, President George Bush continued to encourage congressional legislation that would return control of education to the states. He appointed John Chubb, a political scientist from Stanford University and a well-known proponent of President Reagan's positions on education, as full-time presidential adviser on education as well as an education advisory committee to examine educational reform in the context of innovation, accountability, and flexibility.

President Bill Clinton has carried forward some of the educational agenda of the previous administration. Although this is unusual, as governor of Arkansas he had an important role in drafting Goals 2000 and pushed for its passage in Congress. However, Clinton has also created his own education agenda, appointing Bill Riley, a former South Carolina governor with a reputation for educational reform, as his secretary of education. In his first two years as president, more educational enactments passed Congress than in the previous two decades (see chapter 5, pp. 192–212).

> It has been too long—at least three decades—since a President has come and challenged Americans to join him on a great national journey, not merely to consume the bounty today but to invest for a much greater one tomorrow. . . .
>
> Our nation needs a new direction . . . We all know that Head Start, a program that prepares children for school, is a success story. We all know that it saves money, but today it just reaches barely over a third of all the eligible children. Under this plan every eligible child will be able to get a head start. . . .
>
> We have to ask more in our schools of our students, our teachers, our principals, our parents. Yes, we must give them the resources they need to meet high standards, but we must also use the authority and the influence and funding of the Education department to promote strategies that really work to increase learning in our schools.
>
> We have to recognize that all of our high school graduates need some further education in order to be competitive in this global economy. So we have to establish a partnership between business and education and the government for apprenticeship programs in every state in this country to give our people the skills they need.
>
> Lifelong learning must benefit not just young high school graduates but workers, too, throughout their career . . . We must develop a unified, simplified, sensible, streamlined worker-training program so that workers receive the training they need regardless of why they lost their jobs or whether they simply need to learn something new to keep them. . . .
>
> I want to push education reform . . . not just to spend more money but to really improve learning. Some things work and some things don't. We ought to be subsidizing the things that work and discouraging the things that don't. . . .
>
> (Clinton, State of the Union Address, February 17, 1994)

### U.S. DEPARTMENT OF EDUCATION

In 1979 the **U.S. Department of Education**, headed by the U.S. secretary of education, was elevated to a cabinet-level agency. It was originally established in 1867 as the Federal Department of Education to formalize the government's effort in education. In 1953 it became the U.S. Office of Education and was a part of the cabinet-level Department of Health, Education, and Welfare. In 1979, after extensive lobbying by the National Education Association, whose membership

---

## *Cross-Cultural Perspective*

### The Renaissance Woman: An Interview with Rosa Jervolino

Rosa Jervolino takes on Italy's meshlike bureaucracy, antiquated legal system, and top-heavy Parliament as minister of education in this often Orwellian republic. . . . During a 30-year political career, she has been a senator from Rome, minister of special issues, and minister of social issues. Last October, she became president of the Christian Democrat Party, the first woman ever to hold that post. The problems she faces—budget cuts, political squabbles, and the slow mechanics of reform—will sound familiar everywhere. What's surprising is her willingness to try radical solutions and her tireless quest to keep Italy an agile member of the new world order.

**Q:** *What is your main objective as Italy's new minister of education?*

**A:** To get children all over Italy interested in school again. Our dropout rate is highest in poor areas. I believe that through our children we'll make our world's future—I never think only about my country. My programs include raising the obligatory schooling age from 14 to 16 and updating the curriculum in the high school, which is regulated by a law that's 50 years old. . . .

As a lawmaker, my goals are to bring the democratic process to the schools. I think parents should elect a parent representative, and students should elect students that together with the teachers have a say in school activities. . . .

**Q:** *What are the problems you're facing as minister?*

**A:** My biggest problem is a lack of funding—I have a large budget, 60 thousand billion lire (44 billion dollars at the current exchange of 1 dollar = 1,350 lire), but I have 1,200,000 teachers in 9,000 townships to pay. I've already had problems in my first three months because we've had to close schools where there were too few students.

I'd like more money for more sports facilities, to eliminate architectural barriers for the handicapped, and to improve school buildings. I'd like to build language labs, and I'd like to pay teachers more. . . .

**Q:** *You've been involved in Catholic affairs since the beginning of your career. Do you find yourself clashing with the Vatican in your views or objectives?*

**A:** No. . . . I had to laugh when I became minister of education and the press asked me if I were in favor of sex education. I said yes, when it's taught together with values such as non-violence in the family, and they accused me of being out of step with the Vatican. They hadn't considered the Episcopalian Conference of 1980—the Italian church is in favor of sex education. Of course, between the Pope and the bishops, there are different schools of thought. But I've had only support from the Vatican.

**Q:** *How big of a problem are drugs in Italy, and can you give me some specifics of your campaign against drugs?*

**A:** Up until 20 years ago the problem was unknown—limited to small circles of urban artistic people. Now drugs are used in all of Italy, in all levels of society. My philosophy incorporates prevention and reform.

I think it's really important to educate young children to the danger of drug use. Our new campaign is airing next month—we gambled our budget not on an advertising firm this time, but on schoolchildren—we asked them to come up with the ads. Some were quite chilling, others funny, but it really demonstrated that they had absorbed the message and understood how to render it to others.

From: C. Lynch, "The Renaissance Woman: An Interview with Rosa Jervolino," *Hemispheres*, January 1993, 17–19.

was to make up 10 percent of the delegates to the 1980 Democratic National Convention, President Jimmy Carter established the U.S. Department of Education as a separate cabinet-level department.

The U.S. Department of Education has three separate departments and establishes policy for, administers, and coordinates almost all federal assistance to education, regulating over one hundred different programs ranging from services for Native American students to projects for dropouts. The Office of Educational Research and Improvement is responsible for conducting research, developing innovative educational techniques, and securing grants. The National Center for Education Statistics prepares the *Digest of Education Statistics* and *The Condition of Education.* These two annual publications are compilations of data about enrollment, finances, outcomes of education, teachers, students, and schools at all levels of education. The Information Services Department provides information to the two other departments, the public, and the media.

In recent years, the department has assumed its role as voice of the president through the publication of numerous reports and through speeches of the secretary. For example, during the Reagan administration, Education Secretary William Bennett wrote two major reports suggesting that schools should be more concerned with excellence than with equality. Lauro F. Cavazos, education secretary during the first two years of the Bush administration, wrote two books publicizing Bush's contention that parental choice will help make schools excellent. President Clinton's secretary of education, Bill Riley, was the first to deliver a State of American Education Address (February 15, 1994), explaining the administration's approach to educational reform.

> The time has come to move from the negative crisis of education to a positive solution. All children can learn, if we have higher expectations of them and give them opportunities. This is why we must move from the reform of just a few schools and the reform efforts of a few states to an entirely different scale, to include the reform of all schools for every student. The main challenge of those of us who work in public policy is to take good ideas to scale. . . . Goals 2000 is our way to do it.

In addition to the Department of Education, other federal agencies influence state and local education policies. For example, the Office of Civil Rights and the Equal Opportunity Commission have reviewed claims of discrimination in public schools and initiated suits against school districts not in compliance with civil rights laws. School districts can face termination of federal assistance if they do not comply with federal regulations.

## U.S. SUPREME COURT AND EDUCATION

Article III of the U.S. Constitution provides that "the judicial power of the United States shall be vested in one Supreme Court, and in such inferior courts as the Congress may from time to time ordain and establish." These courts adjudicate all cases arising out of the Constitution, Acts of Congress, and U.S. treaties.

The **U.S. Supreme Court** interprets the Constitution and, therefore, can have significant influence on public education. In fact, during the 1960s, the Supreme Court had such extensive influence that it was called the "black-robed school board." Between 1954 and 1970, 2 thousand cases involving education were brought before the Court, compared to 2 hundred cases prior to 1954. A classic illustration of its policy-making potential is a decision based on the Fourteenth Amendment. The *Brown v. Board of Education of Topeka et al.* (347 U.S. 483, 1954) case established the role of the public schools in the desegregation of society (see chapter 5, pp. 181–183, for a complete discussion). Although segregation in public schools still continues today (66 percent of all African American children attend schools with mostly minority students, according to a 1993 study by the National School Boards Association), the *Brown* decision set educational policy for public schools and contributed to a changing social attitude.

Another important case was *Tinker v. Des Moines Independent Community School District* (393 U.S. 503, 1969), which involved the First Amendment and focused on the school board's refusal to allow students wearing black arm bands to protest casualties in the Vietnam War. The Court ruled that students had a constitutional right to protest their government's policies and that the wearing of arm bands simply represented one method of free speech (see chapter 15, pp. 597–598).

This decision and a number of others established students' First Amendment rights, even in public schools. Students now had the right to voice their opinions, even if they were opposed by the majority of school officials.

### *Changes in the Supreme Court's Interpretation of the Constitution*

Despite the fact that decisions of the Supreme Court are based on the Constitution and its amendments, the political composition of the Court changes over time. Supreme Court justices are appointed by the president for life and confirmed by the Senate. These changes in personnel, influenced by politics and policies of the White House, are reflected in the decisions of the Court. (See chapter 15, pp. 592–595, for an analysis of how the Court has dealt with educational issues and with censorship in education.)

---

**13-1**

**POINTS TO REMEMBER**

- Since the power to influence education is not delegated to the federal government by the Constitution, the Tenth Amendment affirms it is the province of the states.

- Congress influences public education by passing bills to which funding and specific criteria for obtaining the funding are attached.

- The president affects education indirectly through his legislative agenda to Congress.

- The U.S. Supreme Court rules on education cases related to the U.S. Constitution. Court rulings can be extremely influential and affect educational policy.

---

## Role of the States in Public Education

Since the U.S. Constitution does not mention education specifically, it is left to each state to determine how its schools will be governed and maintained. Consequently, there is great variety in the organization and governance of schools from state to state. Utah's constitutional provisions for education, for example, require a "uniform" school system: "The Legislature shall provide for the establishment and maintenance of a uniform system of public schools, which shall be open to all children of the State, and free from sectarian control." In contrast, Virginia's provisions do not require that the state's public schools be uniform but merely that they be free for all children: "The General Assembly shall provide for a system of free public elementary and secondary schools for all children of school age throughout the commonwealth, and shall seek to ensure that an educational program of high quality is established and continually maintained." Differences such as these in the states' constitutional provisions lead to differences in how the schools are governed and maintained within each state.

## GOVERNORS

The role of the governors in public education is indirect. Like the U.S. president, they primarily set the legislative agenda for their constituency. In all states except North Carolina, the governor also has the right to veto legislation passed by the state legislature.

In the late 1980s, however, the states' governors began to take a more active role in public education. All fifty formed the Education Commission of the States. This commission, together with the National Governors' Association and the Council of Chief State School Officers, developed seven task forces to examine teaching, leadership and management, parental involvement and choice, readiness, technology, school facilities, and college quality. This commission gave the governors a more active voice in educational decision making within the states. In *Time for Results: The Governors' 1991 Report on Education,* the governors state, "Still, state constitutions and laws establish the basic framework for how we operate the schools. So we [the governors of the states] can *change* the way we attract and keep the best possible administrators and teachers. We can change the way our colleges educate our future principals and teachers . . . and we can *change* the way we assess performance" (1986, 5). Since then the governors have published three additional reports attempting to define the goals and establish the roles of the federal government, state governments, and local communities in setting standards and reaching goals (*Every Child Ready for School: Report on the Action Team on School Readiness,* 1992; *The Debate on Opportunity to Learn Standards,* 1993; *Kids and Violence,* 1994).

In February 1990 the National Governors' Association set six major goals for education that influenced President Bush's proposals known as America 2000 and later President Bill Clinton's Goals 2000: Educate America Act (P.L. 103–227), which was passed by Congress in 1994. Although the National Governors' Association set an agenda for reaching the goals and the U.S. Congress passed an act to assist in funding the setting of standards to help reach the goals, the governors' suggestions will only be enacted if passed into law by each state legislature, defined by each state board of education, and implemented by each state office of education.

## STATE LEGISLATURES

State legislatures have broad power to pass laws regarding public education. State and federal courts have affirmed state legislative authority to create and design school districts, raise revenues and distribute funds, control teacher certification,

Charter schools are publicly financed experimental schools that generally operate independently of local school districts. They are accountable to taxpayers and subject to state and federal health, safety, and civil rights laws and desegregation orders, but offer parents another option to the neighborhood public school. These students are taking a reading class at Academy Charter School in Castle Rock, Colorado.

prescribe and evaluate curriculums, mandate attendance laws, and regulate other aspects of school administration. All states require students to attend school between specified ages, typically six to sixteen.

State legislatures may not delegate law-making powers to subordinate agencies. However, legislatures may establish agencies to carry on the administrative functions of the schools and implement the laws.

*Charter Schools*  An interesting move to reform public education by reducing state requirements and mandates is state charter schools. Proposed by President Bush as part of America 2000, **charter schools** are public schools chartered and designed by groups of teachers, parents, or other groups or individuals. They are free from most state statutes and rules applying to public schools. Financing differs considerably from state to state. In some states charter schools get complete state funding, but are treated as stand-alone districts; in some they get no local funding and no state funding requiring local levy matches; in others the states negotiate with the school districts to determine the funding. These schools, operated under their own charters, have the freedom to innovate, use different teaching strategies and materials, and seek outside funding, but they are accountable to local school boards of the states for their results.

By 1994 eleven states had charter school laws and six others were considering them. Only Massachusetts and Connecticut allowed charter schools to be run by private corporations. Minnesota was the first state to enact a charter law in 1991. In 1993–1994, Philadelphia had 110 charter schools serving 25,500 students.

## STATE BOARDS OF EDUCATION

Since it is impossible for legislatures to include in state statutes all the details for administering public schools, most states have boards of education whose role is to set policy and to supply the structure and details necessary for carrying out broad legislative mandates. For example, the legislature might determine that all public school teachers must be tested prior to certification. The state board must determine how and by whom this mandate will be implemented. In some states, members of the board of education, which range in number from seven in nine states to twenty-one in one state and serve between two and four years, are appointed by the governor and, in others, elected by the citizenry.

Today, Wisconsin is the only state without a state board of education. Hawaii's state board is also its district board of education because it is all one school district. Florida is the only state in which the governor's cabinet is also the state school board. Figure 13.2 illustrates the levels of educational control.

## CHIEF STATE SCHOOL OFFICERS

In addition to the state board of education, all states have a designated chief school officer, usually called the superintendent of public instruction or commissioner of education. The duties of the state school officers tend to be regulatory. In some states they may be required to adjudicate educational controversies. The chief state school officer may also be involved in such activities as long-range planning and educational research.

FIGURE 13-2

## Hierarchy of Educational Control

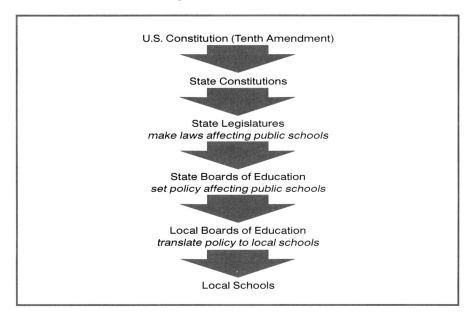

The local schools are subject to legislation based first on the U.S. Constitution and secondly on their own state constitutions. Thereafter, policies and procedures are set by state legislatures and state boards of education, and are processed through the local boards of education to the schools.

In more than half the states (twenty-six), the chief state school officer is selected by the state school board. In other states, he or she may be appointed by the governor (nine) or elected by the people (fifteen).

## STATE EDUCATION AGENCIES

State education agencies, often called the state department of education, provide assistance to the public schools and oversee the implementation of legislative enactments and state board policies. They do not set policy and, therefore, do not exert direct control. Most also conduct research and development to improve public education in the state. These agencies consult with the state board, the chief state school officer, the local school board, and, frequently, colleges and universities that offer teacher training. The state education agencies might recommend policy to the state board, which enacts this policy. For example, the state agency that requires teachers to take tests prior to certification might also participate in the following: consultation with the state board and chief state school officer, evaluation of existing tests or development of a new test, field trials of the test, evaluation of the success of the field testing, suggesting to the state board cutoff scores for passing the test, implementation of the statewide testing, recording and monitoring each certification candidate's test results, and working with teacher-training institutions to help prepare students to take the test. Twenty-seven states have met legislative mandates by requiring that applicants take the National Teachers Examination (NTE), a nationally normed, core battery of three tests: general knowledge, communication skills, and professional knowledge. Many states also require that future teachers take a specialty area test that is designed to measure understanding of the content and methods of a specific subject.

*Curriculum Decisions*   Most states make numerous decisions about their instructional programs. A few write standards regarding instruction into their statutes. However, most state legislatures delegate this authority to the state board of education, which sets broad guidelines and delegates the authority to set specific standards to the state education agency. They are integrated into the curriculum by local school districts.

A few states, however, have more centralized control over curriculum. In North Carolina, for example, a legislative statute requires the state board of education to adopt a course of study for the schools, which is then developed and monitored by the state education agency. The local schools are required to implement this course of study. Such decision making is the exception rather than the rule.

## STATE COURTS

State courts are established under the constitutional provisions of each state. Therefore, the structures of judicial systems are remarkably different. They usually include trial, or circuit, courts; courts of special jurisdiction such as juvenile courts; appellate, or appeals, courts; and a supreme court. In the Illinois state court system, for example, the supreme court, with seven judges, hears appeals from the appellate courts. The five appellate courts hear appeals from the circuit (trial) courts. Illinois is divided into twenty-one circuit court districts, which include, among others, chancery-divorce, law, probate, juvenile, criminal, municipal, and county.

All state court systems provide some type of administrative appeal for individuals involved in disputes regarding the internal operation of the schools. Although state court systems vary, all require that internal administrative sources of appeal be utilized prior to bringing a case to the courts. Dr. Hurwitz, for example, in the opening anecdote, first used the administrative offices of his school to appeal his case before he brought it before civil court. (See also chapter 6, p. 219, for a discussion of Bishop Knox, a principal who was suspended in 1993 for allowing school prayer, and chapter 15, p. 610, for the case of Adele Jones, a teacher who was accused of failing too many students.)

*State Courts and Constitutional Law*   In addition to appeals from cases heard in the lower courts, state supreme courts, like the U.S. Supreme Court, rule on cases having to do with the constitutionality of legislative actions. In 1989, for example, the Kentucky Supreme Court ruled in *Rose v. The Council for Better Education, Inc.* (Ky., 790 S.W.2d 186, 1989) that the legislature should "re-create and re-establish" the state's precollegiate education system. In the case, brought by sixty-six property-poor school districts, the justices ruled five to two that

Kentucky's entire system of school governance and finance violated the state constitution's mandate for an "efficient system of common schools." The court ruled that inequities in state spending for schools violated every student's right to a common education. This court ruling struck down not only the state's financing system but the common-school laws that created school districts, school boards, the state department of education, and laws regarding teacher certification and school construction. (See chapter 14, pp. 565–566, for more about the Kentucky school funding debate.)

*Appealing Cases to the U.S. Supreme Court* A state supreme court ruling is final unless the case involves an issue related to the U.S. Constitution. If the case is appealed to the U.S. Supreme Court, it may either uphold or overturn the state court's decision. State courts are subservient to decisions of the U.S. Supreme Court, as illustrated in 1954 in *Brown v. Board of Education* (347 U.S. 483, 1954) when the U.S. Supreme Court ruled that laws of twenty-one states requiring or permitting racial segregation were in violation of the equal protection clause of the Fourteenth Amendment.

## STATE ATTORNEYS GENERAL

The state attorney general may issue an official opinion regarding the schools when consulted by a local authority. For example, if a local school board has a question about the appropriate use of state funds for the purchase of school buses, it might consult the attorney general, who will research legal questions through statutory law, state and federal law precedents, and state board policy. The opinion will then be forwarded to the official who requested it. How much weight the opinion of the attorney general has in such a case when it is brought to court varies from state to state and case to case, but it can be important in determining public school policy.

# Local Education Agencies

Although the states control public education, the local education agencies (LEA) or school districts administer local public schools. An LEA may be a county, a city, or a district within a large city. Specific decision-making powers are granted to local school boards, which then appoint school administrators to carry out the policies and decisions adopted by the board.

The amount of power given to LEAs varies from state to state. In states with long histories of local control, particularly the New England states, local school boards have a great deal of responsibility for making administrative decisions. In states with centralized control of education, particularly the southern states, local boards function within a strict framework of state legislative mandates. Hawaii makes all decisions regarding the schools under its jurisdiction on the state level as do Washington, D.C., Puerto Rico, American Samoa, Guam, Northern Marianas, and the Virgin Islands.

### STATES AND LEAs

The state, in giving administrative responsibility to LEAs, does not relinquish control of the state's public schools. In fact, the state may withdraw, through legislative action, any power or authority granted to an LEA. The state may also create LEAs and alter the boundaries of existing school districts.

We can see evidence of how the states redistricted the public schools in the consolidation efforts of the 1950s through the 1970s. The number of LEAs in the United States decreased from 94,426 in 1947 to 31,705 in 1964 in a major reorganization of schools due to consolidation of small districts into larger districts. By 1992–1993 the number of LEAs was only 15,025 (U.S. Department of Education 1994, 3). Consolidation represented the states' attempt to bring better and more equitable services and efficient funding to each LEA. In 1993 the one hundred largest school districts in the United States served 23 percent of all public school students (9,823,729 of nearly 42 million students). The largest school district in the United States was New York City with 962,269 students and 1,008 schools; the average school district had five schools and 2,568 students (telephone interview with Vance Grant, U.S. Department of Education, July 22, 1994).

An interesting example of a state's authority to withdraw administrative power from an LEA occurred in Jersey City, New Jersey, in 1989. The New Jersey state board of education authorized a full state takeover of the Jersey City schools, citing evidence of the district's "total educational failure." This takeover became possible following the passage of a 1988 New Jersey law authorizing state officials to take control of school systems deemed to be what they called "academically bankrupt" and unable to provide a "thorough and efficient" education for the students of the district. In 1994 the state still controls the Jersey City schools.

More typically than taking over school districts, states have begun giving more local control to districts and individual schools, the trend over the past two decades being to move educational management closer to each school. Many states have passed laws in which individual schools have **site-based management** in which the state gives the school control of such things as curriculum development, budgeting, staffing, and student distribution. Advocates of site-based management suggest that schools are more likely to reform from within if they have more control over decisions that make reform possible. For example, a school with site-based management might decide to realign teachers in order to make changes in the curriculum; whereas a school without site-based management might be unable to change the curriculum because realignment of staff is not allowable under state regulations. Critics of site-based management often point out the advantages of more centralized systems of school governance. For example, Hawaii, which serves as both the state and local education agency, was the first to apply for and receive federal funds to develop a statewide school reform plan under Goals 2000: Educate America Act. Hawaii was able to act quickly because the decision could be made by a single agency rather than a group of local agencies.

### LOCAL SCHOOL BOARDS

The local school board is the immediate governing body of an LEA and holds those legal powers granted to it by the state. Its chief responsibilities are to develop and improve the district's educational program, to supply staffing for the schools, to provide and maintain educationally efficient school buildings, to obtain adequate financial resources, to maintain two-way communication with the community, to select a superintendent as the school's chief executive, and to work cooperatively with the superintendent.

School boards usually vary in size from five to nine members with staggered terms, and its members serve without pay or with a nominal salary. School boards must act as a body; individual members cannot make policy on behalf of the board.

*Problems of School Boards*   School boards have numerous and diverse responsibilities that they often cannot achieve, including setting goals and developing strategies to achieve them, defining measures of success and accountability, guaranteeing equitable distribution of resources, communicating progress toward goals to the community, and providing avenues for community input (Danzberger, 371).

According to the Institute for Educational Leadership studies of school boards in urban, suburban, rural/small town districts from 1985 to 1992, they get high marks for having district goals and low marks in communicating progress toward these goals to the community. Boards in each type of district were dysfunctional due to conflicts between members resulting in their inability to "chart clear direction for their school systems" (Danzberger 1994, 370). Many school board members were frustrated by the inability to shift from solving immediate problems and crises to providing educational leadership for their communities.

According to these studies, the problems of school boards are often the responsibility of the states because of "the proliferation of mandates, regulations, and prescriptive requirements," limiting the board's ability to make policy (p. 371).

## SUPERINTENDENTS

The superintendent is the chief executive officer of a school district and is usually appointed by the board of education. The superintendent is responsible for the educational and business administration of all the schools in the LEA, including curriculum, selection and improvement of teachers and key administrators, gathering data on issues of interest to the school board, preparing the school budget, implementation of the budget, implementation of the school board's goals and policies, evaluation of curricular and instructional programs, maintenance of buildings, safety of students and personnel, and transportation of students to and from the schools. In addition, the superintendent is the LEA's primary liaison with the community. Most school districts have a central office with deputy or associate superintendents and a professional staff to assist in these responsibilities.

The delineation of responsibilities can again be seen in the chapter's opening anecdote. Dr. Hurwitz, whose actions brought him into conflict with the local superintendent whose responsibility was to carry out the policies of the board, was eventually relieved of his post as a high school principal. When Hurwitz's appeals to the superintendent did not produce the results Hurwitz desired, he took the next logical step and made a further appeal to the local school board. As is the board's right, it suggested a compromise, including a second hearing before a civil court.

Despite the difficulties of the job and a rapid turnover in many school districts, most (68 percent) of the nation's approximately 14 thousand superintendents are satisfied with their profession, according to a 1992 American Association of School Administrators study. Forty-three percent of the superintendents surveyed for the study reported that they had left their last position to become a superintendent of a larger district; less than 17 percent cited problems with school board members; less than 3 percent cited problems with district consolidation, union conflict, or desegregation conflict.

## POLITICS AND LEAs

A 1993 report from the Public Agenda Foundation, commissioned by the Charles F. Kettering Foundation, provides fascinating examples of problems within school districts. Researchers studied the politics in four diverse school districts, a New York City suburban district, a midwestern, a southern, and a western district, all of which were in untroubled communities with strong middle-class participation and resources. Although they were diverse in geography and population, similarities in their politics were found. According to the report, in all four districts what began as a good-faith effort to work together on school reform became a "tug of war over turf" (p. iv). The goals of various constituencies were the same, improved education, but poor communication, widespread suspicion, and outright anger led to parochialism, which caused the reform to collapse.

The report concluded that the problems were not the individuals involved (superintendents, school board members, principals, teachers, parents, and business leaders), but something about the system itself that encouraged conflict rather than cooperation. The unity of shared mission was destroyed by "narrowly partisan modes of interaction within districts" (p. iv). In each community, constituent groups were "organized around narrow interests, competing to influence policy and trying to deflect initiatives adverse to their own special interests" (p. 1). The southern superintendent referred to his school district as "a giant dysfunctional family." Another superintendent complained that individual school board members tended to adopt one or two schools as their own, avoiding the others. One parent said that the only way to get things done was to form a group and complain. Parents felt they had to struggle to be heard. Although some said administrators listened to their problems if the discussion was face-to-face rather than by phone, many said they did not know who was accountable for policy decisions in the district. Teachers, on the other hand, argued that administrators made decisions by fiat to head off resistance by parents.

In all four districts communication across the educational hierarchy was considered poor. Teachers were more likely to receive educational news from the press than from administrators, resulting in rumor and speculation rather than real information. They not only felt isolated from administrators, but also from colleagues in their own school and in other schools in the district. Business leaders claimed the schools were out of touch with the realities of the times, and were frustrated by the bureaucracy and mandates under which they operated. On the other hand, many educators complained that the business leaders did not understand the complexities and difficulties facing the schools. Although they appreciated the involvement of business, they were not sure how far the involvement should extend.

The researchers concluded that there is politics in school districts, but since politics is how change occurs and consensus is reached, the challenge is in preventing a descent into pettiness and parochialism. In addition, the researchers suggested that enormous energy and resources need to be invested in communications. (For additional information on how to solve many of these problems, see chapter 7.)

# Role of Professional Organizations in Education

Professional organizations for educators serve two purposes: securing political power and providing professional development.

## POLITICAL POWER

The National Education Association (NEA) and the American Federation of Teachers (AFT) are the political arms of the profession. Over 80 percent of all public school teachers belong to either the NEA or the AFT. These two organizations research issues related to education, take public stands on these issues, lobby for federal and state legislation, defend members in school-related legal cases, organize local chapters, and bargain with school boards for improved benefits for teachers.

*Viewpoint*  Milwaukee Teachers Back in Fold

The 6,200 teacher members of the Milwaukee Teachers Education Association (MTEA) have voted overwhelmingly to reaffiliate with NEA and its Wisconsin affiliate, the Wisconsin Education Association Council (WEAC).

Reaffiliation will take effect September 1 pending confirmation by the WEAC Representative Assembly, which will vote in early May. If approved, the Milwaukee local will become NEA's fourth largest affiliate, and WEAC's membership roster will expand to more than 74,000 statewide.

The Milwaukee teachers, who have been unaffiliated with any state or national organization for the past 20 years, voted two-to-one for the reaffiliation.

"The results clearly indicate that unity and the protection of public education is paramount to the teachers of Milwaukee," notes Richard Terry, WEAC's director of affiliate relations. "Our unity will increase the power of each organization at a time when power is exactly what we need."

"Our members have already been receiving services," says MTEA Executive Secretary Don Ernest. "But with issues like privatization hitting Wisconsin, members have realized that, in the long run, they'll need strength at the state level. Reaffiliating was the best way to gain that strength."

WEAC and MTEA have been working toward reaffiliation for three years. MTEA members who work as substitutes, aides, and accountants won't be affected by the agreement.

From: *NEA TODAY*, May 1994.

*(continued on p. 529)*

**TABLE 13-1**

## NEA and AFT: Similarities and Differences

| Similarities | Differences |
|---|---|
| 1. Promote professional excellence among educators and excellence in all aspects of education. | 1. NEA opposes merit pay based on performance; AFT supports it if politics are left out and evaluations are fair. |
| 2. Support national education goals. | 2. AFT has relationship with AFL-CIO; NEA is an independent organization. |
| 3. Support National Board of Education standards on what students should know and be able to do. | 3. AFT membership includes noneducational workers such as nurses, custodians, clerical staff, and social workers; NEA membership does not. |
| 4. Work for increased salaries and increased fringe benefits for teachers. | 4. NEA has a national staff of 600; AFT's staff is 50. |
| 5. Work for increased state and federal financial support. | 5. NEA works closely with school administrators, including them in membership; AFT contends that affiliation with administrators interferes with collective bargaining. |
| 6. Support the concept of a licensed educator in every position. | 6. AFT has a permanent national leadership (Albert Shanker has been president since 1973); NEA's president is eligible to serve two, three-year terms. |
| 7. Support the development of a diversity of programs: developmentally disabled; special education; global and multicultural education; sex, drugs, and AIDS education; adult education; vocational and career education; fine arts; counseling; athletics and health; pre-Kindergarten education. | 7. AFT has larger membership in larger cities; NEA's membership is in smaller cities and suburban and rural areas. |
| 8. Work toward teacher autonomy and empowerment in making decisions affecting classroom technique, class size, workloads, selection of instructional materials, and objective evaluation procedures. | 8. NEA opposes standardized testing of teacher competency and student achievement; AFT believes both are necessary. |
| 9. Oppose legislation related to tuition tax credits and vouchers to subsidize private schooling. | |
| 10. Include higher education faculty. | |
| 11. Have a professional code of ethics. | |
| 12. Oppose private enterprise management of public schools. | |
| 13. Promote continued intellectual development of teachers through in-service and advanced degrees. | |
| 14. Promote use of instructional materials and activities related to cultural diversity in classrooms. | |
| 15. Use of collective bargaining rights, due process, and grievance procedures for teachers. | |
| 16. Exercise of academic and professional freedom to explore and discuss divergent viewpoints. | |
| 17. Support career ladder plans in principle (i.e., different levels of compensation for different responsibilities). | |
| 18. Support elected officials that have strong education platforms. | |
| 19. Publish monthly journals and express views in other professional literature. | |

The National Education Association (NEA) and the American Federation of Teachers (AFT) are the two primary organizations that represent teachers in negotiations with the school board, conduct research on policy issues, and lobby the legislature for improved school policies. While they have more similarities than differences, the differences may be crucial to your selection of one or the other to represent you.

Both the NEA, established by Congress in 1906, and the AFT, organized in 1916 by the American Federation of Labor, have similar national education legislative agendas but significant differences in their membership and approaches (see table 13.1). In 1994 the two organizations focused greater efforts on merger, attempting to work out their differences. Both organizations will vote on the issue in the near future.

In 1994 the NEA's legislative agenda included support for: model language for state-level gender equity laws similar to Title IX of 1972, state and local affiliates to develop and maintain academic and disciplinary standards, programs for high-risk students, establishment of a coalition to implement strategies to ensure against discrimination, and adoption of a single-payer health-care plan for all U.S. citizens. In addition the NEA opposed attempts by private corporations and individuals to establish schools for profit.

The 1994 legislative agenda of the AFT focused on some of the same issues. The members supported health-care reform proposed by President Bill Clinton, more Chapter I resources to be targeted for poor children, professional development initiatives, Even Start programs to help low socioeconomic families, Goals 2000: Educate America Act, collective bargaining practices that bar employers from offering preferential benefits and treatments to workers who cross picket lines, and the School-to-Work Opportunities Act. The AFT opposed federal legislation allocating funds for vouchers and private school choice.

## PROFESSIONAL DEVELOPMENT

Organizations primarily devoted to the professional development of teachers include the National Council of Teachers of English (NCTE), International Reading Association (IRA), National Science Teachers Association (NSTA), National Council of Teachers of Mathematics (NCTM), National Council for the Social Studies (NCSS), National Middle Schools Association (NMSA), Association of Childhood Education International (ACEI), Association of Supervision and Curriculum Development (ASCD), etc. They publish journals and books, fund research, conduct conferences and meetings, provide teachers with instructional materials, sponsor special interest groups that publish opinion statements, give awards and scholarships, sponsor state or local chapters, suggest criteria and standards for teacher certification, evaluate teacher certification programs through the National Council of Accreditation of Teacher Education (NCATE), and develop teaching and curriculum standards for the grade levels and subject areas they represent. They also survey teachers to determine trends, publish directories of leaders in the profession, and distribute press releases related to educational issues. Membership in these organizations is voluntary. (See appendix pp. xx-xxi for a list of professional organizations and addresses).

Following are some examples of the work of these organizations.

- In 1989 the National Council of Teachers of Mathematics (NCTM) published *Curriculum and Evaluation Standards* to help mathematics teachers better understand when to use technology such as computers and calculators in teaching mathematics.

- In 1990 NCTM developed Standards for the Improvement of Mathematics Education by the year 2000. They were related to the national goals for education endorsed by President Bush and the fifty governors.
- In 1991 NCTM adopted standards for the teaching of mathematics.
- In 1988 the National Middle Schools Association (NMSA) conducted a survey of the educational approaches, practices, and trends in the nation's middle schools and published a summary of their findings in *Education in the Middle Schools.*
- In 1990 the National Science Teachers Association (NSTA) worked jointly with the Association of Science Education and the NCTM to establish specific goals for classroom teachers for the improvement of both mathematics and science education by the year 2000.
- In 1990 the National Council of Teachers of English (NCTE) approved a policy advocating a class size of twenty and a daily work load of not more than eighty students for English and language arts teachers. NCTE proposed legislation that required that school districts applying for categorical funds have a plan to reduce class size and teaching loads for English and language arts teachers.
- In 1993 NCTE developed voluntary national standards for teaching and learning English/language arts.
- In 1990 the Association for Childhood Education International (ACEI) developed new initiatives to increase parental involvement in education. In particular, ACEI developed activities for collaboration with the Parent Teachers Association (PTA) in addressing problems related to parents and the education of young children.
- In 1993 the National Association for the Education of Young Children (NAEYC) distributed its position paper on violence in the lives of children.
- In 1993 the National Art Education Association (NAEA) developed standards for teaching art.

## Role of Businesses and Foundations in Education

During the 1980s and 1990s, businesses and foundations have significantly increased their influence over public education. Corporate America has historically stood aloof from public schools while complaining about the quality of education.

In 1990 the Business Roundtable (BRT), a group representing the chief executive officers (CEOs) of 213 corporations, made a ten-year commitment to the restructuring of education at the state level. Under the leadership of then IBM Chairman John Akers, BRT members volunteered to work with governors, state political leaders, and other interested parties to identify key educational problems, develop strategies for dealing with them, and implement new policy, regulatory, and funding initiatives. BRT sponsored a series of CEO-governor dialogues in an effort to support state reform efforts.

One of the more controversial elements of President George Bush's America 2000 plan, endorsed by President Bill Clinton, was the involvement of business in education. Bush suggested that first, business must establish a list of job-related skill standards to be taught to students. Second, a group of business leaders headed by Paul O'Neill, CEO of Alcoa, pledged to raise at least $150 million to fund research and development teams to work with schools to develop innovative approaches to education. By the mid-1990s this had developed into Outcome-Based Education, ironically vehemently opposed by fundamental Christian groups who provided a major political support base for Bush's presidency (see chapter 8, pp. 305–307).

Despite critics' concerns that this gave business too great a role in public education, it was just the beginning. In only three years since the first edition of this text, business' involvement in public education has grown from an informal influential role to one of direct control in many school districts around the nation.

## BUSINESS IN THE SCHOOLS

Business and industry have become directly involved in the management of public education, some think to an alarming extent through the increased number of charter schools and a provision in Goals 2000: Educate America Act that allows states to use federal dollars to experiment with school privatization.

In 1991 President Bush asked business leaders to use their resources and talents to "create schools that would help all American students make a quantum leap in learning and that would restore American education to world preeminence" (1992, 293). As a result, CEOs of many of the nation's largest companies joined forces in New American Schools Development Corporation (NASDC). An independent, umbrella nonprofit corporation headed by executives on loan from business and government, NASDC has awarded $20 million in planning grants, funded by major corporations, to eleven design teams made up of individuals from education, business, technology, public leadership, social services, science, and humanities to design and test new school models that would reform public education and meet three challenges:

- to help all students meet new national standards in five core subjects . . . and to prepare students for responsible citizenship, further learning, and productive employment
- to be able to operate on a budget comparable to that of conventional schools
- to seek fundamental institutional change in American schooling (Rundell, 294)

NASDC is not involved in direct management nor does it make a profit from its work in the public schools. However, other business-school ventures are both direct and profit-making.

*Private Funding for Public Education*     The Edison Project, established by Christopher Whittle, CEO of Whittle Communications (the creator of Channel One, the controversial commercial network that broadcasts news programs into U.S. classrooms) and headed by Benno C. Schmidt, Jr., former president of Yale University, attempted but failed to design a national chain of profit-making schools. Whittle's original goal was to "invent the new American school" by creating innovative models in one hundred, for-profit private schools by 1995.

Students in about four hundred schools got the news along with commercials for candy, razors, and cheese snacks as the advertiser-supported classroom program Channel One aired for the first time in March 1990. Chris Whittle, whose company Whittle Communications funds the program, watches the first broadcast with an honors English class at Powell High School in Knoxville, Tennessee.

Due to some business failures, Whittle could not raise the necessary $2.5 billion and in 1993 shifted his strategy to partnership with existing public schools. The increasing number of charter schools and the involvement of Deborah McGriff, former Detroit superintendent, have paved the way for the Edison Project's entry into public education. Called the Edison Project because Thomas Edison did not simply hot-wire a candle, but started over creating an entirely new design, their model is based on Mortimer Adler's Paideia Proposal (see chapter 1, p. 46, and chapter 6, pp. 248–249) and includes high academic standards, an extended school year (210 days as compared to 180 days), and significant use of technology.

Since Massachusetts passed a charter school law in 1993 that allows public schools to be run by corporations, the Edison Project will implement its ideas in three Massachusetts charter schools and two of its elementary public schools beginning in 1995.

Education Alternatives, Inc., another for-profit attempt to manage public schools, is based in Minneapolis, Minnesota, and headed by CEO John T. Golle. Since 1991 they have operated twelve schools in Baltimore and one school in Dade County, Florida. In 1994 EAI assumed management of all thirty-two schools in Hartford, Connecticut, the first and only complete school district in the nation under for-profit management. EAI differs from the Edison Project in that its goal is not to reinvent the school but to redesign existing schools, curriculums, and policies. The firm believes in investing in improved facilities, computers, and teacher training to improve education. Like the other for-profit projects, the corporation's markets are in the growing number of charter schools and some states' experimentation with privatization encouraged under Goals 2000: Educate America Act.

***Business Funds Public Education***    Although the funding of projects for public education is no longer the only role of business in the public schools, it is still an important one. According to the Council for Aid to Education, an organization that tracks corporate support for education, corporate gifts to K–12 education totaled $2.4 billion in 1992. Below are some examples:

1. AT&T funded grants to teams that included a school district, a teacher's college, and a teacher's union to improve teaching in inner-city schools.
2. DeWitt-Wallace Readers' Digest funded sixty summer fellowships for rural teachers to improve the teaching of English and contributed $3 million to the National Board for Professional Standards to hold thirty-six state and regional forums to inform teachers about national certification.
3. General Electric donated a $5 million plant to the Cleveland Board of Education for students to work on assembly lines and be paid for their work.
4. McDonnell-Douglas Corporation conducts management seminars for administrators and courses in computer science and mathematics for teachers.
5. People's Energy, a natural gas firm in Chicago, sends employees to the public schools to tutor students in reading and mathematics.
6. Nike donated $1 million to the National Foundation for the Improvement of Education to create dropout prevention programs for teachers. The "Just Do It" grants gave $5,000 to $25,000 to teachers for creative programs to motivate students to stay in school.
7. The Tandy Technology Scholars Corporation awards a $2,500 stipend to one hundred outstanding mathematics, science, or computer science students annually. They also grant $1,000 scholarships to a second group of one hundred students.
8. Apple Computers donated computers to educators and the schools through the Apple Education Grants Program. The program has granted more than $2 million annually in equipment to needy schools nationwide.
9. The Cleveland business community formed a partnership with the Cleveland public schools to provide a scholarship to every student who earns it. All students in grades seven through twelve earn deposits toward scholarships for grades in core subjects: $40 for an A, $20 for a B, and $10 for a C. Each grading period students receive a statement of earnings.
10. The Computer Science Corporation, Hazelton Laboratories, Martin-Marietta, and other local businesses in Alexandria, Virginia, contributed $4 million in high-tech equipment to Thomas Jefferson Magnet High School for Science and Technology.
11. With a $2 million commitment from 3Com Corporation, an information highway will link 345 Santa Clara County, California, schools.

*(continued on p. 536)*

# SHOULD U.S. PUBLIC SCHOOLS BE PRIVATIZED?

## PRO Benno C. Schmidt, Jr.

Contrary to the dreary prognoses for America's children that fill our nation's press, we at the Edison Project see something far more promising going on in communities across the country. Concerned parents, civic leaders, and educators are actively seeking to change their schools in profound and exciting ways—and are increasingly turning to the private sector for assistance. . . .

The Edison Project and other like-minded enterprises offer school districts several distinct advantages to aid them in their reform efforts: . . .

• A New Vision. The Edison Project is one of a small number of programs that attempts to weave together all the disparate strands of the endeavor that we think of as school into something new and exciting.

• Investment. The Edison Project has invested millions of dollars in developing our school design, curriculum, and school organization. In addition to that research, we bring millions more to a school via direct investment in professional development and technology.

• Accountability. If a business is poorly managed, it goes bankrupt. . . .

Accountability energizes the entire culture of a school. The Edison Project seeks five-year relationships with school districts, and we will spell out the results expected of us and the benchmarks and timetables by which progress will be monitored.

• Competition. Preliminary evidence indicates that the advantages of competition, spurred by public-private partnerships, are already being felt. In Wichita, Kan., where the school board recently voted unanimously to entrust three of its schools to a partnership with the Edison Project, one board member said the endeavor has already "fostered some positive, healthy competition" with other schools in the system. . . .

• Breaking the Logjam. It is no longer tenable to argue that the morass of regulations that burden our public schools is helping us achieve our nation's educational goals. In a great many cases, efforts such as the Edison Project are helping jump-start long-overdue reconsiderations of the regulations that govern our schools. . . .

We at the Edison Project have now heard from thousands of concerned educators and parents, and we've come to some pretty clear conclusions. People are tired of the same old arguments as to why schools can't change. They want alternatives, and private providers can help deliver those alternatives. Competition, freedom of opportunity, and a diversity of choices serve the causes of progress and human dignity.

> From: B. C. Schmidt. "A Very Different Kind of School," *Education Week* (June 22, 1994), 42–43. Benno Schmidt was formerly the president of Yale University and when this article was written was an officer with the Edison Project.

## POSTSCRIPT

Neither Schmidt's nor Shanker's positions on the privatization of public education are surprising. Schmidt had been the president of one of the most prestigious private universities in the country and supports the idea of private funding for public good. Shanker, on the other hand, is suspicious of any group of private citizens who maintain they can do a better job educating American children than the teachers he represents.

# SHOULD U.S. PUBLIC SCHOOLS BE PRIVATIZED?

## CON  Albert Shanker

The Edison Project schools would be important, Whittle said, . . . because of the influence these schools would have on U.S. education. . . .

Since Edison schools would offer fresh ideas, existing schools would be able to learn from them (and perhaps purchase their teaching programs, hardware, software, consulting services, etc.). So while he was making money, Whittle would be helping schools that were already out there.

But Whittle's real message seemed to be that there was no point in thinking of fixing public education; it would have to be replaced with something entirely different. He often compared the difference between our current schools and the ones he would invent to the difference between a candle and Thomas Edison's incandescent light. And, as he said, there is no way to make a light bulb out of a candle. . . .

But Whittle and Benno Schmidt . . . have run into financial trouble. They have not been able to raise the $2.5 billion needed for the first 100 schools. Moreover, it turns out that they made a disastrous miscalculation about how much money it would take, not just to run the new schools but also to build them or rent space for them. So the Edison Project's mission has been totally rewritten. Instead of creating a revolutionary new system, it will concentrate, as Whittle recently announced, on managing existing schools.

This ideological about-face raises some serious questions about Whittle's credibility. Whittle said that the entire education system had to be dismantled and built again according to a new model. But now, . . . he's saying, "If you want to hire us, we can run the old system. . . ." And instead of insisting that only inventing the light bulb will be good enough, he is saying he can make candles that will do just fine.

What is it Whittle now sees that makes him claim he can salvage an education system that he claimed, a short time ago, was irredeemable? What all he said just adtalk? And is that what it is now?

The idea Chris Whittle was selling—and that he has now given up . . . is to replace public education with a private system. . . . [O]ther industrialized countries all over the world . . . have fine public systems. There is no reason why we should not have one too.

From: A. Shanker. "Edison's Candle," *New York Times* (August 30, 1993), E9. Albert Shanker is the long-time president of the American Federation of Teachers (AFT). Both the AFT and the NEA have taken a stand against the privatization of public education.

Although they are both discussing the Edison Project, they could be examining any approach to corporate funding and control of public education. Schmidt maintains that if we put together great minds from across society and give them free rein, we will be able to reinvent the schools in the way Edison reinvented light when he did more than redesign the candle. Shanker's point is that it is neither possible nor necessary to redesign public education.

## FOUNDATIONS AND THE SCHOOLS

Foundations, legally chartered funds administered by independent boards of control, are increasingly involved in financing educational projects. Some major recent foundation projects are listed below.

1. The Annie E. Casey Foundation selected five cities to receive a total of $10 million each for programs designed to reduce the number of school dropouts. The five selected cities were required to match the funds of the foundation with equal funds from other sources.
2. The Pew Charitable Trust Foundation gave $16.5 million to Philadelphia's 110 charter schools. In 1994 this represented the largest single donation ever given by a foundation to a single school district.
3. The Matsushita Foundation is spending $850,000 a year in no more than ten school districts on five- to ten-year school improvement plans that are designed to restructure schools. Teachers and principals must be involved in the process.
4. The W. K. Kellogg Foundation has set up a twenty-year program with three Michigan communities to address the developmental needs of children.
5. The Ford Foundation is assisting twenty-one cities with a total of $2.3 million to reduce the number of school dropouts.
6. The Lily Endowment has appropriated funds to ten cities to improve middle schools and involve teachers in the planning.
7. The Lily Endowment has given up to $5 million to a coalition of business, political, and educational leaders for educational reform in Indianapolis.
8. The John D. and Catherine T. MacArthur Foundation has contributed $40 million in grants over ten years to support educational improvement and community involvement in the schools.

Today, business's control of public education is both indirect, through foundations and grants, and direct, through redesign and management of for-profit, public schools. It is likely that in the next decade business's role in public education will continue to increase, despite the objections of the largest teachers' organizations and many other educators. The success (or failure) of these quasi public-private ventures is likely to be an important topic for some time to come.

# Role of Religious Organizations in Education

The principle of separation of church and state is based on the establishment clause of the First Amendment to the U.S. Constitution, which prohibits state establishment of religion and requires separation of church and state, and the Fourteenth Amendment, which guarantees and safeguards personal liberty from state action impairing it. Since public education is the province of the state, the courts have based most twentieth-century decisions in church-state controversies on the Fourteenth Amendment. It is the principle of separation of church and state and the fundamental concept of personal liberty that have kept public education secular and also have allowed for the development of parochial schools. However, because of the importance of religion in the foundation of the country and its influence on the culture of the nation, the separation of church and state continues to be a complex and controversial issue.

In 1963 the Supreme Court ruled in a landmark school prayer case, *Abingdon School District v. Schempp* (374 U.S. 203) that even voluntary reading of the Bible and recitation of the Lord's Prayer violated the rights of non-Judeo-Christian public school students (see chapter 6, p. 219). More recently in 1994 the Supreme Court's decision in *Kiryas Joel Village School District v. Grumet* (93 U.S. 517) upheld the separation of church and state principle. In 1989 the New York legislature created the Kiryas Joel special education district in a community of all Satmar Hasidic Jews. This allowed Kiryas Joel Village to receive special education funds from the state to educate their special needs children within the community rather than in the neighboring Monroe-Woodbury district where the children were being ridiculed for their distinctive dress and hair. Other Kiryas Joel children attended private religious academies. The New York courts struck down the district as an impermissible union of church and state, and the U.S. Supreme Court, in a six-to-three decision, upheld their ruling.

Although the courts have consistently ruled that religion has no place in public education, the schools, private and political interest groups, and religious organizations regularly challenge these rulings. Many public schools still have prayers at special ceremonies including graduations, and some even allow prayer as part of each school day (see chapter 15, pp. 600–601, and a discussion of principal Bishop Knox, chapter 6, p. 219). A large proportion of public schools, probably a majority, still celebrate religious holidays, particularly Christmas.

During the 1990s the role of religious organizations in public education, particularly fundamental Christian groups, has increased significantly. Although their role remains informal, their impact on public education should not be underestimated.

In 1992, according to an article in *Time Magazine,* candidates supported by conservative Christian groups won in approximately 40 percent of the 5 hundred local and state races, including school board races, contested nationwide (Smolowe 1993, 34). This has given them considerable influence over the curriculum and selection of textbooks and library books.

For example, in Greenville, South Carolina, three fundamental Christians were elected to the twelve-member school board in 1992. At that time, the board was discussing a new curriculum called "Framework for Learning," designed to strengthen reasoning skills, which fundamental Christians claimed was an effort to "sabotage home-taught moral and religious values" (Smolowe, 34). Also, conservative Christians gained a majority on the school board in Vista, California, hoping to influence voters to pass Proposition 174, a school-choice initiative that would have entitled parents to a $2,600 voucher per child for private or parochial school tuition. (The proposition was defeated.)

Numerous curricular attacks have been made by religious groups in an attempt to control what is taught in the public schools. Attacks on sexuality education curriculums, for example, have been made by both fundamental Christians and Roman Catholics who object to references to contraception, abortion, and/or homosexuality. Roman Catholic groups support programs that are "abstinence-based" and teach "sex respect," a program that was found to be "medically inaccurate and marred by sectarian content" by a state judge in Caddo Parish, Louisiana (Boston 1994, 6). Despite these challenges, sexuality education is either recommended or required in forty-seven states (see chapter 11, pp. 461–463). However, there is no doubt that these religious groups have either curtailed or modified some of these curriculums.

Other curricular attacks have been made on Outcome-Based Education (OBE) and school science curriculums. Nancy Schaeffer, president of Family Concerns, an Atlanta-based conservative Christian group, says, "OBE is a plot cooked up by the federal government to seize control of education" (see chapter 8, pp. 305–307 for an extended discussion of OBE). What effects these attacks will have is still undetermined. Even though the Supreme Court ruled in *Edwards v. Aguillard* (107 U.S. 2573, 1987) that public schools may not require the teaching of creationism, fundamental Christian groups continue to promote the concept of creationism in public school curriculums and textbooks. Many textbook publishers, according to an article in *Church and State,* now water down or remove the teaching of evolution using such words as "equal time," "abrupt appearance," and "intelligent design" (Boston 1994, 9).

Frequently, publishers or school districts have decided to either change the content of the books or remove them from the adoption lists rather than face censorship. For example, in Texas a Christian rights group insisted that the state board of education accept a series of changes to sexuality education books being considered for adoption. A total of 4 hundred changes were made by the publisher, but when the group was still not satisfied and threatened to lobby the state legislature, the publisher (Holt, Rinehart & Winston) voluntarily withdrew the books. Literature and reading series have frequently come under attack from religious rights groups. For example, "Impressions" (Harcourt Brace Jovanovich), a children's literature and reading series, has been opposed by the religious right as promoting witchcraft. The books contain fantasy and fairy tales by such children's authors as L. Frank Baum, C. S. Lewis, Dr. Seuss, and A. A. Milne. A three-judge panel in an Illinois Circuit Court of Appeals ruled in favor of the use of the books in the curriculum (*Fleischfresser v. Directors of School District 200*).

The fundamental Christians have attempted to initiate a new professional organization for teachers and parents. The Association of American Educators (AAE) according to director Gary Beckner, represents teachers who believe in traditional values and academic excellence. It promotes a curriculum based on Judeo-Christian values of respect for the law, human life, and self; integrity; cooperation; compassion; and self-discipline. He claims that the main objective of AAE is to refocus public education away from a political agenda to academics (staff, *American Family Association Journal* 1994, 8). There is no doubt that the influence of religious organizations on public education is increasing in spite of the courts' consistent rulings continuing the principle of separation of church and state. In the next five to ten years, it will be interesting to observe how different religious organizations attempt to influence public education legally, legislatively, and practically. It is likely that religious organizations other than fundamental Christians will begin to take a more active role in electing their own candidates to school boards, influencing legislatures through lobbying, and actively seeking influence over curricular matters.

# Nonpublic Schools

The first schools in the United States were private. Even after the establishment of a U.S. public school system, private schools continued to exist, and have grown in numbers from colonial times to the present. The reasons for this growth relate to the nature of nonpublic schools, to the country's democratic creed ("freedom of choice"), societal needs, religious orientations, ethnic and racial concerns, and governmental forces.

## WHAT ARE NONPUBLIC SCHOOLS?

Nonpublic schools are of several types: parochial or church-related schools, secular private schools, and independent schools. Parochial schools are funded by churches or other religious communities. Independent schools are "a collection of accredited private schools not supported generally by public funds, religious communities or great bureaucracies" (Esty 1984, 1). Like independent schools, private schools are not supported by public funds or religious communities, but they may be funded by special interest groups and, unlike independent schools, are frequently not accredited by the regional agencies that accredit nonpublic schools. Most nonpublic schools belong to one of at least twenty-one school membership associations such as the National Catholic Education Association with 8,672 member schools, the Association of Christian Schools International (1,923 schools), American Association of Christian Schools (1,360 schools), National Association of Independent Schools (1,284 schools), and

Nonpublic or private schools have always been one educational choice available to some parents and their children in this country. They may be supported by a special-interest group, a church, or a particular segment of society. Because private schools are not supported by either the federal or state government, they are free to pursue their own curriculums and use their own methods of instruction.

Lutheran Schools-Missouri Synod (1,218 schools).

In recent years more and more schools have focused on the concerns and needs of special groups. For example, by 1991 there were approximately 350 Afrocentric schools with an enrollment of 50 thousand students emphasizing African and African American culture. These schools cite an objective of greater self-esteem and higher test scores for their students, not racial separation. Ivy Leaf Middle School in Philadelphia is an example of a successful Afrocentric school. The students wear green blazers in this academy that emphasizes basic skills and boasts that 60 percent of its students score above the national average in reading and mathematics.

*Enrollment* In 1994, 12 percent of all students enrolled in school from kindergarten through grade twelve attended a nonpublic school. The student population in nonpublic schools totaled 1.7 million in 1920, climbing to a high of 6.3 million in the 1960s, dropping to 5.2 million in the 1980s, and climbing to 5.6 million in 1993–1994. Nonpublic school enrollment is expected to increase to 6.1 million by the year 2000 (U.S. Department of Education, National Center for Education Statistics 1993, 12).

Researchers have attempted to explain why enrollment has fluctuated in nonpublic schools. The increased number of Irish and Italian immigrants caused the number of Roman Catholic schools "to grow from about one hundred in 1840 to about three thousand in the 1880's." Nonpublic school enrollments increased substantially in some parts of the country in the late 1950s and 1960s due to implementation of forced busing for public schools (Kliebard 1969).

In another study to determine why enrollments in fundamentalist Christian schools increased from 160 thousand to 347 thousand in the late 1970s and 1980s, parents explained why they withdrew children from public school: "Poor academic quality, lack of discipline, and the fact that public schools were promoting a philosophy of secular humanism inimical to their religious beliefs" (Butts 1978). Other parents cite the academic success rate of students attending nonpublic schools.

A 1992 study of the National Catholic Educational Association conducted by the Gallup Organization of 1,239 adults including 492 Catholics found that a majority of the general population rated Catholic schools better than public schools in areas such as discipline, small class size, development of moral and ethical behavior, environment that provides less chance for involvement with drugs and alcohol, and safety (1992, 2). Public schools were rated better than Catholic schools on the number and variety of extracurricular activities, a wider range of students from different backgrounds, programs for special needs students, and variety and number of academic courses offered (p. 10). The study also found that 70 percent of all surveyed and 80 percent of Catholics surveyed favored a voucher system to provide parents funds allowing them to select private over public schools for their children.

Catholic school children score higher on standardized tests than public school children. Sociologist James Coleman determined that 3.4 percent of children in Catholic schools drop out of school compared to 14.3 percent of public school children. In addition, 83 percent of Catholic school children attend college compared to 50 percent of public school students. Some contend that these statistics are due to the selective nature of Catholic schools. However, the National Catholic Educational Association insists that Catholic schools enroll 90 percent of all students who apply for admission, and once admitted few are expelled. Albert Shanker, president of the American Federation of Teachers (AFT), claims that it is that 10 percent who make the difference. "Any teacher will tell you that the problem is one or two kids, not everybody" (Rachlin and Glastris 1989, 62). Many nonpublic schools, particularly Catholic, Lutheran, and independent, have attempted to increase their minority enrollment while still remaining selective. In Catholic schools, for example, minority enrollment increased from 11 percent of its student population in the 1970s to 23 percent in 1991. Increases in minority enrollment have occurred in other nonpublic schools at a less significant rate since nonchurch supported schools tend to be significantly more expensive to attend.

## RELATIONSHIP BETWEEN STATES AND NONPUBLIC SCHOOLS

Through a U.S. Supreme Court ruling in 1925 (*Pierce v. Society of Sisters,* 268 U.S. 510, 1925), states have been given general authority over nonpublic schools with respect to compulsory attendance, health, safety, and quality of instruction. The "quality of instruction" component of this ruling caused problems in the late 1970s, when some states attempted to enforce legislative mandates requiring the successful completion of minimum competency tests as a requirement for high school graduation. Most nonpublic schools refused to become involved in minimum competency testing on the grounds of separation of church and state. Nonpublic schools were unwilling to fund the administration of the tests in their schools. In 1992 forty states required competency testing at various grade levels with either state or local agencies setting the standards. Although many nonpublic schools require some type of testing, frequently sponsored by their school membership association, only a few require the same tests taken by public school students in the state (U.S. Department of Education, National Center for Education Statistics 1993, 149). Since nonpublic schools are not directly funded through tax money, they contend that they are not required to meet legislative mandates, particularly when complying with these mandates requires additional funding that they will not be provided through legislative apportionment.

To date the U.S. Supreme Court has not clarified the scope of the state's authority and duty to regulate the means by which all children receive an education, and state courts have provided conflicting opinions on state regulation of private schools. In 1980 the Ohio Supreme Court, on the grounds of free exercise of rights, invalidated comprehensive state regulations governing all aspects of education in nonpublic schools. Also in 1980 the Kentucky State Supreme Court struck down state regulations of nonpublic schools stating that the regulations interfered with the state constitutional guarantee that parents cannot be required to send their children to a school to which they are conscientiously opposed. However, the Supreme Courts of Hawaii, Iowa, Michigan, Nebraska, North Dakota, and Vermont have upheld state minimum requirements, such as teacher certification standards, prescribed courses, and maintenance of public records on the grounds of the state's obligation to ensure an educated citizenry (McCarthy and Cambrone-McCabe 1992, 43–44).

Many individuals, groups, agencies, and branches of government affect U.S. education. Although the U.S. Constitution gives control and operation of the public schools to the states through the Tenth Amendment, federal and local

## 13-2

### POINTS TO REMEMBER

- State control of public schools is established in each state's constitution. Therefore, how schools are governed differs from state to state.
- The governor's role in education is indirect, whereas the state legislature's role is direct. The governor sets a legislative agenda. The legislature passes laws that directly affect the governance and administration of schools within the state.
- Legislatures delegate authority to state school boards to translate state statutes into policy. State boards give the policy to state education agencies or departments to develop curriculums. Chief state

school officers serve a regulatory function to ensure that local education agencies are implementing state policy.

- Each state has a supreme court, which is the final authority of constitutional law within the state judiciary. The appellate courts hear appeals from the circuit or trial courts. A case related to education is usually heard first by the circuit courts and later appealed to appellate and supreme courts.
- Local school boards are usually elected and oversee the implementation of state policy within the local education agency or school district. The board appoints the superintendent, who is the chief administrative officer of the local school district.

- In recent years business has had an increasing role in the public schools, moving from indirect influence of funding special projects to direct control by funding and managing individual public schools. The role of business has increased, in part, due to the passing of charter school laws in several states.
- The role of religious organizations, particularly fundamental Christian groups, has increased in public education through lobbying and election of members to state and local political office including school boards.
- Twelve percent of all students enrolled in school attend non-public schools and this percentage is expected to increase, providing diversity to U.S. education.

governments and all levels of the courts are involved in and have some degree of control over education. In addition, nongovernmental agencies, professional organizations, religious organizations, and businesses indirectly influence education through funding, lobbying, and creating task forces to study controversial issues in education. The direct role of business in public education has increased through charter school laws and business' direct funding and control of some public schools. Similarly the direct role of some religious organizations has increased as they have used their strength to elect public officials to such offices as school board memberships. Education in the United States is thus public in its broadest sense—involving government, the courts, and agencies and businesses; however, many point with concern to what they consider to be the privatization of public education. Ironically, others worry that governance of public education is becoming increasingly federalized, shifting control from states and local school districts to the U.S. Congress and courts.

## For Thought/Discussion

1. How would you balance the rights of the nonreligious with the rights of Christian fundamentalists in determining school curriculum?
2. Do you believe it is appropriate for a state legislature to assume control of a school district? Why or why not?
3. Do you see the role of business in education as a positive or negative factor? Explain.

## For Further Reading/Reference

Blair, L. H., Brounstein, S. L., Hatry, H. P., and Morley, E. 1990. *Guidelines for school-business partnerships in science and mathematics.* Lanham, MO: Urban Institute Press. A discussion of obstacles to and successes of twenty-four school-business relationships across the United States; recommendations for beginning a school-business partnership are presented.

Chubb, J. E., and Moe, T. M. 1990. *Politics, markets, and American schools.* Washington, DC: Brookings Institute. Views of why and how governmental controls present problems for schools; discussions of the author's proposal of parent-school choice as a remedy for school reform.

Hurwitz, H. L. 1989. *The last angry principal.* Portland, OR: Halcyon House. An elaboration of the chapter's opening anecdote that details the author's battle against a school system; a discussion of what the author believes must be done in disciplined schools of excellence.

Jennings, J. F. 1992. Lessons learned in Washington, D.C. *Phi Delta Kappan. 74* (4), 303–307. The author examines the importance of Congress and the president working together when education bills are proposed, particularly on providing adequate funding to support legislative change.

Staff. April, 1994. Theme issue on the separation of church and state. *Church and State. 47* (4). This entire issue, in a journal published by Americans for Separation of Church and State, is dedicated to the constitutional principle. Several articles deal with specific examples of how fundamental Christian groups are affecting public schools.

Joel Pett

Cullum/Copley News Service

**CHAPTER OBJECTIVES**

After studying this chapter, you should be able to:

- Discuss the politics of funding for education.
- Describe how local governments fund education.
- Describe how state governments fund education.
- Explain why school districts are not equally funded.
- Explain how public/private partnerships could equalize funding for public education.
- Analyze how litigation and legislation are affecting state funding for public education.

- Discuss how courts and legislatures are attempting to equalize funding.
- Discuss the federal role in funding education.
- Define block grants.
- Discuss the variety of ways in which nonpublic schools are funded.
- Examine the controversy of public funding for nonpublic education.

# Chapter 14

# FUNDING EDUCATION

*N*EWTON, MASS.—Lauren Bisceglia has stopped buying the sturdy canvas out of which her home-economics students have always made tote bags. "We can't afford that anymore," the Brown Junior High School teacher says.

These days, the totes are cut from cheaper cloth she buys by the pound at a factory-outlet store.

Despite the rising cost of such materials and an increase in the number of students she teaches, Ms. Bisceglia has only $1,800—the same amount she has received for each of the past four years—to buy sewing goods and food supplies for her 300 students.

As long as the students carry a light load in the elegantly stitched bags, Ms. Bisceglia explains, they will hold up fine. But if they use the totes as book bags, the cloth will tear.

While Ms. Bisceglia's forced economies on tote bags are of relatively minor importance in the scheme of things, they epitomize the plight of the school district that employs her. By scaling back on expenditures, both the home-economics teacher and the Newton public schools are getting the job done, but the financial stress is causing the fabric to fray.

In each of the past three years, district officials have been forced to make cutbacks in staffing, services, and programs in order to erase a budget deficit. . . .

Like most school districts in Massachusetts—and throughout New England for that matter—Newton's financial vitality has been sapped by the region's distressed economy.

Irwin Blumer, superintendent of the Newton schools, contends that the nation's public schools can no longer rely on the vagaries of local property taxes and undependable state revenue for their funding.

"It goes beyond Newton and Massachusetts at this point," he said. "There's something wrong with the whole process." . . .

Linda Puretz and her husband moved to Newton in 1977—primarily because of the educational system.

"Imagine our feeling 13, 14 years later . . . of being in a situation where the school system is not what we had hoped for," Ms. Puretz said.

A memorandum from the principal of Bowen Elementary School, where Ms. Puretz's children attend school, outlines what they have to look forward to next year: no room for a computer lab, resulting in limited student access; no room for a nurse's office, meaning reduced nursing support; and 5th-grade classes with 28 students and 6th grades with 29 students.

"The large class sizes have shocked people in a way that other cuts haven't, primarily because this is very visible to people," Ms. Puretz said. . . .

Two years ago, the district started charging $25 user fees for high-school students who wanted to play sports. This year, the school committee voted to raise the fee to $50 and to introduce a $25 fee at the junior-high level. Junior-high students will also pay a fee for some music and drama programs. Later this month, the school committee will vote on a $100 user fee for high-school students. . . .

"We're saying, 'Parents, you pay for what the public used to think was for the public good,' " said Jerold Katz, principal of Bowen Elementary.

From: K. Diegmueller, May 29, 1991, 1, 10.

As he sat in the living room of his white-frame home on this city's hardscrabble, mostly Hispanic west side, Demetrio P. Rodriguez spoke intensely about how poor schoolchildren have been robbed by the Texas Legislature.

The state doesn't give property-poor school systems enough money, leaving them at a disadvantage, he complained. "We want no more or no less than our fair share," said Mr. Rodriguez, a quiet-spoken 67-year-old retired sheet-metal worker. "But people have been so greedy and uncaring."

It is a lament that Mr. Rodriguez has uttered many times in the more than 25 years that he has been the name and face behind the nation's longest-running lawsuit over state funding for public schools. . . .

Three times he has won verdicts from the Texas Supreme Court, which in turn has ordered the State Legislature to overhaul the state school funding formula. But each plan has been contested by Mr. Rodriguez's lawyers.

"Sometimes when I think about it all, I get depressed," said Mr. Rodriguez, who says he dropped out of school to join the Navy and realized the importance of education too late to save himself.

Mr. Rodriguez recalls the days when rocks were thrown through the windows of his home and anonymous telephone callers threatened him. Even fellow workers at Kelly Air Force Base derided him. But Mr. Rodriguez continues fighting for well-financed schools. To that end, he appears at virtually every court hearing (and to date they have run into the hundreds).

From: W. Celis 3d, April 10, 1994, 30.

In the past few years, angry parents and school district officials have turned increasingly to state courts to right the wrongs wrought by unequal school financing from district to district.

In Missouri, for example, 25 schoolchildren and 89 school districts sued the state for not providing all students with an equal opportunity for a good education.

During a three-week trial, Circuit Judge Byron Kinder heard testimony about the state's complicated formula for distributing money to schools. The formula's result: Annual spending per student ranges from $2,653 in some districts to $9,750 in others.

In January, Kinder ruled that education is a fundamental state right and that Missouri's method of paying for public schools "does not pass constitutional muster." School facilities, he said, vary "from the golden to the god-awful." The disparities come not from differing student needs, Kinder wrote, but from differing local property values. Some disparities are "simply irrational," he said.

"The amount of money available for schools can and does make a difference in the educational opportunities that can be provided to Missouri children," Kinder wrote in his 100-page decision.

School finance experts call the Missouri decision a landmark ruling—particularly because Kinder said that education is a fundamental right and that the finance system is irrational. The state is expected to appeal.

From: R. M. Jennings, May 27, 1993, 119.

---

*W*hile most citizens of this country believe in the democratic ideal of equal education for all, the reality is that the quality of education is hardly equal for all children in all school districts. Because the system of educational funding is so heavily dependent on state and local tax revenues, which in turn are so dependent on the economy in various areas of the country, schools even within the same state receive unequal allotments of money. In this chapter we will examine how funding contributes to quality of education, how the courts and legislatures have responded to inequality in funding, and how nonpublic education is funded.

## Funding Public Education

How public schools are funded varies from state to state. Some schools receive most of their funding from the local government rather than state or federal sources. For example, 89 percent of New Hampshire's revenues for public schools comes from local sources. On the other hand, over 90 percent of Hawaii's public school revenues come from the state. New Mexico and Washington receive more than 70 percent of their revenue from the state (Walters 1994, 2–3). Although the percentage of federal funding for schools also varies, most states receive less than

10 percent of their education revenues from the federal government (see map #15 in Student Atlas, p. 584).

## EDUCATIONAL FUNDING AND POLITICS

We might want to think that educational funding is not affected by politics. Unfortunately, this is not so. In 1978–1979, during the Carter administration, for example, 9.8 percent of all the money spent on U.S. public education came from the federal government, 45.6 percent from the states, and 44.6 percent from local sources. By 1988 there had been a shift in the percentage of funding received from each of the three sources: 6.3 percent came from the federal government, 49.5 percent from state funds, and 44.1 percent from local sources (U.S. Department of Education 1990b, 80). In the first two years of Bill Clinton's presidency more federal education legislation was passed than during the entire previous decade. It is likely that this legislation will translate into a larger percentage of federal dollars in the education funding equation.

Why shifts in federal funding for education occur is an interesting political phenomenon. The more politically liberal the federal government, the greater the likelihood of more centralized funding for education because state and federal aid programs equalize educational opportunity for students in all schools. The usual method of funding education, local property taxes, is necessarily unequal since the tax base of richer communities is much larger than that of poorer communities. Hence, when politically liberal administrations gain power, the funds for education generally are equalized by augmenting the tax base of local communities with federal and state grants. On the other hand, the more politically conservative the federal government, the greater will be decentralized funding for education. Decentralization occurs because of a belief in home rule, keeping the center of government as close to the population as possible.

## LOCAL FUNDING OF EDUCATION

Property taxation originated on the U.S. frontier, where wealth was measured in land. It remains a widely used form of taxation because it produces a fairly stable rate of collection and is difficult to evade. Property taxes are also used to fund other municipal services, such as police, fire, parks, libraries, and municipal roads. Most states have laws that place limits on the property tax rates local school districts can levy—a greater rate requires approval by the voters of the district.

Today, local taxation provides the majority of the school funds in half the states. On an average, 43.9 percent of school revenues come from local sources. Ninety-eight percent of that local school revenue is generated from property taxes, which are based on the assessed value of real estate (residential and commercial land and buildings) and personal property (automobiles, jewelry, stocks, and bonds).

When funding for schools is primarily based on local property taxes, significant inequities develop. The richer the district, the higher the assessed property values; the larger the tax base, the greater the funding for local schools. For example, assume that local school district A has an assessed valuation of $100 million and a one-thousand-student school population and that local school

**TABLE 14-1**

## The Massachusetts Supreme Court recently invalidated wide disparities in local education spending

Figures for Wellesley and Lowell, Mass., school districts (FY '93 unless noted)

| Wellesley | | Lowell |
|---|---|---|
| 3,057 | Total enrollment | 14,098 |
| $1,042,000 | Value of assessed taxable property, per student | $208,000 |
| $11.45 | Property-tax rate (per $1,000 assessed value) | $17.72 |
| $6,797 | Revenue per student raised from local property taxes | $1,803 |
| $46,985 | Average teacher salary | $31,987 |
| 82% | Percentage of teachers with master's degrees | 47% |
| 191 | Number of students per guidance counselor | 252 |
| $171 | Library spending per student (FY '92) | $3.50 |

Note: *USN&WR*—Basic data: Lowell Public Schools, Wellesley Public Schools, Massachusetts Teachers Association.

From: *U.S. News & World Report,* August 2, 1993, p. 45.

**The figures in this table clearly indicate the disparity in school funding between the Wellesley and Lowell, Massachusetts, school districts. The Massachusetts Supreme Court recently invalidated these wide disparities at the same time that courts in at least four other states found their systems of funding education with local taxes unconstitutional. The movement to more equitable funding, and thus more equitable educational opportunities, has begun.**

district B has an assessed valuation of $50 million for one thousand students. A tax rate of $2 per $100 of assessed valuation produces $2 million in school district A and $1 million in school district B. Hence, the schoolchildren in district B receive only half the funding from local property taxes that the children in district A receive. (A good example of this can be seen in table 14.1.)

Other local funding sources for schools include local sales taxes and special room taxes in hotels and motels, if the voters decide to implement them. However, poorer districts are likely to have less flexibility assessing these forms of taxation because few nonresidents spend money there. Therefore, district A is likely to be able to raise more revenue from these types of taxation than district B, making funding of education even more unequal. According to Alan Hickrod, director of the Center for the Study of Educational Finance at Illinois State University, if school funding remains dependent on property tax, larger and larger differentials in funding per pupil will occur, resulting in significant differences in resources and facilities available to students. According to Hickrod, a move away from property tax to fund public schools will mean the loss of some local control, but "on a tradeoff, the voter would probably go for property tax relief and not local control" (phone interview, August 3, 1994).

There are numerous examples of what can happen when school districts within a state are unequally funded. In spring 1992, after voters rejected property tax increases three times, the Kalkaska, Michigan, public schools closed three months early for summer vacation. Kalkaska administrators said they had run out of money to operate the schools, which were funded at a level of $3,800 per pupil. Neighboring Bloomfield Hills schools were funded at a level of $10,000 per pupil. In 1994, when an existing tax was defeated by voters in Buncombe County, North Carolina, eliminating $300,000 from the school budget, superintendent Frank Yaeger filed a suit against Buncombe County commissioners over the distribution of sales tax money to the schools. In addition, he joined a group of other North Carolina school districts challenging the way the state pays "low wealth" (property tax poor) equalization funds to poor counties.

### *Viewpoint* Laying a Firm Foundation

In a small town in western Missouri, some bighearted people have taken the germ of an idea and developed it into impressive funding for their local school district. Community members in Lexington, a town of fewer than 6,000 people, organized the Minutemen Academic Foundation, Inc., which in less than three years has raised more than $96,000 in pledges and materials for the approximately 1,100 students in its district. . . .

[Terry] Thompson [foundation secretary-treasurer and bank president] said members of the newly formed foundation sat down with administrators and the school board to determine needs. The initial focus was on the high school. [Marvin] Misemel [founder of the foundation] provided the 15-member group, which casually refers to itself as "the committee," with a list, saying, "These are the basic needs in every department. You tell me how you want to go with it." The committee decided that replacing the school's 1960s chemistry tables was a top priority.

The cost of new tables was estimated to be $30,000. New biology tables, also badly needed, would cost an additional $7,000, most of the high school's equipment budget that year. The committee contacted the local hospital, and, over a two-year period, the Lafayette Regional Health Center donated $34,000 worth of tables, a centrifuge, a spectrometer, a high-resolution microscope, and other laboratory equipment.

The hospital contribution got the ball rolling. The next priority was replacing the school's eight-year-old computers. The estimated cost to provide a new lab—$60,000. Committee members were able to find enough people to make $1,000 commitments, payable over five years, to pay for the new lab. The high school earned a vocational discount by agreeing to offer vocational-oriented business courses, and the local vocational school agreed to pay half of the remaining bill.

After its initial success, the committee decided to begin looking to the future, setting up an endowment for the district.

> From: S. Buchholz, "Laying a Firm Foundation," *School & Community,* Spring 1993, 14–15.

### STATE FUNDING OF EDUCATION

Depending on the formula used, state aid may help equalize funding among local school districts, which receive, on average, 49.8 percent of their funds from the state. Usually funding is allocated by the state legislature and administered through state departments of education. Often, however, state allocations still do not make up for inequities in local property taxes.

State funds for education come from a variety of tax sources, including one or a combination of the following: sales, income, inheritance, gift, use, and occupation taxes; franchise and license fees; and state lotteries. It is not only the amount of revenue collected that affects the funding of schools but also how that revenue is allocated to local districts.

*State Aid Formulas*     The allocation of state revenue to local districts occurs through state aid formulas, the three most common of which are a flat grant, equalization grant, and foundation grant. **Flat grants** are usually based on the district's average daily attendance during the previous school year; each district receives the same amount for each student in attendance. Flat grants do not take into consideration variations among school districts in local taxing ability. Adjustments are made, however, for special students, such as the disabled, and, in some cases, for school districts with large fluctuations in student population during the school year. **Equalization grants** provide the same guaranteed yield to rich and poor districts, which tax themselves at the same rate. Equalization formulas require rich districts to give the state surplus tax revenue above the state per pupil funding level and thus guarantee that this money is distributed to poor districts to make up the difference between the guaranteed per pupil yield and actual lower tax yield. **Foundation grants** ensure a minimum level of revenue per pupil by targeting state aid to poor districts. The state prescribes the required foundation level per pupil and a minimum tax effort to be made by the district. If the district is willing to make the prescribed tax effort but fails to raise the foundation amount because of low property valuation, the state makes up the difference with a foundation grant.

Recent polls such as the 1993 Phi Delta Kappa/Gallup Poll show that the majority of the public recognizes the inequality of funding for public education that exists within their state (54 percent), believes that educational opportunities are not equal throughout their state (62 percent) and the amount of funding affects the quality of education (68 percent); contends that more should be done to improve the quality of education in poorer school districts (90 percent); and would be willing to pay higher taxes to improve the quality of education in poorer states and communities (68 percent). Finally, the majority say that the money allocated in their state should be the same for all students whether in poor or rich districts (88 percent). However, these beliefs do not always translate into the actions of the citizens (see taxpayers' revolts, pp. 563–564).

After the Kalkaska public schools closed their doors, the Michigan legislature eliminated the property tax as the main source of funding for public education, replacing it with increases in sales tax, cigarette tax, and state income tax. This new plan calls for a minimum of $4,260 per pupil funding, increasing the level of funding for Kalkaska's schools. Not surprisingly, the residents of such affluent communities as Bloomfield Hills did not like the idea of paying higher state taxes to increase the funding of schools in Kalkaska and other poor communities.

Some states set qualifying or minimum local tax rates, which districts must levy in order to qualify for state funds. This is to prevent wealthy districts from using state equalization funds rather than local funds for public education. Conversely, some state constitutions or laws set ceilings for the amount of local

*(continued on p. 554)*

TABLE 14-2

## Direct General Expenditures Per Capita of State and Local Governments for all Functions and for Education, by Level and State: 1990–1991

| | | Education expenditures per capita | | | | | | | |
| | | Total | | Elementary and secondary education | | Higher education | | Other education[2] | |
| State | Total, all direct general expenditures per capita[1] | Amount | As a percent of all functions | Amount | As a percent of all functions | Amount | As a percent of all functions | Amount | As a percent of all functions |
| 1 | 2 | 3 | 4 | 5 | 6 | 7 | 8 | 9 | 10 |
| United States | $3,587.33 | $1,226.53 | 34.2 | $863.06 | 24.1 | $312.28 | 8.7 | $51.20 | 1.4 |
| Alabama | 2,942.29 | 1,067.18 | 36.3 | 615.79 | 20.9 | 351.14 | 11.9 | 100.25 | 3.4 |
| Alaska | 9,776.41 | 2,285.59 | 23.4 | 1,696.74 | 17.4 | 493.32 | 5.0 | 95.53 | 1.0 |
| Arizona | 3,421.61 | 1,228.87 | 35.9 | 795.53 | 23.3 | 397.07 | 11.6 | 36.28 | 1.1 |
| Arkansas | 2,439.92 | 978.47 | 40.1 | 619.43 | 25.4 | 281.24 | 11.5 | 77.79 | 3.2 |
| California | 3,978.45 | 1,268.68 | 31.9 | 872.23 | 21.9 | 350.42 | 8.8 | 46.03 | 1.2 |
| Colorado | 3,418.99 | 1,280.41 | 37.4 | 854.20 | 25.0 | 401.31 | 11.7 | 24.90 | 0.7 |
| Connecticut | 4,443.02 | 1,320.65 | 29.7 | 1,052.47 | 23.7 | 212.01 | 4.8 | 56.18 | 1.3 |
| Delaware | 4,092.90 | 1,490.19 | 36.4 | 845.01 | 20.6 | 536.13 | 13.1 | 109.06 | 2.7 |
| District of Columbia | 6,935.39 | 1,188.62 | 17.1 | 1,021.45 | 14.7 | 167.17 | 2.4 | – | – |
| Florida | 3,412.17 | 1,113.97 | 32.6 | 834.52 | 24.5 | 228.30 | 6.7 | 51.16 | 1.5 |
| Georgia | 3,213.36 | 1,085.82 | 33.8 | 801.73 | 24.9 | 234.78 | 7.3 | 49.31 | 1.5 |
| Hawaii | 4,597.48 | 1,118.06 | 24.3 | 690.03 | 15.0 | 411.16 | 8.9 | 16.87 | 0.4 |
| Idaho | 2,852.09 | 1,104.90 | 38.7 | 726.61 | 25.5 | 334.57 | 11.7 | 43.72 | 1.5 |
| Illinois | 3,293.58 | 1,101.26 | 33.4 | 759.95 | 23.1 | 284.48 | 8.6 | 56.83 | 1.7 |
| Indiana | 2,993.85 | 1,236.50 | 41.3 | 816.49 | 27.3 | 370.01 | 12.4 | 50.00 | 1.7 |
| Iowa | 3,416.89 | 1,322.94 | 38.7 | 820.10 | 24.0 | 450.34 | 13.2 | 52.51 | 1.5 |
| Kansas | 3,199.99 | 1,234.66 | 38.6 | 803.64 | 25.1 | 390.79 | 12.2 | 40.23 | 1.3 |
| Kentucky | 2,946.69 | 1,012.40 | 34.4 | 623.03 | 21.1 | 303.76 | 10.3 | 85.61 | 2.9 |
| Louisiana | 3,350.68 | 1,049.65 | 31.3 | 714.54 | 21.3 | 276.29 | 8.2 | 58.81 | 1.8 |
| Maine | 3,628.44 | 1,279.86 | 35.3 | 962.95 | 26.5 | 268.55 | 7.4 | 48.36 | 1.3 |
| Maryland | 3,716.45 | 1,323.32 | 35.6 | 875.59 | 23.6 | 396.49 | 10.7 | 51.24 | 1.4 |
| Massachusetts | 4,104.51 | 1,059.31 | 25.8 | 807.21 | 19.7 | 205.58 | 5.0 | 46.53 | 1.1 |
| Michigan | 3,603.62 | 1,385.97 | 38.5 | 945.93 | 26.2 | 404.46 | 11.2 | 35.59 | 1.0 |
| Minnesota | 4,250.02 | 1,412.03 | 33.2 | 963.78 | 22.7 | 384.92 | 9.1 | 63.33 | 1.5 |
| Mississippi | 2,695.87 | 1,002.40 | 37.2 | 633.69 | 23.5 | 316.82 | 11.8 | 51.89 | 1.9 |
| Missouri | 2,663.86 | 1,034.57 | 38.8 | 761.71 | 28.6 | 239.19 | 9.0 | 33.66 | 1.3 |
| Montana | 3,503.02 | 1,304.97 | 37.3 | 918.86 | 26.2 | 260.05 | 7.4 | 126.06 | 3.6 |
| Nebraska | 3,266.98 | 1,345.02 | 41.2 | 889.57 | 27.2 | 409.48 | 12.5 | 45.97 | 1.4 |
| Nevada | 3,740.07 | 1,193.04 | 31.9 | 917.67 | 24.5 | 250.63 | 6.7 | 24.74 | 0.7 |
| New Hampshire | 3,057.74 | 1,132.66 | 37.0 | 884.26 | 28.9 | 216.79 | 7.1 | 31.60 | 1.0 |
| New Jersey | 4,093.46 | 1,357.98 | 33.2 | 1,081.39 | 26.4 | 237.93 | 5.8 | 38.66 | 0.9 |
| New Mexico | 3,358.76 | 1,318.69 | 39.3 | 831.26 | 24.7 | 438.44 | 13.1 | 48.99 | 1.5 |
| New York | 5,457.12 | 1,540.66 | 28.2 | 1,211.17 | 22.2 | 268.91 | 4.9 | 60.59 | 1.1 |
| North Carolina | $3,035.26 | $1,179.96 | 38.9 | $777.16 | 25.6 | $364.72 | 12.0 | $38.08 | 1.3 |

| State | Total, all direct general expenditures per capita[1] | Education expenditures per capita | | | | | | | |
|---|---|---|---|---|---|---|---|---|---|
| | | Total | | Elementary and secondary education | | Higher education | | Other education[2] | |
| | | Amount | As a percent of all functions | Amount | As a percent of all functions | Amount | As a percent of all functions | Amount | As a percent of all functions |
| 1 | 2 | 3 | 4 | 5 | 6 | 7 | 8 | 9 | 10 |
| North Dakota | 3,541.28 | 1,337.35 | 37.8 | 771.06 | 21.8 | 508.76 | 14.4 | 57.53 | 1.6 |
| Ohio | 3,194.63 | 1,139.78 | 35.7 | 804.51 | 25.2 | 290.85 | 9.1 | 44.41 | 1.4 |
| Oklahoma | 2,908.26 | 1,080.35 | 37.1 | 751.13 | 25.8 | 286.79 | 9.9 | 42.42 | 1.5 |
| Oregon | 3,631.26 | 1,333.60 | 36.7 | 898.86 | 24.8 | 390.27 | 10.7 | 44.47 | 1.2 |
| Pennsylvania | 3,192.89 | 1,124.23 | 35.2 | 856.17 | 26.8 | 177.84 | 5.6 | 90.22 | 2.8 |
| Rhode Island | 3,867.15 | 1,207.95 | 31.2 | 841.51 | 21.8 | 277.13 | 7.2 | 89.31 | 2.3 |
| South Carolina | 3,138.01 | 1,190.03 | 37.9 | 801.18 | 25.5 | 329.45 | 10.5 | 59.40 | 1.9 |
| South Dakota | 2,949.53 | 1,063.21 | 36.0 | 775.83 | 26.3 | 243.65 | 8.3 | 43.73 | 1.5 |
| Tennessee | 2,757.08 | 918.72 | 33.3 | 572.11 | 20.8 | 291.92 | 10.6 | 54.70 | 2.0 |
| Texas | 2,895.44 | 1,147.87 | 39.6 | 802.98 | 27.7 | 318.92 | 11.0 | 25.97 | 0.9 |
| Utah | 3,015.33 | 1,273.66 | 42.2 | 773.28 | 25.6 | 454.43 | 15.1 | 45.95 | 1.5 |
| Vermont | 3,864.55 | 1,588.00 | 41.1 | 1,043.91 | 27.0 | 443.46 | 11.5 | 100.64 | 2.6 |
| Virginia | 3,318.70 | 1,265.32 | 38.1 | 887.49 | 26.7 | 328.14 | 9.9 | 49.70 | 1.5 |
| Washington | 3,810.26 | 1,417.77 | 37.2 | 971.72 | 25.5 | 382.34 | 10.0 | 63.71 | 1.7 |
| West Virginia | 2,865.60 | 1,096.81 | 38.3 | 754.88 | 26.3 | 287.87 | 10.0 | 54.05 | 1.9 |
| Wisconsin | 3,672.24 | 1,423.04 | 38.8 | 956.80 | 26.1 | 412.37 | 11.2 | 53.88 | 1.5 |
| Wyoming | 5,063.84 | 1,824.46 | 36.0 | 1,261.23 | 24.9 | 497.57 | 9.8 | 65.65 | 1.3 |

[1] Includes state and local government expenditures for education services, social services and income maintenance, transportation, public safety, environment and housing, governmental administration, interest on general debt, and other general expenditures. Includes intergovernmental expenditure to the federal government.

[2] Includes assistance and subsidies to individuals and private institutions for elementary, secondary, and higher education, as well as miscellaneous education expenditures.

– Not applicable.

Note: Per capita amounts are based on population figures as of April 1, 1991, and are computed on the basis of amounts rounded to the nearest thousand. Because of rounding, details may not add to totals.

Source: U.S. Department of Commerce, Bureau of the Census, Governments Division, Government Finances: 1990–91, Series GF/91-5. (This table was prepared February 1994.)

From: U.S. Department of Education, National Center for Education Statistics, *Digest of Education Statistics* (1994) (NCES94-293). Washington, D.C.: U.S. Government Printing Office, 39. Courtesy of Vance Grant.

**Each state has its own formula for equalizing spending on education in its districts. There is not, however, any formula for equalizing spending among the states. Thus, the states vary greatly on the amount they spend on education.**

tax dollars that can be spent on public schools. Thus, if districts are below the upper limits, they may authorize new taxes on property; districts whose spending has reached the maximum may not levy new tax monies for schools. Both minimums and maximums are designed primarily to help equalize educational spending across districts within a state. There is, however, no formula for equalizing funding among the states where great diversity still exists. For example, in 1990–1991 Alaska spent over $1,600 per capita on public education, whereas Alabama spent $615 per capita (see table 14.2 on p. 552). Some of this differential can be attributed to the relative cost of living in each state, but large differentials exist even between states with similar costs of living.

*Fluctuating State Funding*   The level of state support for public education fluctuates depending on the level of federal and local funding available. Until 1930 more than 80 percent of public school revenue came from local districts. However, the percentage of local dollars as compared to state and federal dollars spent on education decreased steadily after 1930. From 1930 through 1960 the states' share of educational funding increased from 16.9 to 39.1 percent of all dollars spent on public education. The percentage of state dollars compared to local and federal dollars spent on education remained relatively constant from the mid-1940s through the mid-1970s. The states' share of educational spending then increased from 42.2 percent in 1974–1975 to a high of 49.7 in 1986–1987. We can better understand how substantial this increased share is by looking at figure 14.1 on page 555. While a similar 7.5 percent increase in states' share of educational funding occurred in both time frames, the first occurred over a nearly thirty-year period and the second over only a twelve-year period. When the states' share of educational funding increases, the federal and local shares decrease. It is interesting to note that beginning in 1991–1992 (see figure 14.1), the trend began to shift with a slightly larger percentage of funding for public education coming from local dollars. It is likely that as states move toward equalization and foundation funding this trend will again reverse. A larger share of funding for public education is likely to come from federal dollars in the next several years as the education bills of the Clinton administration are put into law.

*Private Alternatives to State and Local Funding*   In 1994 eleven states had passed laws (six others were considering them), allowing schools or school districts to be chartered by groups of citizens, including businesses and foundations. These schools can then develop new innovative management and educational strategies including creative ways to fund public schools, often through public-private partnerships (see chapter 13, pp. 530–535). It is too early to tell the effect these new school organizations will have on funding for public education. In 1992 only $0.3 billion of $1.8 billion in private funding for K–12 education went to public schools; the rest went to nonpublic schools (Council for Aid to Education). However, in the future the funding and organizational structure of charter schools and other public-private partnerships may provide an answer to the problem of inequality of funding in a limited number of school districts in which these partnerships are possible.

The largest charter school program in 1994 was Philadelphia's Schools Collaborative, funded in part with more than $16 million ($8.3 million for the first three years and $7.8 million for the next three years) from the Pew Charitable Trust, headquartered in Philadelphia. The funding from this grant goes to

FIGURE 14-1

## Sources of Revenue for Public Elementary and Secondary Schools: 1969–1970 to 1991–1992

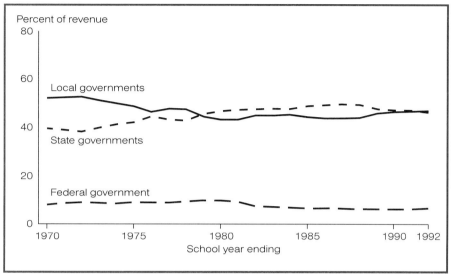

Source: U.S. Department of Education, National Center for Education Statistics, *Statistics of State School Systems; Revenues and Expenditures for Public Elementary and Secondary Education;* and Common Core of Data surveys. 1990–1992 data obtained from table prepared in April 1994.

From: U.S. Department of Education, National Center for Education Statistics, *The Condition of Education,* Vol. I (1991). Washington, DC: U.S. Government Printing Office, 88.

**Most school systems receive funding from local or state sources. While the states differ in the amount of funding derived from local, state, and federal sources, most states receive less than 10 percent of their funds from the federal government.**

Philadelphia's comprehensive high schools, institutions attempting to educate primarily disadvantaged and minority students who do not attend one of the city's twelve special-admissions high schools, which attract the best students. The Schools Collaborative, in operation since 1988, has attempted to break down the "anonymity of the neighborhood high schools by creating 'charters,' or semiautonomous schools, within their walls" (Bradley 1992, 17). Each charter serves between 2 hundred and 4 hundred heterogeneously mixed students and has a team of ten to twelve teachers who together plan curriculum and instruction, which is often interdisciplinary.

"What Pew's money has purchased . . . is enriching professional opportunities for seasoned teachers that have spiced the charters with academically rich programs" (Bradley, 18). From the district, charter schools receive discretionary funds for materials and release time for charter coordinators to plan programs. The goal of Philadelphia's charter schools is not to provide equitable funding for disadvantaged schools and students, but, instead to reform a languishing, urban school system. However, the funds from Pew have the effect of equalizing funding. It will be interesting to see if the funding from Pew and/or other private sources continues in Philadelphia, and if it does not, how the schools will continue to implement the reforms that have begun during the period of the

556 CH. 14 FUNDING EDUCATION

grant. This, of course, is one of the major controversies surrounding public-private partnerships for public education. Will businesses and foundations provide long-term fiscal support for the schools they adopt?

## FEDERAL FUNDING OF EDUCATION

The U.S. Congress has no obligation to provide funding for public education but does so voluntarily. Federal aid to education comes through grants from several federal agencies: the U.S. Department of Education, the Office of Economic Opportunity, the National Science Foundation, the National Endowment for the Humanities, and the National Endowment for the Arts, among others (see figure 14.2). Funds flow directly from federal agencies and indirectly through state agencies. For example, funding for an educational project for an interdisciplinary program in the humanities might come directly from the National Endowment for the Humanities. This constitutes **direct federal aid**. However, the National Endowment also provides significant funding to each state's endowment, and funding for this same program might come, then, from the state humanities council. This is **indirect federal funding**.

Federal funds are not meant to support the schools but rather to improve and equalize educational opportunities for all students, and to encourage innovative programs within the public schools.

Federal funds frequently take the form of matching or seed-money grants. These require that state and local districts either match the amount supplied by the federal grant or extend the project funded by the federal government beyond the granted period. In this way, the federal government ensures state and local involvement in the project and its funding.

Many federal grants are **categorical**, meaning they must be spent for specific purposes. Hence, if money is received by a local school district to fund a Chapter I reading program through the Elementary and Secondary Education Act, the district must use the money to support this program and no other.

In 1981 Congress enacted the Educational Consolidation and Improvement Act (ECIA), which consolidated over forty categorical educational funding programs. Two-thirds of these funds had been distributed competitively. However, under ECIA, these funds are now awarded based on each state's share of the nation's school-aged population. Because of adjustments made for small states and territories, no state receives less than 0.5 percent of the total. Eighty percent of the funds flow through the state to local education agencies, rather than directly to local districts, and these must be distributed according to enrollment. The remaining 20 percent can be distributed by the states for discretionary use. These **block grants** are of two types: **basic grants**, which are available to any school district with at least ten poor students, and **concentration grants** for school districts in communities with high concentrations of poverty-level students.

Many groups, particularly the Children's Defense Fund and the Lawyers' Committee for Civil Rights, have been critical of this consolidation, particularly the two types of block grants. They contend that in the years following the consolidation program, services for underprivileged children under Chapter I of the Elementary and Secondary Education Act (ESEA) declined because of decreased funding, decreased staff to monitor how funds were used, and increased flexibility in how states and school districts can use the funds. Part of the reason for

**FIGURE 14-2**

### Federal Funds for Education, by Agency: Fiscal Year 1994

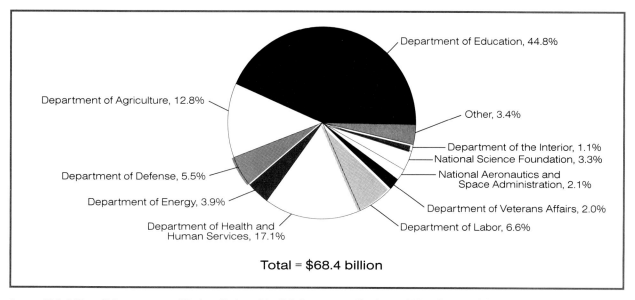

Department of Education, 44.8%

Department of Agriculture, 12.8%

Other, 3.4%

Department of the Interior, 1.1%
National Science Foundation, 3.3%

National Aeronautics and
Space Administration, 2.1%

Department of Defense, 5.5%

Department of Energy, 3.9%

Department of Veterans Affairs, 2.0%

Department of Health and
Human Services, 17.1%

Department of Labor, 6.6%

Total = $68.4 billion

Source: U.S. Office of Management and Budget, *Budget of the U.S. Government, Fiscal Year 1995;* and National Science Foundation, *Federal Funds for Research and Development, Fiscal years 1992, 1993, and 1994.*

From: U.S. Department of Education, National Center for Education Statistics, *Digest of Education Statistics* (1994) (NCES 94-293). Washington, DC: U.S. Government Printing Office, 361. Courtesy of Vance Grant.

> **Several federal agencies voluntarily provide funding for public education, either directly, or indirectly through the states. Federal funds are basically intended to improve and equalize educational opportunities for all students.**

this problem is that only 10 percent of Chapter I funds are reserved for concentration grants for poor communities, whereas 90 percent of the funds can go to virtually any community through the basic grants program. According to a 1994 study conducted by *U.S. News & World Report,* some of the richest communities in the country receive the largest amount of funding per poor student (students eligible for the federal free lunch program) and the poorest districts the least. The highest funded per student school district is Bolton, Connecticut, which has only one poor student. Therefore, Bolton is funded a rate of $53,109 per poor student. One of the lowest per student funded Chapter I districts is Morgan City, West Virginia, which has 617 students who qualify for the federal free lunch program. Therefore, per student Chapter I funding in Morgan City is $44 per qualified poor student (Johnson and Loeb, July 18, 1994, 26). ESEA has been reauthorized by the House and Senate. President Clinton signed the Elementary and Secondary Education Amendment of 1993 in the fall of 1994. President Clinton attempted to move more of the funding into concentration grant programs (telephone interview with Andy Hartman, staff member, House Committee on Education and Labor, August 5, 1994). Proponents of ECIA contend that the block grant program cuts down on waste by reducing staff needed to monitor programs and gives states and districts more local control over federal funds.

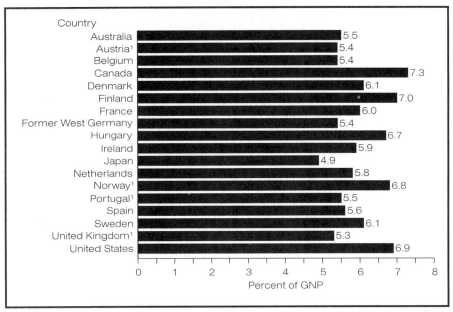

*Cross-Cultural Perspective*

## Public and Private Expenditures for Education as a Percentage of Gross National Product: Selected Countries, 1991

¹Public expenditures only

Source: Organization for Economic Cooperation and Development, *Education at a Glance,* and unpublished data. (The data for this figure were prepared May 1994.)

From: U.S. Department of Education, National Center for Education Statistics, *Digest of Education Statistics* (1994) (NCES 94-293). Washington, D.C.: U.S. Government Printing Office, 412. Courtesy of Vance Grant.

**When comparing expenditures for education as a percentage of the Gross National Product, when the expenditures include both private and public funds, the United States ranks third among these selected countries of the world.**

To receive federal funds, even block grants, school districts must comply with federal regulations and guidelines. For example, if the federal government believes there are civil rights violations in a district receiving federal funds, the government may withhold these funds until the alleged violations have been investigated and remedied. Therefore, it can be said that federal funding is the carrot used to encourage school districts to comply with federal standards and guidelines.

In some cases, however, the federal government does more than extend a carrot. It seeks to enforce regulations even in educational institutions that do not receive federal categorical aid for specific programs. For example, Hillsdale College is a private institution in Michigan that has, since its founding in 1844, refused to accept any federal funds. Nonetheless, the U.S. Department of Health, Education, and Welfare (HEW) instituted legal proceedings against Hillsdale College for refusing to submit an "Assurance of Compliance" with Title IX, which is designed to prevent sex discrimination in federally assisted education programs and activities. HEW claimed that although Hillsdale College did not receive direct federal aid, its students received financial aid through four federally funded programs. Hence, according to HEW, Hillsdale indirectly received federal aid and, therefore, must comply with Title IX requirements. In August 1978 an Administrative Law Judge (ALJ) denied HEW's request for an order terminating federal financial assistance to Hillsdale's students, ruling that the regulations relating to the prohibition of sex discrimination in employment were invalid. However, the ALJ found that Hillsdale was a recipient of federal financial assistance because the money provided to Hillsdale's students by the federal government would have otherwise been provided by the college. Both the college and HEW filed exceptions to the ALJ's initial decision. In October 1979 the Reviewing Authority denied Hillsdale's exceptions and granted HEW's exceptions (*Hillsdale College v. Department of Health, Etc.*, 696 F.2d 418, 1982). This case exemplifies the control exerted by the federal government in education.

---

**14-1**

**POINTS TO REMEMBER**

- The share of local, state, and federal funding shifts depending on politics. The more liberal the federal government, the more likely it will assume a larger share of educational funding; the more conservative, the more likely it will assume less.

- Local governments assume a large share of the funding for public education, which is raised by property and personal property taxes.

- States use aid formulas to fund education. Flat grants are based on average daily attendance; equalization grants provide a guaranteed yield to rich and poor districts, which tax themselves at the same rate by requiring rich districts to give the state surplus tax revenue to poor districts; foundation grants ensure a minimum level of revenue per pupil.

- School districts are not equally funded because poorer districts are unable to provide the same level of funding for education as wealthier districts. Often state formulas do not equalize the funding.

- Public-private partnerships for funding and managing public schools, such as charter school programs, offer some hope for equalizing funding. However, many fear the funding will be short-lived.

- The federal government has no responsibility to fund education but does so voluntarily through legislation.

- Current block grant consolidation programs are controversial because basic grants, representing 90 percent of the funds, can to go any community with at least ten poverty-level students; concentration grants, representing only 10 percent of the funds, must be used in areas of high poverty concentration.

---

## COURTS, LEGISLATURES, AND EQUALIZATION OF FUNDING

In the past two decades, state and federal courts have examined inequities in school funding based on property taxation in thirty-nine states and have come to various conclusions about the constitutionality of the inequalities of educational opportunities that result. In most of these cases, plaintiffs have argued about funding disparities due to assessed taxable property between wealthy and poor districts (see table 14.1, p. 549) and that education is a fundamental right

*(continued on p. 562)*

# WILL REFORMING SCHOOL FUNDING REMOVE INEQUALITY?

## PRO  Ruth Sidel

In 1989 both the Martin Luther King Junior High School and the East St. Louis Senior High School [Illinois] had to be closed after sewage flowed into the kitchen and from the toilets. The same week more than 500 school employees were laid off. The remaining teachers face constant shortages of chalk and paper, the sports facilities are in tatters and the science labs are thirty to fifty years out of date. One teacher states, "I have done without so much for so long that if I were assigned to a suburban school I'm not sure I'd recognize what they were doing. We are utterly cut off."

East St. Louis sets the tone for *Savage Inequalities: Children in America's Schools* by Jonathan Kozol. . . .

Not only is the U.S. Public Education system virtually separate but it is grossly unequal.

Report after report has shown that the poorest districts in New York receive significantly lower allocations than the wealthier districts and that per-pupil expenditures within the city of New York ($5,500 in 1987) are dramatically lower than comparable expenditures in the affluent suburbs surrounding the city (more than $11,000 in some of the affluent communities on Long Island). The same differen-

tials exist, of course, in all the metropolitan areas Kozol examines. . . .

Ultimately, Kozol addresses the central issue of educational equity in a country that prides itself on equal opportunity. As he points out, funding education, particularly during a time of federal cutbacks to human services and extreme reluctance to raise taxes, is a zero-sum game. Additional money for Chicago schools is likely to mean less money for Winnetka students. Improved facilities for students in the rest of the Bronx will, in all likelihood, mean fewer resources for students in Riverdale. Since 1989, when the Texas Supreme Court struck down the old school-financing system based primarily on property taxes, Texas political leaders have searched for a method of attaining school equity [see pp. 562–563]. . . .

The issue is not likely to disappear. The publication of *Savage Inequalities* will insure that the injustice and incredible shortsightedness of American educational policy are vividly and compassionately brought to the forefront of the public's consciousness and the agenda of policymakers.

> From: R. Sidel. "Separate but Unequal," *The Nation* (November 18, 1991), 620–622. Ruth Sidel is a professor of sociology at The Hunter College of the City University of New York.

## Postscript

Ruth Sidel and Peter Schrag do not disagree with Jonathan Kozol's conclusion that American public schools are unequal. Nor do they denigrate the quality of his arguments in his book *Savage Inequalities: Children in America's Schools*. What they do disagree about is how to reform the schools so that all students receive quality educations. Sidel suggests that it is critical that schools develop more humane policies for funding public education (although

# WILL REFORMING SCHOOL FUNDING REMOVE INEQUALITY?

## CON  Peter Schrag

It's a moving book [Jonathan Kozol's *Savage Inequalities*]—about filthy schools where roofs leak and halls are flooded each time it rains, where three or four classes have to share a gym or cafeteria because there aren't enough rooms, where teachers have outdated textbooks or none at all. It's also a reminder that a lot of those kids really want to learn, aren't on drugs, and understand that this is a society that treats white suburban children a lot better than it treats black inner-city kids. . . .

The rationale of the equalizers is simple: unequal spending among schools denies children equal protection of the laws. A poor community with a weak tax base simply can't spend as much on each child's education as a wealthy one, even if it raises rates to the breaking point, and that's patently unfair.

But is equalization of all spending—which, in addition to increasing the spending in poor districts, means capping the spending of affluent or motivated districts—really the solution? Consider California, the only major state where equalization has been thoroughly tried. . . . The results have been a wondrous illustration of the law of unintended consequences.

The most obvious of those consequences is that equalization sharply reduced local incentives to raise school taxes. . . .

School equalization might have taken decades to achieve had it not been for the fortuitous passage of Proposition 13 in 1978. By slashing and capping local property tax revenues, Prop 13 shifted the burden of school funding to state income and sales taxes, which made equalization a lot easier to realize. But because of 13, the state's spending on schools has also slipped precipitately—from sixth or seventh in the nation to twenty-fifth or twenty-sixth. California now spends less per child than any other major industrial state, and less than the national average. . . .

With the power to appropriate funds having shifted from local boards to the state government, it is no longer possible to know who is responsible for the financial problems of the local schools—the board that allocates the funds and overspends or mismanages them or the governor and legislature that fail to pony up enough to begin with. . . .

Kozol says, correctly, that poor children are trapped in awful inner-city schools, while the middle class has choices. But he refuses to give poor children the chance to escape to better public schools, through choice. . . .

But the fact remains that equalization—any way you formulate it—tends to destroy local accountability and erode the supports and sense of mission that make strong schools possible.

From: P. Schrag. "Savage Inequalities: The Case Against Jonathan Kozol," *The New Republic* (December 16, 1991), 18–20. Peter Schrag is the editorial page editor of *The Sacramento Bee.*

she does not suggest a method). However, she agrees with Kozol that humane policies are not enough; society must take responsibility for providing an adequate standard of living for all its children. Schrag claims that the more humane funding policies tried by states such as California have failed miserably and cannot work. Instead, according to Schrag, the only funding reform that will be successful is school choice.

of all children. Defendants have countered that local control is the reason for the disparities, that the states' constitutions do not require equal expenditures per child, and that every district has sufficient funds to meet basic requirements. The courts' decisions have been influenced by their interpretations of the states' constitutional clauses using such terminology for goals of public education as "thorough and efficient" and "uniform and basic," evidence presented in the cases, existing laws, and the jurisdiction the court defines for itself. Hence, the wide variety of decisions.

In the California Supreme Court case of *Serrano v. Priest* (5 C.3d 584, 487 P.2d 1241, 96 Cal. Rptr. 601, 1971), the plaintiffs contended that California's heavy reliance on property taxes to fund public education violated the students' Fourteenth Amendment, or equal protection, rights. Property taxes in Baldwin Park, for example, provided $577 per pupil, whereas the property taxes in Beverly Hills provided $1,232 per pupil. The court ruled in favor of the plaintiffs, stating:

> The California public school financing system . . . conditions the full entitlement to [education] on wealth, classifies its recipients on the basis of their collective affluence and makes the quality of a child's education depend upon the resources of his school district and ultimately upon the pocketbook of his parents. We find that such financing system as presently constituted is not necessary to the attainment of any compelling state interest. . . . [I]t denies to the plaintiffs and others similarly situated the equal protection of the laws.

The court instructed the California state legislature to revise the school finance system to ensure its **fiscal neutrality** where educational funds would not be tied to local property wealth. In 1976 the California Supreme Court reviewed the case (*Serrano v. Priest II,* 557 P.2d 929, 939 Cal., 1976), relying solely on state constitutional provisions. The court again instructed the legislature to determine how to reduce revenue disparities across school districts. The legislature enacted a complicated equalization program that was essentially overturned by voters a year later when they approved Proposition 13, a tax limitation measure almost eliminating the use of property tax for funding public education and shifting nearly full financial responsibility to the state. Although since 1976 California has achieved a fair measure of spending equality among school districts, the desired effect of improved educational opportunities has not been achieved.

In *San Antonio Independent School District v. Rodriguez* (411 U.S. 1, 1973), the U.S. Supreme Court disagreed with the first *Serrano* decision. The Court ruled that a funding system based on the local property tax, even though it provides only minimal educational opportunities to all students through a minimum foundation program, does not violate the equal protection clause of the Fourteenth Amendment. Justice White, supporting the majority opinion of the Court, stated:

> The method of financing public schools in Texas, as in almost every other state, has resulted in a system of public education that can fairly be described as chaotic and unjust. It does not follow, however, and I cannot find, that this system violates the Constitution of the United States.

Despite the U.S. Supreme Court's ruling in the *Rodriguez* case, the Texas Supreme Court later found that the state's method of funding public schools violated its constitution in *Edgewood Independent School District v. Kirby* (777

S.W.2d, 391 Tex. 1989) because minimum foundation aid did not provide school districts with sufficient funding to meet the state's mandated requirements, which are to "establish, support, and maintain an efficient system of public free schools." According to the court, "Property-poor districts are trapped in a cycle of poverty from which there is no opportunity to free themselves. School districts must have substantially equal access to similar levels of tax effort." This ruling effectively overturned the 1973 *Rodriguez* decision in Texas by requiring the legislature to establish a new funding system or the court would close the state's schools. However, each state has to decide if its own system of funding public education is inequitable based on its own constitution, since the U.S. Supreme Court's ruling in the *Rodriguez* case moved jurisdiction in these matters to the state courts (see opening anecdote, p. 546).

Numerous state legislatures have had to deal with the problem of providing equal educational opportunity in all districts. In Texas, for example, the legislature complied with the court's ruling and in 1991 passed legislation whereby school districts with high property values shift money to districts with low property values within regional taxing districts. The wealthy districts opposed this legislation, stating that taxes were levied without voter approval and millions of dollars were being taken from their excellent schools. The Texas Supreme Court ruled in favor of the wealthy districts (*Edgewood v. Carrollton-Farmers Branch Independent School District,* D-1469 Tex. 1992), overturning the 1991 funding legislation as unconstitutional based on the principle of taxation without representation and requiring the legislature to come up with an equitable funding plan or close the state's schools. In 1992 it passed a two-part plan in which funding would be based on a statewide lottery and annexation of the wealthy districts' shopping malls, power plants, and other nonresidential properties. In 1993 the (*Edgewood v. Lionel R. Meno,* 250 Dist. Ct., Austin, Texas 362, 516) case was brought to the court to overturn this new funding plan as unconstitutional. A decision on this case is expected some time in late 1994 or early 1995. Texas and New Jersey have the longest running series of school finance court cases in the country.

*Taxpayers' Revolt* New Jersey's school funding system has been challenged in the judicial system and turned over to the legislature for action numerous times in the past two decades. The New Jersey Supreme Court ruled in 1973 (*Robinson v. Cahill*, 287 A.2d 87, Sup. 118 N.J. Super. 223, 1973) that there were disparities both in property wealth and tax rate among the poor and wealthy districts. Legislative action in 1975 called for a new state income tax to decrease disparities. However, it did not equalize funding between poor urban and wealthy suburban districts. Therefore, in 1990 the New Jersey Supreme Court ruled (*Abbott v. Burke,* 575 A.2d 359,119 N.J. 287) that the state's school funding system violated the "thorough and efficient and equal protection" clauses of the state constitution as well as the state's laws against discrimination. The legislature passed the Quality Education Act of 1990 allocating an additional $1.5 billion to the state's public schools, the majority going to the poorest urban districts (Camden, East Orange, Jersey City, Trenton, and Newark).

As in California, New Jersey's taxpayers objected to this legislation that funneled money primarily to poorer districts and was paid for by increased income and sales taxes. To counter this objection, the legislature shifted $360 million from the school aid fund (30 percent) to municipal tax relief to help lower local property taxes rather than to equalize funding in rich and poor school

Demetrio P. Rodriguez has fought for equitable funding in all school districts in Texas for more than twenty-five years. A retired sheet-metal worker whose five children graduated from the Edgewood Independent School District, Rodriguez regrets that the courts have yet to establish a plan that would give the schools in his district the same funds as all other districts in Texas. He continues to appear at every court hearing on equitable funding, now numbering into the hundreds. "He can be a pain in the neck," said Earle H. Bolton, the district's deputy superintendent. "But he's the district's icon."

districts. As a result, poor school districts had less money to spend on education, and the spending gap between poor and wealthy districts widened rather than narrowed. In 1994 the New Jersey Supreme Court found that the state's school funding formula was unconstitutional since it was not providing an adequate education for all by meeting the special needs of poor children (*Abbott v. Burke,* 643 A.2d 5.573.136 N.J. 1994).

These types of taxpayers' revolts have occurred in numerous other states as well. State and local taxes have increased faster than personal income since 1982. In the 1980s every state enacted some tax increases, and several enacted another in 1990. Nine states increased tax revenue by at least 5 percent, and six states increased sales taxes for school funding. The total increase in taxation exceeded $10 billion, according to the National Association of State Budget Officers, the highest in history. Consequently, tax protesters have attempted to defeat public officials who voted for these tax increases.

## *In the Classroom*

Camden, New Jersey, is the fourth-poorest city of more than 50,000 people in America. In 1985, nearly a quarter of its families had less than $5,000 annual income. Nearly 60 percent of its residents receive public assistance. Its children have the highest rate of poverty in the United States.

Once a commercial and industrial center for the southern portion of New Jersey—a single corporation, New York Shipyards, gave employment to 35,000 people during World War II—Camden now has little industry. There are 35,000 jobs in the entire city now, and most of them don't go to Camden residents. The largest employer, RCA, which once gave work to 18,000 people, has about 3,000 jobs today, but only 65 are held by Camden residents. Camden's entire property wealth of $250 million is less than the value of just one casino in Atlantic City.

The city has 200 liquor stores and bars and 180 gambling establishments, no movie theater, one chain supermarket, no new-car dealership, few restaurants other than some fast-food places. City blocks are filled with burnt-out buildings. Of the city's 2,200 public housing units, 500 are boarded up, although there is a three-year waiting list of homeless families. As the city's aged sewers crumble and collapse, streets cave in, but there are no funds to make repairs.

What is life like for children in this city?

To find some answers, I spent several days in Camden in the early spring of 1990. Because the city has no hotel, teachers in Camden arranged for me to stay nearby in Cherry Hill, a beautiful suburban area of handsome stores and costly homes. The drive from Cherry Hill to Camden takes about five minutes. It is like a journey between different worlds.

On a stretch of land beside the Delaware River in the northern part of Camden, in a neighborhood of factories and many abandoned homes, roughly equidistant from a paper plant, a gelatine factory and an illegal dumpsite, stands a school called Pyne Point Junior High.

In the evening, when I drive into the neighborhood to find the school, the air at Pyne Point bears the smell of burning trash. When I return the next day I am hit with a strong smell of ether, or some kind of glue, that seems to be emitted by the paper factory.

The school is a two-story building, yellow brick, its windows covered with metal grates, the flag on its flagpole motionless above a lawn that has no grass. Some 650 children, 98 percent of whom are black or Latino, are enrolled here.

The school nurse, who walks me through the building while the principal is on the phone, speaks of the emergencies and illnesses that she contends with. "Children come into school with rotting teeth," she says. "They sit in class, leaning on their elbows, in discomfort. Many kids have chronic and untreated illnesses. I had a child in here yesterday with diabetes. Her blood-sugar level was over 700. Close to coma level. . . ."

A number of teachers, says the nurse, who tells me that her children go to school in Cherry Hill, do not have books for half the students in their classes. "Black teachers in the building ask me whether I'd put up with this in Cherry Hill. I tell them I would not. But some of the parents here make no demands. They don't know how much we have in Cherry Hill, so they do not know what they're missing." . . .

Camden High School, which I visit the next morning, can't afford facilities for lunch, so 2,000 children leave school daily to obtain lunch elsewhere. Many do not bother to return. Nonattendance and dropout rates, according to the principal, are very high.

In a twelfth grade English class the teacher is presenting a good overview of nineteenth-century history in England. On the blackboard are these words: "Idealism . . . Industrialization . . . Exploitation . . . Laissez-faire. . . ." The teacher seems competent, but, in this room as almost everywhere in Camden, lack of funds creates a shortage of materials. Half the children in the classroom have no texts.

"What impresses me," the teacher says after the class is over, "is that kids get up at all and come to school. They're old enough to know what they are coming into." . . .

"President Bush," says Ruthie Green-Brown, principal of Camden High, when we meet later in her office, "speaks of his 'goals' and these sound very fine. He mentions preschool education—early childhood. Where is the money? We have children coming to kindergarten or to first grade who are starting out three years delayed in their development. They have had no preschool. Only a minute number of our kids have had a chance at Head Start. This is the *most* significant thing that you can do to help an urban child if your goal is to include that urban child in America. Do we *want* that child to be included?" (Kozol 1991, 137–142)

Jonathan Kozol's book, *Savage Inequalities: Children in America's Schools* (1991) recounts the conditions he found in poor schools he visited in such cities as East St. Louis, New York, San Antonio, and Camden. It is basically a plea for fairness and decency in the way we pay for the education of our children. Earlier, Kozol's book *Death at an Early Age* (1967) won a National Book Award, and *Rachel and Her Children* (1989) won the Robert F. Kennedy Award.

***Successful Funding Reform*** In states in which governors, legislators, and the courts have done a good job explaining why increased taxes are needed for school reform, little or no taxpayers' revolt has occurred. Kentucky is probably the best example. In 1989 a group of property-poor school districts filed suit alleging that the state school finance system violated its constitutional requirement that the General Assembly provide for "an efficient system of common schools throughout the state" (*Rose v. Council for Better Education, Inc.,* Ky., LEXIS, June 8, 1989).

The court ruled for the plaintiff saying Kentucky's "entire system of common schools was infirm." Significant funding disparities were found resulting in "unequal educational opportunities" despite the state foundation and equalization formula. In addition to invalidating the state's funding system, the court invalidated all state education statutes and regulations. Likewise, the court not only examined disparities in funding inputs, but also in educational outcomes. The court noted, for example, that achievement test scores were lower in poorer districts and generally lower than in other states; Kentucky ranked in the lower 20 to 25 percent in virtually every category used to evaluate national educational outcomes. Similarly the court noted that Kentucky ranked fortieth in per-pupil expenditures of fifty states. Finally the court defined what it meant by an "efficient" system saying that it must provide children with at least these "capacities": oral and written communication skills; knowledge of economic, social, and political systems; understanding of governmental processes; sufficient self-knowledge of her or his mental and physical wellness; sufficient cultural and historical heritage; sufficient training and preparation for academics and career; and sufficient levels of academic or vocational skills. By applying these standards to the existing public school system, the court had no problem finding it inadequate and inefficient.

The breadth of this decision helped the state legislature enact the Kentucky Education Reform Act of 1990, which was financed by a state income tax increase. This reform act dealt not only with finances but also with improving Kentucky's total educational system. It included school-based decision making, preschool programs for at-risk students, rewards tied to school performance, a statewide performance assessment program, a new curriculum, a guaranteed level of per-pupil funding, and a method for raising poor districts to the spending level of wealthier districts. Since many of these reforms have been implemented, there has been no taxpayer revolt. Many Kentucky districts have raised local tax rates and received corresponding increases in state aid with which they have initiated preschool programs, extended-day tutorial programs, and ungraded primary classrooms.

## Funding Nonpublic Schools

Providing state aid to nonpublic schools is a complicated issue because historically it relates to the establishment clause of the First Amendment, barring government action in the establishment of religion. However, in *Everson v. Board of Education* (330 U.S. 1, 1947), the U.S. Supreme Court ruled that state aid for services such as transportation and guidance counseling for nonpublic schools primarily benefits nonsectarian students and not the institution and, therefore, does not violate the principle of separation of church and state. Many states' courts, though, have ruled that providing public aid to nonpublic schools violates their own states' constitutions. Recently the Supreme Court ruled in *Kiryas Joel Village School District v. Grumet* (93 U.S. 517, 1994) that when state aid benefits a religious school, such as the special education school set up for Satmar Hasidic

Kiryas Joel Village was established in 1989 by the New York state legislature as a special education district for those children of the Satmar Hasidic Jews who had disabilities ranging from speech problems to neurological disorders. This authorized the school to receive special education funds from the state. In 1994, however, the U.S. Supreme Court upheld the principle of separation of church and state (*Kiryas Joel Village School District v. Grumet* [93 U.S. 517]) and the school was denied state public education funds.

Jewish children in Kiryas Joel Village, New York, the establishment clause is violated, even when the support is only for special education services provided for under Chapter I, or state handicapped funding programs that traditionally have provided services for students attending nonpublic schools (see chapter 13, pp. 536–537).

Funding of nonpublic schools is accomplished with tuition, fees, gifts, contributions, grants from churches and sponsors, endowments, and in a few instances from public funds and tax support. But the single most important way federal policy affects the financing of nonpublic schools is through legislation allowing private schools to receive tax deductible gifts and providing them a tax-exempt status. For this reason, funding of nonpublic schools is filled with complexities.

In 1988, after the U.S. Supreme Court decided that providing compensatory education and remedial services on private school premises was unconstitutional (*Aguilar v. Felton,* 473 U.S. 402, 1985), the Congress passed P.L. 100–297 (Augustus F. Hawkins–Robert T. Stafford Elementary and Secondary School Improvement Amendments) authorizing funding to school districts for the cost of noninstructional goods and services used to provide Chapter I services at neutral sites (mobile vans, portable classrooms, public libraries, public school classrooms, community centers) to children attending nonpublic schools. Since 1989–1990 the states have received about $82 million from the federal government to cover Chapter I services for these students (U.S. General Accounting Office 1993, 1–3).

Other federal funding programs include the National School Lunch Act (P.L. 79–396), providing free milk and low-cost lunches to students from low-income families; the Education for Handicapped Act (P.L. 94–142), providing appropriate education for disabled, nonpublic school students; and the Individuals with Disabilities Act (P.L. 102–119), providing early intervention programs for these students.

Several states, particularly those with large nonpublic school populations such as New York, Ohio, and Pennsylvania, routinely provide public aid to private schools. In addition to Chapter I services, these states provide such things as transportation, textbooks, state-required testing program support, special education for disabled students, and guidance counseling. In 1992, $1.5 billion in private funding went to nonpublic schools with $700 million going to the National Association of Independent Schools, $260 million to Catholic schools, $350 million to other private nonsectarian schools, and approximately $190 million to other religious schools (Council for Aid to Education as reported in *Education Week,* January 12, 1994, 13). It is expected that in the late 1990s some nonsectarian schools will be selected for funding from Edison Projects or the New American Schools Development Association, for-profit school corporations that are involved in financing and managing some public schools (see chapter 13, pp. 531–534).

Most educational funding issues in the United States relate back to questions of equity and excellence. How can all schools provide excellent education for all students no matter how property-poor the school district in which the students dwell? The question itself is complex and the answers difficult. Courts and legislatures have attempted to solve the problem of equitable funding with only minimal success.

Public-private partnerships to fund education may offer some solutions, but most educators worry that the solutions will only be short term. Providing equitable and excellent education for all students is a problem that you will no doubt confront in your own career as an educator.

---

**14-2**

**POINTS TO REMEMBER**

- Courts and legislatures are struggling to equalize educational funding. In some cases, the courts have ruled that property taxes are constitutional for funding schools; in others they have ruled them unconstitutional.

- Many schools are inadequately funded, but the issue of how to fund them equitably is complicated. Property-rich districts are reluctant to levy taxes and give the money to property-poor districts; property-poor districts cannot levy more than citizens can pay.

- Most court and legislative solutions have fallen short of reaching their goal of equitable funding; many have resulted in taxpayers' revolts.

- Most educational funding court cases, beginning with *Serrano v. Priest* in 1971 in California, have been heard based on the states' constitutional clauses regarding education.

- The funding of nonpublic schools comes from a variety of sources, including tuition, fees, gifts, contributions, grants from churches and sponsors, endowments, and, in a few instances, from public funds and tax support.

- Whether or not to fund nonpublic schools with public funds has been a controversial issue resulting in many court cases. Most have been tried based on the establishment clause of the First Amendment, barring government action in the establishment of religion.

## For Thought/Discussion

1. Do you believe educational opportunities would be better equalized in all school districts if the federal government controlled all revenue allocated to the schools, or if each state controlled its own revenue?

2. What problems would you anticipate if all schools became "chartered" and thus were able to pursue programs of their own choosing?

3. If public education depends on business for its funding, what would the consequence be if a particular business failed or decided to end its financial backing to schools?

4. Can equalization of funding be guaranteed if all schools were financed by different businesses throughout the country? For example, would McDonalds be a better corporate sponsor than Mystic Pizza? Midas Muffler better than J. C. Penney?

## For Further Reading/Reference

Educational Testing Service, 1991. *The state of inequality.* Princeton, NJ: Author. This book examines state-school litigation in three states and provides examples of school funding inequities within some of the states.

Gerstner, J. V., Jr., Semerad, R. D., Doyle, D. P., and Johnston, W. B., 1994. *Reinventing education: Entrepreneurship in America's public schools.* NY: Dutton. The chairman and CEO of IBM, Louis V. Gerstner, Jr., examines numerous issues in public education, suggesting new partnerships between private enterprise and public schools.

Hartman, W. T. 1988. *School district budgeting.* Englewood Cliffs, NJ: Prentice-Hall. Identification of varying aspects of budgeting at the local level from conception to adoption, from practical to political, together with choices that must be weighed, made, and implemented. The author also discusses how budgeting affects the classroom teacher.

Honeyman, D., Wood, C., and Thompson, D. (Special Eds.). 1988. *Journal of Education Finance* 13 (4), 349–511. This special edition has thirteen articles on school funding in selected states and in the province of Manitoba. Disparities in district spending are discussed in two articles.

Kozol, J. (1991). *Savage inequalities: Children in America's schools.* New York: Crown. This well-known school reformer discusses inequality of schools and relates these inequities to school funding differentials between property-rich and -poor districts.

Webb, L. D., McCarthy, M. M., and Thomas, S. B. (1988). *Financing elementary and secondary education.* Columbus, OH: Merrill. This textbook provides a thorough explanation of local, state, and federal funding of education. Special attention is given to the funding of education for special needs students and to financing nonpublic education.

# Primary Teacher Salaries Indexed to Per Capita GDP

Teacher Salary Index (per capita GDP = 100)

| | Norway | Italy | Denmark | Sweden | Belgium | Finland | United States | Austria | France | Netherlands | Australia | Germany | Scotland | Canada | England | Switzerland | Japan |
|---|---|---|---|---|---|---|---|---|---|---|---|---|---|---|---|---|---|
| Max | 125 | 138 | 144 | 153 | 156 | 161 | 165 | 168 | 172 | 177 | 178 | 178 | 195 | 197 | 200 | 209 | 228 |
| Mid | 116 | 108 | 138 | 132 | 130 | 158 | 150 | 155 | 148 | 139 | 178 | 165 | 195 | 186 | 192 | 186 | 168 |
| Start | 100 | 89 | 113 | 103 | 100 | 103 | 97 | 90 | 90 | 96 | 122 | 135 | 112 | 108 | 106 | 138 | 93 |
| Years | 16 | 40 | 19 | 23 | 27 | 20 | 16 | 17 | 25 | 26 | 10 | 21 | 13 | 11 | 10 | 24 | 32 |

Note: This chart uses the following data: Finland–c46; Denmark–Rate VI; Australia–New South Wales; Canada–Saskatchewan; Switzerland–Basel city

This table compares teacher salaries of selected industrialized countries to the per capita gross domestic product (GDP). The index is created by dividing the teacher salary figure by the per capita GDP and multiplying by 100. Beginning teachers in the United States earn 97 percent of the per capita GDP. Starting teachers in Norway, Italy, Belgium, Austria, France, the Netherlands, and Japan have indexes in the 90–100 range. By contrast, German and Swiss teachers,

with an index of 135, start at pay levels exceeding 35 percent of per capita GDP. At mid-career, the U.S. index is 150, with seven countries having lower indexes and eleven having higher. At the maximum salary level, the United States ranks only above Italy and the northern European countries of Norway, Sweden, and Denmark. Finland pays about the same as the United States.

Average Teacher Salary, 1992–1993

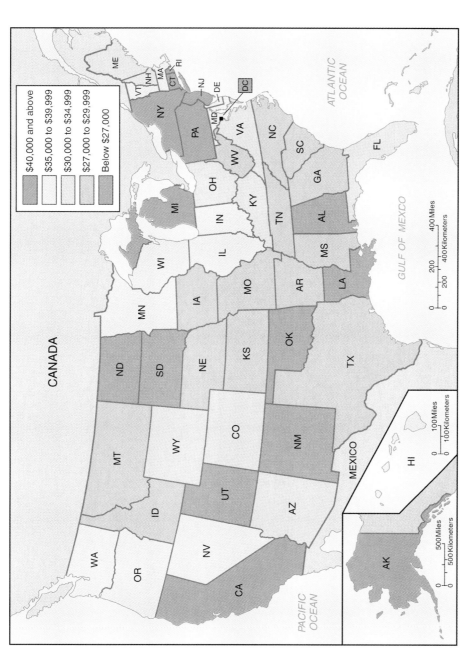

**Legend:**
- $40,000 and above
- $35,000 to $39,999
- $30,000 to $34,999
- $27,000 to $29,999
- Below $27,000

In 1992–1993 public elementary and secondary schoolteachers in the United States earned an average salary of approximately $35,104, an increase of 3.2 percent over the previous year. Alaska, New York, New Jersey, Michigan, Pennsylvania, Connecticut, the District of Columbia, and Rhode Island all had average salaries over $40,000—about 15 to 30 percent above the national average. South Dakota ranked last with an average salary of $24,291. When compared to annual earnings in the private sector, Rhode Island ranks first with a ratio of 1.78 compared to the national average of 1.43. Several states with relatively high teacher salaries, including New York and New Jersey, rank in the middle of the list of states when compared to the private sector pay ratio, and the District of Columbia, with the eighth highest teacher pay in the nation, ranks last.

## Average Teacher Salary Increase, 1980–81 to 1992–93

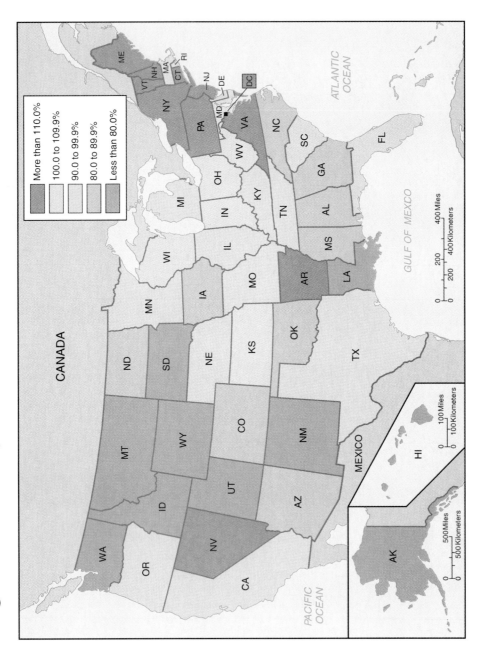

**Legend:**
- More than 110.0%
- 100.0 to 109.9%
- 90.0 to 99.9%
- 80.0 to 89.9%
- Less than 80.0%

Despite substantial gains over the inflation rate during the 1980s, teacher salary growth in most of the nation has barely kept pace with the growth in personal income. The ratio of the national average of teacher salary growth to the per capita personal income is 1.77, about the same as it was in 1990–1991, but well below the ratio of 1.85 in 1986–1987. Only Michigan, Rhode Island, Pennsylvania, West Virginia, and Alaska have ratios of 2.00 or better. In the past twelve years the average teacher salary grew by about 180 percent in Connecticut, by about 170 percent in Vermont, and by about 150 percent in New Hampshire, compared to the national average of 100 percent. Average salaries improved no better than 65 percent over the same time period in Louisiana (57 percent), Utah (60 percent), New Mexico (57 percent), Alaska (61 percent), and Wyoming (62 percent).

# Percentage of Children in Poverty

**4**

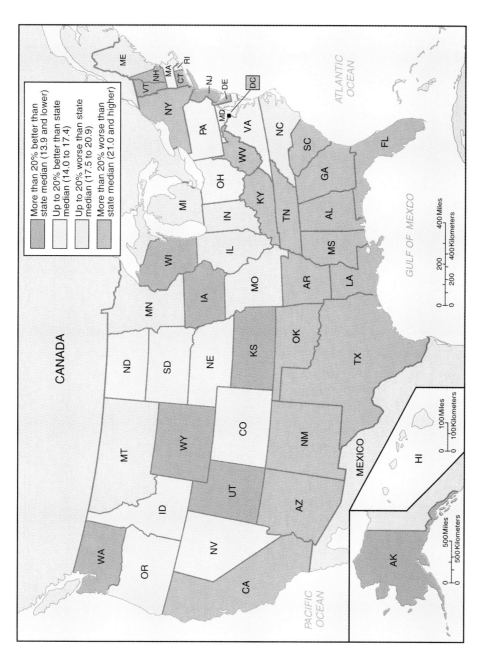

**Legend:**
- More than 20% better than state median (13.9 and lower)
- Up to 20% better than state median (14.0 to 17.4)
- Up to 20% worse than state median (17.5 to 20.9)
- More than 20% worse than state median (21.0 and higher)

The percentage of children in poverty refers to those related children under the age of eighteen living in families with incomes below the U.S. poverty threshold as defined by the U.S. Office of Management and Budget. In calendar year 1990, the poverty threshold for a typical family of four persons was $13,359. The data shown here represent an average from 1989 through 1993. According to the U.S. Census Bureau, a quarter of all children under the age of six are living in poverty. Related children in the household include the family head's children by birth, marriage, or adoption, as well as nieces or nephews. The percentage of children in poverty is the most global indicator of childhood well-being, with direct parallels to negative situations in health, education, emotional well-being, and delinquency.

5

## Juvenile Violent Crime Arrest Rate Ages Ten through Seventeen

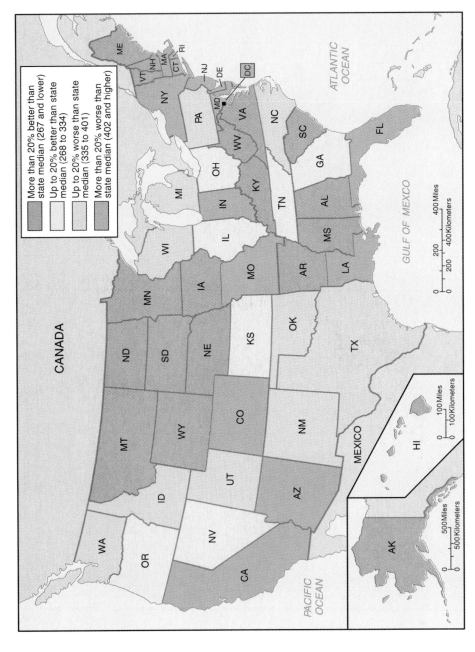

**CANADA**

**Legend:**
- More than 20% better than state median (267 and lower)
- Up to 20% better than state median (268 to 334)
- Up to 20% worse than state median (335 to 401)
- More than 20% worse than state median (402 and higher)

ATLANTIC OCEAN

GULF OF MEXICO

PACIFIC OCEAN

MEXICO

The figures on this map indicate the number of arrests per 100 thousand persons under the age of eighteen for violent crimes such as homicide, forcible rape, robbery, or aggravated assault. Nationally, the rate increased from 305 per 100 thousand in 1985 to 457 per 100 thousand in 1991. The data shown here represent three-year averages, so that these 1991 figures are an average of data from 1990, 1991, and 1992. Because a small number of local law enforcement agencies do not submit their data to the FBI, the number of juveniles arrested was adjusted to compensate for these groups. However, the data must be tempered by the fact that criminal activity is generally perpetrated by relatively few people, that violent crime in this age group has actually decreased slightly since 1991, and arrest rates may reflect changes in police activity or public policy.

574

# Percentage of All Births to Single Teens

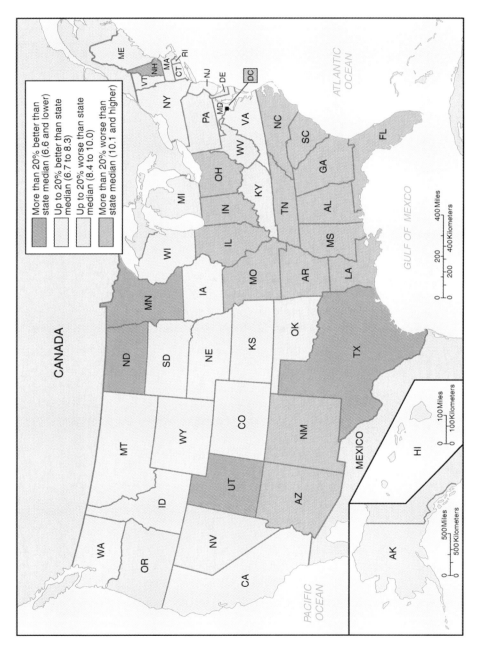

**Legend:**
- More than 20% better than state median (6.6 and lower)
- Up to 20% better than state median (6.7 to 8.3)
- Up to 20% worse than state median (8.4 to 10.0)
- More than 20% worse than state median (10.1 and higher)

CANADA

ATLANTIC OCEAN

GULF OF MEXICO

PACIFIC OCEAN

MEXICO

0   200   400 Miles
0   200   400 Kilometers

0   100 Miles
0   100 Kilometers

0   500 Miles
0   500 Kilometers

This map reflects the percentage of live births occurring among unmarried women under age twenty. That percentage rose from 7.5 percent in 1985 to 9.0 percent in 1991. Of the fifty states, only Maryland and New Jersey experienced a decrease in the same time period and New York and Texas showed no change. According to the Center for Health Statistics, during 1991 "increases in non-marital birth rates brought each age-specific rate to the highest level ever reported during the fifty-one years for which this information has been available" (*Family Planning Perspectives* (26)1, 43. Alan Guttmacher Institute, New York, NY). These infants face difficult odds. A single teen parent is often undereducated, has difficulty finding employment, and thus generally lacks the reserves to provide the child what it needs for successful development.

Percentage of Children in Single-Parent Families

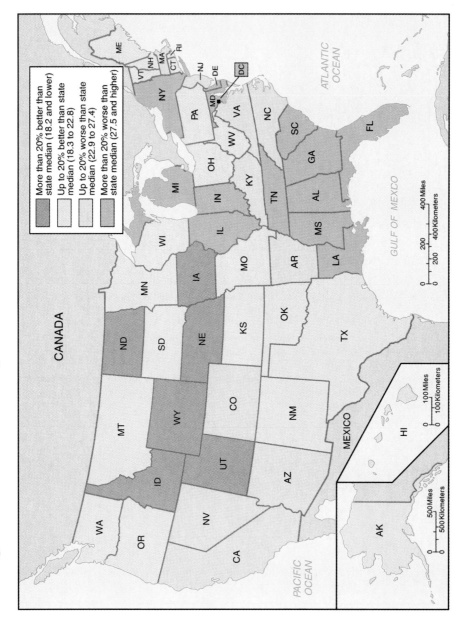

Single-parent families are identified as those households headed by either a male or a female without a spouse present, with related children under age eighteen in residence. Related children include the family head's children by birth, marriage, or adoption as well as nieces and nephews. The percentage of children in single-parent families has risen steadily from 22.7 percent in 1985 to 25.1 percent in 1991. These figures represent an average of the five years from 1989 through 1993. All but six states

recorded an increase. The resulting greatest problem is that of poverty, where the rate is 42 percent for single-parent families compared to 8 percent for two-parent families. Neither is poverty eliminated by public assistance programs. As an example, even with the combination of AFDC and Food Stamps, family income of single-parent families is below the poverty line in every state and under 75 percent of the poverty line in thirty-eight states and the District of Columbia.

# Teen Violent Death Rate, Ages Fifteen to Nineteen

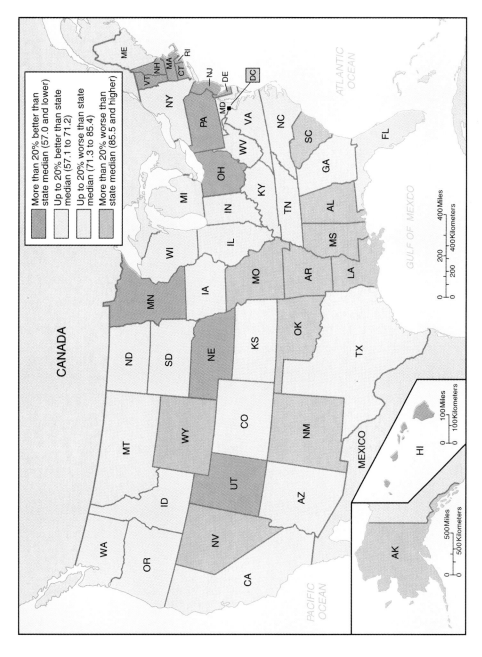

The teen violent death rate reflects deaths from homicide, suicide, and accidents. In 1991 this rate rose to 71.1 per 100 thousand, a 13 percent increase over the 1985 rate of 62.8. Since auto-related fatalities have declined in this age group, the overall growth in this indicator is due almost entirely to homicide. The increase in the numbers of handguns available to teens is one cause of this rise in violent deaths. Between 1979 and 1991, there were nearly 40 thousand deaths of teenagers aged fifteen to nineteen. (Deaths are reported by place of residence, not where they occurred.)

# Hurdles to Success for Teenagers

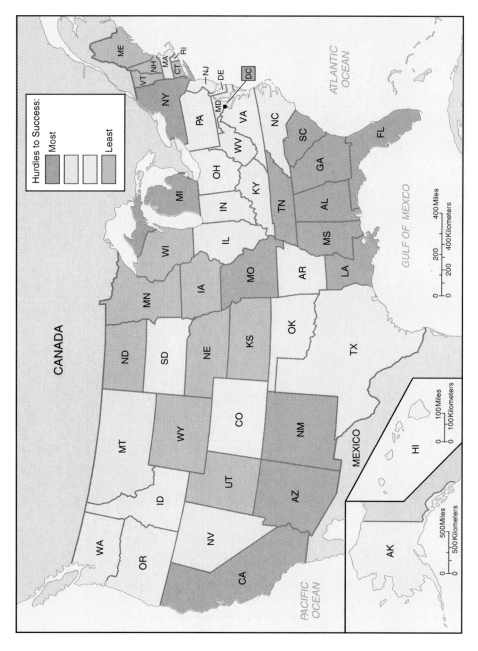

Hurdles to Success:
Most
Least

CANADA

MEXICO

AK

HI

100 Miles
100 Kilometers

500 Miles
500 Kilometers

PACIFIC
OCEAN

GULF OF MEXICO

ATLANTIC
OCEAN

0    200    400 Miles
0    200    400 Kilometers

WA, OR, CA, NV, ID, MT, WY, UT, AZ, NM, CO, ND, SD, NE, KS, OK, TX, MN, IA, MO, AR, LA, WI, IL, MI, IN, OH, KY, TN, MS, AL, GA, FL, SC, NC, VA, WV, PA, NY, ME, VT, NH, MA, CT, RI, NJ, DE, MD, DC

Young people face more hurdles to success in some states than in others. In a study by the *New York Times*, each state was ranked on six factors that affect the lives of the teenagers who live there. The factors considered were: The percentage of all births to single teenagers; the violent crime arrest rate among juveniles; the percentage of teenagers graduating from high school; the percentage of teenagers not in school and not in the labor force; the violent death rate; and the percentage of children living below the poverty level. The composite score of the factors was one way of evaluating those states where teenagers face the most obstacles.

# 10 Percentage of Change in Public Elementary and Secondary School Enrollment by State, Fall 1987 to Fall 1992

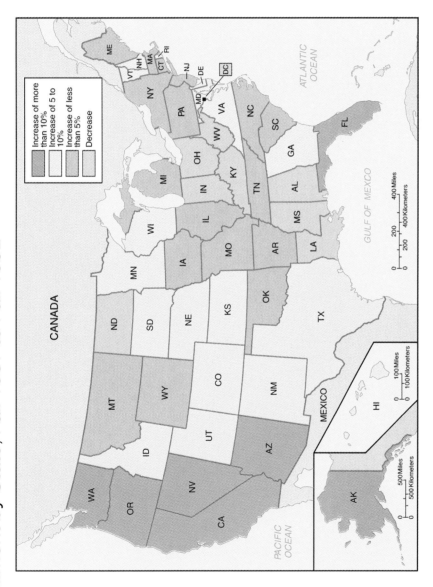

**Legend:**
- Increase of more than 10%
- Increase of 5 to 10%
- Increase of less than 5%
- Decrease

In fall 1985, public elementary and secondary school enrollments increased for the first time since 1971. Enrollment has continued to rise, resulting in an increase of 7 percent from 1985 to 1992. The greatest growth in public elementary and secondary school populations from fall of 1987 to fall of 1992 occurred primarily in the western states of Arizona, Nevada, California, Oregon, Alaska, and Washington, and in the state of Florida. By contrast, the states that had the least population growth were clustered along the Gulf Coast (Louisiana, Mississippi, and Alabama) and in the upper Midwest states of Indiana, Ohio, West Virginia, and Kentucky. In

contrast to the declining elementary and secondary school enrollments during the 1970s and early 1980s, preprimary education enrollment grew substantially. Between 1970 and 1980, preprimary enrollment of three- to five-year-olds rose by 19 percent; between 1980 and 1992, it increased an additional 31 percent. An important feature of the increasing participation of young children in preprimary schools is the increasing proportion in full-day programs. In 1992 about 38 percent of the children attended school all day, compared with 32 percent in 1980 and 17 percent in 1970.

**11** Percentage of Minority Population Change, 1980–1990

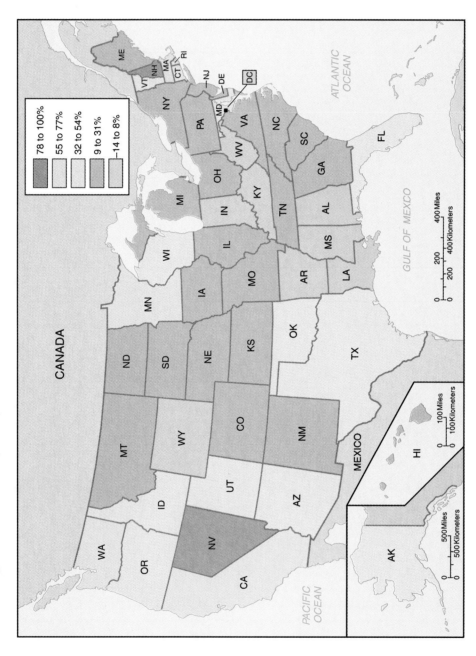

**Legend:**
- 78 to 100%
- 55 to 77%
- 32 to 54%
- 9 to 31%
- –14 to 8%

Minority populations shown on this map include African Americans, Asians, Hispanics, and other races. In the ten years from 1980–1990, Nevada and New Hampshire had the greatest percentage of growth in minority populations primarily because, proportionally, they had the greatest percentage of change in the general population, with Nevada growing at 50.1 percent and New Hampshire at 20.5 percent. The District of Columbia and West Virginia actually lost minority population at the same time that they lost total population. Of the 25.6 percent of the population under the age of eighteen, 30.9 percent are minorities. By 2010 it is projected that Ohio and Pennsylvania will decline in total youth population and only minimally increase their minority populations, while California, Texas, and Florida will gain 1-8 million youths, over half of them nonwhite.

580

# Ethnic Groups in the United States

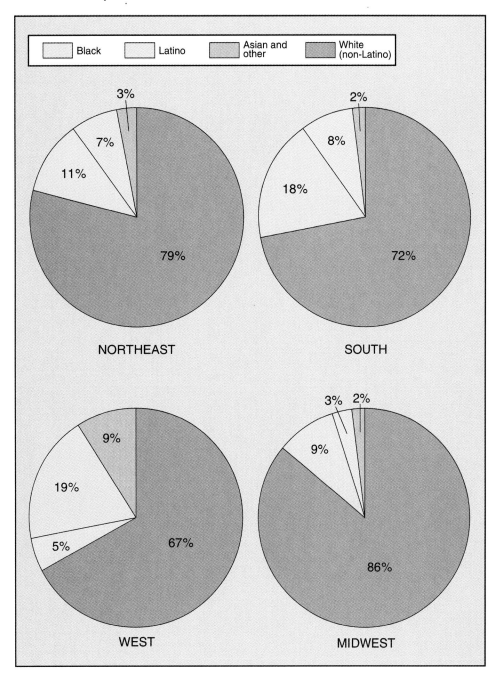

**Legend:** Black | Latino | Asian and other | White (non-Latino)

**NORTHEAST**
3%
7%
11%
79%

**SOUTH**
2%
8%
18%
72%

**WEST**
9%
19%
5%
67%

**MIDWEST**
3% 2%
9%
86%

In the Midwest nearly 86 percent of the population is descended mainly from British, Irish, German, Scandinavian, and Slavic people. The West has a high percentage of Latinos and Asians, and the South still has the largest percentage of African Americans. Educators are becoming aware of the need to account for other cultures in their curriculums and teaching strategies in order to accommodate different learning styles and in order to give students an appreciation of their culture. Diversity rather than melting pot has become the theme in U.S. schools in the 1990s.

# Projected Change in the Number of High School Graduates, 1989–1990 to 1999–2000

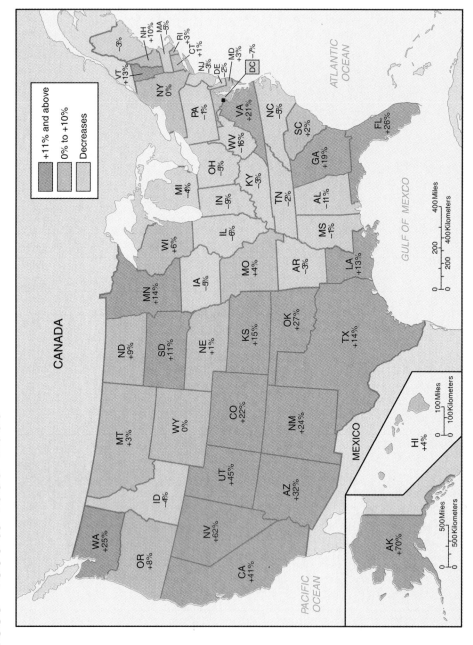

**Legend:**
- +11% and above
- 0% to +10%
- Decreases

CANADA

**State values:**

VT +13%
NH +10%
MA –5%
RI +3%
CT +3%
NJ +1%
DE –3%
MD +3%
DC –7%
NY 0%
PA –1%
VA +21%
NC –5%
SC +2%
GA +19%
FL +26%
WV –16%
OH –5%
KY –3%
TN –2%
AL –11%
MS –1%
MI –4%
IN –9%
IL –6%
MO +4%
AR –3%
LA +13%
WI +6%
IA –5%
MN +14%
ND +9%
SD +11%
NE +1%
KS +15%
OK +27%
TX +14%
CO +22%
NM +24%
MT +3%
WY 0%
UT +45%
AZ +32%
ID –6%
NV +62%
WA +25%
OR +8%
CA +41%
HI +4%
AK +70%

MEXICO

ATLANTIC OCEAN
GULF OF MEXICO
PACIFIC OCEAN

0 200 400 Miles
0 200 400 Kilometers

0 100 Miles
0 100 Kilometers

0 500 Miles
0 500 Kilometers

As the U.S. population increases through the next two decades, the youth population will decline after the year 2000. The eldest baby boomers, now 48, will begin to retire in great numbers after the year 2000. The youngest are now in junior high school and are most apparent in California, Texas, and Florida. There is no significant boomlet in most of the U.S. heartland and the mid-Atlantic states, as this map makes clear.

**14** Projections of Minority Public High School Graduates, 1995

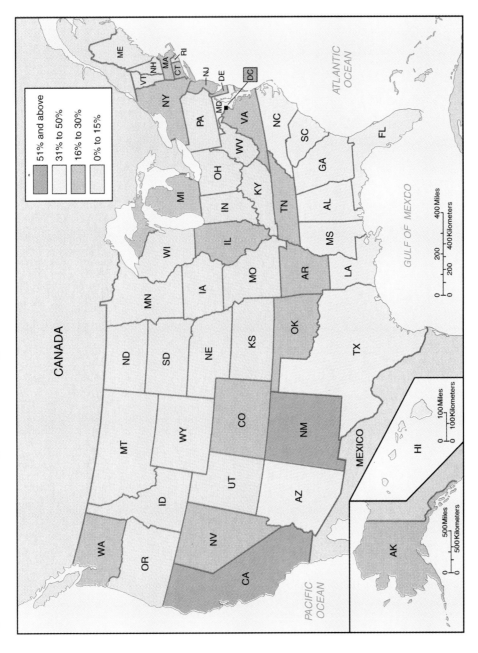

Since 1970 the United States has become more ethnically diverse. In 1940 African Americans were the only statistically significant minority group and occupied states primarily in the Deep South. Such states as New York, California, Texas, and Florida have gained population rapidly, primarily because of an influx of minority groups. These states are projected to have 21 million of the nation's total youth population, or one-third of all youths aged one to seventeen by the year 2010. As a consequence, other states will have relatively smaller minority populations. Maine is projected to have only a 3.1 percent and Vermont only a 5.4 percent minority population in 2010 (up from 2.8 percent and 2.4 percent, respectively, in 1990). The projections of minority graduates in 1995 shown on this map bear out this statistic.

# Sources of Funding for Public Schools

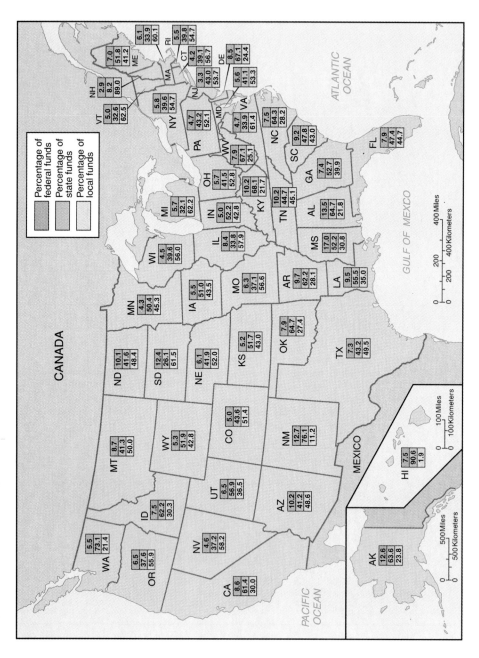

**Legend:**
- Percentage of federal funds
- Percentage of state funds
- Percentage of local funds

CANADA

| State | Federal | State | Local |
|---|---|---|---|
| WA | 5.5 | 73.1 | 21.4 |
| OR | 6.5 | 37.6 | 55.9 |
| CA | 8.6 | 61.4 | 30.0 |
| NV | 4.6 | 37.2 | 58.2 |
| ID | 7.5 | 62.2 | 30.3 |
| MT | 8.7 | 41.3 | 50.0 |
| WY | 5.3 | 51.9 | 42.8 |
| UT | 6.5 | 56.9 | 36.5 |
| AZ | 10.2 | 41.2 | 48.6 |
| CO | 5.0 | 43.6 | 51.4 |
| NM | 12.7 | 76.1 | 11.2 |
| ND | 10.1 | 41.6 | 48.4 |
| SD | 12.4 | 26.1 | 61.5 |
| NE | 6.1 | 41.9 | 52.0 |
| KS | 5.2 | 51.7 | 43.0 |
| OK | 7.9 | 64.7 | 27.4 |
| TX | 7.3 | 43.2 | 49.5 |
| MN | 4.3 | 50.4 | 45.3 |
| IA | 5.5 | 51.0 | 43.5 |
| MO | 6.3 | 37.1 | 56.6 |
| AR | 9.7 | 62.2 | 28.1 |
| LA | 9.5 | 55.5 | 35.0 |
| WI | 4.5 | 39.6 | 56.0 |
| IL | 8.4 | 33.8 | 57.9 |
| MI | 5.7 | 32.1 | 62.2 |
| IN | 5.0 | 52.2 | 42.8 |
| OH | 5.7 | 41.5 | 52.8 |
| KY | 10.2 | 68.1 | 21.7 |
| TN | 10.2 | 44.7 | 45.1 |
| MS | 17.0 | 52.2 | 30.8 |
| AL | 13.5 | 64.7 | 21.8 |
| GA | 7.4 | 52.7 | 39.9 |
| FL | 7.9 | 47.4 | 44.7 |
| SC | 9.2 | 47.8 | 43.0 |
| NC | 7.5 | 64.3 | 28.2 |
| WV | 7.9 | 67.1 | 25.1 |
| VA | 5.6 | 41.1 | 53.3 |
| MD | 4.7 | 33.9 | 61.4 |
| DE | 8.5 | 67.1 | 24.4 |
| PA | 4.7 | 43.2 | 52.1 |
| NJ | 3.3 | 43.0 | 53.7 |
| NY | 5.8 | 39.6 | 54.7 |
| VT | 5.0 | 32.6 | 62.5 |
| NH | 2.9 | 8.2 | 89.0 |
| ME | 7.0 | 51.8 | 41.2 |
| MA | 6.1 | 33.9 | 60.1 |
| RI | 5.5 | 39.8 | 54.7 |
| CT | 4.2 | 39.1 | 56.7 |
| HI | 7.5 | 90.6 | 1.9 |
| AK | 12.6 | 63.6 | 23.8 |

ATLANTIC OCEAN

GULF OF MEXICO

PACIFIC OCEAN

MEXICO

Scale bars: 200 / 400 Miles, 200 / 400 Kilometers; 100 Miles / 100 Kilometers; 500 Miles / 500 Kilometers

584

Nationwide, property taxes have been a chief source of local school funding since the 1820s. However, a reliance on local property taxes has resulted in great disparities in per pupil spending between districts in most states. In Michigan, for example, Kalkaska spent about $38 hundred per pupil in 1994, while Bloomfield Hills spent more than $10 thousand per pupil. Local school districts are thus turning to the state income tax or the sales tax as sources of revenue. New Hampshire has the highest level of local support at 89 percent and New Mexico the lowest at 11.2 percent. But as property taxes rise, and the quality of education remains in doubt, many communities are turning to state funding to solve their school financing problems.

## 16    National Index of Public Revenue per Student in Relation to Per Capita Personal Income by State, 1991–1992

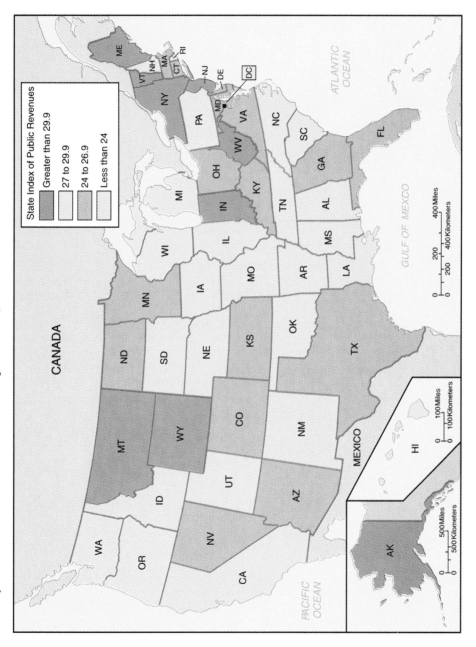

State Index of Public Revenues

- Greater than 29.9
- 27 to 29.9
- 24 to 26.9
- Less than 24

The national index of public education revenues reflects monies raised to educate the average student relative to the taxpayer's ability to pay. Between the school years ending 1930 and 1972, the elementary and secondary index increased 11.7 points from 10.6 to 22.3. Between school years ending 1972 and 1984, the index remained fairly stable. Since then, the national index has increased just over three points to 25.5. In the school year 1991–92, elementary and secondary per pupil state revenues ranged from $3,007 in Mississippi to $8,639 in Alaska. The state index ranged from below 21 in Arkansas and Tennessee to above 34 in Alaska, Vermont, Wyoming, and West Virginia.

**CHAPTER**

**OBJECTIVES**

After studying this chapter, you should be able to:

- Explain who is covered by state compulsory attendance laws.
- Describe how the states are involved in the development of curriculum.
- Discuss ways in which curriculum has been challenged.
- Explain how court rulings on censorship have changed since the 1970s.
- Describe the courts' rulings in First Amendment freedom of expression and assembly cases.

- Explain how courts have interpreted First Amendment freedom of religion rights of students.
- Define the due process rights of teachers.
- Define teachers' freedom of expression and academic freedom rights.
- Define tort liability, negligence, and intentional tort.
- Discuss how teachers can use ethical decision-making techniques.

# Chapter 15

# LAW AND THE SCHOOLS

The Supreme Court first gave a specific standard for protection of students' First Amendment rights in the *Tinker* case [*Tinker v. Des Moines Independent School District*, 393 U.S. 503 (1969)]. This grand protector of student press rights didn't involve a student newspaper at all. It dealt instead with high school and junior high school students from Des Moines, Iowa, who wore black armbands to school in protest of the United States' involvement in Vietnam. Still, the Supreme Court's decision in *Tinker* set the legal standard for student free expression rights in newspapers, yearbooks, and other publications for the next 19 years.

*Tinker* began on a snowy Saturday, Dec. 11, 1965. A large group of students met at the home of Christopher Eckhardt in Des Moines to make plans for a school protest against the Vietnam War. After long discussion, they decided to wear black armbands to school on Thursday, Dec. 16, and to continue wearing them until New Year's Day, 1966.

On Dec. 14, the principals of the Des Moines school system, having learned of the students' plan to wear armbands, adopted a policy that all students wearing armbands to school would be asked to remove them. If they refused, they would be suspended until they were willing to return without the armbands.

Most of the original group of students who had planned to protest backed out when they realized their records and their chances for college entrance and scholarships might be threatened.

On Dec. 16, Christopher Eckhardt, 16, a student at Theodore Roosevelt High, and 13-year-old Mary Beth Tinker, a student at Warren Harding Junior High and family friend, wore their homemade black armbands, complete with peace signs, to school. Mary Beth's 15-year-old brother, John, wore his the following day to North High School.

The three were suspended. They did not return until after New Year's Day, when the planned period for wearing the armbands expired.

More than two decades later, Christopher Eckhardt remembers what happened as if it were yesterday. "I wore the black armband over a camel-colored jacket." There were threats in the hallway. "The captain of the football team attempted to rip it off. I turned myself in to the principal's office, where the vice principal asked if 'I wanted a busted nose.' He said the seniors wouldn't like it. Tears welled up in my eyes because I was afraid of violence.

"He called my mom to get her to ask me to take the armband off." Christopher's parents were peace activists; his mother refused. "Then he called the girls' counselor in. She asked if I wanted to go to college, and said that colleges didn't accept protesters. She said I would probably need to look for a new high school if I didn't take the armband off.

"The year before they allowed everyone to wear black armbands to mourn the death of school spirit . . . but on Dec. 15 the gym coaches said that anyone wearing armbands the next day had better not come to gym class because they'd be considered communist sympathizers.

"My former subversive activities had included being president of the student council in elementary and junior high school, membership in the Boy Scouts, listing on the honor roll, delivering *The Des Moines Register* and shoveling snow for neighbors."

Unlike her friend Christopher, Mary Beth Tinker remembers very little about the events of 1965 and the court cases that followed, although she thinks she attended all three court hearings.

"I think I've blocked a lot of it out. I didn't realize the significance of the case for years," she says. "I had just moved to St. Louis when the decision was announced in 1969. I was a high school junior, and I just wanted to fit in, blend in with the crowd. Suddenly, *Newsweek* and *Time* were descending on the school, wanting to take pictures of me.

"Plus we'd gotten a lot of threats [in 1965]. A man who had a radio talk show threatened my father on the air. Red paint was thrown on our house. A woman called on the phone, asked for me by name, and then said, 'I'm going to kill you!'

"I realized how hateful, how irrational people could be. Subconsciously there was a part of me that withdrew. I got a little bit protective of myself and our family."

(For information about the courts' decisions in the *Tinker* case, see Freedom of Expression and Assembly, pp. 597–598.)

From: *Death by Cheeseburger: High School Journalism in the 1990s and Beyond*, The Freedom Forum (1994), 95–96.

## Students and the Law

In any society, the rights of the individual need to be protected. Thus, in the very special microcosm of society that is the classroom, both the rights of students and the rights of teachers are determined and legislated by court rulings and legal statutes. In this section of the chapter we will discuss students who as vulnerable minors are typically protected by the law. However, the law also maintains that students have the responsibility to follow school rules and state and federal statutes.

**Law** refers to our system of jurisprudence, which defends our rights and secures justice in the courts. When we talk about the law, we are discussing first, the law of the land, which is set forth in the U.S. Constitution, and second, the law of each state, which is established in that state's constitution. These comprise **constitutional law. Statutory law** refers to statutes or laws passed by federal and state legislatures.

As can be seen from the chapter's opening anecdote, statutes and court rulings apply to students' rights and responsibilities. First and foremost, all students regardless of race, ethnic origin, citizenship, or gender have the right to attend a school that provides each of them an equal educational opportunity. Some educators contend that students also have the right to achieve at a predetermined minimal level as established by the state. Students' rights to freedom of expression, of assembly, of privacy, and of religion are protected by the First Amendment, as well as the right to due process in decisions of suspension or expulsion. The parents of students under the age of eighteen have the right of access to their children's school records. Along with these rights, however, students have the responsibility to ensure that their health and behavior do not endanger others. To this end, the state and the school establish laws and rules of discipline and behavior that must be enforced.

## EQUAL EDUCATIONAL OPPORTUNITY

The Fourteenth Amendment of the U.S. Constitution guarantees in part that "no State shall . . . deny to any person within its jurisdiction, the equal protection of the laws." Since the 1954 *Brown v. Board of Education of Topeka* (347 U.S. 483, 1954) case, the Supreme Court has ruled that this equal protection clause applies to education. In recent decades, the group referred to as "all students" has been broadened to apply to undocumented immigrant children (*Phyler v. Doe,* 457 U.S. 202, 1982). Chapter 5 (pp. 180–202) discusses at length the courts' and legislatures' interpretation of equal educational opportunity.

## SCHOOL ATTENDANCE AND STUDENT HEALTH

All fifty states have compulsory attendance laws that include penalties for noncompliance. The laws require that all students, including undocumented immigrant children up to a specified age, be educated whether they attend a private or public school or whether they are tutored or taught in informal settings such as home schools, provided the instructors are qualified by the state. Most states do not require attendance after age sixteen, but a few states, such as West Virginia, have enacted legislation (upheld by the West Virginia Supreme Court in *Means v. Sidiropolis,* 401 S.C.2d 447 W. Va., 1990) to encourage high school graduation by connecting the ability to obtain a driver's license to school attendance for students under age eighteen.

Although home schooling has existed since the Colonial period, it has gained new legal status in the last decade. In 1994 the Home School Legal Defense Association reported that thirty-four states had statutes or regulations authorizing home education. Thirty states required standardized testing of home-schooled students; however, only two states, Iowa and Michigan, required home tutors to be certified by the state, and two other states, Arizona and Louisiana, required them to pass an examination. Nine states required home tutors to have a high school diploma or a Graduate Equivalency Degree (GED).

***Student Health*** In most states, schools have the right to require that all students be in good health so as not to endanger others. For this reason states have the right to require that all students have specific immunizations.

Even though decisions about whether students can attend school for health reasons are made by boards of education and the states, parents often object to them. In AIDS cases, for example, some parents have questioned whether children with the disease should be allowed to attend school. For this reason, the federal Centers for Disease Control and Prevention have established guidelines that have been used as the basis for numerous state policies. The guidelines stress that AIDS is transmitted only through contact with infected blood or semen and not through ordinary contact with an infected person; therefore, they recommend, and the courts have agreed, that most AIDS victims be allowed to attend school with all the rights, privileges, and services accorded to other students. According to these guidelines, decisions about students infected with HIV (human immunodeficiency virus) should be made on a case-by-case basis, relying on the best available scientific evidence and medical advice. (For more information on AIDS and AIDS education, see chapter 11, pp. 460–463.)

Although some school boards have attempted to bar AIDS victims from attending school, the courts have held that AIDS-infected students are protected by federal law barring discrimination against individuals with disabilities. Therefore, the courts have required that schools enroll AIDS students upon certification by health officials that they pose minimal risk of infecting others. The courts and laws, however, have little control over people's emotions, especially when they involve children and a fatal disease, as demonstrated by the highly publicized cases of Ryan White and the Ray brothers. In Kokomo, Indiana, thirteen-year-old Ryan White, a hemophiliac infected with the AIDS virus, was banned from school. He moved to Cicero, Indiana, where the school and his new classmates welcomed him. In Arcadia, Florida, on August 28, 1987, the home of the Rays was burned to the ground by local people angered that the three HIV-infected hemophiliac sons were being sent to the public schools. Other children infected with AIDS, however, are welcomed into the schools. In Swansea, Massachusetts, an HIV-infected hemophiliac was not only accepted into the school but supported by his friends and neighbors. In Wilmette, Illinois, the parents of a boy with AIDS won over other parents by inviting them into their home and asking for their help. In Chicago, the Mexican American parents of children in Pilsen Academy initially demonstrated against the school system's decision to allow an anonymous HIV-infected child to attend. Later, however, after receiving information about AIDS from principal William Levin, the parents approved the decision of the board.

Because the issue of AIDS is such an emotional one, many communities have been unable to solve the problems it causes without the involvement of the courts. In some cases, nervous school officials have been unwilling to admit HIV-infected students into the school without a court order. In the White case in Kokomo, for example, the courts ruled that Ryan had to be readmitted. Almost unanimously, judges have ruled in favor of the right of the child with AIDS to attend school (McCarthy and Cambron-McCabe 1992, 74).

## CURRICULUM

The courts have ruled that the states not only have the right to develop a curriculum as long as federal constitutional guarantees are respected, but also have the right to monitor whether that curriculum is being implemented in the public and private schools of the state. Although few states have constitutional curriculum mandates, most require the state legislatures to make specific curricular determinations. These include:

- Specific topics such as the federal Constitution
- Certain subjects such as U.S. history
- Specific subjects appropriate for the grade level
- Vocational and bilingual education
- Special education for students with disabilities
- Specific subjects required for high school graduation
- Minimal acceptable performance levels for high school graduation

Most legislatures assign the actual development of the curriculum to the state education agency. State statutes usually require that local boards of education offer the state-mandated minimum curriculum and allow them to supplement it based on local needs unless there is a statutory prohibition. The state education agency usually monitors the board's delivery of the curriculum in local schools.

*Challenges to the Curriculum* Parents have frequently challenged the curriculum and materials used by the schools, especially when they deal with sexuality education (see chapter 11, pp. 461–463). A North Carolina survey of health educators revealed, for example, that 50 percent of school health coordinators had been challenged by a parent or told by a school official that particular subjects such as contraception and birth control were inappropriate and should not be taught (People for the American Way 1990). However, the courts have typically ruled in favor of the board's right to establish (not the teacher's right to teach if the board has not established) such courses based on the state's interest in the health and welfare of its children (*Aubrey v. School District of Philadelphia,* 63 Pa. Cmwlth. 330, 437 A.2d 1306, 1981). Likewise, the right to teach *mandatory* sexuality education courses has been upheld even when parents have maintained that they violated their religious beliefs (*Cornwell v. State Board of Education,* 314 F. Supp. 340, D., Md., 1969 and *Smith v. Ricci,* 446 A.2d 510 N.J., 1982). However, a recent case in Caddo Parish, Louisiana, ruled that the sexuality education curriculum for grades seven through twelve adopted by the school board violated a Louisiana state law (LRs 17:281). According to the court, some passages pertaining to premarital sex, contraception, and sexually transmitted diseases in the adopted curriculum violated the state statute, although not intentionally. The court required the school district to examine adopted materials for factual accuracy (*Coleman v. Caddo Parish School Board,* La. App. 2 Cir. 635 So. 2d 1238, 1994).

Although most states do not select a single text for each subject area, most develop a list of acceptable books from which local districts may adopt books. Many cases have challenged the right of local boards to prescribe textbooks. One of the best-known cases, in part because of the violence surrounding it, took place in Kanawha County, West Virginia, in 1974. Parents protested the board's adoption of an English series they considered to be godless, communist, and profane. The federal court upheld the school board's right to select books to be used in the schools (*Williams v. Board of Education of County of Kanawha,* 388 F. Supp. 93, S.D., W. Va., 1975). (See pp. 592–595 for other cases related to censorship of school-related material; chapter 13, pp. 537–538 for a discussion of the religious right's attempts to censor textbooks; and For Further Reading/Reference for a description of J. Moffett's book dealing with the Kanawha case.)

The courts have ruled against curricular requirements they believe limit an individual's constitutional rights. For example, courts have ruled against legislatures that have attempted to ban specific courses from the curriculum. The first such case occurred in 1923, when the U.S. Supreme Court ruled that the state of Nebraska could not prohibit the teaching of a foreign language in any private or public schools to children who had not yet completed eighth grade. According to the Court, the teacher's right to teach private elementary school students reading in German, the parents' right to employ the teacher, and the children's right to learn were protected under the due process clause of the Fourteenth Amendment (*Meyer v. Nebraska,* 262 U.S. 390, 1923). In 1968 the Court ruled against an Arkansas law that prohibited teaching Darwin's theory of evolution in the public schools, as a violation of the teachers' and students' First Amendment rights (*Epperson v. Arkansas,* 393 U.S. 97, 106, 1968).

*Censorship: Supreme Court Decisions* Few things affect the public school's curriculum more than censorship. According to People for the American Way, an organization monitoring censorship cases, incidents of attempted censorship reached a twelve-year high in 1993–1994 with 462 reported cases in forty-six states (up from 395 the previous year), with 42 percent of the challenged materials and books removed or restricted. There are many reasons why censorship incidents have increased. The primary reason is that groups, particularly from the political far right or far left, want control over the school curriculum and have become active in this pursuit. Far left groups attempt to limit the use of books or materials considered to be racist or sexist; far right groups attempt to remove materials considered to be religiously, politically, or sexually offensive. Professional organizations such as the American Library Association and the National Council of Teachers of English, recognizing the potential danger of a curriculum controlled by special-interest groups, have attempted to provide their members with tools and techniques for avoiding censorship before it occurs and limiting its sting after it occurs. The tools include sample book and material selection policies and forms to use when materials are questioned. The techniques include the setting of selection policies, involving the widest constituency possible in the selection, providing parents with options for individual children, and setting policies for how questioned books and materials will be reviewed. Ironically, another reason for the increase of censorship incidents lies in recent court censorship decisions.

Changes in how the Supreme Court has ruled in censorship cases make attempts at censorship more likely and at the same time provide protection for school districts that establish policies for selection and review of classroom books and materials. In 1957, for example, the ruling by the Supreme Court in the case of *Roth v. United States* (354 U.S. 476, 1957) established a precedent for censorship cases that prevailed until the early 1970s. The majority decision in *Roth* stated, in part, "All ideas having even the slightest redeeming social importance—unorthodox ideas, controversial ideas, even ideas hateful to the prevailing climate of opinion—have full protection of the First Amendment guarantees unless excludable because they encroach upon . . . more important areas."

In 1973, however, the Supreme Court handed down a decision in *Miller v. California* (413 U.S. 15, 24, 1973) that provided a new set of guidelines to determine obscenity:

1. Whether the "average person, applying contemporary community standards" would find that the work, taken as a whole, appeals to prurient interest.
2. Whether the work depicts or describes, in a patently offensive way, sexual conduct specifically defined by the applicable state law.
3. Whether the work, taken as a whole, lacks serious literary, artistic, political, or scientific value.

These guidelines make it very difficult to determine whether a work is obscene. Who is the "average person"? How do we determine "community standards"? What does "contemporary" mean? Who decides?

The *Miller* decision, however, does give increased control to the community and the schools in determining obscenity in censorship cases. Justice William O. Douglas, in a dissenting opinion, expressed concern about this increased control.

> What we do today is rather ominous as respects librarians. The anti-obscenity net now signed by the court is so finely meshed that taken literally it could result in raids on libraries. . . . Libraries, I had always assumed, were sacrosanct, representing every part of the spectrum. If what is offensive to the most influential person or group in the community can be purged from a library, the library system would be destroyed.

The courts, possibly realizing the difficulty in determining a work's obscenity, have moved from an earlier attempt to examine the quality of a work to an examination of an individual's or group's right to select a book. In earlier cases the courts examined the work to determine its appropriateness. In *Keefe v. Geanokos* (418 F.2d 359, 361–362, 1st Cir., 1969), a teacher assigned his students an article from the *Atlantic Monthly* that dealt with student revolts of the 1960s in which the word *mother-fucker* was used several times. The Massachusetts Supreme Court ruled in favor of the teacher, saying that the article was acceptable since it was written in a scholarly manner and the word was an integral part of its thesis. In a similar case, a short autobiographical story, containing the phrase *white mother-fuckin' pig,* was read to a class of tenth graders by teacher Stanley Lindros. In reversing a decision of a lower court, the California Supreme Court said that by reading the story Mr. Lindros was pursuing a "bona fide educational purpose" and no disruption was created by the reading of the story. In more recent cases, however, especially since *Miller,* the courts' decisions have been based not on the applicability of the work, but rather on the board of education's right to select material or to remove it from use.

The U.S. District Court in Strongsville, Ohio, in *Minarcini v. Strongsville (Ohio) City School District* (541 F.2d 577, 6th Cir., 1976), found that the board of education had not violated the First Amendment freedom of speech rights of its faculty when it rejected the faculty's recommendations for books to be ordered for the school library. The U.S. Court of Appeals upheld the decision, saying that the board's decision was neither "arbitrary" nor "capricious." As in most cases since 1973, the books were not on trial; obscenity was not the issue. Instead, the court based its decision on the legal right of the board of education to decide. In a similar case, *Cary v. Board of Education of Adams-Arapahoe (Colorado) School District* (28-J, 598 F.2d 535, 544, 10th Cir., 1979), the court ruled that the local school board had the right to rule on course content. The case involved a board-approved elective English course in contemporary literature for juniors and seniors. The books for the course were selected by the teacher and the students, but the board objected to several of the choices. In its decision the court agreed that English teachers and students should be permitted to conduct an open discussion of free inquiry. "The student must be given an opportunity to participate openly if he is to become the kind of self-controlled, individually motivated, and independent thinking person who can function effectively as a contributing citizen." However, according to the court, free inquiry was not the issue at hand; authority to select appropriate materials for the curriculum was. The court decided in favor of the board, claiming that when teachers submit to a collectively bargained contract, they agree to allow the board to decide everything, including the materials to be used in the classroom.

The actual removal of books already in school libraries has been the issue in several court cases. One that was first heard in 1972, appealed to the U.S. Court of Appeals, and argued before the Supreme Court in 1979 is *President's Council Dist. 25 v. Community School Board No. 25* (457 F.2d 289, 2d Cir., 1972, cert. denied, 409 U.S. 998, 1972). In this case Piri Thomas's *Down these Mean Streets* was removed from all junior high school libraries in a New York school district. The appellate court upheld the lower court's ruling that the power to remove books is in the hands of the board. A similar question was argued in 1979 in Vermont in *Bicknell v. Vergennes Union High School Board of Directors* (475 F. Supp. 615, D.V.T., 1979). The board of education, in ordering two books removed from the school library, called them "obscene, vulgar, immoral, and perverted." The court ruled in favor of the board although it did not agree with the board's opinion of the books (again, the books were not on trial); it affirmed the authority of the elected board to control all curricular matters, including the removal of library books. Librarians, on the other hand, according to the court, do not have the right to control the library collection under the "rubric of academic freedom" (the right to speak freely about what one teaches).

In 1986 the Supreme Court also ruled in favor of the school board in a seven-to-two decision in *Bethel School District No. 403 v. Fraser* (106 S. Ct. 3159, 1986). School officials in Spanaway, Washington, had suspended a student for using sexual metaphors in describing candidates for a student government election. Chief Justice Burger wrote in the majority opinion, "Surely it is a highly appropriate function of public school education to prohibit the use of vulgar and offensive terms in public discourse. . . . Schools must teach by example the shared values of a civilized social order."

In January 1988 the Supreme Court, in a five-to-three ruling, upheld a high school principal's right to censor a student newspaper. In the case *Hazelwood School District v. C. Kulmeir et al.* (U.S. 86-836, 1988), Justice Byron White, writing for the majority, said that, while the First Amendment prevented a school from silencing certain kinds of student expression, it did not require a school to promote such expression in plays and publications under the school's auspices. He said that educators may exert editorial control in such instances "so long as their actions are reasonably related to legitimate pedagogical concerns."

**TABLE 15-1**

## Most Frequently Challenged Books and Materials
## 1982–1994

Books
 *Of Mice and Men,* John Steinbeck
 *The Catcher in the Rye,* J.D. Salinger
 *The Chocolate War,* Robert Cormier
 *Scary Stories to Tell in the Dark,* Alvin Schwartz
 *The Adventures of Huckleberry Finn,* Mark Twain
 *Go Ask Alice,* Anonymous
 *I Know Why the Caged Bird Sings,* Maya Angelou
 *The Witches,* Roald Dahl
 *The Bridge to Terabithia,* Katherine Paterson
 *A Light in the Attic,* Shel Silverstein
Materials
 *Impressions* [textbook series]
 *Pumsy in Pursuit of Excellence* [self-esteem program]
 *Quest* [self-esteem program]
 *Developing Understanding of Self and Others* [self-esteem program]
 *Rolling Stone* [magazine]
 *YM* [magazine]
 *Michigan Model for Comprehensive School Health Education*
 *Romeo and Juliet* [film]
 *Junior Great Books Series* [reading texts]
 *Sports Illustrated* [magazine]

From: People for the American Way, *Attacks on the Freedom to Learn: 1992–1993* (1994), 223–224.

**Rather than deciding censorship cases on the quality of the work, courts today focus on the right of those in authority to make decisions about the school's curriculum. These books and materials have been challenged by various groups for classroom use more frequently than any others.**

It is clear, then, that the opinions of the courts have shifted in censorship cases related to education. Earlier cases were decided on the quality of the work, whereas more recent ones have been determined on the right of those in authority to make decisions about the school's curriculum (revised from Reed 1994). Therefore, although these rulings make many books and other materials potential targets of censors (see table 15.1), they also mean that school boards who develop selection and review policies are likely to have their decisions protected by the courts.

## STUDENT ACHIEVEMENT

Since the states have been given the right to require attendance at school and to establish and monitor the curriculum, the public has also demanded that schools assume greater responsibility for student achievement. This **accountability** has

The Mendota Unified School District of California, composed primarily of Spanish-speaking migrant workers, has been accused of shortchanging the education of its students. A federal investigation found that the district violated the Civil Rights Act of 1964 by discriminating against students on the basis of race and national origin. A group of parents were instrumental in bringing these charges against the district. Among them was Maria Larios Gomez, far left, who said that her children, seated with her, never had homework and often played hookey without teachers or principals telling her about it.

led to an increased number of educational malpractice suits in which the schools are considered liable for nonachievement of students, which often is determined by minimum competency testing programs.

For example, in *Peter W. v. San Francisco Unified School District* (60 Cal. App. 3d 814, 131 Cal. Rptr. 854, 1976), a student maintained that the school was negligent in teaching, promoting, and graduating him since he read at only a fifth-grade level. He claimed that his lack of achievement was misrepresented to his parents, who didn't know of his deficiency until he was tested by a private agency after graduation. However, both the trial court and appellate court dismissed charges against the school, based on the complexities of the teaching and learning process, making it impossible to place the entire burden of student learning on the school. This, so far, has been the tenor of all educational malpractice decisions.

Although the schools are unlikely to be held accountable by the courts for specified levels of student achievement, they can be expected to be held accountable for accurately diagnosing student needs and keeping parents informed of student progress. Furthermore, in cases dealing with students with disabilities, the courts have ruled that the school must be able to prove that it is providing them appropriate services.

Another result of public outcries for academic accountability has been the implementation of competency testing. These proficiency exams, which are now administered in most states, are designed to show that students have achieved basic verbal and computational skills at the time of high school graduation.

Because competency tests were developed to ensure that all students were getting at least a basic education, it is ironic that in the court cases involving competency tests, people have claimed that the tests are discriminatory. For example, in Florida, ten black students who failed the test challenged the law authorizing the test, claiming that the test discriminated against minority students. According to evidence presented in the case, 77 percent of black students failed the math portion of the test compared to 24 percent of white students. Likewise, 26 percent of black students, compared to 3 percent of white students, failed the communication section of the test. The students further claimed that they were not given enough warning to prepare for the test. The court ruled that the test could be used for remedial purposes but not as a prerequisite for graduation until a phase-in period was implemented to prepare students for the test. Although the court disallowed the competency test for graduation purposes, it upheld the state's right to establish academic standards.

## FREEDOM OF EXPRESSION AND ASSEMBLY

First Amendment constitutional guarantees of free speech extend to students, as well as to teachers. The U.S. Supreme Court overturned the rulings of the U.S. District Court in Iowa and the U.S. Court of Appeals for the 8th Circuit in a landmark free speech decision, *Tinker v. Des Moines Independent School District* (393 U.S. 503, 1969), in which the plaintiffs, three public school students, could not be suspended from school for wearing black armbands to class to protest the government's policy in Vietnam. The decision stated that school officials could infringe on students' free speech rights only when the students' opinion and expression thereof materially and substantially interfered with the operation of the school. This includes such behavior as excessive noise, agitation, sit-ins, deliberate disruption of school functions, blocking halls, boycotts, and speech intended to incite disruptive action. Justice Abe Fortas, writing for the majority, penned the principle that has guided the courts in subsequent cases, "Neither students nor teachers shed their constitutional rights to freedom of speech or expression at the school house gate." The courts have further established that any regulation prohibiting student expression must be specific, publicized, and uniformly applied without discrimination. The ruling in the *Tinker* case became a precedent for other freedom of expression cases that dealt with issues such as distribution of controversial literature and publication of controversial topics in school newspapers.

In recent years the courts have ruled in favor of the school's right to edit or limit student free expression when students are participating in school-sponsored events. These decisions have focused on an educator's right to control the "style and content of student speech in school-sponsored expressive activities so long as their actions are reasonably related to legitimate pedagogical concerns" (*Hazelwood School District v. Kuhlmeier*, 484 U.S. 260, 1988). In the Hazelwood case, the school principal had forbidden students to print two pages of a school paper, produced as a part of a journalism class, that dealt with student pregnancy and drug use. The Supreme Court ruled that this action did not offend the First Amendment free speech rights since the principal had the right to exercise "editorial control over class material." While delivering a speech as a candidate for student council president, a Tennessee high school student made fun of a school administrator. The principal removed the student's name from the school's ballot.

The U.S. Supreme Court in *Tinker v. Des Moines Independent School District* (393 U.S. 503, 1969) ruled that the school's right to restrict a student's freedom of expression extends only to behavior that substantially interferes with the normal operation of the school. Mary Beth Tinker and her brother John were instrumental in bringing about this decision when they and three other students wore black armbands to school to protest the government's policy in Vietnam and to mourn the war dead.

The courts ruled that the principal was exercising appropriate control over student expression in a school-sponsored event (*Poling v. Murphy*, 872 F.2d 757, 6th Cir., 1989). However, in a 1991 New Jersey decision a state appellate court upheld a lower court ruling that a local school official violated the First Amendment rights of a junior high school student when he censored his reviews of two R-rated movies, "Mississippi Burning" and "Rain Man," in the school newspaper (*Desilets v. Clearview Regional School District*, CIV. No. C-23-90, 1991).

### *Viewpoint* Missing Graduation as a Matter of Principle

Lynn Steirer has a 3.0 grade-point average, but she will not graduate in June with her classmates in Bethlehem, Pa.

The Liberty High School senior, who has spent hours coaching sports and volunteering for Meals on Wheels and the Girl Scouts, is protesting her school district's requirement that students complete 60 hours of community service before they receive their diplomas.

Ms. Steirer says her decision to serve others must be based on personal values and should not be imposed upon her by the school system. So she has decided to forgo a high school diploma.

"The program is slavery. You do not have to work for free unless you are a criminal," she said.

Ms. Steirer, 17, has been battling the district's mandate, adopted in 1990, in federal court throughout her high school years. She lost in both the district and appellate courts, and last fall the U.S. Supreme Court declined to review the case.

"My friends are shocked. They thought I would've caved in by now," she said last week. "If I did, I wouldn't have been able to look at myself in the mirror."

Last week, she flew to Washington with her parents to lend moral support to two students who have just filed similar suits in New York and North Carolina.

**Philosophical Difference**

Phyllis Walsh, the coordinator of the community-service program at Liberty High, said she respects Ms. Steirer's decision to opt out of the program, but philosophically disagrees with her. Service mandates are designed to educate students about citizenship and career opportunities, not impart values, Ms. Walsh said.

Ms. Steirer will be allowed to attend the senior prom and other events. She said she may go to the graduation ceremony to cheer on her friends unless she is "too depressed."

And even without a diploma, Ms. Steirer was admitted to Pennsylvania State University in the fall based on her grades and test scores. She plans to major in criminal justice and psychology.

She said she hopes that the "odyssey" she has been through will convince school administrators that community service should be elective. "My parents are there to instill their values, not the school district," she said.

From: J. Portner. "Missing Graduation as a Matter of Principle," *Education Week* (April 27, 1994), 7.

The courts have also upheld students' right to assembly, based on First Amendment freedoms. This has generally been interpreted to mean that, as long as the operation of the school is not disrupted, students have the right to meet in groups and distribute petitions. School officials can control the time and place of student meetings and circulation of materials, and these rules must be specific, publicized, and uniformly applied.

For example, in *Healy v. James* (408 U.S. 169, 1972) a group of college students, following guidelines, petitioned to have a local chapter of the controversial national organization SDS recognized by the college. (Students for a Democratic Society was an organization actively involved in the student demonstrations of the 1960s and 1970s.) The Student Affairs Committee approved their application, but it was rejected by the college president. The group took its case to court based on the denial of First Amendment rights of expression and association arising from denial of campus recognition. Two lower courts ruled that the college had a right to refuse recognition to any group "likely to cause violent acts of disruption" (319 F. Supp. 113, 116). However, the Supreme Court reversed the decision, ruling that not recognizing the group was a violation of the students' rights of free expression and association.

## FREEDOM OF RELIGION

The First Amendment provides two protections of religious freedom. First, the government may not enact legislation establishing a religion and, second, may

*(continued on p. 602)*

# SHOULD PRAYER BE PERMITTED AT PUBLIC CEREMONIES IN PUBLIC SCHOOLS?

## PRO  Anthony M. Kennedy

School principals in the public school system of the city of Providence, Rhode Island, are permitted to invite members of the clergy to offer invocation and benediction prayers as part of the formal graduation ceremonies for middle schools and for high schools. The question before us is whether including clerical members who offer prayers as part of the official school graduation ceremony is consistent with the Religion Clauses of the First Amendment.

These dominant facts mark and control the confines of our decision: State officials direct the performance of a formal religious exercise at promotional and graduation ceremonies for secondary schools. Even for those students who object to the religious exercise, their attendance and participation in the state-sponsored religious activity are in a fair and real sense obligatory, though the school district does not require attendance as a condition for receipt of the diploma. . . .

The policy of the city of Providence is an unconstitutional one. . . . The government involvement with religious activity in this case is pervasive, to the point of creating a state-sponsored and state-directed religious exercise in a public school. . . . It is beyond dispute that, at a minimum, the Constitution guarantees that government may not coerce anyone to support or participate in religion or its exercise, or otherwise act in a way which "establishes a [state] religion or religious faith, or tends to do so." The State's involvement in the school prayers challenged today violates these central principles.

From: A. M. Kennedy. "States Cannot Exact Religious Control Conformity from a Student," *The Washington Post* (June 25, 1992), 26. In his opinion for the majority in the U.S. Supreme Court case *Lee v. Weisman,* Justice Kennedy examines the constitutional principles of separation of church and state.

# POSTSCRIPT

The arguments of Justices Kennedy, for the majority, and Scalia, for the dissent, differ from the norm in that one bases his argument on the First Amendment of the Constitution, specifically the establishment of religion clause, whereas the other focuses on the importance of historical tradition. More typically both opinions are constitutionally based. Kennedy suggests that when a school principal

# SHOULD PRAYER BE PERMITTED AT PUBLIC CEREMONIES IN PUBLIC SCHOOLS?

## CON Antonin Scalia

Three terms ago, I joined an opinion recognizing that the Establishment Clause must be construed in light of the "government policies of accommodation, acknowledgment and support for religion that are an accepted part of our political and cultural heritage." That opinion affirmed that "the meaning of the Clause is to be determined by reference to historical practices and understandings." . . .

These views of course prevent me from joining today's opinion, which is conspicuously bereft of any reference to history. In holding that the Establishment Clause prohibits invocations and benedictions at public-school graduation ceremonies, the Court—with nary a mention that it is doing so—lays waste a tradition that is as old as public-school graduation ceremonies themselves, and that is a component of an even more longstanding American tradition of nonsectarian prayer to God at public celebrations generally. . . .

Today's opinion shows more forcefully than volumes of argumentation why our Nation's protection, that fortress which is our Constitution, cannot possibly rest upon the changeable philosophical predilections of the Justices of this Court, but must have deep foundations in the historic practices of our people. . . .

The history and tradition of our Nation are replete with public ceremonies featuring prayers of thanksgiving and petition. . . . In addition to this general tradition of prayer at public ceremonies, there exists a more specific tradition of invocations and benedictions at public-school graduation exercises. . . . The invocation and benediction have long been recognized to be "as traditional as any other parts of the school graduation program and are widely established. . . ."

The Court presumably would separate graduation invocations and benedictions from other instances of public "preservation and transmission of religious beliefs" on the ground that they involve "psychological coercion." . . . The Court's argument that state officials have "coerced" students to take part in the invocation and benediction at graduation ceremonies is, not to put too fine a point on it, incoherent.

From: A. Scalia. "States Cannot Exact Religious Control Conformity from a Student," *The Washington Post* (June 25, 1992), 26. Justice Scalia, writing the dissenting opinion for the Court, suggests that historical traditions must be considered when making rulings on issues of public prayer.

selects a member of the clergy to deliver a prayer at a public school ceremony, it is tantamount to the state, in the person of the principal, coercing youngsters to participate in a prayer, which may violate their own beliefs and values. On the other hand, argues Scalia, prayer at public ceremonies is a time-honored tradition in the United States that should itself be valued and maintained.

*Cross-Cultural Perspective*

## India's Supreme Court Upholds Secularism

Declaring secularism a "basic feature of the Indian Constitution," India's Supreme Court has ruled that the president has the right to dismiss any state political unit that mixes religion and government.

According to News Network International, the high court decision stems from an action in 1993 declaring "President's rule" in three Indian states led by a Hindu nationalist party called Bharatiya Janata. Fundamentalist Hindu governments in the states of Madhya Pradesh, Rajasthan and Himachal Pradesh were replaced after Hindu militants demolished a Muslim mosque in December of 1992. The action led to riots between Hindus and Muslims in parts of India.

"Any act by a political party or government of a state in furtherance of its policies and programs to mix religion with politics is violative of not only the law, but the constitution," declared the Indian high court. In a concurring opinion, Justice S. R. Pandian wrote that any attempt by a state government to subvert secularism can "lawfully be deemed to give rise to a situation where the government cannot be carried on in accordance with the law."

Following the March 11 ruling, leaders of India's Christian minority issued a statement calling on the federal government to end religiously based discrimination and increase security at Christian churches. The leaders also pledged to uphold secularism as the lifeline of the Indian Constitution.

From: "India's Supreme Court Upholds Secularism," *Church & State* (June 1994), 47 (2), 21.

not interfere with an individual's right to practice her or his religion. The courts have interpreted these freedoms in the schools by ruling that reciting prayers and reading the Bible in school constitute an attempt on the part of the state to establish a religion and violate the religious freedom of those students who oppose the practice.

In 1963 two separate families challenged a Pennsylvania law requiring the reading of ten biblical verses and the recitation of the Lord's Prayer in school, even though their children could be excused from the exercise. In *Abington School District v. Schempp* (374 U.S. 203, 1963) and *Murray v. Curlett* (374 U.S. 203, L. Ed. 2d 844, 83 S. Ct. 1560, 1963), the Supreme Court ruled that it is unconstitutional for a state law to promote religion on school grounds, even when participation is not compulsory.

The decisions in these two cases, however, did not help resolve whether or not students could initiate religious activities in schools. This continues to be a controversial issue. The arguments have revolved around the constitutionality of state statutes permitting silent prayer or meditation in public schools. In 1985 the U.S. Supreme Court ruled that Alabama's statute calling for a moment of silence did violate the Constitution since it was passed with the intent of bringing prayer back into the schools (472 U.S. 38, 1985). Likewise, in 1992 the Supreme Court ruled in *Lee v. Weisman* (112 S. Ct. 2649, 1992) that nonsectarian benedictions and invocations at graduation were unconstitutional because they coerced students into participating in religious activities, which violated the government establishment of religion clause of the First Amendment (see Taking Sides, pp. 600–601). However, in 1994 six states had laws allowing "nonsectarian, voluntary student led prayers at school-related events." In some of these states, the laws have been upheld by the courts. In 1993 the 5th Circuit Court of Appeals held that "student initiated" prayer at a Texas commencement was legal because Texas statute permitted it. This ruling also applied to Mississippi and Louisiana (*Jones v. Clear Creek Independent School District,* CAS (Tex.) 977 F.2d., 963, 1992). Since these cases have been heard based on the legality of state statute, it is likely that the U.S. Supreme Court will rule on the constitutionality of the other statutes by 1996.

### *Viewpoint* The Contested Prayer

O God, we are grateful to You for having endowed us with the capacity for learning which we have celebrated on this joyous commencement.

Happy families give thanks for seeing Your children achieve an important milestone. Send Your blessings upon the teachers and administrators who helped prepare them.

The graduates now need strength and guidance for the future; help them to understand that we are not complete with academic knowledge alone. We must each strive to fulfill what You require of us all: to do justly, to love mercy, to walk humbly.

We give thanks to You, Lord, for keeping us alive, sustaining us and allowing us to reach this special, happy occasion. Amen.

From: R. Marcus. June 25, 1992. This is the benediction delivered by Rabbi Leslie Gutterman at the Nathan Bishop Middle School, Providence, Rhode Island, graduation in June 1989 that became the focus of the Supreme Court case of *Lee v. Weisman.*

## ACCESS TO STUDENT RECORDS

The U.S. Supreme Court has maintained that a right to "liberty" includes a right to "privacy." What this means in terms of students' school records has been the source of controversy.

In many cases the courts have ruled that potentially damaging information must be expunged from the student's record. In 1974 the U.S. Congress passed the Buckley amendment to the Family Educational Rights and Privacy Act (FERPA), also called the "sunshine law," which stipulates that federal funds may be withdrawn from schools that (1) fail to provide parents with access to their child's records or (2) disseminate information to third parties without parental permission. Parents must also be given the right to a hearing to challenge what is in their child's permanent record. However, a teacher's daily records pertaining to student progress are exempted from the law, as long as they are in the sole possession of the teacher and do not become part of a permanent record.

Some states have enacted legislation regarding the privacy of student records. For example, an Indiana law requires that school boards maintain a list of individuals and agencies who have access to personal files, that they furnish prior notice if information is to be disclosed to a third party, and that they inform students and parents of their right to access and to contest accuracy or appropriateness of material in the file. However, if a student is transferring to a new school and the parents or responsible adults are notified, the files can be routinely transferred. In 1983 a Maryland appeals court ruled against parents who said their child's rights had been violated when a file containing psychological reports was released to the child's new school (*Klipa v. Board of Educ. of Anne Arundel County*, 460 A.2d 601, Md. Ct. Sepc. App., 1983).

Federal legislation, known as the Hatch amendments (Education Amendments of 1978, P.L. 95–561), also requires that parental consent be given prior to a student's participation in any federally supported program involving psychiatric or psychological examinations, testing, or treatment designed to reveal sensitive information including sexual behavior or attitudes, mental or psychological problems, antisocial behavior, or political affiliation. In addition, the Hatch amendments give parents the right to examine instructional materials used in experimental programs. This part of the legislation is very controversial. Although most professional organizations support the privacy protection provided by this law, they object to the parental right of examination of materials, claiming that this gives special-interest groups an opportunity to attempt to control public school curriculum (McCarthy and Cambron-McCabe 1992, 96).

## STUDENT DISCIPLINE

The law is clear in authorizing the state and the schools to establish and enforce rules that protect the property rights of students, to ensure that all students can learn, and to protect students' rights and freedoms. But, historically, the courts have rarely reviewed school disciplinary action. They have instead upheld the right and duty of educators to maintain reasonable discipline. But they have provided guidelines defining appropriate standards for student discipline. In *Public School Law: Teachers' and Students' Rights* (1992) Martha M. McCarthy and Nelda H. Cambron-McCabe summarize these guidelines:

1. Any conduct regulation adopted should be necessary in order to carry out the school's educational mission; rules should not be designed merely to satisfy preferences of school board members, administrators, or teachers.
2. The rules should be publicized to students and their parents.
3. The rules should be specific and clearly stated so that students know which behaviors are prohibited.
4. The regulations should not impair constitutionally protected rights unless there is an overriding public interest, such as a threat to the safety of other students.
5. A rule should not be *ex post facto* [formulated after the fact]; it should not be adopted to prevent a specific activity that school officials know is being planned or has already occurred.
6. The regulations should be consistently enforced and uniformly applied to all students without discrimination.
7. Punishments should be appropriate to the offense, taking into consideration the child's age, sex, mental condition, and past behavior.
8. Some procedural safeguards should accompany the administration of all punishments; the formality of the procedures should be in accord with the severity of the punishment. (p. 202)

## CORPORAL PUNISHMENT

The U.S. Supreme Court has held **corporal punishment** (physical contact such as striking, paddling, or spanking of a student by an educator) to be constitutional where state law and local board policy permit it (*Ingraham v. Wright*, 430 U.S. 651, 1977). However, the number of states and districts abolishing corporal punishments and professional education associations seeking legislation to eliminate it has increased significantly in recent years. According to the National Coalition to Abolish Corporal Punishment in Schools, by 1994 twenty-seven states (up from three in the late 1980s) and more than half the school districts in another eleven states had statutes or policies prohibiting corporal punishment in schools (pp. 2–3). Most professional education associations oppose corporal punishment and seek legislation to eliminate it, as does the National Association of Elementary School Principals in this resolution:

> The practice of corporal punishment in the schools should be abolished. Research indicates corporal punishment may adversely affect a student's self-image and his or her school achievement, and it may contribute to disruptive and violent student behavior. Principals should utilize alternative forms of discipline.
>
> Therefore, NAESP urges all educators, in cooperation with parents and other concerned citizens and associations, to promote legislation that would prohibit all forms of corporal punishment in schools and would provide resources for the development of positive alternatives for disruptive students. (NAESP 1994, 5)

Challenges to the school's right to use corporal punishment on the basis that it violates a student's Fifth or Fourteenth Amendment due process rights are rarely successful since the courts typically rule, as they did in *Ingraham v. Wright,* that even though applying corporal punishment may implicate students' constitutional rights, they are able to bring assault and battery suits against the school. These cases are usually handled by state courts. For example, a sixth-grade student was paddled twice by a coach after he was found playing dodgeball when he had been told not to. The coach had warned the student twice and administered the punishment with two witnesses present. A doctor found no physical injury to the student. However, the father filed suit against the coach. The lower court and the appeals court found no substantive due process violation (*Wise v. Pea Ridge School Dist.*, 855 F.2d 560, 8th Cir., 1988). Even in a case in which doctors found that the children involved had suffered bruises, the courts ruled in favor of the school. In *Cunningham v. Beavers* (858 F.2d, 5th Cir., 1988), kindergarten students were paddled twice, once by the teacher and once by the principal, for refusing to stop "snickering." After the second paddling they missed six days of school. However, the courts found that their due process rights were not violated.

## SEARCH AND SEIZURE

Search and seizure is an area in which the courts have generally ruled in favor of the school rather than the student despite the Fourth Amendment, which protects "individuals against arbitrary searches by requiring state agents to obtain a warrant based on probable cause prior to conducting a search." According to most court decisions, a locker is school property, and a student does not have exclusive possession of it. Therefore, under the view of joint control, school officials have been allowed to inspect school lockers and have even consented to their search by law enforcement officials both for educational purposes and for contraband (particularly alcohol, drugs, and weapons) that would disrupt the operation of the school. However, the courts have also ruled that the search must be based on reasonable suspicion.

For example, *New Jersey v. T.L.O.* (469 U.S. 325, 1985) concerned a student whose purse had been searched for cigarettes. When marijuana and evidence that the student was selling drugs were found, the school imposed sanctions on her. Even though her attorney sought to have them removed on the grounds that they violated the student's Fourth Amendment rights, the Supreme Court affirmed the right of the school to search a student based on "reasonable suspicion." The Court further maintained that searches must be "reasonably related to the objectives of the search and not excessively intrusive in light of the age and sex of the student and the nature of the infraction."

Reasonableness is determined by the search methods employed by the school and the extent to which the search is personally intrusive. Bodily searches and searches of locked cars on school grounds require stricter standards. In *Jennings v. Joshua Indep. School Dist.* (869 F.2d 870, superseded, 877 F.2d 313, 5th Cir., 1989), dogs were used to search for drugs in the school parking lot. When one of the search dogs sniffed out a car, the well-publicized policy stated that the student would be asked to open it. If the student refused, a parent would be summoned. If the parent refused, the police would be called. When, after these steps were followed, one student's father refused to open the car, the police took over. After a search warrant was issued and the car searched, nothing was found. The father subsequently sued the school and the police officer. A district court dismissed the complaint against the school, and a jury returned a verdict in favor of the police officer.

Since drug tests involving the use of urine or blood specimens constitute a search under terms of the Fourth Amendment, the courts have been called to rule in cases involving drug tests of interscholastic athletes. In *Schaill v. Tippecanoe County School Corp.* (679 F. Supp. 833, N.D., Ind., 1988), the court upheld the right of the school to administer drug tests to students wishing to compete in interscholastic athletics. In this case, the courts did not require that reasonable suspicion exist, as in other search cases. However, other courts have ruled differently in this controversial area of school law. In *Acton v. Vernonia School District* (47 J. Dor., 796 F. Supp. 1354, 1994), a U.S. Court of Appeals ruled that an Oregon school district's policy of testing student athletes for illegal drugs violated students' rights under the U.S. and state constitutions. The parents of a seventh-grade prospective football player refused to sign a consent form for drug testing, and the student was suspended from athletics. The family filed suit and won, arguing that the school's policy violated the boy's Fourth Amendment right of prohibition against unreasonable search.

Although the courts have ruled in favor of the administration in many search and seizure cases, they have done so for different reasons. In some instances, the courts have ruled that school officials are not state agents but private individuals, and therefore, the Fourth Amendment is not applicable. In other cases, school officials have been considered state agents, but the courts have applied the rule of *in loco parentis,* meaning that the school has rights in place of parents. In still other cases, the courts have considered lockers joint property and, therefore, permitted searches.

Despite court rulings supporting administrators in searching lockers and personal effects, McCarthy and Cambron-McCabe maintain that schools should adhere to the following guidelines before conducting searches:

1.  If police officials are conducting a search in the school, either with or without the school's involvement, it is advisable to ensure that they first obtain a search warrant.
2.  Students and parents should be informed at the beginning of the school term of the procedures for conducting locker searches and personal searches.
3.  Any search conducted should be based on "reasonable suspicion" that the student possesses contraband that may be disruptive to the educational process.
4.  The authorized person conducting a search should have another staff member present who can verify the procedures used in the search.
5.  School personnel should refrain from using strip searches or mass searches of groups of students. (1992, 227)

---

**15-1**

**POINTS TO REMEMBER**

• All students, including illegal immigrants, are subject to state compulsory attendance laws, most of which require students to attend school until age sixteen. In addition, states and local boards have the right to decide who can attend school based on health and immunization. The AIDS epidemic has required that school boards carefully examine their policies.

• States have the right to develop and monitor implementation of the curriculum in public and private schools.

• Controversial aspects of the curriculum are frequently challenged by parents and special-interest groups; sexuality education is the area most frequently targeted.

• Recent court censorship cases make censorship attacks more likely because the courts have refused to rule on the appropriateness of texts and material; the rulings also protect schools against censorship when board policies have been established for selection and review.

• The courts have consistently ruled that schools cannot promote religion, including reading the Bible and reciting prayers in the classroom and at public events.

• Students, based on recent court rulings, have the right to expect at least a basic level of achievement. In addition, parents have the right to obtain access to their children's school records.

• In earlier court decisions, the courts tended to rule in favor of the students' right to freedom of speech. Recently, however, courts have ruled in favor of educators' rights to limit free speech if it is judged to be potentially disruptive.

• In search and seizure cases, particularly those related to drugs, the courts have ruled in favor of the right of administrators to conduct searches if there is reasonable suspicion.

---

## Teachers and the Law

Teachers, like students, are both protected by the law and responsible for upholding it. It is critical that teachers understand their rights and responsibilities in order to protect themselves and the students. Too frequently teachers are unclear about what is meant by law (see p. 589). Take the North Carolina middle school teacher who said, "I have to use this reading book, it's state law. To supplement it I've been xeroxing short stories from an anthology by young adult writers." In the first instance the teacher is incorrect; in the second he may be violating the law. First, North Carolina has no statute requiring the use of state adopted textbooks. In fact, many school districts replace textbooks with approved children's books or adolescent novels. Next, the teacher may be violating copyright laws by xeroxing stories for student use. In fact, he could be sued for doing so. Understanding the law can help you avoid making similar, potentially costly, mistakes.

## CONTRACT LAW

State statutes grant to the local school board the decision to employ, assign, or transfer a certified teacher within the school district. In most states, only the local board can make such an offer, and it must be approved by a majority of board members in a properly called meeting. A **contract** is an agreement between two or more competent parties to legally create, alter, or dissolve a relationship. A teacher's employment is based on a contract between the teacher and the school board, usually in writing. In order to be valid, contracts must meet certain requirements specified by state law and must have five basic elements: (1) an offer and acceptance, (2) competent parties, (3) consideration, (4) legal subject matter, and (5) proper form. These requirements constitute *contract law.*

In order to be considered competent, parties must have the legal capacity to enter into a contract. These include a legal school board and a teacher who meets state certification requirements.

Consideration is what one party pays in return for services rendered by the other party. Teaching contracts include a designated salary, a period of time, and identified duties and responsibilities as part of this consideration before a contract is considered valid.

In a South Dakota case, for example, a teacher was extended an offer by the superintendent and chair of the school board pending approval of the board in two weeks. During that time, the teacher experienced problems in the classroom and the board refused to extend a contract. The teacher filed suit for breach of contract, but the state supreme court ruled that no contract had existed between the teacher and the district because the procedure mandated by state statute had not been met (*Minor v. Sully Buttes School Dist.,* No. 58-2,345 N.W.2d 48, S.D., 1984).

## AFFIRMATIVE ACTION

The U.S. Commission on Civil Rights has defined affirmative action as "steps taken to remedy the grossly disparate staffing and recruitment patterns that are the present consequences of past discrimination and to prevent occurrence of employment discrimination in the future" (McCarthy and Cambron-McCabe, 334). School boards must adopt and implement affirmative action plans for recruiting and retaining teachers and staff from underrepresented groups.

Although affirmative action plans have been widely supported, they have been challenged by the courts under the equal protection clause of Title VI as causing reverse discrimination (discrimination of nonminorities resulting from efforts to remedy prior bias). The U.S. Supreme Court, for example, struck down a Michigan school district's collective bargaining agreement protecting minority teachers from layoffs (106 S. Ct. 1842, 1986). However, a federal court ruled that a school district under court order to eliminate the effects of prior segregation was justified in temporarily hiring and assigning quotas to achieve integrated faculties and ensure students' rights to equal educational opportunities (*Morgan v. Burke,* 926 F.2d 86, 1st Cir., 1991).

## DUE PROCESS

All U.S. citizens have the constitutionally guaranteed right to **due process**, which protects us from arbitrary governmental action and unreasonable or discriminatory practices.

These rights are protected by the Fifth and Fourteenth Amendments. The Fifth Amendment states that "no person shall be compelled in any criminal case to be a witness against himself, nor be deprived of life, liberty, or property without due process of the law." The Fourteenth Amendment guarantees that no state shall "deny to any person within its jurisdiction the equal protection of the laws."

Frequently, due process decisions deal with the nonrenewal of teaching contracts. Between 1985 and 1988, in 3 hundred of the nation's school districts, representing 2 percent of the districts and 6 percent of the pupils, ninety-four cases were filed by employees against the schools in the area of professional negotiations (Imber and Thompson 1991). In a famous precedent-setting case, *Board of Regents v. Roth* (408 U.S. 564, 1972), the U.S. Supreme Court ruled that nontenured teachers who were dismissed at the end of a specified contract had no right to a statement of reasons or a hearing as long as regulations set by the institution and the state were followed.

**Tenure** is a contractual relationship between a teacher and a school board that can be terminated only for adequate cause and with due process. It is usually awarded after a specified probationary period, usually three to seven years, during which teachers are evaluated by administrators and/or peers. Tenure laws are determined by the states and give discretionary power to local school boards. Tenure is a statutory (by law) right rather than a constitutional right, and therefore, protections and procedures vary among states. It does not give absolute job security to teachers; they may be dismissed for adequate cause, gross misconduct, neglect of duty, mental or physical incapacity, moral turpitude, or financial emergency. These causes are clearly identified by state law. In tenure cases the courts have attempted to protect the rights of the teachers and at the same time maintain some flexibility for school districts in personnel matters.

Since grounds for dismissal are statutorily determined, it is difficult to generalize tenure laws. In many states one of the legal causes for dismissal of tenured teachers is incompetency, but this has been broadly interpreted by the courts. For example, in Pennsylvania the courts upheld the dismissal of a teacher who had been disruptive in school, could not control students, and failed to maintain composure in dealing with students, parents, and other professionals. The court interpreted incompetency to mean deficiencies in personality, composure, judgment, and attitude (*Hamburg v. North Penn School Dist.,* 484 A.2d 867, Pa. Commw. Ct., 1984). In a Delaware court case (*Jones v. Indian River School Board,* Proto. 94 MO2 002, 1994), incompetence was related to the failure of large numbers of students to pass an Algebra II class taught by the teacher. Adele Jones, a tenured mathematics teacher, was dismissed on the grounds of incompetence because 42 percent of her students failed Algebra II and another 21 percent received Ds. The year prior to her dismissal she was put on an individual improvement plan by her principal. Under Delaware statute, judges can examine such cases only in terms of whether correct procedures were used in the firing of the teacher, not on the merits of the case (see Viewpoint below).

### *Viewpoint* The Case of Adele Jones

A Delaware Superior Court judge has ordered the Indian River school board to take another vote on whether to dismiss Adele Jones, the mathematics teacher whose firing last year attracted national media attention.

In a Jan. 19 ruling, Judge T. Henley Graves said the board had erred in voting to dismiss Ms. Jones without fully reviewing all the exhibits in her case. And he ruled that a board member whose children had fared poorly in Ms. Jones's class had a conflict of interest and should not have voted on her firing.

Ms. Jones, who taught algebra at Sussex Central High School in Georgetown, was fired because she had a record of giving many of her students D's and F's. The official charges against her were incompetence and insubordination. (*See Education Week, Sept. 15, 1993.*)

Ms. Jones argued that she had high standards, requiring students to keep notebooks, to pay attention in class, and to do their homework. Those who did so, she said, generally passed her class.

But district administrators said her students' "negative grades" damaged their self-esteem, turned them off from studying mathematics, and were the result of poor teaching methods.

She appealed her firing with legal assistance from the Delaware State Education Association.

*　　*　　*　　*　　*

The Indian River, Del., school board voted last week to reinstate Adele Jones.

The 5-to-4 vote came after a Delaware Superior Court judge ordered that the school board take another vote on Ms. Jones's case. The board's first vote, the judge ruled, violated procedures because members failed to review all of the documents in the case.

The vote to fire Ms. Jones in June 1993 was 6 to 4. Since that time, three new members have joined the board, all of whom voted for reinstatement.

Ms. Jones will resume teaching at Sussex Central High School as soon as she finishes duties associated with her part-time jobs, the state union president said. She will receive full back pay.

From: Ann Bradley. "Board in Del. Ordered to Review Case of Ousted Algebra Teacher," *Education Week* (February 9, 1994), 8.

——. "Board Votes to Reinstate Ousted Algebra Teacher," *Education Week* (March 23, 1994), 11.

Court cases based on an individual's due process rights attempt to establish fair procedures related to life, liberty, or property. For example, in *Board of Regents v. Roth,* the Court ruled that a state university, which did not provide a pretermination hearing for a nontenured teacher hired on a fixed contract for one academic year, did not violate his due process rights. According to the Court, the life, liberty, or property interests of this individual were not impaired, since he did not have property rights based on tenure or length of service.

However, in *Perry v. Sindermann* (408 U.S. 593, 1972), the Court ruled in favor of the plaintiff, who had taught in the Texas state college system for ten years without tenure. Sindermann, who was denied a due process hearing, claimed that he was dismissed because he publicly criticized the college administration. He further claimed that due to his length of service he had de facto tenure. The Court upheld Sindermann's right to a hearing with a statement that, if a case involved freedom of speech, a hearing must be provided. Furthermore, the Court agreed with Sindermann that he had valid property rights based on de facto tenure deriving from length of service.

Hence, the courts have ruled that teachers are entitled to due process of the law prior to dismissal if property rights or an infringement of liberty can be established. Roth established neither; Sindermann established both. Property rights, according to court rulings, are based on tenure, implied tenure, or contract. A liberty issue involves potential damage to the teacher's reputation.

## FREEDOM OF EXPRESSION

The First Amendment to the U.S. Constitution guarantees every citizen the right to freedom of speech, including the right to criticize government agencies, policies, and actions. In *Pickering v. Board of Education* (391 U.S. 563, 1968), the U.S. Supreme Court clearly defined a teacher's First Amendment free speech rights.

Marvin Pickering, a high school teacher, published a letter criticizing the school board and superintendent about the way school funds were raised and spent. The school board claimed that his letter damaged its professional reputation and was detrimental to the administration and the operation of the school. Pickering was dismissed. An Illinois court ruled in favor of the school board. Pickering contended that he was protected by the First Amendment and took his case to the Supreme Court. The Court ruled that, although not all Pickering's contentions were correct, his expression of his opinions did not impede his teaching or the operation of the school, and he was reinstated.

This case firmly established the right of teachers to express their opinions about schools and administrators publicly or privately. However, the case did not give teachers the unrestricted right to interfere with the operation of a school system. In cases of freedom of speech, the courts consider whether the action impedes the teacher's performance, undermines his or her effectiveness, or can be considered libelous or slanderous. According to the Pickering decision, "certain forms of public criticism of the superior by the subordinate would seriously undermine the effectiveness of the working relationship between them." Hence, the Court concluded that discipline might be appropriate in such cases.

In a recent case, two Washington D.C. biology teachers were threatened by their principal for criticizing the school's science curriculum and the practice of requiring teachers to teach courses for which they were not certified (*Sexius et al. v. Dist. of Col.*, 88–2104, 1992). They won a permanent injunction prohibiting the principal and city school officials from threatening to fire them, downgrading their positions, or forcing them to transfer to a junior high school.

## ACADEMIC FREEDOM

Academic freedom, protected by the First Amendment, is the right of teachers to speak freely about what they teach, to experiment with new teaching ideas or techniques, and to select appropriate material even though it may be controversial.

The Alabama case *Parducci v. Rutland* (316 F. Supp. 352, Mo., Ala., 1970) established guidelines for academic freedom. Marilyn Parducci assigned Kurt Vonnegut's "Welcome to the Monkey House" to her eleventh-grade class. After the assignment had been made, she was asked by the school administration not to teach the story. Parducci contended that it was of high literary quality, and she had the responsibility to teach it. Parducci was dismissed for assigning "disruptive" material and refusing the advice of her administrators. She claimed that her right to academic freedom was violated.

A federal court found that the school board "failed to show either that the assignment was inappropriate reading for high school juniors or that it created a significant disruption to the educational process." Because Parducci's First Amendment rights were violated, the court ruled that she be reinstated.

However, neither this case nor subsequent cases have guaranteed complete academic freedom. Teachers and school librarians must be able to prove that the material or the methods they use do not interfere with school discipline and that they are appropriate to the age of the students and the objectives of the course. In fact, in many recent cases the courts have ruled in favor of the administration. For example, the court upheld the dismissal of a Fairbanks, Alaska, teacher who included materials related to homosexual rights in a unit on American minorities because the teacher had not obtained the required approval from the superintendent prior to using the supplementary materials (*Fisher v. Fairbanks North Star Borough School Dist.,* 704 P.2d 213, Alaska, 1985).

However, a teacher in Kingsville, Texas, was reinstated by the court because he was able to prove the methods he used were age-appropriate, important to course objectives, and did not disrupt school discipline (*Kingsville Indep. School Dist. v. Cooper,* 611 F.2d 1109, 1113, 5th Cir., 1980). Some parents complained that the teacher's use of a simulation to teach post–Civil War history aroused racial tensions, and the school board asked the teacher to stop using it. The teacher refused, stating it helped students meet course objectives, it was appropriate for the age of the students, and there was no evidence that the simulation interfered with school discipline. The board dismissed the teacher, who then filed suit in a Texas federal court. Because the teacher had been able to justify the methods used, the court ruled that the board's action had violated the teacher's academic freedom rights. (See also chapter 13, pp. 522–523.)

## SEXUAL HARASSMENT

Sexual harassment is related by statute to discrimination based on gender. Title VII of the Civil Rights Act of 1964 (P.L. 88–352) makes such discrimination an unlawful employment practice, and Title IX of 1972 (P.L. 92–318) bars gender discrimination against participants in federally funded programs. According to Title VII, employers may not hire, discharge, or discriminate against any individual with respect to compensation, terms, conditions, or privileges of employment

Frank Catrambone, an elementary school principal in Belleville, New Jersey, was cleared of sexually assaulting two young students. Here he is welcomed back by students when he returned for the first time in a year.

because of race, color, religion, sex, or national origin. Sexual harassment, as defined by this act, is unwelcomed sexual advances, requests for sexual favors, and other verbal or physical conduct of a sexual nature.

Individuals have the right to bring suit against institutions to force them to comply with Titles VII and IX. Although cases based on discriminatory employment practices have been won by plaintiffs, the U.S. Office of Civil Rights and the U.S. Department of Education report that it is difficult to prove sexual harassment as defined by statute because investigations of complaints often result in evidence that consists of one person's word against another. In addition, the actions and words of a person can be misinterpreted; what is appropriate behavior to one individual may be offensive to another.

Most sexual harassment cases in education have been filed by students against teachers. Although the number of such cases has increased significantly in the past five years, many educators are concerned that far too many are unfounded. According to Karl Pence, president of the Maryland State Teachers Association, some students file false sexual harassment charges as a way to get revenge on a teacher for some perceived wrong (see In the Classroom, next page). Therefore, it is crucial for teachers to protect themselves against false accusations by seeking help in dealing with difficult students, avoiding behavior that may appear to be inappropriate, and avoiding situations in which the teacher is alone for a lengthy period of time with a student, particularly of the opposite sex.

*In the Classroom*

Albert Thompson just wanted to give something back to his community.

What he got in return was a nightmare.

Six weeks into his stint as a substitute teacher in the Chicago public schools last spring, and after just one day at Fuller Elementary School, 10 students there accused Mr. Thompson of molesting them.

The accusations turned out to be false, but the story made headlines across the nation because of reports that one of the 4th graders had paid nine of her classmates to join her in accusing Mr. Thompson. School officials now say the reports of bribery were incorrect.

No criminal charges were ever filed, and Mr. Thompson was cleared to teach again by the city's school board.

But that did not save his reputation. It also did not protect his dream of becoming a black male role model for inner-city schoolchildren from shattering under the glare of the media spotlight.

Mr. Thompson, who is in his early 40's, has spent most of his professional life as a college administrator. Most recently, he was the director of student activities for Chicago State University.

But as someone who got his master's degree in politics and education from Teachers College, Columbia University, he was always interested in—and critical of—public schools.

So, he figured, he should put himself in the system before he did more bashing.

On May 9, he took over a 4th-grade class of about 30 gifted and talented students at Fuller Elementary on Chicago's South Side.

He acknowledges that they were an unruly class and that he disciplined them. He says he told them he was going to leave a note about their misbehavior for the regular teacher. He knows some of them were worried about the impending bad report.

"It was a rough day for me," he said in a recent interview.

The next day, the children leveled the accusations against him. He first learned of the allegations a day later when a local reporter appeared at his door.

Mr. Thompson said he has forgiven the children and is not bitter.

But, he said, "There is nothing I could've done in that class that would warrant my life being put on a block."

"It's the worst type of charge to clear," he added. "Molesting children to me is the worst thing anyone can do in society."

Mr. Thompson said he will not go back to K–12 teaching and is looking for a job in higher education. . . .

Each of the children was suspended for 10 days and had to write a 10-page composition on the seriousness of their actions.

The school's principal, Judith Riggins, said there is no way to know exactly what happened in Mr. Thompson's class. But, given the outcome of the investigation, she had to send a strong message to the children. . . .

During the suspension, the students received counseling. But the parents, who were outraged at the punishments for honor-roll children who were not known discipline problems, refused to let the children write letters of apology to Mr. Thompson, Ms. Riggins said.

The principal faults Mr. Thompson for not seeking assistance from other school staff members to control the students and for allegedly shutting the hallway door to the chaotic classroom.

She said teachers have to learn "not only to avoid evil, but to avoid the appearance of evil."

From: Millicent Lawson, "False Accusations Turn Dream Into Nightmare in Chicago" (August 2, 1994), *Education Week*, 16.

## TORT LIABILITY

A civil wrong perpetrated on the private rights of citizens is defined as **tort liability** and consists of three types: negligence, intentional torts, and strict liability. **Negligence** is unacceptable conduct or care that results in personal injury. **Intentional torts** involve assault, battery, desire to inflict harm, and defamation. **Strict liability** occurs when injury results from unusual hazards. For example, strict liability might occur in a science laboratory in which chemicals are improperly stored and one or more students are injured as a result. Most school-based court cases deal with negligence. In fact, according to the study "Developing a Typology of Litigation in Education and Determining the Frequency of Each Category," conducted by Michael Imber and Gary Thompson, more negligence suits were filed by students than any other kind. Between 1985 and 1988 in 3 hundred school districts, 821 negligence suits were filed by students and 131 by teachers (1991).

*Negligence*  Negligence may occur when a teacher fails to use proper standards and reasonable care to protect students or doesn't foresee potential harm in a situation and correct it. Negligence is contingent upon the age of the students, the environment, and the type of instructional activity.

Teachers can be found negligent if four things are proved: (1) The teacher had a responsibility to protect the student from injury. (2) The teacher failed to use due care. (3) The teacher's carelessness caused the injury. (4) The student sustained provable damages. Most states have laws that permit school boards to buy insurance to cover negligence assessed against the school district. Likewise, teachers are able to purchase their own liability insurance.

There are many examples of tort cases dealing with negligence. In New York, an appellate court ruled that a school district was negligent for an injury occurring in an unsupervised schoolyard prior to the beginning of school. Although school officials were aware students began to congregate and play on the grounds as early as 7:30 A.M., they were unsupervised until 8:30 A.M., and therefore, school officials were liable (*Chan v. Board of Educ. of City of New York,* 557 N.Y. S.2d 91, 1990). In 1992 an appeals court in Louisiana ruled in *Glankler v. Rapides Parish School Bd.* (610 So. 2d 78) that care commensurate with the age of the children is a reasonable standard of care and supervision. According to the court, there is no reason to have each child under constant scrutiny.

In another case a California student left school without permission and was struck by a motorcycle several blocks from the school. In *Hoyem v. Manhattan Beach School Dist.* (150 Cal. Rptr. 1, 585 P.2d 851, Cal., 1978), the trial court ruled that the school's responsibility ended when the child became truant. However, the California Supreme Court reversed the decision in saying that proper supervision might have prevented the student's truancy and serious injury.

Many negligence cases deal with teachers failing to use due care. In *Landers v. School Dist. No. 203, O'Fallon, Illinois* (383 N.E.2d 645, Ill. App., 1978), an Illinois appeals court ruled that a physical education teacher did not use a reasonable standard of care in requiring an overweight student to perform a backward somersault that resulted in injury. In *Brod v. School Dist. No. 1* (386 N.Y.S.2d 125, App. Div., 1976), a teacher was found negligent when a student was injured trying to complete a high jump at a level considerably higher than he had been able to complete before.

Teachers have successfully defended themselves against negligence suits when they have been able to prove that the child was aware of or should have been aware of the consequences of the actions, but nonetheless participated in the activity. This is known as *contributory negligence.* In these cases the courts attempt to determine whether the teacher has provided due care in anticipating dangers and in warning students against them. In North Carolina, for example, an industrial arts teacher was found not liable when a deaf student injured his eyes while trying to add oil to a hydraulic lift. The court ruled that the teacher did not owe this student greater due care because of his deafness, and since the teacher had instructed the student in the rules of safety, he had provided an appropriate standard of care. The student should have known, based on the teacher's instruction, that the hydraulic lift was to be left alone (*Payne v. Department of Human Resources,* 382 S.E.2d 449, N.C. Ct. App., 1989).

However, in a 1989 New York case the court found that a teacher did not meet the standard of acting as a prudent parent when she did not escort a twelve-year-old fifth grader from a third floor classroom to a fifth floor classroom. En route the child was accosted and raped by three students. The court ruled that, while recognizing that the school is not the insurer of student safety, it was liable for damages to this student because of absence of supervision in a school in which student discipline was so bad that two aides and two security guards were assigned to each floor (*Logan v. City of N.Y.,* 543 N.Y.S.2d 661, App. Div., 1980).

Another example of negligence resulting in tort liability is the failure of teachers to report cases of suspected child abuse. The Child Abuse Prevention and Treatment Act of 1974 (P.L. 93–247), amended in 1989 (P.L. 101–126), required all states to pass legislation to combat child abuse in order to qualify for federal funding. Among the required provisions is the mandatory duty of "service professionals" to report known or suspected cases of child abuse, which according to federal legislation, is the physical or mental injury, sexual abuse or exploitation, or negligent treatment of a child. Service professionals include teachers, principals, counselors, and school nurses. In some states, service professionals are more broadly defined as all school personnel or all educators. According to the National School Boards Association, all states and courts have construed this mandatory duty to report as related to occupation, regardless of the relationship with the abused child such as friend or relative that may exist (1994, 34). Every state has mandated penalties, from fines to jail sentences, against mandated reporters who "wilfully or knowingly" fail to report child abuse. Likewise, all states provide immunity from civil liability and criminal penalty for mandated reporters who do report child abuse cases in good faith (National Center for Child Abuse 1992, 10).

In a Taylor, Texas, case (*Doe v. Taylor Independent School District,* 975 F.2d. 137, 5th Cir., 1992), a fourteen-year-old female student reported to her principal that she had been sexually molested by her coach. Several other female students also reported suspicions about the coach to the principal. The principal claimed that "the coach just had a way of flirting with girls." The girl filed suit, and the court ruled against the school district saying that they had failed to adequately investigate the child abuse charges and that the principal and superintendent had ample evidence of a pattern of child abuse.

*Intentional Torts*    Although negligence is the most common tort case filed against schools and educators, cases of assault and battery are not uncommon. In most instances they involve corporal punishment, but no actual physical contact need take place. *Assault* is an overt attempt to cause fear of physical harm; when assault leads to physical injury, **battery** is committed.

If, however, a teacher uses reasonable force with students, the courts will often rule in favor of the teacher. For example, in *Simms v. School Dist. No. 1* (508 P.2d 236, Ore. App., 1973), a teacher held the arms of a student, leading him toward the door after he refused to leave the room. The student swung at the teacher, thereby breaking a window and injuring his arm. The court ruled that the teacher had used reasonable force with the student and, therefore, had not committed assault or battery. In other cases a court has ruled in favor of the student. In *Frank v. Orleans Parish School Bd.* (195 So. 2d 451, La. App., 1967), for example, a teacher was convicted of assault and battery, and the court assessed damages against him when he shook a student against bleachers in a gymnasium and the student sustained a broken arm. The court ruled that the teacher's actions were unnecessary to discipline the student or to protect himself. Similarly, the Supreme Court of Connecticut awarded damages to a twelve-year-old student who suffered a fractured clavicle after a teacher threw him against a moveable chalkboard, then pushed him into a wall (*Sansone v. Bectel,* 429 A. Wd. 820, Conn., 1980).

The basic premise of tort law is that all individuals are liable for the consequences of their conduct resulting in injury to others. Thus, teachers can also file tort cases against abusive students who intentionally harm them. In 1983 a Wisconsin appellate court awarded a teacher both compensatory and punitive damages in a suit against a student who punched and kicked the teacher while the teacher was taking him to the school office for violating a school nonsmoking rule (*Anello v. Savignac,* 342 N.W.2d 440, Wis. Ct. App., 1983). In Oregon where the law stipulates that parents are financially responsible for damages caused by intentional torts of their children, a teacher was awarded $23 thousand in damages because a student struck the teacher while the teacher was attempting to prevent him from leaving the classroom (*Garrett v. Olsen,* 691 P.2d 123, Or. Ct. App., 1984).

## Copyright Law

In 1978, General Revision of the Copyright Law (P.L. 94-553) completely amended Title 17 of the United States Code (Title 17 USC-copyrights), which was adopted in 1909. This recent federal statute has important implications for teachers and schools.

*(continued on p. 619)*

TABLE 15-2

## Guidelines for Photocopying Material

### I. Single Copying for Teachers

A single copy may be made of any of the following by or for a teacher at his or her individual request for his or her scholarly research or use in teaching or preparation to teach a class:

A. A chapter from a book;

B. An article from a periodical or newspaper;

C. A short story, short essay or short poem, whether or not from a collective work;

D. A chart, graph, diagram, drawing, cartoon or picture from a book, periodical, or newspaper.

### II. Multiple Copies for Classroom Use

Multiple Copies (not to exceed in any event more than one copy per pupil in a course) may be made by or for the teacher giving the course for classroom use or discussion, provided that:

A. The copying meets the tests of brevity and spontaneity as defined below; and,

B. Meets the cumulative effect test as defined below; and,

C. Each copy includes a notice of copyright.

*Definitions*

*Brevity*

i(i) Poetry: (a) A complete poem if less than 250 words and if printed on not more than two pages, or (b) from a longer poem, an excerpt of not more than 250 words.

(ii) Prose: (a) Either a complete article, story or essay of less than 2,500 words, or (b) an excerpt from any prose work of not more than 1,000 words or 10 percent of the work, whichever is less, but in any event a minimum of 500 words.

[Each of the numerical limits stated in *i* and *ii* above may be expanded to permit the completion of an unfinished line of a poem or of an unfinished prose paragraph.]

(iii) Illustration: One chart, graph, diagram, drawing, cartoon or picture per book or per periodical issue.

(iv) "Special" works: Certain works in poetry, prose or in "poetic prose" which often combine language with illustrations and which are intended sometimes for children and at other times for a more general audience fall short of 2,500 words in their entirety. Paragraph *ii* above notwithstanding, such "special works" may not be reproduced in their entirety; however, an excerpt comprising not more than two of the published pages of such special work and containing not more than 10 percent of the words found in the text thereof, may be reproduced.

*Spontaneity*

i(i) The copying is at the instance and inspiration of the individual teacher, and

(ii) The inspiration and decision to use the work and the moment of its use for maximum teaching effectiveness are so close in time that it would be unreasonable to expect a timely reply to a request for permission.

*Cumulative Effect*

ii(i) The copying of the material is for only one course in the school in which the copies are made.

i(ii) Not more than one short poem, article, story, essay or two excerpts may be copied from the same author, nor more than three from the same collective work or periodical volume during one class term.

(iii) There shall not be more than nine instances of such multiple copying for one course during one class term.

[The limitations stated in *ii* and *iii* above shall not apply to current news periodicals and newspapers and current news sections of other periodicals.]

**III. Prohibitions as to I and II Above**

Notwithstanding any of the above, the following shall be prohibited:

A.  Copying shall not be used to create or to replace or substitute for anthologies, compilations or collective works. Such replacement or substitution may occur whether copies of various works or excerpts therefrom are accumulated or reproduced and used separately.

B.  There shall be no copying of or from works intended to be "consumable" in the course of study or of teaching. These include workbooks, exercises, standardized tests and test booklets and answer sheets and like consumable material.

C.  Copying shall not:
    (a)  substitute for the purchase of books, publishers' reprints or periodicals;
    (b)  be directed by higher authority;
    (c)  be repeated with respect to the same item by the same teacher from term to term.

D.  No charge shall be made to the student beyond the actual cost of the photocopying.

---

From: House Judiciary Committee, House Report 94-1476, *Congressional Record* (Washington, DC: U.S. Government Printing Office, September 22, 1976), 68–70.

**The intent of the copyright law is to protect both the rights of students to learn and the rights of artists and writers who produced the work. The concept of fair use allows reasonable dissemination of the work. Guidelines for interpreting fair use have been established by the House Judiciary Committee.**

The intent of the copyright law is to promote the creation and dissemination of knowledge and ideas. This intent was established in the U.S. Constitution, Article I, Section 8, Clause 8. Today the phrase "to promote the progress of science and useful arts, by securing for limited times to authors and inventors the exclusive right to their respective writings and discoveries" is broadly interpreted to mean that those individuals who produce artistic and intellectual work should have their financial interests protected by prohibiting others from copying or misusing the work.

The law attempts to balance the interests of the copyright owner and those of the public. The difficulty is in balancing the rights of authors, artists, and scholars who desire to protect their works with the rights of teachers and librarians to disseminate the works. If the law balances these interests, then it encourages both creation and dissemination, but conflicts often arise.

To ensure the fair dissemination of knowledge and ideas, the 1978 copyright law established the concept of **fair use**, which is the right to use copyrighted material in a reasonable manner without the permission of the author. The statute established four criteria for determining whether fair use applies to a particular instance of copying:

1.  the purpose and character of the use, including whether such use is of a commercial nature or is for nonprofit educational purposes
2.  the nature of the copyrighted work
3.  the amount and substantiality of the portion used in relation to the copyrighted work as a whole

4. the effect of the use upon the potential market for or value of the copyrighted work. (Section 107 of P.L. 94–553)

Because of the general nature of these particular criteria, the House Judiciary Committee report (House Report 94–1476) established guidelines for interpreting fair use (see table 15.2).

The fair use concept was tested in the case of *Marcus v. Rowley* (695 F.2d 1171, 1983). In this case a home economics teacher, Eloise Marcus, wrote a thirty-five-page booklet on cake decorating. She copyrighted the booklet and sold most of the 123 copies she had made for $2 each to students in her adult education cake-decorating class. Shirley Rowley took Marcus's class and later developed a Learning Activities Package (LAP) for her high school food-service career classes. Fifteen of the pages in Rowley's twenty-four-page unit were copied from Marcus's booklet without permission. Rowley had fifteen copies made to use with her students on a nonprofit basis. Marcus sued for copyright infringement. The appellate court concluded, "The fair use doctrine does not apply to these facts. . . . Rowley's LAP work, which was used for the same purpose as plaintiff's booklet, was quantitatively and qualitatively a substantial copy of plaintiff's booklet with no credit given to plaintiff. Under these circumstances, neither the fact that the defendant used the plaintiff's booklet for nonprofit educational purposes nor the fact that plaintiff suffered no pecuniary damage as a result of Rowley's copying supports a finding of fair use."

Applying the 1978 copyright law to computers, audiovisual materials, and off-the-air taping is another complex issue. In 1980, amendments dealing with the copyright of computer software were added to the law. Making even a single copy of a computer program that is designed for a single user, without a license to do so, violates the law. Even booting up a series of microcomputers with one disk, enabling numerous students to access a program intended for a single user, is illegal as it is to make a copy of a software program acquired for preview purposes. However, computer software owners are permitted to make a single copy of a disk for archival purposes.

To understand which uses of audiovisual materials are permitted under the copyright law, teachers must know the meaning of the terms *display* and *perform*. **Display** means to show individual frames of a film or videotape, while **perform** means to run the entire work through a projector or recorder. Teachers may display individual images or perform a work for nonprofit educational purposes as long as the copy was not unlawfully made. To be displayed or performed legally, a work must be part of the instruction by teachers or guest lecturers in an educational, face-to-face setting with students, and it must be a legitimate copy. If, however, a videotape displays the label, "Warning: For Home Use Only," it may be used only in the home.

In 1981 the House Subcommittee on the Courts, Civil Liberties, and the Administration of Justice developed guidelines for off-the-air recording of broadcast programs. Videotaping can be done only if the faculty member requests permission from the source in advance. The major limitations for use of videotapes in educational settings are that they can be kept for not more than forty-five calendar days after the recording date, at which time the tapes must be erased. They may be shown to students only within the first ten school days of the forty-five day period.

## The Teacher's Ethical Role

Most of us would like to avoid becoming embroiled in a legal issue related to our contract, teaching, or students. Although it is not always possible to prevent problems from escalating to conflict and suit, understanding the law, working toward the development of policies that protect teachers and students, using common sense in dealing with potentially damaging situations, and learning how to make ethical decisions can help keep problems from moving beyond the classroom into courtrooms.

In dealing with social problems affecting students, the classroom, and the school, teachers are often required to make decisions they would rather not make. They require a great deal of thought and an understanding of the principles that are the foundation of the teacher's ethical role. The following situations, for example, require ethical decision making:

- Students in your social studies class have been studying democracy. They want to have a demonstration at the next school board meeting to change a requirement that nominations to the student council require the endorsement of at least two teachers. Students argue that this keeps those off the council who do not conform to school rules, and they think this is unfair. Although you understand the students' point of view, you also understand the history of the rule and are not convinced that a demonstration at the board meeting is a good idea. What do you do?
- You know that there is one child in your class who instigates the misbehavior of the rest of the children. However, you cannot determine who it is. You decide that the next time the misbehavior occurs you will punish the whole class and suggest that the punishment will be rescinded if they tell you who the culprit is. Before you even initiate this action, you begin to wonder if it is fair.
- You know that Sam has violated the team's rules by drinking on Saturday night. One of your students told you he saw Sam drunk, and when you confront Sam, he confirms it. You know that if you tell the coach, he will kick Sam off the team. But he has been doing much better since he made the team; he's in school every day, does his homework, and participates in class. You know that if he is kicked off the team, he's likely to go back to his far less positive behavior. What do you do?
- You are planning a field trip for the children in your class. Two of your students have a physical disability. You learn that the location of your field trip is not equipped to handle those with disabilities, and you are asked to leave them in school. You believe that it is unfair to exclude these students, but you also believe the others will benefit from the field trip that is important to the unit you have been teaching. What should you do?
- You are in the hallway of your school and you notice Reggie walking down the hall scraping the eraser end of his pencil along the wall. Reggie never sits or walks quietly; he is always tapping on his desk or moving his feet. However, you know that Reggie needs to keep moving; he learns better when he is constantly active. You also know that Reggie is very musical. He always has a song in his head, and you've been encouraging him to

develop his talent. One of the guidance counselors sees Reggie, calls him over, and begins to reprimand him loudly. You are upset because you believe that if Reggie had been white, the guidance counselor would not have confronted him. What should you do?

• Juan tells you confidentially that one of the coaches is sexually abusing some of his players. At first you don't believe it, but you overhear other students talking about it. You ask one of them about it, and he says, "It's a well-known fact that Coach is a pervert." You ask the student, "Why don't you report him?" The student replies, "Are you crazy? Not only would our asses get kicked off the team, but we'd be dead meat." What should you do?

It is the unusual teacher who is not faced with at least some ethical decisions. All these decisions are difficult. No matter what you do there will be consequences for you, the students, and others who are involved. In all these situations what is right and what is wrong is not obvious. How would you handle these very difficult situations?

## ETHICAL DECISION MAKING

Kenneth A. Strike in "The Ethics of Teaching" says, "Ethical issues concern questions of right and wrong—our duties and obligations, our rights and responsibilities" (1988, 156). Strike suggests that ethical decision making has a unique vocabulary that includes such words as *ought, should, fair,* and *unfair.* He further suggests that, although facts are important in making ethical decisions, facts alone are not enough. Nor is knowing the consequences of our actions. For example, in the situation in which the teacher wants to punish the entire class for the behavior of one in order to find the culprit, the consequences might reveal the culprit. However, is the teacher's action an ethical one if all students are punished for the action of one?

Ethical questions are distinguished from values; a value is an idea or object an individual regards as worthy, important, or significant. It may also refer to a system of personal attitudes and beliefs. One individual, for example, might value a work of art, and another may not; the one, however, is no less ethical than the other. Or an individual may value the family unit of two parents and children; whereas another might value his or her independence from a family unit. Again, the individual may choose what he or she values. Ethics, on the other hand, deal with how people should act—What is good? What is right? What is wrong? What is my duty? In the situations just described we must decide the right or fair course of action.

Strike believes that ethical decision making involves two stages. The first stage requires applying ethical principles to cases, and the second requires judging the adequacy or applicability of the principles (p. 156). We will deal with both these stages in the discussion of particular codes of ethics that follows.

## CODES OF ETHICS

Most of the major professional associations have codes of ethics that help teachers deal with difficult decisions. The codes give teachers some principles they can apply to problems with ethical questions.

*The NEA Code of Ethics*    The National Education Association's (NEA) Code of Ethics was adopted by its representative assembly in 1975. The preamble of the NEA states that its membership will recognize the worth and dignity of each individual and the importance of nurturing democratic principles and pursuing truth and excellence.

The first principle of the code is commitment to students. This principle states that no student should be subjected to embarrassment or disparagement, nor be unfairly excluded from participation in any program, denied any benefit, or granted any advantage based on race, color, creed, sex, national origin, marital status, political or religious beliefs, family, social, or cultural background, or sexual orientation. It states that educators will not use professional relationships with students for personal advantage or disclose information about students except for compelling professional purposes or when required by law. As part of this principle, teachers are expected to preserve the confidentiality of students, if possible, and make every effort to preserve the student's safety and health.

All the ethical dilemmas posed in the situations discussed on pages 621–622 involve a teacher's responsibility to students. According to Strike, teachers must apply this principle to each case as the first step of ethical decision making. Let's take the case of Juan. First, if Juan is telling the truth, we are dealing with the preservation of a student's health and safety. The case is also one of potential child abuse for which we have a legal responsibility to report or risk being negligent (see p. 616). We are also dealing with a situation in which the coach may be using students for his own benefit. But we are not sure how to determine if Juan is telling the truth.

The second principle of the NEA code is commitment to the profession. This principle states that educators will respect other educators' reputations, refuse gifts or favors that appear to influence professional decisions, and prevent unqualified persons from entering the profession.

This principle represents the other side of the Juan dilemma. If Juan is not telling the truth, what are the consequences for the other teacher? Since the overriding ethical concern must be for the student and we have a legal responsibility to report cases of suspected child abuse, we cannot let the matter drop, but we must proceed in a way that will protect both the student's right to confidentiality and the teacher's right to protection against false accusation. In addition, if what Juan has said is true, the coach is not qualified to teach. Hence, we must use ethical decision making to protect the rights of everyone concerned. Most school districts have procedures to follow in reporting cases of suspected child abuse, which protect the rights of the student, the reporter, and the potential abuser. We must determine what these procedures are and follow them.

*The Canadian Psychological Association Code of Ethics*    The Canadian Psychological Association (CPA) in 1986 developed a code of ethics based on moral principles. This code has been widely accepted in Canada and has helpful principles for all teachers. The code is in hierarchical order. Hence, when principles within the code seem to be in conflict, the higher principle takes precedence. The four basic principles of the code are:

> Principle I: Respect for the Dignity of Persons
> Principle II: Responsible Caring
> Principle III: Integrity in Relationships
> Principle IV: Responsibility to Society

Larry Eberlein in "Ethical Decision Making for Teachers" (1989) points to the value of the CPA code for teachers and suggests ways in which each of the principles applies to education. According to Eberlein, the first principle, which is much like the first principle of the NEA code, suggests that teachers must respect the worth of all students and that individual differences should neither enhance nor decrease this dignity, which includes a moral right to privacy, self-determination, and autonomy. Furthermore, teachers have the greatest responsibility to protect the dignity of the most vulnerable students. The younger the student, the more precarious these rights; thus the more carefully they should be protected by the teacher.

Let's examine the field trip question, mentioned earlier, using this principle. Because it is the teacher's responsibility to protect the dignity of the most vulnerable, the students with disabilities must be considered first. Therefore, according to this principle, we should consider alternatives to this particular field trip and explain to the students the reason for the decision.

The principle of responsible caring states that the teacher must be competent and not be involved in activities that are harmful to society. A teacher's first concern must be the welfare of the students; secondarily the teacher must be concerned about responsibility to parents, schools, school boards, and the public. Since students are rarely given the right to consent in selected school activities, Eberlein suggests, teachers must be especially mindful of protecting them. In selecting activities, teachers must weigh the likely risks and benefits and choose activities in which the benefits predominate. If harmful effects occur, the teacher must take responsibility for correcting them. According to Eberlein, this assumes that "incompetent action is, by definition, unethical." Competence requires continuous growth in knowledge and evaluation of teaching. Competent teachers are concerned with "both short-term and long-term physical and psychological factors in their students. These include self-worth, fear, humiliation, an interpersonal trust, as well as physical safety, comfort, and freedom from injury" (p. 113).

Since teachers must be concerned about the dignity and worth of students and must demonstrate a caring responsibility, the decision making in Sam's case involves these two principles. We know that Sam has been drinking. Beyond Sam's involvement in athletics, we must be concerned about drinking's potential harm to Sam himself. Therefore, we must help him deal with his drinking problem. The first step is probably to discuss the problem confidentially with him. Beyond this we might suggest that he needs to get help from outside sources. Whether we should tell the coach is a decision that should be made first based on what is best for Sam, second on our mutual respect for the coach, and third on our professional responsibility to school rules. If we believe that it is best for Sam not to tell the coach, this should govern our actions.

All professional relationships formed by teachers require mutual integrity. Expectations of integrity, according to Eberlein, include fairness, impartiality, straightforwardness, avoidance of deception, avoidance of conflict of interest, and the provision of accurate information (p. 113). This principle can be in conflict with the first two. At times, teachers must decide that straightforwardness, for example, is not appropriate if responsible caring is to occur. Because these principles are hierarchical, responsible caring should take precedence. Professional integrity requires accountability for the quality of the work done by the teacher.

Take Reggie's case, for example. We assumed that the guidance counselor was acting out of prejudice because Reggie is black. But there could be another explanation. Given the importance of honoring the guidance counselor's integrity, could we handle this situation in a way that would protect the guidance counselor and also ensure the dignity of Reggie? The first step might be discussing the incident with the counselor. Perhaps this will help us better understand the counselor's actions and will lead to a resolution of the problem. If, however, we believe that the guidance counselor is acting out of prejudice, we must let our next actions be governed by what we believe is best for Reggie.

Teaching, as clearly established in this chapter, exists within the context of society. Therefore, the teacher's final responsibility is to use knowledge to benefit society and, thereby, support the first three principles. Teachers should recognize that because social structures have evolved over time, they must convey respect for these and avoid "unwarranted or unnecessary disruptions." The pursuit of changes in the social structure should be carried out only through the educational process. However, according to Eberlein, if social structures ignore the first three principles of the code, "it would be irresponsible for teachers to work within these social structures and not be critical of them" (p. 113).

An examination of the student council dilemma might make this principle clearer. Although our first responsibility is to the students, we do not always have to agree with their opinions in order to respect their dignity. Sometimes the responsibility of caring requires that we teach students things they would rather not learn. Perhaps a demonstration at the board meeting is a good idea, but first they must have the facts. They must examine the rule: its history, its potential positive effects, and its potential negative effects. They must also determine who made the rule and who has the authority to change it. They should examine the process of changing a rule within the system and should understand the consequences of working outside it. Once the students have accomplished all this, they can determine the best course of action. We have honored the dignity of the students, have shown an attitude of caring, have clearly valued the integrity of a professional relationship with the students, have upheld the integrity of a professional relationship with other professionals, and have acted responsibly toward society.

There is no doubt that the social problems analyzed in chapter 11 and the schools' responses to those problems discussed in chapter 12 lead to the increased involvement of teachers in students' lives. Teachers can no longer be concerned with teaching only content and skills. This is neither possible nor is it ethical. Contemporary teachers must deal with the social issues affecting their students both in and out of the classroom. To do this, protect the rights of the students, and to protect themselves from the legal problems addressed in this chapter, teachers must develop or adopt a strong code of ethics and learn how to use that code in dealing with ethical as well as legal issues.

**15-2**

**POINTS TO REMEMBER**

- Constitutional law is based on the U.S. and state constitutions; statutory law is based on legislation.
- Contract law relates to agreements between two or more competent parties. Teachers enter into contracts with boards of education when they are employed.
- Due process protects teachers from arbitrary action or discriminatory practices of school administrators or boards. School boards have the right to dismiss tenured teachers for reasons determined by state statute as long as due process procedures are followed.
- Academic freedom, related to the First Amendment right of free speech, is the right to speak freely about what to teach and to experiment with new teaching techniques.
- Tort liability is a civil wrong. Negligence is one type of tort liability that relates to unacceptable conduct or care resulting in personal injury. Negligence is the most common case brought against teachers. Teachers can also file intentional tort cases against students.
- Copyright law is designed to both protect and disseminate knowledge and ideas. Teachers must balance their right to disseminate knowledge with the obligation to protect copyrighted material.
- Applying a code of ethics to difficult professional decisions can help teachers make decisions that protect the rights of students and other teachers.

## For Thought/Discussion

1. If you feel uncomfortable in the presence of someone with AIDS, and if a child with AIDS was assigned to your class, how would you deal with the child to make him or her feel comfortable and welcome? How would you deal with the rest of the class?

2. If *Pickering v. Board of Education* guarantees a teacher's First Amendment rights, how far could you go in publicly criticizing the administration in your school?

3. If you were on duty in the school yard during recess carefully watching the students and one child tripped another, resulting in a chipped front tooth, would you be considered negligent? Why or why not?

4. If you suspect one of your students is selling illegal drugs during lunchtime, what steps would you take to see that it stopped?

## For Further Reading/Reference

Del-Fattore, J. 1992. *What Johnny shouldn't read: Textbook censorship in America.* New Haven, CT: Yale University Press. Examines special-interest groups on the political right and left who are objecting to textbooks in elementary and secondary schools.

The Freedom Forum. 1994. *Death by cheeseburger: High school journalism in the 1990's and beyond.* Arlington, VA. Discussion of court cases affecting students' freedom of expression in student newspapers; particular emphasis on *Hazelwood School District v. Kuhlmeir.*

Moffett, J. 1988. *Storm in the mountains: A case study of censorship, conflict, and consciousness.* Carbondale: Southern Illinois University Press. A study of the 1974 Kanawha County, West Virginia, censorship case, in which Moffett was a major player as one of the coauthors of the attacked language arts series. He describes the case from the viewpoints of the administrators, the parents, the community, and the other coauthors of the series.

Thomas, S. B. (Ed.). 1994. *The yearbook of education law, 1990.* Topeka, KS: National Organization on Legal Problems of Education (NOLPE). An annual yearbook that describes relevant legal cases related to the schools, teachers, and students from the preceding year. The yearbook has been published since 1971 and allows teachers to keep up with the legal aspects of education.

Zirkel, P. A. 1993–95. De Jure. *Phi Delta Kappan.* Each issue of the *Kappan* has a column by Zirkel focusing on court cases related to the schools; circumstances surrounding the case and the author's opinion about each case are presented.

Randy Glasbergen in *Phi Delta Kappan*

*"The following is a test from the Emergency Broadcasting System: What is 197 divided by 18? What is the capital of Nebraska? Who was the ninth President of the United States?"*

## Major National Education Organizations and Their Professional Journals

American Alliance for Health, Physical Education,
  Recreation and Dance (AALR)
1900 Association Drive
Reston, VA 22091
(703) 476-3400
*Journal of Physical Education, Recreation, and Dance*

American Alliance for Theatre and Education (AATE)
  Theatre Department
  Tempe, AZ 85287-3411
  (602) 965-6064
  *The Drama/Theatre Teacher*

American Council on the Teaching of Foreign Languages
  (ACTFL) (Classical and Modern)
  Six Executive Plz.
  Yonkers, NY 10701
  (914) 963-8830
  *ACTFL Newsletter*

American Federation of Teachers AFL-CIO (AFT)
  555 New Jersey Avenue, NW
  Washington, DC 20001
  (202) 879-4400
  *American Educator*

American Home Economics Association (AHEA)
  1555 King St.
  Alexandria, VA
  (703) 706-4600
  *Journal of Home Economics*

American Speech-Language-Hearing Association (ASLHA)
  10801 Rockville Pike
  Rockville, MD 20852
  (301) 897-5700
  *Language, Speech, Hearing Services in Schools*

Association for Childhood Education International (ACEI)
  11501 Georgia Ave., Suite 312
  Wheaton, MD 20902
  (301) 942-2443
  *Childhood Education*

Bridging the Education Scene for Teachers of Tomorrow
  (BESTT)
  Mary Davis, BESTT Coordinator
  Region I Education Service Center

Edinburg, TX 78539
(512) 383-5611

Council for Exceptional Children (CEC)
  1920 Association Drive
  Reston, VA 22091
  (703) 620-3660
  *Exceptional Children*

International Reading Association (IRA)
  800 Barksdale Rd.
  P.O. Box 8139
  Newark, DE 19714
  (302) 731-1600
  *Reading Teacher*
  *Journal of Reading Research*

International Technology Education Association (ITEA)
  1914 Association Drive
  Reston, VA 22091
  (703) 860-2100
  *Journal of Technology Education*

Music Teachers National Association (MTNA)
  617 Vine St., Ste. 1432
  Cincinnati, OH 45202
  (513) 421-1420
  *American Music Teacher Magazine*

National Art Education Association (NAEA)
  1916 Association Drive
  Reston, VA 22091
  (703) 860-8000
  *Art Education*

National Association for Gifted Children (NAGC)
  1155 15th St., NW, Ste. 1002
  Washington, DC 20005
  (202) 785-4268
  *Gifted Child Quarterly*

National Association for the Education of Young
  Children (NAEYC)
  1834 Connecticut Ave., NW
  Washington, DC 20009
  (202) 232-8777 (800) 424-2460
  *Young Children*

National Association of Biology Teachers (NABT)
11250 Roger Bacon Drive, No. 19
Reston, VA 22090
(703) 471-1134
*American Biology Teacher*

National Association of Multicultural Education
3135 Gary Blvd, Ste. 275
San Francisco, CA 94118
(415) 750- 9970
*Multicultural Education*

National Business Education Association (NBEA)
1914 Association Drive
Reston, VA 22091
(703) 860-8300
*Business Education Forum*

National Council for the Social Studies (NCSS)
3501 Newark St., NW
Washington, DC 20016
(202) 966-7840
*Social Education*

National Council of Teachers of English (NCTE)
1111 Kenyon Rd.
Urbana, IL 61801
(217) 328-3870

*The Council Chronicle*
*English Journal*
*Language Arts Journal*

National Council of Teachers of Mathematics (NCTM)
1906 Association Drive
Reston, VA 22091
(703) 620-9840
*Mathematics Teacher*
*Arithmetic Teacher*

National Education Association (NEA)
1201 16th Street, NW
Washington, DC 20036
(202) 833-4000
*NEA-Today*

National Middle Schools Association (NMSA)
4807 Evanswood Dr.
Columbus, OH 43229
(614) 848-8211
*Middle School Journal*

National Science Teachers Association (NSTA)
1742 Connecticut Ave., NW
Washington, DC 20009
(202) 328-5800
*Science and Children*

Source: Daniels, P. K., and Schwartz, C. A. (Eds.). (1994). *Encyclopedia of Associations* (28th Ed.). (Volume I, Part 1; Volume II, Part 2). Detroit, MI: Gale Research, Inc.

## Other Selected Professional Journals and Newspapers

*The Clearing House* (Middle/Secondary)

*The Computing Teacher* (K–12)

*Education Digest* (K–12 abridged articles)

*Education Week* (Weekly newspaper of current U.S. K–12 education)

*Educational Leadership* (K–12)

*Elementary School Journal* (K–8)

*Equity and Excellence in Education*

*High School Journal* (Secondary)

*Instructor* (K–6)

*Journal of Learning Disabilities* (K–12)

*Learning* (K–6)

*Phi Delta Kappan* (K–12)

Source: Katz, B. and Katz, L. S. (1992). *Magazines for Librarians.* New Providence, NJ: R. R. Bowker.

# GLOSSARY

**Ability grouping** Assigning students to groups based on their ability to learn. **155**

**Academy** A secondary school established in the early nineteenth century for middle class students, offering a wide range of subjects. **155**

**Accommodation** A cognitive process by which children change or develop new schemes when a new concept cannot be assimilated into existing schemes (Piaget). **368**

**Accountability** The schools' responsibility for ensuring student achievement. **595**

**Accreditation** Certifying that consistent standards, procedures, and policies are met for operating quality teacher-education programs. **102**

**Advanced organizers** Providing external motivation for learning by beginning a lesson with overall aims, giving examples, and relating the learning to past learning and experiences (Ausubel). **393**

**Aesthetic need** The human need for beauty (Maslow). **369**

**Aesthetics** The study of values in the realm of beauty and art. **218**

**Affective development** The development of values. **71, 185**

**Age of the common man** The years between 1812 and 1865 when tracts of land were free and open to all, resulting in equality of economic and political opportunity. **151**

**Alternative approaches** Varied nontraditional, teacher-training approaches that strive to reduce some of the barriers to entry into teaching. **106**

**Analytic approach to discipline** Discipline approaches that attempt to identify the cause of student misbehavior and then treat the cause(s). **83**

**Anecdotal observations** Informal observations that focus on a specific classroom event, a student, or teaching for a specified period of time. **95**

**Animism** A young child's infusing of the inanimate world with conscious attributes (Piaget). **368**

**Assertive discipline** A classroom management approach in which teachers determine structure and routine, expect appropriate student behavior, develop appropriate consequences for misbehavior, and receive support from administrators and parents. **83**

**Assimilation** A cognitive process by which children integrate new stimuli into an existing scheme (Piaget). **367**

**Authoritarian model of discipline** A teacher-dominated discipline approach in which the teacher sets the rules and requires the students to submit to the teacher's authority. **83**

**Autonomy** Teacher discretion in making decisions related to teaching, curriculum course material, discipline, and evaluation of student work. **20**

**Axiology** A category of philosophic thought dealing with the nature of values. **218**

**Basic grant** A block grant available to any school district with at least ten poor students. **556**

**Battery** An assault that leads to physical injury. **617**

**Behaviorism** An educational theory based in the philosophical schools of realism and philosophical analysis, that stresses the scientific method, objectivity, immediate results, efficiency, and positiveness. **245**

**Behaviorist** A scientist who bases conclusions exclusively on the observation of behavior. **389**

**Behavioristic approach to discipline** A classroom management approach in which students are reinforced for good behavior. **86**

**Bell curve** A bell-shaped symmetrical distribution in which most performance scores or human attributes fall near the mean (average). **308**

**Belonging or love need** The human need to feel wanted and loved (Maslow). **369**

**Blended families** Families joined together by the marriage of divorced adults in which one or both have children from previous marriages. **435**

**Block grants** The 20 percent of federal public education funds distributed by the states to the schools for their discretionary use (Education Consolidation and Improvement Act, 1981). **556**

**Career ladder** A hierarchy of levels in a teaching career, each with additional responsibilities and salary; promotion to the next level is based on evaluation of teaching performance and increased responsibilities and levels of education. **30**

**Categorical grants** Federal grants that must be applied for. **556**

**Certification** A specified set of state requirements (such as coursework, fieldwork, examinations) that prospective and inservice teachers must complete in order to teach. **92**

**Charter schools** Public schools chartered and designed by groups of teachers, parents, or other groups or individuals. **520**

**Child abuse** The physical and/or sexual abuse and the physical neglect and/or emotional maltreatment of children by adults. **442**

**Child-centered psychology** The study of the stages of children's physical, intellectual, and behavioral development. **298**

**Child-centered teaching** A teaching style in which the curriculum emerges from the children's interests. **73**

**Classical conditioning** The development of a conditioned stimulus by pairing a neutral stimulus (no effect) with an unconditioned stimulus (effect) (Pavlov). **389**

**Cognitive development** The development of concepts. **71, 185**

**Common school** The ideal of publicly supported education for all students espoused by nineteenth-century educators and businessmen. **154**

**Compensatory education** The schools' effort to individually compensate for the unequal learning and experiences that students bring to the classroom. **199**

**Competency** An element of knowledge that is essential if the student is to master the content of the discipline. **305**

**Competency-based model** A teacher-training approach that requires the development of specific, measurable competencies over a specified period of time. **103**

**Computer-assisted instruction (CAI)** Computer programs that allow students to progress at their own rate by completing a series of complex tasks, each of which receives immediate feedback. **390**

**Concentration grant** A block grant earmarked for school districts in communities with high concentrations of poverty-level students. **556**

**Concrete operational period** A period of cognitive development that occurs between the ages of seven and eleven during which children develop the ability to solve problems through reasoning and to think symbolically with words and numbers (Piaget). **368**

**Conditioned stimulus** The pairing of a neutral stimulus (no effect) with an unconditioned stimulus (effect) to produce the desired effect even after the unconditional stimulus is removed (Pavlov). **389**

**Conservation** The cognitive ability to recognize equivalent volume, regardless of the size of the container (Piaget). **369**

**Constitutional law** The law of the land set forth in the U.S. Constitution and each state's constitution. **589**

**Content-centered teaching** A teaching style which employs lecturing and formal discussion as a means to cover content coherently and systematically and measure student learning objectively. **71**

**Content-student-centered learning style** A learning style that balances the objectives of the material to be learned with the needs of the students. **75**

**Contract** An agreement between two or more competent parties to create, alter, or dissolve a relationship legally. **608**

**Conventional moral reasoning** Moral judgments that are based on the approval of others, on family expectations, traditional values, laws of society, and loyalty to country (Kohlberg). **371**

**Cooperative planning** A teaching style in which teachers and students plan together. **74**

**Corporal punishment** Physical contact such as striking, paddling, or spanking of a student by an educator. **605**

**Dame schools** Seventeenth-century schools held in private New England homes in which several children gathered to be taught by the woman of the household. **144**

**De facto segregation** A subtle but legal means of ensuring that segregation is continued. **184**

**Decenter** A cognitive process in which a child learns that his or her perspective is only one perspective (Piaget). **369**

**Deduction** Logical reasoning that moves from the general to the specific. **220**

**Deductive teaching** Presenting a lesson in an organized sequence from the general to the specific (Ausubel). **393**

**Differentiated staffing** Differing levels of responsibility, education, and professional achievements leading to increased professional status and pay. **30**

**Direct federal aid** Funding that flows directly from federal agencies to the schools. **556**

**Discipline** The training that leads to the development of self-control, an internal conscience that acknowledges appropriate behavior. **83**

**Discovery learning** Learning by oneself through discovery rather than through prepared and teacher-presented information (Bruner). **392**

**Display** To show individual frames of a film or videotape. **620**

**District schools** Schools formed by groups of people as they moved away from the towns. They hired their own schoolmaster and set the length of their term. **145**

**Due process** A constitutionally guaranteed right protecting citizens from arbitrary governmental action and unreasonable or discriminatory practices. **609**

**Effective teaching research** The study and examination of classroom teaching behaviors, mainly those that positively influence student performance. **60**

**Egocentric** Seeing the world as revolving around oneself. **368**

**Elementary and Secondary Education Act (ESEA)** A federal act to improve educational opportunities for socially and economically disadvantaged students. **188**

**Emotional disturbance:** A condition that adversely affects educational performance over a long period of time. May include one or more of the following characteristics: inability to learn that cannot be explained by intellectual, sensory, or health factors; inability to build or maintain personal relationships; and/or inappropriate types of behavior or feelings. **346**

**Enculturation** Everything the child does under the guidance of an adult, including formal schooling. **141**

**English language academy** An eighteenth-century prototype for contemporary secondary schools offering practical and vocational courses such as commerce, English, oratory, politics, and mathematics. **150**

**Epistemology** A category of philosophic thought that deals with the nature and universality of knowledge. **218**

**Equalization grants** A state funding formula for public schools that provides those districts with higher property values less state money than those districts with lower property values. **551**

**Equilibrium** A sense of balance that is achieved through the assimilation of new experiences into an existing scheme (Piaget). **367**

**Essentialism** An educational theory based in the philosophical school of realism, asserting that the primary function of the school is the transmission of essential facts. **239**

**Esteem need** The human need for self-respect, achievement, and status. **369**

**Ethics** The study of moral values and conduct. **218**

**Existentialism** A philosophical school that contends that reality is lived existence and final reality resides within the individual self. **232**

**Expository learning** Learning that occurs from general to specific, from rule to example (Ausubel). **393**

**Expository style** A teaching style focusing on content and sequence of subject matter, usually from a text; lecturing, direct questioning for student recitation, and structured assignments predominate. **71**

**Extinguish** The disappearance of a response if reinforcement does not occur (Pavlov). **389**

**Fair use** The right to use copyrighted material in a reasonable manner without the permission of the author. **619**

**Fieldwork** Observing, participating, and teaching in classrooms during a teacher-training program. **93**

**Fiscal neutrality** A system of educational funding that is not tied to local property wealth. **562**

**Five-year degree model** An undergraduate-graduate five-year approach to teacher training. **104**

**Flat grants** A state funding formula for public schools based on the district's average daily attendance during the previous school year; each district receives the same amount for each student in attendance. **551**

**Formal control** That power delegated to individuals or groups through statute or law. **511**

**Formal operational period** A period of cognitive development that occurs between ages eleven and adulthood during which abstract, logical, and hypothetical reasoning are developed (Piaget). **369**

**Foundation grants** Ensure a minimum level of revenue per pupil by targeting state aid to poor districts. **551**

**Freedmen's Bureau** Established by Congress to work with voluntary organizations to provide basic education for blacks who had been slaves. **162**

**General education** Education for all, but not necessarily equal education. **142**

**Grammaticus** The second level of Roman education for boys, held at the home of the teacher. **136**

**Head Start** A federally funded, comprehensive child development program for three- to five-year-olds from low-income families. **185**

**Hornbook** The first elementary notebook made of transparent paper from flattened cattle horns, used for teaching the alphabet, syllables, and the Lord's Prayer. **144**

**Idealism** A traditional philosophical school that contends that reality consists of an idea, a nonphysical essence, and that the development of the mind and self are primary. **223**

**Incentive pay** Increased compensation for success in teaching, and for additional responsibilities and levels of education; also called performance-based. **27**

**Indirect federal funding** Federal funding that flows first through state education agencies and then to the schools. **556**

**Individual education program (IEP)** An individually designed educational program for physically, mentally, and emotionally handicapped students, and for those with special learning disabilities. **191**

**Induction** Logical reasoning that moves from the specific to a general conclusion. **220**

**Infant schools** Seventeenth-century schools for young children, ages two to six, whose mothers worked in factories. **154**

**Inferential style** A teaching style that stimulates and encourages student participation, self-direction, and independence through the use of a variety of techniques such as inquiry, discovery, simulations, and experimentation. **73**

**Informal influence** Attempted control exerted by individuals or groups who have no legal authority, but who have a strong interest or commitment to schools, and who try to sway opinions of those who have the formal power to control. **511**

**Instructor-centered teaching** A teaching style in which the teacher is the ego ideal and socializing agent, modeling ways that learners should approach a particular field or subject. **71**

**Instrumental learning** An organism is able to repeat a response if reinforcement (food, money, praise) occurs; also called operant conditioning (Skinner). **390**

**Integrated** An approach that unifies a number of subjects or fields of study into one topic. Also known as core approach. **313**

**Intentional torts** A type of tort liability that involves assault, battery, desire to inflict harm, and defamation. 615

**Interview** A planned fact-finding technique in which an attempt is made to obtain information through direct questioning. 96

**Knowledge or understanding need** The human need to understand one's environment (Maslow). 369

**Latchkey children** Children who come home from a school to a house without adult supervision. 492

**Latin grammar school** A seventeenth-century Boston classical secondary school established for young men. 144

**Law** The U.S. system of jurisprudence and the courts, which are utilized in defending one's rights and securing justice. 589

**Law of effect** If an act leads to a satisfying change in the environment, the likelihood that the act will be repeated in similar situations increases; but if the act does not lead to a satisfying change, the likelihood that the act will be repeated decreases (Thorndike). 390

**Learning disability:** A disorder in one or more of the basic psychological processes involved in understanding or in using spoken or written language, which may manifest itself in an imperfect inability to listen, think, speak, read, write, spell, or do mathematical calculations. 346

**Learning outcomes** Learning skills that can be categorized into four types of results: attributes, motor skills, verbal data, and cognitive strategies (Gagne). 393

**Learning style** The manner in which various elements in one's environment affect learning. 401

**Learning-centered teaching style** A teaching style that strives to balance concern for students, curriculum, and materials to be covered. 75

**Liberal arts model** A teacher-training approach that requires an arts and sciences major, general education course work, and a professional education component; emphasis is on the development of thinking skills. 103

**Linguistic analysis** A branch of philosophical analysis that deals with language, particularly grammar and structural linguistics, and logic. 235

**Logic** A category of philosophic thought dealing with the nature of reasoning. 220

**Logical empiricism** A branch of philosophical analysis based on experimentation and observation. 234

**Magnet schools** Schools with focused themes, such as the arts, math and science, and multiculturalism; commonly designed for purposes of integration and parental choice. 202

**Mainstreaming** Participation of handicapped students in regular educational programs. 191

**Major premise** A general statement or fact from which logically inferred conclusions are deduced. 220

**Master teachers** A group of teachers who are given increased leadership responsibility, including leadership of a team working on curriculum and instruction and guiding new teachers; also called mentor, lead, or head teachers. 31

**Maxim** A commonly held belief. 218

**Mental disability** A below-average intellectual functioning that exists concurrently with deficits in adaptive behavior; it manifests itself during a child's developmental period, adversely affecting his or her educational performance. 347

**Merit pay** An annual bonus or reward given to selected teachers and other school personnel for recognized professional achievement. 29

**Metaphysics** A category of philosophic thought that speculates on the nature of ultimate reality, searching for the principles of human existence. 217

**Minor premise** A particular fact. 220

**Modeling** A theory of observational learning in which a child learns through imitation and observation of adults (Bandura). 392

**Monitorial schools** A system whereby master teachers train advanced students to teach beginning students, thus making it possible to educate large numbers of children efficiently and inexpensively. 155

**Multiple intelligences** Gardner's theory of plurality of intellect that suggests that each of seven intelligences has equal claim to priority. 395

**Multitudinousness** The historical concept of breadth of educational opportunity. 140

**National Assessment of Educational Progress (NAEP)** A congressionally mandated periodic testing program of the level of student learning. 412

**Naturalism** An educational philosophy that claims that environment plays a crucial role in individual development and that it could be shaped through reason and science. 137

**Negligence** A type of tort liability that involves unacceptable conduct or care that results in personal injury. 615

**Neutral stimulus** A stimulus that has no effect on the responder (Pavlov). 389

**Normal schools** Teacher training schools established in the early to mid-nineteenth century. 152

**Object permanence** A cognitive skill that allows young children to recognize that an object may exist even though it cannot be seen (Piaget). 368

**Operant conditioning** The operation of an organism on its environment during learning; also called instrumental learning (Skinner). 390

**Paidocentric** A child-centered psychological theory developed by G. Stanley Hall. 298

**Pais, paidas** A Greek word for the upbringing of the child. 298

**Parochial schools**   Schools supported by religious organizations; they originated in the Middle Atlantic colonies during the seventeenth century. **148**

**Parsons schools**   Endowed free schools for women in parishes or districts of the Southern colonies in the seventeenth century. **146**

**Perennialism**   An educational theory based in the philosophical schools of idealism and realism that stresses the great works of the intellectual past and the ability to reason. **238**

**Perform**   To run the entire work through a projector or recorder. **620**

**Performance-based**   Increased compensation for success in teaching and additional responsibilities and levels of education; also called incentive pay. **27**

**Philos**   A Greek word meaning love. **217**

**Philosophical analysis**   Analysis which classifies and verifies phenomena in order to define reality. **234**

**Physiological need**   The human need for food, health, warmth, and shelter (Maslow). **369**

**Politicization**   The historical concept that schools are a force for political change. **140**

**Popularization**   The historical concept of schooling for all. **140**

**Postconventional moral reasoning**   Socially agreed-upon standards of individual rights and democratically determined laws that are the basis of moral behavior (Kohlberg). **371**

**Pragmatism**   A philosophical school that contends that humans and their environment interact, both being responsible for that which is real. **230**

**Preconventional moral reasoning**   Moral judgments that are based on the expectation of rewards and punishment (Kohlberg). **371**

**Preoperational period**   A period of cognitive development that occurs between the ages two and seven during which children acquire language and learn to represent the environment with objects and symbols (Piaget). **368**

**Principle of inclusion**   A cognitive process of the concrete operational stage in which the child can reason about the relationship between classes and subclasses (Piaget). **368**

**Private schools**   Schools supported by private rather than by public funds; they originated in the Middle Atlantic colonies during the seventeenth century. **148**

**Private venture training schools**   Schools developed in the late seventeenth century by businesses and trades in the Middle Atlantic colonies to train skilled workers such as navigators, surveyors, accountants, and printers. **148**

**Progressive movement**   A late nineteenth-century educational movement based on the educational theory of progressivism, which attempted to bring the disenfranchised into the schools. **159**

**Progressivism**   An educational theory, based on the philosophical school of pragmatism, believing that curriculum and teaching methodologies should relate to students' interests and needs. **240**

**Realism**   A philosophical school that seeks knowledge and understanding about the nature of reality and of humankind and attempts to interpret people's destiny based on that nature. **225**

**Reconstructionism**   An educational theory, based on the philosophical school of pragmatism, contending that the purpose of education is to reconstruct society. **241**

**Reinforce**   The occasional presentation of the unconditioned stimulus with the neutral stimulus to encourage the continuation of the desired effect (Pavlov). **389**

**Reinforcement**   A reward (such as food, money, praise) used to encourage a direct response. **390**

**Republicanism**   A political theory founded on the principle that government arises from the consent of the governed. **150**

**Reversal**   A cognitive process that allows children to work a problem backwards (Piaget). **369**

**Safety need**   The human need to feel safe (Maslow). **369**

**Scheme**   An organized pattern of behavior or thought that children formulate as they interact with parents, age-mates, teachers, and the environment (Piaget). **367**

**Scholasticism**   A method of logical reasoning that asks questions to determine the validity of issues. **136**

**Schoolmen**   Medieval philosophers who advocated educational methods of open-ended questioning, independent learning, and sensory learning. **136**

**Self-actualization**   Reaching one's highest potential (Maslow). **369**

**Sensorimotor period**   A period of cognitive development that occurs between birth and two years and is marked by the development of reflexes and responses (Piaget). **368**

**Seven cardinal principles**   A 1918 National Education Association report that recommended a nonclassical secondary curriculum for noncollege-bound students. **158**

**Sexual harassment**   Unwanted and unwelcomed sexual behavior that interferes with one's job or one's studies. **461**

**Shared identity**   Teachers and students share similar characteristics, making teaching easier. **55**

**Single-parent family**   A family group headed by one parent. **430**

**Site-based management**   Procedure where the state gives the school control of such things as curriculum development, budgeting, staffing, and student distribution. **524**

**Social disintegration**   A belief of social reconstructionists that society is in a severe crisis, caused by the unwillingness of humans to reconstruct institutions and values to meet existing needs. **244**

**Socratic method**   A teaching method that uses systematic doubt and questioning to get at underlying, universal meanings. **135**

**Sophists**   The earliest of Greek educators who taught grammar, logic, and rhetoric to educate the citizenry so they could become legislators. **134**

**Sophos**   A Greek word meaning wisdom. **217**

**Statutory law** Statutes passed by federal and state legislatures. 589

**Strict liability** A type of tort liability that occurs when injury results from unusual hazards. 615

**Structured observations** Objective, formal observations of a predetermined classroom event, student, or teacher; data recorded using a prepared format such as a checklist. 95

**Student-centered approaches of discipline** Classroom management approaches of discipline that give students maximum freedom within limits; the teacher provides the appropriate environment and resources commensurate to the children's stage of development. 86

**Student-centered teaching** A teaching style in which instruction is tailored to the needs of the student. 72

**Subject-centered teaching** A teaching style similar to content-centered in that it focuses on covering the subject matter; differs in that student learning is not central. 72

**Sunday school** A church-sponsored, nineteenth-century school held on Sundays for children who worked at low-paying jobs during the week, designed to teach them basics of reading, writing, and religion. 154

**Synectics** Making the strange appear familiar, and the familiar appear strange; usually carried out in a small group setting in which students attempt to solve complex problems. 499

**Systematic observation** Planned, objective, goal-oriented observation of different classroom situations over an extended time period. 95

**Task-oriented** A teaching style in which materials, competencies, and appropriate levels of students' progress are prescribed. 71

**Tax credit** An amount equal to a percentage of school tuition that can be subtracted from federal and/or state income taxes. 486

**Teacher accountability** Personal responsibility for instructional quality as measured by such things as observations and student progress on standardized tests. 28

**Teacher empowerment** Teacher autonomy in making decisions that affect students, teachers, and schools; including selection of texts, promotion and retention of students, selection of teachers and administrators, etc. 22

**Teachers' college model** A teacher-training approach that emphasizes teaching methodology and fieldwork in an education specialty such as middle school mathematics; emphasis is on the development of teaching skills. 102

**Teacher-student interaction approach to discipline** A discipline approach in which the teacher and student work together employing structured discussion to find causes of student misbehavior. 86

**Teacher-student-centered learning style** A learning style in which both the teacher and student share equally in the planning of instruction. 74

**Teaching style** The unique way that teachers organize instruction, based on their philosophy of teaching and learning. 67

**Tenure** A contractual relationship between a teacher and a school board that can only be terminated for adequate cause and with due process procedures. 609

**Theory of verification** A branch of philosophical analysis that states that empirical propositions may be verified either directly or indirectly. 234

**Time-on-task** A strong focus on attention to the completion of tasks related to clearly stated instructional objectives. 262

**Tirocinium fori** A year of apprenticeship for aristocratic Roman sixteen-year-old boys. They learned the duties of senators. 136

**Tort liability** A civil wrong that pertains to the private rights of citizens and consists of three types: negligence, intentional tort, and strict liability. 615

**Town schools** Seventeenth-century schools established to provide elementary education for all New England children. 144

**Tracking** Ability grouping that places students based on academic performance, which includes school-based performance and scores on standardized achievement tests. 184, 358

**Unconditioned response** An untaught response to a stimulus (Pavlov). 389

**Unconditioned stimulus** A stimulus that automatically provokes a response (Pavlov). 389

**U.S. Department of Education** A cabinet-level governmental agency representing a formalized federal effort in education, with three major divisions: the Offices of Educational Research and Improvement, the National Center for Education Statistics, and the Information Services Department. 516

**U.S. Supreme Court** A body of judges, nominated by the president and confirmed by Congress, who interpret the Constitution and thereby can have significant influence on public education. 517

**Vernacular schools** Schools established by the New Amsterdam Dutch settlers during the seventeenth century to teach reading and writing in their native language. 148

**Vouchers** A receipt equal to the average per-pupil cost for educating a child in a specific area's public schools that can be redeemed from the government by the school in which the child is enrolled. 486

# REFERENCES

Adler, J. 1994. Kids growing up scared. *Newsweek* (January 10), 43–50.

Adler, M. J. 1982. *The Paideia proposal: An educational manifesto.* New York: Macmillan.

___. 1983. *Paideia problems and possibilities.* New York: Macmillan.

Alan Guttmacher Institute. 1994. *Sex and America's teenagers.* New York: Author.

American Association of Colleges for Teacher Education. 1990. *Rate IV teaching teachers: Facts and figures.* (Research about Teacher Education Project). Washington, DC: Author.

___. June 1989. *Alternative preparation for licensure: A policy statement.* Washington, DC: Author.

___. June 1989. *Rate III teaching teachers: Facts and figures.* (Research about Teacher Education Project). Washington, DC: Author.

American Association of School Administrators. 1993. *Women and racial minority representation in school administration.* Arlington, VA: Author.

___. 1992. *How schools shortchange girls.* Washington, DC: Author.

American Association of University Women Educational Foundation. 1993. *Hostile hallways: The AAUW survey on sexual harassment in America's schools.* (Researched by Louis Harris and Associates). Washington, DC: Author.

American Broadcasting Company (ABC). June 10, 1991. "Morning News," "Deaths resulting from crime in New York City," and "Deaths in the Persian Gulf War."

American College Testing Program. 1993. *1993 ACT assessment results: Summary report national.* Iowa City, IA: Author.

American Federation of Teachers, AFL-CIO. 1990. *Constitution of the American Federation of Teachers, AFL-CIO.* Washington, DC: Author.

___. 1993. *Survey and analysis of salary trends.* Washington, DC: Author.

___. January–July 1994. *On the hill: Reports and AFT legislative fact sheets.* Washington, DC: Author.

American Student Council Association. 1990. *NAEP Survey of Student's Beliefs.* Alexandria, VA: Author.

Anderson, R. 1993. *Computers in education study.* Department of Sociology, Minneapolis, MN: International Education Association.

Andrew, M. D. 1990. Differences between graduates of 4-year and 5-year teacher preparation programs. *Journal of Teacher Education, 41*(2), 45–51.

___. 1994. [March 31 telephone interview: Status of five-year degree education program]. Durham, NH: University of New Hampshire.

Annie E. Casey Foundation. 1994. *Kids count data book: State profiles of child well-being.* Greenwich, CT: Author.

Apple, M. 1985. Making knowledge legitimate: Power, profit, and the textbook. In *Current thought on curriculum,* Ed. A. Molnar, 75. Alexandria, VA: Association for Supervision and Curriculum Development.

Apple, M., and King, N. R. 1977. What do schools teach? In *Humanistic education,* Ed. R. H. Weller, 29–63. Berkeley, CA: McCutchan.

Aristotle. 1899. *The politics,* Trans. B. Jowett. New York: Colonial Press.

___. 1984. Politics, book VIII. In *The complete works of Aristotle.* Vol. 2, Ed. J. Barnes, 2121. Trans. B. Jowett. Princeton, NJ: Princeton University Press. Original work published 310 B.C.

Arons, S. 1994. The threat to freedom in Goals 2000. *Education Week* (April 6), 40, 52.

Ashby, S., Larson R., and Munroe, M. J. 1989. *Empowering teachers: The key to school-based reform.* Paper presented at annual Association of Teachers and Educators meeting, St. Louis, MO. ERIC Document Reproduction Service No. ED 182 465.

Atkin, J. M. 1989. Can educational research keep pace with education reform? *Phi Delta Kappan, 71*(3), 200–205.

Austin-Martin, G., Bull, D., and Molrine, C. 1981. A study of the effectiveness of a pre-student teaching experience in promoting positive attitudes toward teaching. *Peabody Journal of Education, 58*(3), 148–153.

Ausubel, D. F. 1986. *Educational psychology: A cognitive view.* New York: Holt, Rinehart and Winston.

Ayers, William. 1990. Rethinking the profession of teaching: A progressive option. *Action in Teacher Education, 12*(1), 1–6.

Bailyn, B. 1960. *Education in the forming of American society: Needs and opportunities for study.* New York: Vintage.

Banks, J. A. 1988. *Multiethnic education: Theory and practice,* 2nd ed. Boston: Allyn and Bacon.

___. 1989. Integrating the curriculum with ethnic content: Approaches and guidelines. In *Multicultural education: Issues and perspectives,* Ed. J. A. Banks and C. A. M. Banks, 189–207. Boston: Allyn and Bacon.

___. March 1, 1991. Multicultural imperative. Paper presented at Conference on Cultural Diversity, University of North Carolina at Asheville.

___. 1991. Multicultural literacy and curriculum reform. *Educational Horizons* (Spring), 69(3), 135–140.

___. 1991. *Teaching strategies for ethnic studies,* 5th ed. Boston: Allyn and Bacon.

___. 1993. Approaches to multicultural curriculum reform. In *Multicultural education: Issues and perspectives,* 2nd ed., Eds. J. A. Banks and C. A. M. Banks. Boston: Allyn and Bacon.

___. 1994. *Multiethnic education: Theory and practice,* 3rd ed. Boston: Allyn and Bacon.

Barber, L. W. 1993. Prayer at graduation: A survey. *Phi Delta Kappan, 72*(2), 125.

Barnow, B. 1973. *Evaluating project Head Start.* Madison, WI, Madison Institute for Research on Poverty. ERIC Document Reproduction Service No. ED 106 404.

Barringer, M. D. 1993. How the national board builds professionalism. *Educational Leadership, 50*(6), 8–22.

Barth, R. 1991. Restructuring schools: Some questions for teachers and principals. *Phi Delta Kappan, 73*(2), 123–128.

Bastian, A., Fruchter, N., Gittrell, M., Greer, C., and Haskins, K. 1986. *Choosing inequality.* Philadelphia: Temple University Press.

Beane, J. A. 1993. Problems and possibilities of an integrative curriculum. *Middle School Journal, 51*(1), 18–23.

Becker, S. 1962. The nature of a profession. In *Education for the professions: The sixty-first yearbook of the National Society for the Study of Education,* Pt. 2, Ed. N. B. Henry, 4–42. Chicago: University of Chicago Press.

Bennett, C. I. 1990. *Comprehensive multicultural education: Theory and practice.* Boston: Allyn and Bacon.

Bennett, W. J. 1986. *First lessons: A report on elementary education in America.* Washington, DC: U.S. Government Printing Office.

___. 1987a. *James Madison High School: A curriculum for American students.* Washington, DC: U.S. Government Printing Office.

___. 1987b. *What works: Research about teaching and learning,* 2nd ed. Washington, DC: U.S. Government Printing Office.

___. 1988. *James Madison Elementary School: A curriculum for American students.* Washington, DC: U.S. Government Printing Office.

Bergquist, W., and Phillips. S. R. 1975. *A handbook for faculty development.* Washington, DC: Council for the Advancement of Small Colleges.

Berliner, D. C. 1989. The executive functions of teaching. In *The effective teacher,* Ed. L. W. Anderson. New York: Random, 105–112.

Bestor, A. 1955. *The restoration of learning.* New York: Alfred A. Knopf.

___. 1985. *Educational wastelands: The retreat from learning in our public schools,* 2nd ed. Chicago: University of Illinois Press.

Bierlein, L., and Mulholland, L. 1993. *Charter school update: Expansion of a viable reform initiative.* Tempe, AZ: Morrison Institute for Public Policy, School of Public Affairs, Arizona State University.

Bigge, M. L. 1982. *Educational philosophies for teachers.* Columbus, OH: Merrill.

Biklen, S. K. 1983. *Teaching as an occupation of women: A case study of an elementary school.* Syracuse, NY: Education Designs Group.

Block, H. 1993. Improving child care quality and supply. *Young Children, 48*(6), 32–34.

Bloom, B. S., et al. 1956. *Taxonomy of educational objectives, handbook I: Cognitive domain.* New York: David McKay.

___. 1968. *Learning for mastery.* Los Angeles: Center for the Study of Evaluation.

___. 1981. *All our children learning: A primer for parents, teachers, and other educators.* New York: McGraw-Hill.

___. 1984. The search for methods of group instruction as effective as one-to-one tutoring. *Educational Leadership, 42*(9), 5.

Blue, T. 1986. *The teaching and learning process.* Washington, DC: National Education Association.

Boe, E. C. April 9, 1990. *Teacher incentive research with SASS.* Paper presented at the meeting of the American Education Research Association. Boston, MA.

Bohannan, L. 1966. Shakespeare in the bush. *Natural History, 75*(7), 28–33.

Bond, H. M. 1966. *The education of the Negro in the American social order.* New York: Octagon Books.

Boocock, S. S. 1980. *Sociology of education: An introduction.* New York: Macmillan.

Borich, G. D. 1992. *Effective teaching methods,* 2nd ed. New York: Merrill.

Bossert, S. T. 1985. Effective elementary schools. *Reaching for excellence: An effective school's sourcebook,* Ed. R. M. Kyle, 39–53. National Institute of Education (No. 400-81-0004). Washington, DC: U.S. Government Printing Office.

Boston, R. 1994. Public schools under siege. *Church & State* (April), *47*(4), 4–8, 20.

Bourne, R. S. 1916. *The Gary schools.* Boston: Houghton Mifflin.

Bouvier, L. F., and Agresta, A. J. 1987. The future Asian population of the United States. In *Pacific bridges: The new immigration from Asia and the Pacific islands,* Ed. J. T. Fawcett and B. V. Carino. New York: Center for Migration Studies.

Bradley, A. 1992. Reforming Philadelphia's high schools from within. *Education Week* (November 18), 17–19.

___. 1993. Not making the grade: Teacher's firing spurs debate over standards, expectations for students. *Education Week* (September 15), 1, 19–21.

___. 1994. Board in Del. ordered to review case of ousted Algebra teacher. *Education Week* (February 9), 8.

___. 1994. Board votes to reinstate ousted Algebra teacher. *Education Week* (March 23), 11.

Brameld, T. 1950. *Ends and means in education: A midcentury appraisal.* New York: Harper Brothers.

___. 1971. *Patterns of educational philosophy: Divergence and convergence in culturological perspective.* New York: Holt, Rinehart and Winston.

Brandis, B. 1993. A primer of educational philosophy. *Education Forum, 57*(2), 209–214. (First published in *Education Forum, 31*(4), May 1967).

Brandt, R. 1992/1993. On outcome-based education: A conversation with Bill Spady. *Educational Leadership* (December/January), *50*(4), 66–70.

___. 1993. What do you mean "professional"? *Journal of the Association for Supervision and Curriculum Development, 50*(6), 1.

Bredekamp, S. 1994. Reflections on Reggio Emilia. *Young Children, 49*(1), 13–17.

Bredekamp, S. and Rosegrant, T. 1992. Reaching potentials of linguistically diverse children. In *Reaching potentials: Appropriate curriculum and assessment for young children.* Vol. I, Eds. S. Bredekamp and T. Rosegrant, 137–138. Washington, DC: National Association for the Education of Young Children.

Brookover, W., et al. 1977. *Schools can make a difference.* East Lansing, MI: College of Urban Development, Michigan State University.

Brophy, J. 1974b. *The Texas Teacher Effectiveness Project: Presentation of non-linear relationships and summary discussion* (Research Report No. 74-6). Austin: University of Texas, R&D Center for Teacher Education. ERIC Document Reproduction Service ED 099 345.

___. 1976. *Learning from teaching: A developmental perspective.* Boston: Allyn and Bacon.

Brophy, J., and Evertson, C. 1974. Process-product correlations. In *Texas effectiveness study: Final report* (Research Report No. 74-4). Austin: University of Texas, R&D Center for Teacher Education. ERIC Document Reproduction Service No. ED 091 0943.

Brophy, J., and Good, T. 1984. *Looking into classrooms,* 3rd ed. New York: Harper and Row.

___. 1986. *Teacher behavior and student achievement.* In *Handbook of research on teaching,* 3rd ed., Ed. M. C. Wittrock, 328–375. New York: Macmillan.

Brown, B. F. 1984. *Crisis in secondary education: Rebuilding America's high schools.* Englewood Cliffs, NJ: Prentice Hall.

Brubacher, J. 1966. *A history of problems in education,* 2nd ed. New York: McGraw-Hill.

Brumbaugh, R. S. 1964. *The philosophers of Greece.* New York: Thomas Y. Crowell.

Bruner, J. S. 1960. *The process of education.* New York: Vintage.

Buchholz, S. 1993. Laying a firm foundation. *School and Community, 79*(3), 14, 15.

Bull, B. L. 1990. The limits of teacher professionalism. In *The moral dimensions of teaching,* Ed. J. I. Goodlad, R. Soder, and K. A. Sirotnik, 87–129. San Francisco: Jossey-Bass.

Bull, B. L., Fruehling, R. Y., and Chattergy, L. 1992. *The ethics of multicultural and bilingual groups.* New York: Teachers College Press.

Bullock, H. A. 1967. *A history of Negro education in the South: From 1619 to the present.* Cambridge, MA: Harvard University Press.

Buncombe school board to sue county, state for "fair share." *Asheville Citizen Times* (June 3, 1994), 1A.

Bush, R. N. 1967. The science and art of educating teachers. In *Improving teacher education in the United States,* Ed. S. Elam, 35–62. Bloomington, IN: Phi Delta Kappan.

Butler, J. D. 1966. *Idealism in education.* New York: Harper and Row.

Button, H. W., and Provenzo, E. F., Jr. 1983. *History of education and culture in America.* Englewood Cliffs, NJ: Prentice Hall.

Butts, R. F. 1978. *Public education in the United States: From revolution to reform.* New York: Holt, Rinehart and Winston.

Campbell, F. A., and Ramey, C. T. 1993. *Mid-adolescent outcomes for high risk students: An examination of the continuing effects of early intervention.* (Carolina Abecedarian Project). (Paper presented at the biennial meeting of the Society for Research in Child Development, March 26, 1993, New Orleans, LA).

Campbell, R. F., Cunningham, L. L., Nystrand, R. O., and Usdan, M. D. 1985. *The organization and control of American schools,* 5th ed. Columbus OH: Charles E. Merrill.

Cannell, J. J. 1989. *How public educators cheat on standardized tests: The "Lake Wobegon" report.* Albuquerque, NM: Friends of Education. ERIC Document Reproduction Service No. ED 314 454.

Canter, L., and Canter, M. 1977. *Assertive discipline.* Santa Monica, CA: Canter and Associates.

Carlsson-Page, N., and Levin, D. 1993. A constructivist approach to conflict resolution. *The Education Digest, 58*(7), 10–15.

Carnegie Corporation of New York. 1994. *Starting points: Meeting the needs of our youngest children.* New York: Author.

Carnegie Council on Adolescent Development, Carnegie Corporation of New York. 1989. *Turning points: Preparing American youth for the 21st century.* Washington, DC: Author.

Carnegie Forum on Education and the Economy. 1986. *A nation prepared: Teachers for the 21st century* (Report of the Task Force on Teaching as a Profession). New York: Author.

Carnegie Foundation for the Advancement of Teaching. 1988. *An imperiled generation: Saving urban schools.* Lawrenceville, NJ: Princeton University Press.

Carnegie Foundation for the Advancement of Teaching. 1990. *The condition of teaching: A state-by-state analysis.* Princeton, NJ: Author.

Carnegie Foundation for the Advancement of Teaching. 1992. *School choice: A special report.* (With a Foreward by Earnest Boyer). Princeton, NJ: Author.

Carnoy, M., and Levin, H. M. 1985. *Schooling and work in the democratic state.* Stanford, CA: Stanford University Press.

Cartwright, M. with D'Orso, M. 1993. *For the children: Lessons from a visionary principal.* New York: Doubleday.

Casper, L. M., Hawkins, M., and O'Donnell, M. 1994. *Who's minding the kids? Child care arrangements.* (1991, U.S. Bureau of the Census, Current Population Reports, 70–36). Washington, DC: U.S. Government Printing Office.

Cassidy, D. J. 1993. NC B-K certificate guidelines. *North Carolina Association for the Education of Young Children News.* Raleigh, NC: NC-aeyc.

Castaneda, A., and Gray, T. 1974. Bicognitive processes in multicultural education. *Educational Leadership, 32*(4), 203–207.

Celis, W. 1994. A long-running saga over Texas schools. *New York Times* (April 10) [*Education Life*], 30, 31.

Center for Population Options. 1993. *Adolescents, HIV, and other sexually transmitted diseases (STD).* Washington, DC: Author.

Center for Population Options. 1993. *Condom availability in schools: A guide for programs.* Washington, DC: Author.

Center for the Study of Social Policy. 1992. *Child poverty up nationally and in 33 states.* Washington, DC: Author.

Centers for Disease Control and Prevention. 1989. *Someone at school has AIDS: A guide to developing policies for students and staff members who are infected with HIV.* Atlanta, GA: Author.

___. 1991. *Sexually transmitted disease surveillance.* Atlanta, GA: Author.

___. 1991. *Youth risk behavior study.* Atlanta, GA: Author.

___. 1992. *Youth suicide prevention programs: A resource guide.* Atlanta, GA: Authors.

Chabator, K. J., and Montgomery, S. H. 1972. *Second year evaluation of an American management association pilot program: Adapting and testing business management development programs for educational administrators.* Syracuse University. Maxwell Graduate School of Education. ERIC Document Reproduction Service No. ED 072 543.

Chance, W. 1986. " . . . *The best of educations": Reforming America's public schools in the 1980's.* Chicago: John D. and Catherine T. MacArthur Foundation.

Chastko, A. M. 1993. Field experiences in secondary education: Qualitative differences and curriculum change. *Teacher and Teacher Education, 9*(2), 169–181.

Chenfield, M. B. 1987. *Teaching language arts creatively,* 2nd ed. San Diego: Harcourt Brace Jovanovich.

Chester, D. T., Ed. 1994. *Secretary Riley delivers first state of American education address.* Department of Education Reports (February 21), 1–4. Washington, DC: Feistritzer Publications.

Children's Defense Fund. 1994. *Giving children a Head Start now: Leave no child behind.* Washington, DC: Author.

Children's Defense Fund. 1994. *State of America's children yearbook.* Washington, DC: Author.

Children's Defense Fund and Northeastern University's Center for Labor Market Studies. 1992. *Vanishing dreams: The economic plight of America's young families.* Washington, DC: Children's Defense Fund.

Chira, S. 1990. Princeton student's brainstorm: A peace corps to train teachers. *New York Times* (June 20), A1, B7.

___. 1991a. Bush presses bill allowing parents to choose schools. *New York Times* (April 19), A1, B7.

___. 1991b. Bush's education vision. *New York Times* (April 20), 1, 8.

___. 1991c. The rules of the marketplace are applied to the classroom. *New York Times* (June 12), A1, B5.

Chubb, J. E., and Moe, T. M. 1990. *Politics, markets, and America's schools.* Washington, DC: Brookings Institution.

Cities in Schools. 1994. *Cities in schools works.* Charlotte, NC: Author.

Clinchy, C. 1993. Magnet schools matter. *Education Week* (December 8), 28.

Clinton, W. 1994. State of the union address. In *Public papers of presidents of the United States,* 67–82. Washington, DC: U.S. Government Printing Office.

Coburn, C. 1992. Stress and trauma compound school problem for immigrants. In *New Voices, 2*(3), 1, 2. A newsletter from the National Center for Immigrant Students. Boston: National Coalition of Advocates for Students.

Cohen, D. L. 1989. Middle schools gain "focus" on child. *Education Week* (June 21), 1, 20.

Cohen, D. 1993. The parenting trap: Forgotten fathers. *Education Week* (November 3), *12*(9), 16–19.

Cohen D. 1994. Head Start measure appears to be on congressional fast track. *Education Week* (April 27), 14.

Cohen, R. M. 1991. *A lifetime of teaching: Portraits of five veteran high school teachers.* New York: Teachers College Press.

Cohen, S. A., Ed. 1978. *Education in the United States: A documentary history,* Vols. 1–3. New York: Random House.

Coleman, F. 1994. Political power is only half the battle in Norway. *U.S. News & World Report* (June 13), 58.

Coleman, J. 1966. *Equality of educational opportunity.* Vol. 1. Washington DC: U.S. Government Printing Office.

College Board. 1993. *1993 Profile of SAT and achievement test takers.* Princeton, NJ: Educational Testing Service.

Comenius, J. A. 1897. The great didactic. In *The great didactic of John Amos Comenius,* Ed. and trans. M. W. Keatinge. London, England: Adam Black. (Original work published 1657).

___. 1956. *The school of infancy,* Ed. E. M. Eller. Chapel Hill: The University of North Carolina Press. (Original work published 1633).

___. 1968. Orbis Pictus. In *The Orbis pictus of John Amos Comenius,* Ed. C. W. Bardeen. Detroit, MI: Singing Tree Press. (Original work published 1659).

Committee for Economic Development. 1991. *The unfinished agenda: A new vision for child development and education.* New York: Author.

Committee on Education and Labor, U.S. House of Representatives. 1991. *A report on shortchanging children: The impact of fiscal inequity on the education of students at risk.* Washington, DC: U.S. Government Printing Office.

Compton, N., Duncan, M., and Hruska, J. 1987. *How schools can help combat student pregnancy.* Washington, DC: National Education Association.

Conant, J. B. 1948. *Education in a divided world.* Cambridge, MA: Harvard University Press.

___. 1962. *Thomas Jefferson and the development of American public education.* Berkeley: University of California Press.

Conrath, J. 1992. Effective schools for discouraged and disadvantaged students: Rethinking some sacred cows of research. *Contemporary Education* (Winter), *63*(2), 137–141.

Cook, J. 1994. *Child poverty: A crisis.* [Research report from the Center on Hunger, Poverty, and Nutrition Policy at Tufts University]. Medford, MA: Center on Hunger, Poverty, and Nutrition, Tufts University.

Coreaga, R. 1994. [June 3 telephone interview on enrollment in LEP classes]. Washington, DC: National Clearing House for Bilingual Education.

Corey, S. J. 1944. The poor scholar's soliloquy. *Childhood Education, 64*(3), 150–151.

Cornett, L. M., and Gaines, G. F. 1993. *Incentive programs: A focus on program evaluation.* Atlanta: Southern Regional Education Board.

Counts, G. 1969. *Dare the schools build a new social order?* New York: John Day. (Original edition published 1932).

Covaleskie, J. E. 1992. Discipline and morality: Beyond rules and consequences. *The Education Forum, 56*(2), 173–183.

Craig, A. 1993. Tech prep and youth apprenticeship: Opening new doors to success. *Palmetto Administrator* (Winter), 31–33.

Creighton, L. L. 1993. Kids taking care of kids. *U.S. News & World Report* (December 20), 26, 31.

Cremin, L. A. 1951. *The American common school: A historical conception.* New York: Teachers College Press.

___. Ed. 1957. *The republic and the school: Horace Mann on the education of free men.* New York: Bureau of Publications, Teachers College, Columbia University.

___. 1964. *The transformation of the school: Progressivism in American education, 1876–1957.* New York: Alfred A. Knopf.

___. 1970. *American education: The colonial period, 1607–1783.* New York: Harper.

___. 1977. *Traditions of American education.* New York: Basic Books, Inc.

___. 1980. *American education: The national experience, 1783–1876.* New York: Harper.

___. 1988. *American education: The metropolitan experience, 1876–1980.* New York: Harper and Row.

___. 1990. *Popular education and its discontents.* New York: Harper and Row.

Cress, K. 1992. Why not ask the students? Urban teenagers make the case for working. *Phi Delta Kappan, 74*(2), 172–176.

Crowley, J. C. 1970. Letter from a teacher. *Massachusetts Teacher* (September–October), 34–38.

Cubberly, E. P. 1919. *Public education in the United States.* Boston: Houghton Mifflin.

___. 1920. *Readings in the history of education.* Boston: Houghton Mifflin.

___. 1925. *An introduction to the study of education and to teaching.* Boston: Houghton Mifflin.

Daly, S. 1994. [July 8 telephone interview on the status of home schooling]. Washington, DC: Children's Defense Fund.

Danzberger, J. P. 1994. Governing the nation's schools. The case for restructuring local school boards. *Phi Delta Kappan, 75*(5), 367–363.

Darling-Hammond, L. 1988. Accountability and teacher professionalism. *American Educator, 1*(1), 8–13, 38–43.

___. 1992. *Standards of practice for learner-centered schools.* New York: National Center for Restructuring Education, Schools, and Teaching.

Darling-Hammond, L., and Berry, B. 1988. *The evolution of teacher policy.* Santa Monica, CA: RAND.

Darling-Hammond, L., and Goodwin, A. L. 1993. Progress toward professionalism in teaching. In *Challenges and achievements of American education: 1993 yearbook of the association of supervision and curriculum development,* Ed. G. Cawelti, 19–52. Alexandria, VA: Association and Curriculum Development.

Delaney, S., and Delaney, B. with Hearth, A. H. 1993. *Having our say: The Delaney sisters' first one hundred years.* New York: Kodansha America.

Delattre, E. J. 1992. Condoms and coercion: The maturity of self-determination. *Vital speeches of the day* (April 15), *58*(13), 412–416.

deMauro, D. 1989–1990. *Sexuality education 1990: A review of state sexuality and AIDS education curricula.* New York: Sex Information and Education Council of the United States (SIECUS).

Denham, C., and Lieberman, A., Eds. 1980. *Time to learn. A review of the beginning teacher evaluation study.* (Report No. EA 12 947). Washington, DC: National Institute of Education (DHEW). ERIC Document Reproduction Service No. ED 192 454.

Dewey, E., and Dewey, J. 1915. *Schools of tomorrow.* New York: Dutton.

Dewey, J. 1902. *The child and the curriculum.* Chicago: University of Chicago Press.

___. 1915. *The school and society.* Chicago: University of Chicago Press.

___. 1928. *Democracy and education.* New York: Macmillan.

Dickens, C. 1960. *A tale of two cities.* New York: New American Library. (Original work published 1859).

Diegmueller, K. 1991. A case in point: District fears quality is suffering as it cuts closer to the bone. *Education Week* (May 29), 1, 10, 11.

___. 1993. Charter schools gaining converts in legislatures. *Education Week* (July 14), 18.

___. 1993. NCATE analysis of education schools to help forge partnerships with states. *Education Week* (March 24), 27.

Donohue, W. A. 1990. *The new freedom: Individualism and collectivism in the social lives of Americans.* New Brunswick, NJ: Transaction Publishers.

Douglass, F. 1962. *The life and times of Frederick Douglass.* New York: Macmillan. (Original work published 1850).

___. 1970. *My bondage and my freedom.* Chicago: Johnson Publishing. (Original work published 1855).

Downing, J., and Harrison, T. C., Jr. 1990. Dropout prevention: A practical approach. *School Counselor, 38*(1), 67–73.

Downs, R. B. 1974. *Horace Mann.* New York: Twayne.

Drake, D. E. 1993. Student diversity: Implications for classroom teachers. *The Clearing House, 66*(5), 264–266.

Duke, D. L. 1984. *Teaching: The imperiled profession.* Albany: State University of New York Press.

Dunn, R. 1990. Rita Dunn answers questions on learning styles. *Educational Leadership, 48*(3), 15–19.

Dunn, R. S., and Dunn, K. J. 1979. Learning styles/teaching styles: Should they . . . can they . . . be matched? *Education Leadership, 26*(4), 238–244.

___. 1993. *Teaching secondary students through their individual learning styles: Practical approaches for grades 7–12.* Boston: Allyn and Bacon.

Dunn, R., Gemake, J., Jalali, F., and Zenhauser, R. 1990. Cross-cultural differences in learning styles of elementary-age students from four ethnic backgrounds. *Journal of Multicultural Counseling and Development, 18*(2), 68–93.

Dye, T. R. 1985. *Politics in states and communities,* 5th ed. Englewood Cliffs, NJ: Prentice Hall.

Easterbrook, R. 1992. Constellation building: Leadership for effective schools. *Contemporary Education, 63*(2), 91–92.

Eberlein, L. 1989. Ethical decision making for teachers. *Clearing House, 63*(3), 125–129.

Eby, J. W. 1992. *Reflective planning, teaching, and evaluating for the elementary school.* New York: Merrill.

Eck, A. 1993. [September 22 telephone interview: Number of adults changing careers]. Washington, DC: Bureau of Labor Statistics.

Edmonds, R. 1979. Effective schools for the urban poor. *Educational Leadership, 37*(2), 15–27.

Education Commission of the States. 1992. *At the cross-roads: Linking teaching to school reform.* Denver, CO: Author.

___. 1993. *Improving teacher preparation.* Denver, CO: Author.

___. 1993. *School finance litigation: A historical summary.* Denver, CO: Author.

___. 1993. *A shared vision: Policy recommendations linking teacher education to school reform.* Denver, CO: Author.

___. 1993. *State education governance structures.* Denver, CO: Author.

Educational Testing Service. 1990a. *The U.S. history report card: The achievement of fourth-, eighth-, and twelfth-grade students in 1988 and trends from 1986 to 1988 in the factual knowledge of high-school juniors.* (Project of the National Center for Education Statistics, U.S. Department of Education). Princeton, NJ: Author.

___. 1990b. *The writing report card, 1984–88: Findings from the nation's report card.* (Project of the National Center for Education Statistics, U.S. Department of Education). Princeton, NJ: Author.

___. 1991. *The state of inequality.* (A Policy Information Report). Princeton, NJ: Author.

___. 1994. *Testing in America's schools.* (A Policy Information Report). Princeton, NJ: Author.

Egan, K. 1990. Ethical codes: A standard for ethical behavior. *NASSP Bulletin, 74*(2), 59–62.

Einstein, A. 1954. *Ideas and opinions.* New York: Crown.

Eisner, E. W. 1985. *The educational imagination: On the design and evaluation of school programs,* 2nd ed. New York: Macmillan.

___. 1993. Why standards may not improve schools. *Educational Leadership, 50*(5), 22–23.

Elam, S. M. 1990. The 22nd annual Gallup poll of the public's attitudes toward the schools. *Phi Delta Kappan, 72*(1), 41–55.

Elam, S. M., Rose, L. C., and Gallup, A. M. 1992. The 24th annual Phi Delta Kappa poll: Of the public's attitudes toward the schools. *Phi Delta Kappan,* 137–141.

___. 1993. The 25th Phi Delta Kappa/Gallup Poll. *Phi Delta Kappan, 75*(2), 137–152.

Ellison, L. 1990/1991. The many facets of school choice. *Educational Leadership, 48*(4), 37.

Epstein, J. 1990. *School programs and teacher involvement in inner-city elementary and middle schools.* Baltimore, MD: Johns Hopkins University Press.

Erasmus, D. 1904. Depueris instituendis. In *Erasmus concerning education.* Cambridge MA: Cambridge University Press. (Original work published 1518).

Erikson, E. H. 1963. *Childhood and society,* 2nd ed. New York: W. W. Norton.

Espinosa, L. 1992. The process of change: The Redwood City story. In *Reaching potentials: Appropriate curriculum and assessment for young children.* Vol. I, Eds. S. Bredekamp and T. Rosegrant, 159–166. Washington, DC: National Association for the Education of Young Children.

Evertson, C. M., and Green, J. L. 1986. Observation as inquiry and method. In *Handbook of research on teaching,* 3rd ed., Ed. M. C. Wittrock, 162–213. New York: Macmillan.

Fadely, J. L., and Hosler, V. N. 1983. *Case studies in left and right hemispheric functioning.* Springfield, IL: Charles C. Thomas.

Fagan, T. W., and Heid, C. A. 1991. Chapter I program improvement: Opportunity and practice. *Phi Delta Kappan, 72*(8), 582–585.

Farkas, S. 1993. *Divided within, besieged without: The politics of education in four American school districts.* New York: The Public Agenda Foundation.

Farley, C. J. 1993. Without a prayer: The debate over religion in public schools is born again in Mississippi. *Time* (December 20), 41.

Feiman-Nemser, S., and Floden, R. E. 1986. The cultures of teaching. In *Handbook of research on teaching,* 3rd ed., Ed. M. C. Whittrock, 505–526. New York: Macmillan.

Feinberg, W. 1990. The moral responsibility of public schools. In *The moral dimensions of teaching,* Ed. J. I. Goodlad, R. F. Soder, and K. A. Sirotnik, 155–187, San Francisco: Jossey-Bass.

Feistritzer, E., and Chester, D. 1992. *Alternative teacher certification: A state by state analysis.* Washington, DC: The National Center for Education Information.

Fenstermacher, G. D. 1990. Some moral considerations on teaching as a profession. In *The moral dimensions of teaching,* Ed. J. I. Goodlad, R. F. Soder, and K. A. Sirotnik, 130–151. San Francisco: Jossey-Bass.

Findley, D., and Findley, B. 1992. Effective schools: The role of the principal. *Contemporary Education* (Winter), *63*(2), 102–104.

Firestone, W. A. 1991. Merit pay and job enlargement as reforms: Incentives, implementation, and teacher response. *Education Evaluation and Policy analysis, 13*(3), 269–288.

Fischer, B. B., and Fischer, L. 1979. Styles in teaching and learning. *Educational Leadership, 26*(4), 245–254.

Fiske, E. B. 1991. *Smart schools, smart kids. Why do some schools work?* New York: Simon and Schuster.

Flanagan, A. 1994. Beleaguered principal faces more charges, delayed hearings: Trouble started with whole language curriculum. *The Council Chronicle* (June), *3*(5), 1, 6.

Flanders, N. 1970. *Analyzing teacher behavior.* Reading, MA: Addison-Wesley.

Flavel, J. H. 1982. Structures, stages, and sequences in cognitive development. In *The concept of development: The Minnesota symposia on child psychology.* Vol. 15, Ed. W. Collins. Hillsdale, NJ: Erlbaum.

Flexner, A., and Bachman, F. 1918. *The Gary schools.* New York: General Education Board.

Ford, B. F. 1992. Meeting the educational needs of America's homeless children. *The Delta Kappa Gamma Bulletin* (Summer), *58*(4), 11–16.

Fox, C. L., and Forbing, S. E. 1992. *Creating drug free schools and communities.* New York: HarperCollins.

Franklin, B. 1978. Proposals relating to the education of youth in Pennsylvania. In *Education in the United States: A documentary history.* Vol. 1, Ed. S. Cohen, 495–504. New York: Random House. (Original work published 1744).

Frazier, C. R. 1993. A shared vision: Policy recommendations for linking education to school reform. Denver, CO: Education Commission of the States.

Freedom Forum. 1994. *Death by cheeseburger: High school journalism in the 1990s and beyond.* Arlington, VA: Author.

Freidson, E. 1986. *Professional powers: A study of the institutionalization of formal knowledge.* Chicago: University of Chicago Press.

French, W. M. 1964. *America's educational tradition.* Boston: Heath.

Frick, W. 1994. A teacher examines school choice reform. *Childhood Education* (Summer), *70*(4), 194–195.

Froebel, F. 1889. *The education of man,* Trans. W. Hailman. New York: Appelton.

Futrell, M. H. 1989. *An open letter to America on schools, students, and tomorrow.* Washington, DC: National Education Association.

Gage, N. L. 1978. *The scientific basis of the art of teaching.* New York: Teachers College Press.

___. 1990. Dealing with the dropout problem. *Phi Delta Kappan, 72*(4), 280–285.

Gage, N. L., Belgard, M., Dell, D., Hiller, J., Rosenshine, B., and Unruh, W. 1968. *Explorations of the teacher's effectiveness in explaining* (Tech. Rep. No. 4). Stanford, CA: Stanford University, Center for Research and Development in Teaching.

Gagne, R. M. 1970. *The conditions of learning,* 2nd ed. New York: Holt, Rinehart and Winston.

Gagne, R. M., and Briggs, L. J. 1965. *Principles of instructional design,* 2nd ed. New York: Holt, Rinehart and Winston.

Gallup, A. M. 1990. The 22nd annual Gallup Poll of the public's attitude toward the schools. *Phi Delta Kappan, 72*(2), 41–55.

Gallup Organization. March 1991. *Teenage suicide study.* Princeton, NJ: Author.

___. 1994. *National youth survey: Attitudes and expectations regarding society, education, and adulthood.* Princeton, NJ: Author.

Garcia, J., and Pugh, S. L. 1992). Multicultural education in teacher preparation programs: A political or an educational concept? *Phi Delta Kappan, 74*(3), 214–219.

Garcia, R. 1978. The multiethnic dimension of bilingual-bicultural education. *Social Education, 42*(6), 492–493.

Gardner, D. P. 1983. *A nation at risk: The imperative for educational reform.* Washington, DC: U.S. Government Printing Office.

Gardner, H. 1991. *The unschooled mind: How children think and how schools should teach.* New York: Basic Books.

___. 1993. *Multiple intelligences: The theory in practice.* New York: Basic Books.

Gardner, J. W. 1961. *Excellence: Can we be equal and excellent too?* New York: Harper and Row.

Garibaldi, A. M. 1992. Preparing teachers for culturally diverse classrooms. In *Diversity in teacher education: New expectations,* Ed. M. E. Dillworth, 23–39. San Francisco: Jossey-Bass.

Gauss, J. 1962. Evaluation of Socrates as a teacher. *Phi Delta Kappan* (January, back cover).

Gay, G. 1993. Ethnic minorities and educational equality. In *Multicultural education: Issues and Perspectives,* 2nd ed., Eds. J. A. Banks and C. A. M. Banks, 177–194. Boston: Allyn and Bacon.

Gelman, D. 1990. A much riskier passage. [Special issue]. *Newsweek* (Summer/Fall), 10–17.

Gelman, R., and Gallistel, C. R. 1978. *The young child's understanding of numbers: A window on early cognitive development.* Cambridge, MA: Harvard University Press.

Gibbs, N. 1993. How should we teach our children about sex? *Time* (May 24), 60–65.

Gilligan, C. 1988. Adolescent development reconsidered. In *Mapping the moral domain: A contribution of women's thinking to psychological theory and education,* Ed. C. Gilligan, J. V. Ward, J. M. Taylor, and B. Bardige, vii–xxxix. Cambridge, MA: Center for the Study of Gender Education and Human Development.

Gilman, D. A. 1992. This issue: Correlates of a defective school. *Contemporary Education* (Winter), *63*(2), 89, 90.

Glass, G. V. 1993. A conversation about educational research priorities: A message to Riley. *Educational Researcher, 22*(6), 17–22.

Glasser, W. 1969. *Schools without failure.* New York: Harper and Row.

Glenn, M. 1982. *Class dismissed: High school poems.* New York: Ticknor and Fields.

Gloeckler, L. C., and Cianca, M. 1986. Expectations for quality and achievement in special education. *Educational Leadership, 44*(1), 31.

Goeller, K. A. 1992. Here, effective is spelled . . . extraordinary. *Contemporary Education* (Winter), *63*(2), 153–156.

Golden, T. 1992. Mexicans look askance at textbooks' new slant. *New York Times* (September 21), 20.

Good, T. L., and Brophy, J. E. 1986. School effects. In *Handbook of research on teaching,* 3rd. ed., Ed. M. C. Wittrock, 570–602. New York: Macmillan.

Good, T. L., and Grouws, D. 1975. *Process-product relationships in fourth-grade mathematics classrooms* (Final Report: National Institute of Education Grant NIE-G-00-3-0133). Columbia, MO: University of Missouri, College of Education.

Goodlad, J. I. 1983. The problems of getting markedly better schools. In *Bad times, good schools,* Ed. J. Frymier, 59–77. West Lafayette, IN: Kappa Delta Pi.

___. 1984. *A place called school: Prospects for the future.* New York: McGraw-Hill.

___. 1990a. The occupation of teaching in schools. In *The moral dimensions of teaching,* Ed. J. I. Goodlad, R. Soder, and K. A. Sirotnik, 3–34. San Francisco: Jossey-Bass.

___. 1990b. *Teachers for our nation's schools.* San Francisco: Jossey-Bass.

Goodsell, W. E. 1931. *Pioneers of women's education in the United States: Emma Willard, Catherine Beecher, Mary Lyon.* New York: AMS Press.

Gordon, E. W. 1974. The political economics of effective schooling. In *Equality of educational opportunity,* Ed. L. P. Miller and E. W. Gordon, 445–459. New York: AMS Press.

___. 1989. An interview with Nancy Rabianski-Carriuolo on learning styles in different cultures. *Journal of Developmental Psychology, 62*(6), 18–19.

Gordon, W. J. J. 1971. *Synectics.* New York: Collier Books.

Gorney, C. 1985. The bilingual education battle. *Washington Post National Weekly Edition* (July 29), 6–10.

Goslin, D. A. 1965. *The school in contemporary society.* Chicago: Scott, Foresman.

Gould, J. 1994. [June 13 telephone interview on status of teacher retirement]. Washington, DC: American Federation of Teachers.

Goya, S. 1993. The secret of Japanese education. *Phi Delta Kappan, 75*(2), 126–129.

Graham, E. 1990. Bottom-line education: A business-run school in Chicago seeks to improve learning without a big rise in costs. *Wall Street Journal* (February 9), R24, R26–R27.

Grant, G. 1985. Schools that make an imprint: Creating a strong positive ethos. In *Challenge to American schools,* Ed. J. D. Bunzell, 127–143. New York: Oxford.

Grant, V. 1990. [July 19 telephone interview on the number of teachers leaving the profession]. National Center for Education Statistics. Washington, DC: U.S. Department of Education.

___. 1993. [September 15 telephone interview on the number of teachers leaving teaching]. Washington, DC: U.S. Department of Education.

___. 1994. [April 19 telephone interview on the U.S. government's definition of minority]. Washington, DC: U.S. Department of Education.

___. 1994. [July 22 telephone interview on number of school districts in the U.S.]. Washington, DC: U.S. Department of Education.

Grasha, A. F. 1972. Observations on relating goals to student response styles and classroom methods. *American Psychologist, 27*(8), 144–147.

Greenhouse, S. 1993. If the French can do it, why can't we? *The New York Times Magazine* (November 13), 59–62.

Grossman, H., and Grossman, S. H. 1994. *Gender issues in education.* Boston: Allyn and Bacon.

Grube, G. M. A. 1935. *Plato's thought.* Boston: Beacon Press.

Gushue, K. Not a loser. *The Boston Globe Magazine* (February 6), 50, 51. [Special issue by and about urban youth].

Gutek, G. L. 1968. *Pestalozzi and education.* New York: Random House.

___. 1988. *Philosophical and ideological perspectives on education.* Englewood Cliffs, NJ: Prentice Hall.

Gutman, A. 1987. *Democratic education.* Princeton, NJ: Princeton University Press.

Haberman, M. 1988. *Preparing teachers for urban schools* (Fastback 267). Bloomington, IA: Phi Delta Kappan Educational Foundation.

Haberman, M., and Post, L. 1992. Does direct experience change education students' perceptions of low-income minority students? *Mid-Western Educational Researcher, 5*(2), 29–31.

Haffner, D. 1992. HIV/AIDS education: SIECUS study on HIV/AIDS education for schools finds states make progress but work remains. *SIECUS Report, 21*(2).

Haley, J. F. 1993. Teaching—a profession. *The Education Forum, 57,* 204–208.

Hall, A. G. 1981. Points picked up: One hundred hints on how to manage a school. In *Teaching school: Points picked up,* Ed. E. W. Johnson, 209–216. New York: Walker.

Hall, G. 1993. Field reviews accreditation standards. In NCATE Quality Teaching (Fall), *3*(1), 1–3.

Hamilton, J. G. D., Ed. 1926. *The best letters of Thomas Jefferson.* Boston: Houghton Mifflin.

Hanby-Sikora, C. February 19, 1991. *Technology in teacher education at the Center for Excellence in Education at Indiana University.* [Telephone interview with authors].

Hand, K. 1990. Style is a tool for students, too! *Educational Leadership, 48*(2), 13, 14.

Harbaugh, M. 1985. Who will teach the class of 2000? *Instructor, 94*(1), 31–36.

___. 1990. Celebrating diversity. *Instructor, 100*(2), 44–48.

Harlan, L. R. 1972. *The Booker T. Washington papers* address to the Cotton States Exposition in Atlanta, 1895, Vol. 3, 621. Urbana: University of Illinois Press.

Harris, L. 1990. *The Metropolitan Life Survey of the American teacher: Preparing schools for the 1990's.* New York: Author.

Harris, L., and Associates. 1988. *The Metropolitan Life survey of the American teacher: Strengthening the relationship between teachers and students.* New York: Metropolitan Life Insurance Company.

Harris, W. T. 1898. *The theory of education.* Syracuse, NY: Bardeen.

Hartman, A. 1994. [August 5 telephone interview on the status of reauthorization of ESEA]. Washington, DC: House Committee on Education and Labor, U.S. Congress.

Hays, K. 1994. Topeka comes full circle. *Modern Maturity* (April/May), 34.

Heafford, M. 1967. *Pestolozzi: His thoughts and its relevance today.* London: Methuen.

Hechinger, F. M. 1992. *Fateful choices: Healthy youth for the 21st century.* New York: Carnegie Council on Adolescent Development.

Heitz, T. 1989. How do I help Jacob? *Young children, 45*(1), 11–15.

Heller, K., Holtman, W., and Messick, S. (Eds). 1982. *Placing children in special education: A strategy for equity.* Washington, DC: National Academy of Sciences Press.

Helm, V. M. 1986. *What educators should know about copyright. Fastback 33.* Bloomington IN: Phi Delta Kappan Educational Foundation.

Hemphill, C. 1993. [November 4, 5 telephone interview on the number of hours in different areas for teacher certification in various states]. Washington, DC: Council of Chief State School Officers.

Hennig, M., and Gardin, A. 1977. *The managerial woman.* Garden City, NY: Anchor Press.

Henry, M. 1988. The effect of increased exploratory field experiences upon the perceptions and performance of student teachers. In *Action in teacher education: Tenth-year anniversary issue, commemorative edition,* Ed. J. Sikula, 93–97. Reston, VA: Association of Teacher Educators.

Henry, T., and Kelly, D. 1993. Policy of inclusion under fire. *USA Today* (December 16), 1D, 2D.

Herbart, J. F. 1970. Outlines of educational doctrine. In *Foundations of education in America: An anthology of major thoughts and significant actions,* Ed. J. W. Noll and S. P. Kelly, 205–208. New York: Harper. (Original work published 1901).

Herndon, J. 1971. *How to survive in your native land.* New York: Simon and Schuster.

Hickrod, A. G. 1994. [August 3 telephone interview on using property taxes for school funding]. Normal, IL:

Center for Study of Educational Finance, Illinois State University.

___. 1994. *Status of school finance constitutional litigation.* Normal, IL: Center for the Study of Educational Finance, Illinois State University.

Hill, J. C. 1985. The teacher as an artist: A case for peripheral supervision. *The Educational Forum, 46*(2), 215–217.

Hill, P. T., Foster, G. E., and Gendler, T. 1990. *High schools with character.* Santa Monica, CA: RAND Corporation.

Hilliard, A. 1989. Teachers and cultural styles in a pluralistic society. [Special edition]. *Today: Issues '89* (January), 65–69.

Hirsch, E., Jr. 1987. *Cultural literacy: What every American needs to know.* Boston: Houghton Mifflin.

___. 1987/1988. Restoring cultural literacy in the early grades. *Educational Leadership* (December), *45*(4), 26–27.

Hodgkinson, H. L. 1989. *The same client: The demographics of education and service delivery systems.* Washington, DC: Institute for Educational Leadership, Center for Demographic Policy.

___. 1992. *A demographic look at tomorrow.* Washington, DC: Center for Demographic Policy, Institute for Educational Leadership.

Hofstadter, R. 1963. *Anti-intellectualism in American life.* New York: Alfred A. Knopf.

Hollingsworth, P., and Hoover, K. 1991. *Elementary teaching methods,* 4th ed. Boston: Allyn and Bacon.

Holmes Group. 1986. *Tomorrow's Teachers.* East Lansing, MI: Author.

___. 1989. *Work in progress: The Holmes Group one year on.* Lansing, MI: Author.

Holt, J. 1964. *How children fail.* New York: Pitman.

___. 1967. *How children learn.* New York: Dell.

___. 1970. *What do I do Monday?* New York: Dutton.

___. 1972. *Freedom and beyond.* New York: Delta.

Home School Legal Defense Association. 1994. *Home schooling in the United States: A legal analysis.* Paeonian Springs, VA: Author.

Hood, J. 1993. Caveat emptor: The Head Start scam. *USA Today* (May 12), 75–78.

Horenstein, M. A. 1993. *Twelve schools that succeed.* Bloomington, IN: Phi Delta Kappa Educational Foundation.

House Judiciary Committee, 1976. House report 94–1476. *Congressional Record.* Washington, DC: U.S. Government Printing Office.

House of Representatives Report 103–275. 1993. *Conference report to accompany HR 2519,* 6.

Howard, M., and Partners. 1993. *Racial attitudes of North Carolinians.* (Sponsored by Z. Smith Reynolds Foundation, Winston, NC). Raleigh, NC: Authors.

Howey, K. R., and Zimpher, N. L. 1989. *Profiles of preservice teacher education: Inquiry into the nature of programs.* Albany: State University of New York Press.

Hudgins, H. C., Jr., and Vacca, R. E. 1985. *Law and education: Contemporary issues and court decisions,* 2nd ed. Charlottesville, VA: Mitchie.

Hunter, E. 1983. Under constant attack: Personal reflections of a teacher educator. *Phi Delta Kappan, 67*(3), 222–224.

Hunter, M. 1984. Knowing, teaching, and supervising. In *Using what we know about teaching: 1984 yearbook for Association for Supervision and Curriculum Development,* Ed. P. Wofford. Alexandria, VA: Association for Supervision and Curriculum Development.

Hurwitz, H. L. 1988. *The last angry principal.* Portland, OR: Halcyon House.

Hutchins, R. M. 1936a. *Higher learning in America.* New Haven, CT: Yale University Press.

___. 1936b. *No friendly voice.* Chicago: University of Chicago Press.

___. 1968. *The learning society.* New York: Praeger.

Imber, M., and Thompson, G. 1991. Developing a typology of litigation in education and determining the frequency of each category. *Educational Administration Quarterly, 27*(2), 225–244.

India's supreme court upholds secularism. 1994. *Church & State* (June), *47*(2), 21.

Instructor Magazine. 1986. *Instructor Curriculum Attitude Study Report.* New York: Scholastic Inc.

An international agenda for children. 1990. *New York Times* (October 1), A10.

Jackson, P. W. 1968. *Life in classrooms.* New York: Holt, Rinehart and Winston.

___. 1986. *The practice of teaching.* New York: Teachers College Press.

Jalengo, M. R. 1985. When young children move: Manolo's new country. *Young children, 40*(60), 51–56.

James, W. 1948. *Some problems of philosophy: A beginning of an introduction to philosophy.* New York: Longmans, Green and Company.

___. 1958. Talks to teachers on psychology: And to students on some of life's ideals, Ed. P. Woodring. New York: Norton.

Jefferson, T. 1781–1785. *Notes on the state of Virginia, Query XV,* 94.

___. 1936. Letter to Nathaniel Burwell. From Missouri Historical Society, 1936. Correspondence of Thomas Jefferson, 1788–1826, Vol. 3. In S. K. Padover, *The complete Jefferson,* 1985. New York: Duell, Sloan & Pierce. (Original work published March 14, 1818).

___. 1943. Notes on Virginia and other writings. In *Alexander Hamilton and Thomas Jefferson,* Ed. F. C. Prescott, 134. New York: American Book Company. (Original work published 1781–1785).

___. 1954. Bill 79 of 1779 for the more general diffusion of knowledge. In *The papers of Thomas Jefferson,* Ed. J. P. Boyd, 526–543. Princeton, NJ: Princeton University Press. (Original work published in 1779).

Jencks, C. 1972. *Inequality: A reassessment of family and schooling in America.* New York: Basic Books.

Jennings, R. M. 1993. From the "golden to the god-awful": Tale of two states. *Congressional Quarterly Report* (May 27), 119.

___. 1993. The next education crisis: Equalizing school funds. *Congressional Quarterly Report* (May 27), 117–122.

Johnson, C., and Loeb, R. 1994. Stupid spending tricks. *U.S. News & World Report* (July 18), 26.

Johnson, L. B. 1965. President Lyndon Johnson's call upon Congress to pass elementary and secondary education act. *89th Congress, 1st Session* (House Document No. 45). Washington, DC: U.S. Government Printing Office.

Johnson, P. 1992. High unemployment triggers cycle of poverty. *Asheville Citizen Times* (May 27), 8A.

Johnston, J. S., Jr., Spalding, J. R., Paden, R., and Ziffren, A. 1989. *Those who can: Undergraduate programs to prepare arts and sciences majors for teaching.* Washington, DC: Association of American Colleges.

Johnston, L., Bachan, J. G., and O'Malley, P. M. 1990. *Monitoring the future study: Drug abuse among high-school seniors.* (Conducted for the National Institute on Drug Abuse). Ann Arbor: University of Michigan's Institute for Social Research.

Johnston, L. D., O'Malley, P. M., and Bachman, J. G. 1993. *National survey results on drug use from monitoring the future study, 1975–1992.* Washington, DC: U.S. Government Printing Office.

Jones, S. 1993. Adolescent childbearing: Whose problem? What can we do? *Phi Delta Kappan* (Kappan Special Report), *75*(3), K1–K11.

Joyce, B. R., Hersh, R. H., and McKibbin, M. 1983. *The structure of school improvement.* New York: Longman.

Joyce, B., and Weil, M. 1972. *Models of teaching.* Englewood Cliffs, NJ: Prentice Hall.

Kant, I. 1956 [1788]. *Critique of practical reason,* Trans. L. W. Beck. New York: Bobbs Merrill.

___. 1959 [1785]. Foundations of the metaphysics of morals. In *Fundamental principles of the metaphysics of ethics,* Trans. L. W. Beck. New York: Bobbs Merrill.

Kantrowitz, B., and Wingert, P. 1993. No longer a sacred cow: Head Start has become a free-fire zone. *Newsweek* (April 12), 57.

Katz, J. 1974. *Education in Canada.* London, England: David and Charles.

Katz, M. B. 1968. *The irony of early school reform.* Cambridge, MA: Harvard University Press.

Kauchak, D., and Eggen, P. D. 1989. *Learning and teaching: Research based methods.* Boston: Allyn and Bacon.

Kean, P. 1993. Building a better Beowulf: A new assault on the liberal arts. *Lingua Franca* (May/June), 22–25.

Kemper, V. 1993. Rebuilding the schoolhouse: Author Jonathon Kozol talks about education reform, choice, and Chelsea's school. *Common Cause Magazine* (Spring), 24–28.

Kennedy, A. M. 1992. States cannot exact religious control conformity from a student. *Washington Post* (June 25), 26.

Kennedy, J. 1962. President's message on education to the Congress of the United States. In *Public papers of the presidents of the United States,* 101–117. Washington, DC: U.S. Government Printing Office.

Kennedy, M., Birman, B., and Demaline, R., Eds. 1986. *The effectiveness of Chapter I services.* Office of Educational Research and Improvement. Washington, DC: U.S. Government Printing Office. ERIC Document Reproduction Service No. ED 281 919.

Keogh, B. K. 1983. Classification, compliance and confusion. *Journal of learning disabilities, 16*(1), 25.

Keppel, F. 1966. *The necessary revolution in American education.* New York: Harper and Row.

Kerr, M. E. 1983. *Me, Me, Me, Me, Me; Not a novel.* New York: Harper and Row.

Kidder, T. 1989. *Among school children.* Boston: Houghton Mifflin.

Kilbourn, A. 1993. Derrick White, a Memphis teenager, groping for a road map out of the projects. *New York Times* (April 23), A1.

Kilpatrick, W. 1933. *The educational frontier.* New York: Arno Press.

Kimball, B. 1988. The problem of teachers' authority in light of structural analysis of professions. *Educational Theory, 38,* 1–9.

Kirp, D. 1989. *Learning by heart: AIDS and schoolchildren in America's communities.* New Brunswick, NJ: Rutgers University Press.

Kirp, D., and Epstein, S. 1989. AIDS in America's schoolhouses: Learning the hard lessons. *Phi Delta Kappan, 70*(8), 584–593.

Kirp, D., Epstein, S., Franks, M. S., Simon, J., Conway, D., and Lewis, J. 1989. *Learning by heart: AIDS and school-children in America's communities.* New Brunswick, NJ: Rutgers University Press.

Kirp, D., and Yudof, M. G., Eds. 1974. *Educational policy and the law: Cases and materials.* Berkeley, CA: McCutchan.

Kleinfeld, J., and Noordhoff, K. 1988. *Teachers for Rural Alaska (TRA) program assessment report* (Report No. RC 017 045). Fairbanks: Alaska University, Center for Cross-Cultural Studies. ERIC Document Reproduction Service No. ED 306 055.

Kneller, G. F. 1964. *Introduction to the philosophy of education.* New York: John Wiley and Sons.

Knight, E. February 20, 1991. *Status of a masters degree for initial teacher certification.* [Telephone interview with authors].

Knight, G. R. 1982. *Issues and alternatives in educational philosophy,* 2nd ed. Berrien Springs, MI: Andrews University Press.

Koerner, J. D. 1968. *Who controls American education?: A guide for laymen.* Boston: Beacon Press.

Kohl, H. R. 1969. *The open classroom.* New York: Random House.

Kohlberg, L. 1981. *Essays on moral development: The philosophy of moral development: Moral stages and the idea of justice,* Vol. 1. New York: Harper and Row.

Kohn, A. 1990. The ABCs of caring. *Teacher Magazine Reader* [Special issue], 6–12.

Kozol, J. 1991. *Savage inequalities: Children in America's schools.* New York: Crown.

Kramer, R. 1991. *Ed school follies: The miseducation of America's teachers.* New York: Free Press.

Krathwohl, D. R., Bloom, B. S., and Masin, B. R. 1964. *Taxonomy of educational objectives, handbook II: Affective domain.* New York: David McKay.

Kurtz, P. Ed. 1966. *American philosophy in the twentieth century: A source book from pragmatism to philosophical analysis.* New York: Macmillan.

Labaree, D. F. 1992. Power, knowledge, and the rationalization of teaching: A genealogy of the movement to professionalize teaching. *Harvard Educational Review, 62*(2), 123–154.

Lacey, A. R. 1976. *A dictionary of philosophy.* London: Routledge and Kegan Paul.

Ladson-Billings, G. 1992. Culturally relevant teaching: The key to making multicultural education work. In *Research and multicultural education,* Ed. C. A. Grant, 106–121. Washington, DC: Falmer.

Lagemann, E. C., and Graham, P. A. 1994. *Lawrence A. Cremin: A biographical memoir* [Unpublished manuscript]. Chicago, IL: The Spencer Foundation.

Larke, P. T. 1992. Effective multicultural teachers: Meeting the challenges of diverse classrooms. *Equity and Excellence* (Winter), *25*(2–4), 133–138.

Lawton, M. 1992. Teach for America may be facing $3-million budget deficit. *Education Week* (August 4), 14.

___. 1994. More students falsely charge teachers with abuse. *Education Week* (August 2), 1, 16.

Lee, M. 1993. Asian Americans don't fit their monochrome image. *Christian Science Monitor* (July 27), 9, 10.

Lerner, B. 1985. Our black-robed school board: A report card. In *Challenge to American schools,* Ed. J. H. Bunzell, 169–187. New York: Oxford University Press.

Let states handle funding. 1994. *USA Today* (March 21), 10A.

LeTendre, M. J. 1991. Improving Chapter I programs. *Phi Delta Kappan, 72*(8), 577–580.

Levine, D. U., and Havighurst, R. J. 1989. *Society and education,* 7th ed. Boston: Allyn and Bacon.

Levine, D. U., and Lezotte, D. W. 1990. *Unusually effective schools: A review and analysis of research and practice.* Madison, WI: National Center for Effective Schools Research and Development.

Lewis, A. C. 1993. *Changing the odds: Middle school reform in progress, 1991–1993.* New York: Edna McConnell Clark Foundation.

Lewis, M. 1993. [November 3 telephone interview on colleges and universities in the United States having state-approved teacher certification]. Washington, DC: American Association of Colleges for Teacher Education.

LH Research. 1993. *Testing assumptions: A survey of teachers' attitudes toward the nation's school reform agenda.* (Study # 930012). New York: Author.

Lieberman, M. 1986. *Beyond public education.* New York: Praeger.

___. 1993. *Public education: An autopsy.* Cambridge, MA: Harvard University Press.

Lindner, B. 1988. *Drawing in the family: Family involvement in the schools.* Denver, CO: Education Commission of the States.

Little, J. W. 1990. Teachers as colleagues. In *Schools as collaborative cultures: Creating the future now,* Ed. A. Lieberman, 165–193. New York: Falmer.

___. 1992. Opening the black box of professional community. In *The changing contexts of teaching: Ninety-first yearbook of the national society for the study of education,* Ed. A. Lieberman, 157–178. Chicago: University of Chicago Press.

Lochhead, C. 1988. Homeless in America: All alone, with no home. *Insight* (May 16), 8–18.

Locke, J. 1964. *John Locke on education,* Ed. P. Gay. New York: Teachers College Press.

Lockwood, A. T. 1990. Restructuring schools for effective education. *Focus in Change, 2*(3), 6.

___. 1992. Rethinking professionalization: An interview with Kathleen Densmore. *Focus in Change, 9,* 12–14.

Lodge, R. C. 1970. *Plato's theory of education.* New York: Russell and Russell.

Loman, B. 1985. Improving public education: Recommendations from recent study commissions. *Popular Government* (Winter), 14–16.

Lortie, D. C. 1975. *Schoolteacher: A sociological study.* Chicago: University of Chicago Press.

Louv, R. 1990. *Childhood's future: Listening to the American family, new hope for the next generation.* Boston: Houghton Mifflin.

___. 1993. *Father Love.* New York: Pocket Books.

Lynch, C. 1993. The Renaissance woman: An interview with Rosa Jervolino. *Hemispheres* (January), 17–19.

MacCracken, M. 1976. *Lovey: A very special child.* New York: J. B. Lippincott.

Macionis, J. J. 1991. *Sociology.* Englewood Cliffs, NJ: Prentice Hall.

Macrorie, K. 1984. *Twenty teachers.* New York: Oxford University Press.

Maerhoff, G. I. 1988. A blueprint for empowering teachers. *Phi Delta Kappan, 69*(7), 472–477.

Manatt, R. P. 1981, November. *Manatt's exercise in selecting teacher performance evaluation criteria based on effective teaching research.* Albuquerque, NM: National Symposium for Professionals in Evaluation and Research.

Mann, H. 1867. *Lectures and annual reports on education (1837–1848).* Cambridge, MA: Cornhill Press.

Manning, A. 1994. Texas trims touchy subjects. *USA Today* (February 15), A1.

Manning, M. L. 1993. *Developmentally appropriate middle level schools.* Wheaton, MD: Association for Childhood International.

Marklein, M. B. 1993. Kids rise to the challenge. *USA Today* (December 15), 5D.

Marland, S. P., Jr., 1972. *Education of the gifted and talented,* Vol. 1. Report of the Congress of the United States by the U.S. Commissioner of Education, 2. Washington, DC: U.S. Government Printing Office.

Marriott, M. 1990. A new road to learning: Teaching the whole child. *New York Times* (June 13), A1, B7, B8.

Marsiglio, W. 1988. Commitment to social fatherhood: Predicting adolescent males' intentions to live with their child and partner. *Journal of Marriage and the Family, 50*(2), 427–441.

Martin, L. S. 1992. Implementing the effective school model. *Contemporary Education, 63*(2), 151–152.

Maslow, A. 1970. *Motivation and personality.* New York: Harper and Row. (Originally published 1954).

Massie, R. 1994. [July 6 telephone interview on *State appropriations for preschools/Head Start*]. Washington, DC: Children's Defense Fund.

Mastain, R. K., Ed. 1991. *Manual on certification and preparation of educational personnel in the United States.* National Association of State Directors of Teacher Education and Certification. Dubuque, IA: Kendall/Hunt.

Mathews, J. 1988. *Escalante: The best teacher in America.* New York: Henry Holt.

___. 1992. Escalante still stands and delivers. *Newsweek* (July 20), 58–59.

Matyas, M., and Kahle, J. 1986. "Equitable precollege science and mathematics: A discrepancy model." 1. Paper presented at the Workshop on Underrepresentation and Career Differentials of Women in Science and Engineering. Washington, DC: National Academy of Sciences.

McAshan, H. A. 1979. *Competency-based education and behavioral objectives.* Englewood Cliffs, NJ: Educational Technology Publications.

McCart, L., Ed. 1994. *Kids and violence.* Washington, DC: National Governor's Association.

McCarthy, B. 1990. Using the 4MAT system to bring learning styles to school. *Educational Leadership, 49*(2), 31–36.

McCarthy, M. M., and Cambron-McCabe, H. 1992. *Public school law: Teachers' and students' rights,* 3rd ed. Boston: Allyn and Bacon.

McIntosh, P., and Style, E. 1993. *The S.E.E.D. project on inclusive curriculum: Seeking educational equity and diversity.* Wellesley, MA: Wellesley College Center for Research on Women.

McIntyre, D. J., and Pape, S. 1993. Using video protocols to enhance reflective thinking. *Teacher Education, 4*(1), 2–10.

McLaughlin, M. W., and Shields, P. M. 1988. Involving low-income parents in the schools: A role for policy? In *Drawing in the family: Family involvement in the schools,* 5–12. Denver, CO: Education Commission of the States.

McMillen, M. M. April 19, 1990. *Characteristics of public and private school teachers.* Paper presented at the meeting of the American Educational Research Association, Boston, MA.

McNeil, J. D. 1977. *Curriculum: A comprehensive introduction.* Boston: Little, Brown.

McQueen, T. 1992. *Essentials of classroom management and discipline.* New York: HarperCollins.

Medley, D., and Mitzell, H. 1963. Measuring classroom behavior by systematic observation. In *Handbook of research on teaching,* Ed. N. L. Gage, 247–328, Chicago: Rand McNally.

Menacker, J., Weldon, W., and Huritz, E. 1989. School order and safety as community issues. *Phi Delta Kappan, 71*(1), 39–56.

Mendler, A. N. 1993. Discipline with dignity in the classroom: Seven principles. *The Education Digest, 58*(7), 5–9.

Mentell, E. J. 1993. What to do to stop sexual harassment at school. *Educational Leadership, 51*(3), 96–97.

Mernit, S. 1990. Kids today. *Instructor, 100*(2), 44–48.

Merrow, J. 1989. *Learning in America series. Part III: A transcription.* Overland Park, AR: Strictly Business.

Messerli, J. 1972. *Horace Mann: A biography.* New York: Knopf.

Metropolitan Life Insurance Company. 1985. *The Metropolitan Life survey of former teachers in America* (conducted by Louis Harris and Associates) (fieldwork: April–June 1985). New York: Author.

___. 1988. *The Metropolitan Life survey of the American teacher: Strengthening the relationship between teachers and students.* New York: Author.

___. 1989. *The Metropolitan Life survey of the American teacher, 1989.* New York: Author.

___. 1990. *The Metropolitan Life survey of the American teacher, 1990.* New York: Author.

___. 1991. *The Metropolitan Life survey of the American teacher: The first year, new teachers' expectations and ideals.* New York: Author.

___. 1992. *Ready or not: Grade level preparedness: Teachers' views on current issues in education.* New York: Author.

___. 1993. *The American teacher 1993: Teachers respond to President Clinton's proposals.* New York: Louis Harris and Associates.

___. 1993. *Violence in America's schools.* New York: Louis Harris and Associates.

Metzger, M.T., and Fox, C. 1986. Two teachers of letters. *Harvard Educational Review, 56*(4), 351–354.

Metzger, M., and Ringwall, C. F. 1986. Friendly persuasion: How do you convince a doubting beginner to remain in the classroom? *Teacher Magazine Reader, 1*(1), 1–5.

Miller, J. 1983. *The educational spectrum.* New York: Longman.

Milwaukee teachers back in fold. 1994. *NEA Today* (May), 7.

Ministry of Education and Science (MOW). 1988. *Newsletter on freedom of education in the Netherlands.* Dociform 22 E. Zoetermeer: Ministrie van Onderwizs au Wetenschappen (MOW).

Mitchell, A. 1989. Old baggage, new visions: Shaping policy for early childhood programs. *Phi Delta Kappan, 70*(9), 664–672.

Montenegro, X. 1993. *Women and racial minority representation in school administration.* Arlington, VA: American Association of School Administrators.

Moore, G. E. 1953. The defence of common sense. In G. E. Moore, *Some main problems of philosophy.* London: Allen and Unwin.

Moore, M. T., Walker L. J., and Holland, R. P. 1982. *Finetuning special education finance: A guide for state policymakers.* Princeton, NJ: Educational Testing Service.

Morris, V. C. 1961. *Existentialism in education: What it means.* New York: Harper and Row.

Morrow, L. 1988a. Through the eyes of children: Bianca. *Time* (August 8), 49–51.

Morrow, L. 1988b. Through the eyes of children: Josh. *Time* (August 8), 55–57.

Mosher, E. K. 1977. Education and American federalism: Intergovernmental and national policy influences. In *The politics of education,* Ed. J. D. Scribner, 94–124. Chicago, IL: National Society for the Study of Education.

Mouat, L. 1994. Year of the family aims to shore up society. *Christian Science Monitor* (April 4), 16.

Moulton, M. M., and Ransome, W. 1993. Helping girls succeed. *Education Week* (October 27), 23.

Munis, R. 1994. [March 11, telephone interview on the status of bilingual education]. Bilingual Education and Minority Affairs, U.S. Department of Education.

Murphy, J. T. 1992. Apartheid's legacy to black children. *Phi Delta Kappan, 73*(5), 369–374.

Murray, C. R. 1992. Teaching as a profession: The Rochester case in historical perspective. *Harvard Educational Review, 62*(4), 494–518.

Nai-Lin Chang, H. 1993. *Affirming children's roots: Cultural and linguistic diversity in early care and education.* San Francisco, CA: California Tomorrow.

National Association of Education of Young Children. 1994. NAEYC position statement: A conceptual framework for early childhood professional development. *Young Children, 49*(3), 68–77.

National Association of Elementary School Principals. 1994. *NAESP platform for 94-95: Corporal punishment.* Alexandria, VA: Author.

National Association of State Boards of Education. 1988. *Right from the start: A report on the NASBE task force on early childhood education.* Washington, DC: Author.

National Board for Professional Teaching Standards. 1989. *Toward high and rigorous standards for the teaching profession: Initial policies and perspectives of the National Board for Professional Teaching Standards.* Washington, DC: Author.

National Catholic Education Association. 1992. *The people's poll on schools and school choice.* Washington, DC: Author.

National Center for Education Statistics, U.S. Department of Education. 1989b. *Digest of education statistics,* 25th ed. (NCES 89-643). Washington, DC: U.S. Government Printing Office.

___. 1990a. *The condition of education. Vol. 1: Elementary and secondary education* (NCES 90–681). Washington, DC: U.S. Government Printing Office.

___. 1990b. *Digest of education statistics.* (NCES 90-660). Washington, DC: U.S. Government Printing Office.

___. 1991. *Digest of education statistics* (NCES 91–096). Washington, DC: U.S. Government Printing Office.

___. 1992. *Digest of education statistics* (NCES 92–097). Washington, DC: U.S. Government Printing Office.

___. 1992. *Projections of education statistics to 2003* (NCES 92–218). Washington, DC: U.S. Government Printing Office.

___. 1993. *America's teachers: Profile of a profession* (NCES 93–025). Washington, DC: U.S. Government Printing Office.

___. 1993. *The condition of education* (NCES 93–290). Washington, DC: U.S. Government Printing Office.

___. 1993. *Digest of education statistics* (NCES 93–098). Washington, DC: U.S. Government Printing Office.

___. 1993. *Youth indicators 1993: Trends in the well-being of American youth.* Washington, DC: U.S. Government Printing Office.

National Center for Immigrant Students, National Coalition of Advocates for Students. 1993. *Achieving the dream: How communities and schools can improve education for immigrant students.* Boston: Author.

National Center on Child Abuse, U.S. Department of Health and Human Services. 1992. *The role of educators in the prevention and treatment of child abuse and neglect.* Washington, DC: Author.

National Coalition for the Homeless. 1993. *The problem of homelessness: Causes and trends, #4.* Washington, DC: Homelessness Information Exchange.

National Coalition of Advocates for Children. 1988. *New voices: Immigrant students in U.S. public schools.* Boston, MA: Author.

National Coalition of Advocates for Students. 1988. *New voices: Immigrant students in U.S. public schools.* Boston, MA: Author.

___. 1991. *The good common school: Making the vision work for all children.* Boston: Author.

National Commission for Excellence in Education. 1983. *A nation at risk: The imperative for educational reform.* Washington, DC: U.S. Government Printing Office.

National Commission for Excellence in Teacher Education. 1985. *A call for change in teacher education.* Washington, DC: American Association of Colleges for Teacher Education.

National Commission on AIDS. 1994. Preventing HIV/AIDS in adolescents. *Journal of School Health, 64*(1), 40–45.

National Committee for the Prevention of Child Abuse. April 1991. *Current trends in child abuse reporting and fatalities: The results of the 1990 annual 50 state survey.* Chicago, IL: Author.

___. 1994. *Scared silent: Ways to save our children from child abuse.* Chicago, IL: Author.

National Council for Accreditation of Teacher Education. 1990. *NCATE Standards, procedures, and policies for the accreditation of professional education units.* Washington, DC: Author.

___. 1993. *Proposed refinement of NCATE's standards for accreditation of professional education units.* (Unpublished document). (June 16), 5.

National Council of Teachers of English. 1994. Feds fail to understand English standards. *The Council Chronicle* (June), 1. Urbana, IL: Author.

National Council of Teachers of English. 1994. NCTE/IRA say standards efforts to continue. *The Council Chronicle* (June), 1, 4. Urbana, IL: Author.

National Council of Teachers of English. 1994. Wholistic language arts curriculum. *The Council Chronicle.* Urbana, IL: Author.

National Council of Teachers of Mathematics. 1992. *Professional standards for teaching mathematics.* Reston, VA: Author.

National Education Association. 1977. *The new copyright law: Questions teachers and librarians ask.* Washington, DC: Author.

___. 1989. *NEA handbook, 89–90.* Washington, DC: Author.

___. 1990a. *Estimates of school statistics, 1989-90.* Washington, DC: Author.

___. 1990b. NEA supports nontraditional routes to teacher licensure. *Proceedings of the 128th Annual Meeting of the National Education Association.* Press release July 3–8, 1–2. Kansas City, MO: Author.

National Education Association, Commission on the Reorganization of Secondary Schools, 1918. *Cardinal principles of secondary education.* Washington, DC: U.S. Bureau of Education.

National Education Commission on Time and Learning. 1994. *Prisoners of time.* Washington, DC: U.S. Government Printing Office.

National Education Goals Panel. 1992. *The national education goals report: Building a nation of learners.* Washington, DC: U.S. Government Printing Office.

National Foundation for the Improvement of Education, National Education Association. 1992. *Curriculum, technology, diversity: A paper of the Christa McAuliffe institute for educational pioneering.* Washington, DC: Author.

National Governors' Association. 1986. *Time for results: The governors' 1991 report on education.* Washington, DC: Author.

___. 1987a. *Making America work: Bringing down the barriers.* Washington, DC: Author.

___. 1987b. *Making America work: Productive people, productive policies.* Washington, DC: Author.

___. 1990a. *Educating America: State strategies for achieving the national education goals* (Report of the Task Force on Education). Washington, DC: Author.

___. 1990b. *Report of the task force on education.* Washington, DC: Author.

___. 1990c. *The state of the states' children.* Washington, DC: Author.

___. 1990d. *An overview of state policies affecting adolescent pregnancy and parenting.* Washington, DC: Author.

___. 1992. *Every child ready for school: Report of the action team on school readiness.* Washington, DC: Author.

___. 1994. *The debate on opportunity-to-learn standards.* Washington, DC: Authors.

National Middle School Association. 1992. *This we believe.* Columbus, OH: Author.

National School Boards Association. 1990. *A survey of public education in the nation's urban school districts, 1989.* Alexandria, VA: Author.

Natrello, G., and Zumwalt, K. K. 1992. Challenges to an alternative route for teacher education. In *The changing contexts of teaching: Ninety-first yearbook of the national society for the study of education,* Ed. A. Lieberman, 59–78. Chicago: National Society for the Study of Education.

Natriello, G., McDill, E. L., and Pallas, A. M. 1990. *Schooling disadvantaged children.* New York: Teacher's College Press.

Nelson, C. L. 1991. The national S.E.E.D. project. *Educational Leadership, 49*(4), 66.

Nelson, F. H. 1991. *International comparison of public spending on education.* Washington, DC: American Federation of Teachers, AFL-CIO.

Nelson, F. H., and O'Brien, T. 1993. *How U.S. teachers measure up internationally: A comparative study of teacher pay, training, and conditions of service.* Washington, DC: American Federation of Teachers, AFL-CIO.

Nevi, C. 1987. In defense of tracking. *Educational Leadership, 44*(60), 24–26.

The new teens: What makes them different? 1990. [Special issue]. *Newsweek, 115* (Summer/Fall), 27.

Nicholas, A. 1988. Hidden minorities. *Instructor, 98*(2), 51.

Nicklin, J. 1991. Alternative teacher education project draws mixed reviews in first year of placing recent college graduates in schools. *The Chronicle of Higher Education,* A21.

Noordhoff, K., and Klienfeld, J. 1993. Preparing teachers for multicultural classrooms. *Teaching and Teacher Education, 9*(1), 27–39.

North Carolina Department of Public Instruction. 1989. "Task force on excellence in secondary education." Raleigh, NC: Author. (Unpublished report).

Nzelibe, J. 1994. A foreign view: U.S. schools too cushy. *USA Today* (January 13), 9A.

Oakes, J. 1985. *Keeping track: How school structures inequality.* New Haven, CT: Yale University Press.

Office of Special Education Programs, U.S. Department of Education. 1993. *To assure the free appropriate public education of all children with disabilities: Fifteenth annual report to Congress on the implementation of Individuals with Disabilities Education Act.* Washington, DC: Author.

Office of the Federal Register, National Archives and Records. 1990. *Code of federal regulations: Education, 34,* Parts 300–399. Washington, DC: Author.

Olsen, L. 1994. Bridging the gap. *Education Week* (January 26), 1, 22–26.

Olsen, L., and Mullen, N. A. 1990. *Embracing diversity: Teachers' voices from California's classrooms.* San Francisco: California Tomorrow.

O'Neil, J. 1993. Can national standards make a difference? *Educational Leadership, 50*(5), 4–8.

Orlich, D. C., Harder, R. J., Callahan, R. C., Kracas, C. H., Pendergrass, R. A., and Keogh, A. J. 1985. *Teaching strategies.* Lexington, MA: D. C. Heath.

Ornstein, A. C. 1990. *Strategies for effective teaching.* New York: Harper and Row.

Ornstein, A. C. 1992. The textbook curriculum. *Educational Horizons, 70*(4), 167–169.

Ornstein, A. C., and Levine, D. U. 1989. Class, race, and achievement. *Journal of Teacher Education, 40*(5), 17–23.

Ovando, C. J. 1989. Language diversity in education. In *Multicultural education: Issues and perspectives,* Ed. J. A. Banks and C. A. M. Banks, 208–227. Boston: Allyn and Bacon.

Pang, V. O. 1990. Asian American children: A diverse population. *Educational Forum, 55*(1), 50–64.

Parnell, D. 1978. *The case for competency-based education.* Bloomington, IL: Phi Delta Kappan.

Parshall, J. 1993. Outcomes based education: Toxic teaching? *Family Voice, Concerned Women for America, 15*(4), 14–15.

Partnership for Academic and Career Education. 1993. *PACE and Tech Prep Programs.* Pentleton, SC: Author.

Pearson, J. 1989. Myths of choice: The governor's new clothes? *Phi Delta Kappan, 70*(10), 821–823.

Peddiwell, J. A. 1939. *The saber-tooth curriculum.* New York: McGraw-Hill.

Peirson, C. A. 1993. Leadership in teacher education. *Childhood Education, 69*(5), 288k.

People for the American Way. 1994. *Attacks on the freedom to learn: 1992–1993 report.* Washington, DC: Author.

People for the American Way in N.C. 1990. *Censorship and sex education: A survey of North Carolina Health Educators.* Raleigh, NC: Author.

Perelmann, L. J. 1992. *School's out: Hyperlearning, the new technology, and the end of education.* New York: William Morrow and Company.

Perrin, J. 1990. The learning styles project for potential dropouts. *Educational Leadership, 48*(2), 23–24.

Perrone, V. 1991. On standardized testing. *Childhood Education, 67*(3), 131–142.

Persell, C., and Cookson, P., Jr. 1982. The effective principal in action. In *The effective principal: A research summary,* 42–53. Reston, VA: National Association of Secondary School Principals.

Pestel, B. C. 1990, June. Teaching is not an art, it is a science. *Journal of Chemical Education, 67*(6), 490.

Peterkin, R. S. 1990–1991. What's happening in Milwaukee? *Educational Leadership, 48*(4), 50–51.

Peterson, D. 1990. Pinning down empowerment: Eight teachers speak out on education's hottest topic. Ed. D. Dillon. *Instructor, 99*(5), 26–36.

Pettijohn, T. E. 1989. *Psychology: A concise introduction,* 2nd ed. Guilford, CT: Dushkin.

Phillips, J. C. 1978. College of, by, and for Navajo Indians. *Chronicle of Higher Education* (January 16), *15,* 10–12.

Piaget, J. 1952. *Child's conception of number.* London: Humanities Press.

Planchon, P. 1990. *Highlights of minority data from the schools and staffing survey, 1987–88.* Washington, DC: U.S. Department of Education, National Center for Education Statistics.

Plevin, A. 1988. *Education as a career.* Washington, DC: National Education Association.

Pollard, D. S. 1993. Gender and achievement. In *Gender and education: Ninety-second yearbook of the National Society for the Study of Education,* Eds. S. N. Biklen and D. D. Pollard. Chicago, IL: University of Chicago Press.

Population Reference Bureau, Inc. 1993. *What the 1990 census tells us about women: A state fact book.* Washington, DC: Author.

Portelli, J. P. 1993. Exposing the hidden curriculum. *Journal of Curriculum Studies, 25*(4), 343–358.

Portner, J. 1994. Missing graduation as a matter of principle. *Education Week* (April 27), 7.

Private funding of education, 1992. 1994. *Education Week* (January 12), 13.

Public Agenda Foundation. 1993. *Divided within, besieged without: The politics of education in four American school districts.* New York: Charles F. Kettering Foundation.

Public schools under siege. 1994. *Church & State* (April), *47*(4), 10.

Puglisi, D. J., and Hoffman, A. J. 1978. Cultural identity and academic success in a multicultural society: A culturally different approach. *Social Education, 42*(6), 495–498.

Pulaski, M. A. S. 1971. *Understanding Piaget: An introduction to children's cognitive development.* New York: Harper and Row.

Pulliam, J. D. 1991. *History of education in America,* 5th ed. New York: Macmillan.

Purcel, T. L., and Menaghan, E. C. 1994. Early parental work, family social capital, and early childhood outcomes. *American Journal of Sociology, 99*(4), 972–1009.

Purdy, M. 1994. Budding scientist's success breaks the mold. *New York Times* (January 30), 1A, 17A.

Purkey, S. C., and Smith, M. S. 1983. Effective schools: A review. *Elementary School Journal, 83*(2), 427–453.

Purpel, D. E. 1989. *The moral and spiritual crisis in education: A curriculum for justice and compassion in education.* Granby, MA: Bergin and Garvey Publications.

Quintilian. 1970. De Institutione Oratoria. In *Foundations of education in America: An anthology of major thoughts and significant actions,* Ed. J. W. Noll and S. Kelly, 41–45. New York: Harper and Row. (Original work discovered A.D. 96 and first published 1416).

Rabianski-Carriuolo, N. 1989. Learning styles: An interview with Edmund W. Gordon. *Journal of Developmental Education, 13*(1), 18–20, 22.

Rachlin, J., and Glastris, P. 1989. Of more than parochial interest. *U.S. News and World Report* (May 22), 61–62.

Rafferty, M. 1962. *Suffer little children.* New York: Signet.

___. 1963. *What they are doing to your children?* New York: New American Library.

Ralph, E. G. 1993. Beginning teachers and classroom management: Questions from practice, answers from research. *Middle School Journal, 76*(2), 60–64.

Ramsey, P. G. 1987. *Teaching and learning in a diverse world.* New York: Teachers College Press.

Rasinski, T. Y., and Padak, N. D. 1990. Multicultural learning through children's literature. *Language Arts, 67*(6), 576–580.

Ravitch, D. 1983. *The troubled crusade.* New York: Basic Books.

___. 1984. A good school. *American Scholar, 53*(4), 480–493.

___. 1985. *The schools we deserve.* New York: Basic Books.

Raynes, M., Snell, M., and Sailor, W. 1991. A fresh look at categorical programs for children with special needs. *Phi Delta Kappan, 73*(4), 326–331.

Reagan, R. January 25, 1988. State of the union address. In *Public papers of the presidents of the United States: Ronald Reagan,* 79–80. Washington, DC: U.S. Government Printing Office.

Recruiting New Teachers, Inc. 1993. *State policies to improve the teacher workforce: Shaping the profession that shapes the future.* Belmont, MA: Author.

Reed, A. J. S. 1994. *Reaching adolescents: The young adult book and the school.* New York: Holt, Rinehart and Winston.

Reed, S., and Sautter, R. C. 1990. Children of poverty: The status of 12 million Americans. *Phi Delta Kappan, 71*(10), K2–K11.

Reiff, J. C. 1992. *Learning styles: What research says to the teacher.* Washington, DC: National Education Association.

Reinhartz, J., and VanCleaf, D. 1986. *Teach-practice-apply: The TPA instructional model, K-8.* Washington, DC: National Education Association.

Renzulli, J. S. 1977. *The enrichment triad model: A guide for developing defensible programs for the gifted and talented.* Mansfield Center, CT: Creative Learning Press.

Rich, J. M. 1993. Discipline and moral development. *The High School Journal, 40*(4), 139–144

Richmond, G. 1989. The future school: Is Lowell pointing us toward a revolution in education? *Phi Delta Kappan, 71*(3), 232–236.

Rider, T. M. 1993. Students help business partner grade instruction manual. *Tech Prep News VI* (Fall), (1), 31.

Rierden, A. 1994. The age of high school and motherhood. *New York Times* (March 6), Section 13, 1, 7.

Rimer, S. 1990. Slow readers sparkling with a handful of words. *New York Times* (June 19), B1, B34–36.

Robinson, S. L., and Lyon, C. 1994. Early childhood offerings in 1992: Will we be ready for 2000? *Phi Delta Kappan, 75*(10), 775–778.

Rogers, C. 1983. *Freedom to learn for the 80's.* Columbus, OH: Merrill.

Rohde, D. 1994. Judge orders equal opportunity. *Christian Science Monitor* (March 7), 7.

___. 1994. Racial code in high school: Tolerance, not integration. *Christian Science Monitor* (March 8), 2.

Rosenholtz, S. J. 1986. Career ladders and merit pay: Capricious fads or fundamental reforms? *Elementary School Journal, 86*(4), 513–527.

Rosenshine, B., and Furst, N. 1971. Research in teacher performance criteria. In *Research in Teacher Education,* Ed. B. O. Smith, 37–72. Englewood Cliffs, NJ: Prentice Hall.

Rosenthal, R., and Jacobsen, L. 1968. *Pygmalion in the classroom: Teacher expectation and pupils' intellectual development.* New York: Holt.

Ross, P. O. 1993. *National excellence: A case for developing America's talent.* U.S. Office of Education. Washington, DC: U.S. Government Printing Office.

Rothman, R. 1988a. "Computer competence" still rare among students, assessment finds. *Education Week* (April 13), 1, 20.

___. 1988b. Teachers vs. curriculum in Philadelphia. *Education Week* (March 27), 1, 20, 26.

___. 1990. Ford study urges new test system to "open the gates of opportunity." *Education Week* (May 30), 1, 12.

Rousseau, J.-J. 1979. [1762]. *Emile, or on education,* Trans. A. Bloom. New York: Basic Books.

Rubenstein, C. 1994. A confident generation. *Working Mother Magazine, 70*(4), 38–42.

Rubin, L. J. 1985. *Artistry in teaching.* New York: Random House.

Ruggles, S. 1994. The origins of the African-American family structure. *American Sociological Review, 59*(1), 136–151.

Rundell, C. R. 1992. NASDC: A businessman's experience. *Phi Delta Kappan, 74*(4), 290–295.

Runes, D. D., Ed. 1983. *Dictionary of philosophy.* New York: Philosophical Library.

Russell, A. M. 1991. The twelfth annual working woman salary survey: Women vs. men. *Working Woman* (January), 66–71.

Russell, B. 1903. *The principles of mathematics.* Cambridge, MA: Cambridge University Press.

___. 1926. *Education and the good life.* New York: Boni and Liveright.

Ryan, M. 1994. All he needed was a chance. *Parade* (February 20), 32–33.

Ryle, G. 1946. *The concept of the mind.* Chicago: University of Chicago Press.


Sadker, M., and Sadker, D. 1994. *Failing at fairness: How America's schools cheat girls.* New York: Macmillan.

Sartre, J.-P. 1956. *Being and nothingness,* Trans. H. E. Barnes. New York: Philosophical Library.

___. 1957. *Existentialism and humanism.* New York: Philosophical Library.

Scalia, A. 1992. States cannot exact religious control conformity from a student. *Washington Post* (June 25), 26.

Schetter, W. 1987. *The Netherlands in perspective: The organization of society and environment.* Leiden: Martinus Nijhof.

Schlafly, P. 1993. What's wrong with outcome-based education? *The Phyllis Schlafly Report* (May), *26*(10), 1–4.

Schmidt, B. 1994. Private enterprise. *Education Week* (May 25), 27–30.

___. 1994. A very different kind of school. *Education Week* (June 22), 42–43.

Schmidt, P. 1993. Seeking to identify the gifted among L.E.P. students. *Education Week* (May 26), 1, 12–13.

Schraq, P. 1991. Savage equalities: The case against Jonathon Kozol. *The New Republic* (December 16), 18–20.

Schubert, W. 1993. Curriculum reform. In *Challenges and achievements of American education: 1993 yearbook of the Association for Supervision and Curriculum Development,* Ed. G. Cawelti, 79, 96. Alexandria, VA: Association for Supervision and Curriculum Development.

Schuhmann, A. M. 1992. Learning to teach Hispanic students. In *Diversity in teacher education,* Ed. M. E. Dilworth, 93–111. San Francisco: Jossey-Bass.

Schumacher, E. F. 1980. *Good work.* New York: Harper and Row.

Select Committee on Children, Youth, and Families, U.S. House of Representatives, 101st Congress, 1st session. September 1989. *U.S. children and their families: Current conditions and recent trends, 1989.* Washington, DC: U.S. Government Printing Office.

Sex Information and Education Council of the U.S. 1993. *Future directions: HIV/AIDS education in the nation's schools.* New York: Author.

___. 1993. *Unfinished business: A SIECUS assessment of state sexuality education programs.* New York: Author.

Shade, B. J., and New, C. A. 1993. Cultural influence on learning: Teaching implications. In *Multicultural education: Issues and perspectives,* 2nd ed., Eds. J. A. Banks and C. A. M. Banks. Boston: Allyn and Bacon.

Shanker, A. 1987. The making of a profession. In *Education 87/88: Annual editions,* Ed. F. Schultz, 196–204. Guilford, CT: Dushkin.

___. 1990. Restructuring the teaching profession and our schools. In *What teachers need to know,* Ed. D. A. Dill, 203–224. San Francisco: Jossey-Bass.

___. 1991. A new national strategy: Education 2000. *New York Times* (April 21), E7.

___. 1993. Edison's candle. *New York Times* (August 30), E9.

___. 1993. Where we stand: Outrageous outcomes. *New York Times* (December 26), E7.

Shaw, G. B. 1903. Maxims for revolutionists. In *Man and superman: A comedy and a philosophy,* 203. New York: Brentano's.

___. 1916. *Pygmalion.* London: Constable and Company.

Shepard, L. A. 1991. Will national tests improve student learning? *Phi Delta Kappan, 73*(3), 232–238.

Shevin, M. S. 1989. Mild disabilities: In and out of special education. In *Schooling and disability: Eighty-eighth yearbook of the National Society for the Study of Education, Part III,* Ed. D. Biklen, D. Fergusen, and A. Ford, 77–105. Chicago: University of Chicago Press.

Shurtleff, N. B., Ed. 1853. Massachusetts school law of 1647. *Records of the governor and company of Massachusetts Bay in New England.* Vol. 2, 6–7. Boston: Order of the Legislature.

Sidel, R. 1991. Separate and unequal. *The Nation* (November 18), 620–622.

Sizer, T. R. 1984. *Horace's compromise: The dilemma of the American high school.* Boston: Houghton Mifflin.

___. 1992. *Horace's school: Redesigning the American high school.* Boston: Houghton Mifflin.

Skinner, B. F. 1968. *The technology of teaching.* New York: Appleton-Century-Crofts.

Slavin, R. E. 1987. *Mastery learning reconsidered.* Report No. 7. Baltimore, MD: Johns Hopkins University. Center for Social Organization of Schools. ERIC Document Reproduction Service No. ED 294 891.

Slavin, R. E., Karweit, N. L., and Madden, N. A. 1990. *Effective programs for students at risk.* (Center for Research on elementary and middle schools, Johns Hopkins University). Boston: Allyn and Bacon.

Sleeter, C. E. 1992. *Keepers of the American dream: A study of staff development and multicultural education.* Washington, DC: Falmer.

Sleeter, C. E., and Grant, C. A. 1988. A rationale for integrating race, gender, and social class. In *Class, race, and gender in American education,* Ed. L. Weiss, 144–160. Albany: State University of New York Press.

Smith, A. 1993. [December 21 telephone interview on concept of inclusion and status of Head Start]. Washington, DC: Children's Defense Fund.

Smith, L. G., and Smith, J. K. 1994. *Lives in education: A narrative of people and ideas,* 2nd Ed. New York: St. Martin's Press.

Smith, M. H. 1847. "The ark of God on a cart" [a sermon]. In *The Bible, the rod, and religion in the common school.* Boston: Redding.

Smith, M. S. 1993. [December 28 telephone interview on status of Chapter I national assessment]. Washington, DC: U.S. Department of Education.

Smolowe, J. Crusade for the classroom. *Time* (November 1), 34–35.

Soars, R., and Soars, R. 1973. *Classroom behavior, pupil characteristics and pupil growth for the school year and summer.* Gainesville: University of Florida, Institute for Development of Human Resources.

___. 1978. *Setting variables, classroom interaction and multiple pupil outcomes* (Final Report Project No. 6-04332). Washington, DC: National Institute of Education.

Sockett, H. 1990. Accountability, trust, and ethical codes of practice. In *The moral dimensions of teaching,* Ed. J. I. Goodlad, R. F. Soder, and K. A. Sirotnik, 224–250. San Francisco: Jossey-Bass.

Solman, P. 1989. *Learning in America series. Part III: A transcription.* Overland, AR: Strictly Business.

Sommerfeld, M. 1993. Corporate gifts to K–12 education up 15% in 1992. *Education Week* (September 29), 10.

Sontag, D. 1993. A fervent "No" to assimilation in new America. *New York Times* (June 29), A10.

Southern Regional Education Board. 1986. *Major reports on teacher education: What do they mean for the states?* Atlanta, GA: Author.

___. 1991. *Linking performance to rewards for teachers, principals, and schools: The 1990 SREB career ladder clearinghouse report.* Atlanta, GA: Author.

Spady, W. G. 1988. Organizing for results: The basis of authentic restructuring and reform. *Educational Leadership, 46*(2), 4–8

Spencer, H. 1927. *Education: Intellectual, moral, and spiritual.* New York: D. Appleton.

Sperry, R. 1968. Hemisphere deconnection and unity in conscious awareness. *American Psychologist, 23*(4), 723–733.

Spring, J. 1972. *Education and the rise of the corporate state.* Boston: Beacon.

___. 1986. *The American school: 1642–1985.* New York: Longman.

Spruill, Julia C. 1972. *Women's life and work in the Southern colonies.* New York: Norton.

Stallings, J., Cory, R., Fairweather, J., and Needles, M. 1977. *Early childhood classroom evaluation.* Menlo Park, CA: SRI International.

___. 1978. *How to change the process of teaching basic reading skills in secondary schools.* Menlo Park, CA: SRI International.

Stallings, J., and Kaskowitz, D. 1974. *Follow-through classroom observation evaluation, 1972–1973* (SRI Project URU-7370). Stanford, CA: Stanford Research Institute.

Stedman, D. 1991. Re-inventing the schools of education: A Marshall Plan for teacher education. *Vital Speeches of the Day* (April 15), *57*(13), 354–358.

Steller, A. W. 1988. *Effective schools research: Practice and premise.* Bloomington, IN: Phi Delta Kappan Educational Foundation.

Stevens, L. J., and Price, M. 1992. Meeting the challenge of educating children at risk. *Phi Delta Kappan, 74*(1), 18–23.

Stigler, J., and Stevenson, H. 1994. The Asian connection: Popular stereotype blown out of the waters. *Educational Vision* (Spring), *2*(2), 19.

Stinnett, T. M., and Huggett, A. J. 1963. *Professional problems of teachers,* 2nd ed. New York: Macmillan.

Strike, K. 1988. The ethics of teaching. *Phi Delta Kappan, 70*(2), 156–158.

Su, Z. 1989. People's education in the People's Republic of China. *Phi Delta Kappan, 70*(8), 614–618.

Swalley, G. 1992. Gary Swalley: Social studies teacher. In *1992 Reader's Digest American Heroes in Education,* Ed. M. Terry, 11. Pleasantville, NY: Reader's Digest Association.

Swan, E. T., and Nixon, S. 1992. School improvement took off when we used the effective school model. *Contemporary Education,* (Winter), *63*(2), 125–129.

Swick, K. J. 1991. *Discipline: Toward positive student behavior.* Washington, DC: National Education Association.

Swisher, K., and Deyhle, D. 1989. The styles of learning are different, but the teaching is just the same: Suggestions to teachers of American Indian youth. *Journal of American Indian Education* (August), 1–13.

Taba, H. 1962. *Curriculum development.* New York: Harcourt.

Tanner, D., and Tanner, L. 1975. *Curriculum development.* New York: Macmillan.

___. 1980. *Curriculum development: Theory into practice,* 2nd ed. New York: Macmillan.

Teachers' organization alternative to NEA. 1994. *American Family Association Journal* (August), 8.

Thomas, K. 1994. Learning at home: Education outside school gains respect. *USA Today* (April 6), 5D.

Thomas, S. B., Ed. 1993. *The yearbook of education law, 1993.* Topeka, KS: National Organization on Legal Problems of Education.

Thompson, L. H. 1991. *Within school discrimination: Inadequate Title VI enforcement by Education's Office for Civil*

*Rights.* Washington, DC: U.S. General Accounting Office.

Thompson, M., and Harrington, H. 1993. *Student motivation and case manual.* Boone, NC: Appalachian State University.

Thomson, W. S. 1992. Using videotape as a supplement to traditional student teaching supervision. *The North Carolina Journal of Teacher Education,* 5(2), 20–26.

Thorndike, E. L. 1931. *Human learning.* Cambridge, MA: MIT Press.

___. 1932. *The fundamentals of learning.* New York: Teachers College Press.

Tifft, S. 1989a. The fight over school choice. *Time* (March 13), 54.

___. 1989b. The lure of the classroom, *Time* (April 19), 69.

Timm, J. T., and Marchant, G. J. 1993. Using a structured observational instrument in observational settings in teacher education. *Teaching Education,* 5(1), 65–70.

Toch, T. 1991. Wired for learning: Does computer technology have the power to revolutionize schooling? *U.S. News & World Report* (October 28), 76–79.

___. 1993. Violence in our schools. *U.S. News & World Report* (November 8), 31–35.

Toch, T., and Levine, A. 1991. Schooling's big test. *U.S. News & World Report* (May 6), 63, 64.

Toch, T., and Wagner, B. 1992. Schools for scandal: A U.S. News inquiry finds widespread cheating on standardized tests. *U.S. News & World Report* (April 27), 66–72.

Toch, T., and Wright, A. 1993. Public schooling's opportunity gap. *U.S. News & World Report* (August 2), 45.

Tomas Rivera Center. 1993. *Resolving a crisis in education.* Claremont, CA: Author.

Tower, C. C. 1987. *How schools can help combat child abuse and neglect,* 2nd ed. Washington, DC: National Education Association.

___. 1992. *The role of educators in prevention and treatment of child abuse and neglect.* Washington, DC: U.S. Department of Health and Human Services, National Center on Child Abuse and Neglect.

Towers, R. 1987. *How schools can help combat student drug and alcohol abuse.* Washington, DC: National Education Association.

Troike, R. C. 1975. *Improving conditions for success in bilingual education programs.* In *A report of the compendium,* 2. Arlington, VA: Center for Applied Linguistics.

Tryneski, J. 1990/1991. *Requirements for certification of teachers, counselors, librarians, administrators.* 55th ed. Chicago: University of Chicago Press.

Tse, Tomen. 1994. Hope in a feather. In *In our own words: Special issue by and about urban youth* (February 6). Boston: Boston Globe Magazine.

Turner, R. 1979. The value of variety in teaching styles. *Educational Leadership,* 36(4), 257–258.

___. 1990. An issue for the 1990's: The efficacy of the required master's degree. *Journal of Teacher Education,* 41(2), 38–44.

U.S. Bureau of the Census. 1990a. *Money income and poverty status in the United States, 1989.* Current population reports, Series P-60N0168. Washington, DC: U.S. Government Printing Office.

___. 1990b. *Per capita income in 1987, ranked by state.* Washington, DC: U.S. Government Printing Office.

___. 1990c. *School enrollment—social and economic characteristics of students: October 1988 and 1987,* Series P-20, No. 443. Washington, DC: U.S. Government Printing Office.

___. 1991. Thirteenth Annual Report to Congress on the Implementation of the Individuals with Learning Disabilities Education Act. *To assure the free appropriate public education of all children with disabilities.* Washington, DC: U.S. Government Printing Office.

___. 1992. *Current population reports: Population projections of the United States, by age, sex, race, and Hispanic origin: 1992-2050.* Washington, DC: U.S. Government Printing Office.

___. 1992. *Marital status and living arrangements* (P20–468). Washington, DC: U.S. Government Printing Office.

___. 1993. *Number of non-English language speaking Americans.* Washington, DC: U.S. Government Printing Office.

___. 1993. *Statistical abstract of the United States.* Washington, DC: U.S. Government Printing Office.

___. 1994. *Current population reports.* (Series P67). Washington, DC: U.S. Government Printing Office.

U.S. Department of Education. 1994. Minority students in the nation's hundred largest districts. *Department of Education Reports* (June 20). Washington, DC: Feistritzer Publications.

U.S. Department of Education, National Center for Education Statistics. 1990. *Characteristics of private schools: 1978-88.* (NCES 90-080). Washington, DC: U.S. Government Printing Office.

___. 1991. *Private schools in the United States: A statistical profile, with comparisons to public schools.* Washington, DC: U.S. Government Printing Office.

___. 1991. *Trends in academic progress: Achievement of U.S. students in science, 1969-70 to 1990; mathematics, 1973 to 1990; reading, 1971-1990; and writing, 1984 to 1990.* (Prepared by Educational Testing Service under contract with National Center for Education Statistics). Washington, DC: U.S. Government Printing Office.

___. 1993. *NAEP mathematics report card for the nation and the states.* (Prepared by the Educational Testing Service under contract with the National Center for Education Statistics). Washington, DC: U.S. Government Printing Office.

___. 1994. *Characteristics of the 100 largest public elementary and secondary school districts in the United States.* Washington, DC: U.S. Government Printing Office.

U.S. Department of Education, National Center for Education Statistics and Educational Testing Service. 1993. *NAEP 1992 reading report card for the nation and the states.* Washington, DC: U.S. Government Printing Office.

U.S. Department of Education, Planning and Evaluation Service. 1994. *Educational innovation in multiracial contexts: The growth of magnet schools in American education.* Washington, DC: U.S. Government Printing Office.

U.S. Department of Labor, Bureau of Labor Statistics. 1992. *Employment and earnings, 1991.* Washington, DC: U.S. Government Printing Office.

U.S. General Accounting Office. 1993. *Compensatory education: Additional funds help more private students receive Chapter I services.* Washington, DC: Author.

___. 1993. *School-age demographics: Recent trends pose new educational challenges.* (GAO/HRO-93-105BR). Washington, DC: Author.

___. 1994. *Foster care: Parental drug abuse has alarming impact on young children.* Washington, DC: Author.

Urschel, J. 1991. Why not let teachers really teach? *USA Today* (October 4), 11A.

Usdansky, M. L. 1994. Midwest's working moms are trendsetters. *USA Today* (June 4), 2A.

Wadsworth, B. J. 1984. *Piaget's theory of cognitive and affective development,* 3rd ed. New York: Longman.

Walberg, H. J., Schiller, D., and Haertel, G. D. 1979. The quiet revolution in educational research. *Phi Delta Kappan, 61*(4), 179–183.

Waldman, S. 1994. Taking on the welfare dads: Teen parenthood. *Newsweek* (June 20), 34–38.

Wall Street Journal staff. 1986. Governors opt for choice of schools. *Wall Street Journal* (August 26), 14.

Walsh, M. 1994. Beginning in 1995, Edison Project to manage two schools in Wichita. *Education Week* (May 18), 14.

Walter, D. M. 1992. Tech-prep curriculum. *Partnership for Academic and Career Education.* Pendleton, SC: PACE.

Walters, L. S. 1993. Edison Project turns to public schools. *Christian Science Monitor* (October 22), 13.

___. 1993. Influx of immigrant students strains state educational resources. *Christian Science Monitor* (July 16), 1, 4.

___. 1994. Goals 2000 act broadens federal role. *Christian Science Monitor* (April 11), 14.

___. 1994. States seek fairer share of funding. *Christian Science Monitor* (March 28), 2, 3, 30–31.

Wang, M. C., Haertel, G., and Walberg, H. J. 1993/1994. What helps students learn?: Synthesis of research. *Educational Leadership* (December/January) *51*(4), 74–79.

Wang, M. C., Reynolds, M. C., and Walberg, H. J. 1986. Rethinking special education. *Educational Leadership, 43*(1), 26–31.

Warner, W. L., Havighurst, R. J., and Loeb, M. B. 1944. *Who shall be educated?* New York: Harper and Row.

Watters, E. 1988. A test that never fails. *The Progressive* (August), *52*(18), 12, 13.

Wesson, L. H. 1993. Vocational education: Tech prep. *Clearing House, 66*(4), 197, 198.

Western Interstate Commission for Higher Education (the College Board). 1991. *The road to college.* Boulder, CO: Author.

Westinghouse Learning Corporation. 1969. *The impact of Head Start: An evaluation of the effects of Head Start on children's cognitive and affective development.* Athens: Ohio University. ERIC Document Reproduction Service No. ED 036 321.

White, E. E. 1902. *Report of the U.S. commissioner of education,* 1247–1250. Washington, DC: U.S. Government Printing Office.

White, M. 1987a. Japanese education: How do they do it? *Principals* (March), 19–20.

___. 1987b. *The Japanese educational challenge: A commitment to children.* New York: Free Press.

Whitehead, A. N. 1959. *The aims of education and other essays.* New York: Macmillan.

Wickerson, I. 1993. First born, fast grown: The manful life of Nicholas, 10. *New York Times* (April 4), A1, A20.

Wilbur, G. 1991. *Gender-fair curriculum.* Wellesley, MA: Wellesley College Center for Research on Women.

William T. Grant Foundation Commission on Work, Family, and Citizenship. 1988a. *The forgotten half: Non-college youth in America.* Washington, DC: Author.

___. 1988b. *The forgotten half: Pathways to success for America's youth and young families.* Washington, DC: Author.

Williams, J. 1994. Integration turns 40: The new segregation. *Modern Maturity* (April/May), *37*(2), 24–36.

Williams, K. 1991. Multicultural music: The need, the action, and the future. *Delta Kappa Gamma Bulletin, 57*(2), 15–18.

Wilson, D. L. 1993. Producing computer-literate teachers: Austin Peay State U. aims to make its education graduates users of the machines. *The Chronicle of Higher Education* (December 1), A21.

Wirth, A. G. 1992. *Education and work for the year 2000: Choices we face.* San Francisco: Jossey-Bass.

Wise, A. E., Darling-Hammond, L., McLaughlin, M. W., and Bernstein, H. T. 1984. *Case studies for teacher evaluation: A study of effective practices.* Santa Monica, CA: Rand.

Witkin, G., with Hedges, S. J., Johnson, C., Guttman, M., Thomas L., and Moncreiff, A. 1991. Kids who kill. *U.S. News & World Report, 110*(13), 26–31.

Wolery, M., Strain, P. S., and Bailey, D. B. 1992. Reaching potentials of children with special needs. In *Reaching potentials: Appropriate curriculum and assessment for young children.* Vol. I, Eds. S. Bredekamp and T. Rosegrant, 92–113. Washington, DC: National Association for the Education of Young Children.

Wolf, J. S., and Stephens, T. M. 1989. Parent/teacher conferences: Finding common ground. *Educational Leadership, 47*(2), 28–31.

Wood, D. B. 1993. As students return to class, Los Angeles school district faces a make-or-break crisis. *Christian Science Monitor* (September 7), 3.

Wood, D. R. 1992. Teaching narratives: A source for faculty development and evaluation. *Harvard Educational Review, 62*(4), 535–550.

Woodward, A., and Elliott, D. L. 1990. Textbook use and teacher professionalism. In *Textbooks and schooling in the United States: Eighty-ninth yearbook of the National Society for the Study of Education (Part 1),* Eds. D. L. Elliott and A. Woodward, 178–193. Chicago, IL: University of Chicago Press.

Woodward, W. H., Ed. 1904. *Erasmus concerning education.* Cambridge: Cambridge University Press. (Original work published 1522).

Woolfolk, A. E. 1987. *Educational psychology,* 3rd ed. Englewood Cliffs, NJ: Prentice Hall.

Worsnop, R. 1991a. How choice plans operate in the states. *CQ Researcher, 1*(1), 269.

___. 1991b. School choice: Would it strengthen or weaken public education in America? *CQ Researcher, 1*(1), 253–276.

Wright, C., and Nuthall, G. 1970. Relationships between teacher behaviors and pupil achievement in three experimental elementary science lessons. *American Educational Research Journal, 83*(6), 67–75.

Wynne, E. 1981. Looking at good schools. *Phi Delta Kappan, 62*(5), 377–381.

Young, M. F. D. 1971. Knowledge and control. In *Knowledge and control,* Ed. M. F. D. Young, 30. London: Collier-Macmillan.

Zeichner, K. N. 1993. *Educating teachers for cultural diversity* (April). (Paper presented at the annual meeting of the American Educational Research Association). Atlanta, GA.

Zettel, J. J. 1979. Gifted and talented education over a half-decade of change. *Journal for the Education of the Gifted, 13*(6), 14–37.

Zimpher, N. L., and Ashburn, E. A. 1992. Countering parochialism in teacher candidates. In *Diversity in teacher education,* Ed. M. E. Dillworth, 40–62. San Francisco: Jossey-Bass.

Zirkel, P. A. 1990. Know your copy rights: Teachers have special freedom and responsibilities. *Teacher Magazine, 1*(8), 68, 69.

Zirkel, P. A., and Richardson, S. N. 1988. *A digest of Supreme Court decisions affecting education,* 2nd ed. Bloomington, IN: Phi Delta Kappa Educational Foundation.

# INDEX

# CREDITS

**Chapter 1** p. 4 © Joel Gordon; p. 9 Gloria Woodson; p. 18 J. F. Haley. 1946. "Teaching—A Profession," *The Educational Forum, 11*(1). Reprinted in 1993, *The Educational Forum, 57* (Winter), 204–208 by Kappa Delta Pi, an International Honor Society in Education; p. 19 A. T. Lockwood. 1992. "Rethinking Professionalization: An Interview with Kathleen Densmore," *Focus in Change, 9,* 12–14. Reprinted with permission of the National Center for Effective Schools, School of Education, University of Wisconsin, Madison; p. 22 © Elizabeth Crews—The Image Works; p. 23 D. Peterson, *Instructor.* 1990. Copyright © 1990 by Scholastic Inc. Reprinted by permission of Scholastic Inc.; p. 25 © Robert Finken—The Picture Cube; p. 32 Table 1-2 E. Boe. Graduate School of Education, The University of Pennsylvania, "Teacher Incentive Research with SASS"; p. 33 American Federation of Teachers. 1993. *Survey and Analysis of Salary Trends;* ix; p. 34 American Federation of Teachers. 1993. *Survey and Analysis of Salary Trends;* p. 36 American Federation of Teachers. 1993. *Survey and Analysis of Salary Trends;* p. 39 Table 1-3 H. L. Hodgkinson. 1992. *A Demographic Look at Tomorrow,* Washington, DC: Center for Demographic Policy Institute for Educational Leadership, 2. Based on information in U.S. Census Bureau as cited in *American Demographics,* May 1989; p. 41 © Elizabeth Crews; p. 42 Olsen and Mullen. 1990. Reprinted with permission of California Tomorrow.

**Chapter 2** p. 50 Walter Migdale—Stock •Boston; p. 51 Excerpt from *Lovey: A Very Special Child,* by Mary MacCracken. Copyright © 1976 by Mary MacCracken Inc. Reprinted by permission of HarperCollins Publishers, Inc.; p. 52 *Escalante: The Best Teacher in America,* by Jay Matthews. Copyright © 1988 by Jay Matthews. Reprinted by permission of Henry Holt and Company, Inc.; p. 54 AP/Wide World; p. 55 © Elizabeth Crews; p. 57 Excerpts from Grant. 1992. "Multicultural Education," Falmer Press; p. 65 © Jim Pickerell—Stock•Boston; p. 68–69 Pamela Carley; p. 76 Sally Morrison; p. 80 Reprinted with permission of the author and *The Public Interest,* No. 76 (Summer) 1984, 87–101 © 1984 by National Affairs, Inc.; p. 84 Reprinted by permission. Lee Canter & Associates; p. 85 John F. Covaleskie. 1992. "Discipline and Morality: Beyond Rules and Consequences," *The Educational Forum, 56*(2) (Winter). Copyright © 1992 by Kappa Delta Pi, an International Honor Society in Education. Reprinted by permission.

**Chapter 3** p. 88 © Elizabeth Crews; p. 89 Jack Crowley. 1970. "Letter from a Teacher," *Massachusetts Teacher;* p. 95 Courtesy of Diane Shaffer, Rio Grande City High School; p. 97 Fritz Hoffmann for *The Chronicle of Higher Education;* p. 100 © Elizabeth Crews; p. 106 "How U.S. Teachers Measure Up Internationally," by F. Howard Nelson and Timothy O'Brien, 1993; p. 110 © 1991 Scott Humbert; J. L. Nicklin, copyright © 1991, *The Chronicle of Higher Education.* Reprinted with permission; p. 116 D. J. Stedman. 1991. "Re-inventing the Schools of Education: A Marshall Plan," *Vital Speeches of the Day, 57*(13) (April 15); p. 117 Edited and reprinted with the permission of The Free Press, an imprint of Simon & Schuster, from *Ed School Follies: The Miseducation of America's Teachers* by

Rita Kramer. Copyright © 1991 by Rita Kramer; p. 126 © Harriet Gans—The Image Works.

**Chapter 4** p. 132 The Bettmann Archive; p. 133 The Bettmann Archive; p. 138 The Bettmann Archive; p. 144 The Bettmann Archive; p. 145 The Bettmann Archive; p. 153 Library of Congress; p. 155 The Bettmann Archive; pp. 161 and 162 *Having Our Say,* by Sarah and A. Elizabeth Delany with Amy Hill Hearth. Published by Kodansha America Inc. © by Amy Hill Hearth, Sarah Louise Delany, and Annie Elizabeth Delany; p. 163 Library of Congress; p. 164 E. D. Hirsch Jr., December 1987/January 1988. "Restoring Cultural Literacy in the Early Grades," *Educational Leadership, 45*(4); p. 165 Condensed from James A. Banks. 1991. "Multicultural Literacy and Curriculum Reform," *Educational Horizons, 69*(3) (Spring), 135–140. Reprinted with permission of *Educational Horizons,* a quarterly journal published by Pi Lambda Theta International Honor and Professional Association in Education, Bloomington, IN 47407-6626.

**Chapter 5** p. 170 © Hazel Hankin—Stock•Boston; p. 171 Excerpts from *Me Me Me Me Me, Not A Novel,* by M. E. Kerr. 1983. New York: Harper and Row Publishers, 147–150, 154–155; p. 178 The Bettmann Archive; p. 181 Kristen L. Hays. 1994. "Topeka Comes Full Circle," *Modern Maturity* (April/May), 34; p. 182 Jerome T. Murphy. 1992. Excerpts from "Apartheid's Legacy to Black Children," *Phi Delta Kappan* (January), 369–374; p. 186 Children's Defense Fund. 1994. *Giving Children a Head Start Now: Leave No Child Behind,* 4, 7, 10, 14; p. 187 Reprinted from *USA Today* magazine, copyright © May 1993 by the Society for the Advancement of Education; p. 189 © Joel Gordon, 1988; p. 193 AP/Wide World; p. 197 Educational Testing Service, Policy Information Center. 1991. *The State of Inequality,* Princeton, NJ; p. 198 Therese Frare for the *New York Times.*

**Chapter 6** p. 215 J. Gauss, "Evaluation of Socrates as a Teacher," © 1962, Phi Delta Kappan, Inc.; p. 216 The Bettmann Archive; p. 223 Betty Brandis. 1967. Reprinted with permission of the publisher, Kappa Delta Pi, an International Honor Society in Education. "A Primer of Educational Philosophy," *The Educational Forum, 31*(4) (May). Reprinted in *The Educational Forum.* 1993. *57*(2) (Winter), 209; p. 225 The Bettmann Archive; p. 226 Laura Bohannan. 1966. "Shakespeare in the Bush," *Natural History* (August/September); p. 240 Bob Daemmrich—The Image Works; p. 242 "Students Help Business Partner Grade Instruction Manual," written by Tracie M. Rider, 1993 graduate of Westside High School, Anderson, SC, for *Tech Prep News* (Fall 1993), a publication of the PACE Consortium in Pendleton, SC, and A. Craig. 1993. "Tech Prep and Youth Apprenticeship: Opening New Doors to Success," *Palmetto Administrator* (Winter), 31, 33; p. 243 P. Kean. 1993. "Building a Better Beowulf: The New Assault on the Liberal Arts," *Lingua Franca* (May/June), 22–25; p. 244 The Image Works.

**Chapter 7** p. 254 Gale Zucker—Stock•Boston; p. 255 Excerpts from *Among Schoolchildren* by Tracy Kidder. Copyright © 1989 by

p. 489 L. J. Perelman. 1992. *School's Out: Hyperlearning, the New Technology, and the End of Education,* New York: William Morrow; p. 492 John Sotomayor/*New York Times;* p. 497 Peter Schmidt. "Seeking to Identify the Gifted Among L.E.P. Students," *Education Week, 1,* 12–13. Reprinted with permission; p. 500 Excerpts from Michel Marriott. 1990. "A New Road to Learning: Teaching the Whole Child" (June 13). Copyright © 1990 by the New York Times Company. Reprinted by permission; p. 501 John Coleman/NYT Pictures.

**Chapter 13** p. 508 AP/Wide World; p. 509 H. Hurwitz. 1988. *The Last Angry Principal,* Halcyon House; p. 512 Figure 13-1 E. K. Mosher. 1977. "Education and American Federalism: Intergovernmental and National Policy Influences," *The Politics of Education,* J. D. Scribner, Ed., Chicago: University of Chicago Press. p. 516 C. J. Lynch. 1993. "The Renaissance Woman: An Interview with Rosa Jervolino," *Hemispheres* (January), 17–19; p. 520 Brian Brainerd for the *New York Times;* p. 527 *NEA Today,* May 1994; p. 534 B. C. Schmidt. 1994. "A Very Different Kind of School," *Education Week, 13*(39) (June 22), 42–43. Reprinted with permission; p. 532 AP/Wide World; p. 535 Excerpted from Albert Shanker. 1993. "Edison's Candle," *New York Times* (August 30). Copyright by Albert Shanker; p. 539 Suzie Fitzhugh—Stock•Boston.

**Chapter 14** p. 545 Karen Diegmueller. 1991. "A Case in Point: District Fears Quality Is Suffering as It Cuts Closer to the Bone," *Education Week, 10*(36) (May 29), 1, 10. Reprinted with permission; p. 546 William Celis 3d. 1994. "A Long-Running Saga Over Texas Schools" (April 10). Copyright © 1994 by the New York Times Company. Reprinted by permission; p. 547 R. M. Jennings. 1993. "The Golden to the God-Awful," *Congressional Quarterly* (May 27);

p. 549 Table 14-1 Rod Little. *U.S. News & World Report;* p. 550 S. Buchholz. 1993. "Laying a Firm Foundation," *School & Community* (Spring), 14–15; p. 560 R. Sidel. 1991. "Separate but Unequal," *The Nation* (November 18), 620–622; p. 561 Excerpted by permission of *The New Republic,* © 1991, The New Republic, Inc; p. 563 Craig Stafford for the *New York Times;* p. 564 J. Kozol. 1991. *Savage Inequalities,* New York: Crown, 137, 142. Copyright © 1991 by Jonathan Kozol. Reprinted by permission of Crown Publishers, Inc.; p. 565 AP/Wide World; p. 567 AP/Wide World.

**Chapter 15** p. 586 © Elizabeth Crews; p. 587 "Death by Cheeseburger: High School Journalism in the 1990s and Beyond." 1994. *The Freedom Forum,* 95–96; p. 595 Table 15-1 People for the American Way. 1994. *Attacks on the Freedom to Learn: 1992–1993,* 223–224; p. 596 Darcy Padilla for the *New York Times;* p. 598 UPI/Bettmann; Jessica Portner. 1994. "Missing Graduation as a Matter of Principle," *Education Week, 13*(31) (April 27), 7. Reprinted with permission; p. 600 © 1992 *Washington Post.* Reprinted with permission; p. 601 © 1992 *Washington Post.* Reprinted with permission; p. 602 Reprinted with permission from *Church & State,* the monthly magazine of Americans United for Separation of Church and State; p. 603 © 1992 *Washington Post.* Reprinted with permission; p. 610 Ann Bradley. 1994. "Board in Delaware Ordered to Review Case of Ousted Algebra Teacher," *Education Week, 13*(20) (February 9), 8 and Ann Bradley. 1994. "Board Votes to Reinstate Ousted Algebra Teacher," *Education Week, 13*(26) (March 23), 11. Reprinted with permission; p. 613 John Sotomayor/*New York Times;* p. 614 Millicent Lawson. 1994. "False Accusations Turn Dream into Nightmare in Chicago," *Education Week, 13*(40) (August 2), 16. Reprinted with permission.